AMERICA!

A CONCISE HISTORY

AMERICA!

A CONCISE HISTORY

W. J. RORABAUGH
UNIVERSITY OF WASHINGTON

DONALD T. CRITCHLOW
SAINT LOUIS UNIVERSITY

WADSWORTH PUBLISHING COMPANY

BELMONT, CALIFORNIA

A DIVISION OF WADSWORTH, INC.

History Editor: Brian Gore
Development Editor: John Boykin
Editorial Assistant: Jennifer Deming
Production Coordinator/Copyeditor: Tina Samaha
Print Buyer: Randy Hurst
Designer: Laurie Anderson
Photo Researcher: Photosynthesis/Laurel Anderson
Cartographer: Parrot Graphics/Patti Isaacs
Cover Design: Laurie Anderson
Cover Painting: George Luks, "Armistice Night, 1918." Courtesy of Laurie Platt
          Winfrey, Inc.
Signing Representative: Jay Honeck
Compositor: Graphic World, Inc.
Printer: R.R. Donnelley, Crawfordsville

*This book is printed on
acid-free recycled paper.*

I$\bigcirc$P ™

International Thomson Publishing
The trademark ITP is used under license

Printed in the United States of America

1   2   3   4   5   6   7   8   9   10   98   97   96   95   94

Library of Congress Cataloging-in-Publication Data

Rorabaugh, W. J.
    America! : a concise history   /   W.J. Rorabaugh, Donald T.
Critchlow.
        p.   cm.
    Includes bibliographical references and index.
    ISBN 0-534-13614-1 (alk. paper)
    1. United States — History.   I. Critchlow, Donald T., 1948 –
II. Title.
E178.1.R67   1994
973 — dc20   93-37768

IN MEMORY OF ALICE RORABAUGH—W.J. RORABAUGH

TO PATRICIA, AGNIESZKA, AND MAGDALENA
—DONALD T. CRITCHLOW

W. J. RORABAUGH
is professor of history at the University of Washington in Seattle. A native of
Kentucky, he received his Ph.D. from the University of California, Berkeley.
He has written extensively on the nineteenth century and is the author of *The
Alcoholic Republic* (1979), *The Craft Apprentice* (1986), and *Berkeley at War:
The 1960s* (1989).

DONALD T. CRITCHLOW
is professor of history and chair of the Department of History at Saint Louis
University. He received his Ph.D. from the University of California, Berkeley.
He has taught at the University of Notre Dame and been a guest scholar at the
Woodrow Wilson Center for International Scholars and the Brookings Insti-
tution. A founding editor of the *Journal of Policy History*, he is the author of *The
Brookings Institution, 1916-1952* (1985) and the editor of four books.

PREFACE

American history consists of such a blizzard of facts and events that students can easily become overwhelmed and disoriented by it all. A major goal of this book, therefore, is to keep students focused on the *ideas* that hold the facts together. We tried to accomplish that goal in several ways.

First, we confined each discussion to the minimum information necessary to understand what happened, why it happened, and why it matters. Second, we begin each major section of each chapter with a preview of the main ideas that will be developed in that section. Third, rather than use cryptic headings that mean little to students (e.g., "Jackson and the Second National Bank"), we wrote headings that highlight main ideas and help carry along the narrative (e.g., "Jackson Wrecks the Banking System and the Economy"). Besides giving students a conceptual framework within which to understand the narrative, these features also help in reviewing for exams.

We sought to integrate the latest scholarship in social, cultural, and political history in this brief volume. In the process, we tried to capture the rich and often amusing character of the American people. The story of the United States is a tale not only of triumph and tragedy, but also of foible and unexpected consequences. We did not hesitate to bring out that side of any story.

Writing a concise history requires leaving out a great deal of interesting and important material. Still, we have made a point of discussing as often as possible how women and minorities were involved in, and affected by, the various major events and issues under discussion.

We also made room for something rarely found in introductory history texts: a glossary. We recognize that terms such as *impressment, free silver, mercantilism,* and *trust* or the difference between *nationalism* and *nationalization* can be confusing. Glossary terms are printed in bold at their first appearance in a chapter; the glossary itself is at the end of the book.

Also at the end of the book is a timeline to help students keep track of key events. At the end of each chapter is a list of recommended readings. Because we believe that students should, when possible, read actual historical documents, we have included primary materials in the reading lists.

A picture is worth a thousand words. You will find maps that portray, pinpoint, and illuminate every key episode.

Among the things we deliberately left out of the book are expensive color illustrations. Sharing our students' concerns about high textbook prices, we wanted to keep costs—and therefore the price—to a minimum. We wanted a book of high quality that every student could afford.

At every point we, the authors, have collaborated on this venture, arguing over nuances and details and debating how best to work often-shapeless social history into a political history framework. To satisfy the curious, though, we must confess that Rorabaugh wrote Chapters 1-15; Critchlow, Chapters 16-30.

ACKNOWLEDGMENTS

We would like to thank the editors at Wadsworth Publishing Company who participated at various stages of this project, including Peggy Adams, Diane Honigberg, and Brian Gore. We owe special thanks to John Boykin, developmental editor and to Tina Samaha, production editor. We also want to thank Thomas F. Curran at Saint Louis University for his work on the Instructor's Manual. W.J. Rorabaugh would like to thank his colleagues at the University of Washington, including Richard R. Johnson and Richard White. Donald Critchlow wishes to acknowledge the assistance of his students in an undergraduate senior history seminar at Saint Louis University who helped with research on the photographs, including Kelly Kirchner, Kara Madden, Veronica Manahan, Tanya Manse, Catherine Platt, Heather Proefrock, Scott Schoneman, Andre Smith, and Andrew Timko.

REVIEWERS

Ralph E. Shaffer, California Polytechnic State University
Kenneth Scherzer, Middle Tennessee State University
Elizabeth Ansnes, West Valley College
John Snetsinger, California Polytechnic State University
Carol Petillo, Boston College
Robert Hooper, David Lipscomb University
George McJimsey, Iowa State University
Allan R. Jones, Grinnell College
Nelson Woodward, California State University, Fullerton
Roger L. Nicols, University of Arizona
Ron Yoshimo, California Polytechnic State University
Randolph Roth, Ohio State University
Wilton B. Fowler, University of Washington
James Whitaker, Iowa State University
Neil Rabitov, California State University, Los Angeles
Gregory W. Bush, University of Miami
Elizabeth Dunn, Auburn University of Montgomery
Harold Wilson, Old Dominion University
Richard Jensen, University of Illinois, Chicago
Donald Whatley, Blinn College
Tim Johnson, David Lipscomb University
George Neilsen, Concordia University
Stephen Weisner, Springfield Technical Community College
Ward Vinson, Bucks County Community College
Pat McLatchy, Skagit Valley College

CONTENTS

1

—— ✂ ——

A BIG COUNTRY

CHAPTER OVERVIEW: America's first inhabitants came from Asia thousands of years ago, introduced agriculture, and developed complex civilizations. However, they were ill-prepared for contact with the Europeans, who arrived in 1492. In the early 1500s the Spanish seized control of the Caribbean islands, Mexico, and South America and explored much of North America, especially Florida. Meanwhile, the French entered Canada, and soon France and Spain battled for control of Florida, which Spain won. The English came late to the party. As the conquests of the 1500s drew to a close, the English had to settle for a futile search for the nonexistent Northwest Passage to Asia and a failed colony at Roanoke Island, North Carolina.

Prehistory and the First Americans

Human beings spread themselves across the earth and came to the western hemisphere rather late, less than 40,000 years ago. After a period of hunting and gathering, the native Americans in about 6000 B.C. developed agriculture at about the same time as peoples in the Middle East and Asia, but the crops were different, and the Americans lacked farm animals. Agriculture made possible the first complex cultures, the Mayan and Aztec civilizations. North of Mexico, however, societies remained less developed.

THE FIRST AMERICANS ARRIVE. About 60,000 years ago, as the last Ice Age began, human beings lived in Africa, Europe, and Asia, but none had yet arrived in the Americas. As the temperature of the earth cooled, more and more of the earth's water was stored in the form of ice at the two poles. The oceans shrank, sea level dropped, and about 40,000 years ago, during a brief period of warming within the Ice Age, a habitable land bridge was formed between Asia and North America at the Bering Strait, where Alaska meets Russia today.

A small number of people from Asia, perhaps including as few as four women, crossed this land bridge into North America. Their descendants, fanning across both western continents over thousands of years, became the first Americans. As many as 95 percent of today's native peoples in the western hemisphere may be descended from this first migration.

The warming trend caused the oceans to rise, the land bridge disappeared, and then the Ice Age returned. About 15,000 years ago ice was again stored at the poles, the oceans fell once more, and the land bridge across the Bering Strait reopened. More people from Asia, including ancestors of the Eskimo, Navajo, and Apache tribes, made their way to and through the Americas. It is also possible that then or earlier some migrants came by sea.

HUNTING AND GATHERING IN THE NEW WORLD. We know little about any Americans in this early period, except that they were nomads who primarily hunted big game. The western hemisphere then contained elephant-like woolly mammoths, big-toothed mastodons, saber-toothed tigers, and gigantic buffalo, as well as bear, moose, elk, and deer. The early peoples no doubt supplemented their meat diet with wild berries, fruits, and nuts gathered from the forests.

As time passed, the climate in North America warmed, and either because of climate change or because of overhunting, the big game disappeared. Hunting shifted to smaller animals, and deer became the most important meat in the diet. The warmer climate also caused the number of edible plants to increase, and they became more important. These early peoples did not practice agriculture and had no domesticated animals, except for dogs, which they had probably brought from Asia.

Because the western hemisphere had been separated from the rest of the world for a very long time, its plants and animals had developed quite differently. The Americas had no horses, cows, pigs, or sheep to domesticate. There were no beasts of burden, except for llamas in the mountains of South America and large dogs used to pull sleds in parts of North America. Because the early peoples lacked access to the meat protein and hides of domesticated animals, hunting and fishing remained crucial to survival. Wild game, however, required a low population density, and low density, in turn, prevented the development of complex civilizations.

TURNING TO AGRICULTURE, 6000 B.C. The Americas did provide plants that could be cultivated. About 8000 years ago, in the tropics of Central America, native peoples began to plant maize (corn), beans, and squash. Meanwhile, inhabitants of South America started growing white and sweet potatoes. None of these plants existed in the rest of the world. About the same time people in the Middle East began to cultivate wheat, and Asians grew rice. Corn was as nutritious as wheat and furnished yields that were double the food value per acre. Unlike rice, which required wet paddies, corn could be farmed under widely different conditions.

The early Americans discovered that corn and beans could be planted together. The bean plants literally climbed up the cornstalks. Corn or beans alone lacked certain nutrients, but the combination provided a balanced diet. Both plants required a long growing season and for centuries were planted only in tropical or near-tropical areas. Gradually, American farmers developed types of corn and beans that matured more rapidly, and these fast-ripening varieties then spread throughout North America, reaching what became the American Southwest in 2500 B.C. and as far north as present-day southern Canada by 500 A.D.

The turn to agriculture had a profound effect upon the American peoples. For most, hunting became less important, and wherever soil and climate encouraged crops, the need to maintain vast, unpopulated areas for wild game declined. At the same time, the cultivation of crops made nomadic life impossible and forced people to remain, at least until the harvest, in one place.

Farmers, however, found that corn rapidly depleted the soil, and they learned to put nutrients back into the soil by burning their fields after each crop. These burned fields also produced an abundance of certain plants, which just happened to provide food for deer. After ten or so years, however, the soil became poor, and corn fields had to be abandoned. Native peoples then had to move to clear new parts of the forest for fresh fields. In addition, inhabitants seasonally migrated to places that provided different food sources.

Thus, the population never became as stationary as in Europe, where animal dung was used as fertilizer and where crop rotation was practiced, or in Asia, where annual flooding replenished the nutrients in the rice fields.

AGRICULTURE PRODUCES MORE COMPLEX CULTURES. A larger, easier-to-obtain food supply almost certainly led to increased population. In those areas where agriculture had developed first, such as Central America, the division of labor into specialized tasks produced the highly complex Mayan and Aztec civilizations. From around 300 to 900 A.D. the Mayans in the southern Mexico-Guatemala area built cities with pyramid-like temples, wrote with word-pictures, and knew astronomy.

The later Aztecs, who flourished in central Mexico from 1300 to 1500, built large cities, maintained armies, collected tribute, worked silver, and constructed complex irrigation systems. They also appealed to their gods with bloody human sacrifices.

By 1500 Mexico and Central America had about 25 million people. In contrast, the population north of Mexico, where agriculture was less important and relatively new, ranged from one to thirteen million people. Although scholars disagree sharply about the population, recent estimates have tended toward the higher figure.

Though people in North America depended increasingly on agriculture, hunting did not entirely disappear. Wild animals, especially deer, continued to be an important part of the diet. Low population density meant that tribal bands were small in numbers, and the search for land suitable for new corn fields brought peoples into contact and, one may surmise, conflict. For many, war was an important part of the culture.

Some of these North American cultures became complex within the limits of their technology. For example, inhabitants of the area that is now Boston trapped fish as early as 2500 B.C. in a complicated **weir** that covered nearly two acres. Stone tools were common and sometimes elaborate. Arrowheads made by the early Americans are still found frequently in many parts of the United States.

On the other hand, native peoples did not work iron and used copper to only a limited extent, since smelting ore was unknown. They made clay pottery, often simple and undecorated. Nevertheless, a few surviving elaborate pieces from the Ohio River valley suggest that these cultures achieved considerable artistry. Trade was extensive surprisingly early. By 2000 B.C. copper from the Great Lakes was being sent south, and conch shells from the Gulf of Mexico had reached present-day Ontario, Canada.

A fascinating legacy comes from the southeastern woodlands, where the inhabitants developed elaborate rituals concerning death. We know nothing about the rites directly, but between about 700 and 1600 A.D. these peoples constructed enormous ceremonial mounds. Used for the ritualized burial of people and objects, the mounds were often hundreds of feet wide and long. Many of these mounds, as well as similar mounds built in the Ohio River valley under conditions as yet unknown, are still visible.

North American Indians in 1500

Indian tribes were small and often fragmented. Gender roles were rigid, religion involved worship of nature or animals believed to contain spirits, and dexterity was shown despite limited technology.

Inhabitants survived by different means in different regions. Northeastern tribes depended more upon hunting, while southeastern Indians had a more complex culture. Plains tribes lived by hunting buffalo without horses or guns. Pueblo dwellers in the Southwest farmed on the desert, and natives on the Pacific coast harvested shellfish and salmon.

INDIAN CULTURES AT THE MOMENT OF WHITE CONTACT, 1500. By 1500 the Indians, as they were misnamed by Christopher Columbus, had created complex and sophisticated cultures that Europeans found curious and strange. Although genetically closely related, the Indian peoples spoke hundreds of languages and thousands of dialects. North of Mexico, there were more than 300 separate languages. Social units of organization were governed by complex rules that recognized the primacy of the family-based clan, yet tribes frequently ignored clan loyalty to split into new tribes.

Europeans thought of tribal chiefs as kings, but few chiefs held absolute power. Although they often inherited their positions, they could easily be deposed. Chiefs generally ruled by following the consensus that emerged from tribal councils. Political discussion and negotiation, both within councils and between tribes, included many rituals, and leaders sealed agreements by passing around and smoking a tobacco-filled peace pipe.

Gender roles were extremely rigid. Men hunted, made war, participated in political councils, and led religious observances. Women planted and har-

Map 1.1. Location of Native Peoples around 1500

vested corn, prepared food, made clothes, and looked after children. Their labor produced as much as 90 percent of a tribe's caloric intake.

In many tribes women owned property, including houses, but they commonly were required to live apart from the community during their menstrual periods. Kinship was often matrilineal, that is, calculated through female descent, and the relatives of one's mother were more important than those of one's father. In this type of kinship system, a mother's brother was more important than a father.

Premarital sex was common, extramarital sex was accepted, divorce was easy, and yet marriage was a solemn institution. Child care had, in European eyes, its own peculiarities. In a practice found throughout North America, mothers bound babies to cradle boards so that they developed flattened heads, both front and back. Adults indulged children to the point of wildness, while young men were expected to endure physical pain inflicted by enemies.

No North American peoples were literate or wove cloth. Despite these limitations, they had developed many technological skills. They made digging tools for gardening by using animal skins to bind sharpened stones to wooden sticks. Bows for hunting were light but strong, and arrows were often tipped with sharp stones.

INDIAN PEOPLES VARY REGIONALLY, 1500. Indian cultures showed great regional variations. In the Northeast, with long winters and a short growing season, corn was less important in the diet than game and fish. The Algonquin and Iroquoian tribes built snug wooden houses up to 90 feet long. Each long house had a series of rooms and held a number of nuclear families. To protect against enemies, these Indians built their houses inside villages walled with wooden palisades.

In the Southeast, the warmer climate and longer growing season enabled the Creek and Choctaw to plant two corn crops a year. Plentiful food led to denser populations, larger villages, and more powerful chiefs. In this region natives designed housing to let in breezes during the hot summers as well as to protect against winter storms. Families lived one to a dwelling, but villages were usually fenced.

Among the Creek, young men from rival clans played a ball game similar to modern lacrosse, to which it is related. The game involved using a stick with a loop at the end to put a ball through a goal. All the men from two clans played at the same time, so that hundreds of players crowded the field. As violent as football, the game had no team strategy. Each warrior-player sought individually to put the ball through the goal. Severe injuries, even deaths, occurred. Games sometimes lasted eight hours. Spectators and players placed many bets, and a clan that lost several matches in a row might disband in humiliation.

European artists often portrayed American Indians in fanciful ways, as in this drawing of natives sowing seeds. (Bettmann Archive/Theodore De Bry)

In 1500 the area of the plains was sparsely populated by Arapaho and Pawnee buffalo hunters. Having neither horses nor guns yet, they captured buffalo with cunning, including attacks that led the animals into self-destructive stampedes. These nomadic Indians lived in teepees made of buffalo skins and wooden poles. Teepees could be put up and taken down quickly.

In the dry Southwest the Pueblo tribes, such as the Hopi and Zuñi, built adobe houses into dense villages and grew corn using dry farming techniques. The most stationary of all the tribes in North America, they developed elaborate rituals, including rain dances and sun worship, that revolved around the desert landscape. They conducted religious rites in underground ceremonial chambers called kivas. The town of Acoma, New Mexico, was established at or near its present site in 900 A.D. and has been continuously settled since 1075, making it the oldest community in the United States.

Along the Pacific coast from northern California to southern Alaska lived a number of Salish-speaking peoples devoted to salmon fishing. They also harvested shellfish, ate berries and other wild plants, and lived in boxy wooden houses. They had a ceremony called potlatch, in which they gave away possessions and property. The donors obtained high status for giving; those who received the gifts had to reciprocate or lose face.

Europeans Explore and Exploit
the Americas

Although the Vikings briefly settled in North America around 1000 A.D., their colony had been forgotten by the time Christopher Columbus sailed to the West Indies in 1492. Columbus's four voyages set off a European race for colonial empires in the Americas. The Pope tried to divide the New World between Spain and Portugal, but other countries, particularly France and England, ignored the papal decree and sent out their own explorers. The Spanish, however, gained the lead in the early 1500s.

VIKINGS AND OTHERS SAIL BEFORE COLUMBUS. In all probability the first Europeans to visit America were Scandinavians who sailed across the North Atlantic. The Vikings, most likely under Leif Erickson between 1000 and 1010 A.D., maintained a colony at a place they called Vinland. Archeologists have recently located this site in present Newfoundland, opposite Labrador on the shore of eastern Canada.

The Vikings were a seafaring people who sailed from Norway in the 900s and 1000s to colonize Iceland, Greenland, and Vinland in succession. The Iceland settlement survived, but the Greenland colony died out after about 400 years, and the Vinland settlement was quickly abandoned after encounters with native peoples, whom the Vikings called Skrelings.

By the 1400s this early Viking settlement had been forgotten, but growing commerce throughout Europe had led to increased exploration in search of trade. It also led to the construction of larger and better ships, more likely to withstand the rigors of crossing the Atlantic Ocean. These ships, however, were small and boxy by today's standards. Even in the late 1400s it was unusual for a ship to be more than 70 feet long. Furthermore, vessels tended to maneuver poorly in storms, to go dead in the water because their sails could not catch wind, and to be tossed in storms because their anchors were too light.

In the 1400s the Portuguese became Europe's premier maritime explorers. They sailed along the African coast, settled the Azore Islands, and eventually passed around Africa's Cape of Good Hope and made contact with India and the Africa-India-Middle East trade. According to some historians, as early as the 1480s sailors from Bristol, England, may have begun to exploit the rich fishing banks off Newfoundland, Canada. They preceded, or perhaps followed, French fishermen from Brittany. At the time, fishermen from various nations cooperated with each other without the national rivalries that later marked the 1500s.

COLUMBUS LEADS SPAIN TO THE AMERICAS, 1492-1504. The Spanish, too, became interested in exploration. King Ferdinand V and Queen Isabella commissioned Christopher Columbus to sail west from Spain in search of a short route to Asia and its spices. On October 12, 1492, Columbus found instead what Europeans called the **New World.** Mistaking the islands of the Caribbean for outposts off the Asian mainland, he called the area the Indies and the native peoples Indians. Both names stuck, although people eventually called these islands the West Indies to distinguish them from the East Indies, which really were off the coast of Asia.

Columbus's failure to recognize what he had discovered not only produced confusion, but also cost this sailor from Genoa, Italy some of his fame. When mapmakers first drew in the new continent, they named it America, in honor of another early explorer, Amerigo Vespucci, who had understood the true nature of the discovery almost immediately.

Spain had several advantages in the early exploration of the New World. The Spanish government did not publicize all the information gained from Columbus's four voyages between 1492 and 1504. In addition, compared to other European countries, Spain enjoyed both closer physical proximity to the New World and a more favorable sailing route. In 1492 Columbus had sailed out on the Canaries current and the northeast trade winds and had returned by a northern route along the Gulf Stream current and the westerly winds. England and France lacked easy access to this particular route, which became the lifeline to Spain's American empire.

THE RACE FOR EUROPEAN CONQUEST BEGINS, 1493-1524. In the late 1400s Europe was in ferment. Trade flourished, economies grew, and demand soared for exotic imports such as pepper or cinnamon from faraway places, like China or Asia's spice islands.

At the same time Europeans rediscovered much learning from the ancient Greek world that had been lost for centuries. This rebirth of knowledge, called the Renaissance, led Europeans to gain self-confidence, to express a belief in their own superiority, and to seek ways to impose their rule on other parts of the world.

Johann Gutenberg invented printing around 1456, and his invention promoted everyday languages in place of Latin. Books published in Italian, French, German, or English bound together those who read the same language and led to a rising sense of **nationalism.**

Throughout Europe fragmented, localized **feudalism** gave way to powerful, centralized monarchy in the form of the modern nation-state. Soon the Protestant Reformation, started by Martin Luther in 1517, would shake the Catholic church's hold on Europe. By the early 1500s commercial interests, nationalism, and religious strife had unleashed unprecedented energies, many of which found expression in the conquest of the New World.

In 1493 the Pope, under Spanish influence, used his power as head of the Catholic church to reserve the New World for Catholic Spain. He gave a small slice called Brazil to Catholic Portugal. A year later Spain and Portugal signed a treaty confirming this division, although the agreement gave Portugal a slightly better deal. Other European countries, whether Catholic, like France, or in the process of becoming Protestant, like England, ignored both the **papal edict** and the treaty. Actual possession was to be the only way to hold a claim in the New World.

Accordingly, other European nations almost immediately began exploration. In 1497 the English sent John Cabot, an Italian who had previously sailed for the Portuguese, along the North Atlantic coast. He may have reached as far south as Long Island Sound off New York. A year later Cabot was lost at sea while on another expedition. From 1500 to 1502 two brothers, Gaspar and Miguel Corte Real, explored the coast at Newfoundland and Labrador under a Portuguese flag. Both vanished at sea. In 1524 Giovanni da Verrazano, an Italian sailing for the French, followed the Atlantic coast from South Carolina to Rhode Island and en route discovered New York harbor.

Building the Spanish Empire, 1513-1542

Spanish explorers moved quickly both to expand the empire and to gain personal profit. In 1513 Vasco Núñez de Balboa discovered the Pacific Ocean, and in 1519 Ferdinand Magellan began to sail around the world. Meanwhile, Hernando Cortés conquered Mexico, and Francisco Pizarro seized Peru. These Europeans brought diseases that killed millions of Indians. In 1540 Francisco Vásquez de Coronado explored the Southwest. Florida attracted Juan Ponce de León in 1521, Álvar Núñez Cabeza de Vaca in 1528, and Hernando De Soto in 1539.

CONQUISTADORS SEEK FAME AND FORTUNE. Despite European nations' rival expeditions, the Spanish maintained their lead in exploring the New World. In 1513 Vasco Núñez de Balboa crossed the isthmus of Panama and became the first European to see the western ocean, which he named the Pacific because it appeared to be so calm.

Six years later Ferdinand Magellan set out from Spain to find a route to Asia around the southern tip of South America. He did find a route, and his

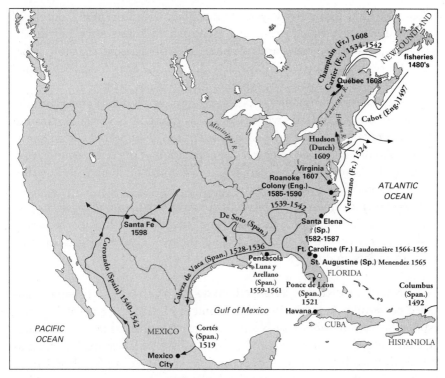

Map 1.2. European Explorations in North America

expedition became the first to sail around the world, but the rocky, stormy Strait of Magellan did not prove to be a viable trade route to Asia.

In 1519 Hernando Cortés and 600 men conquered the Aztec empire in Mexico. The wealth of the Aztecs, especially in the form of gold and silver, quickly fell into Spanish hands and whetted the conquistadors' appetites for more riches. Then, in the 1530s, Francisco Pizarro conquered the Inca empire in Peru and gained fabulous wealth in the form of silver mines.

Largely because of the silver and other valuables, the Spanish decided to colonize the New World. Although they sent out settlers, the Spanish were more concerned about protecting their valuable income-producing property from other Europeans, and so they sent many soldiers, as well as **Jesuit** priests to convert the native peoples to Christianity.

EUROPEAN DISEASES KILL INDIANS. The Indians, however, died in epidemics from exposure to diseases brought by the Spanish and other Europeans. The native peoples had no resistance to measles, smallpox, or bubonic plague, and death rates in particular epidemics reached as high as 95 percent.

Sometimes within a few days of first contact with Europeans, dozens of Indians in a village would sicken and die. Epidemics were physically debilitating, politically disruptive, and psychologically devastating, the more so because Europeans seldom died. The only disease that may have been passed from Indians to Europeans was syphilis, but this is not certain.

On the island of Hispaniola, today's Dominican Republic and Haiti, the nearly four million Arawaks whom Columbus found in 1492 had declined to 15,600 people in 1518. They had almost entirely disappeared within a generation. According to one estimate, the population of the Aztec empire, covering much of present-day Mexico, fell from about 25 million at or just after Spanish contact to 750,000 a century later.

It would take hundreds of years for the native population to regain its precontact level. Although wars and Spanish mistreatment of Indians, including enslavement, hastened population decline, the major cause was lack of resistance to European diseases.

CORONADO PLUNDERS THE SOUTHWEST, 1540-1542. Having established powerful bases in the West Indies and in Mexico, the Spanish began to explore the vast interior of the North American continent. Francisco Vásquez de Coronado, living in Mexico and hearing rumors of fabled wealthy cities to the north groaning with gold, marched into the American Southwest from 1540 to 1542. He was unimpressed by the Pueblo villages in present-day New Mexico and Arizona that he found and, to some extent, plundered. The major consequence of his expedition was to introduce horses to North American Indians.

PONCE DE LEON VISITS FLORIDA, 1521. Meanwhile, the Spanish had concluded that the easiest sailing route for sending silver and trade goods from the New World to Spain was through the straits between Cuba and Florida. The area, however, proved dangerous, for ships sometimes went aground on coral reefs, and hurricanes were common. In consequence, the Spanish showed a keen interest in establishing forts and settlements along the Florida coast.

Juan Ponce de León, who had first landed in Florida in 1513, led a major expedition to that peninsula in 1521. He had his own private reasons for the trip. Although the commander said that he was looking for the fountain of youth, which made a nice cover story, in reality he hoped to find wealth comparable to that previously discovered and plundered in Mexico. No riches were found. Wounded by natives in Florida, Ponce de León retreated to Havana, Cuba, and died.

CABEZA DE VACA LIVES TO TELL QUITE A TALE, 1528-1536. Despite Ponce de León's failure, the Spanish sent another exploring expedition to Florida in 1528. Led by Pánfilo de Narváez, it ended in disaster as a hurricane tore up the ships along Florida's northwestern gulf coast. A few survivors, including Álvar Núñez Cabeza de Vaca, made their way west along the coast through what became Louisiana and Texas. Cabeza de Vaca spent several years among the Indians in Texas, first as a slave, then as a trader and medicine man.

Eight years after landing in Florida, he and three other men from the original party, including a man of African ancestry, joined one of the southwestern Indian trading parties that routinely bartered with the Spanish in northern Mexico. From there the four traveled to Mexico City and then back to Spain, where they retold their bizarre adventure.

DE SOTO TOURS FLORIDA AND THE SOUTHEAST, 1539-1542. As other European powers became more keenly interested in the New World, the Spanish grew uneasy. They saw Florida as a key base to protect the Spanish shipping lanes. Thus, in 1539 Hernando De Soto and 600 men set out to explore Florida more thoroughly. He treated the inhabitants harshly, and since word of his movements preceded his expedition, he often found villages deserted. His troops lived off the land — eating much of the Indians' corn from their fields. He also brought ashore pigs, which became Florida's wild boars.

Finding nothing of value on the Florida peninsula, De Soto, like Coronado, moved northward in 1540. Wherever he wandered, the Indians assured him that they had no wealth, but that rich tribes lived in remote places further inland. The natives told these stories to encourage De Soto to move on quickly, and he did so in eager pursuit of wealth. Frequently, he took captives, put them in chains, and made them carry his expedition's equipment or act as guides until he entered another tribe's land.

In what is now South Carolina, he and his men were entertained by a great Indian queen, whom the Spanish called the Lady of Cofitahequi. Amid elaborate ceremony, the Lower Creeks carried their queen on a litter into De Soto's presence. After exchanging gifts, De Soto decided to march into the mountains, but, as was his habit, he took the queen along as a captive. In the middle of the night, however, she escaped.

Finding little of interest in the Appalachian Mountains, De Soto then turned west through present-day Alabama and Mississippi, where he wintered in 1540-1541. He reached the Mississippi River and built barges to cross. Thousands of Indians watched from canoes, but they disappeared without attacking. Moving west through Arkansas, De Soto sent scouts far enough west to encounter buffalo-hunting plains tribes.

De Soto and his dwindling band, reduced by disease, remained in Arkansas, where they wintered inside a stockade in 1541-1542. He retreated to the Mississippi and, after preparing barges, died of a fever. The remnants of the expedition then floated down the river and sailed along the Gulf to Mexico, which they reached in 1543.

France and Spain Become Rivals in North America

While the Spanish explored the Southwest and Southeast, the French investigated Canada. There they found neither a passage to China nor gold, but the Indians were eager and willing to trade valuable furs. An early attempted settlement, however, failed. Soon the French eyed Florida, which guarded the Spanish treasure ships. In 1564 the French colonized Florida, but the Spanish attacked the settlement and ruthlessly murdered the Protestant inhabitants. The Spanish then built a fort at St. Augustine and later colonized New Mexico.

CARTIER EXPLORES CANADA, 1534-1542. While the Spanish roamed the Southeast and Southwest, the French began to concentrate on the mainland further north, nearest to the Newfoundland fishery. In 1534 Jacques Cartier explored the St. Lawrence Gulf, hoping to find a passage to China. A year later he discovered and named the St. Lawrence River, explored the river as far as what is now Montréal, where more than a thousand natives greeted him, and then wintered at a site near present-day Québec city in a well-constructed fort. Cartier traded knives and trinkets for the local Indians' furs. The high quality of the furs, as well as the absence of gold or silver, led the French to pursue explorations to extend trade with fur-gathering Indians in the colder portions of North America.

On a third expedition in 1541, Cartier explored the St. Lawrence valley beyond Montréal and again wintered near the site of Québec city. In 1542 he returned to France, and Jean François de la Roque, seigneur de Roberval, brought 200 settlers to the St. Lawrence valley. The winter proved more severe than anticipated, and many of the French died of scurvy. The following year the French abandoned the colony.

At the time the area was inhabited by Iroquoian-speaking Indians. When the French finally did establish a permanent settlement at Québec in the St.

Lawrence valley under Samuel de Champlain in 1608, these Indians had been pushed out by Algonquian-speakers from the north. This major shift in Indian populations, in less than a century, shows the fluid and often hostile nature of relationships among native peoples prior to European contact. Indeed, Europeans often played off rival native peoples against each other. The Indians, in turn, learned to do the same to Europeans from different nations.

EUROPEANS FIGHT OVER FLORIDA, 1559-1587. The potential for conflict among Europeans centered more and more on Florida. To the Spanish, holding the Florida peninsula was necessary to guarantee the safety of the Spanish ships that carried wealth from the New World to Spain. To other Europeans, and especially to the French and English, Spanish control of Florida not only secured Spain's wealth and role as a great power but also threatened the interests of other Europeans in furs and fish further north. As part of this contest, in 1559 Tristán de Luna y Arellano established a Spanish colony at Pensacola Bay, but two years later it was abandoned.

The English and French increasingly preyed upon Spanish shipping along the Atlantic trade route. This business was lucrative but dangerous. During wartime — and there were many wars throughout this century — well-armed private ships, called **privateers,** carried government letters authorizing them to seize enemy merchant ships. During peacetime many of these same ships operated without legal authority as pirates.

In 1562 the French moved aggressively. Jean Ribault explored the Atlantic coast from the St. John's River in north Florida to Port Royal, South Carolina. He built a fort at Port Royal, but the soldiers mutinied and turned to cannibalism before being rescued by an English privateer in 1563.

The following year the French under René Goulaine de Laudonnière planted a colony of Huguenots (French Protestants) in Florida at a site on the St. John's River, near what is now Jacksonville. Although ostensibly peaceful in purpose, the Fort Caroline colony was clearly intended to provide privateers with a safe haven.

At first Fort Caroline appeared to prosper, but soon the settlers had trouble with the Indians, who may have resented the colonists' increasing appetite for Indian corn. Then the Spanish under Pedro Menéndez de Avilés arrived and created an international incident by slaughtering virtually all the French after they had surrendered. The ruthless Menéndez considered the Protestant French to be heretics deserving only death.

In 1565 the Spanish under Menéndez built their own permanent settlement in Florida on the Atlantic coast at St. Augustine, which soon included a substantial fort. The Spanish designed this outpost, supported by Mexican revenues, both to protect their sealanes from English and French privateers and to discourage the other European countries from trying to establish colonies on the North American continent. From 1572 to 1587 the Spanish also maintained the Santa Elena colony, at what is now Parris Island, South Carolina.

SPAIN COLONIZES NEW MEXICO, 1598. Somewhat later, the Spanish also moved into the Pueblo Indian country in the Southwest. In 1598 they colonized the area around Santa Fe, New Mexico, and in 1610 they built an administrative capital at Santa Fe. They sent Jesuit missionaries to the nearby Indians. In 1680 the Indians suddenly massacred the priests and settlers and drove the remaining Spaniards south to the Rio Grande. It was 1692 before the Spanish reconquered New Mexico.

England Comes Late to the Party

By the time the English were prepared to explore North America, they found the French and Spanish already there. The seafaring English then turned to seek the Northwest Passage to Asia. No such passage existed. The English, under the brilliant leadership of Queen Elizabeth, also challenged the Spanish empire by sending privateers to seize Spanish treasure ships. Francis Drake used one such expedition to sail around the world and return home triumphantly. Spain retaliated with the Armada, an attempt to invade England that failed. In 1584 the English planned the Roanoke colony in today's North Carolina. By 1590 intrigue, poor planning, and international politics had doomed this colony.

SEEKING THE NORTHWEST PASSAGE, 1576-1610. While the Spanish secured power in Mexico and Peru by establishing outposts in southern North America, the French and English jockeyed for position along the North Atlantic coast. Neither country, however, was able to make a permanent settlement, in part due to a series of wars that raged in Europe in the late 1500s.

Much of the English effort went into the search beyond Newfoundland for a northern sea route to Asia, called the Northwest Passage. Such an opening, everyone agreed, would enable England to bypass Spain's control of South America and give the English an exclusive direct link to the profitable Chinese market. Martin Frobisher made three northern voyages between 1576 and 1578; Sir Humphrey Gilbert sailed in 1583 and in 1584, when he was lost at sea; and John Davis explored the far north between 1585 and 1587. These explorers experienced howling snowstorms and saw icebergs, but found no Northwest Passage.

After 1600 faith in the existence of the Northwest Passage dwindled, but Henry Hudson pursued this quest in four voyages from 1607 through 1610. In 1609, on the one trip he made for the Dutch, he found the river that he named for himself and reached present-day Albany, New York. In 1610 he sailed much further north, to Hudson Bay, where his sailors mutinied and cast him adrift in a small boat, never to be seen again. Hudson's failure ended the quest for the nonexistent Northwest Passage.

ENGLAND CHALLENGES SPAIN, 1560-1588. Queen Elizabeth of England hated Spain, and perhaps with good reason. Her father, Henry VIII, had had a Spanish wife, Catherine of Aragon, but when she failed to produce a male heir, Henry decided to divorce her. The Pope, under Spanish influence, blocked the divorce in 1529, and Henry responded by becoming a **Protestant,** declared himself the head of the **Church of England**, seized Catholic property in England, and annulled his own marriage. Five more wives followed, but the only male heir, the intensely Protestant Edward VI, proved sickly and barely outlived Henry.

In 1553 Mary, Henry's daughter by Catherine of Aragon and a staunch Catholic, gained the English throne. She married King Philip II of Spain and began to burn Protestants as heretics. When "Bloody Mary" died in 1558, the crown passed to her half-sister, Elizabeth, who was Protestant. The queen had little choice about her religion, since the Catholic church, as well as the Spanish, had never recognized Henry's divorce and therefore considered her illegitimate.

Perhaps religion would not have mattered, or an accommodation might have been made, but Spain was then the world's greatest power, and its power appeared to be the direct result of the treasure extracted from its colonial empire. England, a poor, weak nation in comparison, became insanely jealous, and because the English as islanders were naturally a seafaring people, they hungered to gain an empire like Spain's, or at the least to plunder the Spanish. The brilliant, wily Elizabeth used every trick in the book to gain advantage, and during the course of her long reign (1558-1603), she raised her country to new prominence.

Queen Elizabeth considered Spain to be a threat to England's security, and to weaken the Spanish while strengthening her own kingdom, she authorized privateering expeditions, which the Spanish considered to be pirates, against the Spanish silver shipments from the Americas. In the 1560s John Hawkins turned privateer in the West Indies, traded in African slaves, and was soon joined, as a sponsor, by Walter Raleigh, one of the queen's favorites.

Although Elizabeth enjoyed the benefits conferred by the "sea dogs," as the privateers were called, she did not wish England to be known as a nation of pirates. Thus, she kept her government's distance from the actions of her subjects and stood ready to condemn to the Spanish ambassador the very pirates she had approved in private.

Leaving England late in 1577, the privateer Francis Drake sailed along the South American coast, passed through the Strait of Magellan, and entered the Pacific Ocean. He then surprised and seized Spanish ships along the western coast of South America, explored as far north as Drake's Bay in California, and returned to England in 1580 via the Pacific. His ship groaned with wealth, and the voyage created a sensation and whetted appetites for more booty. The first Englishman to sail around the world, a task accomplished by Magellan's expedition in 1522, Drake was welcomed home as a hero and knighted.

King Philip II of Spain tired of Elizabeth's game. He decided to end the English harassment of Spanish shipping once and for all by invading England with a massed fleet called the Armada. The Spanish sailed in 1588 but, due to better English ships and skills, as well as stormy weather (sardonically called the "Protestant Wind"), failed disastrously. After the Armada's destruction, the English gained a stronger position to challenge the Spanish in the New World than at any previous time.

ESTABLISHING THE ROANOKE COLONY, 1584-1590. Even before the Armada sailed, Sir Walter Raleigh, acting "for gold, for praise, for glory," had received from Queen Elizabeth in 1584 a royal grant to plant an English colony along the Atlantic coast. He sent out an exploring party and chose a spot for settlement in what was then called Virginia but is now North Carolina, at Roanoke on the Outer Banks. The location was chosen perhaps more for military reasons — both its closeness to Spanish Florida and its convenient access for passing English privateers — than for its promise as a place for settlement.

In 1585 the queen, knowing that war with Spain was coming, prohibited Raleigh from leaving England, and the Roanoke colony was started without its founder. That year Ralph Lane and about a hundred settlers, most of them soldiers, reached Roanoke and built a fort. Relations with the local Indians were spotty, and the colony nearly starved.

In 1586 Francis Drake visited the colony and found it in poor condition. Lane prepared to evacuate part of the colony on Drake's ships, but a storm ruined this plan. In the end Lane and a few colonists accompanied Drake to

England. Raleigh sent a relief ship that same year, but it arrived after Drake's visit and found the settlers gone. The ship returned to England.

Later that year a new expedition brought 150 to 200 additional colonists, but no one was at Roanoke, and the expedition returned to England, leaving only 15 or 18 men at the fort. Later it was learned that Indians had attacked these men, who had set sail in a small boat and vanished.

In 1587 another 110 colonists arrived under John White. Opposed by other leaders in his plan to relocate the colony to Chesapeake Bay, White reluctantly agreed to remain at Roanoke. Meanwhile, he cultivated good relations with the Indians at nearby Croatoan Island. The colonists fared poorly, and White returned to England to get supplies. He left behind, as a kind of guarantee for his own return, his daughter, his son-in-law, and his granddaughter, Virginia Dare, the first English child born in North America.

An attempted rescue in 1588 failed when pirates attacked White's small ships en route and forced the party back to England. Meanwhile, war had broken out between England and Spain, and in preparation for heading off the Armada, Elizabeth prohibited all English ships from leaving port.

In 1590 White took passage on a privateer that promised to stop at Roanoke. He found the fort abandoned. The only sign of the colonists came from two markings on a tree and a door: CRO and CROATOAN. There was no sign of a maltese cross, which was to be used to show distress. To White, the markings indicated, by prearranged signal with the colonists whom he had left behind, that the settlers had voluntarily abandoned the fort and moved to Croatoan Island, where friendly Indians lived. A storm, however, prevented the English from landing at Croatoan, and the fate of the settlers remained unknown.

Years later, in the early 1600s, an English settler in the later Virginia colony reported a story that at least some of the Roanoke party had been given shelter by friendly Indians who had later moved to the Chesapeake. There it was said both Indians and settlers had been massacred in about 1607 under orders of the great Indian leader, Powhatan.

Conclusion

The original inhabitants of the western hemisphere had developed agriculture and complex cultures, but they lacked sophisticated technology, which put them at a compelling military disadvantage against the invading Europeans. Disease devastated millions, but probably even more important in the easy European conquest was the self-confidence and zest that the Europeans, and especially the Spanish, brought to the task. Modern governmental organization in the form of the nation-state was combined with an intense desire to convert the "heathen" to Christianity.

The Europeans squabbled among themselves. In part, these quarrels were those of thieves fighting over booty, but they also involved controversies over religion, government, and the proper forms for colonialism. The Spanish empire exploited native peoples to extract wealth for export to Spain. The French had a more reciprocal relationship with the Indians, but this may have been because the French had to cultivate the natives in order to maintain the fur trade, a renewable resource. The English arrived so late that they could only seize land that no other Europeans wanted, and they had to plant permanent colonies in order to maintain an actual possession.

Recommended Readings

DOCUMENTS: Richard Hakluyt, *The Principal Navigations, Voiages, Traffiques and Discoveries of the English Nation* (3 vols., 1598-1600).

READINGS: (INDIANS) James Axtell, *The European and the Indian* (1981); William Cronon, *Changes in the Land* (1983); Ramón A. Gutiérrez, *When Jesus Came, the Corn Mothers Went Away* (1991); Charles M. Hudson, *The Southeastern Indians* (1976); Francis Jennings, *The Invasion of America* (1975); James H. Merrell, *The Indians' New World* (1989); Neal Salisbury, *Manitou and Providence* (1982); Bruce G. Trigger, *The Children of Aataentsic* (2 vols., 1976); (EXPLORATION) Kenneth R. Andrews, *Trade, Plunder and Settlement* (1984); Stephen Greenblatt, *Marvelous Possessions* (1991); Karen O. Kupperman, *Roanoke* (1984), and *Settling with the Indians* (1980); Samuel E. Morison, *The European Discovery of America* (2 vols., 1971-74); J.H. Parry, *The Age of Reconnaissance* (1963); David B. Quinn, *North America from Earliest Discovery to First Settlements* (1977), and *Set Fair for Roanoke* (1985); Carl O. Sauer, *Sixteenth Century North America* (1971).

2

THE PLANTATION SOUTH,
1607-1771

CHAPTER OVERVIEW: Founded in 1607, Virginia survived by growing tobacco as a cash crop. From 1642 to 1677 Governor Sir William Berkeley promoted the development of a hierarchical society based on inequality. The wealthy got land easily, the poor only with difficulty. White indentured servants provided labor, but Bacon's Rebellion (1675-1676) revealed the instability of this social system.

Virginia planters then turned increasingly to black slave labor. The use of a self-perpetuating labor force led, during the 1700s, to the emergence of a wealthy, powerful, stable elite. The other southern colonies, Maryland, South Carolina, North Carolina, and Georgia, were modeled, with minor variations, on Virginia.

Virginia's Early Days, 1607-1624

The first English settlers arrived in Virginia in 1607. They nearly starved to death, and the colony barely survived. Virginia was saved by growing tobacco, but the colony's success produced conflict with the Indians. In 1618 Virginia adopted the headright system, by which settlers could get free land. This led both to increased population and to rampant speculation. In 1625 Virginia became a royal colony. The king appointed the governor, the governor appointed a council, and property holders elected the House of Burgesses. The state-supported Church of England, through its vestrymen, aided the poor.

FOUNDING THE COLONY OF VIRGINIA, 1607. In 1603 James I succeeded Elizabeth as England's ruler, and the new king quickly patched up the old quarrel with Spain. In return for England's ban on **privateering,** the

Spanish accepted English colonies in North America. Accordingly, in 1606 James granted the Virginia Company of London, organized as a private stock-holding corporation, the right to colonize North America, but in order to obtain title, settlers had to occupy the land. The company's shareholders planned on profiting from land sales, from trade with Indians, and from any gold or other valuable minerals found in Virginia.

In 1607, 13 years before the Pilgrims landed at Plymouth, the company made the first permanent English settlement in North America at James-town, Virginia. Lured to America with promises of adventure and easy wealth, the 105 colonists instead got misadventure and bad health. Virginia held no gold, the local Indians had no furs to trade, and the combination of bad water, bad diet, and fevers killed two-thirds of the colonists within seven months.

The survivors begged, borrowed, or stole food from the Indians, awaited an overdue supply ship from home, and quarreled among themselves. Few were interested in putting food into the common storehouse, but all eagerly withdrew supplies. There was no individual initiative. Finally, sensing disas-ter, Captain John Smith took charge. "He that will not work shall not eat," he declared, ordering food to be given only to those who fished or planted corn. Smith even had one settler who stole corn tied to a tree until he starved to death. The victim also had a wooden pin driven through his tongue. Smith was hated and left the colony in 1609. He spent the rest of his life promoting the settlement of New England.

The Virginia colonists, including a few starry-eyed gentlemen but drawn largely from the poorer farm workers in southern and western England, con-tinued to bicker. Leadership was poor or nonexistent, expectations far ex-ceeded reality, the water was contaminated, and although more settlers had arrived, hundreds died in the "starving time."

In 1610, after a supply ship failed to appear, the 60 survivors, having eaten all the chickens and livestock, including horses, packed their belongings and prepared to abandon Virginia. They boarded a ship and were sailing down the James River to the sea when they met three ships bringing not only supplies but also new colonists. The colony revived.

Virginia, however, did not prosper. In 1616 it had only 380 English resi-dents, and investors in the Virginia Company of London received no profits. With neither gold nor Indian trade, the only hope for the colony was to dis-cover a crop that could be grown in Virginia and sold at a handsome profit in England.

GROWING TOBACCO AS A CASH CROP. An Indian plant, tobacco, saved the colony. In the early 1600s middle-class merchants throughout Europe began to smoke tobacco in their coffee houses. The weed became so popular in England that James I, who hated the smoke, published the world's first antitobacco pamphlet.

By 1614 the Virginians had discovered, with help from the Indians, that the country produced excellent tobacco. There was a ready, growing market in England, and the price in the early years was so high that profits could be enormous.

Tobacco gained such an importance in Virginia's economy that it became the colony's only currency. Residents paid court fines and property taxes in pounds of tobacco, and ministers received their salaries in the same form.

Profits, however, were not automatic. Although land was readily available for planting, labor was difficult to obtain. Tobacco, more than most crops, required intensive labor. A single worker could care for only three acres. The seed had to be started in a bed and then transplanted to a field. Weeding was constant, and tobacco worms had to be removed by hand. At a crucial moment the tobacco leaves had to be cut and then cured.

Europeans were fascinated by the large-leafed tobacco plant, shown here in somewhat exaggerated size in the background. The woman at the lower left is picking leaves, while other workers prepare and hang the leaves in the curing shed. (BETTMANN ARCHIVE)

COLONISTS CONFRONT INDIANS. The rise of tobacco meant that, more and more, the settlers took over Indian lands. Although low population density made the area largely vacant, the native inhabitants resented the colonists' land grab, even when the settlers' cows and hogs did not trample unfenced Indian gardens. The English experimented with enslaving the natives to work on the tobacco **plantations,** but they ran away into the woods.

Powhatan, the powerful local Indian chief, tried numerous strategies, including trade, diplomacy, war, and withdrawal, for dealing with these English settlers. He sent his daughter, Pocahontas, to make contact. Several years later, in 1614, Pocahontas married one of the settlers, John Rolfe. This was one of the few English-Indian marriages. English men preferred to bring over English women, rather than to marry natives, as the Spanish and the French did.

In 1616 the Rolfes visited England, where Pocahontas died. John Rolfe then returned to Virginia and was among those killed by Indians in a sudden attack in 1622. Of the colony's 900 white settlers, 347 died. The colonists used the massacre as an excuse to kill Indians or to drive away even nearby friendly natives. War and disease caused the Indian population in coastal Virginia to decline from 30,000 in 1607 to 2,000 by 1669.

REORGANIZING THE COLONY. Once the Virginia Company of London understood that the colony's future depended upon tobacco, it moved to lure settlers to raise this cash crop. In 1618 the company adopted the **headright system,** by which settlers from England were promised 50 acres of free land for each settler, for each family member, and for each imported worker. Wealthy settlers imported **indentured servants,** who contracted to work for a fixed period in Virginia in return for having their passage paid.

This system made no provision for land for servants after they had gained their freedom, and it allowed **speculators** to accumulate vast acreages. Despite its flaws, the headright system did lead to an increased immigration to Virginia.

In 1619 a Dutch sea captain, active in the slave trade which flourished between Africa and the West Indies, sold the English settlers 20 or more Africans. Although slavery came early to Virginia, many years passed before slaves were numerous or the slave system's legal structure established.

Also in 1619, the Virginia Company of London tottered toward bankruptcy, and the leading planters in Virginia sought to shore up the company's government and to protect their own landholdings by organizing the House of Burgesses as an elected body to pass laws for the colony. Each elected representative was called a **burgess.**

In 1624 the king revoked the company's charter, ending the House of Burgesses, and the next year Virginia became a royal colony. The king's new charter provided a model that other colonies later adopted. The king appointed a royal governor, who ran the colony. A powerful figure, the governor named numerous officers, including judges. He was assisted by a council, which he appointed for life. The members of the council were invariably the wealthiest men in the colony.

After a brief period without an elected representative body, the House of Burgesses was revived in 1628. However, until the 1650s the burgesses and council met jointly. Landed property holders elected the burgesses, who tended to be wealthy. They were the colony's only elected officials. Laws had to be approved by the burgesses, the council, and the governor, whose veto was absolute.

Local government followed the English model, with the governor appointing Justices of the Peace. Exercising both judicial and executive power, they were usually the leading tobacco planters in each locality. The governor also named county sheriffs, although justices recommended the appointees.

From the beginning, the **Church of England** (Episcopal) was the official, tax-supported church in Virginia. The colony regularly recruited English-trained ministers throughout its history. Poor pay and Virginia's remote location, however, often left vacancies. All public officials were required to belong to the established church, and all residents had to attend services at least once a month. The ministers were efficient, however, and sermons never lasted more than 20 minutes. Exemption from attendance was granted to some colonists who belonged to other **Protestant** denominations, but as late as 1705 Virginia had only five dissenting churches.

Each church parish was governed by a body of men called the vestry. They managed church affairs, including welfare for the poor, which was a church rather than executive responsibility. Parish boundaries followed county lines. The gentlemen in the vestry formed a self-perpetuating body that filled its own vacancies. Drawn from the wealthiest and most politically powerful segments in society, vestrymen were often also Justices of the Peace.

Governor Sir William Berkeley's Virginia, 1642-1677

Believing that social order required hierarchy, Governor Sir William Berkeley from 1642 to 1677 sought to create an elitist society based on inequality. Land policy, in particular, favored the wealthy. White indentured servants provided labor. Many of them died before their terms of service had ended, and the survivors found only limited opportunities to own land.

In 1675-1676 these resentments, combined with the greed and ambition of Nathaniel Bacon, led to Bacon's Rebellion against Berkeley's authority. Bacon and his land-hungry followers demanded that Berkeley drive the Indians from the frontier in order to open more land for settlement, but the governor did not want an Indian war. In the end Bacon's Rebellion marked a turning point that left Virginia a stable, hierarchical society.

BERKELEY SHAPES VIRGINIA AS AN ELITIST SOCIETY. In 1642 Governor Sir William Berkeley arrived in Virginia. He remained as governor for most of the next 35 years. Berkeley, more than anyone else, nurtured the colony and shaped its destiny during its most crucial years.

From an ancient prominent and powerful family in England's west country, Berkeley had all the prejudices of his class and region. A sometime student at Oxford University, a soldier with a record for valor, and a passionate royalist during the English civil war of the 1640s, Berkeley brought strong convictions to Virginia.

First and foremost, he believed in **hierarchy.** He held that social and political order required a chain of hierarchical authority. God, Church, and King were at the top of his system. Being governor was only a little bit lower. Then came the **gentry,** followed by other free people and, on the bottom, indentured servants and slaves.

Those set high in the hierarchy not only had the right to wield power but also had responsibility for those below. In return for this patriarchal concern, inferiors owed duty and loyalty to their superiors. The lowly were expected to honor their betters constantly, to obey them cheerfully, and to show deference. One such sign of respect was for people to line up on Sunday to enter church according to social rank.

For Berkeley, his most important task in Virginia was to recreate English life, especially as he knew it in the west country. He designed laws to lure English gentlemen, or their younger sons, to Virginia. After the English Puritan leader Oliver Cromwell gained power and executed King Charles I in 1649, a number of English gentry did immigrate to the colony.

PRESERVING INEQUALITY. Virginia society was based on preserving and maintaining inequality. At the top the gentry, about 10 percent of the population, held 50 to 75 percent of the wealth, including much of the land, most white servants, and nearly all the **slaves.** Another 20 to 30 percent of the population were small-scale farmers who owned their own land and perhaps one or two white servants. The rest of the population included white tenant farmers, poor white laborers, white indentured servants, and black slaves.

As in England, Berkeley expected the gentry to be society's leaders. He did not believe in or practice equal opportunity. Rather, opportunity was gauged according to one's social standing at birth. These ideas enabled hierarchy to be established and order maintained in Virginia.

Berkeley once boasted that Virginia had neither schools nor a printing press. He believed both to be curses, since education and information might lead ordinary people to challenge elite rule and the hierarchical social order. The gentry enjoyed better education than the masses. They hired private tutors, and some sent their sons to Oxford University in England. The poor and middling classes remained unschooled. Even among the landowners, half could neither read nor write.

As Berkeley intended, over time the Virginia elite accumulated power and wealth. The leading several dozen families who arrived after 1660, with names such as Byrd, Carter, Harrison, Lee, Randolph, and Taylor, became known as the First Families of Virginia (the FFV, a phrase still used today to describe these families) and quickly married among themselves. In 1724 all 12 members of the governor's council were related. By 1775 every member was descended from at least one council member serving in 1660.

In the mid-1600s the gentry used their control of high office to enhance their position. This was especially true in the case of land grants. Members of the governor's council and the House of Burgesses regularly voted themselves large acreages from the colony's vast holdings. Back in England, King Charles I pursued a similar policy. In 1649 he gave 5 million acres to one man. This grant, covering five counties, eventually passed to Lord Fairfax, who became the wealthiest Virginian.

The elite protected their interests in other ways, too. Berkeley's government continued the headright system, which allowed anyone to claim 50 acres of land per English settler brought to Virginia. By enticing settlers and paying their passage, in return for a period of indentured servitude, the large planters not only gained labor but also free land. The servant, even at the completion of service, had no easy means to obtain land.

USING THE LABOR OF WHITE INDENTURED SERVANTS. During Berkeley's governorship the main source of labor on Virginia's tobacco plantations was white indentured servants. More than three-quarters were male, and most had migrated from southern and western England, where they had been tenant farmers. Only 25 percent could sign their names. Generally aged 15 to 24, few had **artisan** skills. Some had been kidnapped or were transported for petty crimes. Many were boys or teenagers from poor families. In exchange for the cost of the ocean voyage, they usually agreed to serve a master in Virginia for five to seven years. Of the English immigrants to Virginia in the 1600s, 75 percent came as indentured servants.

In the early years, climate, disease, hard work, and poor diet killed as many as 80 percent before they had been in Virginia a year. If they were lucky enough to have survived the "seasoning" and lasted to the end of their service, they became free men with doubtful prospects. They neither owned land nor had easy means to earn from their labor enough money to buy land.

In the 1630s and 1640s, when 60 percent of indentured servants lived out their term of service, about half of the survivors became landowners. Later, as land prices rose and tobacco prices fell, saving money to buy land became more difficult. A number, of course, moved to other colonies, where land was easier to acquire, and others settled on the frontier, where farms could be worked without formal ownership.

Many former indentured servants became **tenant farmers** renting from the great landowners, just as in the English west country. This is what Berkeley intended, but it did not please the tenants. They dared not complain, however. Deference required that poor people speak only with great respect about their betters. Loose talk by a poor man about a gentleman could bring 30 lashes for "contempt of authority."

Because three-quarters or more of the immigrants were male, their marriage prospects were poor. Land made a man more attractive to a woman seeking a husband. Some men did marry, but most marriages ended with the death of a spouse in less than ten years. Life expectancy was no more than 40 years.

The prospect for children was equally bleak. Of white children born in Virginia, half died before age 20. If a child survived, the parents probably did not. More than three-fourths of children lost at least one parent before the age of 18. Orphans, half-siblings, nieces, and nephews often lived in the same household, making the extended family important.

The contrast with New England is striking. During the 1600s three times as many people migrated from England to Virginia and Maryland as to New England. A milder climate, lucrative tobacco profits, and the ability to get a free passage as an indentured laborer favored these southern colonies. Yet in the year 1700 healthful New England, where nuclear families flourished, had a white population greater than that of the two southern colonies. An even larger number of English settlers had migrated to the West Indies, but the sugar cane growing islands proved even unhealthier than Virginia, and the population there remained small.

BACON REBELS AGAINST BERKELEY, 1675-1676. In the 1670s Governor Berkeley's elitist system increasingly came under attack. To avoid an expensive Indian war, the governor had restricted white settlement to areas near the seacoast. This policy not only sustained a lucrative Indian trade that the governor had developed for his personal profit, but it also helped speculators by driving up the price of farmland.

Berkeley's land policy irritated indentured servants, former servants, and even ambitious large planters who were not politically connected. In addition, the price of tobacco had dropped, and the poor economy, in which many people became burdened with debt, caused tempers to rise.

Finally, in late 1675 and early 1676 Berkeley ignored a series of battles fought along the frontier between Indians and whites. The settlers were led by Berkeley's second cousin, the ambitious Nathaniel Bacon, who had only recently arrived from England. The 29-year-old member of the governor's council was a hothead, and when Berkeley refused to attack the Indians, Bacon raised his own army.

In May 1676, Berkeley publicly declared Bacon a traitor. When Bacon arrived in Jamestown, he was arrested. Then, at a legislative session, the governor forced Bacon to beg pardon on bended knee. Deference being shown, pardon was granted.

Bacon returned home, raised an army of 500 men, and marched his soldiers, who included landless free whites, indentured servants, and some slaves, into Jamestown. He forced Berkeley to commission the troops to fight Indians. As soon as Bacon had left the capital, a furious governor declared Bacon to be a rebel. But Berkeley could rally no troops and fled.

Bacon marched his force to the frontier to attack the Indians and in September 1676, returned to Jamestown. After Berkeley and his supporters retreated, Bacon plundered and burned the capital city. By this time news of the rebellion had reached England, where an alarmed King Charles II had decided to treat Bacon and his accomplices as traitors.

The king sent a thousand royal troops to Virginia, but before they arrived, Bacon died suddenly, either of a fever or, as his supporters charged, by poisoning. Regaining power, Berkeley in 1677 nullified royal pardons for the rebels and executed 23 of Bacon's most prominent supporters. Then, recalled by the crown, the elderly and exhausted Berkeley set sail for England, where he died shortly after landing.

Bacon's Rebellion marked a turning point in the colony's history. Afterward, no Virginia officials defended Indians. Officials also promoted white settlement on the frontier. Opening more land drove down land prices, and the small-scale white farmer, whether formerly an indentured servant or not, was considered to be a positive element in Virginia society.

Hierarchy was preserved, however, as the great planters sought a reliable and docile kind of labor to replace unpredictable and unruly indentured servants.

The Great Planters Turn to Slavery

Africans who arrived in Virginia before the 1660s were not necessarily slaves, and the differences between black slaves and white indentured servants were blurred. By the 1670s Virginia had adopted a clear policy of race-based slavery, and large importations of slave labor replaced indentured servants.

From 1700 to 1760 great planters used the stability provided by a permanent, self-perpetuating, and naturally increasing slave labor force to gain and maintain enormous wealth, power, and social prestige. Planters put on showy displays of their wealth but also feared poor whites, slave revolts, and land hungry frontier settlers. The elite kept control because they had all the wealth and power, dominated the society's existing institutions, and admitted talented white newcomers to their ranks.

VIRGINIA ADOPTS SLAVERY, 1619-1750. Although the first blacks had been brought to Virginia in 1619, as late as 1670 black slaves were only 5 percent of the population. Even in 1700 slaves were only 20 percent. By 1750, however, slaves, mostly African-born, were more than 40 percent of Virginia's population.

In the early 1600s the words "slave" and "servant" were more or less interchangeable. White servants from England and black slaves from Africa were both sold to Virginia tobacco planters. English colonists in the West Indies had previously used both types of labor.

Differences, however, put the two kinds of servants on an unequal basis almost from the beginning. The English servants spoke the same language as the planters, deferred to them, conceived of themselves as free Englishmen no matter how temporarily degraded by service, came under English law that limited terms of service, and practiced Christianity.

In contrast, the Africans spoke no English, were disoriented by their forced removal from Africa, were sold for whatever terms the market dictated, and were considered heathens. Because they were not Christian, they did not have to be treated with Christian charity.

Remarkably, despite these disadvantages, some Africans who arrived in Virginia in the early 1600s managed to attain their freedom. They did so by having their service sold by traders to planters for a short term of years rather than for life. Or they converted to Christianity. In early Virginia a Christian could not lawfully be enslaved for life. Or they arranged with their masters to hire out their labor and use part of the proceeds to buy their freedom.

As late as the 1660s some free blacks had their own plantations. They bought land and worked it with bound labor. These black planters owned both white indentured servants and black slaves, brought lawsuits against whites, and testified against white planters in court.

AFRICAN SLAVERY BECOMES ROOTED IN VIRGINIA. As early as the 1640s, however, Virginia began to move from a society where the distinction was between free persons (mostly white) and unfree persons (whether white or black) to a society where whites were free and blacks were not. The colony established race-based slavery concretely by the 1670s.

Rising life expectancy for both whites and blacks may have played a role in the development of Virginia's particular slave system. The colony's elite feared that large numbers of white former indentured servants could destabilize the colony, and their numbers would grow ever larger if they continued to be imported, survived, married, and had children. In contrast, increased life expectancy for blacks made lifetime slaves a better investment for planters, and slave children promised a perpetual, growing labor supply.

Also important in the rise of slavery in Virginia was the growth of the international slave trade, including the chartering of the Royal African Company in 1672. Between 1600 and 1800, European traders regularly called at ports in West Africa and bought as many as 10 million slaves for shipment to the western hemisphere. During the horrifying Middle Passage, as the trip was called, people were packed so densely aboard ships that as many as one-sixth died.

Most slaves were destined for sugar plantations in Brazil and the West Indies. Because these plantations had to import food, they tried to hold down costs by using only highly productive adult male slaves, who died quickly and were replaced. In contrast, Virginia planters imported both men and women. Although only 4 percent of the Africans shipped to the western hemisphere were sent to North America, their descendants today outnumber the descendants of those sent to Brazil and the West Indies.

The most important reason for the new system, however, was white racism. Englishmen in Virginia believed that the white race was superior to all other races. This idea was not new. It could be traced through English and European history for centuries. To the English, both Christianity and their own high rates of literacy, scientific invention, military prowess, and commercial success proved superiority.

The relative disadvantage of Africans in Virginia also played a role in promoting the slave system. Lacking experience in living in an English society and without economic leverage, Africans were vulnerable to English exploitation. And they were exploited.

By the end of the 1600s few whites in England were willing to migrate to Virginia as indentured servants. The high death rates and the low chances to acquire land and become a planter were well-known in England. New colonies, such as Pennsylvania, offered better opportunities. In addition, the English economy had created more jobs at home.

For Virginia's great planters, African slaves proved a boon. Vast acreages could be worked by a stable, reliable, permanent workforce. This workforce would never become free and would never be able to seek land ownership. The children of slaves would be slaves. If slaves multiplied, as planters hoped and expected, then planters would grow ever richer. Virginia society would resemble English rural society, in which a permanent laboring class supported a landed aristocracy.

THE GREAT PLANTERS ESTABLISH DYNASTIES, 1700-1760. After 1700 the great Virginia planters acquired slaves in large numbers. The ruling elite, established by Governor William Berkeley's land policies, now sustained itself with a permanent labor force to work that land. The result was that the elite became permanent and self-perpetuating. And as the profits from slave-worked tobacco land increased, with larger acreages being worked, the planters bought more slaves and worked yet more land.

As late as 1700 the wealthiest planters in Virginia had owned only a few slaves. Very, very few people owned more than 20 slaves. Plantations were small in scale, and profits were low. Ordinary planters lived in one- or two-room wooden houses, and even wealthy planters had only four- or six-room pine clapboard homes. When planters died, they left remarkably few personal possessions — in some cases only an iron skillet and an iron cooking pot. Even wealthy planters lacked china dishes or silverware. Furniture of local woods such as pine or cherry was crudely made on or near the premises.

By 1750 much had changed. The wealthiest planters often owned hundreds of slaves and worked several large plantations in various parts of the colony. Profits could be enormous, although the lifestyle of a great planter often led to debt. While ordinary planters continued to live in one- or two-room houses, the great planters were beginning to build the mansions that we associate with the South. Houses such as George Washington's Mount Vernon, beautifully situated overlooking the Potomac River, were designed less for comfort than to show off a family's wealth. Washington's house was built of local wood, but the wood was carved so that from a distance it looked like stone.

Planters furnished their new homes with fine mahogany furniture, which was often imported. They ate from the finest English china with silver knives, spoons, and forks. The three-pronged fork for eating was a recent innovation. House servants cooked increasingly elaborate meals and polished the family silver.

Planters' wives held an ambivalent rank. On the one hand, the mistress of the household instructed servants, supervised children, and doctored everyone. She had authority, but her authority was entirely derived from her husband, whom both law and custom required her to obey. To him, she must show the deference due to a superior being. Like her poorer sisters, she was often bearing and burying children.

PLANTERS INTRODUCE FREEWHEELING LIFESTYLES. Great planters displayed their wealth in order to maintain their social and political status. They bestowed alms upon the poor, entertained lavishly, and continued the old English west country custom of keeping an open house. Any respectable traveler could get food and lodging without charge. Some poor gentlemen lived by traveling from house to house.

Planters drank freely. When William Byrd II was a member of the governor's council in the early 1700s, the council frequently got drunk. Sometimes members collapsed under the council table. Virginia gentlemen chased women, both white and black. They forced themselves on servants or slaves without feeling guilt.

They were also notorious gamblers. Horseraces, in particular, both provided entertainment and reinforced the gentry's high status. The races were usually between two horses ridden by their owners for a quarter mile on a dirt track. They often raced after church on Sunday, frequently on a dare, and without preparation. It was illegal for poor people to race horses or to bet on a horse race. In Virginia a man could sue to collect a gaming debt in court.

Ostentacious public display and gambling led many planters to live beyond their means. Foxhunting and hosting lavish dancing balls could also be expensive forms of recreation. Although outwardly successful through ownership of land and slaves, a planter could easily squander his income.

Planters often had a cosmopolitan outlook. They kept in touch with the larger world through conversations with the captains whose ships landed at the plantation dock. Most of the comforts of life and the goods that defined high social status came from England. The ships that picked up the tobacco and hauled it to England for sale also brought English goods, especially fancy cloth and household articles, including books. For example, when George Washington married Martha Custis, he found it necessary to order a long list of imported items for the occasion.

A planter usually ordered goods through his tobacco factor, that is, the person in England who sold the tobacco for the planter's account. Factors sold goods to planters on credit and reimbursed themselves out of the following year's tobacco sales. As a result, many planters owed large debts to their English factors.

PLANTERS FEAR CHALLENGERS. Great planters maintained an uneasy hold on Virginia society. The immigration of white indentured servants in the 1600s had led to a substantial population of small-scale white farmers. Although some of these farmers acquired land, others were tenants. In 1676, 25 percent of free whites were landless. Ignorant and poor, they posed a threat to the gentry's rule. The elite, however, controlled Virginia through a combination of deference by poor whites and a growing emphasis upon white racial solidarity.

As Virginia's slave population grew, the great planters became afraid of slave revolts. In parts of the Tidewater region, nearest to Chesapeake Bay, slaves were more than 60 percent of the population. The colony passed laws to prevent slaves from owning guns, from congregating in groups, from moving freely about the country, or from learning to read, and slaveowners were discouraged from freeing slaves.

A third threat to planter rule came from the Virginia frontier. By the mid-1700s that region had developed its own culture. Although the great planters owned large tracts, the frontier was settled primarily by non-slaveholding white farmers, some of whom were **squatters** rather than owners. Many came from the Tidewater area, but others were Scots-Irish or German settlers who had drifted down the Great Valley of the Shenandoah River from Pennsylvania.

Frontier culture was both more **egalitarian** than that in the Tidewater region and ethnically mixed. The area was also unstable. During any five-year period, 40 percent of all households moved. The English institutions that had been strong in the Tidewater, especially the Church of England, did not take root. Indeed, most frontier parishes lacked ministers, and dissenting Protestants, such as Scots Presbyterians and German Lutherans, were allowed to form their own congregations apart from the Church of England.

PLANTERS KEEP CONTROL. Yet the great planters did keep control of Virginia. They did so because they held most of the society's wealth and power. They had the time and resources to serve in government office. Elections to the House of Burgesses, for example, depended upon the custom of treating the voters with liquor. It was costly to seek public office, and only the wealthy could afford to run. To save money, George Washington once ran without treating. He lost. He learned his lesson and at a later election in 1758 provided each voter with a half gallon of liquor — and won.

The gentry were flexible enough to admit newcomers into their ranks, particularly by marrying daughters to promising, ambitious young men. Yet they insisted on dominating all the institutions of society, and went unchallenged because there were no other organized centers of power. This Virginia gentry produced ten presidents: Washington, Jefferson, Madison, Monroe, both Harrisons, Tyler, and through remote lesser branches, Taylor, Truman, and Carter.

Although the Virginians hated cities and built none, in 1699 they did relocate their colony's capital from Jamestown to a healthier place, Williamsburg. The new town, which had under a thousand residents, was carefully planned to reflect planter values. The public buildings were built of brick. The dominant one was the Governor's Palace, not the Capitol. Also important were Bruton Parish Church and the College of William and Mary, which had been founded in 1693. The broad, straight, empty streets were dotted with small wooden houses and a few taverns and inns that came to life when the fun-loving legislature was in session. Otherwise, the oaks, pines, squirrels, and songbirds of a peaceful rural setting prevailed.

From the beginning, Virginia had been founded upon greed. To this lust for wealth, the great planters had added an emphasis upon politeness. In an often raw frontier society, the elite's good manners had been perhaps the only way to hold the society together. These two traits, greed and politeness, became the hallmarks of southern culture. They did not preclude the exploitation of slavery.

Founding the Other Southern Colonies

With only minor variations, Virginia provided the model for the other southern colonies. Tobacco-growing Maryland, started in 1632, resembled Virginia most closely, but its small size discouraged land speculation, and its religious diversity contrasted with Virginia's uniformity. South Carolina, chartered in 1663, depended from the beginning upon slaves to grow rice. North Carolina, split off from South Carolina in 1729, had fewer plantations and more small farms. Georgia, founded in 1732 as the last colony, at first restricted land ownership and barred slavery and rum, but these policies failed.

MARYLAND, 1632-1750. In 1632 Cecilius Calvert, Lord Baltimore, received a royal charter from King Charles I to establish the colony of Maryland. This was the first **proprietary colony** placed entirely under the control of a single person. The owner or proprietor, Lord Baltimore, was Catholic, and he established his colony as a refuge for Catholics seeking a haven from the religious turmoil then engulfing England.

Although many original settlers at St. Mary's City were Catholic, Maryland soon lost its Catholic character as Protestants, including Scots-Irish Presbyterians and German Lutherans, flooded into the colony. A handful of wealthy Catholic families, however, continued to exert influence.

Map 2.1. American Seaboard Colonies

In 1649 the colony passed the Toleration Act, which allowed all Christians to practice their religion freely. Five years later the Protestants, feeling protected by Oliver Cromwell's **Puritan** government in England, repealed the act. In 1658 Lord Baltimore restored a policy of toleration, but religious strife continued.

Like Virginia, Maryland produced tobacco, and it, too, contained great planters, African slaves, English indentured servants, and small farms owned and operated by former servants. Maryland imported large numbers of slaves even before Virginia did.

Maryland also adopted the headright system that gave 50 acres to each settler for a settler's family member or servant. The colony, however, provided free land to servants after they had completed their service. The result was more small farms than in Virginia.

Because of Lord Baltimore's lesser political influence as well as his religious views, Maryland's boundaries were restricted. The colony was too small in area to support the vast land speculations found in Virginia. And because Maryland sprawled across both sides of Chesapeake Bay, with access to both Virginia and interior Pennsylvania as well as the Atlantic Ocean, the colony early gained commercial importance beyond its size.

Maryland's religious and ethnic diversity made it more like a middle colony, such as Pennsylvania, but its cultivation of tobacco and the widespread use of slave labor on large plantations rooted Maryland in the South. It had long, stormy disputes with Virginia. The Virginians looked down upon Marylanders as latecomers who lived in a place puny in size and inferior in status.

SOUTH CAROLINA, 1663-1750. In 1663 King Charles II, who had gained the throne after the collapse of England's Puritan government in 1660, granted eight wealthy supporters, called the lord proprietors, the right to colonize Carolina, named to honor the king. (The colony originally included both North and South Carolina.)

Carolina was planned both to protect Virginia from Spanish movement northward from Florida and to add a distinctive semitropical agricultural area to the ever-expanding English empire. The philosopher John Locke helped write a bizarre, aristocratic constitution for the colony. The proprietors and settlers ignored most of its provisions, including plans for a titled nobility.

In 1670 settlers arrived near the site of Charles Town (now Charleston). Many great planters came from the English West Indian island of Barbados, where African slaves cultivated sugar at great profit. After a brief period raising grain and cattle to sell to the food-short West Indies, the planters turned the hot, humid swamps along the southern Carolina seacoast into rice plantations. Slaves brought the knowledge of how to grow rice. Later, Carolinians grew indigo, a plant used to produce a blue vegetable dye.

The planters did not debate about where to get labor. The climate in South Carolina was brutal. The English and other Europeans died from malaria and other fevers that did not affect local Indians or Africans, who had gained immunities in Africa. From the beginning, the planters ignored white indentured servants and depended exclusively upon slave labor, both Indian and African.

In the early years local Indian slaves worked the plantations. However, they often ran away, and the planters then undertook a different scheme. They purchased Indian slaves from friendly tribes and sold them to the West Indies in exchange for African slaves. The colony's population became mixed. In 1708 there were 5,300 whites, 2,900 black slaves, and 1,400 Indian slaves.

As the English encroached on Indian lands, tensions grew. Finally, in 1715 many of the local tribes revolted. The Carolinians, with support from the Cherokee, defeated the Yamasees and the Creeks. In terms of the white casualty rate, the Yamasee War was the deadliest Indian war in colonial America. Of 6,000 whites, 400 died. At the end of the Yamasee War, the English in Carolina embarked on a long-term policy of pushing the Indians west and destroying any Indians who remained behind.

From the failure of Indian slavery until just before the American Revolution, a majority of South Carolina's population was black. In many coastal rice-growing areas, the African population exceeded 90 percent. Planters were afraid of slave revolts. In the Stono Rebellion in 1739 a hundred slaves killed several whites and then marched toward Spanish Florida. They were defeated in battle by the white South Carolina militia allied with Indians.

During the malaria season, wealthy planter families fled their plantations and moved to the one healthy spot, Charles Town. Protected from malaria-breeding mosquitoes due to the steady flow of water in its two major rivers, Charles Town developed into a populous outpost of English culture and civilization. By 1750 its 8,000 people made it the only major town in the South, a center of urban culture with many accomplished white and black artisans, especially furnituremakers.

NORTH CAROLINA, 1729-1771. The northern portion of Carolina had a different climate and soil from the area around Charleston. It was also geographically isolated. Finally, in 1729 disputes among powerful land speculators forced Carolina to be split into two colonies. North Carolina developed slowly. It lacked good ocean transportation due to the storms off Cape Hatteras and the barrier islands that prevented ships from reaching the mainland. Furthermore, its coastal areas were largely too swampy to be habitable.

Virginia tobacco planters settled the extreme northeastern portion of the colony on Albemarle Sound as early as 1653. Access to good land on ocean-going sea routes attracted these settlers. Some also went to North Carolina to escape legal problems. They long controlled North Carolina. South Carolinians settled along the South Carolina border. North Carolina, it was said with reference to its two neighbors, was a valley of humility between two conceits.

North Carolina did not prosper until settlement reached the fertile interior. Scots-Irish and Germans came down from Pennsylvania through Virginia's Great Valley. They were not slaveholders, and because North Carolina lacked numerous large plantations along its swampy coast, the colony always had a greater proportion of small-scale white farmers than its neighbors.

The Quakers who settled Greensboro brought commercial skills. In 1753 German Moravians from Bethlehem, Pennsylvania, founded Salem (now Winston-Salem). These highly skilled craftsmen worked iron, wood, and leather and developed an important pottery industry. They also opened the first bank in the South.

For many years these westerners were dominated by the colony's eastern planters. Friction grew, but the planters kept control. They continually moved the colony's capital in search of a locale that had good water. Finally, the capital was fixed at New Bern, which had been founded by Baron de Graffenried as a German-Swiss colony in 1710. New Bern was an oceangoing seaport, even though it was 100 miles from the Atlantic.

In 1767 the royal governor, William Tryon, built a palace at New Bern. Tryon's Palace was conceived both as a governor's mansion, similar to the one in Williamsburg, Virginia, and as a capitol building. Although Tryon provided a chamber for the governor's council, he did not include a meeting room large enough to hold the colonial legislature. The alarmed planters took this as a sign that the governor intended to rule without a legislature.

Tryon imposed a special property tax to pay for the palace. The tax had to be paid in gold or silver, and frontier farmers lacked cash. They grew furious and in 1771, after years of east-west tension, revolted. Although Tryon used eastern militia troops to crush the Regulators, as they were called, many western North Carolinians had no further use for royal government. During the American Revolution the governor fled from the palace to a warship. Tryon's Palace was so hated that the new state legislature refused to use it, and in 1798, unmourned, it burned to the ground.

GEORGIA, 1732–1749. Georgia, the last of the original 13 colonies, was founded in 1732. General James Oglethorpe, an English reformer, obtained a charter to establish a colony for England's poor, including those in prison for debt, which was then a crime. The British government was willing to grant such a charter in order to beat the Spanish (or others) to settlement of the area.

To make the colony a success, Oglethorpe adopted several unique policies. First, all settlers, including the poor, were granted 50 acres apiece. Second, there were no large land grants. Instead, actual settlers could own a maximum of 500 acres. These policies encouraged widespread land ownership and retarded the establishment of the kind of elite that dominated Virginia and South Carolina.

Third, there were no slaves. Slaves, Oglethorpe believed, degraded the value of labor, forced poor whites to compete with slaves, and created an idle slaveholding elite. Fourth, rum was banned, since alcohol caused much poverty.

Oglethorpe built military fortifications at the mouth of the Savannah River and laid out Savannah as a planned city with handsome public squares. Lots were large so homeowners could plant vegetable gardens and keep chickens.

Little came of Oglethorpe's plans, except for the migration to Georgia of a sizeable number of paupers and debtors, who did gain access to land. Rum came in 1742. South Carolina planters began to move into Georgia. They defied the law and brought their slaves. When challenged, they said that the climate required slave labor. Slavery became legal in 1749.

Although great planters dependent upon slave labor quickly gained control of Georgia, the colony did retain two features from its early days. Its white population formed a higher percentage than in South Carolina, which through most of the colonial period had a black majority, and Oglethorpe's land policy did enable many small-scale farmers to own land. Originally granted a 20-year charter, Oglethorpe considered the experiment a failure and returned the colony to royal control before the time expired.

Conclusion

Founding a colony was difficult and dangerous. To succeed, a colony had to have a reason to exist that attracted settlers. Virginia found its purpose in raising tobacco for the overseas market. Growing tobacco required land, which was plentiful in Virginia once the native inhabitants were pushed aside, and labor, which shifted over time from white indentured servants to black slaves. The planters who made the crucial decisions, including land policy, aggrandized acreage, wealth, and power to themselves.

After Bacon's Rebellion, when Virginia's rulers saw that poor whites might threaten their power, planters quickly turned to race-based African slavery. They used the slave system to dominate society both by combining control of land and labor and by rallying poor whites through white supremacy. Elite power, slavery, racism, and cash crops became the hallmark of all the southern colonies.

Recommended Readings

DOCUMENTS: William Byrd II, *The Secret Diary, 1709-1712* (1941); Landon Carter, *Diary, 1752-1778* (2 vols., 1965).

READINGS: (VIRGINIA) T.H. Breen, *Puritans and Adventurers* (1980), *Tobacco Culture* (1985), and with Stephen Innes, *Myne Owne Ground* (1980); A. Roger Ekirch, *Bound for America* (1989); David Galenson, *White Servitude in Colonial America* (1981); Ivor N. Hume, *Martin's Hundred* (1982); Rhys Isaac, *The Transformation of Virginia* (1982); Edmund S. Morgan, *American Slavery, American Freedom* (1975); Darrett B. and Anita H. Rutman, *A Place in Time* (2 vols., 1984); Daniel B. Smith, *Inside the Great House* (1980); Mechal Sobel, *The World They Made Together* (1987); Bertram Wyatt-Brown, *Southern Honor* (1982); (SLAVERY) Philip D. Curtin, *The Atlantic Slave Trade* (1969); Winthrop Jordan, *White over Black* (1968); Gerald W. Mullin, *Flight and Rebellion* (1972); (MARYLAND) Lois G. Carr, et al., *Colonial Chesapeake Society* (1989); Paul G.E. Clemens, *The Atlantic Economy and Colonial Maryland's Eastern Shore* (1980); Allan Kulikoff, *Tobacco and Slaves* (1986); Gloria Main, *Tobacco Colony* (1982); Thad Tate and David Ammerman, eds., *The Chesapeake in the Seventeenth Century* (1979); (SOUTH CAROLINA) David C. Littlefield, *Rice and Slaves* (1981); Peter H. Wood, *Black Majority* (1975).

3

———— ✖ ————

RELIGIOUS NEW ENGLAND,
1620-1760

CHAPTER OVERVIEW: The Pilgrims rejected the Church of England and settled at Plymouth, in what is now Massachusetts, in 1620. At the time England's rising middle classes demanded religious reform, and between 1630 and 1642 many reformers, called Puritans, moved to Massachusetts. Puritan society revolved around the church and its theology. After 1660 religion declined, Massachusetts and English officials quarreled, and 1692 brought the Salem witch trials. By 1700 commerce flourished, and religion revived with the Great Awakening in the 1730s-1740s.

The Pilgrims Found Plymouth Colony, 1620

In 1620 the Pilgrims settled at Plymouth, Massachusetts. They were Protestant religious zealots who considered the Church of England hopelessly corrupt and demanded the right, against government opposition, to worship in their own way.

THE PILGRIMS MOVE TO PLYMOUTH, 1620. As early as 1602, Englishmen had fished off the northeastern shore of North America. They sometimes traded with the local Indians and in the process transmitted diseases. As a result, before 1620 most of the native inhabitants had died in a series of epidemics. Indian villages had been abandoned after being depopulated so rapidly that the dead remained where they fell. In a few years cornfields were covered with scrubby brush. Many Englishmen concluded that God had killed the heathen Indians to enable the Christian English to replant the fields. It was all part of God's plan.

In 1620 English settlers sailed on the *Mayflower* to plant the first colony at Plymouth in what is today southeastern Massachusetts. While still on board the 41 colonists signed the Mayflower Compact. This agreement provided the colony with a government, which soon came under William Bradford's leadership.

The colony barely survived and did not prosper. Summers were warmer than in England, and winters far more severe. Almost half the colonists died in the first year. They avoided starvation only by obtaining food from nearby friendly Indians. Squanto, the last surviving member of a local tribe, taught the English settlers how to plant corn. He fertilized each cornhill with a fish, a technique which the English thought to be Indian, but which Squanto had learned earlier while living in England.

RELIGION LEADS THE PILGRIMS TO NEW ENGLAND. The Plymouth colonists called themselves **Pilgrims.** They had moved to New England because of their religion. In truth, they were fanatics. At that time in England, as in other Christian countries, the government controlled religion and required people to participate in the state-run church.

Beginning in the late 1500s, the Pilgrims thought the **Church of England** impure and corrupt. They disliked its leaders, its practices, and its principles. Rejecting bishops, they demanded both local control by each congregation and less ceremony in church services. They rejected the state church and became separatists.

These fundamentalists thought icons, stained glass windows, and church music evil. Opposed to all practices not found in the Bible, they wanted **communion** to be taken at a plain table and not at an altar covered with a fancy cloth. Ministers ought to wear ordinary clothes and preach long, powerful sermons using the Bible as the text.

Nor were these dissenters silent. Because of their outspoken opposition to the state church, they came under suspicion of treason. The government told them to shut up and worship like everyone else. Instead, some went underground, and in 1608 a number moved to Holland, where the government tolerated them. After 12 years, they found the Dutch grating, and their own children began to lose English ways. In 1620 they decided to resettle in North America.

For ten years this tiny colony existed but barely grew. No new immigrants followed, except for some nonreligious settlers who set up Indian trading posts and fishing villages along the New England coast. The most famous of these settlements was Thomas Morton's Ma-re Mount, founded in what is now Boston in 1627. In the eyes of the Pilgrims, it was devoted to drinking, gambling, and whoring. Worse, Morton traded guns to the Indians. The Pilgrims raided Ma-re Mount and shipped Morton to England.

England in 1620

In 1620 England was beginning to become modern but retained many traditional ways, including a rigid class structure in rural areas. Many members of the rising middle classes demanded change, including reform of the Church of England. Because they wanted to purify the church, these reformers called themselves Puritans.

MAINTAINING THE POLITICAL AND CLASS STRUCTURE. In 1620 England was becoming what we would recognize as a modern country. But ties to olden times were still strong. For example, an elderly person, born in 1550, might remember a grandparent born in 1480. In 1480 England had an overwhelmingly rural populace, numerous Catholic monasteries and feudal rules, no printing presses, little influence in Europe, and a weak government racked by civil war.

During the 1500s royal government was strengthened. Henry VIII (reigning 1509-1547) had declared the country **Protestant,** abolished monasteries, and confiscated the church lands. His daughter Elizabeth I (r. 1558-1603) had defeated Spain's Armada, sent explorers to North America, and provided for uniting the crowns of England and Scotland under her successor, James I (r. 1603-1625). The King James Bible had been published in 1611, printing had flourished, and commercial towns had thrived, especially in East Anglia, the area to the northeast of London. The capital teemed with nearly half a million people.

Despite these changes, England retained many old ways in the early 1600s. Social classes remained rigid, and people generally were born, lived, and died in the same class. At the top was the king and the royal family. Just below were 16,500 high-ranking noble or **gentry** families who owned most of the real estate. Another 85,000 farmers, called **yeomen,** owned their own land.

The remaining one million families included prosperous, nonlandholding craftsmen, farm tenants, farm laborers, servants, and the unemployed. About one-quarter of the five million people could find work only during planting and harvest seasons. Thousands of beggars strolled along the roads.

Although ten percent of the people lived in London and many others in thriving commercial distribution centers called market towns, about three-fourths of the people resided in traditional agricultural villages. English farmers rarely worked individual farms. Rather, from 500 to 1500 people lived together in a village, and each day residents walked to surrounding fields to labor. People rarely moved away and often became related through marriage.

Usually, the entire village with its fields was owned by one person, and this property was called a manor. Most villages had a manor house, where the owner, the lord of the manor, lived and actively managed its affairs. This static, traditional society was undergoing stresses and strains. For one thing, landowners in some areas were beginning to fence in traditional open fields where villagers had herded cows and gathered firewood. This policy of enclosure drove down rural living standards and led to emigration.

Life expectancy was only about 35 years, and two-thirds of all children died before the age of four. Nevertheless, high birth rates matched high death rates, and the population grew steadily. Increased population was difficult to absorb in a society with a rigid class structure, which provided rural residents few new opportunities. People saw England as overpopulated and looked to emigrate.

THE MIDDLE CLASSES RISE. England, however, was richer than many European countries. Although this wealth was highly concentrated, it did stimulate both crafts production and trade. The English wrought iron and wove woolen cloth. They also built ships, filled them with woolens, and sailed to trade with the world. Crafts and commerce encouraged the growth of market towns, especially in East Anglia, which became densely populated. London, too, thrived. Commercial prosperity, in turn, produced work for lawyers, bankers, and accountants.

Many people in these new commercial classes found that they did not fit into the old social system. They owned no land, and their business did not require land, but without land the new middle classes lacked social status or political power. They formed a restless, rootless part of the society.

REFORMING THE CHURCH OF ENGLAND. If the Church of England had not been a state-controlled church dominated by lords of the village manors, perhaps the members of rising new classes might have expressed their discontent in other ways. But the elite used the church to maintain the rigid social structure. Village lords picked the ministers, whose main purpose often was to defend the lord's power. In other cases, a lord's younger son became the village minister, and religious taxes became yet another means to support the landlord's family.

Like other restless groups in other times and places, many people from the new middle classes turned to religion. But the traditional Church of England, which stressed preserving old ways, including the power of village lords, did not meet their needs. In the late 1500s and early 1600s, however, an occasional minister broke with tradition and captured the middle-class imagination by preaching long, inspirational sermons based closely upon the Bible. The Bible, now easily available from the new printing presses, was the key to this movement.

A movement for reform grew inside the Church of England. These reformers called themselves **Puritans,** because they said that, unlike the Pilgrims, they did not wish to separate from the church. Rather, they wished to reform the church by purifying its corrupt, worldly, and ungodly aspects.

As late as the 1620s the Puritans felt optimistic. In many English towns, especially in East Anglia, prosperous middle-class residents had used their new wealth to install Puritan preachers in public lectureships. A number of Puritan lords of the manor had appointed reformers as ministers in their churches. Cambridge University had become a Puritan stronghold, and Puritans could be found in high office in London or among the Church of England's bishops.

Puritanism produced a backlash, however, and — unfortunately for the reformers — the opposition's leader was King Charles I (r. 1625-1649). The king understood keenly the danger of Puritanism. If congregations ran the church from the bottom up rather than the king's bishops from the top down, it would not be long before these same people, in the king's view, challenged the king's divine right to rule.

In 1629 the king dismissed **Parliament,** where support for Puritanism was strong, and ruled alone. Four years later he appointed William Laud as the Archbishop of Canterbury, the head of the Church of England. Laud aggressively purged Puritan ministers from the church.

In the short run this campaign succeeded, but Laud's zeal, together with financial problems that forced Charles I to recall Parliament, led to a growing dispute between Charles I and Parliament over royal power and taxes that produced a civil war between the king and Parliament in the 1640s. The Puritans, under General Oliver Cromwell (r. 1653-1658), won the war, executing Laud in 1645 and Charles I in 1649.

The Puritans Found Massachusetts Bay Colony, 1629-1642

In 1629 the Puritans received a charter for the Massachusetts Bay Company. From 1630 to 1642 as many as 21,000 colonists migrated to Massachusetts, establishing America's first self-governing colony. Drawn largely from the middle classes, the Puritans stressed education. They recreated English ways, including living in villages with outlying fields, a system that discouraged land speculation. Life expectancy was long, and families large. The Puritans comprised the largest single group of Europeans to immigrate to America and exercised more influence on America's development than any other single group.

MASSACHUSETTS BAY COMPANY GETS A CHARTER, 1629. In 1629, as the atmosphere in England began to turn nasty for the Puritans, a number of middle-class religious reformers used political connections to obtain a royal charter for a private joint-stock company to acquire land and trading rights in Massachusetts. The Massachusetts Bay Company's planners selected Massachusetts as a place for settlement because of Indian depopulation and because the area lacked valuable resources that would attract rivals.

The English government saw the Massachusetts Bay Company as a way to claim land in North America that might otherwise fall to the French, the Dutch, or the Spanish. The colony also promised to remove from England a set of well-known, powerful troublemakers.

The **charter** had one curious feature. It did not specify the location of the company's annual meeting. The corporate colony's founders took the charter to Massachusetts and declared that the colonists themselves would meet to select the company's officers. Voters chose both the governor and legislators in annual elections. Thus, the colony became self-governing from the beginning, and later attempts to force the company to surrender its charter were hampered by the fact that the charter was physically in Massachusetts. Under English law actual possession of the physical document guaranteed the holder the rights stated in that document. Courts were reluctant to overturn a charter unless it was produced in court.

THE GREAT MIGRATION, 1630-1642. The Puritan move to Massachusetts in 1630 was the largest single European migration to the New World. More than a thousand settlers arrived in 17 ships. The colonists came mostly in family groups with many women and children, and even a few elderly people. The flow that started in 1630 continued through 1642, by which time 21,000 people had arrived in the area around Boston. Because of the civil war in England, few Puritans migrated after 1642.

These family-oriented immigrants began to reproduce in large numbers. The population doubled every generation, and today more than 16 million Americans can trace their ancestry to the great migration of the 1630s. They include 16 presidents: both Adamses, Fillmore, Pierce, Lincoln, Grant, Hayes, Garfield, Arthur, Cleveland, Benjamin Harrison, Taft, Harding, Coolidge, Franklin Roosevelt, and Bush. In terms of the effect upon the development of American society, this one group played a larger role than any other single immigrant group in American history.

THE PURITANS EMPHASIZE EDUCATION. The Puritans were drawn particularly from England's middle classes. Almost no **titled nobility** immigrated, and most of the gentry who came soon left. On the other hand, the Puritans barred the poor, drifters, laborers, and servants, except for those of a religious temperament with long service in a Puritan family. No indentured servants were sent to New England.

At the high end, the Puritans included some English landowners, essentially yeomen; a few men of greater prominence, like the longtime governor, John Winthrop, whose family had controlled a lesser English manor; and 90 well-educated ministers. At the low end, a majority of Puritans had been town-dwelling craftsmen; in New England most of these mechanics gave up their trades for agriculture. Other settlers were farmers who had leased but did not own land in England.

They were remarkably well educated. Two-thirds of the adult males could sign their names. This was twice the rate among Englishmen. Because the Puritans associated education with religion, and particularly with Bible-reading, they quickly established public schools for both boys and girls. In 1647 Massachusetts required every town with at least 50 families to levy taxes to maintain public schools. (Many towns, however, ignored the law.) School books reflected Puritan values. The widely used *New England Primer* opened with the line: "In Adam's Fall, We Sinned all."

One in every 40 family heads was a college graduate. This was a far higher proportion than in England. No other colony ever began with so many educated people. To maintain this level of learning, Harvard College was chartered in 1636 and opened in Cambridge, Massachusetts, two years later. Instruction was in Latin, and the students — all males — were required to study Hebrew, Greek, and theology. Half of the graduates became ministers.

In 1640 the Puritans established the first printing press at Harvard College, publishing sermons, catechism books, and school primers. It remained the only press in English North America until 1675, when a second printer set up in Boston.

RECREATING OLD WAYS OF LIFE. The settlers were disproportionately from East Anglia. A part of England settled by Danes centuries before, the region's dense population and thriving market towns had combined agriculture with the weaving of woolens. East Anglians conducted a busy trade with

John Winthrop, the long-time governor of the Massachusetts colony. Earnest and serious, he holds the gloves of a gentleman. (CULVER PICTURES)

Holland, and the area had long been noted for religious dissent and rebellion against authority.

East Anglians built wooden saltbox houses, that is, boxy houses with two stories in the front and one in the back covered by a steep-pitched roof with a long rear slope, and so did the colonists. Like the Dutch, the East Anglians preferred to cook by baking, a tradition they carried across the ocean. Pies had been invented in East Anglia, where they were filled with meat. New Englanders filled their pies with fruit.

The Puritans replicated East Anglian life in many ways, but there were differences, including New England's severe winters and strange local foods, such as corn and pumpkins. Other differences included the absence of manor houses, less rigid social classes, and abundant land for new farms. Those who felt constrained by their neighbors could join with a handful of others and create a new town in the wilderness.

The colony's officials granted land not to individuals but to groups of settlers in the form of a town. Settlers often came as a single congregation from England. The town, the basic unit of organization, then deeded property to individuals according to their needs and abilities as farmers. This system discouraged land **speculation**. Towns governed themselves through annual town meetings.

Following the model for English villages, residents lived in a concentrated fashion. Each family was given a lot on the common near the meeting house for a house and garden, as well as several agricultural fields on the village's outskirts. Towns preserved pastures and woodlands for shared use and retained generous acreage for anticipated population growth.

THE PURITANS ENJOY LONG LIFE AND LARGE FAMILIES. New England turned out to be far healthier than England. The soil probably had more nutrients, at least in the early years, and low population density discouraged contagious diseases. Severe winters killed more microbes than people. Few children died, and a majority of adults who reached age 20 survived to 60.

Of those who came in the Great Migration, the average lifespan reached 70; one-fifth attained 80. This was double the life expectancy in Virginia. New England may have been the first society where it was normal to have living grandparents.

Puritan life revolved around families. Practically everyone married, and it was illegal to live alone. Divorce was rare but possible. Men headed households, but women enjoyed a higher status than in England. For example, in contrast with England, wifebeating was a crime. The typical family had seven or eight children. Families consciously replicated themselves: 75 percent of first-born children were given the name of a parent.

The state closely watched family life. Couples who produced a child born less than seven months after marriage were fined or whipped. A woman who gave birth out of wedlock was pressured during delivery by the midwife to name the father. Courts usually accepted the answer, especially if the man named was able to provide child support. Adultery was a capital crime, but only one double execution took place, because juries declined to convict.

Puritan Life Revolves around Religion

Religion was the key to Puritan society. These newcomers restricted church membership and embraced a complex theology
that balanced faith and works and stressed the conversion experience. Rejecting tolerance, Puritans banished dissenters such as
Roger Williams and Anne Hutchinson. Dissidents sometimes
founded new colonies, such as Connecticut. Thus, Puritan beliefs were largely responsible for the spread of colonies around
New England.

ESTABLISHING A SOCIETY BASED ON RELIGION. For the Puritans,
religion was the key to life. All questions, big and small, had to be answered
with reference to the Bible, to the church, to the minister, and to prayer. The
colonists put the church at the center, and yet they did not create a **theocracy,**
that is, a church-run government. Instead, their churches and their government operated along parallel, complementary tracks.

In England the Puritans claimed that they merely wanted to reform the
corrupt state-controlled Church of England. Once in Massachusetts, however, they created churches that resembled those of the separatist Pilgrims in
Plymouth. Indeed, Massachusetts absorbed the Plymouth colony in 1691.

Most important was the concept of congregational church government,
that is, the members of each individual congregation selected their own minister. There were no bishops, and power flowed from the bottom up, not from
the top down.

This democratic tendency was restrained in two ways. First, not everyone
could be a church member, although everyone was expected to attend services. The right to membership had to be earned through religious devotion.
Second, the ministers of the colony met collectively from time to time and
monitored each other's behavior. It was difficult for a congregation to select a
minister not generally approved by all the colony's ministers.

The church was separated from, but connected to, the government. For
example, the Puritans legally prohibited celebrations of Christmas or Easter as
pagan. Government officials, not ministers, performed marriages, which took
place in public buildings rather than in churches. As in England, taxpayers
supported the churches. All local residents paid for the services of a minister,
whose income ranked high in most towns.

Dissent was not tolerated. There was no freedom of religion. During the
1600s the government ordered persons who did not wish to practice Puritan-

ism to conform or leave. People who were banished and returned to the colony ran the risk of being executed. In 1656 four Quakers, members of a radical Protestant sect that later settled Pennsylvania, were hanged.

MAKING RULES FOR CHURCH SERVICES AND MEMBERSHIP. The Puritans kept the sabbath, doing no work from sundown on Saturday until sundown on Sunday. Food had to be cooked ahead of time. Reports of work, play, or any unnecessary activity on Sunday brought condemnation both from the church and from the government.

A church service was long, solemn, and serious, lasting at least two hours. It began with a long prayer, followed by an exposition on a Bible verse and the singing of a psalm without musical accompaniment, featured an hour-long sermon, and concluded with a short prayer and benediction. Each Sunday settlers attended two services.

Both men and women joined the church, and in most towns women formed a slight majority of members. To become a member, a person had to undergo a **"conversion experience"** in which he or she gained confidence in being among the eternally saved. Furthermore, this experience had to be recounted to the minister and, often, to the deacon, who was the leading lay person in the congregation. If they found the experience convincing, the candidate then recounted the conversion to the entire congregation. Only then could membership be granted.

Among those who immigrated in the 1630s, about half joined the church. Almost every family had at least one member. Although members came from all social and economic levels, those higher up the scale were more likely to belong. Only a church member could have a child baptized. More curiously, only male church members had the right to vote in colonywide elections, to hold public office, or to be licensed to operate a tavern.

THE PURITANS PONDER FAITH, WORKS, AND THE CONVERSION EXPERIENCE. At the heart of Puritanism was a concept developed by the Protestant reformer John Calvin: the world was divided into two kinds of people, those whom God intended to save for eternal life and those damned to eternal hell. The very small number of the world's people to be saved were called the Elect or, more commonly, the Saints. The Puritans conceded that they could not know for certain whom God would save. But the Puritans believed that they could devise tests to indicate who would probably be among the Saints.

The most important test was faith, that is, belief in God. Although God might save an unbeliever, the Puritans thought this unlikely. The chances were that those who were to be saved had faith in God. Through faith, God bestowed grace, and grace guaranteed salvation.

For the Puritans, however, this test posed problems. After all, a person could assert faith and either through self-delusion or lies falsely claim grace. So a second test was a matter of works, that is, one's deeds, or how one lived one's life. The chances were that if one had received grace, one would be enabled to live a godly life of charity, honesty, and humility. The danger was that a person could live an outwardly blameless life yet lack true faith, be without grace, and be damned. Thus, works might lead to self-delusion and prevent salvation. Works, therefore, were insufficient.

Thus, the Puritans came to their third test, which was the conversion experience. A person, born a sinner and wishing to be reborn of God and placed among the Saints, not only had to have faith, to receive grace, and to do good works, but also had to undergo an intense, personal religious experience that could be convincingly related to others. Public ratification of this personal experience predicted that the conversion was real and that the person truly was a Saint.

The Puritans recognized that no person could know God's will, but they believed that they had devised a means to gain a likely understanding of the truth. Thus, no Puritan who had had a conversion experience and had been accepted into church membership could claim with absolute certainty to be a Saint, but the probability was high. Anxiety concerning a possible miscalculation, however, produced much tension.

ROGER WILLIAMS EMBRACES ANTINOMIANISM, 1636. The Puritan religious system contained contradictions that caused trouble. In England the Puritans had attacked Archbishop Laud for putting too much emphasis upon works. Such a belief was called Arminianism, after the theologian Arminius. But in Massachusetts the threat came from the opposite direction, from Puritans who ignored authorities' warnings and slipped into putting too much emphasis on faith. This belief was called Antinomianism, derived from a Latin word that meant opposing works.

The congregational system of church government made it difficult to restrain a minister who persuaded his congregation to go in a new direction. Roger Williams was such a minister. Williams began to suspect that many conversion experiences were false. After serious reflection and much prayer, he concluded that few people were truly Saints. His list of Saints kept shrinking, until it included only his wife and himself.

At this point Williams suddenly saw the absurdity of a religious system with only two Saints. Therefore, he reversed himself and concluded that any person could go to heaven. All that was necessary was to have faith and thereby receive grace. Williams's idea of **universal salvation,** which became the basis for the Baptist church in America, alarmed the Puritan authorities. If Williams's idea was accepted, church membership, voting, and public office would have to be open to everyone. Massachusetts society might unravel.

Worse, theologically, Williams's position destroyed Puritanism. Conversion experiences would have no significance, and in a world in which any person could claim salvation, how would self-deluders and liars be stopped? Individual claims of righteousness would lead to the organization of strange new churches. Attempts to stop these churches would fail, because members of each new church would claim to be true believers.

Williams had other unorthodox ideas. He declared that the colonists should buy land from the Indians rather than just occupying it. In 1636 Massachusetts's authorities forced Roger Williams to flee. He founded a new colony at Providence, Rhode Island, chartered by Parliament in 1644 and by the king in 1663. Williams recognized that others did not share all his views, and he soon advocated religious freedom. Thus, Rhode Island became the first American colony founded on the basis of personal religious choice.

BANISHING ANNE HUTCHINSON, 1638. A different kind of Antinomian challenge came from Anne Hutchinson. She had migrated to Boston with her husband and began to hold prayer meetings and religious discussions in her home. Although such activities were a normal part of Puritan life, the ministers and government officials grew uneasy when hundreds of people, including many women, began to attend Mrs. Hutchinson's meetings. To the men who ran the government and the churches, her sessions also seemed unwomanly.

Authorities became gravely concerned about Hutchinson's message. She found the **Holy Spirit** present at her meetings. Though that statement did not challenge Puritan doctrine, church authorities investigated, and she took the witness stand and claimed a direct, personal line to God. He spoke to her "by an immediate revelation."

No Puritan could accept that belief. Such an idea meant that each person, under God's direct input, could declare what was religiously acceptable. The church would lose control of its members, and each individual would constitute a personal church. Religious order would collapse, and since religion was the basis for the state, so would social order. In 1638 Massachusetts's authorities banished Anne Hutchinson. She moved to Rhode Island and then to an English settlement on Long Island, New York, where she was killed by Indians in 1643.

FOUNDING CONNECTICUT, 1636. The Puritan system was fragile, and religious disputes common. The easiest way to keep the peace was to encourage outspoken people to leave. In 1636 Thomas Hooker, a respected but opinionated Puritan minister, led a group into the Connecticut Valley and founded a colony at Hartford. Other Puritans, considered to be the most religiously fervent, arrived from England and founded a colony at New Haven in 1638. In 1662 these colonies, having secured a royal charter, merged as Connecticut.

Not everyone in New England shared the intense religiosity found in Massachusetts. Nonreligious settlements could be found in Rhode Island, on the Massachusetts frontier, such as William Pynchon's colony at Springfield, and in remote areas of Maine and New Hampshire. Massachusetts controlled Maine from 1691 to 1820, but New Hampshire succeeded in organizing separately in 1680.

Troubles Come to Massachusetts, 1660-1692

After 1660 religion waned, despite the Half-Way Covenant and sermons called jeremiads designed to stir up conversion experiences. King Charles II challenged Massachusetts, and the Indian King Philip led the last Indian war against whites in New England, 1675-1676. In 1684 England revoked the Massachusetts charter and in 1686 merged the colony into the Dominion of New England, which lasted three years. In 1691 Massachusetts was rechartered as a royal colony, which limited the colonists' self-government. The next year, in an incident which revealed political, social, and psychological instability, Salem Village hanged 19 witches.

PURITAN RELIGION DECLINES. John Winthrop, the longtime early governor of Massachusetts, had spoken of founding a godly community, a "city upon a hill," and the first generation of Puritans had devoted itself to that cause. But their children, born in Massachusetts, began to drift away from religion. As the number of conversion experiences fell, the percentage of adults in the church dropped from about 50 to 20 percent. Because the founding members' children failed to join, and since only members could have their children baptized, the number of infant baptisms plummeted.

In 1662 some congregations adopted the Half-Way Covenant. An adult child of a church member who had faith and lived a godly life could, without a conversion experience, receive communion, which was normally restricted to church members, and could have children baptized.

Amid religious decline, ministers preached sermons called jeremiads, after the Old Testament prophet Jeremiah. These sermons bewailed the woes that were befalling an ungodly people and demanded mass repentance and multiple conversion experiences as the price for saving Massachusetts from utter destruction as an ungodly society.

The first great New England poet, Anne Bradstreet, had written warmly of family, love, and religion. In her work the three were entwined aspects of a godly whole. In 1662 Michael Wigglesworth, the next great poet, gloomily predicted New England's doom for its sins in "God's Controversy with New England."

CHARLES AND PHILIP MAKE ROYAL TROUBLE, 1660-1676. During Oliver Cromwell's Puritan regime in England, Massachusetts had been left alone, but the installation of the distinctly unpuritanical King Charles II in 1660 put the colony on the defensive and complicated its politics. The English government took an increasing, unwelcome interest in New England's affairs. Massachusetts fared poorly, but Connecticut under the politically shrewd John Winthrop, Jr., in 1662 obtained a royal charter that provided for self-government, and this document lasted until 1818.

On the New England homefront troubles grew in 1675, when the Indian leader Metacom, called King Philip by the settlers, led the Wampanoag tribe in war against the colonists. For years, ever since the minor Pequot War of 1637, Indian-white relations in New England had been peaceful, but by the 1670s the remaining Indians recognized that white population growth was destroying the Indian way of life, which depended upon hunting.

In King Philip's War, 1675-1676, Indians attacked 52 of 90 towns in New England, destroyed 12 of them, killed 600 whites, and took many captives. One of them, Mrs. Mary Rowlandson, wrote a popular account of her ordeal, which became a model for many later narratives.

The colonists fought ruthlessly, losing one of every 16 men of military age. They took advantage of old tribal rivalries and hired Indians to kill other Indians. At the end of the war in 1676, many natives fled west. The remainder settled on **reservations.** King Philip's War was the last Indian-white war in New England.

THE DOMINION OF NEW ENGLAND RISES AND FALLS, 1684-1691. In 1684 the English government, long frustrated by Massachusetts's snubs, lack of cooperation, and smuggling, annulled the old charter and invoked royal rule. The colony's prospects worsened the following year, when King James II

(r. 1685-1688) came to power. A practicing Catholic, James II antagonized Parliament in all sorts of ways, including the appointment of Catholic officers in the army and aggressive management of the country's colonies.

In 1686, under Governor Sir Edmund Andros, Massachusetts was merged with New Hampshire and Maine as the Dominion of New England. Organized in the name of greater imperial administrative efficiency, the Dominion's main effect was to increase both Andros's power and the king's opportunity to exploit America for his own purposes. The next year Andros's Dominion took over Plymouth and Rhode Island, and the governor visited Hartford for the purpose of annexing Connecticut. The clever Yankees, however, defied Andros by hiding their charter in an oak tree.

In 1688 Andros added New York and New Jersey to the growing, unwieldy, and unpopular Dominion, which managed to irritate almost everyone. Land speculators in England and in the colonies, as well as farmers, worried about such a consolidated system, where only the most influential could extract concessions, including confirmation of land titles.

New Englanders also feared an attempt to use taxes to establish the Church of England. The brusque Andros heightened these anxieties when he ordered an Anglican church set up at his administrative capital at Boston. Andros also questioned the legitimacy of the Massachusetts General Court as a governing legislature and the legality of the colony's land grants to towns. That threatened property rights.

In late 1688 James II fled from the throne and was succeeded in the bloodless and, hence, Glorious Revolution by William III (r. 1689-1702) and Mary II (r. 1689-1694), both Protestants. When word of this event reached Boston in early 1689, the local residents overthrew Andros's regime. Many yearned for a return of the godly days of their old charter government.

The English, however, refused to give Massachusetts its former privileges. In a political compromise, a royal charter was granted in 1691. It called for the king to appoint a royal governor, for the people to elect the General Court to pass laws, and for the General Court to elect a council to advise the governor.

Power was to be shared. Although the governor was influential and along with the council controlled spending, the legislature retained the sole right to levy taxes. This system produced much conflict during the 1700s. The right to vote was extended to nonchurch members, based on property, as in England, and Massachusetts was allowed to absorb both Plymouth and Maine.

SALEM VILLAGE HANGS WITCHES, 1692. Amid the unraveling of Puritan society and following immediately on the political chaos of 1684-1691, there occurred one of the strangest episodes in American history, the Salem witchcraft trials. Witch accusations and trials had occurred regularly in Europe for centuries, and at least 30 witches had been executed earlier in colonial New England. What set Salem apart were mass accusations, mass hysteria, and mass hangings.

Salem Village, today the town of Danvers, Massachusetts, was an agricultural area geographically remote from but politically controlled by the seaport town of Salem. The farmers who lived in the village had long been bitterly divided, and one important issue had been the attempt to establish a separate church in Salem Village.

In 1692 two young girls who lived in the household of the town's minister, Samuel Parris, suddenly became hysterical, even convulsive. Parris, as well as the local physician and others, quickly became convinced that a witch afflicted the girls. Accusations of witchcraft were made, accused witches were examined and jailed, and the number of afflicted girls grew to ten. Whenever a witch was jailed, the outcries stopped, but then they returned, as an afflicted girl claimed to be possessed by a new witch.

Eventually, more than 150 persons were jailed as accused witches, and 19 were tried, convicted, and hanged. All but five were women. One man was pressed to death with stones for refusing to enter a plea in court. When the accusations marched up the social scale and included the wife of the Massachusetts governor, officials suddenly halted the proceedings.

Accused witches in Salem, as in earlier New England witchcraft proceedings, tended to be elderly women, especially those without husbands or sons. In some cases inheritance of family property seemed to be an issue. In almost all cases the suspected witch either came from a family where witchcraft had been charged or suspected earlier, had engaged at some time in unseemly or immoral behavior (such as having a child out of wedlock), or was on poor terms with church members.

The Salem trials became so notorious that they inhibited further legal prosecutions of witches. Folkways die slowly, however, and New Englanders continued to believe in witches, an idea rooted deep in the folk culture of East Anglia.

Awakenings, Commercial and Religious, 1700-1760

New Englanders increasingly participated in the larger world, including three wars against France. After 1700 the colonists traded inside the British empire. Shipbuilding and sailing flourished, and urban merchants grew wealthy. The 1730s-1740s brought a series of religious revivals called the Great Awakening, led by the Reverend Jonathan Edwards. These revivals replaced the traditional emphasis on community with an emphasis on individual religion.

NEW ENGLAND THRIVES ON COMMERCE AFTER 1700. After 1700 New England became a more secular society and gained greater contact with the broader world. New Englanders fought alongside England in global conflicts against France in King William's War, 1689-1697; and against both France and Spain in Queen Anne's War, 1702-1713; and again in King George's War, 1744-1748, when New England soldiers captured Louisbourg, Nova Scotia, in 1745. On a per capita basis, this proved the deadliest war in American history.

As the British empire developed, extensive trade grew among England, New England, Virginia, and the West Indies. New Englanders played a prominent role in this trade. Felling great trees in abundant forests, they built and sailed ships. They raised grain and horses for export to the West Indies, where these items were in short supply. New Englanders netted fish for overseas markets and imported both rum and molasses, from which they distilled their own local rum. They carried rum to Africa, where they traded it for slaves, whom they sold in the West Indies and along the southern seacoast.

Commerce became a major part of the New England economy, and as is always the case in commercial societies, merchants in the leading seaports gained great wealth. By the 1750s the richest 5 percent of Boston's population owned half the city's wealth.

Boston and, to a lesser extent, Salem and Newport, Rhode Island, became filled with the mansions of the newly rich. People who cared more about the making of money than the saving of souls dominated the seaport's economy, society, and politics. The Church of England even erected a building in a prominent location in Boston, while the Revere family turned out silver cups and plates as elegant as any crafted in London. Among the new luxuries were forks, table linens, and mirrors.

Rural New Englanders looked upon these changes with both awe and suspicion. Although the glitter of Boston attracted ambitious young people, farm folk suspected that Boston's worldliness and wealth gave proof of the city's ungodliness. As late as 1735 fewer than 4 percent of New Englanders dissented from the established **congregational churches.**

Sticking to the old ways was what farmers and farmer-craftsmen in the countryside did best, and they continued to plow their fields, ply their trades, and lay plans for providing farm lands for their children, if not in the immediate vicinity (which had filled up), then on lands along the frontier.

Meanwhile, if they saw an opportunity to build a mill, to sell some grain to strangers, or to swap some local produce for imported earthenware plates, they took the main chance. They were in transition from being devout, other-worldly Puritans to becoming sharp-eyed, hard-bargaining Yankees.

RELIGION RETURNS WITH THE GREAT AWAKENING, 1741-1742. In the early 1700s New Englanders lacked the intense religious feelings of their ancestors. This began to change as early as 1733, when the Reverend Jonathan Edwards stirred people with his preaching at Northampton, Massachusetts. During the rest of the decade the **revival** spread through all the colonies. From 1739 to 1741 the great English evangelist, George Whitefield, preached from the South to New England. Everywhere he traveled, large crowds turned out. In Boston 19,000 people — far more than the city's population — heard him.

Whitefield preached in a new style, extemporaneously, without notes. His message had great emotional appeal. Among his listeners at one New England meeting was Jonathan Edwards, who wept. After Whitefield's visit, a wave of revivals in 1741 and 1742 flooded across New England in both rural and urban settings.

Soon ministers and others disputed the meaning of these events. Conservatives, or "Old Lights," became suspicious and were especially upset by outbursts of emotion at the revivals. Liberals, called "New Lights" because they believed the revivals brought forth God's light, looked approvingly upon the large number of converts.

In New England the **Great Awakening's** most important figure proved to be Jonathan Edwards. Although his written sermons showed the dryness, quiet logic, and rich use of scripture associated with Puritanism, his oral delivery was closer to Whitefield's. Edwards gazed out across his congregation, his eyes transfixed on the far end of the meeting house, and preached as if the spirit of the Lord was pouring forth from his mouth. Members of Edwards's congregation in Northampton, Massachusetts, burst out in screams of religious ecstacy, and dozens surged to the front of the church to declare their conversions. Edwards rarely challenged these claims. He harvested hundreds of church members.

Important people in Northampton were appalled. Edwards offended their sense of order and threatened their status. The creation of a mass, popular church on a wave of emotion might overturn the town's political, social, and economic order. So Edwards was dismissed. He went into the wilderness, ministered to Indians, and wrote several volumes explaining his theology. In 1757 he moved to Princeton, New Jersey, where he became the president of a college, now Princeton University, founded by Presbyterians in 1746 to train "New Light" ministers. He died in 1758.

The revivals also led Baptists to found the College of Rhode Island (Brown) in 1764, the Dutch Reformed to begin Queen's College (Rutgers) in 1766, and Congregationalists to start Dartmouth as an Indian mission school in 1769.

The Great Awakening was the single most important event in the history of American religion. Although it took place in all the colonies, it had its most pronounced effect in New England. Those who rejected the revival, if they tried to maintain orthodox Puritan views, were left with an emotionally dead, rigid system of predestined salvation for only a handful of Saints that did not appeal to Americans living in and developing a more egalitarian society. John Winthrop, John Calvin, and old-fashioned Puritanism were long dead.

New Englanders, as well as other Americans, were now divided religiously not so much by denomination as by how they regarded the revival. To accept the revival was to admit the possibility of free grace, that is, all persons who had faith could receive grace and be saved. This was the Antinomian idea that Roger Williams had first articulated and that Anne Hutchinson had approached.

As the Puritans had warned, this sort of **evangelical** religion emphasized emotion over reason, heart over intellect, and individual sentiment over communal consensus. Such a religion ran the dangers of emotional excess, of personal eccentricity, and of social disintegration. It was also inherently antiintellectual, which explains why Jonathan Edwards, a transitional figure who tried to combine the old theology with the new style, remains the last great American theologian.

Boston merchants drifted toward the Arminian belief in works. Smugly confident that wealth was a sign of God's favor and reinforced in this belief by charitable acts that suggested salvation through works, they rejected both predestination and the revival. During the 1700s their branch of congregational religion evolved into Unitarianism, which stressed reason and social justice, as evidenced through works. They clung to intellect without emotion.

Since the Great Awakening no one in America has been able to put the two halves of religious experience — theology and reason versus faith and feeling —together again, and the country has more or less regularly oscillated between periods of rational, secular activity and periods of intensely emotional religious revivals.

Conclusion

Puritan religion shaped both New England society and America as a whole. The Puritans were unusual immigrants — middle class, educated, resourceful, and fanatical. While trying to replicate English village life, they emphasized church and family. The church and state together monitored, regulated, and controlled people's lives, imposing conformity as well as high standards.

After 1660, religion lost preeminence, and New Englanders became commercially engaged with the rest of the world. During these years friction between England and Massachusetts led the colonists to assert local, democratic rights and to distrust authorities in faraway London. By the early 1700s England's benign neglect and the colonies' prosperity had temporarily cured these resentments. During the Great Awakening, religious fervor returned. It provided the foundation for modern American religion and indicated the development of a belief system reflecting a truly American psyche.

Recommended Readings

DOCUMENTS: William Bradford, *Of Plymouth Plantation* (1952); Anne Bradstreet, *Works* (1967); Samuel Sewall, *Diary* (2 vols., 1973).

READINGS: (PURITANISM) Charles L. Cohen, *God's Caress* (1986); Richard Godbeer, *The Devil's Dominion* (1992); Philip F. Gura, *A Glimpse of Sion's Glory* (1984); Edmund S. Morgan, *Visible Saints* (1963); David Stannard, *The Puritan Way of Death* (1977); Harry S. Stout, *The New England Soul* (1986); (NEW ENGLAND) Richard L. Dunn, *Puritans and Yankees* (1962); John F. Martin, *Profits in the Wilderness* (1991); Roger Thompson, *Sex in Middlesex* (1986); Laurel T. Ulrich, *Good Wives* (1982); (COMMUNITIES) Richard L. Bushman, *From Puritan to Yankee* (1967); John Demos, *A Little Commonwealth* (1970); Philip J. Greven, Jr., *Four Generations* (1970); Christine Heyrman, *Commerce and Culture* (1984); Stephen Innes, *Labor in a New Land* (1983); Kenneth A. Lockridge, *A New England Town* (1970); Michael Zuckerman, *Peaceable Kingdoms* (1970); (INDIANS) Russell Bourne, *The Red King's Rebellion* (1990); Calvin Martin, *Keepers of the Game* (1978); Richard White, *The Middle Ground* (1991); (EMPIRE) Michael G. Hall, *Edward Randolph and the American Colonies* (1960); Richard R. Johnson, *Adjustment to Empire* (1981); (WITCHCRAFT) Paul Boyer and Stephen Nissenbaum, *Salem Possessed* (1974); John Demos, *Entertaining Satan* (1982); Carol F. Karlsen, *The Devil in the Shape of a Woman* (1987); Richard Weisman, *Witchcraft, Magic, and Religion in Seventeenth Century Massachusetts* (1984).

4

THE DIVERSE MIDDLE COLONIES, 1624-1760

CHAPTER OVERVIEW: The Dutch established New Netherland in 1624, but 40 years later the English captured this diverse, unstable colony and renamed it New York. That colony's political quarrels continued, as did its ethnic diversity. In 1681 William Penn founded Pennsylvania for the Quakers, who were joined by Germans and Scots-Irish. Philadelphia became the most important city in the American colonies in the 1700s. New Jersey and Delaware were closely tied to New York and Pennsylvania, respectively.

The Dutch Found New Netherland, 1624-1664

In 1624 the Dutch founded New Netherland, but few Hollanders wished to immigrate, and so in 1629 the Dutch adopted the patroon plan to settle the colony. This plan failed, and by the 1640s Governor Pieter Stuyvesant's colony held an increasingly diverse population of Dutch, English, Germans, Africans, Jews, Italians, French, and New Englanders.

THE DUTCH SEEK A FUR-TRADING COLONY, 1624-1647. In 1600 tiny Holland (also called the Netherlands) was one of the richest and most powerful countries in the world. Its wealth came from the hand manufacture of textiles and from worldwide trading and commerce. Dutch merchants' ships carried spices for the European market from the East Indies (Indonesia, which became a Dutch colony), shipped slaves from the African coast to the West Indies, and sent Dutch, French, and German textiles, knives, and other products throughout the world.

Wealthy **Protestant** merchants dominated Holland, and in 1588 they had ended the Catholic Spanish king's control over the northern Netherlands and established the Dutch Republic. For a time, the Protestant Dutch and English were allied against the Catholic French and Spanish, but the Dutch competed commercially against the English, and this rivalry grew during the 1600s.

After the English had begun to settle North America, the seafaring Dutch decided to found their own colonies. They were especially interested in trading European goods for Indian furs. Around 1614 the private Dutch East India Company built a fort at what became Albany, New York, to trade with the Mohawks, one of the tribes in the Iroquois confederation.

In 1624 the Dutch, using Henry Hudson's exploration of the Hudson River under Dutch sponsorship as the basis for their claim, founded the colony of New Netherland, on the site of what is now New York. The Hollanders knew that the English would not recognize this claim, so they drew New Netherland's boundaries as large as possible in order to enhance their negotiating position with the English.

The Dutch West India Company planted their main colony on the lower tip of Manhattan Island at a place they called New Amsterdam (today, New York City). In 1625 they built a crude wooden fort, which offered little protection against possible attack by an English fleet. Soon the Dutch decided to farm the whole of Manhattan Island, and in 1626 their leader, Pieter Minuit, bought the island from the local Indians for $24 worth of trading goods.

To capture the interior Indian fur trade, the Dutch built another settlement 140 miles up the Hudson River at the site of the previously established Fort Orange (today's Albany). Outposts were also constructed on the eastern tip of Long Island, on the western bank of the Connecticut River, and on the eastern shore of the Delaware River nearly opposite present-day Philadelphia.

THE DUTCH ADOPT THE PATROON PLAN, 1629. The Dutch realized that unless their own people migrated to the colony they would lose control. In 1629 the Dutch government authorized a plan for the colony that gave huge **land grants** to men called **patroons.** To keep ownership of the land, each patroon had to settle 50 Dutch immigrants within a few years. The immigrants would never gain the right to own their land. They would remain tenants and pay a small annual rent to the patroon.

As it turned out, only one patroon ever met all the terms to establish a patroonship. The Van Rensselaer family gained control of an area near Albany of more than one million acres. However, the manor, called Rensselaerswyck, limped along, much of its land remaining empty, as tenants shrewdly realized that they could buy nearby land rather than remain as tenants. Nevertheless, the Van Rensselaers became a wealthy, powerful family.

For the Dutch the principal problem was that, despite the patroon plan, few Hollanders wanted to leave home, and the colony quickly gained a mixed population. Only half were Dutch. In 1643 the colony's 1600 residents spoke 18 languages. They had no churches, but 17 taverns. Dutch and English merchants, especially in New Amsterdam, joined Jews, Scots, Italians, **slaves** from Africa, **Huguenots** (French Protestants) in Westchester County, Germans along the Hudson River, and New Englanders on eastern Long Island.

PIETER STUYVESANT GOVERNS NEW NETHERLAND, 1647-1664. In 1647 Pieter Stuyvesant, a one-legged military veteran, arrived to become the governor of New Netherland. A shrewd if ruthless politician, Stuyvesant both ignored the impractical instructions that he received from Holland and discouraged ethnic conflict. Against all logic, he declared that Lutheran services conformed with the Calvinist Dutch Reformed church. This policy enabled Germans to claim equality with the Dutch. He also allowed Jewish immigrants to remain so long as they held religious services in their homes and not in a synagogue.

He even made border compromises with the New Englanders, who were known as difficult negotiators. The Hartford Treaty of 1650 gave the New Englanders control of eastern Long Island, where they had already settled, and established Connecticut's present western boundary. Stuyvesant joined his New England rivals to fight a series of wars against their commonly hated foe, the Indians.

Fearing the colony's long-term insecurity, Stuyvesant in 1655 led an expedition to seize the Swedish and Finnish settlements on the Delaware River. He quickly incorporated them into New Netherland. The fur-seeking Swedes, as caught up in the mania for American possessions as other Europeans, had first colonized that area at Fort Christina in 1638. Their one major contribution to American culture was to introduce the first log cabins.

The English Add New York to Their Empire, 1651-1750

Mercantilism led the English government to regulate colonial trade with several Navigation Acts. In a related move, the English in 1664 seized New Netherland and renamed it New York. There the English manor system created a wealthy, powerful elite, which the popular Jacob Leisler nearly toppled in 1689. From 1700 to 1750 New Yorkers quarreled in this ethnically diverse and politically fragmented colony. A libel trial against the newspaper editor John Peter Zenger established a precedent for a free press.

THE ENGLISH USE NAVIGATION ACTS TO REGULATE TRADE, 1651-1725. During the 1600s Europeans did not believe in **free trade** between nations. Instead, they thought that a country's prosperity depended upon controlling colonies and restricting access to markets. According to this system, called **mercantilism**, a mother country could best prosper by gaining control and exclusive trading rights to colonies producing a wide variety of raw materials. Government power, including chartered monopolies, fixed prices, and quotas, was brought to bear upon economic activity, especially overseas trade.

In 1651 the English government under Cromwell passed the first of a series of Navigation Acts. This law required that American colonists trade only with English ships. To be considered English, not only did the ship have to fly an English flag — easy enough to change before arriving at a port — but at least half the crew on a vessel had to be English.

The restoration of Charles II brought more Navigation Acts. In 1660 the law forced English ships to sail with crews that were three-fourths English, and colonists could market certain products, including tobacco and rice, only in England or in other English colonies. In 1663 the English government required that European goods destined for America had to be offloaded in England in order to pay duties. Ten years later duties were charged on some American exports.

In 1675 the English systematized the commercial and political regulation of the American colonies by establishing an agency, the Lords of Trade and Plantations, which increasingly enforced customs duties. This agency, however, proved inefficient, and in 1696 the last of the Navigation Acts created the Board of Trade to regulate the colonies' commerce. It functioned vigorously until 1725, when enforcement became lax.

THE ENGLISH CAPTURE NEW NETHERLAND, 1664. The Dutch and English battled to control both the world tobacco market and the African slave trade. The English hated New Netherland, sandwiched between New England and Virginia, and disliked the Dutch tendency to undercut English merchants by trading with England's American colonies at low prices. Growing commercial rivalry between Holland and England led to a series of wars between the two countries.

In 1664 an English fleet sailed into the harbor at New Amsterdam and captured New Netherland without a shot. At the time the population was about 9,000, of whom 2,000 were New Englanders. The English sought to win over the Dutch settlers by allowing them to practice their own religion and retain their property. King Charles II gave the colony to his brother the Duke of York, the future James II. In honor of the duke, the colony and its capital were renamed New York.

The English found New York difficult to digest. In 1673 the Dutch briefly recaptured the colony, but the English regained control the following year. Unlike New England, with its fanatical Puritans, or Virginia, with its iron rule by the gentry, New York lacked a focal point. It was a colony destined to be dominated by quarrels.

English authorities did not seek to evict any of New York's mixed population. More English merchants did settle in New York City, which became largely English, but the area around Albany remained overwhelmingly Dutch, as did much of the Hudson River valley, and the fur trade remained in the hands of Dutch traders. Settlers from New England on Long Island and in Westchester County found the new English authorities scarcely more accommodating than the Dutch.

The colony's proprietor, the Duke of York, sent a series of political hacks to govern the colony. They used their offices to gain as much wealth for themselves in as short a time as possible before beating a hasty retreat to the comforts of England. The governors were autocrats. From 1664 to 1682 the Duke refused to allow New York's elected assembly to meet.

THE ENGLISH ADOPT THE MANOR SYSTEM. The only way to gain wealth in New York was by controlling land. The Dutch patroon system had failed, but it inspired the English. Governors, their councils, and the elected assembly that the English eventually established adopted the Virginia practice of granting large acreages to themselves. The usual trick was to write the boundaries of the grants so vaguely that a later friendly court might interpret what had at first appeared to be a grant of 2000 acres to be a grant of 200,000 acres.

The English laid out a series of large estates called **manors** along the fertile banks of the Hudson River, especially on the eastern side. By 1703 five families held half the land between Albany and New York. Land made the Schuylers, Livingstons, and Van Cortlandts the wealthiest and most powerful families in New York. By 1750 these large landholders formed a colonial elite second in wealth only to South Carolina's rice planters.

Although they tried to keep tenants on the land, landowners were freewheeling **capitalists,** a characteristic that became a hallmark of New York society, and were willing to sell land outright if that was more profitable. As long-term **speculators,** they kept enormous blocks of land off the market, thereby discouraging settlement, and in the end caused New York's economic development to fall behind that of other colonies. Discouraging newcomers, however, had the effect of preserving this elite's power.

The use of vague descriptions in land grants had one other consequence. From the beginning New York was awash in lawsuits. In many cases original grantees literally did not know what had been granted, and in other cases claims conflicted. The government sometimes gave the same land to two or more sets of people. Sales of land with clouded title to settlers only compounded the problem. Lawyers benefited handsomely. Courts showed little respect for evidence or justice and usually sided with the politically well-connected.

JACOB LEISLER REBELS, 1689. Many New Yorkers hated their government, dominated by an appointed governor, an appointed council of wealthy and powerful land speculators, and a weak, tiny elected assembly composed of the same sorts of people. New York's absorption into the Dominion of New England in 1688 did not make the government more popular. When James II was overthrown in England in 1688, some New Yorkers also feared that local officials would betray the colony to France, where the Catholic James II had fled. Accordingly, colonists moved to replace their government.

With support from German and Dutch farmers, as well as a good many New York City laborers and merchants, a wealthy German merchant and intense Protestant named Jacob Leisler deposed Lieutenant Governor Francis Nicholson in 1689 and declared himself the acting governor. He ruled with a general popularity for more than a year, until, much to Leisler's surprise, an English officer arrived in 1691 and demanded Leisler's surrender. Leisler hesitated before capitulating, and the new governor, Colonel Henry Sloughter, found Leisler's tardy obedience treasonous.

The new government charged Leisler and seven supporters with treason, and they were convicted. Six were pardoned, but Leisler and his son-in-law were hanged, drawn, and quartered. Jeered at the public execution, Leisler warned his enemies that they would live to regret their actions.

Leisler's prophesy proved correct. Four years later **Parliament** pardoned Leisler and restored his confiscated property to his family. Thousands attended his reburial. For more than a generation the lingering bitterness over the execution of the popular Leisler dominated New York politics. In addition, the anti-Leislerians discovered that they not only lacked popular support, but in time lost the influential friends in England who had made them powerful.

NEW YORKERS QUARREL, 1700-1750. Throughout most of the 1700s New York did not thrive. The colony's constant political bickering was not helped by a series of incompetent or corrupt governors. One, Lord Cornbury, was a transvestite, and another, Sir Danvers Osborn, hanged himself within a week of his arrival. A third, George Clarke, arrived poor and retired to England with a fortune of £100,000.

Other issues also produced tension. In 1733 John Peter Zenger established a new newspaper, the *Journal,* in opposition to the government-sponsored *Gazette.* A year later Governor William Cosby, long annoyed by Zenger's barbed attacks, ordered Zenger arrested for libel. The judge, controlled by Cosby, disbarred Zenger's lawyers, and a desperate Zenger finally had to import a brilliant trial lawyer, Andrew Hamilton, from Philadelphia. Hamilton argued a new and important legal theory, namely that criticizing the governor was not a libel, so long as Zenger had told the truth. The jury acquitted Zenger and thereby established truth as a defense against the charge of libel. This set a precedent for a free press.

Slavery presented another troublesome situation. In 1741 New Yorkers discovered a plot by the city's many black slaves — nearly 20 percent of the city's total population of 11,000 — to revolt against their white masters. Riding a wave of hysteria against the alleged slave plot, New York executed 29 slaves and banished 70 others. In this quarrelsome and socially fragmented colony, slavery never seemed secure, and white New Yorkers gradually turned against the institution.

Clouded land titles, large owners who refused to sell, and the resultant high prices discouraged people from settling in New York. Without interior settlement, the marvelous port at New York City was largely a wasted asset. The city stagnated, as Philadelphia grew far more rapidly.

Multiethnic Experimenting in Pennsylvania, 1681-1760

In 1681 William Penn founded Pennsylvania as a refuge for Quakers. Members of this militantly pacifist sect, however, were few, and the colony quickly gained diversity with Germans and Scots-Irish. A Quaker-German alliance long controlled Pennsylvania, which had lush farms that produced a high standard of living.

THE QUAKERS FOUND PENNSYLVANIA, 1681. Quakers, a Protestant group more formally called the Society of Friends, founded and settled Pennsylvania. In 1681 William Penn, a wealthy English Quaker, received from his friend and debtor King Charles II a **charter** for a new colony in North America. Penn became the colony's proprietor, a position that gave him great power and influence over events in Pennsylvania. The king named the colony for Penn's father, an admiral.

Penn planned his colony carefully in order to avoid the mistakes made in

The founder of Pennsylvania, the Quaker William Penn, took the unusual position that the colonists should buy land from the Indians rather than merely seizing it. Penn signed treaties with a number of Indian tribes. These events have long fascinated American artists.
(Culver Pictures/Benjamin West)

earlier settlements. He had the boundaries surveyed to avoid disputes with other colonies. Carefully negotiating treaties with the various Indian tribes, including the friendly Lenni Lenape who lived in the Delaware River valley, Penn insisted that whites could settle only on land that he had purchased from the Indians. Showing great respect for native culture, Penn even learned the local Indian language in order to avoid interpreter's errors.

The founder placed the government in the hands of a governor (the proprietor's designated deputy), an elected assembly, and a council chosen by the assembly. The council both sat as a court and initiated all laws, which had to be ratified by the assembly. This structure failed, and in 1701 Penn's Charter of Privileges established a government with a weak governor, a powerful one-house legislature, and a strictly advisory council. Political bickering, however, continued.

THE SOCIETY OF FRIENDS SEEKS INNER LIGHT. Penn thought of his colony primarily as a refuge for English Quakers, who had suffered from much religious persecution in England. Members of this sect rejected the formal, hierarchical religion of the Church of England, but they also opposed the gloomy **Calvinism** of New England's Puritans. To the Quakers, founded by George Fox during the English civil war in the 1640s, salvation came from an

The Society of Friends, founded in England, was among the first religious groups to allow women to preach. Quakers, as they were usually called, also insisted upon plain, undecorated gray clothing. (BRIDGEMAN ART LIBRARY/BRITISH LIBRARY)

inner light, and religious conversion was mostly an individual experience. This particular doctrine led the sect to tolerance of outsiders, diverse practices within the group, and a tendency toward pacifism.

Quakers rejected family hierarchy, holding all members equal before God. Because men and women were spiritually equal, the sect recognized female preachers. Family life was child-centered, and family members took meals together. Quakers stressed the work ethic, dressed simply in gray, kept austere houses, and ate plain food. Their very simplicity, in the eyes of others, became a form of ostentacious display.

Among the practices that annoyed their neighbors, Quakers refused to bow, kneel, or take off their hats in the presence of their social betters. They insisted on using "thee" and "thou" instead of "you," which they believed to be a term implying spiritual inequality, declined to swear oaths in court, and refused to bear arms. In England, their pacifism often landed them in jail.

PENNSYLVANIA SHOWS ETHNIC DIVERSITY. Penn recognized that the Quakers were not numerous enough to populate an entire colony. To attract other settlers, he promised that Pennsylvanians would pay no taxes to a state church and could worship with few restrictions.

The colony had begun in 1682 with the arrival of 2,000 Quakers personally led by William Penn, but only in the beginning were Quakers a majority, and their proportion of the population constantly declined with further immigration. The Quakers, mainly from England's northern Midlands, were joined by other English immigrants as well as by people from Germany, Wales, Scotland, and Ireland.

By 1755 Pennsylvania was 42 percent German, 28 percent English or Welsh, and 28 percent Scots-Irish. Despite this polyglot population, or perhaps because of it, the Quakers remained influential beyond their numbers. Until the American Revolution they dominated Pennsylvania society, politics, and business.

Quaker control was based on an alliance with Pennsylvania's large German community. The first Germans settled in 1683 at Germantown, now inside Philadelphia. They not only farmed but also engaged in crafts, which thrived in a colony blessed with timber, iron ore, and coal important to heavy industry. Germans preserved their culture with the early establishment of a printing press at Germantown.

In the early 1700s tens of thousands of Protestant Germans migrated to the colony. Some were Lutherans, but many belonged to small Protestant religious denominations that were persecuted in Germany. Their English neighbors called them the Pennsylvania Dutch, a corruption of Deutsch, the German word for Germans. They had nothing to do with Holland. The Pennsylvania Dutch included Calvinists; Moravians, who founded a large colony at Bethlehem; Mennonites, who preached pacifism; the Amish, who clung to tradition; and Dunkers, who baptized by immersion.

Most were farmers, but they avoided the frontier. Instead, they bought out pioneer farms and then greatly improved these farmsteads. Occupying the best land in southeastern Pennsylvania, they became famous for neat farms, large barns, productive orchards, molasses-based shoefly pie, a certain stinginess, and a crabbed suspicion of outsiders. They had little interest in politics, often quarreled among themselves, and stubbornly clung to the German language.

SCOTS-IRISH SETTLE THE FRONTIER. The other large immigrant group were Scots-Irish Presbyterians from northern Ireland. More than 100,000 — one-seventh of the total — Ulster Protestants emigrated, mostly between 1750 and 1800. Disdainful of the Quakers and the Pennsylvania Dutch, they usually headed for the frontier, which they came to dominate, not only in Pennsylvania but also in Virginia and the Carolinas.

Their culture stressed hard drinking, a warrior's ethic of physical courage, egalitarianism within a system of masculine domination, and the preeminence of the extended family as a clan. Rowdy and raucous, they hated Indians, explored the wilderness, lived off wild game, distilled whiskey, cut trees to make farms, and then floated the timber downstream to market. Many remained poor backcountry farmers for generations.

The Scots-Irish always had an eye for the main chance, frequently went into business, and quickly took to politics, where they became the main rivals to the Quaker-German alliance. During the American Revolution they were intense patriots, and with the American victory gained political control of Pennsylvania, which they kept for generations.

The arrival of large numbers of immigrants into the colony destroyed Penn's policy of harmonious relations with Indians. White settlers encroached on native lands, often by squatting, and the Indians resisted during the mid-1700s with increasing violence.

PENNSYLVANIA AS THE BEST POOR MAN'S COUNTRY. Although settled late, Pennsylvania proved remarkably successful during the 1700s. William Penn's policies provided a firm foundation. Religious toleration encouraged the migration of clannish groups who were as devoted to hard work and thrift as to piety. Penn's generous land policies, which bankrupted Penn and put him in debtors' prison, made land readily available to settlers and discouraged large-scale speculation. Penn's policy of buying land from the Indians, instead of merely taking it, reduced military expenses and led families to take up isolated farms scattered across the countryside.

Farm land within 50 miles of Philadelphia was unusually rich and productive, by far the best land for general agriculture along the Atlantic seaboard. The soil was better and the growing season was longer than in New England. Winter feed for animals such as horses and cows was minimal, while the hot summers were shorter, healthier, and more bearable than further south.

Even small farms yielded bountiful crops, which led Pennsylvanians to be well fed. Living standards in the middle colonies were about 40 percent above the average for all the American colonies, ranking considerably above the South and more than double the level in New England, then the poorest region. Overall, Americans enjoyed a standard of living higher than in Scotland or Ireland and similar to that in England.

Because this lush agricultural area lay close to Philadelphia, farmers easily sold their surplus in that city's public market, which grew to occupy five blocks under a covered roof along Market Street. One could buy fresh meat, fish, and produce, as well as clothing, imported clocks, and other luxury goods.

In addition, Pennsylvania exported wheat, beef, pork, and lumber to the West Indies. In the 1750s Americans built, owned, and operated one-third of the ships sailing under the British flag. By 1770 Philadelphia ranked behind London as the second busiest port in the British empire.

Philadelphia Grows and Prospers, 1682-1760

William Penn carefully planned Philadelphia, and his ideas influenced later American cities. During the 1700s this boomtown became the second most populous English-speaking city in the world. Its leading citizen was Benjamin Franklin. Although merchants prospered, laborers, including those with skills, often did not. Many arrived as indentured servants, as signs of poverty increased. The Quakers turned against slavery, but free blacks faced harsh discrimination, and women fared poorly.

PHILADELPHIA AS A PLANNED CITY. From the beginning William Penn's colony was dominated by Philadelphia, America's first planned city. In 1682 Penn carefully picked the site between the Delaware and Schuylkill rivers. He hired a surveyor to lay out a town that was two miles in each direction, with broad, straight streets at regular intervals. Two exceptionally wide streets, Market and Broad, crossed at a square at the center, while each of the city's four sections also held major squares.

The grid concept became a model for most later American cities. Even New York, founded with narrow, twisted streets, eventually adopted a grid that covered Manhattan Island. So did later cities, such as flat Chicago, Salt Lake City, Denver, Phoenix, and Miami, and, improbably, hilly San Francisco and Seattle.

Philadelphia's large blocks enabled householders to combine the advantages of both urban and rural life by having deep lots with gardens, chickens, and fruit trees. Despite the plan, Penn's settlement grew mostly along the Delaware River, where good drinking water could be readily obtained and where oceangoing ships could easily dock.

To prevent a fire like the one that had destroyed most of London in 1666, Philadelphians built houses and shops of brick. Tall, narrow, and deep, most buildings contained a basement with storage, a ground floor with a shop in front and a living area behind, two upper floors with rooms rented to boarders, and an attic for servants.

CULTURE AND SCIENCE FLOURISH IN BENJAMIN FRANKLIN'S PHILADELPHIA. Although founded much later than Boston or New York, Philadelphia grew rapidly during the 1700s, becoming the most populous city in America by the 1760s, when it had about 25,000 people. Philadelphia was then probably second only to London in population in the English speaking world. The city's rich agricultural hinterland provided an unrivaled supply of cheap, plentiful food.

Philadelphia's culture owed much to its most famous resident, Benjamin Franklin. This native Bostonian and former runaway apprentice made his fortune as a printer and retired at age 42. Turning to invention and public service, he invented the Franklin stove and bifocal lenses, tested for electricity with a kite, and founded the first property insurance company and the first volunteer fire department.

He also helped start a private lending library, which became the basis for the idea of a public library, set up a debating club called Franklin's Junto, and organized the American Philosophical Society, which gave the city intellectual prestige, sponsored scientific experiments, and published the results.

Franklin's city was also home to David Rittenhouse, a self-taught astronomer, who invented the orrery, a wooden model that showed how the moon revolved around the earth as the earth revolved around the sun. Newspapers, pamphlets, and almanacs — including Franklin's witty *Poor Richard's Almanac,* which became America's first self-help book — made Philadelphia an important early publishing center.

The Quakers established free schools, so that even poor children could get an education. Like the Puritans, the Quakers expected people to read the Bible. Unlike the Puritans, however, the Quakers had uneducated lay ministers and believed higher education unnecessary to preaching, a hindrance to getting the inner light, and destructive to good business habits. Other Philadelphians established the University of Pennsylvania and a medical school.

DIFFERENCES IN WEALTH GROW. Although Philadelphia thrived throughout the colonial era, as suggested by its rapid population growth, not everyone shared the prosperity. At the top of society, wealthy Quaker merchants did well. They had devised business networks of trustworthy fellow Quakers both in England and in other colonies. Merchants also profited from local real estate speculation. Just 10 percent of the populace owned more than half the city's property.

Craftsmen and other skilled workers had mixed experiences. Some, like Ben Franklin, became self-employed as masters and gained fortunes. Others became master craftsmen, went bankrupt, and had to seek work as **journey-**

men, that is, employees. Although most **apprentices** still expected that they would pass through the journeyman stage and eventually become masters, the odds for success declined after 1760.

Unskilled laborers were usually hired in the morning for one day's work. If a man could not find work after a few days, he was likely to leave Philadelphia and seek his fortune elsewhere. Laborers did not prosper, but so few stayed in Philadelphia that their lack of success made little impact on the city's consciousness.

INDENTURED SERVANTS ARRIVE. During the colonial period many residents of both Philadelphia and the rest of Pennsylvania were **indentured servants.** These servants, unlike Virginia's single males in the 1600s, often arrived in family groups. Perhaps one-third of the Germans immigrated this way. By 1729 about one-fifth of Philadelphia's workforce was indentured servants.

Both males and females who wanted to migrate to North America were often too poor to pay the passage. Some ship captains transported people in exchange for the right to sell the person's labor upon arrival. Usually, these immigrants were teenagers or young adults who were bound as servants for four to seven years.

They were generally not taught trades, and they ended their service as unskilled laborers or servants. About 10 percent successfully ran away. After completing their service, many moved to rural areas. Of those who immigrated to Pennsylvania during the early years, about one-third eventually became landowners.

Over time, the number of indentured servants declined. In the 1770s such servants were only 11 percent of the Philadelphia workforce. Servants who came in these later years fared poorly. Within 20 years of finishing their service almost half ended up on public assistance — a rate four times that for the population as a whole.

From 1730 to 1753 booming Philadelphia had little poverty, with fewer than 1 percent of the city's residents considered poor. Labor shortages led to a growing use of indentured servants. The poor enjoyed cheap food and housing — rent was often only 5 percent of income — but firewood became increasingly expensive, since it had to be brought from greater and greater distances. The preferred wood was walnut, which made a hot fire with little effort.

By the 1760s, when poverty clearly had increased in Philadelphia and other American cities, private charitable assistance and taxes to aid the poor rose substantially. Urban poverty, however, remained rare, since more than 90 percent of Americans lived on farms. Less than 5 percent of the country's populace lived in the five largest cities — Philadelphia, New York, Boston, Charleston, South Carolina, and Newport, Rhode Island.

DIVERSITY INCREASES. Like other ports, Philadelphia attracted sailors, who came from many nations and shared a common language of the sea. Risking their lives on long, dangerous voyages that often lasted many months, they came into port to unwind and to boast of their adventures, bringing both salty talk and curiosities from every part of the world, as well as a little money in search of liquor and women. Jack Tars, as they were called, kept the city from being dull.

Philadelphia also had a number of black slaves. In 1729 they were about one-fifth of the workforce, mostly houseservants or unskilled laborers. In 1758, the Quakers' yearly meeting turned against slavery, and wealthy Quaker merchants eventually freed their slaves. The newly freed blacks, however, usually remained servants. Free blacks in colonial Philadelphia found few occupations other than servant or laborer open to them. By the 1770s slaves had declined to 5 percent of the workforce.

Women lived and worked in their own sphere, marrying, raising children, cooking, cleaning, and sewing clothes. They were not taught male trades. Widows faced difficulties, since only a handful could earn enough money through their labor to support a family. A few lucky widows operated businesses left behind by their husbands. There were female printers and tavernkeepers, but all were widows, and the businesses eventually passed into the hands of sons. Many widows remarried as quickly as possible. Others wound up living on the charity of relatives or made their way to the poor house.

Founding the Other Middle Colonies

In 1664 the Duke of York carved New Jersey out of New York without informing the governor of New York. The result produced so much confusion that New Jersey was long split into East Jersey and West Jersey, which were reunited only in 1702. Delaware fell under the control of William Penn, who recognized it as a separate colony in 1704.

CARVING NEW JERSEY OUT OF NEW YORK, 1664. New Jersey, originally part of New Netherland, became an English colony in 1664, when the Duke of York named two followers, Sir George Carteret and John, Lord Berkeley, its proprietors. Sharing characteristics with both New York and

Pennsylvania, New Jersey was trapped between its two more prominent neighbors. It lacked a good harbor and a major city, which weakened its sense of identity.

Unfortunately for Berkeley and Carteret, the governor of New York — incorrectly assuming that New Jersey still belonged to his province — granted land west of the Hudson River to New Englanders. He had also promised them a representative assembly. Amid this confusion, neither Berkeley nor Carteret made much money, and in 1674 Berkeley's share in the colony passed to the Quakers. In 1676 the dispute among the proprietors led New Jersey to be split formally into two colonies, East Jersey and West Jersey. They were reunited in 1702 as a single royal colony.

East Jersey, the northeastern portion adjacent to New York, had the same polyglot population found on the other side of the Hudson River. New Englanders, who had a habit of multiplying and spreading in all directions, made several important settlements, including one at New Ark (Newark). To produce ministers, they founded the college at Princeton.

East Jersey's politics was so controlled by New York that the local residents were relieved when the two Jerseys were joined together to form a more vigorous, independent colony. From 1702 to 1738 the royal governor of New York was also commissioned separately as the royal governor of New Jersey.

West Jersey, the southwestern portion nearest to Philadelphia, was long dominated by Quaker settlers at Burlington. They had arrived in 1677. The Quakers retained their influence locally longer in that area than in Pennsylvania.

Much of New Jersey had a poor, marshy, and sandy soil little suited to cultivation — the later famous cranberry bogs. Settlers preferred Pennsylvania's better land, and New Jersey remained sparsely populated by poor farmers.

DELAWARE BECOMES INDEPENDENT OF PENNSYLVANIA, 1704. Delaware, a tiny colony just below Philadelphia, was originally part of New Sweden, and then New Netherland, and became part of New York in 1664. Because of its small size and generally poor soil, which made it unattractive to land speculators, Delaware quickly fell under the influence of neighboring William Penn. He gained control in 1682 and recognized it as a separate colony in 1704.

Until the American Revolution the governor of Pennsylvania served as the governor of Delaware. Because Delaware had never been technically annexed to Pennsylvania, it was possible for Delaware to escape Pennsylvania's domination and reassert its separate status during the Revolution.

Conclusion

Unlike the plantation South or religious New England, no single group or idea prevailed in the middle colonies. In both New York and Pennsylvania, ethnic diversity produced disputes over core values that made strong, stable government difficult. New York's quarrels, painfully illustrated by Jacob Leisler's execution, both reflected and reinforced the wealthy manor elite's control. Often politically weak and unstable, they nevertheless ran the colony as they pleased. Pennsylvania settled for the gentler if less effective solution of avoiding giving much power to the government.

New York's land policies, in particular, retarded development and kept New York City poor and sleepy. Philadelphia benefited from Penn's policies as well as from a rich agricultural hinterland that both supplied the city with cheap food and provided commodities for export. The integration of agriculture into the commercial economy and the increasing importance of Philadelphia as a world port inside the growing British empire marked the beginning of sophisticated economic development. By 1760 Americans engaged in such activities were less and less willing to be governed from London. They were no longer rude, primitive colonists automatically doing the mother country's bidding.

Recommended Readings

DOCUMENTS: Daniel Horsmanden, *The New York Conspiracy* [1744] (1971); Peter Kalm, *Travels* [1750] (2 vols., 1937).

READINGS: (GENERAL) Jack P. Greene, *Pursuits of Happiness* (1988); Gary B. Nash, *Red, White, and Black* (1974); Marcus Rediker, *Between the Devil and the Deep Blue Sea* (1987); (NEW YORK) Patricia U. Bonomi, *A Factious People* (1971); Joyce D. Goodfriend, *Before the Melting Pot* (1992); Stanley N. Katz, *Newcastle's New York* (1968); Oliver A. Rink, *Holland on the Hudson* (1986); Robert C. Ritchie, *The Duke's Province* (1977); (PENNSYLVANIA) David H. Fischer, *Albion's Seed* (1989); James T. Lemon, *The Best Poor Man's Country* (1972); Sharon V. Salinger, *To Serve Well and Faithfully* (1987); Stephanie G. Wolf, *Urban Village* (1976); (IMMIGRATION) Bernard Bailyn, *Voyagers to the West* (1986); J.M. Bumsted, *The People's Clearances* (1982); Jon Butler, *The Huguenots in America* (1983); Ned Landsman, *Scotland and Its First American Colony* (1985).

5

—— ✠ ——

THE AMERICAN REVOLUTION,
1750-1783

CHAPTER OVERVIEW: From 1750 to 1763 the American colonists, satisfied with the British empire, helped drive the French out of North America. To pay for that war, the British Parliament then imposed taxes in the form of the Sugar Act (1764), Stamp Act (1765), Townshend Acts (1767), and Tea Act (1773). The colonists rebelled. Their most dramatic protest, the Boston Tea Party, prompted the British to punish Massachusetts with the Coercive Acts (1774), which led to war in 1775. A year later the Americans declared independence. Financing the war proved even more difficult than raising an army. The British won many battles, but lost two armies, at Saratoga in 1777 and at Yorktown in 1781. They recognized American independence in 1783.

Americans Help Maintain
the British Empire, 1750-1763

In 1750 the American colonies belonged to the British empire, prospered commercially, and grew rapidly in population. The colonists, protective of their liberty and wary of concentrated political power, developed a democratic politics based on English Whig principles. The colonists hated Britain's rivals, the French, and joined Britain in war against them in 1754. During the war, George Washington learned a military tactic that would later help him defeat the British in the Revolutionary War. In 1763 Britain won and, to Americans' relief, acquired French Canada. Britain's attempts to force the colonists to help pay for the war set the stage for the revolution.

THE COLONIES IN 1750. By 1750 nearly one and a half million Americans lived along the seacoast in 13 English colonies that stretched from

Maine (then part of Massachusetts) to Georgia. About one-fifth were **slaves** of African descent. Although economic growth had been slow and life hard during the 1600s and early 1700s, the years after 1730 had brought both increased immigration and greater prosperity. Americans then enjoyed the fastest economic growth of any society in the world.

The population doubled every 22 years, with a high birth rate, a relatively low death rate, and continued immigration. Benjamin Franklin shrewdly calculated that in the next century the colonies would have more people than England. In the long run English control appeared doubtful. In 1750, however, no one expressed such doubts.

The British empire was increasing in size, in wealth, and in prestige, with opportunities for commerce and trade expanding on a global scale. As part of the empire, the colonists shared in its benefits. Americans already supplied it with numerous raw materials, raising grain and horses or cutting timber for sale to the West Indies. In time America also promised to become a major market.

Thanks to Indian corn, food was cheap and plentiful in America. The colonists found land and timber for housing easy to come by, too. Skilled laborers usually worked at high wages, but the picture was not entirely rosy. The poor were likely to remain poor.

Immigrants looked for opportunities for their children. In England a rigid social class system limited the prospects of a poor man's son. In many parts of America, education was more readily available than in England, and throughout the colonies a poor boy had a better chance to gain an apprenticeship to a trade without paying a fee than in England.

AMERICA IS RIPE FOR SELF-GOVERNMENT. White male Americans enjoyed more actual political rights than their English or European counterparts. Although in both England and America a man got the right to vote only if he owned property, the colonists found it easier to gain the small amount of real estate needed to qualify to vote. In most colonies a majority of the adult white males could vote. By contrast, in England fewer than 10 percent were eligible.

In England both the poor and the middle class were dominated by a wealthy, landholding **aristocracy.** Dukes, earls, and lords had titles, special privileges, and great wealth. Nobles and knights, who had inherited both titles and money, had little reason to migrate to America. Almost none did.

America lacked titled nobles, and as a new country, had little inherited wealth. Indeed, only a handful of colonists, mostly a few landed families in New York and rice growers in South Carolina, had truly great wealth. Even George Washington, reputed to be the richest American at one point, lived in a relatively modest wooden house — not an ornate stone palace like Versailles.

The colonial middle class — mainly owners of small farms, self-employed craftsmen, and storekeepers — felt much closer to the wealthy, and, indeed, the newly rich in America had often been born into the middle class. From the viewpoint of an English duke, colonial society lacked the leadership provided by aristocrats. From the viewpoint of a colonist, America offered a unique possibility for ordinary people to develop their own political leadership.

AMERICANS ADOPT WHIG POLITICAL IDEAS. Throughout the 1700s both Americans and Europeans embraced the **Enlightenment,** a widespread philosophical movement characterized by a devotion to reason, including science; by a desire to promote learning, including mass education; by an insistence upon testing ideas concretely and empirically; and by a growing skepticism toward religion. In America, Benjamin Franklin, a man both practical and philosophical, epitomized the Enlightenment, as did Thomas Jefferson and John Adams.

As part of the Enlightenment's emphasis on the dispassionate exploration of ideas, both the British and Americans discussed the nature of a just government. Much of this discussion grew out of a general acceptance of the English philosopher John Locke's theory that people came together under a compact of their own making to create a government. All government, in this view, was based on **natural law,** that is, on certain rights that all human beings shared. This concept of rights led most English-speaking people on both sides of the Atlantic to conclude that government had to be based on the rule of law. Otherwise, rulers would trample on rights and become tyrants.

They also agreed that power led to corruption, and they sought to establish a mixed political system in which power was not concentrated but diffuse. In particular, they sought to maintain checks and balances, even though executive, legislative, and judicial powers were not separate.

In Britain, especially after the Glorious Revolution of 1688, power was shared by the king, **Parliament**, and the courts, which became increasingly independent. In the colonies power was shared by the governors (appointed by the king's government), governor's councils (usually appointed by the governor), legislative assemblies (elected), and local courts (appointed).

Some Englishmen, however, worried that, even with built-in safeguards, the political system favored the rich and powerful — especially the king and the aristocrats. Warning their countrymen that they must be ever vigilant lest the government stamp out the liberties of the people, these Englishmen, who ironically included many aristocrats, called themselves **Whigs.**

Not everyone in England agreed with the Whigs. For one thing, some people pointed out, too much liberty could lead to disorder — even to civil war. The purpose of government was to maintain order, and everyone owed allegiance to the government. This allegiance prevented disorder. In this view the king and the Church of England, especially, symbolized proper order. These Englishmen, who included many wealthy merchants and powerful rural gentry disinclined toward change, called themselves **Tories.**

Most Americans were Whigs. Indeed, in a new country where change was common, few people feared disorder. Instead, Americans became obsessed with liberty. They took to heart such English Radical Whigs as John Trenchard and Thomas Gordon, who, in *Cato's Letters* (1720), warned that unless people were vigilant, a corrupt government would trample on people's liberties. Long before the American Revolution, Americans had adopted this position.

Widespread property ownership and voting, the absence of a wealthy aristocracy, and the fluid nature of a rapidly changing society also gradually led Americans to accept the idea of equality. In the 1700s equality did not mean that the wealth should be shared, nor did it mean that each person should have an equal opportunity.

Equality meant that the same law applied to all people — or at least to all adult white males. The colonists did not consider slaves or Indians equal, and in 1750 few would have argued that the concept applied to free blacks or women. Generations would pass before the idea of equality would be expanded to mean an equal opportunity for everyone.

FIGHTING THE FRENCH AND INDIAN WAR, 1754-1763. In the mid-1700s Britain's empire had a great rival — France, which also had an empire, including the important colony of New France (today's Canada). Both the French and the British wished to crush each other's empires and to take valuable colonies. The two countries were at war from 1689-1697, 1702-1713, and 1744-1748. In America, these wars retarded frontier settlement, which drove up land prices, and worsened Indian-white relations (since both sides used Indians to attack colonists).

The British believed that New France threatened the British colonies along the North American seaboard. The French had cultivated good relations with many tribes both to gain beaver skins for the fur trade and to join the Indians in attacking English frontier settlements. Especially in New England, which was geographically closest to New France, the colonists feared the French and clung to England's protection.

The settlers' views were echoed by land speculators both in England and in the colonies. **Land grants** were of uncertain or little value if they could not be sold, and few people wanted to buy property that was likely to become a battleground the next time Britain and France went to war.

In 1754 Britain and France did go to war again in North America. Two years later the war spread to Europe. In most of the world the war was called the Seven Years' War, even though it lasted nine years, but in England's American colonies it became known as the French and Indian War.

Because the British navy controlled the Atlantic Ocean, the American colonies did not face a French threat from overseas. Instead, the French and their Indian allies attacked interior frontier areas with sudden, violent surprise.

The British and the colonists agreed that these raids must cease and that the only way to guarantee peace on the frontier was to remove the French permanently from North America. The British supplied the officers, some of the soldiers, and heavy weapons. The Americans provided armed men and food.

That same year, 1754, colonial leaders met at Albany, New York, to consider defense matters, including a possible coordinated attack on Canada. Nothing came of that scheme. They also discussed a Plan of Union, presented by Benjamin Franklin. Neither the colonies nor British authorities, however, wanted a single, unified American government, and the idea died.

In 1755 an expedition under Britain's General Edward Braddock marched through the woods to take France's Fort Duquesne (later renamed Fort Pitt by the English; today, Pittsburgh). At the Battle of the Wilderness, the French surprised and defeated the British. Although Braddock's soldiers maintained impressive discipline, the French fought Indian-style by shooting from behind the trees. Braddock died from wounds received in this battle. His aide, George Washington, observed the superiority of French methods.

After the French had repulsed attacks against New France, a British army in 1759 defeated the French on the Plains of Abraham at Québec city in New France. Both sides' generals were killed in the battle. In 1760 the British took Montréal and gained control of all New France.

THE BRITISH WIN THE WAR, 1763. In 1763, when Britain and France made peace, the British occupied a strong negotiating position. They demanded and got New France, which they renamed Canada. The numerous French settlers, however, were allowed to remain in Canada under British rule.

Settlers in the American colonies, especially in New England, celebrated. The French threat had been permanently removed. Indian-white relations promised to be more stable, and the frontier made safe for settlement. Land speculators licked their chops. The British, however, looked at matters somewhat differently. In many small ways over the years they had humored the colonists. The French threat had encouraged the British to treat the colonies well. Now that that threat had been removed, the British expected the Americans to show their gratitude by helping their mother country.

First, the war had been very expensive, doubling Britain's national debt. British taxpayers, including wealthy aristocrats, resisted further tax increases. Taxes in the colonies were low. Surely, thought the English, the colonists should pay a portion of the cost of a war that had brought them so much benefit.

Second, there were the Indians. English frontier settlers had constantly battled Indians. The result was that the British had had to post a very expensive army on the frontier. Without the French threat, the English saw no need for a large frontier army. If the Indians could be placated, then the army could be withdrawn. The natives would be peaceful, thought the English, without French guns and without American settlers encroaching on their territory.

In 1763 the British government issued a proclamation that prohibited frontier settlement beyond the ridge of the Appalachian Mountains. Americans reacted with anger and disbelief. Some settlers already lived beyond the proclamation line. Many land **speculators** saw their dreams of fortune evaporate. Besides, America's population was growing rapidly, and how could the increase be provided for within the coastal area left for settlement?

The French and Indian War changed the map of North America. It also changed the political relationship between Britain and the American colonies. Far from being the beginning of a long peace, the end of the war heralded a new age of strife. Seldom has a peace failed so utterly.

The Mother Country Abuses Her Children, 1764-1774

The British Parliament passed a series of acts to tax the colonists to help pay for the French and Indian War. After the Sugar Act (1764) raised little revenue, Parliament passed the Stamp Act (1765). The colonists rebelled. Benjamin Franklin explained that Americans would pay import duties on goods they bought, but not general taxes levied by a Parliament where they were not represented. Parliament's Townshend Acts (1767), contrary to Franklin's argument, found Americans unwilling to pay even import duties. The Tea Act (1773) led to the Boston Tea Party, for which Parliament punished Massachusetts with the Coercive Acts (1774).

LAWS ABOUT SUGAR, CURRENCY, AND QUARTERING, 1764-1765.
In 1764 the British Parliament decided to tax the American colonies. Actually, some small taxes, in the form of **import duties,** had been levied for years. The amounts had been minor, they had been paid mainly by wealthy merchants, and they were frequently evaded by smugglers.

The Sugar Act (1764), which covered many items in addition to sugar, reduced duties for some goods, increased charges for others, and extended levies to a number of items. To make sure that these duties were paid, Parliament authorized the appointment of many new customs officials and provided that disputes would be sent to special British admiralty courts that did not use juries. American juries had routinely declined to convict smugglers.

In another sign of meddling, Parliament passed the Currency Act (1764), which restricted the ability of the American colonies to issue paper money. Since the colonies always ran short of gold and silver, they had long used paper money to supply the credit necessary to keep commerce alive. This measure worsened a postwar depression.

A third measure, the Quartering Act (1765), required the colonies to provide barracks and provisions for the thousands of British soldiers stationed in America. If the colonies did not provide barracks, the law allowed soldiers to use inns or vacant buildings, including barns. New York's assembly defied the law, and Parliament ordered it to comply or be terminated.

THE STAMP ACT OUTRAGES THE COLONISTS, 1765. The British government found that, due to widespread smuggling, the Sugar Act's import duties were raising little money. So Parliament looked for a way to gain additional revenue from a broad-based tax. A stamp tax promised to fill the bill. England already had such a tax, and Parliament reasoned that the colonists should not object to any tax also levied in the mother country.

The Stamp Act (1765) required all colonial court papers, deeds, licenses, pamphlets, or newspapers to be stamped by a government official for a small fee. This measure showed no political sensitivity. It managed to touch most colonists, regardless of class, and its effect on licensed taverns and newspapers guaranteed a noisy response.

The colonists reacted to the changes in the enforcement of import duties and to the Stamp Act with outrage. The truth was that Americans hated taxes. This hatred, a peculiarly American idea, was rooted both in practice and in theory. In a new country built largely on credit, it was difficult to find the cash to pay taxes.

More important, Americans, drawing on popular Whig ideas about power, concluded that the Stamp Act was part of a scheme to deprive Americans of their liberty. In May 1765, Patrick Henry, a young Virginia legislator, introduced resolutions declaring that only the elected House of Burgesses could tax Virginians. Speaking for the Virginia Resolves, as the resolutions were called, Henry compared George III to Caesar and Charles I (who had lost his head). Shouts of "treason!" led Henry to reply, "If *this* be treason, make the most of it."

When British officials in America tried to enforce both the duties and the new stamp law, they were met with smuggling and defiance. To oppose British policy, Americans, including many wealthy merchants, created a secret organization called the Sons of Liberty. In the larger towns the Sons of Liberty forced officials to swear that they would not enforce these laws. Newspapers defiantly printed a skull and crossbones in the space where the Stamp Act required a stamp. In Boston the Sons compelled the local Stamp Act collector to resign, and a mob sacked Chief Justice Thomas Hutchinson's house.

Americans organized a boycott of English imports. No duties could be collected if no goods were imported. The colonists resolved to do without imports and be self-sufficient. This insistence upon self-sufficiency coincided with economic hard times. It was easy for Americans to swear not to buy imports when they lacked the means to buy much of anything. At the same time, as Americans dressed in homespun clothing, their pride swelled at the realization that they were capable of producing everything that they needed for themselves.

In October 1765, nine colonies sent representatives to the Stamp Act Congress in New York. At the suggestion of James Otis, the delegates petitioned both the king and Parliament to repeal the Stamp Act. They argued that only colonial assemblies had the right to levy taxes.

The protests, resistance, violence, and petitions surprised the British government. The prime minister, George Grenville, was of two minds. On the other hand, he did not want trouble from the colonies. On the other hand, he was not prepared to capitulate to American mobs.

FRANKLIN DISTINGUISHES BETWEEN DIRECT AND INDIRECT TAXES. Benjamin Franklin, then a colonial agent in London, and other Americans devised a theory both to explain American anger and to offer a solution. According to Franklin, Americans drew a distinction between indirect taxes, such as import duties, and direct taxes, such as the Stamp Act. The colonists had never objected to Parliament's small import duties, because they were a valid charge to maintain the benefits of the British empire's trading system. Besides, they were easy to evade.

Direct taxes like the Stamp Act, however, were another matter. The colonists, said Franklin, believed strongly that Parliament had no right to levy such taxes. Americans were not represented in Parliament. As Whig political theory had long held, there could be no taxation without representation. Therefore, only the popularly elected colonial assemblies could impose direct taxes on Americans.

Many members of Parliament found Franklin's position appalling. Parliament, including Grenville, believed that it alone held supreme legislative authority throughout the empire. As for the argument that the colonists were not represented in Parliament, members stated that the colonists did enjoy representation. Their virtual representation, like that of any other nonvoters, was derived from the fact that the members of Parliament collectively represented the entire empire. According to the theory of virtual representation, *some* voters elected Parliament, which then represented *everyone.*

This controversy continued, but in 1765 Grenville's Whig government fell for other reasons. The new prime minister was another Whig, the Marquess of Rockingham. The new government was more sympathetic to American concerns, and it sought compromise.

In 1766 Rockingham's government repealed the Stamp Act. Even a Whig-led Parliament, however, rejected the American notion that Parliament had no right to impose taxes on the colonies. The Declaratory Act (1766) accompanying the repeal of the Stamp Act made this point specifically. In addition, while Parliament removed import duties from many products, it kept a small duty on sugar, tea, and a few other items.

The colonists paid these duties without complaint, and the controversy subsided. Under the surface, however, both sides seethed. Parliament noted that very little revenue arrived from the colonies. Sooner or later, ways would have to be found to make the Americans pay more. And the colonists realized that, despite the repeal of the Stamp Act, the Declaratory Act threatened American liberties. Besides, British officials began to enforce import duties more vigorously.

AMERICANS BATTLE THE TOWNSHEND ACTS, 1767-1772. Lord Rockingham's government soon gave way to another Whig government under the Earl of Chatham. When Chatham fell ill, the administration was run by Charles Townshend. In 1767 he decided that the time was ripe to make the colonists pay more taxes. Paying careful attention to Franklin's distinction between direct and indirect taxes, Townshend got Parliament to impose new and higher import duties on the colonists for paper, glass, paint, and tea.

The Townshend Acts (1767) produced an outcry in America. For one thing, Americans perceived correctly that the royal governors intended to use the revenues so that they would not have to get appropriations from the elected colonial assemblies.

Americans then resumed the boycott of imported goods. Women played an important role in organizing this campaign. Little revenue was collected, and smuggling thrived. John Dickinson's widely read *Letters from a Farmer in Pennsylvania* (1767) denied that Parliament had any right to tax Americans. "No taxation without representation" soon became a popular American slogan.

In 1768 British customs officials in Boston seized the *Liberty,* a ship owned by the wealthy merchant John Hancock. A mob attacked customs officials, who fled to an island in the harbor. The British then stationed two **regiments** of troops in Boston.

In 1770 Lord Frederick North, a Tory, became the head of the British government. He recognized the futility of trying to enforce the Townshend Acts. North's government, however, was unwilling to surrender parliamentary power. Besides, the American reaction to the import duties had shown that Franklin's distinction between direct and indirect taxes, even if it had once been true, was no longer accepted by most colonists. From the English viewpoint, the Americans were ungrateful upstarts, cantankerous children who needed to be taught a lesson. In 1770 Parliament repealed the Townshend Acts, but North's government insisted on showing the Americans who was boss. Therefore, the tax on tea was reduced but retained.

That same year British soldiers, popularly called **Redcoats,** angered New Yorkers by cutting down their Liberty Pole. In Boston, where fights between soldiers and local crowds had become common, the Redcoats fired into an angry mob. Five people, including the runaway slave Crispus Attucks, died in the Boston Massacre.

In 1772 a British customs ship, the *Gaspée,* went aground in Rhode Island. After nightfall a mob led by the wealthy merchant John Brown attacked the ship and set it afire. A British investigation failed to uncover what had happened because local residents refused to cooperate.

TEA TIME IN AMERICA, 1773. The following year the British government decided to aid the nearly bankrupt East India Company by passing the Tea Act (1773). This law reduced the import duty on tea sold in America but gave the East India Company a monopoly on American tea sales. Ordinary Americans worried less about the price of tea than about the British show of power. Wealthy merchants who had long sold Dutch tea, whether obtained legally or not, faced ruin.

To the surprise of North's government, the tea tax became a political issue in America in 1773. In Charleston, South Carolina, a tea ship was allowed to unload its cargo after officials agreed not to collect customs duties. The untaxed tea was put into storage. In New York and Philadelphia residents persuaded tea ships to depart without docking.

In Boston the royal governor, Thomas Hutchinson, insisted that the tea be unloaded. He arranged special protection for the tea ship to enter the harbor. Once docked, however, the ship fell prey to a protest organized by Samuel Adams and John Hancock, leaders of the Sons of Liberty. Disguised as Indians, 150 angry colonists went aboard and threw 342 chests of tea into the harbor in an episode that came to be called the Boston Tea Party.

PARLIAMENT COERCES MASSACHUSETTS, 1774. The Boston Tea Party outraged the British government, which decided to make the people of Boston pay for their bad joke. Parliament passed a series of laws designed both to punish Boston and to deter other colonists. Collectively, they were called the Coercive Acts (1774).

The harshest provision closed the port of Boston. Because Boston was essentially a commercial city devoted to trade, closing the port for an indefinite period threatened to wreck the city's economy. This measure, more than any other, united residents in opposition to England.

Closing the port required a **naval blockade** to prevent smuggling, and given the history of Boston, unrest was likely inside the city. So the British sent several thousand soldiers to Boston and in a new Quartering Act required that the city's residents house and feed them, even if it meant that civilians had to take soldiers into vacant rooms in their homes.

The English knew that widespread popular opposition throughout the colony of Massachusetts would cause further trouble. The center of that opposition was the colony's popularly elected assembly and town meetings. Therefore, Parliament ordered that the governor's council be appointed by the crown rather than chosen by the assembly. The royal governor was to control the courts, and town meetings were to be restricted.

The colonists had long used the local courts to harass British officials. Massachusetts juries rarely convicted smugglers and routinely ruled against colonial officials. To prevent these kinds of decisions, Parliament provided that cases could be tried in England rather than in Massachusetts.

The four Coercive Acts were joined by a fifth measure, the Québec Act (1774). This law provided Canada with a government that lacked an elected assembly. In addition, Parliament gave Canada generous boundaries and allowed the French inhabitants to keep their Catholicism and language. To the English colonists, the harsh treatment of Boston contrasted with the generosity shown to the French settlers. Furthermore, the tolerance of nearby Catholics did not set well with many Americans, especially in New England.

Americans Make a Revolution, 1774-1783

In 1774 the crisis intensified, and the next year war began in Massachusetts at Lexington, Concord, and Bunker Hill. In early 1776 Tom Paine proposed independence, which the Continental Congress adopted in July. The Americans' victory at Saratoga in 1777 raised American morale and convinced the French to provide crucial help to the Americans. They desperately needed help, lacking money to finance the war or feed their hungry soldiers. The British army moved south, where they got support from local sympathizers. After a costly campaign in the Carolinas (1780-1781), Lord Cornwallis surrendered to George Washington and the French at Yorktown in 1781. The peace treaty, signed in 1783, left America independent — and financially ruined.

SEEKING A POLITICAL SOLUTION, 1774. By 1774 many Americans had adopted a new view of the proper role between Britain and the colonies. According to this view, Britain and the colonies were distinct political entities. Britain was governed by the king and Parliament. The colonies were to be governed by governors acting as the king's representatives and by popularly elected colonial assemblies. Parliament had no role to play in governing the colonies. Until the 1760s, in fact, this had been the actual way that the colonies had been governed.

The sole connection between the colonies and Britain was to be allegiance to the same king. Many years later, the British government would adopt this formula for the British empire, but in 1774 few people in England accepted the idea of colonial self-government.

In response to the Coercive Acts, leading colonists organized Committees of Correspondence, which created a network to exchange information about current events throughout the 13 colonies. These leaders pushed the colonies to stand together. Otherwise, they believed, the British government would pursue a policy of dividing the colonies and, as evidenced by Boston's recent experience, conquering them one at a time.

Correspondence, however, was not enough. The hated British laws had to be opposed vigorously. For this purpose self-appointed leaders, such as Boston's fiery Samuel Adams, created Committees of Safety. These committees organized mass support and began to arrange with elected legislative leaders and **militia** officers to provide military force if needed against the British.

To coordinate these activities, 12 colonies (Georgia was missing) sent representatives to the First Continental Congress in Philadelphia in September 1774. This congress pledged to continue the trade boycott, authorized coordinated military preparation, and sent a conciliatory petition to the king. The atmosphere, however, was anything but tranquil, as Samuel Adams and Patrick Henry raged, John Adams brooded, and George Washington carefully observed. It became clear that however the controversy with Britain might end, the congress would play a major role in shaping the colonial response to the British challenge.

FIGHTING AT LEXINGTON, CONCORD, AND BUNKER HILL, 1775. In 1775 British officials in America watched events with growing alarm. To maintain British authority, they had to crush the colonists' organized opposition. The greatest threat to British rule came from popular defiance backed by local militias.

Boston, which the British correctly perceived to be the center of the rebellion, offered an important test case. A crackdown there might serve as a warning to rebels elsewhere. The closing of the port had only worsened relations between the people and the occupying British army. Furthermore, the arming of the militia in nearby towns threatened to leave the British soldiers, called Redcoats, trapped inside Boston.

So on April 19, 1775, the British army marched from Boston to Lexington and Concord to challenge the local militia companies and to seize the arms and ammunition stored there. Instead, on Lexington's village green the Redcoats met the local militia, which had been warned by the midnight rides of Paul Revere and William Dawes that the British were coming. Ordered to disband, the militia at first refused. Then they began to disperse. Someone let go a single shot, and the British opened fire — in a "shot heard round the world." The war was on.

The British soldiers did take some arms from Concord and Lexington, but they found themselves so unwelcome that they beat a hasty retreat back to occupied Boston. Along the way snipers harassed them. The Americans saw this episode as a great victory.

The Redcoats were stuck in Boston. The American militia had the city surrounded. Both sides agreed that a pitched battle could lead to a big victory and end the dispute one way or another. When General Thomas Gage, the British commander, prepared to attack Americans outside Boston, the local militia suddenly felt weak.

The residents of Massachusetts appealed for military assistance from the other colonies, which raised troops and sent them to Massachusetts. They became the Continental army and were put under the command of a Virgin-

At the beginning of the Revolutionary War, the British marched to Concord, Massachusetts, where they were fired upon before hastily retreating to Boston. (Bettmann Archive)

ian, George Washington, in order to demonstrate to the English that the Americans were united.

Before Washington took command, on June 17, 1775, British troops left Boston by crossing the Charles River and moved toward Bunker Hill in Charlestown. Americans met the Redcoats at Breed's Hill in the first great battle of the war. Although fought on Breed's Hill, it was remembered as the battle of Bunker Hill.

Redcoats marched in formation up the hill toward the Americans, who hid behind logs and hastily thrown up dirt **breastworks.** The Americans held. The British seemed stunned and recoiled twice under a hail of fire. The Americans, running low on ammunition, withdrew, and the Redcoats captured the hill. But because of heavy British casualties, the Americans claimed a great victory and celebrated.

The British, however, remained in control of Boston. They could repel any direct attack upon their stronghold but were too weak to control the surrounding countryside. Similarly, the Americans could not drive the Redcoats out, although they retained control of areas not under British occupation. Throughout the war the British found it impossible to occupy the entire countryside while the Americans lacked the ability to take British-controlled cities. These two facts predicted a military stalemate.

AMERICANS DISCUSS INDEPENDENCE, 1775-1776. Meantime, the First Continental Congress had given way to the more militant Second Continental Congress. Meeting in May 1775, in Philadelphia — after the shooting had started — delegates for the first time began to question the fundamental political theory of the British empire.

Why should an entire continent be governed by a tiny island? And did it make sense for Americans to fight a war in order to gain the right to be a self-governing part of an empire that had such contempt for Americans that it would not recognize their right to self-determination? In late 1775 the congress debated these matters, even as they scrambled to provide men and arms for Washington's army.

Meanwhile, Parliament decided to get tough with the rebels by passing the Prohibitory Act (1775). This law allowed the British to impose a naval blockade on the colonies and seize American ships on the high seas. Such economic warfare did not hold out compromise, reconciliation, and a peaceful settlement.

In January 1776, Tom Paine, a tailor who had recently immigrated from England to Philadelphia, anonymously published a radical pamphlet, *Common Sense.* It swept through the colonies like wildfire, selling more than 100,000 copies in three months. Paine argued that Americans had a natural, God-given right to independence. Ridiculing monarchy as an archaic system of government, he embraced liberty and equality.

By June 1776, public opinion clearly supported independence. Congress prepared to act by authorizing a small committee, chaired by Thomas Jefferson, to draft a declaration setting forth the reasons why the colonies should be independent.

DECLARING INDEPENDENCE, 1776. Jefferson's Declaration of Independence, adopted by congress on July 2, 1776, and proclaimed publicly two days later, mainly condemned King George III's conduct. Attacking the king was necessary in order to win over to the idea of independence those Americans who still clung to the notion of self-governance within the British empire. The document was also designed to gain foreign support, especially from France.

The Declaration, however, did far more. It said that "all men are created equal." Even though the sentiment did not apply to slaves and women, it was a bold assertion far more radical than anything in any other major political document of its era. Even today, the concept sends shivers of fear down the spines of elitists around the world.

Jefferson defended the right of revolution, maintaining that people had an innate right to overthrow their government any time they decided that the government was unworkable and tyrannical. This, too, was a radical concept — and one frequently cited by later revolutionaries. Linked to the right of revolution was the right of people to form a government based on rules of their own choosing. In other words, as John Locke had suggested, the people had an intrinsic right to draft a constitution in order to frame a new government in place of the one they had overthrown.

Finally, the Declaration stated that people had a right to "life, liberty, and the pursuit of happiness." The right to life and liberty had long been part of the Whig political philosophy. Whigs, however, generally joined these rights with the right to own property. Jefferson instead saw a right to pursue happiness. Property might be one form of happiness, but Jefferson's vision clearly contained the idea that people could seek out whatever made them happy. This notion resonated with a peculiarly American desire for personal satisfaction. Society was to be based on fulfillment of the self.

Not every American accepted the Declaration of Independence. The projected break with the British empire terrified 10 to 20 percent of the colonists. To those who remained loyal to British authority, called **Tories,** the power and order represented by the empire seemed necessary, the link to monarchy wise, and the British restraint on the democratic power of the American rabble desirable.

Tories, or Loyalists, as they called themselves, came from all social classes, but were especially prevalent among officeholders. Although found in all geographical regions, they were most numerous in northern port cities and the Carolina backcountry. By the end of the war about 100,000 Tories, some 3 percent of the population, left the colonies, mostly for Canada. One-quarter of the lawyers fled. The states usually confiscated their property.

Many more Americans, however, were **Whigs,** as the revolutionaries called themselves. They believed in the political ideas expressed in the Declaration of Independence and were determined to make the revolution a success. About 30 to 40 percent of the colonists actively embraced independence, while most of the remainder, the silent near-majority, either gave lukewarm support or simply acquiesced.

THE BRITISH WIDEN THE WAR, 1776-1777. The British came to realize that their military occupation of Boston was meaningless, since a naval blockade could (and did) keep the port closed. The English decided to carry the war to the other colonies that had supported Boston's resistance.

So in March 1776, the British evacuated Boston, regrouped their forces, and returned in July under General Sir William Howe in a massive attack by 32,000 troops, including 9,000 hired Germans, on Long Island, New York. This was the largest military force ever assembled in North America. In contrast, Washington had only 19,000 soldiers, including militia.

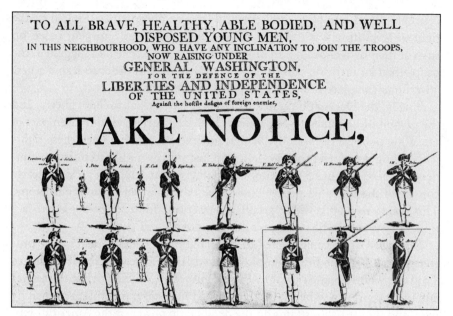

During the American Revolution, the Continental army used recruiting posters to encourage young men to enlist. Both glamor and
patriotism were promoted by the uniform and drill suggested in this
poster. (CULVER PICTURES)

The British strategy was to occupy the major cities — New York, Philadelphia, and Charleston — and to choke off the foreign trade that had seemed so
necessary to sustain the American economy. Redcoats could make punitive
raids into rebel areas near the seaports.

In 1776 Washington's Continental army retreated from the New York
area after a string of minor defeats. During this campaign the British captured
and executed the schoolmaster Nathan Hale as a spy. Facing superior British
forces, Washington retreated across New Jersey.

As the year closed at Christmas 1776, a small number of Washington's
troops crossed the Delaware River to capture an unimportant British garrison
at Trenton. The 900 British-paid German soldiers who occupied Trenton were
surprised amid their Christmas celebrations. This incident, as well as a similar
minor victory at Princeton in January 1777, gave the Americans heart and
suggested that the passionately committed colonists should be able to defeat
hired foreign troops who cared little about the war one way or the other.

In 1777 the British planned to march from Québec, which had remained
loyal to Britain, through upstate New York. This force would give comfort to
New York's many Tories and would link up with another British army that

moved north along the Hudson River from New York City. America would be cut in half, and if the colonists were so stupid as to fight a battle, they would find themselves surrounded by two British armies.

This British strategy failed. First, it overestimated Tory support in upstate New York. Second, it depended on two British armies moving toward one another in a situation without communications. As it turned out, General Howe went south from New York to capture Philadelphia, leaving half the pincers missing.

Consequently, the Americans, under General Horatio Gates, surprised General John Burgoyne's British army coming from Canada. In October 1777, Gates's army surrounded Burgoyne's at Saratoga, New York. The British surrendered.

Saratoga boosted American morale. It also made it possible for Benjamin Franklin, then the American representative in Paris, to negotiate French support for the American cause. In 1778, the French agreed to send a navy, an army, and military supplies to assist the Americans. This help from a great power proved crucial to American victory.

WEAK FINANCES THREATEN RUIN AT VALLEY FORGE, 1777-1778. With the British in control of New York and Philadelphia, euphoria over Saratoga quickly faded and the revolutionaries became demoralized by the lack of further success. Even the Continental Congress had been forced to flee. Congress found it increasingly difficult to raise money to support the war. The congress continued to issue paper currency, but its value began to decline rapidly, partly because many expected a British victory and partly because the sheer quantity of paper money caused inflation to accelerate.

The financier Robert Morris valiantly tried to stabilize the government's finances in 1781. But by the end of the war congress had issued $240 million in paper money and the states another $200 million; the continental dollar had lost 98 percent of its value.

George Washington's army suffered mightily. During the harsh winter of 1777-1778, they camped at Valley Forge just 20 miles from the British in Philadelphia. Although the valley was agriculturally rich, the local German farmers saw little reason to sell their produce to the revolutionaries for worthless paper currency. They could sell provisions for good British money to the Redcoats occupying Philadelphia.

Washington's patience and courage provided the leadership that kept the army and the idea of nationhood alive. While others wrung their hands in despair, Washington stoically wrote letters begging congress to find the money to continue the war. He promised that he would not quit if the means to sustain the cause could be found.

THE WAR MOVES SOUTH, 1778-1781. Meanwhile, the British turned to the South, promising freedom to slaves who would support their cause. A few blacks took up the offer, but most remained suspicious either about British victory or about the prospects for actually attaining freedom.

Beginning in 1778, the British tried a more direct southern strategy. After sending forces under Lord Cornwallis to occupy Georgia, they seized Charleston in May 1780, capturing three American generals and 5,000 troops, the greatest patriot reverse of the war.

In parts of the southern backcountry, Tories were so numerous that more fought for the empire than with Washington's Continental army. In North Carolina, home to Tory Highland Scots long hostile to the Whiggish Scots-Irish, local bands of Loyalists and revolutionaries marauded, burned, looted, and killed each other. This backcountry civil war was by far the most vicious campaign during the revolution.

White southerners, however, generally backed independence. Support was especially strong among Virginia's wealthy tobacco planters. Many were heavily in debt to London merchants, and the revolution provided them with a convenient opportunity to default.

Some planters allowed their slaves to enlist under terms that provided for freedom at the end of the war. About 20 percent of the soldiers who fought on the American side in the revolution were black. After the war, Virginia had a large free black population due to this policy. Other states acted differently. South Carolina refused to arm any slaves, even at the risk of military defeat.

Responding to the loss of Charleston, congress sent troops south under Horatio Gates, the hero of Saratoga. On August 16, 1780, Gates met the British, commanded by Cornwallis, in a major battle at Camden, in western South Carolina. Had the Americans been able to defeat the British so far from Cornwallis's coastal supply base, it surely would have been the end of the war. Instead, Gates relied too heavily upon militia units, and as the battle began, the militia fled. They retreated 75 miles, but Gates rushed away even faster and was finally located 160 miles north at Hillsboro, North Carolina.

More trouble followed. A month later the American General Benedict Arnold sold out to the British. His plan was to deliver the key post at West Point, New York, to the British. Only the timely capture of a British spy, the unfortunate Major John André, prevented Arnold from carrying out his betrayal. André was hanged. Arnold commanded British troops before retiring to London on a fat pension.

In the South, Washington replaced Gates with General Nathanael Greene, a onetime Rhode Island Quaker and blacksmith. Greene divided his forces, as did Cornwallis. A portion of Greene's army defeated a part of Cornwallis's at King's Mountain, North Carolina, in October 1780, and at Cowpens, South Carolina, in January 1781. Both backcountry battles left the British far from their supply lines. After a costly victory over Greene at Guilford Court House, North Carolina, in March 1781, Cornwallis headed for the coast.

THE BRITISH SURRENDER AT YORKTOWN, 1781. In 1781 Cornwallis's Redcoats marched north into Virginia toward Yorktown. This turned out to be a major mistake. The Americans controlled rivers on both sides of Cornwallis's position, and Washington placed his army alongside the Comte de Rochambeau's French army on the neck of land so as to cut Cornwallis off from escape through Virginia.

British supply ships arrived late and faced a naval battle with the Comte de Grasse's French fleet. The French won and thereby prevented either resupply or retreat by sea. After a time, Cornwallis came to see the hopelessness of his situation. On October 19, 1781, he surrendered his army to Washington while, according to tradition, the British band played "The World Turned Upside Down."

By 1781 the British government had lost interest in the American war, which was part of a world struggle that had gone poorly for the British. Maintaining the empire by military force had little appeal because of the expense. A face-saving formula for withdrawal from America, however, could not be found, and peace negotiations dragged on, even after British troops had been evacuated from most of America.

Finally, in 1782, after the Marquess of Rockingham's Whig government replaced North's Tory government, negotiations grew serious. In September 1783, both the Americans and the British signed a peace treaty in Paris as part of a global settlement that recognized American independence. Shortly afterward, the last British troops left New York.

The western boundary of the new republic was generously fixed at the Mississippi River. The British, no doubt, had concluded that American settlers would soon reach the river anyway. To the British, it was more important to keep the Mississippi out of the hands of their enemies, the French, than to resist the encroaching Americans. The French gained nothing from the war, except the satisfaction of seeing the British lose.

The United States began with a bright future — and with massive war debts, a ruined economy, no trade with the British empire, weak political organization, and internal disputes between Tories and revolutionaries.

Conclusion

The British empire did not meet America's needs. When the colonists protested against Parliament's arbitrary decisions, they discovered that their actions had little effect in London, except to produce more bad policies. Once war began, Americans came to realize that they had grown into a separate people, and their capacity for resistance became the basis for declaring independence. This independence existed in Americans' minds long before it was won on the battlefield and finally recognized in a peace treaty.

The war forced a clean break with Britain and gave national identity a heroic mold. The heroes of the American Revolution became both legends in their own time and heroes for all time. Jefferson's idealism and Washington's stoicism proved inspirational, just as the victory at Yorktown appeared providential. God helps those who help themselves, said Franklin. The revolutionaries had lived out Franklin's admonition, convincing themselves that they thereby confirmed both their own worthiness and God's favor upon their enterprise. No other nation was ever born in such self-righteousness.

Recommended Readings

DOCUMENTS: J. Hector St. John de Crevecoeur, *Letters from an American Farmer and Sketches of Eighteenth Century America* (1963); John Dickinson, *Letters from a Farmer in Pennsylvania* (1767); Peter Oliver, *Origin and Progress of the American Rebellion* (1961).

READINGS: (VALUES) Bernard Bailyn, *The Ideological Origins of the American Revolution* (1967), and *The Origins of American Politics* (1968); Ruth H. Bloch, *Visionary Republic* (1985); Jack P. Greene, *Peripheries and Center* (1986), and *The Quest for Power* (1963); Nathan O. Hatch, *The Sacred Cause of Liberty* (1977); Henry F. May, *The Enlightenment in America* (1976); Edmund S. and Helen M. Morgan, *The Stamp Act Crisis* (1953); Jack N. Rakove, *The Beginnings of National Politics* (1979); Gordon S. Wood, *The Creation of the American Republic, 1776-1787* (1969), and *The Radicalism of the American Revolution* (1991); (REVOLUTION) Joy D. and Richard Buel, Jr., *The Way of Duty* (1984); Edward Countryman, *A People in Revolution* (1981); Robert A. Gross, *The Minutemen and Their World* (1976); Linda K. Kerber, *Women of the Republic* (1980); Pauline Maier, *From Resistance to Revolution* (1972), and *The Old Revolutionaries* (1980); Mary B. Norton, *Liberty's Daughters* (1980); Kenneth Silverman, *A Cultural History of the American Revolution* (1987); (WAR) Don Higginbotham, *The War of American Independence* (1971); Robert Middlekauff, *The Glorious Cause* (1982); Charles Royster, *A Revolutionary People at War* (1979); John W. Shy, *A People Numerous and Armed* (1976).

6

— ⚏ —

THE NEW NATION,
1783-1800

CHAPTER OVERVIEW: Any new country must first devise and then develop an appropriate political system. The 1780s began with a weak federal government under the Articles of Confederation, which proved inadequate, and ended with the adoption of the Constitution, which created a much stronger government. In the 1790s President George Washington set the tone and established crucial policies that came to define the American political system. From 1797 to 1801, his unlucky successor, John Adams, was embroiled in almost constant controversy, including foreign troubles and increasingly bitter partisan battles. The century ended with lusty political parties competing for power, a presidential election crisis, and the peaceful passage of power from Federalists to Democrats.

Living under the Articles
of Confederation, 1783-1787

Economically devastated by the Revolutionary War, the new nation entered a depression, which sparked Shays's Rebellion in 1786. The new state governments experimented with democratic constitutions that proved much more effective than the Articles of Confederation, which had provided a weak federal government throughout the 1780s. It accomplished little, but Congress did pass major ordinances governing the western territories. National leaders finally decided to overhaul the federal government.

AMERICANS SUFFER DEPRESSION, INFLATION, AND DEBT. The 1780s brought both economic and political troubles. Massive public debt, worthless paper money, low economic growth, and high unemployment

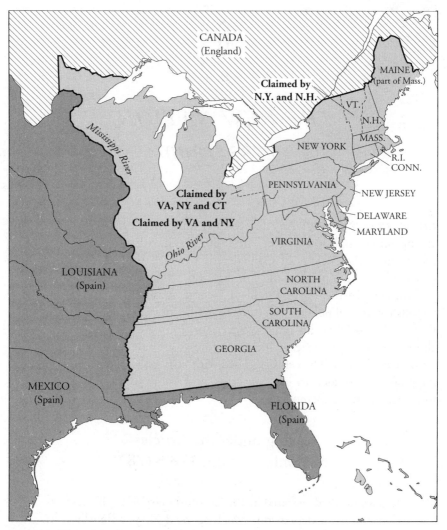

Map 6.1. The United States in 1783

caused political crises, while the inability of the political system to respond worsened these economic problems.

Economic difficulties had many causes. For one thing, the British government punished the United States by cutting off American trade with the British West Indies. Before the revolution, Americans had sold agricultural produce to the West Indies and in return had imported molasses and rum. Much of this profitable trade had been carried in American ships. As these markets were lost, both trade and shipbuilding declined.

On the other hand, Americans were to blame for much of the trouble.

They had paid for the very expensive Revolutionary War largely by borrowing, usually by issuing paper money. The money supply had increased much faster than had the economy, and the result was tremendous wartime **inflation.**

By 1783 most wartime paper money was worthless. State governments generally ceased to issue new paper money, and economic activity declined. People who had borrowed money during the war were now unable to pay their debts. As the dwindling money supply brought a general decline in commerce, **artisans** and farmers found it hard to sell their goods. Economic production dwindled, and the standard of living fell, creating a **depression.**

State governments seemed incapable of solving these problems. Rhode Island continued to issue paper money, even though its paper was held in contempt. This money did not circulate outside Rhode Island, but it was **legal tender** for all debts inside the state and had to be accepted. When debtors approached their creditors with Rhode Island paper, creditors fled to Massachusetts to avoid having to accept the stuff.

States quarreled and pointed accusing fingers across state boundaries. They imposed high **tariff** duties on goods from adjacent states. Although this was popular locally, it caused overall trade to decline.

SHAYS'S REBELLION CAUSES PANIC, 1786. Massachusetts tried to pay off its war debts too fast. The state raised taxes on land and demanded that the new taxes be paid in **specie,** that is, gold or silver. Farmland owners in the western part of the state found few markets for their produce. Therefore, they had no access to specie with which to pay these burdensome taxes.

Threatened with the loss of their land, these farmers, led by Daniel Shays, rebelled in 1786. They sought to prevent the courts from meeting to hear suits brought against debtors. Although Shays's Rebellion failed, and thereby showed the state government's soundness, it produced panic among Boston's wealthy merchants, who saw the revolt, incorrectly, as an attack on private property. Wise politicians understood that the real problem was a bad economy combined with an unresponsive federal government.

ESTABLISHING THE NEW STATE GOVERNMENTS. In the mid-1780s political leaders began to examine the political structure. In contrast with the anemic national government under the **Articles of Confederation,** most state governments established during the Revolutionary War seemed popular and robust. They had been constructed with written constitutions that largely confirmed the colonial practice of dividing power among independent executive, legislative, and judicial branches. The legislative branches had been made more powerful and had been divided into two houses.

In place of royal governors with absolute veto power over legislation, there were now governors elected either by the voters or by the legislators, and the governors had only limited vetos that the legislatures could override. Only Pennsylvania's radical constitution had broken with this concept. Pennsylvania provided for a plural executive council instead of a governor.

Most states had expanded the right to vote, although it was usually restricted to adult white males, and many states still required voters to own property. The minimum amount, however, declined. Property requirements for officeholders had also been reduced. Some states maintained religious requirements for voters. Personal rights also had been expanded. Virginia, for example, no longer used tax money to support churches and in 1785 guaranteed all citizens freedom of religion.

CONFRONTING THE WEAK ARTICLES OF CONFEDERATION. In contrast, the states in 1781 had created a weak central government through the Articles of Confederation. This government, which consisted of little more than a congress appointed by the states, was generally considered a failure. The states had retained too much power, including the right of taxation. The Confederation lacked power to collect taxes. It could only beg money from the states, which often ignored its pleas. The Confederation also could not control interstate commerce.

At the same time, the executive branch was virtually nonexistent. Congress was supposed to run the government, but the delegates seldom agreed on a policy and then only after long debate. Each of the 13 states had one vote in the Congress, and important laws required the consent of nine states. It was hard to find nine votes.

THE CONFEDERATION MAKES PLANS FOR THE WEST. The Confederation's only success concerned land policy west of the Appalachian Mountains and north of the Ohio River. The Land Ordinance of 1785 had provided for surveying these federal lands in six-mile wide by six-mile long townships, for selling land at modest prices to settlers, and for providing one section per township for the support of public schools.

The Northwest Ordinance of 1787 further provided for the organization of territorial governments in the same area. The territories were to be admitted to the union eventually as five states (Ohio, Indiana, Illinois, Michigan, and Wisconsin) on an equal standing with the original states. Furthermore, slavery was prohibited in this area.

NATIONAL LEADERS DEBATE THE ARTICLES. The Articles of Confederation had one fatal flaw. The Articles could be amended only with the consent of all 13 sovereign states. As a practical matter, amendments were almost impossible. Maryland had blocked the settlement of western land claims, in which it had no interest, in order to gain political advantage, and Rhode Island's rum distillers had singlehandedly prevented the Confederation from imposing a duty on imported rum.

Political leaders concluded that the Confederation was unworkable, and that the ability of one state to block any changes made revision of the Articles unlikely. The Articles, unlike the state constitutions, had been too experimental. Not enough attention had been paid to organizing the government in ways supported by political experience. Many concluded that the central government needed to be made more like the successful state governments.

In 1786, therefore, at a meeting in Annapolis, Maryland, Alexander Hamilton persuaded a dozen delegates from five states to call for a general convention to deal with this political problem and, by implication, with the economic problem as well.

Planning the United States Constitution, 1787-1789

In 1787 state legislatures elected delegates to the Constitutional Convention, which drafted a plan for a new federal government. The new Constitution included a number of important compromises. Ratification by the states during 1787-1788 was difficult and controversial. As a condition for ratification, several states demanded that a bill of rights be added.

THE CONSTITUTIONAL CONVENTION MEETS, 1787. Twelve state legislatures sent 55 delegates to meet as a convention in Philadelphia during the sultry summer of 1787. (Rhode Island, still sulking over the attempt to tax rum, declined to send representatives.) It was generally expected that the convention would revise the Articles of Confederation. Although representing different states and diverse interests, these delegates were similar in several respects. All were white males, most owned considerable property, and a large number held **slaves.** Many were planters or large-scale commercial farmers, while others were wealthy merchants. Some were both. A number practiced law. Almost all were politicians with much experience in government.

At the convention, the delegates sought to protect their own property interests, but they also showed a remarkable capacity for larger issues. They understood that future prosperity both for themselves and for the country as a whole required boldness, a grand vision, and a willingness to sacrifice petty personal concerns to larger, national needs.

Above all, they wanted to create a national government that would last. If the new government succeeded, the failure of the Confederation would be overlooked. However, if the new government failed, most Americans would conclude that a strong continental government based upon republican principles was impossible. The country then would either become a centralized despotism or quickly disintegrate into a collection of warring states.

George Washington chaired the convention, and at crucial moments he acted to resolve angry disputes. An old and ill Benjamin Franklin, carried to the convention every day in a litter, retained his wit and kept the other delegates laughing. Alexander Hamilton of New York constantly pushed for a stronger new government, while two Virginians, George Mason and James Madison, continually drew upon political experience in their home state. Two prominent leaders were missing. Ambassadors John Adams and Thomas Jefferson were, respectively, in London and Paris.

DEBATING REPRESENTATION, SLAVERY, AND PRESIDENTIAL ELECTIONS. The Virginia delegates proposed a new constitution with a strong federal government divided among the executive, legislative, and judicial branches. The Congress was to have two branches, both based on state population. The lower house was to be elected by the people, while the upper house was to be elected by the lower house from among men nominated by state legislatures. The Congress was to elect the chief executive, who would resemble a prime minister. The executive and judiciary were jointly to have the right to veto legislation.

The Virginia plan drew much support, but delegates from lightly populated states opposed it. They were afraid that a powerful legislature controlled by a handful of populous states would dominate the new government. Delegates from New Jersey, then small in population, proposed modifying the Articles of Confederation. Congress would gain the power to tax, to regulate interstate commerce, to name a veto-less plural executive, and to pick a supreme court. Each state, regardless of population, would continue to have equal representation in Congress.

Most delegates found the New Jersey plan's revisions too modest. They liked the Virginia plan's boldness, although they felt uncomfortable with the details. Delegates from Connecticut then proposed a compromise, which was adopted. Representation in the lower House of Representatives would be based on population. Each state would have equal representation in the upper house, which the delegates decided to call the Senate.

Another compromise was contained within this compromise. Delegates from the South wanted representation to be based upon total population, but delegates from the North opposed counting the South's slaves, who did not participate in the political process. Finally, it was decided that three-fifths of the slaves were to be counted for the purpose of representation.

The convention also struggled with how to elect the president. Delegates were determined that the chief executive should be politically independent, and thus rejected election either by Congress or by state legislators. Nor did they trust popular election. Ignoring the methods proven effective in the states, they instead provided for an **electoral college** to choose the president.

THE CONSTITUTION'S CHECKS AND BALANCES. The Constitution was an extraordinarily clever political document. It ingeniously set forth a basic framework for government that kept power divided among the executive, legislative, and judicial branches. At every turn, **checks and balances** prevented hasty action or the aggrandizement of power by any single branch.

To become law, a bill had to pass both the House and Senate and then be signed by the president. However, the president's **veto** could be overridden by a two-thirds vote in each chamber of Congress. The president appointed the cabinet and all judges, but the Senate had to approve the appointments. Federal judges were independent because they served for life, but both judges and the president could be removed from office by Congress using the impeachment process. The president negotiated all treaties, but they had to be **ratified** by the Senate.

The Constitution also promised to settle the decade's economic problems. The new government would have the sole right to coin money, interstate tariffs would be prohibited, and an overseas tariff would help protect American manufactures. At the same time, the new federal court system offered merchants engaged in interstate commerce a practical way to resolve disputes that crossed state lines.

The document was written broadly, so that it could evolve with the country. Basic rules were stated emphatically, but specific details were left to later generations of Americans to debate and negotiate in the new political arena. Frequently amended and constantly reinterpreted in the light of changing political and economic conditions, the United States Constitution is today the world's oldest basic government document.

FEDERALISTS BATTLE ANTIFEDERALISTS, 1787-1788. Not all of the delegates to the convention approved of the new Constitution. Only 39 of the 55 delegates signed it. They called themselves Federalists. Most objections came from those, like George Mason, who feared that the document created a too powerful central government at the expense of the state governments and of individual freedom. They took the name Antifederalists.

Proponents were well-organized. Hamilton, Madison, and John Jay defended the Constitution in a series of widely circulated newspaper articles, later collected together as the *Federalist Papers*. They argued that the Constitution would create a vigorous government representing the majority while protecting minority rights.

The convention had provided that the new Constitution would go into effect when ratifying conventions in nine of the 13 states had approved it. The battle for approval moved to the state level. In a few states ratification was quick and easy. Fast approval came from Delaware, afraid of being swallowed by Pennsylvania, and from Pennsylvania, where Philadelphia merchants saw the new Constitution as the key to prosperity. New Jersey, Georgia, and Connecticut rapidly followed.

The first battle over ratification occurred in Massachusetts. The memory of Shays's Rebellion remained fresh, and western Massachusetts sent many delegates to the state convention opposing the Constitution. Opponents, led by the war hero Sam Adams, feared a tyrannical federal government.

Proponents won over Adams and a narrow majority in the convention only by promising that the first Congress to meet under the new Constitution would submit nine amendments to restrict the power of the new federal government. The most important amendment reserved to the states all powers not specifically mentioned in the new Constitution.

Rhode Island voters rejected the Constitution in a popular referendum, while Maryland, South Carolina, and New Hampshire conventions approved. New Hampshire was the ninth state to ratify, but both sides recognized that without support from populous Virginia and New York the Constitution could not work.

The debate in the Virginia state convention was heated. Patrick Henry's opposition was brilliantly met by James Madison's arguments, although to win a narrow victory Madison had to agree to a set of 20 proposed amendments, including a bill of rights. Alexander Hamilton used political pressure to push ratification, 30-27, through the New York state convention.

North Carolina did not ratify until late in 1789, after the new government was established, and Rhode Island was coerced into the Union in 1790 by the threat to impose United States import duties on Rhode Island products.

POPULAR OPINION OPPOSES THE CONSTITUTION. If the Constitution had been put to a popular vote, it would have failed. The document had strong support from planters and from merchants and artisans in the towns and cities along the seacoast, where trade was crucial to economic health. But further inland, and especially among **subsistence farmers,** the predominant view was that the Constitution merely created a new, useless, and expensive layer of government.

To many, this new federal government seemed remote and alien. The average person lived too far from such a government to have any chance to shape its action. Only the socially, economically, and politically prominent were likely to have influence. Such a government seemed suspiciously like the British government that the revolution had overthrown. Americans worried that the new government could not be trusted to respect the liberties of the people.

ADDING THE BILL OF RIGHTS. As the Antifederalists demanded, in 1789 the first Congress passed a series of constitutional amendments called the Bill of Rights. Twelve amendments were sent to the states, and within a short period ten were ratified. (The two that failed concerned detailed provisions about representation and the salaries of members of Congress. In a strange twist, the salary amendment was declared ratified in 1992.)

The most important amendment, the first, provided that Congress could interfere neither with religious freedom nor with freedom of speech, including the press and assembly. The second amendment provided for the right of militiamen to keep and bear their own arms. The fourth through eighth amendments required a warrant before a search, legal due process, a speedy trial, trial by jury, and reasonable bail. The tenth amendment, never much observed in practice, reserved powers not specifically in the Constitution to the states or the people. (See U.S. Constitution in Appendix.)

George Washington's Presidency, 1789-1797

As the first president, George Washington in 1789 established many precedents, setting the tone, organizing the government, and adopting financial policies. Soon, much to Washington's disgust, cabinet members Alexander Hamilton and Thomas Jefferson bickered.

The administration was shaken by the Genêt affair in 1793 when the French ambassador's indiscretions raised anti-French sentiment and by the Whiskey Rebellion in 1794, which tested the government's credibility. In 1795 Washington had mixed results, gaining only a poor commercial treaty with England, but signing treaties in which Indians ceded land in the Great Lakes region and in which Spain confirmed America's southern border. After two terms, Washington retired in 1797.

George Washington achieved a unique status as the living embodiment of the American Revolution. The powdered wig, stern brow, prominent nose, straight mouth, and set jaw conveyed a sense of republican leadership. (BETTMANN ARCHIVE/REMBRANDT PEALE)

SETTING A SERIOUS, DEMOCRATIC TONE. In early 1789 the first electoral college, appointed by state legislatures or elected by the voters in some states, met and unanimously elected George Washington the first president. There was no contest. To give geographical balance, John Adams of Massachusetts was made vice-president, and New York City the capital.

Washington's popularity was matched by respect from important political leaders. In the Revolutionary War, Washington had demonstrated an unusual capacity for humoring quarrelsome rivals, for settling both military and political disputes, and for handling vast flows of bureaucratic paper. These were good qualities for a president.

The new president's first and most important task was to set the tone for the government. Washington strongly believed in **republican** government as opposed to monarchy or aristocracy, but he also believed in order and decorum. He wished to steer a middle course between those, like Alexander Hamilton, who saw the president as an elected monarch and those, like the Constitution's opponents, who wanted no authority symbol at all.

Washington believed that republican government could only succeed if it were based on virtue, which he defined as a solemn, self-sacrificing devotion to duty. He sought to create a government that combined seriousness of purpose with a quiet dignity. The new federal government was to have integrity, to be taken seriously, and never to be a joke. To this day, the federal government has a solemnity found at no other level of government in the United States and in few other governments in the world.

Symbolism was important. Thus, Washington took his oath of office before the public on the balcony of the federal building in New York. A public oathtaking helped make the president a man of the people, but standing on the balcony, surrounded by government officials and both above and beyond the touch of the masses, also conveyed the president's status as a uniquely important national leader.

Washington carefully considered how people should address the new president in person. He agreed with those who held that some title was necessary to show proper respect for the office, but he also understood that most Americans would ridicule any title that smacked of monarchy. So he decided that he, and his successors, should be addressed as "Mr. President."

ORGANIZING THE GOVERNMENT. The administration's first task was to organize the government. Since the Constitution was vague about the internal operations of the executive branch, Washington found it necessary to get Congress to set up the various departments.

The first cabinet had four members. Most important were Secretary of State Thomas Jefferson and Secretary of the Treasury Alexander Hamilton. President Washington took his cabinet seriously. In his view, the president should not make personal decisions. Rather, the president's main duty was to get the cabinet to reach collective judgments that then became the basis of government policy.

The first Congress provided the Supreme Court with six justices as well as a system of lower federal courts. From the beginning, then, this extensive judicial system signalled that the new government was to be actively involved in people's everyday affairs.

THE NEW GOVERNMENT TAKES OVER WAR DEBTS, 1790. In 1790 the Washington administration tackled one of the main issues which had led to the creation of the Constitution — the old war debts and now worthless paper money left over from the days of the Confederation.

Alexander Hamilton wanted the new federal government to take over the Confederation's foreign and domestic debts as well as most of the state war debts. To pay off these debts, the new government would issue **bonds** backed by new federal revenues. The policy would revive economic activity and generate confidence in the new government. It would also encourage bondholders from Boston to Charleston to back the new government.

The assumption of the Confederation debt was generally accepted, although James Madison, then the administration's floor leader in the House of Representatives, protested that many debtholders were **speculators** who had bought the nearly worthless debt at two cents on the dollar. They now stood to make a huge profit. He proposed that the government pay only original debtholders at the full rate. Congress rejected this plan.

The proposed takeover of the state debts unleashed regional rivalries. The southern states had largely paid off their Revolutionary War debts, and they now faced having to pay higher federal taxes in order to help pay the debts of the northern states. Virginians were outraged, and Madison, with his eye on the next election, permanently broke with the administration over this issue and became the opposition leader.

Finally, Thomas Jefferson arranged a dinner between Madison and Hamilton, at which a compromise was reached. The state debts would be assumed, which the North wanted. In return the permanent national capital, which Hamilton had hoped would stay in New York, would be built, as the South wanted, on the Potomac River between the southern states of Maryland and Virginia. In the meantime, the capital was to move to Philadelphia for a period of ten years. Many Pennsylvanians gambled that the government would never leave Philadelphia.

MEETING THE GOVERNMENT'S BANKING NEEDS, 1791. In 1791 Hamilton proposed that the federal government charter the Bank of the United States. A public-private partnership, this mixed venture was to have both government and private directors. This bank, under the control of wealthy private shareholders, was to handle the government's banking needs, which had been greatly enlarged by the assumption of the debts and the issuance of federal bonds.

In the cabinet, Thomas Jefferson protested vigorously. He saw nothing in the Constitution that permitted the federal government to charter a bank. Jefferson developed what became known as a **"strict constructionist"** doctrine of the Constitution: The government could only do those things specifically listed among its powers.

Hamilton took a contrary view. The government, said he, had to be able to carry out its duties. The Constitution could not anticipate all the details needed to deal with different crises. Besides, the Constitution did grant a general power to the federal government in the "necessary and proper" clause giving the government the right to promote the general welfare.

Although Washington had reservations, he sided with Hamilton's " broad interpretation" on this issue. The bill to establish the bank passed Congress and became law.

Hamilton found that the government needed more revenue than import duties could provide. Tariffs on molasses and rum had led rum distillers to protest that such duties were unfair because they made rum more expensive than American whiskey. In 1791 Hamilton persuaded Congress to tax whiskey. Internal revenue agents were sent throughout the country to collect the tax. They met resistance in areas where people lacked money to pay.

HAMILTON AND JEFFERSON FEUD. Hamilton and Jefferson began to quarrel vigorously. Hamilton wrote nasty anonymous articles in John Fenno's *Gazette of the United States,* and Jefferson replied in kind in Philip Freneau's *National Gazette.* Washington wrung his hands in despair. Much of this dispute involved clashing personalities and a natural rivalry for political leadership, but Hamilton and Jefferson also held quite different views about national purpose and about shaping the country's future.

Hamilton, as suggested in his *Report on Manufactures* (1791), believed that government power should be used to develop cities, industries, and trade. Government subsidized manufacturing might provide employment for the poor, and a totally self-sufficient American economy would guarantee national greatness.

This vision appalled Jefferson. In *Notes on the State of Virginia* (1787), he had championed rural life. Personal experience, especially in Paris, taught him that cities generated disease, poverty, and corruption. The backbone of any republic was the independent, small-scale, landholding **yeoman** farm family.

Although Washington was reelected in 1792, his second term brought him much unhappiness. The Hamilton-Jefferson feud continued, despite Washington's attempts at mediation. Because Washington usually sided with Hamilton in policy disputes, in 1793 Jefferson, now firmly allied with Madison, finally resigned from the cabinet.

CITIZEN GENÊT CREATES A FOREIGN POLICY CRISIS, 1793. Meanwhile, the United States became entangled in foreign affairs. The French Revolution, which started in 1789, had turned bloody, and the new French republic was at war with Britain and Spain. Hamilton sought to bring the United States into a closer relationship with Britain, which Jefferson opposed. Washington pursued a neutral course.

In 1793 Edmond Charles Genêt became the French ambassador to the United States. Warmly received, Citizen Genêt, as he called himself in revolutionary fashion, mistook a vague American popular endorsement of the French Revolution for support for himself. The politically indiscreet Genêt then violated American neutrality by commissioning **privateers** to attack British ships off the American coast.

Amid a rising tide of anti-French sentiment whipped up by Hamilton, the administration ordered Genêt to return to France. (Before he could leave, Genêt's enemies came to power in France, and he was allowed to remain in the United States as a political refugee.)

THE WHISKEY REBELLION TESTS THE GOVERNMENT, 1794. At home, frontier settlers grew restless, and in 1794 farmers in western Pennsylvania openly revolted. They defied the federal government's attempts to enforce the whiskey tax. The tax was hated both because people who lived on the frontier perceived the federal government as remote and useless and because frontier residents lacked the cash with which to pay the tax.

Washington, prodded by Hamilton, declared an insurrection and called 15,000 militiamen from adjacent states to crush the rebellion. Hamilton, in a panic, saw the event as a crucial test of the federal government's credibility. He drew up plans to lead the military expedition — and to become a military dictator of the country, if necessary.

The military expedition, however, was led not by Hamilton but by Henry ("Lighthorse Harry") Lee, with Hamilton's assistance. This massive show of force caused the resistance to collapse, and defiance of the whiskey tax resumed its more benign form — hidden stills. Several insurrectionists were charged with treason. Two were convicted and sentenced to be hanged. Washington shrewdly pardoned them.

MAKING THREE TREATIES, 1795. Domestic turmoil led the administration to seek conciliation abroad. In 1794 Washington decided to obtain a commercial treaty with Great Britain and sent John Jay as special **envoy** to Britain. The British, however, showed little interest in trade. They also refused to negotiate about the **impressment** of American seamen, which was the British practice of manning its navy by seizing American sailors from American ships on the high seas. The British offered a mediocre treaty, gaining access to the American market while keeping American goods out of Britain and the West Indies. Jay signed anyway. Jay's Treaty created a furor, and the Senate only reluctantly approved the treaty after an extensive debate in 1795.

The administration had better luck in the Great Lakes region. There General Anthony Wayne had defeated several Indian tribes at Fallen Timbers in Ohio in 1794, and the following year 12 tribes signed the Treaty of Greenville, which led the native inhabitants to cede much of the area to white settlement.

In late 1795 Washington scored a triumph with Pinckney's Treaty with Spain. Thomas Pinckney persuaded the Spanish to confirm America's southern boundary and to give western American farmers the right to ship produce down the Mississippi River to New Orleans, then in Spanish hands.

WASHINGTON RETIRES WITH A FAREWELL ADDRESS, 1796. Despite these successes, Washington by 1796 was tired and frustrated. Yearning for the tranquility of his beloved estate at Mount Vernon, he announced that he would not accept a third term, and this became a precedent that was not broken until Franklin Roosevelt's third election in 1940. Washington is one of only a few world leaders who ever gave up power voluntarily.

Washington decided to issue a Farewell Address. In it he lamented the rise of political parties, which he saw as against the public interest. His view was ignored. He also warned against permanent foreign alliances. Such alliances, he believed, led inevitably to war, and the United States would be better off remaining neutral. This warning more or less became the basis of American foreign policy for the next hundred years.

John Adams's Presidency, 1797-1801

Elected in 1796 in a bitterly partisan election, John Adams took a middle course between Hamilton and Jefferson. Enraged by the XYZ Affair, he found himself in 1798 entangled in the Quasi-War with France but refused to ask Congress to declare war. His support for the Alien and Sedition Acts in 1798 revealed his foolish vanity, and despite an economic boom, he was defeated for a second term in the strange election of 1800. That election resulted in the twelfth amendment, which changed the way presidents were elected.

ELECTION OF 1796. The drafters of the Constitution had not intended to create political parties and, indeed, generally looked upon parties with suspicion as political combinations devoted to special interests rather than the common good. However, the creation of a single powerful office, the presidency, had spurred the creation of parties as the means to that prize, and the electoral college system drove political leaders into a two-party system.

By 1796 two distinct parties had taken shape. The Federalists, led by Hamilton and John Adams, were strongest among merchants in the cities and throughout New England. The Democratic-Republicans, led by Jefferson, Madison, and Aaron Burr (in New York), were strongest among artisans in the cities and throughout the South.

A fierce fight to succeed Washington occurred. In 1796 Adams defeated Jefferson for the presidency by 71 to 68 electoral votes. Under the constitutional provisions then in effect, the runner-up Jefferson became vice-president.

ADAMS FACES THE XYZ AFFAIR, 1797-1798. John Adams was temperamentally ill-suited for the presidency. Talented and hard-working, he had risen from a small farm to the top of the legal profession, but his perfectionism, obsession with detail, Yankee gloom, and a sour suspicion about most of his contemporaries made him neither liked nor likeable. His only joy seemed to come from his marriage to Abigail, which was a lifelong romance and a true partnership. She once teased John that if the new country did not give women their rights that they would lead a revolution.

Almost from the beginning, Adams found himself trapped between the extreme views of Thomas Jefferson and Alexander Hamilton. Hamilton had deeply alienated many people inside his own party and had left the cabinet. For Adams, this only made matters worse, because Hamilton received inside reports about the cabinet meetings and then used this information to undermine Adams.

Adams's first crisis was the XYZ Affair in 1797. The French government had been so angry at the pro-British Jay's Treaty that they had refused to receive Adams's ambassador. The president then sent three special envoys to make amends and to negotiate a trade treaty with France.

The French foreign minister, Talleyrand, sent three special agents to meet the American delegation. The French agents demanded a bribe of $240,000 to present the American case to the French government. The American envoys resisted, negotiations collapsed, and in 1798 a furious, righteous Adams presented the facts, with the names of the French agents identified only as Messrs. X, Y, and Z, to Congress.

American public opinion turned against France. Adams had copied Washington's policy of maintaining neutrality in the ongoing Franco-British war and now faced a severe test. Mobs surged through city streets demanding war with France, and the Hamiltonian wing of the Federalist party vilified Adams.

The fear of war with France drove the pro-French Democratic-Republicans, the followers of Jefferson, into a frenzy. Worried that Adams was plotting such a war in order to crush his domestic political opponents, the Jeffersonians used their newspapers to denounce war, England, and Adams.

PASSING THE ALIEN AND SEDITION ACTS, 1798. In 1798 Adams and the Hamiltonian Federalists, temporarily united and holding a majority in Congress, struck back at the Jeffersonians with a series of four laws. Many leading Jeffersonian newspaper editors were foreign-born, and the Federalists now enacted a new Naturalization Act. It changed the period of residency required for citizenship from five to 14 years. The implication was that noncitizen editors who attacked the government faced deportation.

A companion Alien Act gave the president the authority to deport any noncitizen deemed a threat to public safety. Both of these laws lasted until 1802. An Alien Enemies Act gave the president the right during a declared war to arrest and imprison any person from a country with which the United States was at war.

The Sedition Act was intended to prevent an internal insurrection. It prohibited meetings to plot treason. It also barred "malicious writing" that attacked the reputation of any government official. The law was so loosely drawn that it could be applied to almost any dissent.

In some parts of the country, especially New England, Federalists used the law to crush their political opponents. Ten prominent Jeffersonian newspaper editors were fined or imprisoned. Matthew Lyon of Vermont became a hero in jail and was elected to Congress.

ADOPTING THE KENTUCKY AND VIRGINIA RESOLUTIONS, 1798. The Jeffersonians attacked the Alien and Sedition Acts as despotic and unconstitutional. In their view, these laws violated both the first amendment's protection of free speech and the tenth amendment's limitation upon federal power. In 1798 Thomas Jefferson secretly drafted a series of resolutions, which the Kentucky legislature adopted. That same year Madison framed a similar set for Virginia. The Kentucky and Virginia Resolutions denounced the Alien and Sedition Acts as unconstitutional.

Both sets of resolves insisted that each state should judge for itself how to redress such grievances. Virginia suggested that a state might "interpose" itself to resist such a law, while Kentucky held that a bad law might be "nullified" by a state declaring a federal law invalid inside its borders. Other politicians would adopt these terms in later years.

The underlying issue was difficult and complex. The Constitution had not spelled out clearly how a law might be declared unconstitutional. The Kentucky and Virginia Resolutions suggested one method, but it could produce the awkward result of having some federal laws enforced only in part of the country. Some people suggested as an alternative that the Supreme Court might pass upon a law's constitutionality. The court later adopted this idea.

ADAMS PURSUES QUASI-WAR WITH FRANCE, 1798-1800. From 1798 through 1800 the United States fought an undeclared naval war against France. The Quasi-War, as it was sometimes called, grew out of American anger over the XYZ Affair combined with American insistence upon the right of neutral American merchant ships to trade with whomever they wished.

Adams opposed a declared war, because it might provoke a French invasion. National defenses were decrepit, and the American army was too small to prevent a French landing. Adams did organize a modest navy, and the navy fought well against the French in several battles.

To pay for the war, the federal government imposed taxes on luxuries, such as carriages, and real estate. Opposition to these taxes, especially from those against war with France, was intense. In 1799 John Fries led hundreds of Pennsylvanians in open revolt. Caught, tried, convicted, and sentenced to death for treason, Fries was pardoned by Adams.

In 1800 Adams made peace overtures to the French, and the French accepted. Although Adams's action pleased and surprised the Jeffersonians, his decision angered the Hamiltonian faction of the Federalist party. Adams had badly split the party, which appeared likely to lose the next election.

AMERICANS ENJOY AN ECONOMIC BOOM IN THE 1790S. Adams's political troubles played against a booming economy. Throughout the 1790s the economy had done well. Once the Constitution had been put into operation, opposition to it had all but disappeared, in large part because of prosperity. How much of the improvement was due to Hamilton's refunding of the debt and how much to lucky timing is uncertain.

Real income per person increased during these years for almost everyone, or at least for everyone who participated in the moneyed economy. (It is difficult to believe that the living standards for slaves changed very much, although a prosperous master might have fed his slaves better.)

Because of war in Europe, American farmers enjoyed record exports at high prices. Much of this profit was recycled through the American economy, which became more self-sufficient in manufacturing due to both British and French anti-American trade policies and Hamilton's tariff.

Seaport merchants found the decade especially profitable. Urban artisans, unless they produced luxury goods, did less well than merchants. Many craftsmen concluded that Hamilton's policies favored wealthy merchants, and these mechanics split with the merchant-dominated Federalists to create their own labor unions and Democratic-Republican Societies, which moved into the Jeffersonian political camp.

PROSPERITY PRODUCES FEDERALIST CULTURE. Prosperous, self-confident Federalists frequently adopted British culture that matched pro-British politics. Federalist merchants built mansions that borrowed details from London's houses, as portrayed in contemporary pattern books. The style was neoclassical, featuring Greco-Roman columns made out of delicately carved wood, with modest, graceful, and restrained detail.

Furniture, too, was produced in the same style. American-made from native walnut or cherry or from imported mahogany, wooden chests of drawers and sideboards were gracefully curved, delicately inlaid, beautifully polished, and carefully positioned upon thin, tapered legs. Gilded mirrors topped with fierce, patriotic eagles completed the typical Federalist merchant's drawing room.

Literature, too, as is often true during an economic boom, flourished. Charles Brockden Brown published a series of novels in which he wrestled with the problem of class in an avowedly democratic society. Hugh Henry Brackenridge, an attorney and an active Jeffersonian, wrote *Modern Chivalry,* a scathing satire about Irish immigrants on the western Pennsylvania frontier. A youthful William Cullen Bryant amused himself turning out sarcastic, anti-Jeffersonian verse.

ELECTION OF 1800. Federalist smugness was smashed in the election of 1800. Although the party was split, Federalists saw no alternative to renominating the unpopular Adams. The Democrats, as they increasingly called themselves, had come close to winning with Jefferson in 1796, and so they renominated the Virginian.

It was a dirty campaign. Both the Alien and Sedition Acts and the Quasi-War with France had left bitter feelings. On the other side, the Federalists worried that a Jefferson administration would be too democratic, would pander to the popular will, and would lead the country back toward the chaos of the 1780s.

Jefferson's personal life became an issue. He believed in God but in no particular church and had little to say about Jesus Christ. New England ministers condemned his deism. Federalist newspaper editors raised questions about Jefferson's relationship with his slave, Sally Hemings, who was three-fourths white and was his dead wife's half-sister.

The election was decided on regional lines. The South, along with New York (under Burr's control), voted for Jefferson. Adams got few electoral votes outside New England.

The Constitution had not anticipated a party system, and each member of the electoral college was to vote for two candidates for president. The person with the highest number, provided it was a majority of the electors, was to become president. The runner-up was to be vice-president. In 1800 the disciplined Democrats in the electoral college all voted for both party candidates. The result was a tie between Jefferson and his running mate, Aaron Burr.

In the event of a tie, the Constitution provided that the House of Representatives would elect one of the top candidates from the electoral college. Each state cast one vote, and it was necessary to get a majority of states to win.

The Federalists in the House backed Burr, but the Democrats remained loyal to Jefferson, and a deadlock ensued. To avoid a constitutional crisis, Hamilton told friends that Jefferson should be picked. Burr never forgave Hamilton for this decision and later killed Hamilton in a duel. Finally, on the 36th ballot, Jefferson was chosen.

To prevent a similar problem in the future, the twelfth amendment to the Constitution was adopted in 1804. Each elector was to vote for two people separately, one for president, the other for vice-president.

Although no one knew it then, the election of 1800 marked the end of national power for the Federalists. The party continued to hold power in some parts of the country, especially New England, for another decade, but never regained the presidency or control of Congress. In 1801 power passed peacefully from one political party to another. Although relationships were strained, a major accomplishment had taken place. The ability to transfer power without revolution or revolt is one of the hallmarks of democratic government.

Conclusion

Any new nation can expect growing pains. The trick is to overcome present obstacles in ways that provide for healthy, long-term success. The sick economy and weak Confederation of the 1780s gave way to vigorous economic growth and a robust new federal government in the 1790s. Much of this transformation was due to the wisdom contained in the United States Constitution, the oldest fundamental charter still in use.

A blueprint can only succeed, however, with expert builders. Washington not only set the tone but shrewdly adopted policies in the nation's long-term interest. Hamilton's financial genius was matched by Jefferson's understanding of the American psyche, while Adams sacrificed personal ambition to govern in the way that he believed necessary for the new nation's survival. By 1800 no one doubted that the founders had actually created a nation.

Recommended Readings

DOCUMENTS: Thomas Jefferson, *Notes on the State of Virginia* (1787); Thomas Paine, *The Rights of Man* (1791); Clinton Rossiter, ed., *The Federalist Papers* [1788] (1961).

READINGS: (1780s) Van Beck Hall, *Politics without Parties* (1972); Jackson T. Main, *The Antifederalists* (1961), and *Political Parties before the Constitution* (1973); Peter S. Onuf, *The Origins of the Federal Republic* (1983); David P. Szatmary, *Shays' Rebellion* (1980); (WASHINGTON'S PRESIDENCY) Harry Ammon, *The Genêt Mission* (1973); Joyce Appleby, *Capitalism and a New Social Order* (1984); Richard Buel, Jr., *Securing the Revolution* (1972); Jerald A. Combs, *The Jay Treaty* (1970); Felix Gilbert, *To the Farewell Address* (1961); Thomas P. Slaughter, *The Whiskey Rebellion* (1986); (ADAMS'S PRESIDENCY) Manning J. Dauer, *The Adams Federalists* (1953); Peter Shaw, *The Character of John Adams* (1976); Lynne Withey, *Dearest Friend: A Life of Abigail Adams* (1981).

7

———— ❧ ————

THOMAS JEFFERSON'S
AMERICA, 1801-1829

CHAPTER OVERVIEW: By 1801 Thomas Jefferson had captured America's heart, at least outside New England, by advocating a minimalist federal government and a nation of small-scale, landowning, family farmers. Reality, however, never quite matched Jefferson's vision, and much of the anger against Indians and the British that produced the War of 1812 had its origins in his vision's limitations. By 1816 Americans embraced a harmonious but nonvisionary Era of Good Feelings. Happy talk, however, could not last, and from 1825 to 1829 John Quincy Adams failed to persuade Americans to seek national greatness in new ways.

Thomas Jefferson Envisions a Great, Expanding Nation

Thomas Jefferson's values had been forged in the American Revolution, but they had been tempered under attacks from Alexander Hamilton in the 1790s, and by 1801, like a fine French wine, they were mature. Jefferson's high idealism contrasted with the ugly, undeveloped swamp constituting the nation's new capital, Washington, D.C. His vision of democracy rested upon a republic of small farmers stretched across the continent, in territory that promised the end of slavery, which Jefferson abhorred but did not know how to end. His vision of a great, expanding nation depended on the West. In 1803 he purchased Louisiana and then sent Lewis and Clark to explore what had been bought. Aaron Burr, too, had a western dream, but it was neither Jefferson's nor democratic.

Jefferson found it increasingly difficult to maintain American neutral rights in the Franco-British wars. In 1807 he tried cutting off foreign trade to stop the British and French interfering with American ships, but the embargo only hurt America's own economy and was repealed in 1809. By the time Jefferson retired as president in 1809, his vision seemed terribly limited, a better anchor to the Revolution than a predictor for the future. Passing his last years amid a stream of visitors to his home at Monticello, he was curiously silent about the nation's prospects, except when he shuddered about slavery.

JEFFERSON TAKES OFFICE IN A PRIMITIVE CAPITAL, 1801. On March 4, 1801, Thomas Jefferson was inaugurated as the third president of the United States. He took the oath of office inside the unfinished Capitol building in Washington, D.C., the new capital city. In an attempt to heal wounds, he said, "We are all Federalists, we are all Republicans."

Earlier in the day, John Adams had fled to Massachusetts. Still smarting over losing the election, Adams was relieved to be leaving swampy, humid, and uncivilized Washington. Abigail Adams had frequently hung out the family's wash to dry in the still unfinished East Room of the Executive Mansion.

More than a mile separated the Capitol from the president's house. Although Pennsylvania Avenue had been partially cleared, travelers on horseback still had to pick their way through swamp and forest and sometimes got lost. Most people refused to make the trip after dark. Washington was called, sarcastically, the city of magnificent distances. There was little magnificent about it.

The city's sprawling layout, planned by the French immigrant Pierre L'Enfant, had led each branch of the government to be physically separated. Congress met only a few months each year, and congressmen lived in ramshackle boarding houses within walking distance of the Capitol. They usually voted with their boarding housemates rather than with fellow party members or other representatives from the same state. After all, a vote against the majority view within the boarding house could cause severe repercussions when dishes were passed at table.

The Supreme Court also had its boarding house near the Capitol, and Chief Justice John Marshall governed both meals and the court in patriarchal fashion. Marshall, a staunch Federalist, tolerated no dissenting opinions. Much to Jefferson's annoyance, the chief justice had been appointed to this lifetime post in the last days of Adams's term.

Jefferson's cabinet and other members of the executive branch lived near the president's house, where Jefferson conducted the affairs of state with a personal staff composed of one secretary. The president employed few servants and once shocked the British ambassador by personally opening the front door wearing his houserobe.

Jefferson's dinner parties became famous. He served fine food, French wine, and ice cream. Guests included members of the cabinet, congressmen, diplomats, and visiting dignitaries. Conversation could turn to any subject, since Jefferson's interests ranged from politics to philosophy, from agricultural experiments to Indian languages, from violin playing to architecture.

JEFFERSON'S FAITH IN DEMOCRACY. Jefferson's life was rooted in paradox. A wealthy, slaveholding Virginia tobacco planter, this complex man insisted that poor farmers and mechanics were the backbone of society. The sole heir to a fortune in land accumulated by his speculating father, he favored equal inheritance among all children and insisted that effort rather than luck brought the greatest rewards.

Jefferson was a democrat in part because he was an incurable optimist. The world was improving, and progress inevitable. Everywhere he saw barbarism, superstition, and ignorance yielding to civilization, reason, and enlightenment.

Because of his democratic values, he believed that education could transform people's lives. He strongly supported public schools and late in life founded the University of Virginia. He hired its faculty and designed its campus, his greatest architectural achievement.

His faith in democracy came from two observations. One was that talented people often emerged from poor backgrounds. Democracy gave such people opportunities to improve themselves, and it gave society as a whole the benefit of their talents. No other system enabled talent to be developed so readily. He sometimes said that he favored an aristocracy of talent, or, in other words, a meritocracy.

At the same time, democracy prevented a permanent ruling class from aggrandizing power and wealth solely for its own benefit. Monarchy, **aristocracy,** and dictatorship were inherently flawed, because they concentrated power in the hands of a few people who were disconnected from the masses and could easily grow out of touch with society's needs. The French Revolution had resulted from just such a situation.

Democracy served the common good because it gave power to those who enjoyed popular support and shared values with the masses. Power was held only so long as the people approved, and since public opinion was inevitably fickle, there would be no permanent ruling class.

Jefferson also saw democracy as the greatest protector of liberty. The temporary nature of democratic leadership made leaders respect liberty, since if they fell from power, which was likely, liberty would protect them from their successors. Liberty, moreover, also celebrated the right of the average man to property, to opportunity, and to personal advancement based upon merit.

Jefferson expressed his devotion to democracy and liberty in his architecture. The Virginia State Capitol at Richmond was the first neoclassical public building in America. Jefferson modeled the structure on an ancient Greek temple, because Greece was the birthplace of democracy. This style, with its memorable columns, became the predominant one for American public buildings.

Jefferson's democratic ideas resonated with the public mood, especially along the western frontier. The Democratic party expressed Jefferson's values, and the West became staunchly democratic and Democratic. In that most egalitarian region, depopulated of Indians and devoid of wealthy planters and their **slaves,** small-scale white farm families lived out the dream of a free, democratic society that Jefferson envisioned.

JEFFERSON HATES SLAVERY — IN THE ABSTRACT. On no subject was Jefferson more eloquent than on slavery. He hated it. He thought the institution degrading and inhumane, applauded its abolition in the North, and fought successfully to ban it in the Northwest Territories. He urged Virginia to consider gradual emancipation and supported ex-slaves voluntarily moving to Africa.

At the same time, race both fascinated and terrified him. He speculated that skin color might change with exposure to a different climate over several generations. Perhaps someday the South's slaves might turn white! Meanwhile, he believed, one must keep the races legally separate. Suspecting black inferiority, he believed that the white race had the right to dominate. He was a racist.

He was also a slaveowner. Although he freed a few of his own slaves at his death, most remained in bondage. Worse, he had accumulated massive debts in his last years, mortgaging his slaves in order to maintain the rural hospitality for which he was famous. Slaves had to be sold, with families broken, in order to settle the estate. This prospect tormented him.

For Jefferson, however, slavery was a given, a fixture of life, an age-old institution that was only beginning to crumble. Like others of his generation, he believed in halfway measures. Results were less important than intentions. In the fullness of time he believed that slavery would fall. He worked for its doom even as he received its fruits.

THE SUPREME COURT TAKES ON A NEW ROLE. Jefferson's presidency began with his enemies, the Federalists, in firm control of the judiciary. After an attempt to use the Constitution's **impeachment** powers to remove a Federalist Supreme Court justice failed, Jefferson and his supporters reluctantly backed down. As a result, the judiciary became independent of the executive in practice as well as in theory.

In 1803 John Marshall's Supreme Court issued a landmark ruling. At the end of his term in 1801 President John Adams had appointed William Marbury as a justice of the peace for the District of Columbia. The commission, however, had been held up by Secretary of State James Madison on President Thomas Jefferson's instructions.

When Marbury sued for his commission, the Supreme Court issued a remarkable ruling. John Marshall dismissed the suit on the grounds that the court lacked jurisdiction. This result pleased Jefferson. Marshall, however, went on to assert that the law under which Marbury had been commissioned contained an unconstitutional provision. Thus, for the first time *Marbury v. Madison* held that the Supreme Court could pass on the constitutionality of federal laws.

JEFFERSON PURCHASES LOUISIANA, 1803. Jefferson's most notable achievement as president was the Louisiana Purchase. He had sought to buy New Orleans and the right for western farmers to navigate and ship produce on the Mississippi River. The French, shrewdly observing the ongoing American migration to the western frontier, decided instead to sell all their American holdings. Besides, the sale would deprive the British of the territory.

For $15 million the size of the United States was doubled. Exactly what had been purchased beyond New Orleans was not known. Louisiana had vague boundaries running westward as far as the imagination could roam. Jefferson had enough constitutional misgivings about the purchase that he asked Congress to enact a constitutional amendment allowing it. Congress, however, chose to ignore this request and merely appropriated the purchase funds.

Jefferson believed that enough land had been acquired to allow his beloved country of small-scale **subsistence farmers** to multiply for 50 or 100 generations by expanding into the West. When thinking in this fashion, Jefferson gave little thought to the West's native inhabitants. Thus, the Louisiana Purchase was part of the long-term strategy of building and nurturing white democracy.

LEWIS AND CLARK EXPLORE THE WEST, 1804-1806. Intrigued by the mystery of the new territory, Jefferson in 1804 sent a large exploring party led by Meriwether Lewis and William Clark into the western region. They were instructed to make sketches, to collect soil, plant, and animal specimens, to cultivate Indians in order to build future trade relations, and to seek a water or land route across the region to the Pacific Ocean.

Setting out from St. Louis, the expedition made its way up the Missouri River. Much of this region was well known to fur traders. Lewis and Clark found a woman from the western Shoshone tribe, Sacajawea, who interpreted and guided them to her ancestral home in the Rocky Mountains.

The expedition then crossed the mountains and floated down the Columbia River to its mouth on the Pacific Ocean. After wintering on the coast, Lewis and Clark split into two parties for further explorations on their return trip. In 1806 they reached St. Louis and soon after personally reported to President Jefferson, who bubbled with excitement and enthusiasm.

BURR PLOTS TREASON IN THE WEST, 1806-1807. Not all was tranquil at home. In 1804 Aaron Burr, Jefferson's vice-president, had killed Alexander Hamilton in a duel. Burr, as interested in the West as Jefferson, withdrew from electoral politics and began to plot the establishment in the Mississippi River valley of a new western republic with himself at its head.

Burr sought support from the British, from the Spanish, and from the American western military commander. In 1806 Burr and an adventurer named Harman Blennerhasset, who lived on an island in the Ohio River, organized a military expedition. The plot failed. Burr was caught and in 1807 tried for treason, at Jefferson's orders, in Richmond, Virginia. Although acquitted under Chief Justice John Marshall's strict definition of treason, Burr was ruined, and the West, for the time being, was secure to the United States.

ASSERTING NEUTRAL RIGHTS AND THE EMBARGO OF 1808. In 1807 Britain and France were again at war, and the fighting threatened American neutrality. Americans, especially farmers, had profited from selling surplus goods, including grain, to overseas customers. These goods were carried in American ships, which also profited from the trade.

Both the French and the British seized American ships that they suspected of trading with the enemy. The French, however, had a small navy and caused less trouble. The British stopped American vessels in the Atlantic Ocean, confiscated cargo that they believed destined for France, and took American seamen that they claimed were British. Some were, but many were not. The desperate British had found a reliable way to man their fleet.

In 1807 a British frigate, the *Leopard,* stopped an American frigate, the *Chesapeake,* just outside American territorial waters. When the American ship refused the British the right to search for four deserters, the British attacked, won the battle, killed three Americans, and removed the alleged deserters. The *Chesapeake* incident soured relations and was not settled until 1811.

Unprepared for war with Great Britain, Jefferson decided to reduce the risk of war by cutting off American overseas shipping. In late 1807 Congress passed an **embargo** against all foreign trade. The Embargo Act was a disaster. During 1808 prices plummeted, as foreign markets disappeared. Shipping merchants in the seaports went bankrupt, and their collapse dragged down other businesses. Urban unemployment soared, and people faced starvation. This manmade catastrophe provoked a political backlash.

JEFFERSON RETIRES TO MONTICELLO. In 1809 Jefferson followed Washington's example and retired after two terms. He returned to his beloved mountaintop plantation, Monticello. There he performed agricultural experiments, including an unsuccessful attempt to grow French wine grapes.

Many guests came to visit the Sage of Monticello. He showed them his inventions: his collapsible music stand, his chair with a built-in writing desk, his dumbwaiter for bringing wine from the cellar to the dining room, his eight-day clock in the central hall, and his three-panel windows that opened into doors. On a clear day he could see 40 miles around, including the University of Virginia and James Monroe's house at Ashlawn.

Best known as the author of the Declaration of Independence, Thomas Jefferson was also an architect, inventor, university founder, and third president of the United States. (INDEPENDENCE PARK/L.P. WINFREY; CHARLES WILLSON PEALE, 1791)

Jefferson's presidency did not live up to the grandeur of his vision. This may have been because Jefferson was at his best in theoretical speculation, or it may be that he was a shrewd enough practicing politician to understand that one cannot try to implement a grand vision and remain successful in politics.

Friction with Britain Leads to the War of 1812

James Madison, who succeeded Jefferson in 1809, also had trouble staying neutral, especially when the British seizure of American seamen was matched by Indian attacks in the West.

In 1812 Congress pushed Madison into war against Britain and her Indian allies. The Americans crushed the Indians, but the British burned Washington, and antiwar New England threatened to secede. The peace treaty produced no gains, but Andrew Jackson won a victory at New Orleans making him a hero. An odd consequence was the ruin of the nation's finances and the establishment, contrary to Jeffersonian principle, of the second Bank of the United States.

MADISON TAKES OVER, 1808. The embargo disaster took place just as the Democratic party quarreled over Jefferson's successor. In those days the party's members of Congress picked the nominee. Some favored James Madison; others, James Monroe or George Clinton. Jefferson wanted Madison, and Madison got the nod. Despite the embargo, he won the election of 1808 against Charles Pinckney and a dying Federalist party.

Jefferson and Madison had been political collaborators for two decades. Their philosophies were complementary but not identical. Jefferson was more theoretical, more ethereal, more other-worldly. Madison preferred concrete things, and he viewed politics more pragmatically as the art of the possible. Encumbered by a dark, brooding distrust of those who held power, he also profoundly respected the law. Nevertheless, he shared Jefferson's democratic vision.

In early 1809 Congress repealed the embargo and enacted the Non-Intercourse Act. Trade was resumed with all nations except Britain and France, which could regain trade rights by promising to respect American neutrality. Regardless of the risk of war, the United States had learned that it could not afford a policy of total isolation.

GROWING DISPUTES WITH BRITAIN, 1809-1811. As American foreign trade resumed in 1809, after the embargo's failure, the dispute with Britain turned bitter. Madison reopened trade with Britain after the British ambassador indicated that Britain would soon revoke its Orders in Council (1807), which had banned American or other neutral trade with France. Unfortunately, the ambassador misspoke, the Orders continued, and he was recalled. Madison then reinvoked the Non-Intercourse Act against Britain.

In 1810 Congress passed Nathaniel Macon's Bill No. 2, which authorized the president to reopen trade with either Britain or France. If either country repealed its laws against neutral commerce by early 1811, then the president could temporarily ban trade with the other country, which had three months to follow suit to gain back its trade.

France's Emperor Napoleon played a double game. He used the excuse of the Non-Intercourse Act to seize American ships in French ports. At the same time he indicated that he was prepared to accept the terms laid down in Macon's bill. Madison rushed to reopen trade with France. Only later did he learn that Napoleon had not actually changed his policy with regard to neutrals.

During 1811 Madison pressured Britain to withdraw the Orders in Council, but Britain resisted the appearance of giving in to American pressure. British **impressment** of American sailors continued, and American relations with Britain grew steadily worse. An American frigate, the *President,* attacked a smaller British ship, the *Little Belt,* which was mistaken for a ship that had impressed an American seaman.

BRITAIN SUPPORTS INDIAN RAIDS, 1811. That same year, 1811, the Indians of the Old Northwest, with support from the British, grew restless. The Shawnee chief Tecumseh, assisted by his brother, the Prophet, began to unite diverse native peoples over the issue of white encroachment onto native lands. Tecumseh dreamed of creating a powerful Indian political and military combination that stretched from the Northwest to the Southwest. Indian frontier raids increased, and white settlers became frightened.

William Henry Harrison, the governor of Indiana Territory, moved to take the Indian capital on Tippecanoe Creek. Just before Harrison's troops reached the settlement, the Indians launched a surprise attack. Neither side won a decisive victory at Tippecanoe, but the battle raised Harrison's military stature and persuaded many frontier residents that war with Britain, which had backed the Indians, was necessary.

CONGRESS DECLARES THE WAR OF 1812. The new Congress that met in late 1811 included a large number of new, young members. Cocky, proud, and fiercely patriotic, these **"war hawks,"** as they were called by John Randolph, clamored for war against Britain. The hawks included Henry Clay, John C. Calhoun, and Felix Grundy. Although a minority, these southerners and westerners were able to elect the charismatic Clay as speaker of the house.

In 1812 Madison found it impossible to resist the pressure for war. The hawks demanded war as a matter of honor, and the only way to avoid war, a British repeal of the Orders in Council, took place too late for news of it to reach the Congress before war was declared.

It was a sorry war. The United States had no military objective except to seize Canada. The British captured parts of the United States in order to gain political influence. The American army, led by elderly officers from Revolutionary War days, showed incompetence. The government suffered the same lack of bureaucratic capacity shown in the earlier war, and finances again created a problem.

In 1812 Detroit surrendered without firing a shot, and Indians under British direction massacred the garrison at Fort Dearborn (Chicago). The American invasion of Canada failed, in part because of a battle lost when the New York militia refused to cross over the border. As the humiliated soldiers retreated across upstate New York, they were greeted with hoots and jeers.

In contrast, the navy enjoyed surprising success against the renowned British fleet. Stephen Decatur and Oliver Hazard Perry became war heroes, and the *Constitution* was dubbed "Old Ironsides" for taking hits so well. In 1813 Perry took control of Lake Erie and declared, "We have met the enemy and they are ours."

INDIANS JOIN THE WAR, 1813-1814. In 1813 General William Henry Harrison beat a combined British-Indian force in Canada at the battle of Thames River. Colonel Richard M. Johnson of Kentucky distinguished himself in the attack, but the battle's major event was the death of Tecumseh, which ended the dream of a pan-Indian western empire.

By 1814 the action shifted to the South. General Andrew Jackson led the Tennessee militia in a war against the Creek nation, whom Tecumseh had brought into the British-Indian alliance. After Jackson's victory at Horseshoe Bend, Alabama, the Creeks surrendered. The Treaty of Fort Jackson ceded more Indian land than any treaty in history. Most of what became Alabama and Mississippi passed into white hands.

THE WAR ENDS SLOWLY, 1814-1815. The British marched on Washington and humiliated Madison, who was forced to flee. The president's wife, Dolly, managed to save a favorite portrait of Washington. The Capitol and president's house were torched. Afterwards, the Executive Mansion, stained by smoke, was painted white and renamed the White House.

Baltimore was the next British target, but the local residents had, unlike Washington's, arranged proper defenses. Fort McHenry's guns kept the enemy at bay. A nighttime bombardment failed, although the spectacular sight did move Francis Scott Key to write "The Star-Spangled Banner." The poem was set to the music of a popular Anglo-American drinking song.

Meanwhile, sentiment against the war had grown ever stronger in New England. Generally Anglophilic and hostile to the frontier war hawks, **Yankees** wanted and needed British trade. Smuggling thrived. As the war continued and threats of invasion grew, many people in the Northeast questioned the value of the federal Union.

In late 1814 disaffected New England Federalists met secretly in Hartford, Connecticut. The Hartford Convention called for new laws and constitutional amendments to restrict federal power. Privately, the group threatened secession if the war continued. Their meeting, considered treasonous by many, destroyed the influence of an already waning Federalist party.

Almost simultaneously, American and British negotiators, meeting in Ghent, Belgium, had reached agreement to end the war. The American delegates, John Quincy Adams and Henry Clay, disliked the terms, but Clay at least had the satisfaction of beating the British delegates at poker. Neither country gained territory, impressment and neutral rights were not mentioned, and the United States lost the use of the fisheries off the Newfoundland coast.

Before news of the treaty could reach the United States, General Andrew Jackson won a spectacular victory at the battle of New Orleans on January 8, 1815. Repelling a British attack across an open field, Jackson hid his troops behind carefully thrown up **breastworks** and waited until the British were quite close before raking the enemy with murderous fire. British casualties were 2,036, including the commander. Eight Americans were killed. Jackson became a hero.

The end of the war left the country in a shambles. New England was talking secession, the federal government had proved barely capable of survival, and the economy was a mess. War debts threatened to create the same kind of economic trouble that had prevailed in the 1780s.

The Era of Good Feelings, 1816-1824

The luckiest of presidents, James Monroe presided over a period so tranquil it became known as the Era of Good Feelings. Successful treaties in 1818 with Britain and in 1819 with Spain were matched in 1823 by the vigorous Monroe Doctrine, which asserted American supremacy in the western hemisphere. At the same time, John Marshall's Supreme Court upheld the sanctity of contracts, encouraged commerce, and increased the court's own power.

The Missouri Compromise of 1820 proved that the political system could even deal with the nation's most difficult problem, slavery. Only a debate about the constitutionality of the federal financing of internal improvements disturbed the calm, at least until the election of 1824 produced a five-way battle for the presidency, which ended the Good Feelings.

MONROE DRAWS NEW BOUNDARIES. Virginia's domination of the presidency continued in 1816 with the election of James Monroe against a weak Federalist party. Monroe's constitutional views were more flexible than Madison's, and his desire for political compromise and harmony led his eight years in office to be called the Era of Good Feelings.

Foreign affairs took a decided turn for the better. In 1818 the United States and Britain fixed the Canadian boundary at the **49th parallel** as far west as the Rocky Mountains. The two countries also agreed to joint occupation of the Oregon country (today's Oregon, Washington, Idaho, and British Columbia).

The next year Spain turned over Florida to the United States in return for the American government's assumption of American citizens' claims against Spain. In the Adams-Onís Treaty the Secretary of State John Quincy Adams and the Spanish ambassador drew a boundary between the United States and Mexico all the way to the Pacific Ocean. Spain gave up claims to the Pacific Northwest in return for American recognition that Texas was not part of Louisiana.

One of the most significant events of Monroe's presidency was the Monroe Doctrine. In 1823 the United States declared that no new European colonies could be established in the western hemisphere. The breakup of Spain's empire in Mexico and Latin America had whetted appetites. Although issued under Monroe's name, this militant, nationalistic document had actually been crafted by Secretary of State John Quincy Adams.

MARSHALL'S SUPREME COURT MAKES MAJOR RULINGS, 1819. On the domestic front the Supreme Court in 1819 issued two important rulings. In the *Dartmouth College Case*, in which the eloquent Daniel Webster represented the college, Marshall's court held that New Hampshire could not revoke a college **charter** that it had granted years earlier. The state must continue to honor its contracts. This ruling strengthened private entities, including businesses, that had received special charters from state legislatures.

Marshall's court also considered banking. The Bank of the United States had come to an end when its charter had expired in 1811, but the War of 1812 had proved so difficult for government finances that Congress and Madison chartered the second Bank of the United States in 1816.

In *McCulloch v. Maryland* the court ruled the Second Bank constitutional through a broad, Hamiltonian interpretation of the general welfare clause. The court also prohibited Maryland from taxing the federally chartered bank. "The power to tax involves the power to destroy," declared Marshall.

MISSOURI COMPROMISE LIMITS SLAVERY, 1820. The Good Feelings even extended to Congress. In 1819 Missouri petitioned to be admitted to the Union. A northern congressman persuaded the House to adopt an amendment to the admission bill. It prohibited the introduction of any new slaves into Missouri and provided that the children of any present slaves born after statehood would become free at age 25. The Senate, however, rejected this amendment.

The debate continued into 1820. Finally, Congress compromised. Missouri was to enter the Union as a slave state, but to maintain the balance in the Senate between slave and free states, Maine was to be set off from Massachusetts and admitted as a new free state. In addition, slavery was to be barred in the remaining Louisiana Purchase territory north and west of Missouri above 36° 30′ latitude. This compromise barely passed the northern-dominated House.

Despite the Missouri controversy, Monroe's popularity remained high, and in 1820 he was reelected with only one electoral vote cast against him. (The dissenting elector explained that Washington deserved to be the only president elected unanimously.) The Federalist party had totally disappeared.

CONTEMPLATING INTERNAL IMPROVEMENTS. Although Monroe was more willing than Madison to approve laws that gave the federal government broad powers, he shared the general Jeffersonian suspicion of the federal government. Thus, in 1822 he vetoed the Cumberland Road Bill on the grounds that the Constitution did not specifically give the federal government the right to build highways. Monroe cheerfully proposed a constitutional amendment allowing federal funding of national improvements. Members of Congress chafed, wondering what was the difference between the Second Bank, which the Supreme Court had upheld, and the Cumberland Road. Monroe declined to offer any explanation.

THE FIVE-WAY ELECTION OF 1824. The collapse of the Federalist party along with Monroe's erratic course of trying to please everyone created political confusion. The result was a bitter five-way battle to succeed Monroe as president in 1824.

The leading candidate was Secretary of State John Quincy Adams. Tradition favored Adams, since both Madison and Monroe had served as secretary of state immediately before becoming president. Adams, on the other hand, was personally cold and aloof. Nor was he fully trusted as the son of a Federalist and as a Yankee suspected of being unsympathetic to slavery. He said little about policy but could be considered a supporter of Monroe's approach.

Another strong candidate was Secretary of the Treasury William H. Crawford of Georgia. Southerners, especially those devoted to Jefferson's doctrine of a strict interpretation of the Constitution, liked Crawford, who called himself a states'-rights man. He had strong support in Congress, and the Jeffersonian Democrats traditionally had picked their presidential candidate in a congressional caucus.

Secretary of War John C. Calhoun also enjoyed support. He, too, appealed to white southerners, since as a South Carolinian he was considered sound on slavery. Unlike Crawford, however, Calhoun in this phase of his career was a broad constructionist, an enthusiastic nationalist, a federal road builder, and a proponent of a large military establishment.

Crawford's supporters undermined Calhoun, whose friends retaliated. The jousting among Monroe's cabinet officers gave outsiders a chance. Henry Clay, the charismatic House speaker from Kentucky, calculated that he might prevail, especially, as seemed possible, if the **electoral college** did not produce a majority, and the House decided the outcome.

Clay countered Crawford's Jeffersonian views with his own American System. He proposed a high tariff to protect American manufacturing, which pleased the East, along with massive federally financed internal improvements, which pleased the West.

Eager for Clay to be the western candidate, Clay and his friends urged the Tennessee legislature to support his election. To everyone's surprise, the Tennesseeans instead nominated General Andrew Jackson, the war hero and a man almost totally unknown in Washington politics.

Calhoun, playing the Scots-Irish ethnic card, carefully engineered a large convention in Pennsylvania, where the Scots-Irish dominated politics, to endorse his candidacy. Much to his amazement and consternation, the convention instead backed the other Scots-Irish candidate, Andrew Jackson.

Calhoun then reassessed his chances. Adams had a lock on the nationalist constituency in the North, and Calhoun seemed destined to lose the South to Crawford over states' rights. Clay and Jackson were likely to divide the West. Calhoun withdrew and announced that he would accept the vice-presidency. He was unopposed.

The previously important congressional caucus endorsed Crawford, but so few representatives attended that the action was meaningless. More significantly, Crawford suffered a paralyzing stroke, which his friends tried, unsuccessfully, to keep secret. The stroke ruined his chances, but he refused to withdraw.

Legislators picked electors in some states; voters did so in other states. When the **electoral vote** was counted, Jackson had 99; Adams, 84; Crawford, 41; and Clay, 37. The popular vote was similar, although Clay had a slight edge over Crawford.

Since no candidate had a majority in the electoral college, the election went to the House of Representatives, as Clay had calculated. Crawford's third place electoral college finish, however, destroyed Clay's chances, since the Constitution provided that the House could only elect one of the top three electoral vote getters, and Clay had placed fourth.

Clay found it easy to ignore Jackson's claims. Although clearly popular, Jackson lacked a majority. More voters had cast ballots for other candidates. Besides, Clay suspected Jackson of states'-rights' views, and both were rivals for leadership of the West.

Adams, on the other hand, appealed to Clay. The two had utterly different personalities but shared a common political vision of a great national republic bound together by a vigorous federal government exercising strong political leadership. Besides, Clay's West and Adams's North could provide a long-term political combination every bit as strong as Jefferson's South and Burr's New York.

Clay's support for Adams in the House guaranteed Adams's election. It also enraged Jackson and his supporters, who charged that Jackson should have been picked because he got the largest number of both popular and electoral votes. After Adams appointed Clay as his secretary of state (and heir-apparent to the presidency), Jackson charged that Adams had bought the presidency in a "corrupt bargain." The Era of Good Feelings was over.

John Quincy Adams's Presidency, 1825-1829

John Quincy Adams's yearning for national greatness yielded nothing, in part because the cold, impersonal Yankee lacked the common touch, and in part because the country was confused. Parochial Americans still insisted on borrowing almost everything from others, whether from the ancient Greeks, from the modern British, or from their own decaying revolutionary heroes. Adams's policies never rose above this confusion and quickly descended into pork-barrel politics, producing the Tariff of Abominations in 1828. In the end, he fell before Andrew Jackson, who created a new, popular vision for America.

ADAMS PROMOTES NATIONAL GREATNESS. John Quincy Adams was out of touch with the nation's mood. When he asked Congress to establish a National University in Washington, he was merely ignored. But when he suggested a National Observatory, which he unfortunately called a "lighthouse of the skies," his poetic whimsy led to scorn and ridicule.

Adams was a wealthy, urbane, cosmopolitan man. An avid book collector, he read 14 languages and conversed in eight. He had lived abroad much of his life. He understood, more than most Americans of his era, the vast potential for the United States, but he also recognized that the realization of national greatness required determination, effort, and the ability to transcend the limits imposed by past visions, including Thomas Jefferson's vision.

To Adams, facts were facts, and a nostalgic longing for a republic of small-scale farmers replicating themselves ever westward to the Pacific represented a refusal to face facts. The world was changing, and the rise of industry was a reality. The only question for the United States was whether the country was going to remain predominantly rural and, hence, backward while under Britain's economic domination, or whether Americans would harness the continent's vast resources for national prosperity, strength, and glory.

Adams hated slavery because it discouraged slave initiative while it promoted slaveholder indolence. Worse, the defense of slavery caused slaveholders to fear all change. The Jeffersonian vision of rural virtue, small farms, and states' rights was a vision that condoned and even celebrated the dominance of slaveholding planters as society's natural leaders. National greatness, to Adams, meant renouncing this outmoded institution. Just as Europeans, in order to make progress, would have to give up monarchy for democracy, Americans would have to replace slavery with a free market labor system.

Adams found only his native New England ready for the modern age. There, government provided mass public education, industry flourished, banks were sound, cities grew, and commerce thrived. Surplus rural population moved west, as in the South, but it was also drawn to the cities, and the rural birthrate was falling. All of this could be a model for the rest of the country, which was at least a generation behind New England.

AMERICANS BORROW CULTURE. Although Adams talked of national greatness, he, like most Americans, remained within the Jeffersonian tradition. He, too, admired neoclassical architecture, which continued to be the prevailing style for public buildings in the 1820s. Even more than before,

Americans modeled themselves consciously on the citizens of the ancient Greek democratic city-states. The fact that the Greeks had held slaves did not go unnoticed in the South.

For many visitors, the American tendency to borrow cultural values was the country's least endearing trait. Americans seemed, in this era, peculiarly incapable of expressing a uniquely American vision. Even a genius as bold and as bright as Thomas Jefferson had not been able to provide a sustainable vista. Having all but invented modern republican politics in the revolutionary era, Americans of the next generation — represented by John Quincy Adams, Clay, and Calhoun — found it impossible to construct a culture that both resonated with and built upon the values of the Founders.

In 1820 the *Edinburgh Review,* a well-known Scottish magazine, ridiculed American pretensions. "In the four quarters of the globe," sarcastically asked the author, "who reads an American book? or goes to an American play? or looks at an American picture or statue?" Indeed, who did?

JOHN QUINCY ADAMS PURSUES CONTRADICTORY POLICIES. The visionary but impractical Adams nearly drove Henry Clay crazy. Adams refused to remove any federal employees from office, unless they were guilty of corruption. This policy, Clay pointed out, both deprived the administration of a patronage network and left in place Jackson-Crawford supporters who actively used their positions to destroy the administration.

In 1826 the Senate, under the influence of Vice-President John C. Calhoun and Senator Martin Van Buren, confronted Adams over a projected American delegation to a western hemisphere conference in Panama. Although Congress eventually approved American participation, it humiliated Adams in the process.

Tariff policy concerning imports became controversial during Adams's presidency. Jefferson had established modest tariffs to raise revenue rather than high protective tariffs that kept out foreign goods, protected American manufacturers, and raised no money.

With the rise of American manufacturing during and after the War of 1812, especially in textiles, producers had gradually succeeded in getting **tariff** duties increased. An attempt to raise duties on wool and textiles failed in 1827, because other interests felt left out.

In 1828 Congress considered higher duties on many items, including textiles, wool, hemp, and iron. By lumping many special interests into a single bill, proponents were able to pass it. Opponents, mainly southern cotton exporters, called it the Tariff of Abominations. It became a major issue in the 1828 presidential election.

ADAMS LOSES, 1828. Adams lost to Jackson in 1828. The incumbent Adams carried New England and other parts of the Northeast; Jackson, the South and West. The election was decided by Jackson's success in Pennsylvania among his fellow Scots-Irish and in New York. Jackson narrowly won New York because of the Albany Regency, the **political machine** of Martin Van Buren and William L. Marcy. In 1824 Van Buren had backed Crawford. Jackson was to reward Van Buren handsomely for his political conversion.

Conclusion

Circumstances change, and no political vision — even one from a thinker as brilliant as Thomas Jefferson — lasts more than a generation. Jefferson advocated economic and geographical expansion under the watchful eye of a federal government always more active than in Jefferson's rhetoric. The War of 1812 did little damage to the Democratic party, and the so-called Virginia Dynasty of Jefferson, Madison, and Monroe marched on. The Jeffersonians temporarily resolved the controversy over slavery in Missouri in 1820, but rising sectional discord gradually dissolved the Era of Good Feelings amid the bitter personal rivalries in the presidential election of 1824. John Quincy Adams failed to build on the Jeffersonian past, and Andrew Jackson awaited in the wings.

Recommended Readings

DOCUMENTS: Lester J. Cappon, ed., *The Adams-Jefferson Letters* (1959); Merrill D. Peterson, ed., *The Portable Thomas Jefferson* (1975); John A. Schutz and Douglass Adair, eds., *The Spur of Fame: Dialogues of John Adams and Benjamin Rush, 1805-1813* (1966).

READINGS: (JEFFERSON'S VISION) Lance Banning, *The Jeffersonian Persuasion* (1978); Joseph J. Ellis, *After the Revolution* (1979); John C. Miller, *The Wolf by the Ears* (1977); James S. Young, *The Washington Community* (1966); (JEFFERSON'S PRESIDENCY) Richard E. Ellis, *The Jeffersonian Crisis* (1971); Richard Hofstadter, *The Idea of a Party System* (1969); Linda K. Kerber, *Federalists in Dissent* (1970); Drew R. McCoy, *The Elusive Republic* (1980), and *The Last of the Fathers* (1989); R. Kent Newmyer, *The Supreme Court under Marshall and Taney* (1968); Merrill D. Peterson, *Thomas Jefferson and the New Nation* (1970); Norman K. Risjord, *The Old Republicans* (1965); Robert E. Shalhope, *John Taylor of Caroline* (1980); Marshall Smelser, *The Democratic Republic* (1968); (WAR OF 1812) Ronald L. Hatzenbuehler and Robert L. Ivie, *Congress Declares War* (1983); Donald R. Hickey, *The War of 1812* (1989); J.C.A. Stagg, *Mr. Madison's War* (1983); Steven Watts, *The Republic Reborn* (1987).

8

—— ✠ ——

THE MARKET REVOLUTION,
1790-1850

CHAPTER OVERVIEW: From 1790 to 1850, during the course of a single lifetime, the United States underwent a startling transformation. This period of sudden, rapid change is called the Market Revolution. After a century of slow economic growth during the colonial period, the economy grew rapidly, so that per capita income doubled in a single generation.

This economic "take-off" was marked by drastic changes in the way the economy worked. Subsistence agriculture increasingly gave way to sales of produce in the market, handcraft production was reorganized, factories were built, transportation was improved, and great cities emerged. A high birthrate and, after 1840, increasing immigration caused population to soar from four million in 1790 to 23 million in 1850.

Most important to the Market Revolution was the idea of change itself. Prior to 1790 Americans, like people throughout history, had modeled their lives on those of their ancestors. Tried and true patterns of behavior worked best. By 1850 everyone knew that change was the only constant, that old ways had little value, and that each generation faced new challenges.

Textile Manufacturing Starts
the Market Revolution

Before the Market Revolution, clothing was both scarce and expensive, as rural women spent much time handspinning yarn and weaving cloth. In the 1790s water-powered mechanical spinning, a new technology that Samuel Slater brought from England, began to reduce fabric prices. Then the Boston Associates introduced water-powered weaving, in 1813 at Waltham, Massachusetts, and in 1823 at Lowell. These mills provided industrial employment for young women and produced ever greater

140

quantities of low-priced cloth. By 1860 cheap fabrics, increasingly made by poorly paid Irish immigrants, sold in a national market. In textiles, the Market Revolution was complete.

MAKING TRADITIONAL CLOTHING. From the beginning of settlement, white Americans had clothed themselves, as well as their slaves, in European fashion. They had worn shirts, trousers, dresses, and stockings handcut and handsewn from cloth. The making of clothes was a time-consuming task for females in almost every household. Only the well-off could afford professionally tailored clothing.

The process began with yarn made at home. Women and girls in farm families devoted much of their time to converting raw linen plant fibers and fluffy bits of sheep's wool into yarn on their spinning wheels. Many families owned spinning wheels, but if they did not, one of these lightweight, portable devices could be borrowed. Women spent so much time spinning that an unmarried older woman became known as a spinster.

Cloth, commonly a combination of linen and wool called linsey-woolsey, was usually professionally woven on large handlooms. Both men and women did weaving. Because looms were expensive, took up much space, and required special skills, few people tried home production. Weavers usually accepted yarn from a neighborhood and provided cloth in exchange, while retaining a portion of the output. This surplus could then be sold or traded outside the community.

Weavers sometimes dyed the fabric that they made. Butternuts, for example, made a rich golden brown fabric. In some places professional dyers, often women, provided this service, taking their commission in the form of a percentage of the material, while in other areas cloth buyers dyed it themselves, often using ancient, secret family recipes.

Keeping a family in clothes was burdensome and expensive in terms of labor. Wool wore quickly, and children outgrew their clothes. Even though a large amount of household labor went into the production of garments, few people owned many clothes. Adult slaves, for example, had only the coarse, simple clothing they wore, and slave children sometimes were kept naked to save the expense.

In an ordinary white family each person usually had two sets of clothes. A man's set included underwear, a shirt, trousers, long stockings, and a neckerchief (a hat and shoes were extras). A woman's set included underwear, a skirt, a blouse, and an apron. The best set was for Sunday use, and after a year's wear it then became the set worn during the workweek the following year. Thus, clothes were supposed to last two years in annual rotations.

SAMUEL SLATER INTRODUCES MECHANICAL SPINNING, 1790. In the mid-1700s the English invented water-powered machinery that could spin high quality yarn cheaply at enormous profit to the manufacturer. The inventors jealously guarded their machinery. No strangers could see it, and Britain allowed no skilled workers to leave the country.

But one workman, Samuel Slater, disguised himself as a sailor, left England, and moved to Pawtucket, Rhode Island. Carrying the plans for a spinning mill inside his head, Slater in 1790 opened the first American water-powered spinning mill. It was an enormous success.

Other spinning mills soon opened elsewhere in New England and in the Philadelphia area. Professional weavers, many of them English or Irish immigrants, settled near the new spinning mills. Meanwhile, the English had kept their technological lead in textiles by perfecting the more difficult task of using water power for mechanical weaving.

In the early 1800s many American families began to find it cheaper and easier to sell raw wool and buy yarn or cloth to make clothing. The time saved could be spent more productively on other tasks. Indeed, some families quit keeping sheep altogether and produced other items for sale, such as grain, eggs, or honey, from which they could gain a larger profit. Some of the purchased fabric was made from yarn spun at Slater's and other American mills, but much of it, and especially the highest quality which sold for the highest prices, came from the new English mechanical weaving mills.

THE BOSTON ASSOCIATES ESTABLISH THE WALTHAM MILL, 1813. A group of wealthy Boston merchants decided to set up a mechanical weaving mill. Organized as the Boston Associates, they sent one of their number, Francis Cabot Lowell, to England, where he toured the new mills and memorized the highly secret machinery that he saw. Lowell returned to New England, perfected his own machinery, which improved upon the English devices. The Boston Associates then opened the first American combined water-powered spinning and weaving mill at Waltham, Massachusetts, near Boston, in 1813.

During the War of 1812 the United States lost access to British fabrics. Waltham, as well as the rest of the American textile industry, prospered mightily. Cloth was sold at a high profit as fast as it could be produced. Indeed, within a few years, Waltham's production had reached the maximum possible from that site's available water power.

FOUNDING THE LOWELL MILLS, 1823. In 1823 the Boston Associates established a series of textile mills at the new town of Lowell, Massachusetts. Growing rapidly, it became by 1850 the second most populous city in Massachusetts with 33,000 people. Whereas Slater and other early mill owners had employed poor families as workers, the Boston Associates tried a different strategy. They recruited teenaged, single women from New England farm families. Wages for such workers were quite low — only $3.50 a week, about half the rate for an unskilled adult male laborer, who generally earned $1 a day for a six-day week.

To reassure parents that their daughters were safe, the company built boarding houses connected to the mill buildings. The young women lived under enforced curfews and various moral restrictions, including mandatory church attendance on Sunday. To reinforce the virtuous atmosphere, the employers sponsored a morally proper magazine, *The Lowell Offering*, written by and for the workers.

The workers considered the twelve-hour days and six-day weeks tending textile machinery easier than the farmwork at home. Few, however, worked for more than several months, although many returned for additional periods. Women were attracted by the adventure of living in a town and by the chance to find a husband among the mechanics and carpenters employed at the mills and thus escape permanently from farm life. Many also saved a sum of cash, which could be used as a dowry, to attend school, to pay family debts, or to buy fancy clothes.

TEXTILE MILLS SPREAD. From 1830 to 1860 textile mills popped up wherever waterpower could be harnessed. Overall production soared, and as output rose, competition increased, and prices fell. Consumers found cheaper cloth at higher quality. Careless, shoddy producers closed, as did smaller mills that lacked sufficient capital or water power to add new machinery.

By mid-century a national market had developed. Textile production became concentrated in those places, like Lowell, that had access to large sums of capital, abundant waterpower, sophisticated technology, and cheap labor. Mills were located in rural areas away from big cities that lacked waterpower and had expensive labor. Such production centers could and did manufacture more fabric at cheaper prices. Even when shipping costs were added, it was usually cheaper to buy Lowell cloth than to make it locally.

Although the economy as a whole benefited, as did consumers and owners, mill workers did not. Thin profit margins led Lowell's managers constantly to speed up production rates, to reduce wages, or to raise boarding house fees, which amounted to the same thing. When Lowell workers protested by going on strike, as they did in 1834 and 1836, they were replaced.

By 1860 few farm girls worked at Lowell. Instead, the workforce increasingly was composed of desperately poor Irish immigrant families. The men were paid no more than the farmers' daughters had been, and all members of

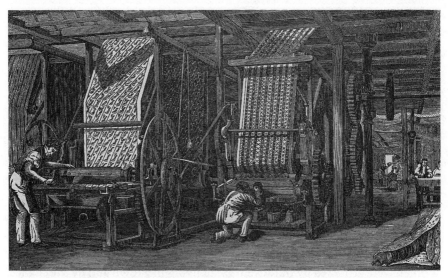

After turning to mechanical spinning and weaving, textile mills by the 1830s were beginning to add the capacity to print designs on cotton cloth. High-speed calico printing revolutionized fashion and taste.
(CULVER PICTURES)

the family had to work in order to make ends meet. They did not, however, live in company boarding houses, and owners no longer required workers to attend church.

Irish immigrants did not complain about their treatment as much as had the New England farm women. The Irish had been abused for centuries in their own country, and most expressed gratitude to be in the United States instead of in famine-ridden Ireland.

King Cotton Drives the Economy

The textile industry needed a raw fiber to spin and weave. Mechanization and vast increases in cloth production were based on a shift from linen and wool to cotton, which became practical only after Eli Whitney invented the cotton gin in 1793. After 1800 high demand for cotton produced both high prices and the march of new cotton plantations rapidly westward across the South.

More than any other crop, cotton was identified with slave labor. Cotton planters boasted that slaves made possible both King Cotton and the nation's prosperity, which depended heavily upon cotton exports to England. Cotton was, in fact, the key to the transatlantic economy, stimulating plantations in the South, textile mills in England and New England, food production in the Midwest, and the export of English capital to America's North and West to finance railroads.

ELI WHITNEY'S COTTON GIN TRANSFORMS COTTON PRODUCTION, 1793. In the 1790s a small number of planters along the South Carolina seacoast grew a speciality crop called sea-island cotton. This particular cotton plant, which did not grow inland, developed an oversized boll filled with loose strands of fluffy, thick, and long white fibers which could be picked from the boll and then spun into a yarn to make a luxury cloth. As late as 1800 only 8 million pounds of sea-island cotton was produced for export.

Inland, planters experimentally planted short-fiber cotton. This plant produced a small, hard boll packed tightly with short white fibers, whose seeds were difficult to remove. One laborer, usually a slave, could pick, deseed, and sort only about one pound of cotton a day. At that rate, short-fiber cotton cost too much to prepare to make cloth.

In 1793 Eli Whitney, an inventor from Connecticut, visited Georgia and, learning about the problem of processing short-fiber cotton, designed a small device to deseed cotton, the **cotton gin.** Whitney's gin, about the size of a breadbox, enabled one worker to process about 50 times as much cotton as could be done by hand.

The device was ingeniously simple. A worker placed raw cotton in the top and then handcranked two comblike metal pieces that separated the fibers from the seeds. The loosened strands of cotton could be prepared for machine spinning , while the irksome seeds dropped to the bottom. Later, they would be pressed into cottonseed oil.

DEMAND FOR COTTON ENCOURAGES SLAVERY. Whitney's gin made processing raw cotton practical, and the new textile mills increasingly demanded cotton, which soon displaced wool as the leading fiber in cloth. Raw cotton production soared:

1810	171,000 bales
1830	731,000
1850	2,133,000
1859	5,387,000

Increased production required two main ingredients: land and labor. The land came from the Cotton Kingdom spreading itself westward across the entire lower South from South Carolina to Texas. Cotton could not move north of this area of mild winters, because it required an exceptionally long growing season.

Slaves provided the labor. Had blacks been free, they might have preferred growing food for their own use in subsistence agriculture, or they might have been reluctant to move so rapidly to the Southwest. But the slaves had no say in the western migration of planters and their plantations. Slave labor made it possible to settle the cotton belt rapidly and to expand production quickly.

As a crop, cotton almost perfectly matched the needs of the slave system. Cotton required little specialized agricultural knowledge, provided near year-round labor, including months of backbreaking weeding, and could employ families, including children of all ages. No other crop in the United States ever made such a full, effective use of slave labor.

In the early 1800s cotton prices were high, and the newly plowed land returned fabulous crops that made planters rich on relatively small invest-ments. By the 1830s increased production, lower cotton prices, and higher land prices brought about by speculation gradually made cotton less profit-able. The price of slaves also rose sharply, and unless a planter had inherited slaves, it was increasingly difficult to find the money to buy or hire the slaves needed to enter the business.

COTTON LEADS THE TRANSATLANTIC ECONOMY. Much of the cot-ton was exported to England, where it was made into cloth and returned to the United States. White southerners gradually became aware that they were part of a vast transatlantic commercial system, and they came to realize that they were engaged in the least profitable part of the business.

The planters made less money than did the cotton brokers (many of them Yankees), the shippers (almost all Yankees), or the textile manufacturers, whether in England, in Lowell, or in the South. Furthermore, planters, whose cotton exports to England provided the positive balance of trade that made imports to the United States possible, had to buy many manufactured goods, which came from either Britain or the Northeast. Duties on imports kept prices high.

Southern cotton exports to the North and to England stimulated manu-facturing in both those areas. Although the South grew much of its own food, and many large plantations were self-sufficient, southerners often found cot-ton so profitable that they preferred to import food from the Midwest, which also shipped food to the Northeast. The English invested in railroads and manufacturing in the Northeast and the Midwest. Every section of the trans-atlantic economy prospered by this increased regional specialization and trade.

Both the American and British economies were, southern planters boasted, beholden to King Cotton. And the key to the success of cotton, white southerners believed, was the institution of slavery. This latter idea was not entirely true, because cotton could be grown without slavery, but much northern guilt about slavery grew out of the perception that the entire nation owed its prosperity to the enslaved producers of cotton. No one asked the slaves for their views.

Improved Transportation Stimulates Commerce

Improved transportation was a key ingredient in the Market Revolution. Only when goods could be shipped cheaply, efficiently, and reliably over long distances could an integrated national economy emerge. The first significant change, in 1807, was the invention of the steamboat, which opened trade in the continent's interior. Then came canals, which in the 1820s enlarged markets by enabling heavy, bulky goods, particularly grain and coal, to be moved at low cost. After 1830 railroads, which were built where steamboats and canals did not go, made it fast, easy, and profitable to ship perishable goods to national markets.

ROBERT FULTON INVENTS THE STEAMBOAT, 1807. The idea of applying steam power to boats was tested in the 1780s, but only in 1807 did Robert Fulton's *Clermont* make a convincing demonstration on the Hudson River between New York and Albany. The idea quickly caught on, and by the 1820s large numbers of steamboats plied America's rivers.

These boats revealed much about the emerging entrepreneurial spirit. Quickly constructed from plentiful cheap green lumber, the average steamboat lasted less than five years. It survived long enough for an owner to make a fortune. Crude but fast boats rode high on the water. They could puff their way up the most shallow streams in search of new business. Boilers were gigantic but inefficient, because wood, used as fuel, was cheap, and the technical knowledge for constructing engines was primitive. Captains were often incompetent, even when sober, and the boilers frequently blew up, sinking the boats and killing the passengers with steam.

STEAMBOATING IN THE MISSISSIPPI AND OHIO VALLEYS. Nowhere did the steamboat make a larger difference than in the Mississippi and Ohio River valleys. Previously cut off by the Appalachian Mountains from the important trade that flowed along the Atlantic seacoast, residents of the interior had developed a self-sufficient, isolated culture.

Although Kentucky and Ohio had good soil and a climate favorable to corn, the lack of a market gave residents little incentive to produce. Lacking both towns and transport to the East, western farmers simply planted less corn and took life easy or turned their corn into whiskey, a form of liquid asset that could be easily stored. Farmers needing cash floated their produce down the Ohio and Mississippi rivers on wooden rafts. At New Orleans they usually sold in a glutted market at low prices, often watched their produce rot on the wharf, and always had to walk home, which took an average of six weeks along robber-infested trails.

The steamboat changed everything. Some farmers found it profitable to load produce on a boat and sell it upstream in drought-stricken areas or in places to the north where crops had not yet come in. Others continued to float produce to New Orleans, but now they returned home safely in less than a week on a steamboat. They also carried goods home on the boat.

Economic activity grew. For example, western farmers had long planted apples and peaches, but these crops had been strictly for home use. Fruit previously had no economic value. Locally, everyone's fruit ripened at the same time, and it would spoil if shipped to faraway places. The steamboat marked the beginning of sales to distant places, where fruit did not grow or ripened at a different time.

From 1817 to 1855 the number of steamboats on western waters rose from 17 to 727. As a result, numerous cities along the heartland's major rivers became inland ports. The Atlantic seaports of Boston, New York, Philadelphia, Baltimore, and Charleston now had western rivals in Pittsburgh, Cincinnati, Louisville, St. Louis, and New Orleans.

Cincinnati, in particular, grew into the leading city in what was then the American West. Founded with Yankee capital, its location just across the Ohio River from Kentucky gave it a southern flavor. Its main fame, however, came from its processing of the numerous hogs that in free, democratic fashion roamed its unpaved streets. Barrelled salt pork and soap were the most famous products of the city that was nicknamed "Porkopolis."

BUILDING CANALS. Canals also improved transportation. Heavy, bulky products such as grain could be shipped cheaply — at 10 percent of wagon rates — on barges that floated on canals while being pulled by horses or mules along the edge. The speed was barely above that of walking, but the animals required little feed, and canals could be kept open more predictably than rivers that dried up in droughts or flooded in storms.

In the early 1800s the Atlantic seaport cities, recognizing that the population was pushing inland, tried to keep control of inland trade and to dominate the hinterlands by building canals. Boston did benefit from the Middlesex Canal, but Washington, D.C., profited little from the canal along the Potomac River. An attempt to build a canal above Richmond along the James River into West Virginia failed due to high construction costs for building locks in the mountains.

THE ERIE CANAL OPENS, 1825. By far the most successful waterway was New York's 300-mile-long Erie Canal, built by Governor DeWitt Clinton. Begun in 1817, this canal crossed the flat area between Albany and Buffalo north of the Appalachian Mountains. When it opened in 1825, it connected New York City, which already enjoyed excellent access to Albany along the Hudson River, with the Midwest's Great Lakes at Buffalo.

The Erie Canal set off a major boom in New York City. Population, manufacturing, and commerce soared, as New York quickly eclipsed Philadelphia and became the most important city in America. The canal brought cheap western food to New York, where it replaced more expensive food previously grown locally. New Yorkers also reshipped food at a profit to other eastern seaports.

Raw materials also came cheaply from the West, and New York manufacturers benefited from that, too. Increased availability of produce and locally made products led more ships to call at the port, and New York boasted the only regularly scheduled ships sailing to England. That, too, led to increased business. Finally, the profits made from trade and manufacturing made New York the center for capital, which could be attained both more easily and at lower interest rates than in other cities. New York quickly became the nation's banking center.

Upstate New York was also transformed. Sleepy towns along the canal route blossomed into a string of important cities that included Utica, Syracuse, Rome, and Buffalo. Rochester, settled almost entirely by New Englanders, underwent rapid change. Flour millers who had started with modest mills became, much to their surprise, wealthy owners of major works.

Rapid economic change was accompanied by the collapse of Rochester's political system, long dominated by the founding families, and a religious **revival,** in which the newly successful suddenly praised God for their fortunes and encouraged their workers to join in. Those who did were more likely to be promoted to junior partners in business.

Philadelphia, New York's desperate rival, planned its own canal system. Central Pennsylvanians, however, already looked upon the Susquehanna

River as leading more naturally to Baltimore. Although several interconnecting canals were built across Pennsylvania, the high cost of crossing the Appalachian Mountains made an effective system impossible.

RAILROADS FORM A NATIONAL TRANSPORTATION NETWORK.
Baltimore and Charleston also recognized the importance of the Erie Canal. These cities were determined not to be left behind. Geography, however, made canals impossible, and so in 1830 both cities borrowed an English invention and opened the first American railroads. Despite the early start, neither became a major rail center.

Railroads could be built far from water, where steamboats or canals could not go, and rail routes could be laid through mountains. The Pennsylvania canal system was eventually completed with a railroad. Railroads, however, posed their own problems. They were hideously expensive to build. During the 1840s one-tenth of all the new capital invested in the United States was spent on building railroads. By 1850 the nation had 8,879 miles of track.

Construction was difficult and frequently dangerous. In the North, Irish immigrants provided most of the labor, as they had for digging canals. Many died from disease and accidents. In the South, some slave labor was used, but the Irish also worked there, because many slaveowners were reluctant to risk the lives of their valuable slaves in such dangerous construction.

Part of the problem in the early years was the brittleness of the iron rails, which frequently broke either while being laid or later in use. The railroad industry tried desperately to solve this technical problem, at first in the 1840s by using a rolling method to make iron rails and later in the 1860s, more successfully, through Bessemer's process for making steel, which led to steel rails replacing iron ones. By 1850 the railroads had created a vast iron industry that rapidly consolidated into large-scale enterprises centered in Pennsylvania.

Railroads were also inherently political. Although some were government-sponsored, including the principal line in Georgia, most were built with private money, often from England. Even with private financing, railroad companies required legislative approval, both for incorporation and for the acquisition of rights of way. As a practical matter, a railroad company had to be able to place its track wherever it wished, even if a property owner did not want it. Thus, railroads had to be given the right of **eminent domain,** that is, the right to take over private property and pay a fair price for it, whether the owner wished to sell or not.

By the 1850s two vast regional railroad systems, one northern and one southern, had been built. Trains could not leave their home system, however, because most of these two systems used different track widths — the southern gauge was three and a half inches wider — and they met at only two points: Louisville, Kentucky, and Washington, D.C. Cities along rail lines had prospered, and towns passed by, like Georgia's capital of Milledgeville, were beginning to dwindle. Some rail junctions, such as Atlanta and Chicago, were already boomtowns.

Railroads both reinforced and changed trade patterns. Overall, commerce grew even more rapidly, as many perishable goods were now shipped quickly to market. Between 1817 and 1852 the time for shipping goods from Cincinnati to New York dropped from 52 days by a handpoled keelboat and overland wagon to six days by rail. Since trains often followed the earlier canal and steamboat routes, trade frequently flowed in familiar ways. But not always.

In 1850, for example, 80 percent of Cincinnati's trade floated on the Ohio River to southern markets. Local political and business leaders dared not offend the South and refused to discuss slavery. Ten years later 80 percent of the city's trade moved on railroads to northern markets. Local leaders then expressed open hostility to slavery.

The Market Revolution Transforms Society

Technology, invention, capital, and improved transportation combined to create an economic revolution in the United States during the early 1800s. Even before the organization of the large industrial corporation or the use of large-scale factories, economic life was transformed. The key was specialization, whether it was farm women who lived near Philadelphia and entered the butter business, Cincinnati's pork processors, or Rochester's flour millers.

The topsy-turvy national market produced both losers, like Philadelphia's traditional shoemakers, and winners, such as Lynn's shoe entrepreneurs. Success came to those who had access to capital. Skilled workers sought protection through labor unions, which generally failed. Limited social mobility drew little protest, because immigrants who arrived on the bottom pushed those born in the United States up the scale. Cities grew rapidly and contained both vast, new wealth and appalling poverty. Everyone angled to make a dollar.

ADOPTING NEW WAYS OF BUSINESS. People gave up old ways, even though they had been followed for centuries, and took up new ones. Inventors played a major role in this change. After Eli Whitney invented the cotton gin, he and Simeon North independently manufactured firearms out of stan-dardized, interchangeable parts. Their idea depended upon fine tolerances that helped develop the machine tool industry. In the 1820s Thomas Blan-chard's gunstock lathe allowed for mass production copied from a single handcarved model. New Englanders patented the largest number of inven-tions, but one of the most successful inventors was the Virginian Cyrus Mc-Cormick, who pioneered the mechanical grain reaper in 1831.

Farm families became less likely to produce at home all that they con-sumed. They tried to specialize in whatever their particular farm could pro-duce best and then traded or sold some of the surplus in order to obtain the items they no longer produced. For many families, the first item to be bought was cloth, which was produced cheaply and efficiently in the new textile mills.

Farm women played a major role in this change. For example, in the rural townships nearest to Philadelphia farm wives and their daughters kept cows and made vast quantities of butter for sale in the Philadelphia market. Many of these women took the butter into the city and sold it at the market on their own account. By tradition, women kept the money from the sales of their own production.

Residents of towns and cities were even more likely to find a special niche in the economy. Different places had different advantages, and local produc-tion became highly targeted for sale in a national market. Thus, the numerous hogs in the vicinity of Cincinnati made that city the center for pickled pork and soap. Similarly, the wheat belt of northern New York led Rochester to become the Flour City. The entire lower South, with its long growing season and its slave labor, became the Cotton Kingdom.

For some Americans the national market offered extraordinary opportuni-ties for economic success. Matthew Baldwin, a modest Philadelphia master ironmonger, began to produce railway locomotives just as that industry was developing. By the 1850s Baldwin had expanded his small shop to more than 500 employees, which made him one of the leading employers in the country. Baldwin's workers, however, had no prospect for following in their boss's footsteps. The capital required to enter the business had grown enormously in just a few years.

FROM SHOEMAKERS TO SHOE ENTREPRENEURS. Philadelphia shoe-makers were major losers. In this ancient craft, an apprentice learned the trade and then became a journeyman who temporarily worked for wages. After sav-ing money, a shoemaker then became a master with his own shop. Tradition-ally, **journeymen** had been able to earn decent wages of up to $2 a day, which had enabled most to become masters. Amid the Market Revolution, however, Philadelphia proved to be a poor place to make shoes from scratch by hand in

While the masses bought cheap shoes from Lynn's factories, the wealthy, like these two customers, continued in the 1850s to buy handmade shoes at fancy shoe stores. (Culver Pictures)

competition with the new system. By the 1840s local shoemakers faced bankruptcy.

The winners were the shoe entrepreneurs of Lynn, Massachusetts. They divided the labor of making a shoe into multiple parts and assigned many of these tasks, such as sewing the shoes or polishing them, to women and children, who performed the work cheaply at their own homes. This system, called **outwork,** reduced the need for highly skilled, highly paid master shoemakers. Awash in capital, Lynn's shoe masters also bought vast quantities of leather cheaply and hired expert cutters to use the leather efficiently.

The subdivision and deskilling of labor, combined with national marketing, led Lynn's shoe entrepreneurs to dominate the American shoe business. The consumer, of course, benefited, since Lynn shoes were incredibly cheap, less than half the price of shoes made by traditional methods. By the 1840s shoemaking had been destroyed as a craft. Only after 1850 did shoe entrepreneurs gradually begin to build factories and use machinery and unskilled immigrant labor to make cheap shoes. The crucial change that made such manufacturing possible was the national market created by the Market Revolution.

PRINTING BECOMES AN INDUSTRY. The printing industry provides another example of how the Market Revolution changed America. In 1816 James Harper finished his apprenticeship to a New York printer. A year later with $1,000 saved from his work as a journeyman and $1,000 borrowed from his father, a Long Island farmer, James Harper and his brother founded a printing company.

The technology was similar to that Benjamin Franklin had used a century earlier. Printers set type by hand and hand-pulled printed sheets of paper for books or newspapers from presses at a maximum speed of 250 copies per hour. By the 1850s Harper Brothers was the largest printer and book publisher in the country, and although typesetters still worked by hand, the firm produced more than a million volumes a year on high-speed steam presses that operated at the rate of 18,000 sheets of paper per hour.

In the 1830s Horace Greeley finished his apprenticeship as a printer and went to New York to seek work. Because of a temporary glut of journeymen printers, he barely made enough to avoid starvation. Eventually, conditions improved, and he saved $1,000, but it took political connections to put together the $10,000 necessary to buy a power press to start the *New York Tribune* in 1841. Greeley became a famous editor.

Ten years later, in 1851, Henry J. Raymond, who had worked for Greeley, founded the *New York Times*. To compete, Raymond needed an expensive high-speed press, invented by Richard Hoe in 1846, and the firm had to be capitalized at $100,000. Able to contribute only $1,000, Raymond never had control and was later forced out of the company. Thus, in one generation the capital required to succeed in printing and publishing had multiplied by 50.

CAPITAL FLOURISHES. The Market Revolution created unprecedented opportunities for capital. A relatively small investment, if combined with favorable local conditions, good transportation, and luck, might generate a comparative advantage that was overwhelming. An entrepreneur could both charge cheaper prices and make higher profits, with the profits providing the new capital that enabled the business to gain further advantage and yet more market share.

Attempts began to be made to measure entrepreneurial activity, and particularly to evaluate businessmen who wanted to borrow money or make deals. The emergence of a national economic market led to the need for a fair measure of individual worth. In 1841 Arthur and Lewis Tappan, two New York City merchants, sent agents to every county in the United States to evaluate all local businessmen. Their credit rating service, the forerunner of Dun and Bradstreet, played a crucial role in economic development by assisting the expansion of credit.

LABOR PROTESTS AS INEQUALITY INCREASES. For skilled labor, the Market Revolution produced mixed results. Some trades, such as iron molding and machinery, prospered enormously with wages rising for scarce skills to as much as $4 a day. In other trades, like printing, work was usually plentiful, but typesetters had to recognize that they would never make more than $2 a day, might be laid off in economic slumps, and could not save enough money to open their own shops. Still other trades, such as shoemaking, simply disappeared. Factory shoeworkers earned about $1 a day, the rate for unskilled labor.

In large cities, the distribution of wealth became more uneven. In 1825 the wealthiest 1 percent in Boston, New York, and Philadelphia, including manufacturers as well as merchants, had owned about a quarter of the wealth; by 1850, they owned half. A new educated middle class of doctors, lawyers, and specialized managers also prospered. Small shopkeepers did about as well as before, while skilled **artisans** shrank both in relative wealth and as a percentage of the population. The ranks of the unskilled, mostly poor and all propertyless, rose from about one-fifth to two-fifths of the population.

These changes did not take place without objection. As early as the 1790s, skilled artisans had attacked nonproducing "drones," such as merchants, bankers, and attorneys. As craftsmen's status and relative income fell in the 1820s and 1830s, the comments grew more bitter. Proclaiming a "producer ideology," artisans denounced people who did not make tangible things for a living. They promoted the "labor theory of value," that is, that only labor created economic value.

Some artisan spokesmen, such as William Leggett and Robert Rantoul, entered politics, often as Democrats. Other radicals broke with mainstream politics to organize the anemic Workingmen's parties in the 1820s. In the long run, skilled workers found that the greatest political influence came through participation in mainstream parties and elections. After 1850 in some cities artisans were elected to high office. For example, the mayors of New Orleans and Lynn, Massachusetts, were respectively a printer and a skilled shoeworker.

Artisans also organized labor unions to promote their interests. Unions were created in the booming 1790s, but few survived past 1800. In the 1830s skilled workers in some trades organized both local and national unions, which advocated a ten-hour day. In Philadelphia these unions succeeded in setting up a city-wide trades council, but no national unions from this period lasted, and the failure to organize beyond local areas as the economy became national proved fatal. Few unions survived the economic Panic of 1837. Organized labor did well during boom years but faded during economic downturns.

Labor's protests were surprisingly ineffective. For one thing, many artisans, perhaps a third, continued to follow custom. These traditionalists drank heavily, skipped work on Monday, which they celebrated as "St. Monday," and cultivated close relationships with their masters — a name the oldtimers preferred to the modern term: employers. Other craftsmen, perhaps half, embraced modern values, including a strong work ethic, but did so through the transforming power of **evangelical** Christianity. Only about a sixth of skilled workers adopted radical political or labor ideas.

AMERICANS FACE LIMITED SOCIAL MOBILITY. In reality, there was little social or economic mobility. Most American children grew up to belong to the same class as their parents. Merchants, artisans, and laborers begat, respectively, merchants, artisans, and laborers. Of those who were wealthy, 90 percent had wealthy parents; only 2 percent were born poor. Relative to others, people were as likely to move down as up.

Few complained, for a variety of reasons. For one thing, the poor, unskilled workers on the bottom were unsettled. They contributed little either to politics or to community consciousness. Most of these unpropertied masses moved from town to town looking for work by the day. They signaled that they wanted jobs by standing in front of the courthouse early in the morning. If they could get no work for a few days, they moved on. In most cities as many as half the people had lived in town less than a year.

Then, too, the Market Revolution had produced a growing economy. Per capita income doubled within a generation, and many people whose *relative* socioeconomic standing was no higher than their parents nevertheless did enjoy higher living standards. For many, even though their *share* of the economic pie stayed the same, their *piece* of pie still grew, because *overall* the pie had doubled in size.

On the whole, Americans preferred to believe that the United States was a country of opportunity. Matthew Baldwin, James Harper, and Horace Greeley were all heralded as proofs that people could succeed on their own. This ideology was reinforced by evangelical Protestantism, which held that people were primarily responsible for looking after themselves. Any success was visible proof of holiness and God's favor.

Many ambitious artisans abandoned their crafts for greater opportunities in commerce. If they were too old to change, then they tried to provide suitable training for their children. The principal demand for the expansion of public education, including high schools, in the early 1800s came from urban artisans. A high school diploma led to employment as a clerk in the booming commercial sector.

Finally, immigration pushed native-born Americans up the social and economic ladder as thousands of unskilled and impoverished newcomers entered at the bottom. To immigrants, especially the Irish, the standard of living in the United States was higher than at home, even if for some people it had declined from what it had been in the United States in earlier years.

LARGE CITIES GROW RAPIDLY. Although the country remained rural, with urban population, defined as living in a community with at least 2500 people, rising from 3 percent in 1790 to only 15 percent by 1850, the emerging national economy quickly led to the creation of several large cities. In a single lifetime the scale and magnitude were transformed. In 1790 New York's 33,000 people had vied with Philadelphia's 42,000 for national leadership. Each of the next three most populous cities, Boston, Charleston, and Baltimore, had fewer than 20,000 residents. By 1850 New York had 515,000 people and its thriving suburb of Brooklyn another 97,000. Philadelphia's metropolitan population was 409,000, while Baltimore, Boston, New Orleans, and Cincinnati were all over 100,000.

Rapid growth and large populations created enormous urban problems. Water was often contaminated, and not until the middle of the century was good water from reliable sources piped in at great expense. Sewer systems were primitive or nonexistent, and epidemic diseases, such as the cholera that struck in 1832, 1849, and 1866, widespread. Every year more city dwellers died than were born.

Measures for public safety did not keep pace with rapid growth. City residents resisted higher taxes to replace unpaid volunteer night watchmen with a professional police force. Only the rise of marauding gangs, highly organized vice, and street robberies finally led in the 1840s to hiring uniformed officers on call day or night. Fire protection long remained a private matter, until people became disgusted when volunteer fire companies frequently fought each other while buildings burned to the ground.

The principal method of getting around the city was on foot. Since most people could not walk more than three miles to work, there was little sprawl. Construction techniques, however, limited buildings to about six stories. Poor transport and low buildings led to incredible congestion and high rents. Large families sometimes lived in a single room, and 10,000 people might live on one block.

As cities grew and became more congested, wealthy residents moved from the commercial centers, where they had traditionally lived behind or above stores, to outlying areas, where they built mansions on landscaped lots and kept horses in private stables. The suburbs flourished, and by the 1850s the middle classes followed the wealthy in commuting to the city by horsedrawn streetcar or steam railway.

Neighborhoods became identified with a particular social class, and this tendency increased when massive immigration began in the 1840s. Class and ethnicity were linked, with the Irish, in most cities, as unskilled laborers, and the Germans as skilled craftsmen. Few immigrants were middle class. No one, it appears, wanted to live near the Irish — sarcastically ridiculed as the Great Unwashed — and Germans formed neighborhoods where everyone spoke their language. One could live in New York's Kleindeutschland or Cincinnati's Over the Rhine without knowing or hearing a word of English.

The American city demonstrated both what was right and what was wrong with the country. Fabulous wealth was generated next to the grimmest poverty. Intense local pride led private donors to establish numerous museums and charities, but public money could seldom be found to improve urban life. Democratic political rights degenerated into corrupt **political machines,** and the ideal of equality contrasted with frequent ethnic riots. Every city puffed itself with expectations of even greater glory in the future, and yet almost no one pondered the price of success.

Meanwhile, there was always a dollar to be made. In the final analysis, that was the message of the Market Revolution.

Conclusion

The Market Revolution produced the single most dramatic change in American history. Textile manufacturing, based on slave-produced cotton, marked the beginning of an industrial revolution that over the long run transformed people's lives in multiple ways. Transportation improvements, in the form of steamboats, canals, and railroads, accelerated economic growth by creating national markets. Business began to be conducted in new ways, as products such as shoes or books were produced on a massive scale. Inequality in wealth increased, labor protests failed, and large cities grew rapidly. The combination of all these changes taking place simultaneously explains why the total result is called the Market Revolution.

Recommended Readings

DOCUMENTS: Joseph G. Baldwin, *The Flush Times of Alabama and Mississippi* (1853); *The Lowell Offering* (1840-1845); Frances Trollope, *Domestic Manners of the Americans* (1832).

READINGS: (GENERAL) Richard D. Brown, *Modernization* (1976); Thomas C. Cochran, *Frontiers of Change* (1981); James A. Henretta, *The Evolution of American Society* (1973);

Charles Sellers, *The Market Revolution* (1991); (TEXTILES) Thomas Dublin, *Women at Work* (1979); Jonathan Prude, *The Coming of Industrial Order* (1983); Philip Scranton, *Proprietary Capitalism* (1983); Cynthia J. Shelton, *The Mills of Manayunk* (1986); Anthony F. C. Wallace, *Rockdale* (1978); Gavin Wright, *The Political Economy of the Cotton South* (1978); (SHOES) Mary H. Blewett, *Men, Women, and Work* (1988); Alan Dawley, *Class and Community* (1976); (LABOR) Herbert G. Gutman, *Work, Culture, and Society in Industrializing America* (1976); Joan M. Jensen, *Loosening the Bonds* (1986); Alexander Keyssar, *Out of Work* (1986); W. J. Rorabaugh, *The Craft Apprentice* (1986); Mary P. Ryan, *Cradle of the Middle Class* (1981); Merritt R. Smith, *Harpers Ferry Armory and the New Technology* (1977); (CITIES) Paul A. Gilje, *The Road to Mobocracy* (1987); Bruce Laurie, *Working People of Philadelphia* (1980); Suzanne Lebsock, *The Free Women of Petersburg* (1984); William H. and Jane H. Pease, *The Web of Progress* (1985); Howard Rock, *Artisans of the New Republic* (1979); Steven J. Ross, *Workers on the Edge* (1985); Christine Stansell, *City of Women* (1986); Charles G. Steffen, *The Mechanics of Baltimore* (1984); Sean Wilentz, *Chants Democratic* (1984).

9

———— ❈ ————

EVANGELICAL RELIGION AND
REFORM, 1790-1850

CHAPTER OVERVIEW: In 1790 most Americans had little interest in religion. Beginning with the American Revolution, many people had put political principles above religion. Despite this apathy, religion was not dead. Going to church remained a favorite activity for many people. Of those Americans who did profess faith, probably 99 percent called themselves Protestant Christians. Catholics and Jews were scarce.

Between the late 1790s and 1830 intense revivals swept across the United States. This evangelical upsurge, similar to the revivals of the 1740s, became known as the Second Great Awakening. The movement began on the southern frontier, where residents developed a religion that combined a belief in universal salvation with emotional display. The northeastern revivals shared these traits, but evangelical Calvinists also stressed reform. Northerners established Sunday Schools and missions; gave up gambling, premarital sex, and liquor; built hospitals, prisons, and schools; and considered women's rights. Not everyone thought that such reforms went far enough, and idealists advocated communes, adopted romanticism, embraced transcendentalism, or worshipped nature.

Southerners Embrace Revivals but Disdain Reform

The Revolutionary War had destroyed the Church of England as an effective force in the South, and afterward the region became largely unchurched. Traveling Baptist and Methodist preachers — uneducated representatives of new denominations — provided some services and began to hold camp meetings on the frontier in the 1790s. These meetings created a new evangelical style in which worshippers, contrary to Calvinist ideas, accepted the belief in universal access to salvation and the need

160

for intense emotional display, including rolling on the ground. In the early 1800s southerners became devout but adopted a form of Protestantism that disdained moral or political reform.

SOUTHERN RELIGION DECAYS AFTER THE REVOLUTION. In no region of the country had organized religion suffered more losses than in the South. Before the Revolution most southerners, white and black, had at least nominally belonged to the **Church of England** (i.e., the Episcopal church). In Virginia it had been the legal, tax-supported state church. In cities and long-settled areas near the seaboard, the church had functioned well, providing not only worship services but also charity for the poor. In inland frontier areas the church existed only in theory. There, even before the Revolution, Baptist, Methodist, and Presbyterian ministers had preached, although few congregations were organized formally.

The Church of England's ministers had been routinely supplied from England, and during the Revolution many of its clergymen were Tories. They returned home. Financial support from England was cut off, and wartime inflation destroyed the value of church investments in America. All of the southern states withdrew their tax support for the church.

The Episcopal church, as it was renamed, emerged from the war with few ministers and meager resources. Although the church continued strong in towns and along the seacoast, it lacked the means to maintain inland missions. Frontier areas went largely without organized religion.

TRAVELING PREACHERS SERVE THE FRONTIER. Beginning in the 1740s, during the **revivals** called the **Great Awakening,** wandering Baptist and Methodist preachers, many with little or no religious training, had circulated throughout the colonies. In the 1790s leaders of these new denominations, along with some Presbyterians, crisscrossed the otherwise unchurched wilderness.

Although the frontier lacked regular churches, once every few years a circuit rider might show up at a farm, have dinner, perform a marriage ceremony for a young farm couple, and baptize their children. The preacher, carrying news and good stories, would read from the Bible and lead a family prayer. He would then move on to repeat his mission with the next family.

Sometimes neighbors would learn about the pending visit of a traveling minister. A makeshift religious service might be held, almost certainly out of doors, since frontier cabins could not hold more than a few people. Such services were popular, and the preachers, who learned the ways of ordinary people as they traveled around, decided that organized events that brought people together would strengthen religion.

HOLDING CAMP MEETINGS. In the late 1790s frontier preachers in western North Carolina, Tennessee, and Kentucky began to hold camp meetings. Weeks in advance the organizers posted signs on trees for miles around, and at the appointed time thousands gathered to hear preaching, to pray, and to sing hymns. In 1801 the largest camp meeting, held at Cane Ridge, Kentucky, attracted an estimated 25,000 people.

Camp meetings were often interdenominational. Baptists, Methodists, and Presbyterians preached and prayed together. Although these **evangelicals** competed to see who could gain the most converts, this cooperation marked a new attitude among American **Protestants.**

The camp meeting ground was laid out as a rectangle. Participants placed the horses and wagons in which they traveled and the tents in which they slept along the outside perimeter. In front of each tent, facing the preaching field in the center, each revivalist built a fire for cooking and light. At some camp meetings rival preaching platforms were built at each end, and ministers vied to see who could get and hold the biggest audience. Sometimes logs served as benches, but many people sat on the ground.

The meetings lasted for three to seven days. Every morning bugles called people from their tents, and the preaching started. After breakfast, there was more preaching and prayer, then a dinner break, followed by more religious activity. This pattern continued all day, and with camp fires burning brightly, often all night as well.

Camp meetings frequently became mass exercises in pandemonium. Participants — including both whites and blacks, of all ages, and perhaps three-fourths of them female — did not politely listen to cogent, logical sermons. Rather, the preachers exhorted their listeners to accept Christ into their lives, to feel their new-found religion, and to express their agony or their joy openly. People responded with shrieks, fainting, praying aloud, rolling in the dirt, and speaking in tongues, that is, by making unrecognizable sounds.

SOUTHERN EVANGELICALS PREACH UNIVERSAL SALVATION. The revivalists specifically rejected the Calvinist idea that God planned to save only a few people whom He had selected. **Salvation,** these evangelicals preached, was open to all. God freely gave everyone the right to be saved. This was a democratic, **egalitarian** religion.

Furthermore, the camp meeting preachers stressed that salvation required no education, no special religious study, and no visible good deeds. Salvation required only faith in Christ as the savior. Faith, and faith alone, guaranteed eternal life.

This simple doctrine had broad appeal, but it posed one problem. How could anyone, even a preacher, tell whether a person was sincere in proclaim-

In the early 1800s, evangelical Protestants' camp meetings often led to outpourings of emotion, which was seen as the sure sign of the beginning of a religious conversion. (BETTMANN ARCHIVE)

ing faith? The ministers looked for outward signs consistent with faith. Hence, the shouts, faintings, and loud prayers became the means by which a person proved faith and being born again in Christ.

Southern evangelicals' staunch belief in the primacy of faith, and their insistence upon measuring faith through visible signs of religious fervor had a profound consequence: this emotionally self-contained kind of religion had little concern for, or connection with, events in the secular world.

Southern churches looked upon secular reform with suspicion or hostility. Attempts to define social issues as moral problems offended southern evangelicals, since morality was the province of the church, and southerners knew that universal faith, repentance, and rebirth for salvation were all that was required to make a perfect society.

The frontier revivals first spread eastward, then throughout the South, and eventually northward into the Midwest. By 1840 the South's leading denomination was Methodism. After the Civil War, the region became the **"Bible Belt,"** the section of the United States where religion was (and still is today) most important. Furthermore, the evangelical Protestantism established during the Second Great Awakening of the early 1800s has continued to prevail. As late as the 1920s about 98 percent of southerners were evangelicals, mostly Baptists, Methodists, or Presbyterians.

Northeasterners Undertake Revivals with Reforms

In the early 1800s the Second Great Awakening also reached rural New England, but local traditions caused the revivals to take a different form. New England had been founded by Calvinist Congregationalists, who believed that God offered salvation through grace to only a small number of people. During the early 1700s, this idea had lost its popular appeal, and by the time of the Great Awakening in the 1740s, it was increasingly ignored.

By 1800 orthodox Calvinists had lost ground to both Edwardseans, who believed in universal salvation, and Unitarians, who emphasized behavior. Then the Calvinists regained the initiative by adopting evangelicalism. The Burned-Over District of western New York, settled by New Englanders, produced much religious fervor as well as new denominations. Throughout the Northeast, evangelicals sponsored Sunday Schools and missions. Faced with a large Irish Catholic immigration, they also expressed a biting anti-Catholicism.

EDWARDSEANS, UNITARIANS, AND ORTHODOX CALVINISTS. The followers of Jonathan Edwards, the great revivalist of the 1740s, moved away from the early colonists' Calvinism, which had held that only a select few people who had had conversion experiences could be saved. These Edwardseans, as they were called, gravitated, like the southern revivalists, toward a doctrine of salvation open to all. In this egalitarian religion, faith and fervor displaced doctrine, although the Edwardseans were never as outwardly emotional as southern evangelicals. (Yankees can't "get down," southerners say to this day.) By the early 1800s many of these Congregationalists had become Baptists, especially strong in poorer rural areas, such as the Maine seacoast.

In the seaports wealthy merchants and professionals had increasingly drifted from Calvinism to Unitarianism, which became the creed of John Adams. Unitarians argued that moral conduct was more important than faith. Their most famous minister, William Ellery Channing, advocated the "perfection of human nature." Wealthy church members gave considerable money and devoted much energy to solve social problems that they believed were rooted in immorality. Over time, Unitarians drew away from Jesus Christ, whom they admired as a noble man but denied as a manifestation of God.

Thus, by 1800 the orthodox Calvinists found themselves under attack from two directions. Increasingly defensive, the ministers of New England's established tax-supported Congregational churches looked on with incredulity and rage as local congregations hired Unitarians or Edwardseans to replace retiring Calvinist ministers.

In 1804, the wealthy and socially prominent Unitarians captured control of the Harvard Divinity School, which, along with Yale, had traditionally educated New England's Calvinist clergy. If Harvard produced only Unitarians for a generation, Calvinists realized, old-style Congregationalism would die. The Calvinists were desperate.

EVANGELICAL CALVINISTS LEAD THE NORTHEASTERN REVIVALS. In the early 1800s a large number of Calvinists suddenly caught the spirit of the Second Great Awakening. Borrowing the revival techniques of the Edwardseans, the evangelical Calvinists, as they now styled themselves, decided to confront both Edwardseans and Unitarians.

Like the Edwardseans, the evangelical Calvinists accepted salvation through faith. Although they declined to emphasize salvation's universal availability in their preaching, their revival was designed to gain mass converts. Like the Unitarians, the evangelical Calvinists emphasized doing good in the world. Deeds, however, were not to be valued for their own sake but as visible outward signs of true faith. Thus, for evangelical Calvinists, unlike southern evangelicals, moral issues, including those from the secular world, had great religious significance.

The leading figure in this movement was Timothy Dwight, a grandson of Edwards and the president of Yale. Dwight trained a generation of evangelical Calvinist ministers, who spread these ideas not only across New England but into those parts of New York and the Midwest where Yankees settled. Among Dwight's students was Lyman Beecher. He became the leading evangelical Calvinist of the next generation, as well as the father of the abolitionist author Harriet Beecher Stowe.

Evangelical Calvinists in Massachusetts were galled at having to send divinity students to Yale, which was in the rival state of Connecticut, and so in 1808 they founded their own seminary at Andover, Massachusetts. Students at Andover found the atmosphere exciting. They talked about establishing foreign missions, publishing Sunday School tracts, cooperating across traditional denominational boundaries, and organizing moral societies to deal with the nation's leading social problems.

REVIVALS SCORCH NEW YORK'S BURNED-OVER DISTRICT. No part of the United States was more influenced by evangelical Calvinism than western New York. Settled almost entirely by New Englanders in the years just after 1800, the region from Utica to Buffalo witnessed so many revivals that it became known as the "Burned-Over District." Lacking the stability found in New England's long settled towns and without older Edwardseans, Unitarians, or traditional Calvinists, western New York was ripe for evangelicals of all types.

One of America's great revivalists, Charles Grandison Finney, carried the evangelical message across the region with incessant travel. In 1830-1831 he spent six months in Rochester and claimed 100,000 conversions. Finney combined charisma with a shrewd sense of organization. Wherever Finney went, he recruited local talent to organize a church after he left.

He also had an eye for technique and published a manual on how to conduct a revival. For example, he advised the preacher to leave the pulpit and exhort among the people. As the minister passed by, he ought to lay hands on people. Amid the great tension of a revival, this physical act would often cause the touched persons to scream and send waves of emotion through the entire gathering. Many converts would follow.

The intensity of feeling in the Burned-Over District led many converts to seek new ways to express religion. Joseph Smith, originally from a poor farm family in Vermont, was converted during the revivals in western New York to Methodism. Dissatisfied with that church's loose doctrine and gripped by a passion for religion, he founded the Church of Jesus Christ of Latter-Day Saints by 1830. Early followers came from among the residents of New York's religiously scorched region. Smith's adherents, called Mormons, lived semi-communally with their own economic institutions, practiced a ritualized religion more given to good deeds than faith, and eagerly sought converts. The Mormons moved to Kirtland, Ohio, and, after alienating non-Mormons, to Missouri and then to Nauvoo, Illinois.

After a mob murdered Joseph Smith in Illinois in 1844, leadership passed to Brigham Young, a Vermont native converted in western New York. This brilliant organizer sent missionaries to Europe to make converts and recruit immigrants. In 1847, after careful planning, he took more than 10,000 Mormons to Utah, then part of Mexico. The most controversial early Mormon doctrine was polygamy. Young had 16 wives and 57 children. The methodical Young maintained each wife in a separate household which he visited in rotation.

Also in the Burned-Over District, William Miller, an uneducated Baptist minister, preached that Christ was about to return to earth. Miller unwisely indicated a precise date in 1844. His followers bought white robes to ascend to Heaven in proper attire and gathered for the appointed day. (Some purchased their robes on credit, rationalizing that Judgment Day would cancel the debt.) When nothing happened, many became disillusioned, but others merely concluded, as did Miller, that his calculations were incorrect. Out of the Millerite movement came the Seventh Day Adventist Church, which rose to prominence under the influence of the religious and dietary prophetess Ellen White.

Western New Yorkers did not always express their yearnings by founding new denominations. If people felt confused, they could turn to advice from their ancestors. So said the Fox sisters, two residents who in the 1840s claimed that they had made contact with the dead through seances. They invented the crystal ball. The popular press reported excitedly on **spiritualism,** which most people eventually came to see as a hoax. To understand the popularity of spiritualism, one must remember the context of the times. Spiritualism was scarcely more fantastic than the newly invented telegraph, which carried sounds over wire for hundreds of miles.

The Burned-Over District's peculiar religious zeal had several causes. The area was newly populated and, hence, unstable. It just happened to be settled at the moment when the Second Great Awakening overtook the entire country. Its residents, native New Englanders, had grown up in a culture that stressed religion. Then, too, the opening of the Erie Canal played a role, as rapid economic growth brought drastic economic, social, and political upheaval to the region. As in other parts of the North, Methodism became the leading denomination by 1840.

CREATING SUNDAY SCHOOLS, TRACTS, AND MISSIONS. Northeastern evangelicals were keen on spreading their version of the Christian gospel. One innovation was the organization of children's Sunday schools. Reformers designed programs, including children's religious literature that was sent all over the country, to entice young people to the revival. Evangelicals adopted the practice of rewarding children who memorized large numbers of Bible verses by presenting them with Bibles.

Revivalists also produced adult religious tracts, many distributed by more than one denomination, by the millions. A sharp decline in the cost of printing in the 1830s made free distribution possible. Tracts not only explained the Bible but also offered advice about personal and social problems. They praised churchgoing and condemned taverns, lauded family life and warned that those who rejected religion would go to hell.

Determined to save the entire world, evangelicals in the early 1800s organized foreign missions to Africa, to India, to China, and to Hawaii. Husband and wife missionary teams were sent overseas, and women in American churches provided the cash and goods that kept the missions going.

Only after overseas missions were established did evangelicals turn to the many unchurched people on the American frontier. Giving special attention to Indians, evangelicals set up missions, such as the one at Walla Walla in the far Northwest, founded in 1836 by the Rev. Marcus and Narcissa Whitman. In 1847 the Whitmans were murdered by native Americans who blamed the missionaries for bringing fatal diseases into the country.

Some of the most important missions took place in large cities. In the 1820s the Unitarians appointed Joseph Tuckerman as a street missionary in Boston. Walking all over the city made Tuckerman familiar with its wretched sailors' drinking halls, its houses of prostitution, and its children living on the street. He organized hot meals and beds in shelters, but his efforts seemed paltry beside the grim and growing needs of the poor.

In New York during the 1850s Charles Loring Brace set up a cheap boarding house for orphans and newsboys, poor children who earned barely enough to eat by hawking newspapers on the streets. The Ladies' Five Points Mission was one of the first large settlement houses located at the center of New York's grimmest Irish slum. The mission offered meals, shelter, second-hand clothes, advice about jobs, emergency travel money, and Protestant tracts. The founders were especially pleased that the site was an abandoned brewery.

Catholic and Jewish immigrants had mixed feelings about these Protestant missions. Although the missions stressed charity, the message of salvation through conversion to evangelical Protestantism was seldom left out, and the missionaries were often condescending if not insulting. Catholic and Jewish religious leaders were downright antagonized. Not only were Protestants trying to steal their members, but the missions suggested that Protestants did not believe other groups capable of providing for themselves. As quickly as possible, immigrants organized their own charities.

NORTHEASTERN EVANGELICALS ATTACK CATHOLICISM. Anti-Catholicism appealed to northeastern evangelicals. Rallying Protestants against the Pope as the Anti-Christ was an old custom. It united people from different denominations who might otherwise have quarreled among themselves. But more was at stake. Protestants worried that Catholic and Jewish immigrants threatened to change the character of the United States. After all, evangelicals believed that their form of Christianity was uniquely suited to America. Their religion nurtured self-improvement, the moral reform of society, and wholesome, democratic politics.

Deeply ignorant and darkly suspicious of Catholics, a Protestant mob in Boston, egged on by the Rev. Lyman Beecher, left church in 1834 to cross the Charles River and burn down the Catholic convent at Charlestown. Boston's wealthy merchants forced Beecher to resign, and he moved to Cincinnati, which he was determined to save. The Pope, according to Beecher, was settling Catholics in Cincinnati in preparation for moving the Vatican there.

In 1836 a visibly pregnant prostitute arrived in New York and persuaded several leading Protestant ministers that she had been impregnated by **Jesuits** while being held against her will in a monastery in Montreal. Calling herself Maria Monk, she became a celebrity, told her story on stage, and was the subject of a bestselling book. Only later was her story generally dismissed as false.

In 1844 Philadelphians burned a Catholic church, and the same thing might have happened in New York, but Archbishop John Hughes vowed that if any Catholic church was torched, the financial district would be set ablaze. When the Pope donated an inscribed building block to be placed inside the Washington Monument, then under construction in the nation's capital, an anti-Catholic mob that saw evil in the papal stone dumped it into the Potomac River. In 1854 an official representative from the Vatican, Archbishop Gaetano Bedini, had to escape New York in the middle of the night to avoid a lynching.

Reformers Tackle Social Problems

The Second Great Awakening, especially in its northeastern evangelical Calvinist form, combined with the impact of the Market Revolution to unleash an unprecedented era of reform, particularly in the Northeast. As economics, politics, and society changed rapidly, reformers rushed with fervor and enthusiasm to reorganize both the country's morals and the ways of doing business. Improvement, both individual and social, became the watchword of the day. Optimistic and self-confident reformers believed that society's problems could be solved if only sufficient reform took place.

EMPHASIZING MORALS AND URGING SEXUAL RESTRAINT. Northeastern evangelicals were determined to remake society in a moral fashion. They lobbied for a law to prohibit the mail from being carried or distributed on Sundays, and they succeeded in establishing stage lines and steamboat companies that refused to operate on the sabbath. Under this attack, state lotteries were abolished. Gambling was immoral because winnings were an unearned windfall. To evangelicals, who believed that faith rather than works was the basis of salvation, winning at gambling was as obscene as sinners attaining salvation without making the effort to gain the faith necessary to attain a second birth.

Sexual practices were also subject to new restrictions. Reformers vigorously attacked prostitution, even in the seaports where it had long been tolerated, and homes for unwed mothers were opened. In addition to shelter, the young women received more than ample moral and religious advice. The percentage of women who were pregnant at the time of marriage dropped from 30 percent in 1790 to 10 percent by 1850.

Much of the effort to restrain sex was directed at young men. Advice books warned against prostitution, which led to disease, and masturbation, which, according to reformers, produced insanity. The only safe solutions for a young man were self-restraint or early marriage. In the absence of a virtuous woman and the financial means for marriage, reformers recommended vigorous physical exercise and cold baths.

Sex within marriage was also subject to restraint. Reformers believed that frequent sexual activity caused the male to lose vigor, to become both sexually and economically lethargic, and to decline into an alarming, nonproductive, premature old age. The female had to protect her mate from this fate by declining his advances.

Reformers also taught that sex excited women, which made them unfit mothers. Besides, childbirth exhausted women, and in congested cities or in long-settled rural areas with scarce, expensive land, where most Americans lived, children had ceased to be economic assets. Coitus interruptus, that is, early withdrawal, was recommended as a form of birth control. (Condoms existed in Europe but were unknown in the United States.) In the rural Northeast by 1860 family size had declined to only three children.

Not all reformers shared these views. In the 1830s Frances Wright, an advocate for labor's rights and founder of a failed abolitionist commune, preached the doctrine of **free love** to New York audiences. According to the Scots-born Wright, men had designed the institution of marriage to control women. If marriage were abolished, a perfect harmony and equality between the sexes might result. Protestant clergymen, almost all men, denounced her from their pulpits. Few people dared to put Wright's theories into practice.

FIGHTING ALCOHOL. The most important reform, both in the eyes of evangelical leaders and in the number of people involved, was the campaign against alcohol. The **temperance movement,** as it was called, combined a religious idea with a secular practice. A born-again Protestant who gave up liquor offered visible outward proof of the proclaimed inner faith. To break a lifelong habit in this fashion provided strong evidence of a true conversion.

At the same time, giving up drink had practical consequences. The ex-

"FATHER, DEAR FATHER, COME HOME WITH ME NOW.
THE CLOCK IN THE STEEPLE STRIKES ONE."

In the mid-1800s, T. S. Arthur's play, *Ten Nights in a Bar Room*, enjoyed popularity throughout the United States. This story of a drunkard and his daughter conveyed well the temperance movement's antiliquor message. (Culver Pictures)

drinker did not frivolously waste time and money sipping whiskey in a tavern, with its temptations to fights, gambling, and prostitution. The abstaining male was expected to work harder and with more enthusiasm, to be more devoted to family, and to use leisure time for self-improvement, Bible-reading, or prayer.

The United States had been one of the heaviest drinking countries in the world, with the typical adult white male drinking about a half pint of whiskey a day. Between 1825 and 1850 alcohol consumption dropped in half. This did not mean that the average American drank half as much. Rather, it meant that the evangelical half of the population took the "teetotal" pledge to stop drinking altogether.

At first, evangelicals were delighted with the progress of the anti-alcohol campaign, but in the 1830s they came to realize that the reform was no longer spreading. The non-religious, as well as Catholics and Episcopalians, never accepted abstinence.

Evangelicals then proposed laws to prohibit the sale of alcohol. The first such law, passed in Massachusetts in 1838, outlawed the sale of hard liquor in quantities under 15 gallons. The theory was that only respectable people could afford to buy that much liquor. Retailers quickly found ways to evade the law. One enterprising seller charged 6 cents for the right to see his blind pig. Viewers got a free drink. This is the origin of the expression "blind pig" to describe an illegal drinking establishment. Within two years the state had repealed the law.

In the 1840s, many states allowed voters to ban alcohol sales in cities or counties, and in 1851 Maine became the first dry state. Pushed through by Neal Dow, the dry Quaker mayor of Portland, the Maine law provoked such a backlash that it was repealed in 1856. Although several states tried **prohibition** in the 1850s, none kept it for long. The evangelical war against liquor was to be resumed after the Civil War. By 1850, however, evangelicals had managed to make abstinence a requirement for middle-class respectability.

PROMOTING HEALTH. The antiliquor campaign led in the 1830s to a more modest movement to ban meat. Vegetarians argued that alcohol and meat made people animalistic, and that spirituality could be enhanced with an all-grain diet. To ensure that such a diet was balanced, the Rev. Sylvester Graham, a leading temperance lecturer turned vegetarian, invented Graham flour, a nutritionally balanced blend of several grains. That flour today is the basis of the Graham cracker.

Many reformers rejected orthodox medicine, which depended heavily upon laudanum, that is, opium dissolved in alcohol, and bleeding patients with leeches. Instead, reformers sought to restore proper bodily balance through water cures, which meant visiting mineral springs, or through homeopathy, an unorthodox branch of medicine that advocated minimal doses of a large variety of natural drugs designed to restore balance.

Another reformer was Amelia Bloomer, who rejected the tight, unhealthy whalebone corsets worn by fashionable middle-class women. Bloomer designed, made, and wore a short skirt combined with loose trousers that were gathered at the ankles. Although some radical women took to wearing bloomers, as the new costume was called, it would be more than a century before respectable women wore pants.

Others thought that health and destiny could be read in the shape of one's head. After an examination, a phrenologist would declare the subject's susceptibility to specific diseases, the nature of his morals, and his financial prospects.

OPENING ASYLUMS FOR THE POOR AND THE MENTALLY ILL. After 1830, many aspects of the reform movement were secular and institutional. Cities and states used profits from the growing economy to build poorhouses. Whereas most poor people, usually old and infirm, had previously received what was called outdoor relief, that is, sporadic, small quantities of food or cash, the poor were now provided with permanent shelter and hot meals. The system cost more money, but it was expected that some of the poor could work indoors and thereby help support themselves. Also, some vagabonds might be discouraged from seeking assistance if they had to live in a government institution without liquor or bawdy activities.

Mental hospitals were also built in large numbers. Previously, families had chained disturbed relatives in the cellar or attic. Now, people with mental problems were considered to be ill and therefore capable of receiving treatment. Treatment began by placing the person in a clean, sanitary, comfortable institution, where doctors and staff could watch after their needs and help them adapt to normal life. Much of the credit for this new policy goes to Dorothea Dix, a tireless reformer who lobbied successfully with numerous state legislatures and city councils to build asylums.

BUILDING PRISONS. Prisons were another innovation. Prior to 1800 criminals were executed, whipped, or fined, but rarely imprisoned. Jails were used only to hold people awaiting trial. By 1830 reformers conceived of prisons as a more humane form of punishment. They were expensive, but reformers believed the expense worthwhile, because prison provided the best way to reform the criminal. Criminals, like sinners, could be reborn and saved.

Exact methods varied. At the Pennsylvania Prison in Philadelphia prisoners served relatively short sentences in solitary confinement. Jailers pushed food into the cell through a trap door, and the prisoner, given a number and ordered to observe total silence, had nothing to do in the cell except read a Bible and contemplate the error of his ways. On Sundays the doors were opened a crack and the prisoners, whether they wanted to or not, heard an evangelical sermon in the hallway. The theory was that lack of contamination by other inmates would enable a large number of criminals to reform their characters. Instead, a high percentage went insane.

New York's Auburn Prison was cheaper to operate than Pennsylvania's, because the prisoners slept alone in tiny cells but spent their days working in a large common room. To avoid criminal contamination, the prisoners were not allowed to talk with each other, and to enforce this rule, guards circled the working inmates with six-foot long whips. Despite brutal beatings, the productive work and the contact with other human beings made the Auburn prison more successful than the one in Philadelphia.

SETTING UP PUBLIC SCHOOLS. Around 1830 reformers demanded the establishment of public schools. Under the reform governor William Henry Seward, New York provided schools upstate and reorganized the charity schools in New York City into a true public school system. Pennsylvania overcame resistance from Germans who believed, correctly, that their language would die out and set up public schools across the state. Even in the South the movement for public schools made some headway. Wealthy planters, however, resisted paying higher taxes to educate poor white children. Their own children were often privately tutored.

Massachusetts, under its brilliant commissioner of education, Horace Mann, set the pace for school reform. Mann concentrated on the quality of education. He stressed that children had to be prepared for a rapidly changing society, one in which industry and commerce demanded workers who were sober, cheerful, obedient, resourceful, and disciplined. Mann expressed a keen interest in the new high schools, which promised to provide clerks and skilled managers to run the emerging industrial economy.

ADVOCATING WOMEN'S RIGHTS. The Market Revolution had upset old ways, and one consequence was that women began to question their role in society. The early 1800s brought the first generation of educated women. In 1821 Emma Willard founded Troy Female Seminary, where women were taught serious, college-level subjects. In 1833 Oberlin College became the first American college to admit female students, and four years later Mary Lyon opened Mount Holyoke as a women's college. Many leaders of the women's rights movement came from this first generation of formally educated women.

The women's rights movement had its origins in certain evangelical churches. Although only a few churches allowed women to preach, most evangelical congregations were preponderantly female. Furthermore, as almost every male minister recognized, women ran church activities, and the pressure of women on husbands, fathers, and sons kept money flowing into church coffers.

The can-do evangelical spirit, combined with everyday experiences of tending to church business, led women to become involved in moral and secular reform movements. Women were active in all the reform movements, especially temperance and the **abolition** of slavery, which is discussed in Chapter 11.

Eventually, some women came to believe that their own position in society should be changed. Started by two breakaway radical religious groups that had given women the right to preach, the Hicksite Quakers and Wesleyan Methodists, the women's rights movement was publicly scorned and mocked during the 1830s. When Sarah and Angelina Grimké dared to become the first women to speak before "mixed" audiences, that is, audiences of both men and women, riots nearly occurred. In 1837 Angelina Grimké broke new ground by debating a man in public. The press generally agreed that she won the debate.

Still, little was accomplished, and in 1848 Lucretia Mott and Elizabeth

Cady Stanton organized a women's rights convention at Seneca Falls, New York. At this meeting the delegates, including women and men, adopted the Female Declaration of Independence. It placed men in the position of a George III, as the hated tyrant, and it mockingly threatened revolution unless male oppression and domination came to an end. Although the Declaration drew some attention, it would be two generations before the women's rights movement became a major force in the United States.

Idealists Seek Change

Some Americans thought that reformers focused too narrowly on changing society's existing institutions and ways. These idealists, often influenced by evangelicalism even when they rejected formal religion, advocated a larger, more philosophical approach that promised to restructure society radically. Some idealists, such as evangelicals in the peace movement, believed that the change of heart required to make a born-again Christian could so transform the human personality that war would become impossible. Pacifism, however, failed. Others, usually more secular, looked to communalism as a way to restructure society, solving all the problems created by the Market Revolution while providing moral uplift. Still others turned to romanticism as an alternative to religion and reform, and yet others embraced the semireligion of transcendentalism or simply worshipped nature. Many women influenced these movements through their writings.

PRACTICING COMMUNALISM. Idealism took many forms, including the advocacy of a shared, communal way of life. Many **communes** were religious. "Mother" Ann Lee, an English immigrant, had brought the Shakers, or Shaking Quakers, to America in 1774. Noted for the simplicity and grace of their architecture and furniture, they thrived during the Second Great Awakening. In more than a dozen colonies, they farmed, worked, and lived communally, with men and women occupying separate dormitories. The Shakers denounced sex, and the men and women saw each other only at religious services, where they did shaking dances. They recruited new members primarily by raising orphans. By far the most successful of the communes, the Shakers survived into the twentieth century.

Other religious communes rarely outlived their founders, and secular communes seldom lasted long. One of the exceptions was the Oneida Community, founded by John Humphrey Noyes in 1848. Strong personal leadership and business sense made the difference. Noyes's advocacy of multiple sexual partners in group marriage gave the colony a scandalous reputation, but Oneida eventually gained economic security through the sale of its well-made, elegant silverware.

The most famous commune was the secular one at New Harmony, Indiana, founded in 1825 by the Scottish immigrants Robert Owen and his son, Robert Dale Owen. The elder Owen had owned a textile mill in Scotland, and the horrors of the sweatshop had revolted him. Selling out, he had founded New Harmony on the theory of communal, socialist ownership and operation. Although both Owens were brilliant speakers, neither could make the commune work. It ended within a few years in disharmony.

Some people argued that the existing communes had failed either because of shallow theory or because of inadequate attention to detail. The French philosopher Charles Fourier proposed fully self-sustaining socialist communities with about 10,000 people per commune. Each commune, which Fourier called a phalanx, was conceived as a giant circle with a village at the center and with fields radiating outward like spokes. The large size enabled the commune to employ people efficiently at specialized work. Land use and economic production could be carefully planned.

The reformer Horace Greeley, publisher of the *New York Tribune* and an enthusiast for many 'isms,' adopted Fourier's ideas in the 1840s. He envisioned settling frontier America with a series of these large circular communes marching across the landscape toward the Pacific Ocean. Greeley provoked much talk but little action, since most Americans, even evangelical reformers, scorned the planned, "beehive" model for society.

ADOPTING ROMANTICISM. Not all Americans responded to the Market Revolution by adopting evangelical Protestantism, by joining various reform movements, or by advocating communalism. Some people became romantics. The **romantic movement,** most closely identified with the English poets Byron, Keats, and Shelley, was a global reaction in the early 1800s against the stiff, logical reason of the Enlightenment.

Romantics believed that life could be understood best and lived to the fullest only by recognizing that emotion rather than reason was the key to personal contentment. Only through living "on the edge" could a person discover the true self. Critics found this attitude both dangerous and self-indulgent, but romanticism had a growing appeal, especially to those in literature and the arts, amid the radical change and cultural confusion caused by the Market Revolution.

Writers such as the southerners Edgar Allen Poe or William Gilmore

Simms, whose work defended the South and its slavery, adopted a romantic attitude. Romanticism could also be seen in the widespread popularity in the South of the novels of Sir Walter Scott, who set his formulaic tales of heroes rescuing heroines from villains in the Middle Ages. Indeed, southern planters, escaping from a reform-minded present that they did not much like, held mock medieval festivals complete with jousts on horseback.

In northern hands, romanticism often included a moral element. By the 1850s women authors were turning out numerous novels, poems, and magazines for women. Both authors and readers were northern, urban, upper-middle-class women. The magazine, *Godey's Lady's Book* had the name of the male publisher in the title, but it was truly the work of its editor, Mrs. Sarah J. Hale. The widowed Mrs. Hale was probably the first woman in America to make her living by the pen.

The poet Lydia Sigourney wrote verse on topics as diverse as nature and, more darkly, the soul. No matter the subject, she presented an emotional, romantic attitude. Lydia Childs was one of the few authors to mix openly a demand for reform with sentiment, and she sold distinctly fewer copies of her books than did Fanny Fern or Mrs. E.D.E.N. Southworth. The latter two's novels, early versions of gothic romances, sold millions of copies. Although little was serious in either Fern or Southworth, their villains inevitably hated evangelical religion and their heroines never deviated from conventional evangelical morals.

ADVOCATING TRANSCENDENTALISM. Ralph Waldo Emerson and other New Englanders embraced the love of nature, called it **transcendentalism,** and turned it into a religion which incorporated the romantic movement and rejected evangelicalism. Through the study, contemplation, and admiration of nature, Emerson argued, people could *transcend* reason and the manmade world in order to approach and commune with God. Nature was, in this view, God's noblest work. Emerson, the most popular public lecturer of his day, expressed his views in small-town **lyceums,** that is, educational lecture series, all over America.

In 1841 some transcendentalists pursued their ideas by founding an experimental commune called Brook Farm, located just outside Boston. The literary Alcott family lived there for a time, and although the commune was a commercial and agricultural failure abandoned in 1847, it did produce a stunning literary magazine, *The Dial,* edited by the talented Margaret Fuller.

EMBRACING NATURE. Many Americans, like Henry David Thoreau, coped with modernity by escaping to embrace nature. In 1845 Thoreau retreated to Walden Pond in Concord, Massachusetts, and when the train whistle intruded there, he moved to the remote Maine woods. Less interested in reforming a rapidly changing society than in escape, Thoreau found America so corrupted by the Market Revolution that only total personal isolation brought him solace. Communing with nature restored the soul and freshened thought, but Thoreau realized that his personal experience had no social significance unless he shared it with others. He did so in *Walden* (1854). His minimalism, his love of nature, and his jaundiced suspicion of **capitalism** found great appeal in later years.

The appeal to nature was also expressed through the growth of the cemetery movement. Before 1830 Americans were typically buried in small, simple graveyards next to churches. Often ill-kept and overgrown with weeds, churchyards had little natural beauty. After 1830 increasing numbers of urban, middle-class Americans were buried in spacious suburban cemeteries. These parklike burial grounds, such as Mt. Auburn Cemetery outside Boston, were professionally landscaped with trees, shrubs, flowers, meandering walks, and occasional ponds. Families spent Sunday afternoons walking through the grounds, often picnicking near their loved ones.

The obsession with nature led to the new profession of landscape architect. Andrew Jackson Downing, the first professional in this field, not only laid out spacious grounds around suburban and rural estates, but he also published books encouraging others to do so. To Downing, the setting was as important as the house, and trees and plants could be used to create a natural environment that pleased the eye, shaded the house, and soothed the spirit.

Wealthy residents in congested, growing cities could not bask in a natural setting, so as a substitute they increasingly hung pictures of nature on their walls. Some of America's greatest oil painters, such as Frederic Church, Thomas Cole, Asher Durand, and George Inness, turned out so many fine landscapes that they became known, because of their favorite subject, as the Hudson River School. These paintings celebrated the grandeur of nature, and if they included any manmade elements, such as a railroad, they were always dwarfed by the mountains, the trees, and the sky. There is no greater clue as to how Americans felt about the industrial age, even as they partook of its profits.

Conclusion

The Second Great Awakening's revivals accompanied the Market Revolution's economic changes. In the South, the revivals produced a type of evangelical Protestantism that embraced universal salvation while rejecting reform. In the North, evangelical Calvinists adopted both revivalism and reform. Reformers tackled social problems by advocating such new ideas as abstinence from alcohol, building public schools, and women's rights. Idealists, some of whom had little use for evangelicalism, experimented with communes, romanticism, transcendentalism, and the worship of nature. By 1850 the country's ideals and institutions had been transformed.

Recommended Readings

DOCUMENTS: Lyman Beecher, *Autobiography* (1864); Horace Greeley, *Recollections of a Busy Life* (1868); Elizabeth C. Stanton, *Eighty Years and More* (1898).

READINGS: (RELIGION) John B. Boles, *The Great Revival* (1972); Jay P. Dolan, *The Immigrant Church* (1975); Paul E. Johnson, *A Shopkeeper's Millennium* (1978); Donald G. Mathews, *Religion in the Old South* (1977); James Turner, *Without God, without Creed* (1985); (REFORM) Carl F. Kaestle, *Pillars of the Republic* (1983); Michael B. Katz, *The Irony of Early School Reform* (1968); Walter D. Lewis, *From Newgate to Dannemora* (1965); W. J. Rorabaugh, *The Alcoholic Republic* (1979); David J. Rothman, *The Discovery of the Asylum* (1971); Ian R. Tyrrell, *Sobering Up* (1979); Ronald G. Walters, *American Reformers* (1978); (WOMEN'S RIGHTS) Barbara J. Berg, *The Remembered Gate* (1978); Nancy A. Hewitt, *Women's Activism and Social Change* (1984); Barbara Welter, *Dimity Convictions* (1976); (CULTURE) Ann Douglas, *The Feminization of American Culture* (1977); Drew G. Faust, *A Sacred Circle* (1977); Leo Marx, *The Machine in the Garden* (1964); Anne C. Rose, *Transcendentalism as a Social Movement* (1981).

10

※

ANDREW JACKSON OF THE WEST

CHAPTER OVERVIEW: The product of the self-reliant, egalitarian frontier, Andrew Jackson brought western democratic principles to national politics. An advocate of voting rights for all white males, frequent elections, and term limits, Jackson adopted policies that rearranged the political landscape and greatly expanded presidential powers. In the 1830s he eliminated the presidential hopes of John C. Calhoun, ended the idea that states could nullify federal laws, wrecked the economy by destroying the second Bank of the United States, and removed Indians from the East.

Jackson isolated Henry Clay, his western rival, as the leader of the hapless Whig party, and named Martin Van Buren as his successor in 1836. Ironically, Jackson's banking policies led to a depression that ruined Van Buren and resulted in the election of the Whig William Henry Harrison in 1840. By then, however, even the Whigs had been forced to accept many of Jackson's democratic ideas.

The Frontier West Gives Birth to Jacksonian Ideals

In the early 1800s frontier culture became nationally important as Americans increasingly moved into the landlocked area west of the Appalachian Mountains in the Ohio and Mississippi River valleys. Pioneer families engaged in gender-divided subsistence agriculture in a society where possessions were few and where most people enjoyed rough equality. Ideals of self-reliance and equality marked the West, and frontier figures such as Andrew Jackson naturally embraced these principles.

THE ISOLATED FRONTIER WEST PRACTICES DEMOCRACY. In 1790 only 1 in 40 Americans lived west of the Appalachian Mountains. By 1810 1 in 7 did, and 20 years later nearly 1 in 3 did. This massive population growth in the Trans-Appalachian West led to growing political power as new states entered the Union. In 1787, 13 states had hugged the Atlantic seacoast. Fifty years later 26 states stretched as far west as Missouri.

In one sense, this migration merely continued the movement of people inland from the seacoast that had begun in the 1600s. In another sense, however, Americans who settled west of the Appalachian Mountains had encountered new challenges. No rivers crossed the mountains, which formed a crucial barrier to trade. A farmer's horse could not carry grain across the mountains worth as much as the horse's feed. Trade often went the long way around. For example, from Bedford, Pennsylvania, to Philadelphia, it cost more to ship goods using the 200-mile overland route than the 2,100-mile water route via Pittsburgh, the Ohio and Mississippi Rivers, and New Orleans.

Although western settlers had brought their culture from the East, the isolation of the West allowed people to develop their own economy, society, and politics. Freed from eastern influence, westerners stressed principles and practices that had been present in weaker form in the East. Over time they shaped a society that, without colonial or English tendencies, was peculiarly American.

Map 10.1. Water vs. Land Transportation

Democracy may not have been born on the frontier, but it certainly reached an earlier maturity there than in the East. A stubborn insistence by white males upon equality among themselves, a giddy expression of the love of freedom, distrust for government and organized institutions — especially if suspected of **elitism** — and an enthusiasm for popular participation in politics became hallmarks of the West.

In 1800 the frontier stretched from Maine to Ohio, through Kentucky and Tennessee to Georgia, and to southern outposts along the Mississippi River. Its exact location is impossible to describe, since the frontier was never fixed. It moved continually westward at a varying rate of 20, 50, or 100 miles a year.

The "frontier" was less a particular place than a state of mind. Beyond the frontier was the "wilderness," where Indian tribes hunted game, planted corn, and moved restlessly, often in conflict with each other. The only whites who lived in the wilderness were fur trappers and traders. To the east of the frontier was "civilization," where white settlers farmed and often shipped their produce for sale in cities, where land had to be bought or rented, where a sheriff might seize a man for failing to pay a debt, where churches, schools, and towns thrived, and where, in the South, slave labor might be used to grow cash crops.

Frontier Americans farmed, too, but they had begun by taming the land. They cut and burned the trees and hacked away the stumps in order to gain a field to plant. This backbreaking labor gave the settlers an intense relationship to the land, even though, paradoxically, the land had been only recently acquired, and many were "squatters" rather than landowners. Lacking any market for their crops, these farmers grew only what they could consume. Nor could they consume anything that they did not grow or make. They were independent, autonomous, subsistence farmers.

THE FRONTIER FAMILY AND GENDER-BASED LABOR. Frontier life meant hard physical labor, and this labor divided along gender lines. Men and boys hunted game, planted, weeded, and harvested the corn and other crops, took care of the family horse, cleared fields, built cabins, barns, and fences, chopped vast quantities of winter firewood, and engaged with the outside world, including swapping produce, goods, and stories.

Women and girls tended chickens, fed hogs, milked cows, made butter, prepared food, kept house, spun thread, arranged for the weaving of cloth, made clothes, and watched the children. The log cabin, although said to be a man's castle, was the wife's domain, as was the medicine cabinet. Except for periods of intense specialized labor, such as harvest, males and females seldom saw each other during the workday.

Because of this division of labor, a farm required the presence of both a man and a woman. This was a family way of life. Furthermore, young people were encouraged to marry early. By the age of 17 or 18, a young man was fully trained and, if strong enough to plow, ready for marriage and a farm of his own. Such a youth might marry a young woman 15 or 16 years old. Parents tried to provide land for the young couple, although sometimes the marriage had to be delayed until the youth had cleared it. While waiting, the young woman might sew clothes for her "hope chest."

Early marriages and economic incentives led to large families. Children cost little to feed in a society based upon subsistence agriculture, and their labor was highly valued in a culture where hired labor virtually did not exist. Even two-year-olds could weed gardens. In fact, they were the only people who actually enjoyed weeding.

Families had eight, ten, or a dozen offspring, each of whom expected someday to live on his or her own farm. For example, James K. Polk — a product of the frontier, Andrew Jackson's friend, and later president — was typical in having more than a hundred first cousins. The inability of Polk and his wife to have children caused Polk considerable embarrassment. Children were considered to be a sign of God's blessing.

PRIMITIVE WAYS PREDOMINATE. Frontier life could be unpleasant. Imagine a dozen people living in a typical one-room log cabin no larger than 18 feet by 24 feet. The window openings lacked glass windows and could only be either open or shuttered. The floor was dirt, the roof leaked, and wind howled through the cracks between the logs where the mud filler had fallen out. Insects crawled and flew everywhere. There was no plumbing, only two paths, one to a springs perhaps a quarter-mile away, and the other to an outhouse, which froze in the winter.

Scarce furniture might consist of a crude, homemade table, a few three-legged stools, and a chest, in which the wife kept her few treasures. There was probably one bed, which took up most of the space in the cabin. The parents slept in it with the younger children. Older children climbed a ladder to sleep upstairs in the loft, where the cured hams hung.

Cooking was done over an open hearth that smoked up the entire cabin. The same food appeared at breakfast, midday dinner, and evening supper. The women prepared corn, the main crop, into hominy or handground it into a crude flour. When combined with water, this flour was made into johnnycakes and fried in pork lard along with pieces of salted pork. The hogs ran wild in the woods and were lured back to the farm with corn, which they loved. To wash down this greasy, salty food, the settlers drank whiskey, also distilled from corn. Except for venison or rabbit from the woods, seasonal peaches or apples, or eggs and milk, this was the diet. People rejected many foods, considering tomatoes, for example, poisonous.

Pioneers needed practical skills. Shooting straight with a hunting rifle was more useful than being able to read the Bible. Chopping wood quickly yielded more prestige than spelling words correctly. Raising a log cabin with a group of neighbors as a cooperative venture while under the influence of whiskey showed character. Being able to cure an illness with herbs and roots plucked from outside the cabin door had more value than did proper medical knowledge based on medicines that could only be bought in Philadelphia.

CREATING DEMOCRATIC PRINCIPLES. Self-reliance led pioneer Americans to a special devotion to liberty, which they defined as a family's right to make its own way in the world. They expected little help from others, especially from the government. Assistance, when offered, was rejected as an interference with basic rights. Sometimes this attitude took extreme forms, as in the case of one woman eating dinner in a frontier tavern. When offered a dish on the other side of the table, she declared, "I helps myself," adding as she reached across, "I don't want no waitin' on." Much of America's devotion to rugged individualism can be traced to frontier culture.

Pioneers also loved equality. An essential social equality pervaded frontier life. Capital was unimportant, and even land had little value without access to labor. Nor were sophisticated skills that might be valuable in more settled areas very useful. The frontier way of life depended upon simple skills easily learned by almost everyone. This reality of equality was matched by an intense devotion to the ideal of equality. Residents resented anyone who put on airs, and they used practical jokes to cut people down to size.

According to the settlers, taking land and turning it into farms not only improved the earth but constituted a moral duty. God had made the land for those who could use it best, and frontier Americans believed that God wanted them to carve farms out of the forest for themselves and their plentiful descendants. Because the population doubled about every 20 years, it was necessary to bring ever more acreage into cultivation. God had willed it, and these pioneers were determined to carry out God's will.

THE FRONTIER PRODUCES ANDREW JACKSON. Andrew Jackson was born in 1767 in a Scots-Irish settlement along the western North Carolina–South Carolina border. Jackson's father died before his birth; his mother and two older brothers died supporting the revolution. In the war, a British officer ordered the teenaged Jackson to clean the officer's boots. When the youth refused, the officer nearly killed Jackson with a sword blow to the head. Jackson wore the scar as a lifelong badge of honor.

After the war young Jackson moved to frontier Tennessee, practiced law, speculated in land, and eventually acquired a plantation and many slaves. He married Rachel Robards, whom he believed to be divorced from Lewis Robards. When this proved to be untrue, the Robardses divorced, and the Jacksons remarried. Jackson, a sensitive man with a hair-trigger temper, resented Charles Dickinson's gossip about Rachel's marital problems, and in 1806 Jackson challenged Dickinson to a duel. Both men were crack shots. When ordered to fire, Dickinson quickly did so, hitting Jackson, who, while suffering intense pain, then calmly and deliberately took aim at Dickinson and killed him.

Frontier experiences shaped Jackson's politics. Involved in a local bank whose paper money proved worthless, Jackson nearly went bankrupt and began to hate banks and, especially, paper money. He also had little use for Indians. Although kind to individual native Americans and even the father of an adopted Indian son, Jackson believed Indians to be a doomed people who used resources unproductively and primitively. When Jackson encountered Indians who had adopted white ways, he shifted the argument. Then, he said, racial animosity and cultural differences made it dangerous for whites and civilized Indians to live in the same vicinity.

Jackson Brings Frontier Democracy to the Nation

As the first western president, Andrew Jackson brought frontier values to the federal government. The Jacksonians promoted egalitarianism, at least among white males. Strong proponents of equal opportunity, they urged such democratic policies as frequent elections, term limits, and the rotation of bureaucrats in and out of office.

JACKSON BECOMES THE FIRST WESTERN PRESIDENT. Riding a wave of popularity, especially in the South and West that followed military victories over both the Creek Indians and the British during the War of 1812, Andrew Jackson defeated John Quincy Adams in the 1828 presidential election. This victory marked a turning point. For the first time, a man whose adult life had been spent west of the Appalachian Mountains entered the White House. Although a planter and a slaveholder, Jackson was much more closely identified, both in his own mind and in the public's, with the western frontier.

He fervently preached his region's rugged individualism and equality. Speaking in a twang — he invited guests to "set in this hare cheer" — and writing an uneducated hand riddled with misspelled words, Jackson unnerved many wealthy, powerful people, who shuddered at his ascension to power.

Jackson, like earlier presidents, had a cabinet composed of political leaders from many states. The new president, however, felt uncomfortable with his cabinet's political philosophy and formal, eastern ways. The cabinet ceased to meet, and Jackson instead turned to a group called the "Kitchen Cabinet." These behind-the-scenes political operators included the frontier newspaper editors Amos Kendall, Francis Preston Blair, and Isaac Hill.

JACKSONIAN DEMOCRATIC IDEALS. Jackson and his friends began to articulate a new political philosophy. Building on Jefferson's ideas, the Jacksonians called themselves Democrats and then refined the term's meaning. To Jefferson, democracy meant a written constitution, the rule of law, equality of persons before the law, and broad participation in the political process. Jackson found these conditions necessary but insufficient to guarantee a democratic society. In refining Jefferson's vision, the Jacksonians looked to the essential equality of frontier life.

The Jacksonians insisted upon adult white male equality. The law must give all white men the same rights. Thus, the law must apply equally to all, and to guarantee this equality, all white men must have the right to vote. Property, literacy, or religion must not be considered, because they tended to produce a privileged, elite electorate. On the other hand, the Jacksonians opposed extending the vote or any other rights to women, to minorities, or to children, because Jacksonians believed these people to be inferiors who lacked the essential equality found among all white men.

Jacksonian Democrats wanted equal opportunities rather than equal outcomes. Blaming the actual inequality that existed among white men on laws that favored the few, Democrats wanted to use the political system to make life into a fair race, with each white youth having an equal position on the starting line. Although the Jacksonians excluded women and minorities, their concept of equal rights could theoretically be expanded to include everyone. Thus, they favored constructing canals, which any farmer might use, and operating public schools for the masses, but they often opposed state universities, which only the well-to-do attended.

JACKSONIAN POLICIES. At the state level, Jacksonians ended medical licensing, because that system gave wealthy, educated people an advantage in becoming physicians. Any person should be able to hang out a shingle, claim to be a doctor, and practice medicine. The public, not elite government officials, would decide a doctor's competency. Similarly, Democrats opposed federal or state bank **charters.** Any person should have the right to operate a bank without a charter or any other regulation.

Democrats believed that frequent elections kept public officials close to voters and preserved democracy. They advocated the election of all officials, including judges, for short terms of office. They also favored limitations on terms, so that officeholders would not look upon elected positions as lifetime jobs. Beginning in 1832, they organized national party conventions in place of congressional caucuses to select presidential candidates.

They practiced "rotation in office," a policy of replacing all appointed government officials after a few years' service. Such a policy ensured that even unelected bureaucrats did not grow arrogant in their positions, and because the Jacksonians believed that all white men had an equal right to any public position, the policy of rotation gave more people the chance to hold office.

Winning an election, Democrats held, gave them the right to replace all government employees. "To the victor belong the spoils," said William L. Marcy of New York. Under the **"spoils system,"** critics charged, talent and merit counted for less than political connections.

Jackson Fights to Preserve the Union

As South Carolina began to assert states' rights, so did Vice-President John C. Calhoun. In 1828 he viewed himself as Jackson's successor, but they quarreled over whether states had a right to nullify federal laws, over Calhoun's role in an attempt to courtmartial Jackson in 1818, and over Peggy O'Neale Eaton's social standing. By 1833, when South Carolina threatened to defy federal authority, Jackson and Calhoun had become such bitter enemies that the president threatened to hang Calhoun.

CALHOUN'S TUNE CHANGES. During the War of 1812 John C. Calhoun of South Carolina had been a strong **nationalist.** Later, as secretary of war, he had advocated increasing military preparedness, including the use of federal funds to build roads and to dredge harbors. Such expenditures could be defended constitutionally as providing for the national defense. In 1824 Calhoun was elected vice-president under John Quincy Adams. Four years later, he gambled that Adams would lose to Jackson, that Jackson would retire after one term, and that he might replace Jackson in 1832. So Calhoun allied himself with Jackson and successfully ran for vice-president under Jackson in 1828.

The political climate in Calhoun's native South Carolina, however, had changed during the 1820s. Cotton prices fell, and so did yields on land that was wearing out. Planters' incomes declined while the prices of manufactured goods rose, due to higher tariff duties on imports. South Carolinians demanded a lower **tariff,** and Calhoun took up the issue. Congress, however, was under the influence of northern manufacturers more than ever, and in 1828 it passed an even higher tariff, which South Carolinians called the Tariff of Abominations.

In 1829, after it became clear that President Jackson did not plan to reduce the tariff, the South Carolinians, led secretly by Vice-President Calhoun, adopted the doctrine of **nullification.** According to this theory, the United States was a compact of sovereign states, and thus any state could use its sovereign powers to declare a federal law null and void inside its own territory. A law's constitutionality would be determined not by the U.S. Supreme Court but separately inside each state. Thus, a federal law might be upheld in some states and overturned in others.

JACKSON CHALLENGES CALHOUN. Jackson disliked the theory of nullification. He also knew the vice-president's role in the scheme. In April 1830, Jackson attended a Democratic party dinner, looked Calhoun square in the eye, and offered a toast: "Our Union: It must be preserved." Taking on Calhoun was risky, and to gain support from the Democratic party's states' rights faction, Jackson a month later vetoed a bill to use federal money to build a road totally inside Kentucky. He said that the federal government should not pay for local roads. The Maysville Road Veto followed Jackson's constitutional principles, but it also blocked a project favored by Jackson's other enemy, Henry Clay. The inconsistent Jackson opposed most federal spending on roads and canals but approved money for improving rivers and harbors.

Jackson and Calhoun became personal enemies. Years before, in 1818, Jackson had provoked an international incident by pursuing the Seminole Indians into then-Spanish Florida. He narrowly avoided being courtmartialed after a discussion within President James Monroe's cabinet. Jackson had long believed that inside the cabinet Secretary of War Calhoun had resisted Secretary of State John Quincy Adams's attacks, and Calhoun had hinted that Jackson's belief was correct. In 1830 Jackson learned that the roles of Calhoun and Adams had been the reverse, that Adams had defended Jackson against Calhoun's rage. Calhoun's position back then bothered Jackson much less than did the vice-president's continuing deceit.

The Peggy O'Neale Eaton affair also rocked Jackson's administration in 1830. Secretary of War John Eaton, an old friend of Jackson's, had shocked members of Washington's social elite by marrying a local barmaid. The wives of the other cabinet members, led by Floridé Calhoun, refused to call on Mrs. Eaton. Jackson, enraged at the insult to a woman, raised the issue at a cabinet meeting and received support only from Martin Van Buren, a widower. The other cabinet officers may well have been afraid to cross their wives in a social matter. In 1831 Jackson reorganized his cabinet and decided to make Van Buren his vice-president in 1832 and his presumptive successor in 1836.

In 1831 an angry and defiant Calhoun supported nullification anew and, in a pamphlet called the Fort Hill Address, proposed a new constitutional arrangement with two sectional presidents, North and South, each with a separate veto. Although Congress reduced the tariff in 1832, the nullifiers gained strength in South Carolina and adopted resolutions nullifying the tariff laws of 1828 and 1832. Calhoun resigned as vice-president and was elected to the Senate.

Jackson was furious. If the South Carolinians persisted in their crazy theories and actually resisted the collection of **customs duties** or other federal laws, then the president would personally lead an army to put down the rebellion. Ordering plans both for an invasion by land and for a naval attack on Charleston, Jackson threatened to burn the city and hang Calhoun.

The president issued a tough proclamation declaring federal **sovereignty.** In 1833 he persuaded Congress to pass the Force Bill, which authorized the use of the military against South Carolina. Meanwhile, Jackson became amenable to reducing the tariff, and Congress adopted a new tariff, arranged by Henry Clay. South Carolina then "suspended" its nullification of the tariff, and the crisis ended.

Jackson Wrecks the Banking System and the Economy

The second Bank of the United States had become a powerful institution. When the bank sought rechartering in 1832, Andrew Jackson vetoed the bill. Jackson's enemies sought to use the issue in the presidential election, but Jackson won. From 1833 to 1836 Jackson waged an unrelenting war to destroy the bank. He succeeded but left the economy in a shambles.

THE SECOND BANK CONTROLS THE ECONOMY. President James Madison, following Jefferson's constitutional view, had allowed the charter of the first Bank of the United States to expire in 1811. The War of 1812, however, had proved the need for some sort of national bank, and in 1816 the nearly bankrupt federal government had chartered the second Bank of the United States. Both the government and private investors owned its stock and had seats on its board.

Headquartered in Philadelphia, the bank had been ably run since 1823 by Nicholas Biddle. He opened branches throughout the country, made sound, nonpolitical loans, managed the money supply properly, and disciplined the nation's numerous local banks. These banks issued their own local paper money, and Biddle's bank fixed the exchange rate that determined their currency's value. By 1830, when the Second Bank had 29 branches and one-third of the nation's deposits, it played such a major role in finance that it had become what economists call a central bank, like today's Federal Reserve system.

Not everyone liked these results. Many local bankers, especially in the South and West, were galled that Biddle could dictate the value of their currency. When he discounted their paper money with unfavorable exchange rates, local economic activity contracted, and if the money was discounted too much, their banks failed. Some people resented the Second Bank because it concentrated power in one place. Supporters of states' rights considered this philosophically wrong; others thought it unconstitutional. New Yorkers disliked the fact that the bank had its headquarters in Philadelphia. Still others suspected that the bank showed favoritism by making loans to members of Congress.

RECHARTERING THE BANK, 1832. The Second Bank's charter was to expire in 1836, and as a practical matter, the bank needed rechartering several years in advance. After Jackson and others in his administration expressed hostility to the bank, Biddle decided in 1832 to ignore the administration and push a rechartering bill through Congress. Several politicians assured Biddle that the bank was so popular that Jackson would not dare veto a rechartering passed in a presidential election year.

Jackson, however, had come to hate Biddle's bank. Long suspicious of all banks and paper money, and doubtful about the Second Bank's constitutionality, Jackson called the bank a "hydra-headed monster" that must be slain. "I will kill it," he swore, as he promised aides that he would veto the recharter bill.

This 1832 **veto**, written by Jackson's aide Amos Kendall, was a masterpiece. It not only set forth Jackson's view that the bank was unconstitutional, but it also asserted that the president, even more than the Supreme Court, had a duty to block unconstitutional legislation. Prior to this time, presidents had used vetoes sparingly. Indeed, Jackson's six predecessors had vetoed a total of only nine bills in 40 years, and most of those bills had been technically

Many people were enraged by Andrew Jackson's use of presidential power. His policies provoked a number of hostile cartoons, which gained wide circulation due to the decline in the cost of printing during the 1830s. (BETTMANN ARCHIVE)

flawed. Jackson eventually killed 12 bills and established the right of the president to stop legislation on grounds of policy. The president's powers were greatly increased.

The bank became the main campaign issue in the presidential election of 1832. Henry Clay, Jackson's main opponent, believed that the public favored the Second Bank. Biddle, of course, was not neutral, but the more he maneuvered to help Clay, the more his actions confirmed the charge that the bank played political favorites. By campaigning for the bank, Clay believed that he could defeat Jackson. Jackson, however, saw matters differently. Some Americans, especially the poor, hated all banks. Others, including those rich enough to own a local bank, hated the Second Bank. The veto made it possible for Jackson to get the support of people holding both views. Jackson won in a landslide.

KILLING THE BANK, 1833-1836. In 1833 Jackson decided to destroy the Second Bank by removing the federal government's deposits. Opposition inside the cabinet delayed this policy for a time, and the president had to fire two treasury secretaries before the policy could be carried out. A third secretary, Roger Taney, agreed to withdraw the deposits and place them in selected local banks. (He was later rewarded by being appointed chief justice of the U.S. Supreme Court.)

The removal of the deposits wrecked the banking system and the economy. In order to keep the Second Bank afloat, Biddle had to stop new loans and refused to renew old ones. As the economy contracted, businesses failed, and so did many local banks. By 1834 the country fell into **recession.** The 23 local banks chosen to receive the federal deposits had been picked for political reasons, not for sound banking practices. Opponents derisively called them the "pet banks." Even when sound, they were too small to manage the financial system. The Second Bank's central banking mechanism had been dismantled, and nothing was put in its place.

Over time, results worsened. In the short run, banks popped up like toadstools all over the country. Some were sound, but many were not. Without the Second Bank to regulate currency exchange rates, a bank could issue as much paper money as it pleased. The money supply grew rapidly, the economy boomed, and **inflation** soared. Eventually, of course, if too many people took paper money to the bank and demanded to be paid in gold or silver (together called **specie**), the bank failed. To avoid being asked for specie, many banks were located in remote areas. They were said to be among the wildcats, and they became known as "wildcat banks."

By 1836 even Jackson recognized that something was wrong. Convinced that paper money was the root of the evil, the president issued the Specie Circular. This proclamation required that all debts to the federal government be paid in gold or silver. Suddenly, postage, customs duties, and western land demanded specie. There was, of course, a tremendous shortage of specie, since so much paper money had been issued. As people clamored to get specie, the wildcat banks collapsed, and so did many of the pet banks. By 1837 the country was deep in **depression.**

Jackson Removes Eastern Indians to Western Reservations

Thomas Jefferson's policy of seeking trade and friendship with Indian tribes had not always succeeded, and in the 1830s Andrew Jackson, with an eye on both peace and land, decided to relocate all Indians from the East to the West. Removal was expensive and devastating, leaving 89,000 native Americans in dependency in Indian Territory (today's Oklahoma). A few tribes, including the Cherokee, tried to resist, but leaders such as John Ross understood the president's determination and in the end succumbed to his demands. To this day, there are few Indians in the East.

FEDERAL INDIAN POLICY BEFORE JACKSON. Thomas Jefferson had been the first president to establish an effective Indian policy. Federal agents offered tribal chiefs special shiny medals, as well as other trinkets, in ceremonies of friendship that stressed how the Great White Father in far-off Washington loved the Indians. Jefferson wanted friendly relations and, particularly, to prevent a British-Indian alliance on the frontier.

Jefferson also established government trading posts. Such posts not only provided the Indians with reliable places to market their valuable furs but also enabled American manufacturers to sell cloth and knives to the natives. These government trading posts failed. Staffed by self-serving political hacks, the posts' American trade goods were inferior to those the British stocked, and independent traders offered the Indians better deals. By the time Jackson became president, Indian policy needed revision.

JACKSON PLANS TO REMOVE INDIANS. Jackson, wishing to avoid further Indian-white wars, concluded that only separation of the races could avoid conflict. Believing that white contact threatened Indians with extinction, Jackson favored moving native Americans away from white areas. Over time, he thought, some Indians might adopt white ways and survive, if they had land reserved for them. He planned to remove all Indians from east of the Mississippi River to federal **reservations** beyond the western frontier.

Other important political considerations contributed to the Indian Removal Act (1830). Jackson knew that opening vast new acreages in the East to white settlement would enhance his popularity. Land hunger was a major political force. At the same time, Jackson's Indian policy was designed to bring Georgia into an alliance with Jackson against Calhoun, South Carolina, and nullification. Georgia planters wanted a low tariff but were not prepared to support nullification, because they did not wish to lose federal support and thus face the Cherokee alone. By allying themselves with Jackson against nullification, Georgians could gain Jackson's support for Cherokee removal from Georgia.

Jackson adopted the idea of large-scale Indian reservations. Such areas could be self-sufficient. Both to avoid destructive white contact and to preserve racial harmony, the reservations should also be remote from areas densely settled by whites. The administration proposed to resettle numerous tribes on separate reservations in a buffer area along the United States-Mexico boundary called Indian Territory. Today it is Oklahoma.

Politicians disagreed about Indian Territory's future. Some believed that the Indians would vanish, and that whites would eventually settle there. Others thought that native Americans would adopt white ways and create a separate Indian nation. Still others, like Jackson's friend Senator Thomas Hart Benton of Missouri, hoped that an Indian state might be admitted to the Union. If there was an Indian state, a few people argued, then someday there might be black states, settled by emancipated slaves.

CARRYING OUT REMOVAL. Jackson's agents used promises, bribes, and threats to persuade the leaders of Indian tribes living east of the Mississippi River to agree to relocate to reservations in Indian Territory. Sales of Indian lands in the East would pay for the move and provide a trust fund to help support the Indians in the early years in their new homes.

Although many tribal chiefs resisted these appeals, most eventually realized that Jackson intended to have them removed with or without their consent. Some Creek, Choctaw, Chickasaw, and Cherokee leaders agreed to removal. The first tribe to move were the Choctaw. A small tribe in Mississippi, they found resistance difficult, although a portion of the Choctaw retreated into a part of Mississippi where the soil was so poor that cotton planters did not want it. Most, however, moved west.

Jackson had boasted that all the Indians could be removed for $4 million, but it cost $5 million just to move the Choctaw. Although the Choctaw removal was hardly a model, conditions during the trip west were better than for some of the later tribes, who virtually starved enroute. The Choctaw reached their new reservation disoriented by the strange setting and its unfamiliar trees, plants, and animals. Like most transplanted Indians, they fell into a permanent condition of dependency upon federal handouts and agents.

THE CHEROKEE RESIST REMOVAL. Jackson's greatest difficulty came from the Cherokee, who lived in northern Georgia and western North Carolina. In 1791 the United States government had signed a treaty with the Cherokee recognizing the tribe both as landowners and as a nation. The Cherokee claim to sovereignty came from sophisticated leaders. A number of white traders had married into the tribe, and their offspring had attained high positions while understanding white ways.

Despite this treaty, the state of Georgia began to sell Cherokee land in north Georgia to whites. Most of the land was bought by speculators rather than settlers, who risked being harassed by the Indians. Meanwhile, the Cherokee had rapidly adopted white ways. Many built log cabins and farmed in white fashion, and the tribal leader Sequoyah, with the help of New England missionaries, devised an alphabet and a written language. In 1820 the Cherokee adopted a **republican** constitution. The tribal legislature passed laws for the Cherokee Nation, erected a capitol building, and established schools. The leading families, like white planters, kept black slaves.

In 1828 Georgia voided the Cherokee laws, and after gold was discovered in north Georgia the following year, the rush of white prospectors into the area doomed Cherokee control. The Cherokee took their case to the U.S. Supreme Court, which ruled in *Cherokee Nation v. Georgia* (1831) that an Indian nation was not truly sovereign but a dependency of the federal government.

In 1830 Georgia ordered all whites living on the Cherokee lands to obtain a state license and swear allegiance to Georgia. Two northern missionaries refused, were arrested, and were eventually sentenced to four years in prison. In *Worcester v. Georgia* (1832) the Supreme Court overturned the convictions and ruled that Georgia's law was unconstitutional, because the federal government had sole jurisdiction over Indians.

This ruling did not help the Cherokee, however, since Georgia simply ignored the ruling, and white Georgians poured ever faster onto Cherokee lands. In the end, the Cherokee were forced to move to the West, except for a small number who remained in a remote mountainous region of North Carolina.

In 1838 the federal government sent 7,000 army troops to escort the Cherokee to Indian Territory. The removal, plagued by fraud, poor planning, inept federal leadership, and rotten foodstuffs, was a disaster. Of the 17,000 Cherokee who moved, about one-quarter are said to have died on the way. The Cherokee recalled their removal as the Trail of Tears.

REMOVAL'S CONSEQUENCES. In the North, Jackson's removal policy led in 1832 to the Sac and Fox Indians fighting the government in the Black Hawk War, which the Indians quickly lost. In the South, many Seminole resisted removal and fled into the Florida swamps. The army gave chase in the Seminole War, which lasted from 1835 to 1843. During that conflict the army captured the great Seminole guerrilla warrior Osceola under a white flag of truce. He died in prison in 1838, and the war continued. Finally, in 1843 the federal government gave up and allowed the remaining Seminole to stay in Florida.

Jackson's policy did change the distribution of Indian peoples. During the 1830s, 80 percent of the Indians living east of the Mississippi River were removed, and a decade later 89,000 Indians belonging to relocated tribes lived in Indian Territory, along with about 170,000 members of western tribes scattered throughout the West.

These changes produced profound consequences. In Indian Territory the original inhabitants did not welcome the newcomers. Incredibly, Jackson's policy had presumed Indian Territory to be unpopulated. Then, too, the relocation of numerous tribes into the concentrated space of Indian Territory led Indians to begin thinking about themselves as Indians rather than as members of specific tribes. In the long run, this change would be important, because it would lead Indians to join together in more effective efforts to demand rights.

Finally, to this day, few American Indians live east of the Mississippi River. As a result, Indian issues are usually western rather than national. Jackson's policy was designed to eliminate Indian-white conflict, as well as to obtain Indian land, but its principal effect may have been to make native Americans less important in national politics.

Jackson Casts a Shadow, 1836-1845

To perpetuate democratic values, Andrew Jackson personally picked Martin Van Buren as his successor. By 1836 a rival party, the Whigs, had been formed around opposition to Jackson and support for a national bank. Although Van Buren won the White House in 1836, depression destroyed his presidency. In the 1840 election the Whigs defeated Van Buren with dazzling public relations. The Whigs had little to celebrate, though, because in 1841 their victorious candidate, President William Henry Harrison, died after 30 days in office and was succeeded by John Tyler, a states' rights Democrat who served until 1845.

THE ELECTION OF 1836 AND THE WHIG PARTY. In 1836 Jackson retired, and his handpicked successor, Martin Van Buren, easily won the Democratic party nomination. Son of a tavernkeeper in upstate New York, Van Buren was one of the wiliest politicians to seek the White House. No one completely trusted the "Little Magician," as he was called, and southern planters strongly suspected that he secretly opposed **slavery.**

By the time of this election Jackson's political enemies, under Henry Clay's leadership, had combined into the Whig party. Always defensive, **Whigs** found it difficult to articulate a positive philosophy, except for support for a national bank, because they disagreed among themselves about almost everything else. An unstable political coalition, they primarily defined themselves as opponents of Jackson and the Democrats.

Although the Whigs, like the Democrats, had a party organization, newspapers, pamphlets, songs, and rallies, they never felt entirely comfortable appealing to the masses in democratic fashion. Despite this limitation, the Whigs became competitive with the Democrats. Almost every state had a two-party system. The Whigs attracted large numbers of well-educated lawyers, doctors, and businessmen to a party favorable to business and devoted to notions of just rewards for those who worked hard. This party of opportunity attracted gifted leaders like Clay, Daniel Webster, and the young Abraham Lincoln.

A northern merchant elite, however, formed the inner core of the Whig party. Never numerous and always maintaining somewhat strained relations with the wealthy planters who led the southern Whigs, these merchants could not control the party but did enjoy an influence beyond their numbers. The party also attracted **evangelical** reformers, who found Whigs more congenial than Democrats in pressing for laws to ban the mail on Sunday or to stop the sale of liquor. Pointing to the Democrats' appointment of uneducated, vulgar men to office under the spoils system, the Whigs claimed to be the party of respectability.

In 1836 the Whigs experimented with the strategy of running different candidates in different parts of the country. This strategy failed, and Van Buren won, but the Whig leaders noticed that William Henry Harrison had run a surprisingly strong race in the Midwest.

MARTIN VAN BUREN FACES DEPRESSION, 1837-1841. Martin Van Buren's presidency was dominated by the depression that began in 1837. A financial panic, set off by Jackson's Specie Circular, led to a full-fledged economic disaster. Unemployment soared, reaching 25 percent in some cities during the winter in early 1838. People faced starvation. Although the worst was over within a year, the economy limped until 1845. It was, with the exception of the 1930s, the worst depression in American history.

Lacking an understanding of economic processes, including business cycles, people looked for villains. Because Jackson had killed the Second Bank, few blamed the bank. Some people, correctly, attacked land **speculators**. Others denounced the increasing concentration of capital. These radicals praised labor unions, approved of the right to strike, and sought more government regulation of the economy. Still other people wanted the economy reorganized, with private businesses replaced by producer and consumer nonprofit cooperatives.

The restlessness even extended to the Supreme Court, where Chief Justice Roger Taney, who had been appointed by Jackson upon John Marshall's death in 1835, began to reshape the court's views. In the *Charles River Bridge Case* (1837), the court overturned a legislative grant of a toll bridge monopoly. In contrast with Marshall's ruling in the *Dartmouth College Case* (1819), Taney held that the sanctity of contract had to yield to competition and equal opportunity.

Practically the only accomplishment of Van Buren's presidency was the establishment of the Independent Treasury in 1840. Van Buren had found a way to manage finances without a national bank by having the government maintain its funds inside the Treasury Department.

ELECTION OF 1840. The depression ruined Van Buren's presidency. By 1840, when Van Buren sought reelection, the opposition was well organized. Following in the footsteps of the Jacksonians, the Whigs nominated a War of 1812 war hero, William Henry Harrison. A native of Virginia, Harrison had been both territorial governor of Indiana and senator from Ohio. Like Jackson, he linked the South and the West.

In a brilliant campaign, the Whigs exploited Van Buren's unpopularity. Their newspapers repeated rumors that the president, amid the depression, had refitted the White House with expensive furniture and carpets. He was said to sup on silver plate with a golden spoon. Van Buren thought these slanders beneath the dignity of a reply. Democratic party denials only led the Whigs to chant, "Van, Van is a used up man."

When a Democratic party editor declared that Harrison was a country hick who had been born in a log cabin and liked to drink hard cider — that is, mildly alcoholic apple juice — Whig papers declared Harrison an ordinary guy. (In reality Harrison came from a prominent family and lived in a 16-room house.) By claiming to be a cider drinker, Harrison appealed both to drinkers and to those who had turned against hard liquor. The Whigs then built miniature log cabins near courthouses all across the country. They distributed campaign tracts with samples of hard cider. Bonfires, barbecues, fireworks, and parades — which included women waving campaign fans and children wearing badges and buttons — marked the Whig extravaganza.

Shouting "Tippecanoe and Tyler, too!" on their way to the polls, the voters elected Harrison, the hero of the battle of Tippecanoe, and his running mate, the eccentric John Tyler of Virginia, in a landslide. Poor Van Buren never had a chance. He had been undone not only by the depression but by the first media and public relations oriented presidential campaign. Turnout reached an astonishing 90 percent of the eligible voters, the highest ever recorded.

HARRISON AND TYLER OPPOSE JACKSONISM, 1841-1845. In 1841 Harrison was sworn in and dutifully accepted a cabinet arranged by the Whig party leader, Henry Clay. But the president spoke too long at his inauguration, caught a cold, and died 30 days later.

John Tyler became president. The Whigs did not trust Tyler, a renegade states' rights Democrat, and some of them suggested that a vice-president who succeeded to the presidency only became an acting president, who had to follow the advice of the cabinet. Tyler ignored this strange theory, fought with his cabinet, and on constitutional grounds vetoed two Whig bills to re-establish a national bank. The cabinet then resigned, and Tyler, read out of the Whig party, governed with the support of southern Democrats, including John C. Calhoun as secretary of state.

Conclusion

Andrew Jackson never forgot his frontier roots. Drawing upon western experiences and values, he brought to national politics a keen belief in white democracy, an intense opposition to nullification, a woefully ignorant belief that banks were evil, and a determination to remove Indians from the path of white advance. His administration defined the major political issues of the era, especially banking, and in doing so created both Democratic and Whig parties, as well as causing a depression. Jackson cast a shadow that lasted through the administrations of Martin Van Buren, William Henry Harrison, and John Tyler.

Recommended Readings

DOCUMENTS: Rebecca Burlend, *A True Picture of Emigration* (1848); Alexis de Tocqueville, *Democracy in America* (2 vols., 1835-1840); Christiana H. Tillson, *A Woman's Story of Pioneer Illinois* [1873] (1919).

READINGS: (FRONTIER) John M. Faragher, *Sugar Creek* (1986); Malcolm J. Rohrbough, *The Land Office Business* (1968), and *The Trans-Appalachian Frontier* (1978); (JACKSON) Robert V. Remini, *Andrew Jackson* (3 vols., 1977-1984); (POLITICS) Lee Benson, *The Concept of Jacksonian Democracy* (1961); Ronald P. Formisano, *The Transformation of Political Culture* (1983); Paul Goodman, *Towards a Christian Republic* (1988); Daniel W. Howe, *The Political Culture of the American Whigs* (1979); Marvin Meyers, *The Jacksonian Persuasion* (1957); Harry Watson, *Jacksonian Politics and Community Conflict* (1981); (NULLIFICATION) John Niven, *John C. Calhoun and the Price of Union* (1988); (INDIANS) Michael P. Rogin, *Fathers and Children* (1975); Ronald N. Satz, *American Indian Policy in the Jacksonian Era* (1975); Bernard W. Sheehan, *Seeds of Extinction* (1973); (VAN BUREN) John Niven, *Martin Van Buren* (1983).

11

THE PROBLEM OF SLAVERY

CHAPTER OVERVIEW: Slavery first came under attack during the American Revolution, which expressed principles of liberty and equality, and northerners adopted gradual emancipation. In the South, slave life revolved around large plantations and, especially, cotton. Supporting abolition but believing that free blacks could not live with whites, colonizationists advocated freeing the slaves and resettling them in Africa. After this idea failed, white southerners defended slavery vigorously. Meanwhile, northern evangelicals opposed slavery as a sin, while militant abolitionists demanded not only abolition but full civil rights for blacks. Northern public opinion gradually turned against the continuation of slavery in the South.

The Revolutionary Generation Attacks Slavery

The revolutionary generation found slavery inconsistent with ideals of liberty and equality. After the revolution, the federal government acted to keep slavery out of the Old Northwest and to end the African slave trade. In addition, the northern states abolished slavery, and some southern states encouraged voluntary emancipation. This program to end slavery failed when southern opposition to slavery declined as the cotton boom began to drive up the price of slaves.

THE REVOLUTIONARIES OPPOSE SLAVERY. In 1776 Americans of African ancestry formed nearly one-fifth of the population in the new United States, and more than 90 percent of African-Americans were **slaves.** Slavery existed in every state, ranging from New England, where slaves were under 3 percent of the population, through Virginia with 40 percent, to coastal South Carolina with a black majority in bondage.

The Revolutionary War eroded slavery in two ways. First, many states, as well as the British, allowed slaves to enlist in the Continental army, in return for freedom at the war's end. In Virginia about 10 percent of the blacks gained freedom in this way, and after the war that state had a sizeable free black population. South Carolina, despite pleas from the Continental Congress, refused to allow slaves to enlist.

More important, revolutionary ideology that emphasized freedom and equality threatened slavery. Many white Americans found it inconsistent to liberate themselves from British bondage while continuing to hold slaves. Thomas Jefferson understood the conflict, and an early draft of the Declaration of Independence condemned slavery, but slaveholders' objections led to the removal of this provision. Thus, the Founding Fathers opposed the idea of slavery, even as they grappled with how to abolish it.

At the time the principal method to **emancipate** slaves was for owners to free their servants through wills. George Washington, for example, used this technique and tried to encourage others to do the same. However, many slaveholders, like Thomas Jefferson, became so trapped in debt that they were unable to release their slaves.

THE FEDERAL GOVERNMENT TAKES MODEST STEPS, 1787-1808. Thomas Jefferson's Northwest Ordinance (1787), which provided the framework for organizing territorial governments in the region west of Pennsylvania and north of the Ohio River, specifically banned slavery from that area. Jefferson believed that keeping the institution from spreading to new territories was more practical than abolishing it where it already existed. He once observed that **abolition** was easy in Pennsylvania, where there were few slaves, hard in Maryland, and would prove still harder in Virginia, where slaveholders dominated the political system. If slavery could be kept out of the West, Jefferson believed, the national influence of slaveholders would wane, and eventually the institution might be ended everywhere.

In 1787 slavery was a major issue at the constitutional convention. The drafters showed their defensiveness by refusing to use the word "slave" in the document. At the same time, they compromised in giving southern planters greater political representation by counting three-fifths of the slaves in the census used to apportion Congress. Another compromise provision gave Congress the right to abolish the African slave trade in 1808. In fact, few new slaves entered the United States after 1787, every state except South Carolina banned the overseas trade, and Congress did abolish this trade in 1808.

THE NORTH ABOLISHES SLAVERY. Even before the end of the revolution the campaign to abolish slavery had gained ground in the North. In Massachusetts, a state with few slaves and with growing public opposition to slavery, the state supreme court ruled that slavery violated the state's constitution, which had been adopted during the revolution.

In other northern states the power of slaveholders led to gradual emancipation. In Pennsylvania, for example, no existing slaves were freed, but children born of slave mothers after 1780 were to become free at the age of 28. New York had many slaves, making up as much as 20 percent of the population on parts of Long Island, and for years its wealthy, influential slaveholders blocked gradual emancipation. A plan similar to Pennsylvania's finally went into effect in 1799. The last northern state to adopt gradual emancipation, New Jersey, still had a few slaves as late as 1846, when human property was abolished outright.

The abolition of slavery in the North did not lead to equality for blacks. Outside New England, blacks generally could not vote, and blacks lost voting rights in Rhode Island in 1822 and in Pennsylvania in 1837 with the tide of Jacksonian democracy that stressed white equality. Most northern states prohibited free blacks from moving into the state, maintained segregated jails, poorhouses, and hospitals, and excluded African-American children from public schools.

When a sympathetic white, Prudence Crandall, attempted to open a private school for black girls in Canterbury, Connecticut, in 1833, local residents destroyed the school and drove Miss Crandall away. Not long after, a Philadelphia mob burned a meeting hall used by abolitionists. Although free, most northern blacks could find work only as unskilled laborers or household domestics, where they increasingly competed with Irish immigrants.

THE SOUTH TRIES VOLUNTARY EMANCIPATION. In the 1790s in Delaware, in Maryland, and to a lesser extent in parts of Virginia — all tobacco-growing areas in economic decline with worn-out land and surplus labor — a campaign for voluntary emancipation enjoyed considerable success. About 90 percent of Delaware's blacks and about half of Maryland's were freed. This movement by slaveholders to renounce slavery was rooted, in part, in economics, but revolutionary values that had led to abolition in the North also played a role. So did the legal system, which encouraged voluntary emancipation and controlled freed slaves under the age of 21 through **apprenticeship.** In addition, a Methodist **revival** had swept the area, especially Delaware, and at the time Methodist leaders disapproved of slavery. Born-again Christians routinely freed their slaves, who often converted at the same time.

After 1800 voluntary emancipation in the South more or less ceased. Revolutionary ideology waned, and the legal system changed. Apprenticeship eroded as a form of control for young blacks, and Maryland learned that slaveholders had freed older slaves incapable of supporting themselves while retaining ownership of vigorous workers. Welfare costs grew, free blacks who drifted to Baltimore competed with poor whites for jobs, and this rivalry produced racial violence. Southern states responded with laws making it increasingly difficult to free slaves. As the religious revival continued, its leaders came from higher social classes, where slavery was accepted, and so religious opposition declined.

At the same time, the economic situation changed, as the Deep South began to plant cotton, which depended upon slave labor. By 1830 three-fourths of all slaves raised cotton. From 1790 to 1860 cotton production soared nearly a hundred-fold, but the slave population increased less than six-fold. Slaveowners in the upper South either moved with their chattels into the cotton belt or sold them to the new cotton states. From 1820 to 1860 as many as two million slaves may have been sold, many in the interstate trade, separating perhaps 300,000 pairs of husbands and wives.

The high demand for slaves to grow cotton led the price of slaves to rise dramatically. A prime field hand, worth $300 in 1790, brought $1,500 by 1860. This period saw little **inflation,** so the difference in price represents an enormous increase in worth. By 1860 the value of the South's slave property exceeded that of all the real property — including factories, stores, houses, barns, farm implements, and animals — put together. This high and growing value of slave property made voluntary emancipation less and less attractive to slaveholders.

Black Life in the South

Most slaves lived on large plantations and worked as agricultural laborers producing tobacco, sugar, rice, and, especially, cotton. In such settings African culture, including language patterns, ways of family life, and music survived. The black church played a special role in bonding African-Americans together. Slaves who worked on small farms or slaves and free blacks who practiced skilled crafts were more assimilated to white ways but faced discrimination that limited their success. By 1850 southern industrialists had begun to use slave labor in factories.

SLAVERY ON LARGE PLANTATIONS. Here is the paradox: a mere one-quarter of the South's white families owned slaves, and most slaveowners held but a few, so that only one-eighth of the slaveholders were planters (defined as holding 20 or more slaves). This tiny elite, 3 percent of the white population, owned a majority of the slaves. Thus, living on a large **plantation** with from 20 to 500 slaves was typical for blacks but rare for whites.

In some areas, particularly along the South Carolina seacoast, large numbers of blacks lived on plantations almost untouched by whites. On such plantations the planter's family and overseer's family were the only whites, and during the malaria season the whites, highly susceptible to the disease, fled to Charleston, leaving the slaves to manage for themselves.

Plantations produced cash crops, including tobacco in Virginia, rice in coastal South Carolina, sugar cane in Louisiana, hemp for rope in Kentucky, and cotton throughout the Deep South. Although some planters assigned laborers daily tasks, others, especially cotton producers, worked slaves in gangs of from six to ten laborers under the supervision of a white overseer or a black driver. They planted, tended, and harvested the crops. Men, women, and children worked together.

To ensure order, overseers carried whips into the fields and whipped slow or lazy workers on the spot. Hands worked daily except Sunday from sunup to sundown, pausing only for meals. Slave women also prepared food and kept clothes in repair; older slave women watched slave infants. Planter-provided cabins had dirt floors and lacked glass windows.

Some planters allowed slaves to plant vegetable gardens for their own use, and many slaves fished and hunted to supplement the limited diet provided by the planter, usually just corn flour and **salt pork.** Although a slave could

These slaves pose for a photograph in front of a wooden structure typical of slave cabins. (The Bettmann Archive)

not legally own or use a rifle, this restriction was often ignored when it came to hunting. Slaves were prohibited from having alcohol, but many planters provided barrels of liquor for a week-long celebration and period of general drunkenness between Christmas and New Year's Day.

THE AFRICAN HERITAGE SURVIVES. Slave culture had strong African roots. In predominantly black areas, such as coastal South Carolina, such influences were striking. The Gullah dialect, still spoken in one area, shows grammatical patterns typical of African languages and includes many words of African origin. Preferences in food, in clothing, and in housing also showed African influences, such as round or eight-sided cabins.

Cultural survivals also occurred in patterns of marriage and child naming. Slaves lived in monogamous family units, although divorce occurred frequently, and planters rarely interfered with these customs. The marriage ceremony consisted of the couple jumping over a broom, followed by joyous dancing. The law did not recognize slave marriages. Many children received African names, which whites generally refused to recognize, or were named in the African fashion: a pretty sound or the first word that came into a mother's head after birth might be given to the child as a name.

As in Africa, black women carried heavy baskets by balancing them on their heads. The slaves wove these baskets by hand in patterns that originated in Africa. Blacks used herbs and roots as medicine, and when African plants could not be found, they borrowed from the Indians. Wealthy planters provided good medical care, resembling a prepaid medical plan. This was self-interest, for a slave who sickened and died cost the owner money.

One striking legacy concerned music and dance. The African-style drum and the banjo — an African word and apparently a modified African instrument — provided the beat and strongly rhythmic melody that became the basis for black music in America — and for modern American rock. This music appeared in its most exuberant form at festive occasions and at Saturday night dances, when slaves moved their bodies in complex rhythmic patterns.

Song always accompanied work in the fields, providing both a work rhythm, another African idea, and pleasurable sounds. Some lyrics were painfully astute. The ex-slave Frederick Douglass recalled singing:

> We raise de wheat,
> Dey gib us de corn;
> We bake de bread,
> Dey gib us de crust;
> We sif de meal,
> Dey gib us de huss;

We peel de meat,
Dey gib us de skin;
And dat's de way
Dey take us in.

When blacks became Christians, they took their music into the church.

ADOPTING BLACK CHRISTIANITY. Black Christianity outwardly resembled its white counterpart, but slave religion served different purposes. Like the religion of other oppressed peoples, such as Irish Catholicism under English rule in Ireland, black churches gave African-Americans as much stability as could be gained under harrowing circumstances. Planters, fearful of plots, prohibited almost all organized black activities, but Christian tradition made it impossible to prevent slave worship.

Although planters tried to get slaves to attend white churches and listen to sermons instructing servants to obey masters, the slaves preferred their own preachers, mostly free blacks. They created powerful new denominations, especially the African Methodist Episcopal church, founded in 1816 by Rev. Richard Allen of Philadelphia.

Black religious services often contained veiled attacks against slavery, including emphases upon blacks seeing themselves as the Chosen People and their desire to reach the Promised Land. Moses leading the Israelites out of bondage in Egypt was a powerful theme.

Delicate matters were presented in a code that the slaves understood, sometimes shouting "Amen" to indicate comprehension, while the white person required by law to be present at all slave gatherings missed the point. Black preachers frequently talked about shepherds, flocks, and sheep, because, as one explained, "We know who has the wool," referring to tightly curled hair.

Services emphasized singing, in which, unaccompanied by instruments, the leader sang out a line and then the audience repeated it. This practice both gave instruction and promoted group solidarity. Black religion also incorporated African beliefs, including voodoo, magic, and conjuring, that is, summoning the assistance of spirits.

BLACKS WORK ON SMALL FARMS AND IN SKILLED CRAFTS. Slaves who lived on small farms had a very different experience from those who lived on large plantations. Deprived of the presence of other blacks, they lost contact with African roots. At the same time, working day by day together with a poor master in a field promoted **assimilation.** However, the relative poverty of many small-scale farmers often made for a harsh life.

Some slaves and free blacks practiced skilled crafts. Planters usually kept slave carpenters, blacksmiths, and shoemakers, the three most common rural trades. Skills were passed down on the plantation from slave to slave. Normally, all young black males became field hands, and a few received training as craftsmen only after they had reached an age where their work as field hands had deteriorated.

In areas with many small-scale white farmers, free blacks often provided skilled work. Local customs varied. In Virginia, where many whites also worked as skilled craftsmen, racial competition produced friction. Blacks were grudgingly allowed to enter the rougher trades, such as blacksmithing, but only whites practiced "high-class" crafts such as watchmaking. On grounds of public safety, laws barred black printers. (A slave printer might print posters announcing a slave revolt.) No southern state allowed slaves to be taught to read, although some learned on their own. In South Carolina, however, where black **artisans** were common, local whites refused to do most skilled work. Except for a few **Yankees** or immigrants, all craftsmen were black, either slave or free.

INDUSTRIALISTS TRY SLAVE LABOR. By 1850 southern industrialists, such as the owners of Richmond's Tredegar Iron Works, had used slave labor successfully. Although less skilled than a northern factory worker and with proportionately lower output, a slave was cheaper. A slave received no wages and cost only $70 a year to house, clothe, and feed, whereas a northern laborer had to be paid as much as $300 in wages, out of which the worker covered his own expenses. Nor did a slave dare strike. Indeed, slaves had first been employed at Tredegar in large numbers as strikebreakers.

Most Southern factory owners did not wish to own slaves, since they wanted to invest capital in machinery, not workers. Besides, if a factory had to be closed during an economic slump, slaves still had to be fed. Industrialists preferred renting slaves by the year, but slaveowners resisted sending their servants into factories, where harsh working conditions and accidents threatened lives.

Colonizationists Urge Abolition with Removal

Colonizationists proposed abolition, but only under the condition that the freed ex-slaves be removed from the United States. In 1822 the American Colonization Society founded Liberia in Africa as a colony for freed slaves, but it proved inhospitable, and slaves declined to go. As a result, by 1830 the colonization movement had died. With no more ideas of what to do with freed slaves, abolitionist sentiment in the South died out, too.

FOUNDING THE AMERICAN COLONIZATION SOCIETY, 1817. After 1800 the idealism of the revolution waned, and it became clear that neither state abolition nor voluntary emancipation would end slavery. Many thoughtful people, including southern slaveholders, believed that emancipation had come to a halt because abolitionists had failed to provide for ex-slaves. Whites feared that large numbers of free blacks would become a culturally unassimilated element that would threaten society.

In 1817 abolitionists founded the American Colonization Society with U.S. President James Monroe as its president. Henry Clay was also a sponsor. The **colonizationists** argued that slaveholders should be encouraged to free their slaves, provided the ex-slaves resettled in Africa. The proposal resembled Jackson's policy of Indian removal.

In 1822 the society established a colony in a swampy area of West Africa and named it Liberia. Its capital was named Monrovia to honor the society's president. Liberia was to be a black, Christian republic. Indeed, the society persuaded **evangelical Protestants** to support the colony in order to christianize Africa. The ex-slaves who migrated were to spread the Gospel throughout the continent.

A number of ex-slaves and free blacks did migrate to Liberia, but they encountered culture shock, deadly disease, and hostile natives, who regarded them as interlopers. The society found it difficult to send blacks and white missionaries at a rate greater than the colony's death rate. Liberia's problems led some blacks to return to the United States, and the pace of migration slackened. Slaves who were offered freedom on condition that they move to Liberia often declined such offers. By 1860 only 15,000 African-Americans had migrated there.

COLONIZATION FAILS. Even if Liberia had succeeded, the colonizationists would have failed. Money was too scarce to send more than a handful of people to Liberia, and there were not enough ships to take the number by which the African-American population was growing each year. So even if blacks had wanted to migrate to Liberia, the plan could not have relocated the entire race. In fact, of course, African-Americans, most of whose families had lived in the United States for several generations, did not want to migrate to Africa.

As late as 1827 there were more antislavery societies in the South than in the North, but by 1830 the idea of colonization had collapsed and so had the

South's antislavery movement. The failure of colonization put slavery's opponents on the defensive in the South. For years, proponents of slavery, while conceding the contradiction between slavery and America's revolutionary values, had argued that preserving the institution was necessary on grounds of security. Law, order, and white supremacy, said these southerners, could only be maintained through slavery. The white South could not control large numbers of free blacks. Colonization's failure led white southerners to accept the proslavery position by default.

Southerners Adopt a Positive View of Slavery

Slave insurrections frightened white southerners and convinced them that a hard line on slavery was the only way to preserve order. After 1832 slavery was no longer even a subject of debate in the South, as southerners turned militant in defending it. The North and South then quarreled, and the major national churches split over the issue. Southerners, united in their belief in slavery, began to see themselves as a distinct society.

SLAVE REVOLTS PRODUCE PANIC. In 1800 a Virginia blacksmith, Prosser's slave Gabriel, planned an uprising. Betrayed by fellow slaves, he and his followers were executed. "Gabriel's Revolt" and the success of the black leader Pierre Toussaint L'Ouverture's revolution against French rule in Haiti in 1804 alarmed white southerners about their own safety.

In 1822 Denmark Vesey, a free black in Charleston who had purchased his freedom and become a preacher after winning a lottery years earlier, planned a sophisticated slave insurrection. Word of the uprising leaked from the slaves, and in the panic that followed, South Carolina executed 37 blacks, including Vesey, and sent others as slaves outside the United States. The Vesey plot led many southerners to conclude that free blacks, especially if educated, posed a grave danger, and laws discouraging emancipation grew stronger. Southern fears were confirmed in 1829, when David Walker, a free black born in North Carolina, published his *Appeal* in Boston. Walker urged abolition, by slave insurrection, if necessary.

Then in 1831 the slave Nat Turner, a preacher and mystic who had learned to read and write, led a rebellion in rural southeastern Virginia. Turner and his 70 or so followers murdered 57 whites in a house-to-house rampage before being captured and executed. Up to 200 blacks lost their lives amid the hysterical reaction.

These revolts led white southerners to conclude that slavery was essential for order, that free blacks would assist slaves in rebellion, and that whites could no longer safely question slavery in public lest the discussion lead blacks to challenge their status.

PROSLAVERY MILITANCY GROWS. The South's last serious public discussion about abolishing slavery took place in Virginia in 1831-1832. The legislature considered gradual emancipation, including compensation to slaveholders. Strongly pushed by delegates from the nearly all-white mountainous western part of the state (today, West Virginia) and vigorously opposed by those from the slaveholding eastern region, the proposal proved controversial. In the end, the fear of bloodshed — in the aftermath of Nat Turner's uprising and the collapse of the belief in colonization — destroyed any chance for abolition. The lower house voted 73-58 to uphold slavery.

After 1832 southern intellectuals led a proslavery crusade. Comparing the South to ancient Greece and Rome, they noted with pride that those democracies had embraced slavery and touted the institution as the basis of civilization. In 1837 John C. Calhoun declared slavery "a positive good." Jefferson Davis said the institution came from "Almighty God." The writer George Fitzhugh contrasted the lives of poor northern whites, often unemployed and all but allowed to starve, with the fate of southern slaves, always cared for by their owners. Southern evangelical ministers played a crucial role in mounting this defense of slavery. Because slavery could be found in the Bible, they said it was morally right. These cheerleaders for slavery staked out the high moral ground, and almost no one in the South dared to disagree.

THE NORTH AND SOUTH QUARREL. White southern militancy produced friction. Northerners were outraged when southerners persuaded the post office to ban antislavery books or pamphlets from the mails. Nor did Yankees approve of South Carolina's laws harassing northern free black sailors who put into port in Charleston, where they faced being sold into slavery.

There was bitter sectional controversy over the *Amistad* case. In 1839 the *Amistad,* a Spanish slavetrading schooner, illegally carried slaves from Africa across the Atlantic Ocean. In the middle of the voyage the slaves, led by a captive named Cinque (pronounced sin-cue), seized the ship. The American navy later found the ship and brought it to New London, Connecticut, where the federal government agreed to return the *Amistad* and its slave cargo to the ship's owners.

The leader of the slave captives, Cinque, then claimed that all the Africans had been kidnapped and should be freed and returned to Africa. Outraged abolitionists sent former president John Quincy Adams to urge the Supreme

Court to release the Africans. Equally outraged southerners protested that releasing the captives would violate sacred property rights. In 1841 the court finally freed Cinque and the other Africans, who returned to Africa.

As northern and southern views diverged, national institutions groaned under the strain. No organizations felt more pressure than the nation's evangelical churches, which split regionally. In 1837 slavery caused one branch of Presbyterians to break apart, and in 1844 the Methodists divided geographically. A year later many southerners formed the Southern Baptist Convention. By the time of the Civil War, only Catholics and Episcopalians maintained national organizations. They did so by ignoring slavery and scorning abolition.

Although proslavery arguments did not play well outside the South, they did unite white southerners, who came to see themselves increasingly as constituting a society distinct from that of the North. The sense of the South as a separate place was based mostly on slavery. That sense was to have tremendous repercussions. More important, white southerners no longer openly discussed slavery, except to proclaim its virtues. Opponents either kept quiet or were driven from the South.

Religious Abolitionists
Call Slavery a Sin

Religious abolitionists came to see slavery as a sin, a moral position that left little room for compromise. The Grimké sisters and Theodore Weld promoted abolition, and after 1834 so did a generation of ministers trained at Lane Seminary and Oberlin College. Weld's abolitionist revivals failed to end slavery immediately, and he retired without realizing how much he had changed northern opinion.

SEEING SLAVERY AS A SIN. During the early 1800s, and especially during the 1830s, northern white evangelical Christians came to see slavery as sinful. Ignoring the existence of slavery in the Bible, reform-minded evangelicals believed that the institution degraded everyone who came into contact with it. A slave kept in a barbaric, inhuman condition found it difficult to undergo a Christian **conversion experience** or to adopt high moral standards.

At the same time, the slaveholder also risked losing his soul, since slavery made the owner arrogant. Lacking humility and Christian feeling, he was apt to indulge in brutality and in sexual exploitation of his female slaves. Interracial sex, often involuntary, was common. "Every woman is ready to tell you who is the father of all the mulatto children in everybody's household," wrote the southern diarist Mary Chesnut, "but those in her own she seems to think drop from the clouds."

The concept of slavery as a sin had profound consequences. A moral issue, unlike a political issue, left little room for compromise. Religious abolitionists, unlike colonizationists, found no support among southern owners, since these abolitionists attacked slaveholding as immoral. They deeply offended their opponents.

At the same time, the position of the religious abolitionists was difficult to attack. The only way to argue against a person who declared slavery a sin was to deny the whole moral argument. In other words, middle ground disappeared. This religious condemnation of slavery gradually led most northerners to support abolition. Otherwise, they would have had to deny that slavery was immoral and, logically, accept the southern view that slavery was moral.

Those who found the institution immoral demanded its immediate abolition. Sin was an absolute concept, and the sinning had to stop instantly. As a practical matter, the movement's leaders recognized that slavery could not be abolished overnight without chaos. However, they loathed the gradual emancipation formulas by which the northern states had abolished slavery after the American Revolution.

Seeking to broaden their support, religious abolitionists urged "immediate emancipation gradually accomplished." Willing to see slaves freed over some unspecified period of time, they nevertheless argued that the sin of slavery required that the abolition process begin immediately. To do otherwise was to implicate the nation and the abolitionists themselves in the continuation of this immoral institution.

THE GRIMKÉ SISTERS AND THEODORE WELD PROMOTE ABOLITION. The religious abolitionists included the important Grimké sisters from Charleston, South Carolina. Daughters of a wealthy lawyer, Angelina and Sarah Grimké had been sent to Philadelphia for a Quaker education. While there they were converted to that religion and became abolitionists. All but banned from their native city, they spent the 1830s traveling around the North explaining the evils of slavery to mostly female audiences.

The Grimké sisters were especially influenced by Theodore Weld, another religious abolitionist who had been converted to evangelical Christianity by Charles Grandison Finney during the revivals in western New York's Burned-Over District. Angelina and Theodore married and later lived in a commune in New Jersey.

As early as 1826, Weld traveled through the South ostensibly as a temperance lecturer but secretly as a recruiter for abolition. He found little sympathy for abolition, although he did make one important convert, James Gillespie Birney. This Alabama planter publicly denounced slavery while outside the South. His home state then declared Birney a traitor and seized his slaves and real estate. Birney dared not return. Becoming a public lecturer in the North, he ran for president as an abolitionist in 1840 and 1844.

Throughout the 1830s the funding for Weld's travels came largely from the American Antislavery Society, headquartered in New York. Founded in 1833, the society by 1840 had 200,000 members in 2000 local organizations throughout the North. The national society, composed of wealthy white businessmen and evangelical ministers, was dominated by two brothers, the New York merchants Arthur and Lewis Tappan. New Englanders by birth, the Tappans had made their fortunes selling cloth made from slave-grown cotton to southern planters. The Tappans felt guilty about these connections to human bondage. Eventually, they withdrew from southern trade, promoted the sale of cloth that traced none of its content to slave labor, and contributed more than one-quarter of the annual budget of the American Antislavery Society.

FROM LANE SEMINARY TO OBERLIN COLLEGE, 1833-1835. In 1833 a number of abolitionists decided that the key western city of Cincinnati, just across the Ohio River from the slave state of Kentucky, could be converted to the idea that slavery was a sin. These religious abolitionists took over Cincinnati's Lane Seminary and invited Rev. Lyman Beecher to head it. Beecher's daughter Harriet accompanied him to Cincinnati. She saw slavery with her own eyes in Kentucky and met and married one of the Lane students, Calvin Stowe. Years later she would use her observations to write *Uncle Tom's Cabin.*

The leading professor at Lane Seminary was the same Theodore Weld who had traveled the South secretly recruiting for abolition. A charismatic speaker whom some students proclaimed "a God," Weld turned the seminary upside-down. While Beecher temporarily left to raise funds, Weld and the students, mostly practicing evangelical ministers in their mid-twenties, held an abolitionist revival. For 18 nights in a row in February 1834, Weld led fervent meetings about slavery. Awash in prayer and song, some sessions lasted all night.

The 54 students included Birney, Stowe, an ex-slave named James Bradley, and Henry B. Stanton, the husband of the future women's rights leader Elizabeth Cady Stanton. All began as opponents of slavery, and they soon came to agree that slavery was a sin, that it must be abolished immediately, and that colonization was inadequate.

The Lane students expressed their views among the residents of Cincinnati, who became alarmed. Cincinnati had a large free black population, and a number of students, noticing for the first time that the city barred black children from its public schools, began to teach these children to read and write. Beecher returned to find the business community, anxious not to offend its southern customers, in an uproar. Merchants demanded that Beecher stop the students' activities, but the students refused to listen to the president's pleas and withdrew from Lane Seminary, which ceased to exist. The mayor led a mob that drove the blacks out of the city and burned down their neighborhood.

The Tappans then made a large donation to Oberlin College in northeastern Ohio's Western Reserve, an area settled mostly by New Englanders. Although Beecher and Weld did not move to Oberlin, many of the former Lane Seminary students did, and Oberlin became the center of religious abolitionist activity in the West for the next generation. In 1835 Oberlin became one of the first American colleges to admit a black student; two years earlier it had been the first male college to admit a woman.

Oberlin's graduates, largely evangelical ministers, preached the message that slavery was a sin from pulpits throughout the upper North for more than 20 years, and their congregations gradually adopted these beliefs. Northern public opinion about slavery was transformed.

WELD CONVERTS THE NORTH TO ABOLITION. The impatient Weld left Lane Seminary to hold abolitionist meetings throughout the North. Called the "most mobbed man in America," Weld patterned his sessions on religious revivals. He usually picked a small town where he enjoyed the support of at least one local minister. This gave him a church to use and guaranteed that someone would keep the abolitionist spirit alive after Weld's departure.

The first night's meeting often brought jeers and rotten fruit, sometimes thrown by public officials and leading citizens, but Weld's evangelical style and the novelty of his message — that slavery was a sin — brought people back for a second night. Usually, there was less hostility the second night. By the third or fourth night, Weld could count on a majority of the audience pledging its opposition to slavery on moral and religious grounds. Weld then took his revival to another town.

Weld exhausted himself and came to realize that his cause would grow only slowly. He also recognized, painfully, based on his earlier travels in the South, that few white southerners had embraced abolition. Although the North seemed well on its way to rejecting slavery, the North had no slaves, so his work showed no promise of freeing any slaves. After the Panic of 1837, the Tappans faced financial difficulty and withdrew their support. Weld, understanding that slavery would not soon be abolished by religious fervor, was tormented by psychological depression and retired from public life.

Although the religious abolitionists failed to convince Americans that sla-very was a sin that needed to be abolished immediately, they did much to change northern attitudes over the long run. Furthermore, the adoption of the moral argument that could neither be compromised away nor easily at-tacked in a society devoted to liberty and equality gave abolitionists the upper hand in the debate over slavery. After the 1830s, defenders of slavery were always on the defensive. Outwardly frustrated and defeated, the religious ab-olitionists actually did more to abolish slavery than they ever recognized.

Militant Abolitionists Denounce Slavery

Militant abolitionists, unlike slavery's religious opponents, fo-cused on how slavery ruined the slave economically, politically, and socially, as well as spiritually. This total degradation, they argued, demanded the institution's immediate destruction. Mil-itants like the white editor William Lloyd Garrison so hated sla-very that they could never bring themselves to compromise. Some, like the black Harriet Tubman, who helped operate the Underground Railroad, risked everything. Others, like Elijah Lovejoy, gave their lives. The eloquent former slave Frederick Douglass focused on the slave's plight. The intense desire to abolish slavery set the militants apart, making them impatient, impolitic, unpopular, and feared.

WILLIAM LLOYD GARRISON FOUNDS A NEWSPAPER, 1831. Like the religious abolitionists, many militants had once been colonizationists. In 1830 the printer William Lloyd Garrison lived in Baltimore, where he helped edit a colonizationist newspaper, the *Genius of Universal Emancipation.* The paper alarmed some Maryland slaveholders, who had Garrison arrested. He could not make bail and had time to think while languishing in jail. He con-cluded, correctly, that white southerners were not ripe for conversion to abo-lition, even in the form of colonization, and he decided to take a much more militant position against slavery. Then the Tappans provided the money to bail him out of jail.

Garrison moved to Boston, the center for American reform movements, and in 1831 began to publish *The Liberator,* a militant abolitionist organ. Promising to be "as harsh as truth, and as uncompromising as justice," he vowed, "I am in earnest — I will not equivocate — I will not excuse — I will not retreat a single inch — AND I WILL BE HEARD."

His first issue denounced both colonization and the religious abolitionists' concept of gradual emancipation. Garrison apologized to the slaves, whom he called his brothers, for his own prior views. He called not only for the immediate end of slavery but for blacks to have full civil rights, including the right to vote, to serve on juries, and to own property.

Although Garrison had fewer than 500 subscribers, predominantly free blacks in the North, his strident language brought immediate notice. In those days, before the Associated Press, newspapers regularly obtained news by exchanging copies. Circulated all over the country, Garrison's paper so angered proslavery editors in the South that they quoted it in hostile editorials — which the northern press then reprinted with their own comments. Within a few years Garrison became notorious.

The man had no tact. Calling the Methodist church, then the largest in the country, a "cage of unclean birds" may have been amusing to some, but burning a copy of the United States Constitution on the Boston Common infuriated people. Garrison held the document in contempt because it allowed slavery. He suggested throwing the South out of the Union. Even in reform-minded Boston, these views angered people, and in 1835 a mob nearly lynched Garrison, who was saved only by the mayor's timely arrival.

MOBS ATTACK MILITANT EDITORS. Other militant abolitionist editors paid dearly for their unpopular views. In Alton, Illinois, a town near St. Louis and just across the Mississippi River from the slave state of Missouri, local mobs three times dumped Elijah Lovejoy's printing presses into the river. Alton merchants hated Lovejoy because he drove away business from Missouri. After losing his third press, and facing financial ruin, the editor vowed to defend his newspaper office. In 1837 a mob destroyed the office and murdered Lovejoy.

In Lexington, Kentucky, Cassius Clay, a cousin of Henry Clay, converted to the antislavery cause. He, too, decided to publish a newspaper expressing these views. Warned against the folly of his enterprise, Clay swore he would kill anyone who interfered with his free speech. Although mobbed at his office, Clay survived, but not without a price. Deprived of sleep by the need for a constant state of alert, he finally realized that he could no longer live in Kentucky. He moved to Ohio and became a powerful antislavery lecturer and organizer.

BLACK ABOLITIONISTS ACT. Many free blacks in the North strongly supported abolition. They largely organized the Underground Railroad, a network of abolitionists who helped smuggle runaway slaves from the South to safe areas in the North or in Canada. A slave who made contact with an agent would be sent north by being passed from person to person, transported at night by wagon under a load of hay, and hidden in secret rooms of the houses that served as waystations.

Harriet Tubman, an escaped slave, made 20 daring return trips to the South to rescue as many as 300 others, including her parents. A legend, she was given the nickname Moses and had a $40,000 price on her head.

Another important black abolitionist was Sojourner Truth. Born in 1797 as a slave in New York state with the name Isabella Baumfree, she learned mystical religious practices from her mother. Freed in 1827 by New York's emancipation law, she took the name Sojourner Truth in 1843 — after conversing with God, she said — and traveled the country to preach a religious message of abolition and women's rights. "I have borne thirteen children, and seen most of 'em sold into slavery," she said, "and when I cried out with my mother's grief, none but Jesus heard me — and ain't I a woman?"

FREDERICK DOUGLASS TELLS HIS STORY. The leading black abolitionist was Frederick Douglass. Son of a white planter and a black slave mother, he grew up in the 1820s as a slave on a Maryland plantation until sent to Baltimore to be trained as a house servant. This bright youth's mistress helped him learn to read and write — developments that alarmed his master — and he mixed with and learned from Baltimore's free blacks in the streets. Sent to a shipyard to learn to be a shipcaulker, he was nearly killed in a fight when a white worker decided to teach this proud, cocky, intelligent black youth about white supremacy.

Concluding that Douglass had been ruined by literacy and by contact with independent-minded free blacks, his owner sent him to a plantation to be broken. Douglass resisted, received frequent beatings, and fled to the North. In 1838 he obtained a free Negro's pass, bought seaman's clothes, and sailed from Baltimore to Philadelphia. Feeling unsafe there, he quickly moved to New England but due to prejudice found no work as a caulker.

One day Douglass attended an abolitionist meeting, told his story, and electrified the crowd. This articulate, self-educated man refuted the argument for slavery merely by his existence. Sent on a speaking tour throughout the North, Douglass told his audiences, "I grew up to manhood in the presence of this hydra-headed monster — not as a master — not as an idle spectator — not as the guest of the slaveholder; but as a *slave*." The most successful of the abolitionist lecturers, Douglass in 1847 founded a major antislavery newspaper, *North Star,* in Rochester, New York. His autobiographical *Narrative* (1845) became an American classic.

Douglass occupied a key position in the abolitionist movement. An astute student of southern culture, both white and black, he believed that northern-

The most prominent black abolitionist was the runaway slave Frederick Douglass. His writing and speaking did much to convince northern audiences that slavery should be abolished. (UPI/Bettman)

ers could do little either to change white southern opinion or to reach the slaves. Therefore, like Theodore Weld, he concluded that more could be accomplished in the North, by converting the masses to abolition.

Like other militants, he advocated full civil rights for all blacks everywhere. Indeed, he frequently pointed out that free blacks in the North like himself lacked many rights, including the right to vote in most states, and were generally treated as second-class citizens. He stressed the importance of education and job training in the race's advancement and, being rather pessimistic about rallying whites to assist, called for black self-help.

Despite his militancy, he maintained good relations with the religious abolitionists, especially Harriet Beecher Stowe. In part, this was due to his calm, which contrasted vividly with Garrison's stridency, and in part because he shared the religious abolitionists' concerns about the practical consequences of immediate emancipation. Mostly, however, they admired him for overcoming the handicap of being born a slave. Douglass's success demonstrated what emancipation might accomplish. Such a message suggested that slavery was not only cruel but also a hoax, a form of exploitation disguised by a racial myth.

Conclusion

The American Revolution started the movement to abolish slavery. State emancipation succeeded in the North, which had few slaves, but failed in the South, where fears of free blacks as well as profits led whites to defend slavery vigorously. Meanwhile, northern evangelicals saw slavery as a sin, even as militant abolitionists demanded its immediate end. By 1850 the issue divided Americans sectionally and, as we shall see, was ripe for entering into politics.

Recommended Readings

DOCUMENTS: Frederick Douglass, *Narrative of the Life* (1845); Frances A. Kemble, *Journal of a Residence on a Georgian Plantation in 1838-1839* (1864); Solomon Northrup, *Twelve Years a Slave* (1853).

READINGS: (GENERAL) David B. Davis, *The Problem of Slavery* (2 vols., 1966-1975); John H. Franklin, *From Slavery to Freedom* (6th ed., 1988); George M. Frederickson, *The Black Image in the White Mind* (1971); Eugene D. Genovese, *Roll, Jordan, Roll* (1974); Peter Kolchin, *Unfree Labor* (1987); Lawrence W. Levine, *Black Culture and Black Consciousness* (1977); Kenneth M. Stampp, *The Peculiar Institution* (1956); (SLAVE LIFE) John W. Blassingame, *The Slave Community* (2nd ed., 1979); Orville V. Burton, *In My Father's House Are Many Mansions* (1985); Charles W. Joyner, *Down by the Riverside* (1984); James Oakes, *The Ruling Race* (1982); Leslie Owens, *This Species of Property* (1976); Albert J. Raboteau, *Slave Religion* (1978); (RELIGIOUS ABOLITION) Robert Abzug, *Passionate Liberator, Theodore Dwight Weld* (1980); Lawrence J. Friedman, *Gregarious Saints* (1982); Leonard L. Richards, *Gentlemen of Property and Standing* (1970); James B. Stewart, *Holy Warriors* (1976); (MILITANT ABOLITION) William S. McFeely, *Frederick Douglass* (1991); Waldo E. Martin, *The Mind of Frederick Douglass* (1984); Benjamin Quarles, *Black Abolitionists* (1969); John Thomas, *The Liberator, William Lloyd Garrison* (1963).

12

———— ✠ ————

AMERICANS AT MIDCENTURY: UNBOUNDED OPTIMISM

CHAPTER OVERVIEW: The years on either side of 1850 formed a kind of turning point in the development of the United States. The year 1845 marked the beginning of an economic boom that lasted a generation, and large numbers of Irish and German immigrants poured into the country. Amid prosperity, the optimistic middle class adopted rigid values, but the more adventurous were prepared to lay claim to the continent. The annexation of Texas produced the Mexican War, which led to the acquisition of New Mexico and California. The only sour note was in politics, where slavery became an agonizingly divisive issue, but optimistic Americans thought they could settle the issue with the ill-fated Compromise of 1850. No piece of legislation ever expressed better the flavor of a period or its limitations. Throughout the era, Americans believed it was their Manifest Destiny to possess the entire continent.

Rapid Growth Reshapes the Country

In 1845 the economy began a long boom. Prosperity brought demands for labor that led to increasing immigration, especially from Ireland and Germany. Although assimilation proved difficult, hostility to immigrants faded due to both good economic conditions and the spirit of optimism.

THE ECONOMY TAKES OFF. The period between 1845 and 1873 saw such unprecedented economic growth all over the world that economists have called it the "Long Boom." Although punctuated by **recessions**, including the Panic of 1857, the downturns never lasted long, were seldom deep, and were followed by vigorous recoveries.

During this boom, American **gross domestic product** — that is, the value of the nation's total economic output — exceeded Great Britain's for the first time. Industrial output grew rapidly in the United States, and world trade blossomed, as railroads and steamships linked hitherto remote areas and brought agricultural produce and minerals such as copper, iron, and tin into a global market.

Many people believed that continued economic growth required access both to new natural resources and to markets. Explorers sought new resources all over the world. Europeans raced to colonize Africa, and Americans, filled with unbounded optimism, became determined to push the boundaries of the United States to the Pacific Ocean.

IMMIGRATION SURGES TO RECORD LEVELS. The growth of the American economy could not have taken place without a large increase in the labor force. Natural resources were plentiful, and so was capital, generated by the textile industry, by profits made through increased trade, and by British investments in the United States. But labor was scarce and expensive.

Immigrants, particularly from Ireland and Germany, poured into the United States in unprecedented numbers during the 1840s and 1850s. Driven from Ireland by famine and from Germany by political turmoil combined with a sense that greater opportunities existed in the United States, the immigrants arrived to face economic exploitation and prejudice, especially if they were Catholic, as many were. Nevertheless, they continued to come.

Of a total population of 31 million in 1860, about 13 percent were foreign-born. Some 1.6 million had been born in Ireland, 1.3 million in Germany, and another 1.2 million elsewhere. Almost all settled in the North, where by 1860 the foreign-born constituted close to one-quarter of the adult population.

In most northern cities, immigrants and their American-born children were a majority. The Irish settled along the East coast, the Germans in the Midwest, where they established, among other things, breweries. Anheuser-Busch, Pabst, Schlitz, and Miller (originally Müller) date from this period. English-style beer all but disappeared. Immigration made the United States a much more diverse society.

Although most immigrants worked as laborers or as skilled **artisans,** they quickly decided that they, or at least their children, would rise into the middle class. Even though artisan labor was becoming less and less needed and valued, these aspirations were realistic. The economy, growing ever more complex as it expanded, generated far more new, specialized, middle-class jobs than the native-born could fill. Learning English, working two jobs, going to night school, pooling funds with relatives, and living frugally to save money to open a family business provided ways for immigrants to join the middle class. At the very least, many embraced middle-class values and claimed respectability even with modest incomes.

A BACKLASH FIZZLES. The arrival of large numbers of upwardly mobile immigrants did not set well with the native-born **Protestant** working class in America's largest cities. As job competition drove down wages, the native born responded by rioting and in 1844 by organizing the American Republican party. Protesting against both the merchant-dominated **Whigs** and the immigrant-oriented Democrats, the American Republicans elected a mayor and city council in New York and a congressman from a working-class district in Philadelphia. The congressman was Lewis Levin, a Methodist street preacher, temperance advocate, and son of a Jewish merchant. The virulently anti-immigrant Levin served three terms before his party, a victim of rising prosperity, disappeared from view. Even **nativism** could not survive the unbounded optimism of the boom.

The Middle Class Adopts Modern Values

By the 1840s, the Market Revolution (Chapter 8) had created, for the first time, a substantial urban middle class. Increasingly, this class's core values — emphasizing thrift, respectability, family life, and separate gender roles — became dominant in the society as a whole. Men competed in the marketplace to earn money; women guarded morality and cultivated family life. Young people carefully trained for future roles. The middle class stressed self-improvement and organized groups to enhance virtue in the community.

DEFINING THE MIDDLE CLASS. In small towns and cities across the United States doctors, lawyers, ministers, many merchants, some master mechanics, and specialized white-collar workers and their families increasingly constituted a new, self-defined middle class. Lacking great wealth, without inherited money, and often without much education, members of these families nonetheless enjoyed above average incomes, a rising standard of living, and homeownership.

At a time when a laborer earned a maximum of $300 a year and a typical skilled artisan $600, a middle-class man made $1,200 or more. Such a man could support a wife who did not work outside the home and several children in a comfortable household, often with a female live-in Irish servant to help with the chores. Perhaps 20 to 40 percent of urban Americans lived in this fashion, and even more people tried, as best as they could, to imitate middle-class ways.

Rigid values and practices marked the middle class, which believed that "there was a place for every thing, and every thing should be in its place." This desire for boundaries, perhaps understandable amid the chaos of a rapidly changing and often unbounded society, led to complex formulas that governed all aspects of life. For example, a widow was expected to wear black mourning clothes for one year after her husband's death. The development of a rigid code of conduct made it possible for new people to join the middle class, since conduct defined membership, while at the same time conformity helped define the class and maintain its cohesion.

GENDER ROLES AND FAMILY VALUES. One important middle-class principle was to separate men and women in all aspects of life. In 1850 men were seen as strivers and doers, by nature aggressive and acquisitive. Accordingly, they ought to employ themselves competitively in business or the professions. If they succeeded, they married, established a home, and enjoyed family life with children. Women were seen as dreamers, by nature passive and fragile, and, thus, fit only to maintain a home as a refuge from the world for husbands and as a place to nurture children. The duty of women, who understood morality better, was to regulate the passions of men. The duty of men, inclined toward worldly success, was to use their earnings to take care of women.

At an early age, middle-class children learned that authority must be respected, that rules must be obeyed, and that men and women performed different life's work. Raising children, a principal duty for middle-class mothers, involved teaching the young to distinguish between right and wrong and to understand the importance of moral principles, as defined by **evangelical** Protestants. Capable of both good and evil, children had to be guided along the correct moral path, which would all but guarantee that they would acquire proper manners, social graces, and practical work skills.

Institutions reinforced family training. Both church-sponsored Sunday schools and public schools, which often included the Bible in the curriculum, repeated values taught at home and provided social contacts in a moral setting. Encouraged to show responsibility, pupils were given assignments that combined learning, discipline, and morals. The new high schools emphasized practical preparation for life and work by teaching boys penmanship, accounting, and geography, all skills valued in the job market. They also stressed order, propriety, and obedience to authority.

Many young men had to carve out a middle-class life for themselves. Sunday school tracts and teenage advice manuals praised upward mobility and urged youths to become "self-made" men. These books both stressed the importance of high morals and favored formal education, especially technical training that made a young man more employable. Honesty, honor, and, perhaps most important, self-restraint gave a youth the character necessary to survive in a world filled with evils that snared the unwary.

Young women learned from sermons, magazine essays, and popular novels to model themselves on their happy, successful mothers or other female relatives. Useful information could be found in household management manuals, such as Catharine Beecher's. A young woman was expected to learn to cook, to sew, to care for children, and to manage household money and servants, but her most important skill was to size-up young men. She was expected to marry and to remain married to the same man. In many ways he would control her life, so it was important for her to resist passion, which might lead her to fall in love with a scoundrel, and to marry a moral, virtuous man capable of earning a living.

THE IMPORTANCE OF THE HOME IN TOWN AND CITY. In small towns and large cities, wives typically set a moral tone in the home for their husbands, for their children, and for their reputations among visitors. Religious or moral newspapers, magazines, and books, including *Harper's New Family Bible,* were piled high in prominent places on tables in the living room. Moral or patriotic lithographs, designed to educate as well as enliven, hung on the walls. These devices added an element of piety and rectitude to the new, elaborate decorative style, which featured luxurious wall-to-wall carpets, lavish wallpaper, heavy drapes, and carved wooden furniture, including red horsehair sofas.

Pianos graced many middle-class living rooms. Although buying a piano might cost a family all of its income beyond the price of necessities for several years, families often made this sacrifice. A skirt carefully covered the piano's legs, which were supposed to be kept hidden. The legs were called limbs. The word *leg* was considered obscene.

After meals, family members adjourned to the piano and sang while a daughter played. A woman's musical skills might attract the attention of an eligible young man. Religious hymns and the melodic songs of Stephen Foster were favorites. No wonder that when the singer Jenny Lind, dubbed the

"Swedish Nightingale," toured the United States in 1850, middle-class Americans rushed to buy tickets at $50 apiece.

The middle class, for the first time, began to eat in a dining room separate from the living room or kitchen. Meals were at fixed times, and every member of the family except for young children was expected to be present. Dining became complex and elaborate, with expensive tablecloths, napkins, china, and silver covering the table. A place setting for silver included many utensils, each designed for a specific purpose. For example, strawberries and raspberries required different spoons. The food, carried from the kitchen by a servant, was simple bu. heaped high on the platter to indicate wealth.

THE MIDDLE CLASS SEEKS SELF-IMPROVING ENTERTAINMENT. Although members of the middle class worked hard, they also enjoyed leisure. They rejected liquor at taverns in favor of ice cream sodas or fruit-flavored drinks with crushed ice at the new soda fountains. Or they organized games, such as baseball, with its elaborate rules. Children played with mechanical toys, including savings banks designed to teach thrift. Family members sat for their portraits before the camera at the new **daguerreotype** photographic studios.

Especially favored was entertainment that provided, or claimed to provide, self-improvement. Thus, middle-class Americans keenly read daily newspapers. By the 1840s every major city had several penny papers, such as James Gordon Bennett's *New York Herald.* The energetic Bennett often scooped the competition, helped organize the Associated Press, and quickly embraced Samuel F. B. Morse's newly invented telegraph, which sent word of James K. Polk's nomination at the Democratic convention in 1844. The whole country was wired rapidly.

Attending lectures at the local **lyceum** promised increased knowledge as well as fun. So did going to P. T. Barnum's American Museum in New York. To attract middle-class audiences, Barnum stressed his establishment's educational mission. He exhibited curiosities from the natural world, but many were fake. Barnum called the theater in his museum an "auditorium" and its live shows "illustrated lectures" in order to appease evangelicals who found theatrical shows sinful.

Despite its absurdities and faults, the middle class had one striking virtue. Surrounded by an atmosphere of evangelical Christianity, the middle class optimistically believed in charity and in doing good in the world. Women, especially, thought that a moral home offered insufficient protection in a largely immoral world. Thus, middle-class women organized moral societies, church welfare groups, and reform organizations to bring virtue to their communities.

Americans Lay Claim
to the Continent

In the 1840s the spirit of unbounded optimism led Americans to see the whole of North America as theirs. Settlers flocked west, to Texas, New Mexico, California, and the Oregon country. The Texas colonists never doubted that Texas would some day join the Union. Early American settlers in New Mexico and California had the same dream. So did the pioneers who trudged along the Oregon Trail. Boosters claimed that America's expansion was God-given Manifest Destiny.

STEPHEN AUSTIN COLONIZES TEXAS. Americans had long looked toward the day when their nation would reach the Pacific Ocean. In 1821, the year Mexico won its independence from Spain, Moses Austin received a Mexican **charter** to establish a colony in Mexico's province of Texas, which had only 3,000 Mexican residents. When Austin died, his son Stephen took over the project. By 1824 as many as 2,000 Americans, some southerners with slaves, had settled in Austin's colony. In 1829 Mexico abolished **slavery,** but the Texans evaded the law by turning their slaves into servants **indentured** for life.

During the early 1830s the Mexican government became so alarmed at the large number of Americans pouring into Texas that it halted further land grants. Mexican officials harassed the Texans about slavery, about **customs duties,** and about their religion — Mexico required the Americans to promise to convert to Catholicism. In 1833, when Austin went to Mexico City to protest, he was jailed. In 1835 General Antonio Lopez Santa Anna declared himself dictator of Mexico — a move that alarmed the democratically inclined Texans — and decided to march an army into Texas to punish the Americans.

In 1836, just as Santa Anna and his army arrived, the Texans declared their independence. A few days later, Santa Anna's forces took the fort called the Alamo in a bloody victory in which all the defenders, including Davy Crockett, were slaughtered. The defenders' defiant refusal to surrender despite hopeless odds became a symbol of courage and honor to the Texans. A month later the Texans, led by Sam Houston, beat the Mexicans at the battle of San Jacinto. Santa Anna was captured and, under threat of execution, signed treaties recognizing Texas's independence and the Rio Grande as the boundary between the Republic of Texas and Mexico. The Mexican congress would later void these treaties as coerced.

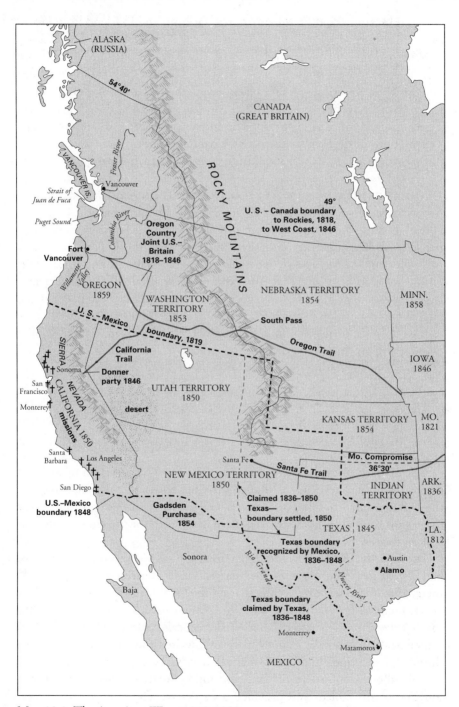

Map 12.1. The American West, 1818-1859

Sam Houston asked President Andrew Jackson, an old friend from Houston's Tennessee days, to annex Texas to the United States, but Jackson wanted to avoid controversy and declined. The Texans continued to maintain their independence from Mexico. In 1836 Texas's population included 30,000 white Americans, 5,000 black slaves (the Republic of Texas quickly reintroduced slavery), and only 4,000 Mexicans. By 1860 only 6 percent of Texas's population was Hispanic. The Indian population is unknown. The Texans killed or drove away the native inhabitants, largely Comanche, and to this day there are only three small Indian reservations in Texas.

TRADERS SETTLE IN NEW MEXICO AND CALIFORNIA. In 1821 the first American traders reached Santa Fe, New Mexico, by using an Indian trail that quickly became the main road from the Midwest to the Southwest. Whereas the Spanish had jealously prohibited trade between the United States and New Mexico, Mexico's newly independent government did not object. This business was so profitable that American traders organized annual caravans, largely to exchange manufactured goods for mules and silver. Soon American merchants set up shop in Santa Fe, a town of about 3,000 people, where they learned Spanish, turned Catholic, and married New Mexican women. Within two decades an Anglo-Hispanic elite dominated New Mexico's politics and economics by exploiting the poorer Hispanic and Indian residents.

As early as the 1820s American ships in the China trade began to barter along the California coast with the Californios, as the province's 4,000 Mexican residents were called. The Americans exchanged both manufactured goods and Chinese tea and silk for fresh water and hides from California's vast rancheros (cattle ranches).

The Spanish priest Junipero Serra had founded 21 Franciscan missions in California in the late 1700s. Although these missions still held some power in the 1820s, a small number of Mexican land grantees increasingly dominated the region. Indians provided virtual slave labor both for the church missions and on the rancheros.

By the early 1840s a few hundred Americans, as well as some Europeans, had settled in California either as ranchers with Mexican grants or as hide merchants in the seaports. While sharing the Californios's contempt for the government in far-off Mexico City, the Americans had no desire for Californio rule, since the **Yankees** considered the locals backward, lazy, dishonest, impractical, and foolish. Many Americans awaited the day when California dropped, like a ripe plum, into American hands.

Talk about California's rich soil and mild climate reached the East, but moving to this fabled land provided a challenge. The only sea route took travelers through dangerous storms around the tip of South America on cargo ships or on whaling ships ill-equipped for passengers. The overland route meant crossing the desert and risking encounters with Indians.

Naive guide books optimistically insisted that the "Yerba Buena River" flowed conveniently on a direct line from Colorado to San Francisco Bay. When knowledgeable explorers denied that there was such a river, they were accused of hiding the truth in order to make money by selling guide services to travelers. In 1846 a group of settlers led by George Donner migrated to California and, using a guide book's faulty map, took a shortcut that left them trapped at Donner Pass high in the Sierra Nevada all winter. Some members of the Donner party froze to death, and others turned to cannibalism to survive.

THE OREGON TRAIL GOES TO GOD'S COUNTRY. In 1834 Jason Lee established a Methodist mission in Oregon's Willamette River valley, and partly due to his lavish praise, American farmers began to settle there almost immediately. By 1836 these settlers already outnumbered the British in the valley, and in 1843 they were sufficiently numerous that they organized a provisional, democratic government.

In the early 1840s many more Americans migrated overland to the Oregon country than to California. The Oregon Trail had more reliable water for horses and cattle, and the Pacific Northwest was under joint British-American occupation rather than Mexican rule. In addition, the climate in the Willamette Valley was nearly as mild as California's, but greater rainfall enabled Americans to grow familiar crops without irrigation.

Travel on the Oregon Trail, which usually took about six months from Missouri with horses pulling a covered wagon at the rate of 15 miles a day, was more arduous than dangerous. Indians approached the trail to make friendly trades rather than to attack. Hundreds, later thousands, of settlers set out from Missouri each spring, usually selling their farms to raise the $600 that it cost a family of four to make the trip. By the mid-1840s the wagons grew so thick on the trail that they stretched as far as the eye could see in both directions and were often a dozen abreast. The ruts from their wheels are still visible today.

BOOSTERS CLAIM MANIFEST DESTINY. As the economy gathered steam in the 1840s, so did promoters of national geographical expansion. Many young men, including Stephen A. Douglas and George N. Sanders, called themselves the Young America movement. Although primarily motivated by the desire to enrich themselves, advocates of expansion preferred to use moral arguments as suited the spirit of the age.

As a "go ahead" people, Americans considered themselves uniquely suited to acquire, develop, and exploit North America's rich natural resources. To do so was a God-given right, wrote the Democratic party promoter John L. O'Sullivan, for the country had a **Manifest Destiny** to spread itself westward to the Pacific Ocean.

The phrase Manifest Destiny ostensibly marked the bold cry of confident Americans announcing to the world that they were God's chosen people destined for national greatness. In reality it masked many other traits, including self-aggrandizement, acquisitiveness, and exploitation of both people and resources. The assertion of American superiority implied the right of white Americans to enslave blacks or to take land from Indians, Mexicans, or anyone else.

In addition, Manifest Destiny suggested a coherent, logical policy for territorial expansion, when the reality was that Americans — and especially those devoted to national glory — sought to expand anywhere and everywhere at whatever price. Such gluttony raised serious questions about the country's stability.

The Texas Question Leads to War with Mexico

Political realists, like Henry Clay and Martin Van Buren, worried that the country's enthusiasm recognized no limits. But the election of 1844, which put the obscure James K. Polk in the White House, proved that Americans were not prepared to accept limits — at least as far as Texas was concerned. In 1846 Polk made peace with Britain over Oregon but fought Mexico over Texas annexation, and in 1848 the Mexican War ended with the United States acquiring California and New Mexico. In 1846 David Wilmot's Proviso reintroduced the slavery issue into politics.

ELECTION OF 1844. As the 1844 presidential election approached, the expected candidates were the leaders of the two parties, the Whig Henry Clay and the Democrat Martin Van Buren. Both were realists rather than unbounded optimists. Although Clay owned slaves, neither man liked slavery, and both believed that a sectional dispute over slavery could wreck their parties and cause a civil war. Therefore, they quietly agreed not to discuss slavery, and both issued public statements opposing the admission of the Republic of Texas into the Union as a new slave state. Among other problems, the **annexation** of Texas invited war with Mexico.

The Whigs nominated Clay, as expected. But southern Democrats, unhappy over their party leader Van Buren's Texas position, sabotaged his candidacy. Going into the national convention, Van Buren held pledges from a majority of delegates, including southerners whose votes had been obtained before he had announced his Texas policy. These delegates killed Van Buren's candidacy by persuading the convention to adopt a rule requiring the nominee to get a two-thirds vote. This provision, retained until 1936, gave southerners a veto over the Democratic party's presidential nomination.

As the southerners knew, Van Buren could not be nominated with the two-thirds rule, and in order to break the deadlock, the Democrats on the ninth ballot picked an obscure former speaker of the House of Representatives, James K. Polk of Tennessee. "Young Hickory," as he was called, enjoyed Andrew Jackson's friendship and support. Polk and the Democrats, unlike Clay and the Whigs, favored annexing Texas. This position guaranteed southern votes, and to get support in the North, the Democrats promised to acquire all of the Pacific Northwest, then under joint British-American control, to the southern boundary of Alaska with the slogan "54° 40′ or fight." The only other issue was the **tariff**, which Polk promised to revise. Southerners said Polk would reduce the tariff; northerners thought he would raise it. Polk did not elaborate.

The Whigs, perplexed by the Democrats' first **"dark horse"** candidate, chanted derisively, "Who is James K. Polk?" The better-known Clay, however, had made many enemies. His pledge against Texas annexation hurt him in the South, and when he tried to retract it, he lost credibility among northerners without gaining any southern support. **Abolitionists**, mostly Whigs, refused to vote for Clay and instead cast ballots for James Gillespie Birney, the Liberty party's antislavery candidate. In an extremely close election that remained in doubt for six days, Polk won by narrowly taking New York state. In that crucial state Polk's margin of victory was less than the number of votes cast for Birney.

POLK INHERITS TEXAS AND MAKES PEACE WITH BRITAIN. After protracted negotiations conducted by outgoing Secretary of State John C. Calhoun, on March 3, 1845, President John Tyler's last day in office, Texas joined the Union. Thus, Polk's presidency began with Texas as a state, but the issue still troubled his administration. Mexico had never recognized Texas's independence, and the new state had an uncertain boundary.

Texans cited a border that ran along the Rio Grande to its headwaters and then straight north to meet the United States in what became Wyoming. They claimed half of New Mexico, including Santa Fe. The Mexicans contended the Texas boundary ran along the Nueces River to its headwaters inside central Texas and then north to meet the United States in what became Oklahoma. Polk faced a war with Mexico over this boundary dispute.

Before tackling that issue, Polk decided to use diplomacy to divide ownership of the Pacific Northwest. The British had suggested extending the United States-Canadian boundary at the **49th parallel** from the Rocky Mountains west to the Columbia River, and then down the river to the ocean. Recognizing that the New Englanders who had begun to settle in Oregon's Willamette valley had given Americans effective control of that area, the British sought to retain the Hudson's Bay Company's Fort Vancouver on the Columbia and the great natural harbors on Puget Sound.

The Americans countered by proposing to extend the 49th parallel boundary to the Pacific Ocean. Wanting peace, the British in 1846 accepted the American proposal with the provision that Vancouver Island be entirely under their control. The United States agreed to this boundary. The island was less important to the British than the navigation rights through the Strait of Juan de Fuca to the Fraser River, which flowed just north of the 49th parallel. The Hudson's Bay Company relocated its headquarters there, to what is now Vancouver, British Columbia.

THE MEXICAN WAR BEGINS, 1846. Polk's diplomacy with Mexico failed, in part because Mexican honor barred yielding territory, and in part because Polk wanted even more land than the Texans claimed. Westward migration, the idea of Manifest Destiny, and the concept of a **transcontinental railroad** focused American attention on Mexico's provinces of New Mexico (which then included what became Arizona, Colorado, Utah, and Nevada) and California, especially on the great natural harbors at San Francisco and San Diego. One or the other of those bays was bound to be the site of the transcontinental railhead. Polk wanted both and offered to buy the largely unpopulated southwestern desert. He knew that the local peoples, whether New Mexicans, Californios, or Indians, despised Mexico. The Mexicans, however, refused to sell.

In 1846 Polk stationed American troops under General Zachary Taylor on the north bank of the Rio Grande, ostensibly to protect Texas, although no American settlers lived anywhere near the border. The Mexican army took Polk's bait and attacked. The president, stating that "Mexico has . . . shed American blood upon the American soil," persuaded Congress to declare war on May 13, 1846.

Taylor quickly occupied Matamoros, on the south bank of the Rio Grande, and Colonel Stephen Kearny took Santa Fe and then marched his army to California. Under secret orders from Polk, Captain John C. Frémont also entered California, and in June 1846, some American settlers at Sonoma, with support from Frémont, declared the independent Bear Flag Republic. In

July, Commodore John Sloat sailed into the harbor at Monterey and annexed California to the United States.

In August, Commodore Robert Stockton occupied Santa Barbara and Los Angeles and declared himself governor, which provoked the southern Californios to revolt against the Americans. Kearny helped quell the rebellion, and then he and Stockton quarreled over the right to govern California. Kearny won the battle for Polk's support and had Frémont, who had sided with Stockton, courtmartialed.

Meanwhile, Taylor's army had captured Monterrey in northern Mexico. Peace talks began but broke off, and in 1847 General Winfield Scott persuaded Polk to try a bold new strategy. When Scott ordered Taylor to hold his position and transfer part of his army to Scott, the suspicious Taylor concluded that he was the victim of political intrigue. Disobeying orders, Taylor marched his troops to Buena Vista and routed a larger Mexican force. Reprimanded for his removal from Monterrey, Taylor resigned and toured the United States as a hero.

Scott's daring plan was to capture the key port of Vera Cruz on the Gulf of Mexico and march directly to Mexico City. After a technically brilliant amphibious assault on Vera Cruz, Scott's army defeated the Mexicans at Cerro Gordo and at Mexico City, which fell on September 14, 1847. United States Marines stood guard over the **Halls of Montezuma.**

THE UNITED STATES BUYS CALIFORNIA AND NEW MEXICO, 1848. After the fall of Vera Cruz, Polk sent Nicholas P. Trist to Mexico on a secret peace mission. In early 1848 Trist, whose legal authority from Polk had expired, persuaded the Mexican government to sign a treaty. The treaty of Guadalupe-Hildalgo recognized the Rio Grande as the Texas boundary and ceded New Mexico and California to the United States in return for $15 million and the assumption by the American government of American citizens' claims against Mexico. Although embarrassed by Trist's unauthorized negotiations, Polk sent the treaty to the Senate, which ratified it, despite objections from those who wanted to annex all of Mexico.

Throughout the war controversy had swirled around the possible acquisition of California and New Mexico. Public opinion no longer doubted, as it had in 1844, the wisdom or indeed the inevitability of American ownership, but now the question Clay and Van Buren had feared was openly raised: should slavery be permitted in the new territory? Northerners opposed slavery, believing that the institution should not be allowed to spread and that because Mexico had abolished slavery, New Mexico and California should remain free. Southerners argued that, having enlisted, fought, and died disproportionately as volunteers in the Mexican War, they had the right to take slave property into newly won territories.

CONGRESS DEBATES DAVID WILMOT'S PROVISO, 1846-1847. After the war had begun in 1846, Congress had considered a military spending bill. In the House, David Wilmot, an antislavery Democrat from Pennsylvania, had proposed an amendment. **Wilmot's Proviso** banned slavery in any territory acquired from Mexico as a result of the war. Added to the bill in the House, where antislavery northerners predominated, the amendment failed in the Senate, where free states and slave states had equal representation and where several northern senators had proslavery views. Finally, the House swallowed the Senate version.

In 1847 Wilmot's Proviso again passed in the House and failed in the Senate; it suffered the same fate a third time. By then it had become clear to everyone, especially after the treaty of Guadalupe-Hidalgo gave New Mexico and California to the United States, that slavery in the new western territories would be the major political issue in the 1848 presidential election.

Adopting the Compromise of 1850

As the election of 1848 approached, unbounded optimism gave way to panic over the threat to the Union posed by slavery. Campaigning without a program, Zachary Taylor won without a mandate. To solve the slavery issue, Clay proposed the grand Compromise of 1850 that aimed to appeal to northerners and southerners alike, but ultimately angered both sides, although it did delay civil war for a decade.

ELECTION OF 1848. In 1848 Polk kept his pledge not to seek reelection, and the Democrats, under southern influence, nominated Lewis Cass of Michigan, the first "dough-face" candidate, that is, a northerner willing to support the South on slavery. The Whigs, badly split over slavery, could not agree on a platform, did not adopt one, and nominated Zachary Taylor for president. This Mexican War hero proved to be an ideal candidate. He had no political record, had never voted, and declined to discuss any issues. Northerners noted that his brother was an abolitionist in Ohio, while southerners observed that his wife had inherited hundreds of slaves in Louisiana.

Martin Van Buren, still bitter over the way he had been cheated out of the Democratic nomination in 1844, decided to teach the southerners a lesson. He accepted the nomination of the **Free Soil** party, which promised not to touch slavery in the South but opposed its expansion into the West. His running mate was the antislavery Whig Charles Francis Adams, the son of John Quincy Adams. Thus, in the strange ways of politics, Jackson's hand-picked successor now allied himself with the son of Jackson's enemy.

On election day southerners gave Taylor a landslide victory, while northerners split their votes. Van Buren's strong showing in parts of the North that had been settled by New Englanders indicated intense opposition to the expansion of slavery, especially among those of Puritan descent touched by the Second Great Awakening.

Taylor's clever strategy for winning the election without taking any positions now backfired. As president, he was bound to disappoint some of his supporters with any action that he took. The temporary military governments in New Mexico and California had to be replaced, and with people pouring into California after gold was discovered there in 1848, the issue had to be settled quickly.

In 1849 Taylor proposed admitting both New Mexico and California to the Union. He dodged the territorial slavery issue by saying that, as states, they could decide for themselves if they wanted slavery. This scheme drew no support. Both northerners and southerners felt cheated. New Mexico did not seem ready for statehood, and southerners knew that California would enter the Union as a free state. For the first time, the number of free and slave states would not be the same, and the slave states would lose their equal representation in the Senate.

CLAY PROPOSES A GRAND COMPROMISE, 1850. Ignoring the stubborn Taylor, Henry Clay, the Whig party leader, began in 1850 to arrange a grand compromise. Wanting legislation that gave each section something concrete, Clay's Omnibus Bill contained six provisions:

• California would be admitted as a free state. This reflected public opinion in California, which had more than enough population to be admitted. It also pleased the North. The Senate, however, would not be unbalanced, because many Californians were former southerners, and it was understood that one California senator would represent them.

• New Mexico would be split into northern and southern territories respectively called Utah and New Mexico. Congress would not bar slavery from these territories, and the territorial legislatures could do as they pleased. Utah, with its large Mormon settlement, would probably keep slavery out, but New Mexico, if later settled by Texans, might adopt slavery. The dry climate, however, made it unsuitable for cotton, and slavery was unlikely to thrive there.

• Texas would cede much of its land, including its claim to half of New Mexico, and in return the United States would take over Texas's enormous debt, which was owed to private bondholders. Many Texas **bonds** were now owned by the Washington banker W. W. Corcoran. He offered the bonds at reduced rates to members of Congress during the discussion of Clay's compromise. Clay knew that the Texas bonds, which would rise sharply in value if his bill passed, would generate votes for the compromise from corrupt congressmen who had recently bought bonds.

• Although slavery would remain in the District of Columbia, the slave trade would end. No longer would antislavery northern congressmen have to watch slave auctions taking place across the street from their offices inside the Capitol. Slaveowners, however, would hardly be inconvenienced, since they could sell their slaves a few miles away in Virginia or Maryland.

• Congress would pledge not to interfere with the interstate slave trade. Slaveholders in some states, especially Virginia, had made enormous profits selling their slaves to cotton growers in other states, and they did not want federal legislation that would ban these sales and thereby reduce the value of their slaves.

• A new Fugitive Slave Law would provide for the speedy return of runaway slaves from the North to their owners in the South. In some parts of the North, where local officials were abolitionists, slaveholders had found it impossible to recover slaves. Now federal officials would be appointed to settle these cases without jury trials. Southerners looked upon this provision in Clay's compromise as the one concrete benefit they expected to receive. They were willing to give up a great deal to obtain an effective law, because a runaway slave represented a major financial loss.

CONGRESS DEBATES AND ADOPTS THE COMPROMISE OF 1850. Clay's attempted compromise produced the greatest debate in Senate history, as the old lions roared for the last time. Daniel Webster of Massachusetts, Clay's rival, endorsed Clay's Omnibus Bill, saying that he spoke "not as a Massachusetts man, nor as a northern man, but as an American" wishing to preserve the Union. But in doing so, he antagonized his constituents, who opposed slavery.

A dying John C. Calhoun of South Carolina denounced Clay's effort and demanded a constitutional amendment giving the South control over its own affairs. Calhoun died even before the debate had concluded, and both Clay and Webster died two years later.

Younger senators, the leaders of the next generation, stridently opposed the bill. Abolitionist Salmon P. Chase of Ohio urged Congress to keep slavery out of the territories, and William H. Seward of New York said a "higher law" than the Constitution led him to oppose slavery's spread. On the other side, Jefferson Davis of Mississippi demanded that southerners have the right to take slave property into *all* federal territories.

Clay could not find enough votes to pass his Omnibus Bill, in part due to Taylor's opposition. But on July 9, 1850, Taylor died suddenly and was succeeded by Millard Fillmore, who enthusiastically endorsed the compromise. An old and tired Clay went on vacation, and a young representative from Illinois, Stephen A. Douglas, then split Clay's bill into five separate pieces of legislation. With support from the new administration and with many members of Congress voting only for portions of the overall compromise, Douglas pushed through all five bills. Only a handful of members voted for the total package. Few northerners favored the Fugitive Slave Law, which had become the compromise's most controversial feature.

LIVING WITH THE COMPROMISE OF 1850. The Compromise of 1850 was the last and greatest contribution of Henry Clay and his generation to American governance. Lacking the devotion to abstract ideals found among the Founding Fathers, Clay's generation struggled to pass imperfect but workable laws while hoping that future events would somehow allow revolutionary principles to be carried out. Meanwhile, it was more important to keep the country together, even when people disagreed on the interpretation of fundamental principles, and even if it was necessary to buy votes from some members with profits from Texas bonds.

Although Clay, unlike the gloomy Calhoun, remained an optimist, even he felt forebodings about the future. He was not sure that leaders like Seward and Jefferson Davis, with their energetic devotion to high-minded principles, could continue to make the political system work, especially with an issue as troubling as slavery. Clay did not feel, as young northerners did, embarrassment at living in a self-proclaimed free society in which some people were enslaved.

Devoted in his own way to a national greatness based on his own American system composed of industry, commerce, and cities, Clay had once been "Young Harry of the West," but he had opposed the annexation of Texas and Polk's unbounded vision of a transcontinental republic. He understood, better than Polk, the power of centrifugal forces in an ever-expanding United States, and he feared that the country, if it grew too fast, would fly apart.

The great compromise, so carefully constructed, solved nothing. It papered over the real problems, which were growing gaps between the North and the South in population, in wealth, in economic development, and in moral principles. In the end both sides felt cheated. Northerners were reluctant to hand over runaway slaves and resented the Fugitive Slave Law that ordered them to do so, while the law's ineffectiveness irritated southerners. California's admission to the Union broke the tradition that the number of free and slave states must be the same, and after 1845 no new slave states were admitted.

Congress's policy to allow Utah and New Mexico to decide about slavery for themselves generated controversy in those territories, and it inadvertently opened the question about slavery in other western territories, where that issue had supposedly been settled. If the compromise had any virtue, it was to prevent a civil war in 1850. Its long-term consequence, however, was not to settle the slavery issue but to invite further controversy.

Manifest Destiny and Filibusters

In 1849 would-be miners swarmed into California in search of gold, but few succeeded. Nonetheless, Americans clung to the notion of Manifest Destiny, either their own or the country's. Some particularly ambitious optimists, such as William Walker, aimed to combine national and personal greatness by trying to take over other countries.

THE LURE OF THE CALIFORNIA GOLD RUSH. At the end of the Mexican War, in 1848, the United States had acquired California. That same year gold had been discovered, and by 1852 California's population had surged to 250,000, about six times the pre-Gold Rush level. Almost 90 percent of Californians were male. About half were Americans from the eastern United States, and the others were Europeans, Mexicans, Chileans, Chinese, or settled Indians.

Of 900,000 young white single men in America, one in ten had rushed to California, mainly to seek gold. Few were lucky. The shrewder ones, like Leland Stanford, quickly realized that more money could be made selling supplies to miners or in agriculture. Levi Strauss, an Alsatian Jew, turned blue tent canvas into tight-fitting pants called jeans that both made his fortune and made popular a uniquely American style of dress.

The price of services grew so high that it was cheaper to have clothes sent to Hawaii to be laundered than to have them washed in San Francisco. Then the Chinese opened laundries and restaurants in San Francisco and soon constituted the bulk of California's unskilled workforce. Almost all the Chinese were male, few married or had children in California, and many returned to China. Within a few years most of the American miners had returned to the East, some with profits, some broke. The dream of the nation's Manifest Destiny, however, lived on.

THE FILIBUSTERERS SEEK FAME, FORTUNE, AND LAND. No men exemplified Manifest Destiny better than the **filibusterers.** They were Amer-

The California Gold Rush attracted people from all over the world, and especially from the eastern United States, during the 1850s. But swinging a pickaxe did not necessarily produce gold, and many left California broke. (Brown Brothers)

ican adventurers who used private armies to overthrow foreign governments so they could seize power for themselves. In 1849 Henry Crabb tried to take Sonora in northern Mexico, while two years later Narciso Lopez invaded Cuba, then a Spanish colony. Both were captured and executed.

The most persistent filibusterer was William Walker. After failing to capture the Mexican provinces of Baja California and Sonora in 1853, this "gray-eyed man of destiny" set out in 1855 to conquer the Central American nation of Nicaragua. Intending to have the country annexed to the United States as a new slave state, Walker landed with 58 men, seized the capital, and proclaimed a government. To gain legitimacy, he had himself "elected" governor, although no election was held. Walker made up the election returns, which he carefully printed in his newspaper. In 1857 he suffered a military defeat and was forced to flee. Three years later the British foiled Walker's self-appointed mission to Honduras, which ended with Walker being shot by a firing squad. Filibustering ceased.

Conclusion

At midcentury Americans lived in a delicate balance, partly in a static world of the Founding Fathers' republican principles and rural virtues — which included slavery—and partly in a dynamic world of markets, industry, cities, immigrants, railroads, and national territorial expansion to the Pacific Ocean. This new world, brought into being by the Market Revolution and awash in evangelical Protestantism and reform; was only beginning to develop its own sense of poise, of rootedness, of self-confidence about the shape of the American future.

At midcentury Americans looked both backward and forward, and they took cues alternatively from those aspects of the society that were age-old and those that were new. Unbounded optimism masked their essential insecurity. This point of ambiguity, however, was about to dissolve, and in the decade that followed Americans, especially young northerners, became fully modern people.

Recommended Readings

DOCUMENTS: Catharine E. Beecher, *A Treatise on Domestic Economy* (1841); George G. Foster, *New York by Gas-Light* (1850); George T. Strong, *Diary* (4 vols., 1952).

READINGS: (SOCIETY) Stuart M. Blumin, *The Emergence of the Middle Class* (1989); Clifford E. Clark, *The American Family Home* (1986); Kenneth Cmiel, *Democratic Eloquence* (1990); Patricia C. Cohen, *A Calculating People* (1982); Hasia R. Diner, *Erin's Daughters in America* (1983); Karen Halttunen, *Confidence Men and Painted Women* (1982); Kerby Miller, *Emigrants and Exiles* (1985); (POLITICS) K. Jack Bauer, *The Mexican War* (1974); Frederick J. Blue, *The Free Soilers* (1973); Charles H. Brown, *Agents of Manifest Destiny* (1980); Albert H. Z. Carr, *The World and William Walker* (1963); Thomas R. Hietala, *Manifest Design* (1985); Robert W. Johannsen, *To the Halls of the Montezumas* (1985); (BIOGRAPHY) Irving H. Bartlett, *Daniel Webster* (1978); K. Jack Bauer, *Zachary Taylor* (1985); Maurice G. Baxter, *One and Inseparable, Daniel Webster and the Union* (1984); Merrill D. Peterson, *The Great Triumvirate* (1987); Charles Sellers, *James K. Polk* (2 vols., 1957-1966); Kathryn K. Sklar, *Catharine Beecher* (1973).

13

THE SECTIONAL CRISIS, 1852-1861

CHAPTER OVERVIEW: The 1850s started with optimism, a booming economy, and political compromise. The decade ended with raw feelings, a soured economy, and the stormclouds of approaching civil war. If only, Americans both North and South agreed, the issue of slavery had never cursed politics. If only, experienced leaders lamented, the political system had not broken down along sectional lines, smashing the old national parties and bringing in their place militant leaders of new, ideologically charged sectional parties. Other people saw the growing sectional crisis in politics as a symptom of a more fundamental problem, the growing divergence of North and South. Whatever its origins, the sectional crisis had a rhythm and momentum all its own.

The Territorial Slavery Issue Returns, 1852-1854

Although the Democrats won a landslide in 1852 by upholding the Compromise of 1850, northern concern over slavery remained high, as evidenced by large sales for *Uncle Tom's Cabin.* The Pierce administration planned a transcontinental railroad, and to make Chicago the eastern terminus, Senator Stephen A. Douglas from Illinois pushed the Kansas-Nebraska Act through Congress in 1854. This measure allowed each territory to vote on slavery, an idea Douglas called popular sovereignty. The act unleashed a firestorm of controversy that splintered the existing parties and resulted in the formation of two new parties, the free-soil Republicans and the nativist Know-Nothings.

ELECTION OF 1852. In 1852 the Democrats nominated Franklin Pierce of New Hampshire for president on a platform upholding the Compromise of 1850. Pierce, a handsome, amiable senator and former minor general in the Mexican War, exuded charm but had little substance. Known best in Washington for having arrived at the theater several times belligerently drunk, Pierce was considered by northerners to be one of their own, although they might have pondered the ease with which he had received southern votes for the nomination.

The **Whigs**, attempting to repeat their success with Zachary Taylor, picked another Mexican War hero, General Winfield Scott. The Whigs, however, quarreled over a platform, with Scott's northern supporters unwilling to endorse the Compromise, and with southerners angered by Scott's cranky statements about slaveholders. The candidate lived up to his military nickname, "Old Fuss and Feathers," not exactly a term of endearment.

Pierce won in a landslide. The election wrecked the Whig party and affirmed popular support both north and south for the Compromise. Despite this victory, the **slavery** issue remained alive. After 1850 northern states responded to the new Fugitive Slave Law by passing personal liberty laws that enabled local elected officials to try to save black residents from the federal law. Slavecatchers operating in the North risked arrest for kidnapping, and abolitionists defied the Fugitive Slave Law to rescue runaways who had been caught. Celebrated incidents took place in New York, Boston, Syracuse, and Christiana, Pennsylvania. Publicity angered northerners, who hated the federal law, and southerners, who cursed northern defiance.

HARRIET BEECHER STOWE PUBLISHES *UNCLE TOM'S CABIN*, 1852. Meanwhile, Harriet Beecher Stowe, daughter of the prominent **evangelical** minister, Lyman Beecher, had published her great antislavery novel, *Uncle Tom's Cabin* (1852). By 1853 sales topped a million copies. It became the best selling book in the United States before 1880, made Stowe famous, and was turned into a popular drama that played before teary-eyed audiences throughout the North in the 1850s.

Stowe's chilling story combined realism and morality in exactly the mix that her middle-class and largely female audience wanted. Based on facts collected from visits to Kentucky during her own residence in Cincinnati as well as material provided by her abolitionist friends, the white Theodore Weld and the black Frederick Douglass, the book succeeded because it insisted that slavery was a sin for Christians. The South banned the book.

PLANNING A TRANSCONTINENTAL RAILROAD. The undercurrent of growing antislavery sentiment escaped the Pierce administration, which pondered the best route for a **transcontinental railroad**. Surveyors scouted various routes, and when they reported that mountains blocked a potential railroad from New Orleans to Los Angeles via El Paso unless the line went through Tucson — a desert town inside Mexico — the administration moved quickly to acquire the area. The Gadsden Purchase, ratified by the Senate in 1854, added what became southern Arizona and New Mexico to the United States and established the present boundary with Mexico.

The administration debated possible western rail routes. Southerners favored an eastern terminus at New Orleans, but northerners wanted Chicago, and many proposed St. Louis as a compromise. No man was more interested in this rail project than the Young America enthusiast and Chicago real estate speculator, Senator Stephen A. Douglas. "The Little Giant," who had recently moved from the House to the Senate, wanted a Chicago railhead, and he decided to use his position as chair of the Committee on Territories to make this happen. All he had to do was organize the land west of Missouri, hitherto popularly known as the Great American Desert, into a new territory and then give a railroad company huge land grants in that territory as the incentive to build the railroad.

STEPHEN A. DOUGLAS PROMOTES POPULAR SOVEREIGNTY, 1854. In 1854 Douglas found that southern senators would support his bill organizing the territory only if he agreed to two changes. The first change created two territories: Kansas, just west of Missouri, and Nebraska, north of Kansas, including what became the Dakotas. The reason for the two territories became clear with the second change, which repealed the provision in the Missouri Compromise of 1820 that no territory north or west of Missouri would ever have slavery. With this repeal, Kansas and Nebraska would be organized, like New Mexico and Utah, on the principle that the territorial residents should decide whether to adopt slavery.

Boasting of his devotion to democracy, Douglas called this concept "popular sovereignty." Many southerners believed that Missourians would settle Kansas and choose slavery. Douglas doubted that outcome, but, unlike Harriet Beecher Stowe or Frederick Douglass, he did not much care about slavery. He was prepared to accept Kansas as a slave state, if that was what its residents wanted. To Douglas, it was important to organize the area so that land grants could be given to build the transcontinental railroad.

This bill generated a firestorm of opposition throughout the North. In early 1854 mass meetings condemned the proposal. Democratic and Whig newspaper editors, long at each other's throats, joined together to denounce the measure, as did governors, legislators, senators, and congressmen.

One devastating attack came from the abolitionist Senator Salmon P. Chase of Ohio. In a pamphlet, "Appeal of the Independent Democrats," he shrewdly rallied those opposed to territorial slavery, whether Democrats or

Whigs, by arguing that slaveholders had plotted to repeal the Missouri Compromise and seize Kansas. This theory of a **Slave Power** conspiracy had popular appeal.

CONGRESS PASSES THE KANSAS-NEBRASKA ACT, 1854. Despite this opposition, Douglas and the Pierce administration persuaded Congress to pass the Kansas-Nebraska Act. The executive branch used its patronage powers shamelessly, although the final vote in the House was close, 113-100. More curious was Pierce's failure to understand the depth of the anger that had been unleashed. A weak, vacillating man, he had become notorious as a president who always agreed with whatever his last caller wanted. Southern politicians played upon his fears, while everyone who saw Pierce took the precaution of demanding his promises in writing, since he broke his word so often. He broke the written pledges, too. The *New York Herald,* which had supported his election, sarcastically ran a daily column called "Poor Pierce."

A few Democrats, recognizing the danger of the territorial slavery issue to the national nature of their party, tried, in Polk-like fashion, to shift the issue to expansion. In October 1854, three American ambassadors in Europe, James Buchanan, John Y. Mason, and Pierre Soulé, met at Ostend, Belgium, and proposed that the United States buy Cuba from Spain. If Spain refused to sell its colony, which had a large slave population, then the ambassadors suggested that Cuba might be acquired through force. The Ostend Manifesto backfired. Instead of diverting attention from slavery, it only led abolitionists to charge that proslavery Democrats were plotting a war against Spain for the purpose of adding new slave states carved from Cuba to the Union.

REPUBLICANS AND KNOW-NOTHINGS EMERGE, 1854. No law ever produced such a disaster for its supporters as did the Kansas-Nebraska Act. Although northern Democratic officeholders believed that the furor would die down, it did not. Instead, antislavery Whigs and Democrats created a new political coalition, known in various places as the Anti-Nebraska movement, the People's party, or the Republican party. They called for repeal of both the Kansas-Nebraska Act and the Fugitive Slave Law, as well as abolition of slavery in the District of Columbia.

By focusing on the territorial slavery issue, antiadministration politicians appealed to both racists opposed to the presence of any blacks in the West and outright abolitionists. In the fall 1854 elections, northern Democrats who remained loyal to Pierce took a pounding, and a majority in the new House opposed slavery in the territories.

The Republicans, as the opponents of Pierce and Douglas increasingly called themselves, would have done even better, if it had not been for the revival of anti-Catholic and antiimmigrant sentiment in the country's cities. Wherever large numbers of immigrants, and especially Irish Catholics, lived, the native-born surged into another new party, called the American party. Demanding lower taxes, reduced immigration, and a 21-year waiting period for citizenship, the American party gave voters yet another way to protest against the administration.

The American party was a semisecret organization that traced its roots to the founding in 1849 of a secret society, the Order of the Star-Spangled Banner. The party's trappings included a special raised-arm, palm-up salute, a **masonic**-style secret handgrip, and the pledge that members, when asked about the organization, would reply, "I know nothing." To an inquiring member, this code phrase revealed a fellow member.

Claiming that the country had been engulfed by a Catholic, immigrant conspiracy, the Know-Nothings, as they were popularly called, operated with a self-selected secret leadership of political amateurs that picked electoral candidates without supporters' consent. Instead of an open party nominating convention, the leaders privately selected the candidates and printed party ballots, which members received already folded and then dropped into ballot boxes without knowing for whom they had voted.

The Jacksonian political system fractured overnight. In the South the Whig party collapsed, and many white southerners — enthusiastic supporters of Pierce's policy — became Democrats. In the North a few conservative Whigs, fearful of civil war, joined the Democrats, while most Whigs became antislavery Republicans or nativist Know-Nothings. A few Democrats remained loyal to Pierce, often for reasons of **patronage** (such as local postmasters), but antislavery Democrats bolted to the Republicans, and some working-class **Protestant** Democrats in the cities backed the Know-Nothings. No one knew how, or even whether, a stable two-party system could be constructed from these various fragments.

Violence Helps the Republican Party, 1854-1856

A fraudulent election and civil war in Kansas, 1854-1856, proved that popular sovereignty was impractical. To many northerners, Preston Brooks's beating of Charles Sumner with a cane on the floor of the Senate in 1856 only confirmed southern arrogance. Democrat James Buchanan won the presidency in 1856, but John C. Frémont ran surprisingly well as the candidate of the new Republican party, while Millard Fillmore, the Know-Nothing, finished a poor third.

KANSAS BLEEDS, 1854-1856. Popular sovereignty provided a formula for settling the question of slavery in the territories, but how such a formula might work in practice had yet to be tested. Kansas was to show Douglas's theory in action, although not with the results he wanted. Both proslavery and antislavery forces recognized that control of the territorial legislature, which would decide the slavery question, depended ultimately upon the views of the majority of settlers.

The proslavery forces, already living close to the border in Missouri, got an early start in filing land claims and actually moving to Kansas. Few of these Kansans owned slaves, but they were of southern stock, had long lived in the slave state of Missouri, and felt an intense loyalty to the southern conception of white supremacy based on slavery. Antislavery northerners responded by organizing the New England Emigrant Aid Company, which founded the town of Lawrence, Kansas, and settled more than 2,000 pioneers in the territory in two years.

This competition produced hard feelings on both sides. In 1854 and 1855, when Kansans held their first territorial elections, thousands of proslavery Missourians crossed the border and either cast ballots or prevented antislavery residents from voting. Ironically, even without this illegal intervention, there was probably a proslavery majority in Kansas at the time.

Governor Andrew Reeder at first resisted this massive fraud, which the northern newspapers widely reported, but in the end, fearful for his life, he recognized the election returns. The proslavery legislature, contemptuous of the cowardly Reeder, met and passed statutes defending slavery and banning discussion of abolition.

Kansas settlers from the free states denounced the election, the legislature, and its laws, held their own election, and organized a convention at Topeka that drew up an antislavery constitution, which free state voters later ratified. By early 1856 Kansas had two territorial governments. Pierce had appointed the proslavery William Shannon as governor to replace Reeder, but the antislavery settlers had then elected Reeder as their territorial delegate to Congress.

On May 21, 1856, "border ruffians" from Missouri joined proslavery Kansans in attacking the antislavery town of Lawrence. They burned the hotel, where prominent abolitionists had slept, and destroyed the presses of Lawrence's two antislavery newspapers. The northern press exaggerated the incident, in which two lives were lost, as the Sacking of Lawrence. In retaliation, three nights later abolitionist John Brown organized a party that raided the homes of several proslavery settlers and executed five men in what became known as the Pottawatomie Massacre.

Full-scale **guerrilla** war broke out. Henry Ward Beecher, son of Lyman

Beecher and the charismatic minister of a large church in suburban Brooklyn, New York, sent rifles to Kansas in crates marked "Bibles." Shannon resigned as governor, and Pierce appointed John Geary, who restored order with help from the army. Kansas still had no government, as a paralyzed Congress fumed, with the Republicans persuading the House to adopt a plan to admit Kansas as a free state under the Topeka constitution, and with the Democrats getting the Senate to pass a bill calling for new elections. Neither side budged.

THE CANING OF SENATOR CHARLES SUMNER, 1856. Congressional debate grew heated, many politicians carried pistols, and the quiet reconciliatory voice of Henry Clay was missed. Senator Charles Sumner of Massachusetts, one of the new breed of staunch **abolitionists,** spoke passionately about "The Crime against Kansas." Bitter and sarcastic, Sumner condemned Senator Andrew Butler of South Carolina. Butler's nephew, Representative Preston ("Bully") Brooks, thought Sumner had insulted Butler. Had Sumner been a southern gentleman, Butler would have challenged him to a duel. Butler, however, considered Sumner no gentleman and decided to teach the abolitionist a lesson.

Approaching Sumner's Senate desk with a heavy cane, Brooks began to beat the tall, massive Sumner savagely. With his legs pinned under the desk, the senator struggled free, breaking the bolts that held the desk to the floor, and then slumped into unconsciousness, as senators pulled Brooks away.

The northern-dominated House, outraged by Brooks's conduct, tried but failed to get the two-thirds majority necessary to expel him. Brooks then resigned and returned to his South Carolina district, which unanimously reelected him. The ladies of Charleston and other southern cities presented Brooks with gold-headed canes. One was inscribed, "Hit him again."

While Brooks received accolades, Sumner nursed his wounds, both physical and psychological. Claiming poor health, he did not return to the Senate for two years but toured Europe instead, angrily brooding on free speech and the arrogance of southern slaveholders. For many Americans, Sumner's empty Senate desk spoke more eloquently than any speech about where matters stood.

In 1856 the chaos in Kansas and the caning of Sumner permeated northern consciousness. Republicans denounced Douglas's plan of popular sovereignty as a scheme that allowed slaveholders to use fraud and violence to seize territory that they could not have lawfully claimed either under the Missouri Compromise or under a fair and impartial implementation of Douglas's own plan.

At the same time, Republicans believed that Brooks's attack upon Sumner revealed the arrogance of the South's rulers. Not content with controlling the federal government and using manipulation, deceit, and violence to take Kansas, southerners could not stand fair and open debate. Their society, thought Republicans, had been so corrupted by proslavery forces which Republicans now called the Slave Power that it was incapable either of political integrity or of decency.

ELECTION OF 1856. Presidential politics moved in strange, new directions. In 1856 the Know-Nothings nominated Millard Fillmore, the former Whig president and supporter of the Compromise of 1850. The Know-Nothings, however, faced internal divisions. The party included both native-born Catholics who hated immigrants, and non-Catholic immigrants, such as the German "Sag Nichts" (Say Nothings), who despised Catholics. The party's failure to oppose the extension of slavery led some northerners to declare themselves "Know-Somethings" and bolt to the Republicans.

The Republicans faced mixed prospects. Whigs had moved en masse into the Republican party in some states, including New York, under the party boss Thurlow Weed. In Ohio, Salmon P. Chase had created a powerful party by merging Whigs, Democrats, and abolitionists, but in Indiana and Pennsylvania, where the Know-Nothings were strong, the Republicans remained weak.

Few Republican leaders expected the party to win the presidency in 1856, and some, fearing a divided North incapable of handling southern **secession,** preferred to lose. Others felt that the Republicans had to avoid the Whigs' two mistakes: becoming identified with business interests and showing hostility to immigrants. Portraying their party as sympathetic both to workers and to immigrants, Republican leaders believed that the Know-Nothing party would collapse and that antiimmigrant voters could then be obtained without offending immigrants. Most Know-Nothings did eventually join the Republican party, which also attracted Protestant immigrants. To this day, the party has retained its ties to business and has lacked enthusiasm for immigrants.

Pledging to keep slavery out of western territories, but also promising not to seek abolition in the South, the Republicans nominated John C. Frémont, the western explorer, sometime soldier in the Mexican War, and son-in-law of Thomas Hart Benton, Missouri's former Jacksonian senator. Adopting the slogan "**Free Soil,** Free Labor, Free Men, Frémont," the Republicans also praised the dignity of labor.

The Democrats adopted a platform upholding both the Compromise of 1850 and the Kansas-Nebraska Act and, passing over candidates embroiled in the Kansas controversy, nominated James Buchanan, a Pennsylvanian who had been out of the country as ambassador to Great Britain. As the only national party, the Democrats promised to hold the country together. Southern-

Table 13.1. 1856 Presidential Election

Candidate	Party	Popular Vote	Electoral Vote	States Carried
Buchanan	Democrat	1.8 million	174	14 slave, 5 free states
Frémont	Republican	1.3 million	114	11 free states
Fillmore	Know-Nothing	.9 million	8	1 slave state

ers vowed that the election of a Republican would be just cause for secession. Buchanan's strategy was to sweep the South and carry a few northern states to win narrowly in the **electoral college**. As election day approached, pro-Fillmore southerners, recognizing that their candidate had no chance in the North, switched to Buchanan.

Buchanan won by carrying the South, the small free states of California, Illinois, Indiana, and New Jersey, and his home state of Pennsylvania amid charges of massive vote fraud.

Although Buchanan enjoyed a large electoral majority, he received only 45 percent of the popular vote. The election was really two separate sectional races. In the South's Buchanan-Fillmore contest, "Old Buck" handily defeated Fillmore, who carried only Maryland. In the North's Buchanan-Frémont race, Buchanan barely won. He ran well only in traditionally Democratic areas where no New Englanders had settled. The Republicans exceeded their expectations, including a landslide in New York, and looked forward to 1860, when the gain of two or three northern states promised victory.

James Buchanan's Presidency, 1857-1861

In 1857 James Buchanan encouraged the Supreme Court to make a definitive ruling about slavery, but the proslavery Dred Scott decision, far from proving definitive, only enraged the North. When proslavery Kansans tried to get Kansas admitted as a slave state in 1857 under the Lecompton constitution, the president backed the effort, despite evidence that most Kansans then opposed slavery. In 1858 angry northerners voted Republican. In 1859 the abolitionist John Brown tried to lead a slave insurrection beginning in Harper's Ferry, Virginia, which succeeded only in producing panic throughout the South. His execution disgusted the North. The four-way election of 1860, fought sectionally as two two-way races, led to Abraham Lincoln's victory in a bitterly divided country. Sectional conflict had reached its limit.

THE SUPREME COURT ISSUES THE DRED SCOTT DECISION, 1857. James Buchanan arrived in Washington in early 1857, and prior to his inauguration he tried to arrange behind the scenes what he hoped would be the final resolution of the slavery controversy. The Supreme Court had just heard a slavery case, and Buchanan urged the justices to use the occasion to make a definitive declaration about slavery in the territories. An emphatic court decision, he reasoned, would end once and for all the sectional political feud by establishing what the Constitution required.

Five of the nine justices, including Chief Justice Roger Taney, held slaves, and Buchanan must have known how that fact would affect the outcome of the case. In 1834 the owner of Dred Scott, a Missouri slave, had taken him into federal territory north of Missouri that was free under the Missouri Compromise of 1820. After four years, Scott returned with his owner to Missouri. Later, the owner died, and in 1846 Scott sued his new owner in the Missouri courts for freedom, on the grounds that he had gained his freedom by living in free federal territory. After the Missouri supreme court ruled against Scott in 1852, he appealed to the federal court in Missouri, which denied jurisdiction. In 1853 *Dred Scott v. Sandford* reached the U.S. Supreme Court.

In considering this case, the justices faced numerous choices. They might have declined to accept it, or they could have overruled the federal court in Missouri and ordered a trial. Either course would be normal. They might have ruled that Scott had waited too long to bring the case or that Scott should have brought the case while living in federal territory. In other words, many technicalities could have been used to rule against Scott. Or the court could have declared that Scott had gained his freedom by being in free territory, without elaborating whether he had gained that freedom instantly upon entering the territory or only after residing there.

The court, however, used this case to resolve several constitutional issues that had not been argued at trial. On the question of Scott's freedom, the court ruled, 6-3, with all five slaveholders in the majority, that Scott's residence in free territory had not made him free upon his return to Missouri, since he had brought suit as a resident of Missouri, which did not recognize his freedom.

By the same margin the court held both the Missouri Compromise and the popular sovereignty provisions of the Compromise of 1850 unconstitutional, since both laws deprived persons from taking their slave property into federal territory in violation of the Constitution's guarantee of property rights under the due process of law. Congress, in other words, could not ban slavery from any territory. This political idea, often called free soil, was unconstitutional.

The court added, by a 3-2 vote, that Scott had no standing to sue in federal court, because no black could be a citizen of the United States or of any state, since all states had recognized slavery at the time of independence. This part of the decision sought to impose white supremacy upon both the federal government and the states.

Far from settling the slavery controversy, the Dred Scott decision worsened the situation. Defenders of slavery now had the court on their side, but they would find it impossible to exercise their theoretical right to take slaves into any federal territory. Northern opponents announced that they would defy the ruling. Noting that slaveholding justices had issued the majority decision, abolitionists refused to accept the ruling's legitimacy. Instead, northerners increasingly saw the Dred Scott decision as proof of the Republican charge that slaveholders through a Slave Power conspiracy controlled the federal government.

KANSAS'S PROSLAVERY LECOMPTON CONSTITUTION, 1857-1858. Trouble brewed again in Kansas. In 1857 the proslavery legislature, which met at Lecompton, ordered a convention to draft a proposed state constitution. The legislature declined to require the new document to be submitted to a popular vote. In protest Governor John Geary resigned, and Buchanan appointed Robert J. Walker as the new governor. Walker supervised fair elections that gave the free-state faction control of the new territorial legislature.

Recognizing that a proslavery constitution would be voted down by the growing antislavery population of the territory, which now formed a large majority, the proslavery Lecompton constitutional convention proposed a state constitution that would not be submitted for ratification. However, the drafters knew that Congress would not admit a state without some kind of vote. So voters could choose to have the Lecompton constitution "with slavery" or "without slavery." If Kansans voted against slavery, slaves already in residence would remain enslaved.

Walker refused to participate in this scheme, and he went to Washington to consult with Buchanan. To Walker's surprise, the president, under the influence of a proslavery cabinet, declined to back Walker, who resigned. Meanwhile, Senator Stephen A. Douglas had announced his opposition to the Lecompton constitution. In Kansas the free state faction boycotted the Lecompton election, and about 4,000 proslavery voters adopted the constitution with slavery. In early 1858 the new territorial legislature, dominated by the free staters, called a second popular election, boycotted this time by the slave staters, in which free staters cast more than 10,000 votes against the document.

Buchanan then asked Congress to admit Kansas as a state under the proslavery Lecompton constitution. An infuriated Douglas, appalled by how the administration had interpreted popular sovereignty, revolted against the administration, which responded by removing Douglas's supporters from federal office. The Senate accepted Kansas as a slave state, but the House balked.

Finally, Representative William English of Indiana proposed a compromise. Kansans would vote directly on the Lecompton constitution. If they approved it, Kansas would be admitted with extra federal land and money. If they rejected it, Kansas would remain a territory. The English bill passed the House, 112-103, and was adopted by the Senate.

Kansans, however, spurned what Republicans called a federal bribe and voted down the proslavery Lecompton constitution by more than five to one. Although Kansas remained a territory technically open to slavery under the Dred Scott decision, public opinion in Kansas kept slaves out.

THE ADMINISTRATION LOSES THE MIDTERM ELECTIONS, 1858.
Buchanan's administration faced other difficulties. The Panic of 1857 plunged the country into a sudden, sharp recession that led to high unemployment and mass suffering, especially in the North's large cities during the winter of 1857-1858. Southerners, noting that cotton prices remained high and that their region went untouched, said that slavery provided economic stability and that unemployed northern white laborers, largely Irish immigrants, faced a harsh reality no enslaved blacks did.

Not everyone accepted this analysis. Hinton Rowan Helper's book, *The Impending Crisis* (1857), argued that slavery had in fact retarded the South's economic development. The author, a native of North Carolina, saw his book banned in the South and was forced into exile in California. Meanwhile, as often happened during hard times, religious **revivals** swept the northern cities, and the upsurge of evangelicalism did the Democrats no good, since evangelicals leaned toward the Republicans.

Northern exasperation and impatience grew, and Republican leaders spoke with a new bluntness as the 1858 congressional elections approached. In New York, Senator William Henry Seward, considered the party's frontrunner for the next presidential election, called the sectional controversy an "irrepressible conflict."

In Illinois, Abraham Lincoln, the Republican candidate for the Senate, warned, "A house divided against itself cannot stand," adding, "I believe that this nation cannot exist permanently half slave and half free." Running

In 1858 Abraham Lincoln ran against the incumbent U.S. Senator Stephen A. Douglas. The contest led the candidates to a series of debates, which were widely reported in the press around the country. Although Douglas won the election, Lincoln gained name recognition. (ILLINOIS STATE HISTORICAL LIBRARY)

against Douglas, Lincoln engaged his better known rival in a series of seven debates.

At Freeport, in a part of Illinois settled by slavery-hating Yankees, Lincoln asked Douglas how popular sovereignty could be reconciled with the Dred Scott ruling. Douglas replied that, despite the court decision, slavery could not exist without local territorial laws and their enforcement. According to Douglas's new Freeport Doctrine, territorial settlers could actually determine whether slavery would exist or not.

On election day Lincoln won the popular vote but lost the Senate seat, because Douglas's supporters held a narrow margin in the malapportioned legislature, which actually picked the senator. Douglas's fame, Illinois's Democratic tradition, and the Freeport Doctrine enabled Douglas to survive. He was one of only a few northern Democrats to win, and the administration lost control of the House to the Republicans. As the Democrats became weaker in the North, the center of gravity inside the Buchanan administration shifted slowly but subtly to its southern base.

JOHN BROWN RAIDS HARPER'S FERRY, 1859. In 1859 John Brown, already notorious for his Kansas killings, conspired with a small group of abolitionists — "the secret six" — to launch a slave uprising. Brown led 18 men, including two of his sons and five blacks, to Harper's Ferry, Virginia, and seized the federal arsenal. He planned to distribute the arms to Virginia's slaves and then march south with an ever-growing band of armed slaves to end slavery once and for all. Brown's scheme so terrified the slaves he tried to recruit that they fled, and the United States military under command of Colonel Robert E. Lee quickly captured Brown and his followers inside the arsenal.

Virginia tried and executed Brown and the others for treason in a public hanging witnessed by more than 10,000 howling, jeering southerners. This public spectacle, and the fears of slave insurrection that it revealed, appalled the northern newspaper reporters covering the event. Meanwhile, in far-off Boston the evangelical clergy, strongly opposed to slavery, ordered church bells pealed. The fervor of the indignation on both sides did not go unnoticed.

SOUTHERNERS GROW FEARFUL, 1860. As 1860 opened, a wave of fear approaching hysteria swept across the South. Sheriffs stopped **Yankee** peddlers and searched them for abolitionist literature or papers indicating that they planned to lead a slave revolt. Schoolmasters from the North were invited to go home. A northern accent was enough to be told to move on. Rumors of slave insurrections in remote places filled the southern press, but when no hard evidence could be produced to show that a particular revolt had occurred, the report was restated to indicate that heroic southerners had blocked an insurrection just in time.

When some editors pointed out that all was quiet, opponents argued that the absence of overt actions proved that secret undertakings were afoot. Meeting in this curdled atmosphere, southern state legislatures passed laws denouncing abolitionists, prohibiting any discussion of slavery, increasing slave patrols, and enhancing the militia.

ELECTION OF 1860. The discredited Buchanan administration, political party decay, sectional differences, southern fear, and northern anger combined to produce a bizarre atmosphere in 1860. The sour mood reflected both political irritation and lingering economic problems. Americans were increasingly frustrated with the large and growing inequality in the distribution of wealth. Compared with other decades in American history, older people were unusually rich, and younger people particularly poor. The 1850s had favored the wealthy and, to a lesser extent, the middle class. In the North the richest 30 percent owned 92 percent of real estate or other kinds of property. Although many Americans had experienced economic failure, they remained a "go-ahead" people who believed in opportunity and success. Then, as now, they tended to blame current problems on the incumbent in the White House.

The Democrats, the one remaining national party, held their convention in Charleston, South Carolina. High humidity and a gallery packed with raucous locals did not deter the party from adopting a platform upholding popular sovereignty. Southern delegates from eight states, led by William Yancey of Alabama, walked out over the convention's refusal to endorse the Dred Scott decision. Yancey knew that such an endorsement would cause the party to lose in the North, but he did not want the Democrats to win the election. Rather, he wanted a Republican victory that would lead to southern secession and his dream of a new slaveholders' confederacy.

Because party rules required a two-thirds majority for nomination, Douglas could not be nominated, in large part because of southern irritation over his Freeport Doctrine, and after 57 ballots the delegates adjourned. A month later the Northern Democrats met in Baltimore and nominated Douglas. Although he knew that he would lose the election, he was determined not to allow the southerners to take over the party.

A few days later the Southern Democrats also met in Baltimore and, adopting a platform calling for slavery in all the territories, nominated John Breckinridge of Kentucky. The Southern Democrats knew that they could not win in the electoral college, but they calculated that they might succeed if the election had to be decided in the House.

Meanwhile, the Constitutional Union party, composed of conservative southern Whigs and Know-Nothings, had also met in Baltimore and nominated John Bell of Tennessee. They declined to adopt a specific platform beyond a pledge to uphold the Constitution.

The Republicans held their convention in Chicago. Seward was the leading candidate, but party leaders from Indiana and Pennsylvania warned that Seward's inflammatory, radical rhetoric made it impossible for him to carry their states. In addition, Seward had tried unsuccessfully to woo Irish votes and, in the process, had antagonized the Know-Nothings. Seeking a candidate with Seward's antislavery views but without his acid-tongued reputation, the party turned to the trial lawyer Abraham Lincoln. His views were nearly identical to Seward's, but he seemed less likely to irritate southerners, immigrants, or nativists.

Although the Republicans stressed free soil, they also pledged to accept slavery in the South, to seek a higher **tariff** pleasing to both manufacturers and their workers, to build a transcontinental railroad, to encourage immigration, and to enact a homestead law giving farmers free federal land in the West. Southerners disliked most of these proposals, but the Republicans saw no reason to humor the South, where they would get no votes, since they were not even on the ballot.

The election had four candidates, but it was really a two-way contest in

Table 13.2. 1860 Presidential Election

Candidate	Party	Popular Vote	Electoral Vote	States Carried
Lincoln	Republican	1.9 million	180	17 free states, split 1 free state
Douglas	N. Democrat	1.4 million	12	1 slave state, split 1 free state
Breckinridge	S. Democrat	.8 million	72	11 slave states
Bell	Constitutional Union	.6 million	39	3 slave states

each region. Lincoln easily defeated Douglas in the North, where "Honest Abe" got 55 percent of the vote. He won at least 50 percent in every northern state except California, New Jersey, and Oregon. He carried all the states that Frémont had won and added Pennsylvania, Illinois, Indiana, California, and the new states of Oregon and Minnesota. Douglas and Lincoln split New Jersey.

Douglas's only victory came in the border slave state of Missouri. By sweeping the North, the nation's most populous region, Lincoln guaranteed a large electoral victory. Breckinridge carried the South, but Bell won Kentucky, Tennessee, and Virginia — states in the upper South where views about slavery were moderate.

Lincoln's electoral total was impressive, but his share of the popular vote was only 40 percent. Three out of five voters had voted against Lincoln, giving him the lowest popular percentage of any electoral college winner in American history.

Lincoln's political position was unenviable. Most Americans who voted for Lincoln's opponents considered his views — far from representing a majority — to be extreme. His strong support from the North had to be weighed against intense opposition, even loathing, in the South. The constitutional structure for presidential elections favored candidates like Lincoln who had concentrated support in several key states over those like Douglas who had thinner support spread across many states, and it provided no mechanism, such as a runoff election, to allow voters to pick a moderate candidate.

Secession Crisis, 1860-1861

Lincoln's election led South Carolina in December 1860, to carry out its threat to leave the Union, and in early 1861, as a lame duck Congress debated how to solve the crisis with compromise, six other cotton-producing states also seceded and formed the Confederacy. President-elect Lincoln could do little but watch and brood, as President Buchanan vacillated between fatalism and toughness. Lincoln's inaugural address was the last hope for saving the Union as it had been. It was not enough.

SOUTH CAROLINA LEAVES THE UNION, 1860. Throughout the campaign southerners had warned that Lincoln's election would lead the South to leave the Union. Oddly, Republican leaders dismissed these pronouncements as election rhetoric. Only after Lincoln's election, as southerners living in the North began to buy arms and pack bags to return to their home states, did alarm grow.

Within weeks of Lincoln's election, on December 20, 1860, South Carolina's special state convention unanimously declared the state an independent nation free from the federal Union. The Carolinians acted to spur on the other southern states, where their agents carefully cultivated a general southern movement for secession to be followed by the organization of a new, slave-oriented southern confederacy. Such a union, the seceders believed, would combine with divided opinion in the North (as revealed by Douglas's vote in the recent election) either to force Lincoln to recognize the new nation without war or — even more deliciously — to lead Lincoln to resign so that the South might again claim its traditional leadership of the United States.

Congress met in a desperate attempt to save the Union. Wearing Henry Clay's mantle, Senator John Crittenden of Kentucky presented a compromise. He proposed a constitutional amendment pledging that Congress would never interfere with slavery in the South and that slavery would be allowed in western territories below 36° 30', the old Missouri Compromise line. Crittenden found little support for his proposal among either northerners or southerners, who were beginning to leave town, and Republicans insisted that no legislation could be introduced without their prior approval. They did not wish to see the southerners manufacture a crisis to overturn the result of the presidential election.

THE COTTON STATES FORM THE CONFEDERACY, 1861. By February 1861, Mississippi, Florida, Alabama, Georgia, Louisiana, and Texas had joined South Carolina in secession. All were cotton-growing states heavily dependent upon slave labor. The seven states moved quickly to form the Confederate States of America. After adopting a constitution that resembled the United States Constitution, with a clause asserting states' rights and providing for a single six-year term for the president, they elected the Mississippi

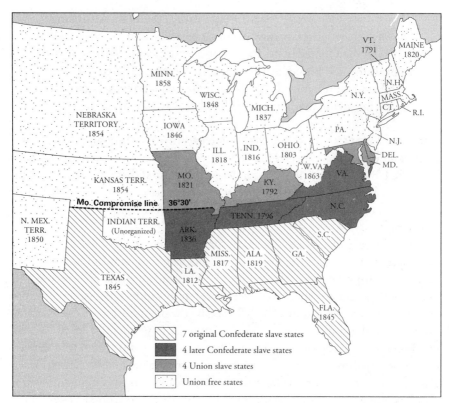

Map 13.1. The United States in 1861

planter and former senator Jefferson Davis as provisional president. The new government's main business was seizing federal property, arming the South, and encouraging secessionists in the upper South.

LINCOLN BROODS AS BUCHANAN VACILLATES, 1861. Lincoln's term did not begin until March 4, and before that date the newly designated secretary of state, William Henry Seward, held negotiations with prominent southerners, particularly Virginians, on the Potomac River. Although Seward expressed a surprising willingness to accommodate the Virginians, whose presence in the Union gave the North many advantages, Lincoln and other Republican leaders feared the appearance of giving away principles under pressure and instructed Seward to break off the talks.

President-elect Lincoln sat quietly in his hometown of Springfield, Illinois. Although he believed strongly that secession was illegal, he avoided comment, because his position gave him no power, and he did not wish to be accused of meddling. Lincoln brought a slender reputation to the presidency. This tall, raw-boned, moody man had less than a year's schooling. A former railsplitter and failed country storekeeper, he had served only one term in Congress. Yet Lincoln had become the West's premier trial lawyer, he had nearly defeated the popular Douglas for a Senate seat, and on an eastern tour in early 1860 he had deeply impressed an important audience in New York. This self-made man, a member of no church but a student of the Bible and Shakespeare, had substance. Even his numerous dirty stories made points.

Meanwhile, President James Buchanan pursued a strange policy. Determined to prevent civil war while still in office, the president allowed members of the administration to negotiate with southerners over federal military facilities in the South. After two southern cabinet members were caught transferring military supplies to the South, they were forced out.

The reorganized cabinet then followed a curious legal theory articulated by Buchanan's attorney general. According to Jeremiah Black, secession was illegal, but so was any attempt by the federal government to coerce states to remain in the Union. Whether intentional or not, this position played into the hands of politicians in the upper South, who asserted that their states would remain in the Union only so long as the federal government did not use force against the states that had left.

In February Lincoln traveled by train from Springfield to Washington. Taking a long route, he gave speeches along the way but had to sneak into Washington in the middle of the night due to the disclosure of an assassination plot in Baltimore. Both cities were infested with secession-minded southerners.

Lincoln agonized over his inaugural address, which he delivered March 4, 1861. He told Americans that he would not touch slavery in the South, that secession was illegal, and that the federal government would not fire the first shot. His policy, designed to keep states like Virginia and Kentucky in the Union, was to wait patiently until the South had returned to reasoned calm and then to welcome the seceding states back into the Union.

Conclusion

The 1850s proved to be uniquely tumultuous for the United States. The apparently stable Jacksonian political structure collapsed. In its place came political chaos and chicanery in the form of the Know-Nothings, and then the earnest morality of the sectionally based Republicans. Both northerners and southerners soured on the Union, with northerners determined to gain control of the federal government for the first time, and with many southerners gradually convincing themselves that they should go their own way rather than live under Yankee rule.

The nation choked on slavery — both its spread into the West and its very existence — as solutions for compromise failed. The Missouri Compromise had divided territory between the two sections, but by the 1840s northerners resisted any new slave territories because they opposed new slave states. Many who did so were racists who wanted a white-only West. Southerners worried that new free states would lead to an antislavery Senate, which, when combined with the populous North's ability to elect a president and a House, might produce a constitutional amendment banning slavery.

Douglas's idea of popular sovereignty was democratic, offered each side hope, and had the advantage of postponing the outcome until some future date when passions ran cooler. Kansas, however, proved the concept unworkable in practice. One might speculate how presidents more competent than Pierce or Buchanan would have handled the controversy. Yet the sense that the crisis was merely a matter of a blundering generation (a view some historians once held) ignores the overwhelming evidence that, no matter who was in charge, the political system could not stand the strain of the issue of slavery and its expansion. Of course, the emergence of such weak leaders as Pierce and Buchanan is itself a comment upon the political structure's difficulties. During the 1850s it seemed as if events, not presidents, were in charge.

Recommended Readings

DOCUMENTS: Hinton R. Helper, *The Impending Crisis* (1857); Robert M. Meyers, ed., *The Children of Pride* (1972); Harriet B. Stowe, *Uncle Tom's Cabin* (1852).

READINGS: (GENERAL) William E. Gienapp, *The Origins of the Republican Party* (1987); Michael F. Holt, *The Political Crisis of the 1850s* (1978); David Potter, *The Impending Crisis* (1976); Richard H. Sewell, *A House Divided* (1988); (1856 ELECTION) Jean H. Baker, *Ambivalent Americans* (1977); Eric Foner, *Free Soil, Free Labor, Free Men* (1970); John R. Mulkern, *The Know-Nothing Party in Massachusetts* (1990); (BUCHANAN'S PRESIDENCY) Stanley W. Campbell, *The Slave Catchers* (1968); David Donald, *Charles Sumner and the Coming of the Civil War* (1974); Don E. Fehrenbacher, *The Dred Scott Case* (1978); Stephen E. Maizlish, *The Triumph of Sectionalism* (1983); Kenneth M. Stampp, *America in 1857* (1990); Mark W. Summers, *The Plundering Generation* (1988); (1860 ELECTION) Benjamin P. Thomas, *Abraham Lincoln* (1952); Glyndon G. Van Deusen, *William Henry Seward* (1967); (SECESSION) Michael P. Johnson, *Toward a Patriarchal Republic* (1977); J. Mills Thornton III, *Politics and Power in a Slave Society* (1978).

14

※

CIVIL WAR, 1861-1865

CHAPTER OVERVIEW: As hope for peace faded, most Americans took comfort in the belief that the coming war would be short and almost bloodless. They were wrong. If 1861 ended the hope for a short war, 1862 brought only frustration. The key year of 1863 marked a turning point in which Union victory began to seem inevitable, but only in 1865 did the Confederacy finally expire. Perhaps it was just as well that no one could see what was coming. If northerners had known the price for saving the Union, they might well have accepted secession; and if southerners had known how much failure would cost, they probably would never have tried to secede. The drama, however, unfolded one act at a time.

The War Begins, 1861

South Carolina's attack on Fort Sumter led Virginia and three other southern states to join the Confederacy, but four border slave states remained in the Union, while patriotism grew in the North. Each side had some key advantages, with the balance favoring the North. Although both northerners and southerners looked for a quick victory, the Union troops' panicky retreat at Bull Run, as well as the Confederates' inability to take advantage of it, predicted a long war.

FORT SUMTER FALLS, 1861. In April 1861, just one month after Lincoln's inauguration, the self-proclaimed sovereign state of South Carolina demanded that the United States army withdraw from Fort Sumter in Charleston harbor. Under orders from President Abraham Lincoln, Major Robert Anderson refused. After learning that the president was sending food to Sumter, the Carolinians decided to attack. On the morning of April 12, Confederate General Pierre G. T. Beauregard's shore guns opened fire, and the following afternoon Anderson surrendered. The Civil War had begun.

Each side had gambled by playing its Sumter card, and the result gave each side hope. The Carolinians believed that their action would force Lincoln into announcing plans to make war against the seceded states, and that his decision would destroy Union sentiment in the South. Wanting to bring the large and important state of Virginia into the Confederacy, the Carolinians tried to stir southern patriotic passions in Richmond. At the time of the attack, a Virginia convention debated leaving the Union, and secessionists had met resistance. Virginia Unionists had taken the Buchanan position, that is, against both **secession** and federal coercion.

Lincoln, over opposition from Secretary of State William Henry Seward and others in his cabinet, had refused to surrender Fort Sumter peacefully, because he felt that northerners would find that cowardly. He did not wish to start a war, but if the Carolinians attacked, he planned to reply in kind.

Psychologically, Lincoln put the Carolinians on the defensive by portraying them as crazed aggressors. This portrayal, he hoped, would keep the upper South's eight remaining **slave** states in the Union. Residents there would surely be reluctant to join a confederacy dominated by the wild, warmongering Carolinians. At the same time, Lincoln believed that the firing on the American flag at Sumter would rally all northerners, even conservative Democrats, to the Union.

VARIED RESPONSES TO FORT SUMTER'S FALL, 1861. Fort Sumter's surrender forced Lincoln's hand. On April 15 he proclaimed a rebellion and asked the states to supply 75,000 volunteers for 90 days' duty to put down the insurrection. Although northern governors quickly rallied, this message received a frosty reception in the upper South. Thus, the Union cause gained popular support in the North but lost ground in the South. On April 17, citing Lincoln's proclamation as evidence of the administration's hostile intentions, the Virginia convention voted, 103-46, to secede.

The Confederates won a great prize. As the home of George Washington and Thomas Jefferson, Virginia had symbolic importance for southerners. More practically, the South needed Richmond's ironworks, and as an added benefit, Virginia's secession led Robert E. Lee, who had turned down Lincoln's offer to command the Federal troops, to join the Confederate army.

Virginia's addition to the Confederacy pushed the new nation further north. This both protected the Deep South from immediate attack and caused the Federals much trouble by threatening the capital at Washington, D.C. In appreciation, the Confederates quickly moved their capital from Montgomery, Alabama, to Richmond, Virginia, which they recognized would be near the center of the coming war. Indeed, many Virginians had been reluctant to secede because they feared, correctly, that a war would largely be fought on their soil.

The secessionists, however, did not get all that they had expected. Although Arkansas, Tennessee, and North Carolina followed Virginia into the Confederacy, many Unionists remained in these states, especially in East Tennessee's mountains.

All the border slave states remained in the Union. Maryland's Unionist governor prevented the secessionist legislature from acting, and a majority of that state's residents, influenced by the large number of Federal troops called to defend Washington, supported the Union. Lincoln used drastic measures, including arrests and the suspension of **habeas corpus,** to secure Maryland.

The Delaware legislature unanimously rejected secession. Kentucky leaders declared their state neutral to prevent war in Kentucky. Missourians quarreled, but Unionists gained control, and the secessionist governor fled. Residents of mountainous western Virginia revolted against the Confederacy and created the new state of West Virginia, which the Union admitted in 1863.

In the North partisanship disappeared, as **Yankees** rallied around Lincoln and the Union cause. Patriotism swept the land, with flags waving everywhere. Senator Stephen A. Douglas denounced secession and vigorously supported war. In the Democratic stronghold of New York City, where Horace Greeley's *New York Tribune* and James Gordon Bennett's *New York Herald* had both clamored for northern concessions and peace during the secession crisis, mobs demanded that these newspapers' offices fly American flags. Greeley, suddenly converted into a war hawk, cheerfully complied. But when the proud, stubborn Bennett resisted, the crowd not only raised Old Glory but forced the publisher to apologize in public.

LOOKING FOR A QUICK VICTORY, 1861. By June, as attitudes hardened and neutrality became virtually impossible, one could calculate each side's advantages and disadvantages in the coming war. The North had 22 million people, an excellent railroad network, numerous factories, and diversified agriculture. Yankees dominated shipping, including overseas trade, and controlled the United States navy. The North did not face physical destruction, since no one believed that the war would be fought on northern soil.

The South had only 9 million people, including 3.5 million slaves, a poor rail grid, little manufacturing, a long coastline with no navy, and agriculture based largely on cotton exports. But the Confederacy did have a few advantages. Southern officers had long predominated in the United States army's combat divisions, so they had valuable experience. Moreover, a war fought in the South would mean that the South's supply lines would be short, that southerners would have excellent knowledge of local conditions, and that they could rally people against invasion.

Although the balance of advantages and disadvantages slightly favored the North, they could be interpreted so as to give the South hope. The North could win only by conquering the South, whereas the South could gain independence, as Americans had during the revolution, merely by holding on until a war-weary enemy gave up. Traditionally, military experts agreed, an offensive force needed a superiority of about three to one in order to win. The North could field more troops than the South, but it was questionable whether the Union's numerical superiority would be sufficient.

The South was physically large, much larger than the North, and the region's mountains, muddy roads, vine-tangled woods, swamps, and poor rail network hampered invaders as much as defenders. To send large armies into the South required an enormous system of support with supply lines running hundreds of miles through hostile territory.

In 1861 many people believed that the war would be decided quickly in a single big battle. Self-delusion aided this belief, since no one wanted a long, bloody war, and people chose to believe that their hopes would be fulfilled. But a few people did fear a long war. Horace Greeley, the reform-minded editor of the *New York Tribune,* spent hours at home on the parlor couch writhing and groaning from the certainty of massive bloodshed. William Tecumseh Sherman privately told government officials that the rebellion could not be put down with fewer than 500,000 soldiers. He predicted huge casualties. The government ignored him, and friends politely suggested he check himself into an insane asylum.

Arrogance also led both sides to a firm conviction in a short war. Yankees recited statistics to prove that the North's advantages made victory inevitable. Residents of New York City boasted that more whites lived inside their city than in all of South Carolina. Just how this fact would enable Lincoln's government to conquer South Carolina went unexplained.

White southerners believed that slavery had taught them how to command, which gave them a military edge. Disdainful of Yankee courage, they also thought that northern leaders would never be able to rally the North's alienated poor whites, especially immigrants, to invade the South.

With a smaller army, the Confederates necessarily chose a defensive military strategy, although at times they did contemplate seizing Washington, D.C. That threat forced the North to deploy troops to guard the capital. The North adopted General Winfield Scott's strategy, called the Anaconda Plan, after the snake that encircles and crushes its victims.

First, the State Department cultivated Britain and France to ensure that they did not recognize the Confederacy. In diplomacy, the South's enthusiasm for slavery in a world opposed to slavery gave the North an edge. Second, the navy planned to blockade the South and cut off both its cotton exports and manufactured imports. This would disrupt the southern economy. Third, the army was to seize important southern cities and then move through the South destroying Confederate arsenals and forces. An early goal was to split the Confederacy by gaining control of the Mississippi River.

YANKEES FLEE BULL RUN, 1861. Northern newspapers and politicians demanded action, and so in July 1861, General Irvin McDowell's Federals marched south from Washington toward Richmond, only 100 miles away. They did not get far. On July 21, at Bull Run, about 25 miles from the capital, McDowell's army of 30,000 men met and fought Beauregard's southern army. Spectators, including members of Congress, took the train from Washington to watch the battle with field glasses. Some even brought champagne for celebrating an anticipated northern victory.

At first the numerically superior Yankees fought well, although Confederate General Thomas J. Jackson refused to budge during a Union assault. Then General Joseph E. Johnston arrived with 9,000 fresh Confederates quickly brought over by rail from the Shenandoah Valley. These soldiers gave the war's first Rebel yell and caused the inexperienced Federal troops to retreat, with increasing panic, to Washington. The spectators fled, too. Amid the chaos, the Confederates might have marched into the capital without opposition. The Rebels, however, were too stunned by their triumph to act.

After Bull Run, called Manassas in the South, both sides recognized that the war would be neither short nor easy. Battles like Bull Run would yield neither southern independence nor Yankee victory. As the northern volunteers' 90-day enlistments expired, Lincoln recognized the difficulties ahead. He reluctantly ordered that new enlistments be for three years. The naval blockade of the South began to take hold, and by late 1861 the navy had captured part of the coastal Carolinas.

On the diplomatic front, the North made limited headway. The British did refuse to allow Confederates to use ports for **privateering.** To avoid war with Britain, however, the North had to release two Confederate agents, James Mason and John Slidell, who had been seized aboard a British vessel, the *Trent,* en route to Britain.

The War Grows Long, 1862

Massive bloodshed and near misses marked 1862. In the West, the war's first big battle took place at Shiloh, Tennessee. In the

East, General George B. McClellan nearly captured the Confederate capital, Richmond, before General Robert E. Lee drove him off. Lee moved into Maryland and was defeated at Antietam on the bloodiest single day of the war, but got away. Lincoln announced plans to free the slaves and enlist black soldiers in the Union army. In 1862 the Confederates adopted a draft. The Federals did so in 1863.

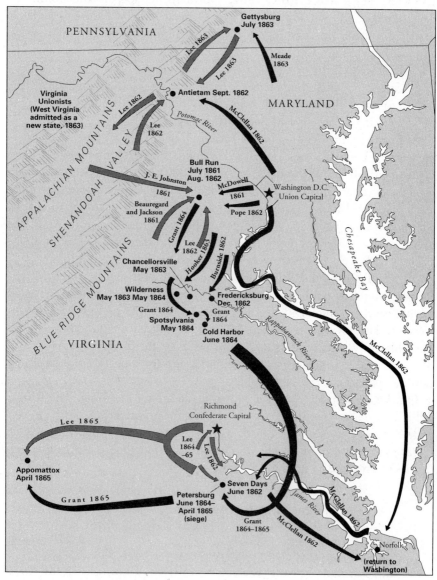

Map 14.1. The Civil War in the East, 1861-1865

THE 1862 CAMPAIGN BEGINS. At the beginning of 1862, during the lull brought on by winter weather, the North held the upper hand. No more states had left the Union, the border slave states had been secured, northern sentiment favored the war, the fighting had moved south, and the area controlled by the Confederacy was visibly shrinking.

In February Union General Ulysses S. Grant, in coordination with a river **flotilla** of gunboats, had captured Fort Henry on the Tennessee River. After nearby Fort Donelson on the Cumberland River fell, the Confederates, under General Albert Sidney Johnston, evacuated Nashville, which Union forces then occupied. In early March a Union victory at Pea Ridge in the Ozarks ended the Confederate military threat to Missouri, although **guerrilla** clashes there continued until the war's end.

JOHNSTON STRIKES GRANT AT SHILOH, 1862. Spring, that most glorious of seasons in the South, sent both sides roaming across the warm, lush

Map 14.2. The Civil War in the West, 1861-1862

landscape. Capturing the Mississippi River and its tributaries, and thus dividing the Confederacy, had been a major northern aim, and in April, following a three-week siege, the Confederates surrendered Island No. 10 in the Mississippi River above Memphis. While some of Grant's troops had been diverted toward this siege, that hard-drinking, cigar-smoking general had taken most of his understrength army further up the Tennessee River toward Alabama.

On April 6 Johnston's Confederates suddenly struck Grant's soldiers in their camp near the country church at Shiloh, Tennessee. A chaotic day of battle ended with Grant's forces exhausted and Johnston dead. During the night Union reinforcements arrived, and the Confederates gained no victory on the battle's second day. They retreated, with northern troops too bloodied for pursuit.

Grant described the field as "so covered with dead that it would have been possible to walk across the clearing, in any direction, without a foot touching the ground." At Shiloh, 13,000 of 63,000 northern soldiers were killed or wounded; the South lost 11,000 of 40,000. In two days more Americans had been killed than in all the country's previous wars put together. Shiloh revealed the sickening reality of civil war.

Toward the end of the month, the Union navy, under Commodore David Farragut, took New Orleans, the Confederacy's largest and most important city, and the key to control of the southern Mississippi River. Army troops under General Benjamin F. Butler occupied the city. Local residents complained about the soldiers' behavior and denounced the general as Butler the Beast. Northerners hoped that the capture of New Orleans predicted, despite Shiloh, an early victory.

MCCLELLAN FLAILS AND FAILS AGAINST RICHMOND, 1862. In the East, the Union cause went less well. The goal, as in 1861, was to take Richmond. Declining to move Federal troops in a direct line south from Washington, General George B. McClellan led his army down the Potomac River, across land near Norfolk, and then up the James River toward Richmond's unguarded back door. At Norfolk, Virginia, the Union ironclad gunship *Monitor* defeated the Confederate ironclad *Virginia,* earlier called the *Merrimac* when in Federal hands, and Norfolk fell to northern control.

By May, McClellan's army had gotten within ten miles of Richmond. Some soldiers heard the city's church bells. However, Confederate General Thomas J. Jackson, now nicknamed "Stonewall" for his stand at Bull Run, kept so many Union troops occupied by his lightning-like maneuvers in the Shenandoah Valley that a portion of McClellan's army had been sent to guard Washington. McClellan, doubting that he had enough men for a successful offensive, also learned that Richmond lacked defenses on its eastern side because the area was an impenetrable swamp.

At the end of the month, General Joseph E. Johnston's Confederates suddenly attacked. (Joe Johnston was not related to Albert Johnston, killed at Shiloh.) McClellan's troops barely avoided a disaster, and, even worse for the Union, Confederate President Jefferson Davis replaced a badly wounded Johnston with the vastly more talented Robert E. Lee as commander. In the Seven Days' Battles beginning on June 26, Lee tried to drive McClellan out of Virginia. Sending Jackson to attack McClellan's flank, Lee struck the Union center. Each day's skirmish ended with the Federals retreating, until they reached a base camp on the James River, protected by gunboats. Although many Confederates died, Lee had driven McClellan from Richmond.

LEE ESCAPES FROM ANTIETAM, 1862. In July Lincoln put McClellan under General Henry W. Halleck's control. Determined to march overland to Richmond, Halleck ordered McClellan to withdraw his army from the Virginia peninsula and return to Washington to go south with General John Pope's army. The concentration of Union troops in Washington left Virginia open and gave Lee the freedom to maneuver. Lee was dangerous when not boxed in. After Jackson destroyed Pope's supply base in northern Virginia, Pope, believing that he faced only Jackson's small army and that Lee remained in Richmond, moved forward to attack.

Using a portion of Lee's troops, General James Longstreet's Confederates struck Pope's flank on August 29, caused a panic, and sent the Federal army across Bull Run to Washington. A Union defeat with heavy casualties, Second Bull Run, also called Second Manassas, cost Pope his command. Bowing to pressure, Lincoln restored the popular McClellan.

Carrying the war into the North for the first time, Lee crossed into Maryland, resupplied his army, and threatened Washington, while Jackson seized military supplies at Harper's Ferry. On September 17 McClellan caught Lee at Antietam, also called Sharpsburg. The bloodiest single day of the war, this Maryland battle produced more than 11,000 casualties on each side. One survivor wrote, "No tongue can tell, no mind conceive, no pen portray the horrible sights I witnessed this morning."

McClellan might have beaten the Confederates or chased them as they retreated into Virginia. Incredibly, however, he did not commit his reserves and settled for a battlefield draw. An exasperated Lincoln wrote McClellan, "If you don't want to use the army, I should like to borrow it for a while." Complaining that the general had "the slows," the president then replaced McClellan with General Ambrose E. Burnside.

Table 14.1. Civil War Commanders

In the East		
Union	Confederate	Battles or Places
Maj. Robert Anderson	Gen. P.G.T. Beauregard	Ft. Sumter, S.C., Apr. 1861
Gen. Irvin McDowell	Beauregard, Gen. Thomas J. Jackson, Gen. Joseph E. Johnston	Bull Run, Va., July 1861
Gen. George B. McClellan	Johnston, Gen. Robert E. Lee, Jackson	Seven Days, Va., June 1862
Gen. Henry W. Halleck, McClellan, Gen. John Pope	Lee, Gen. James Longstreet	Second Bull Run, Va., Aug. 1862
McClellan	Lee	Antietam, Md., Sept. 1862
Gen. Ambrose Burnside	Lee	Fredericksburg, Va., Dec. 1862
Gen. Joseph Hooker	Lee, Jackson	Chancellorsville, Va., May 1863
Gen. George G. Meade	Lee, Gen. Jeb Stuart, Longstreet, Gen. George E. Pickett	Gettysburg, Pa., July 1863
Gen. U.S. Grant	Lee	Wilderness, Va., May 1864
Grant	Lee	Spotsylvania, Va., May 1864
Grant	Lee	Cold Harbor, Va., June 1864
Grant	Lee	Petersburg, Va., June 1864-Apr. 1865
Grant	Lee	Appomattox, Va., Apr. 1865

victors in italics

LINCOLN FREES THE SLAVES, 1862-1863. Since June 1862 the northern cause had been going poorly, and northern opposition to the war was growing. At the same time, as casualty lists grew, Lincoln found it harder to argue that he wanted merely to restore the Union as it had been. **Abolitionists,** in particular, saw the war as a chance to rid the country of slavery once

Table 14.1. Civil War Commanders — cont'd

In the West		
Union	*Confederate*	*Battles or Places*
Gen. U.S. Grant	Gen. Albert S. Johnston	Ft. Henry, Tn., Feb. 1862
Grant	A.S. Johnston	Ft. Donelson, Tn., Feb. 1862
		Pea Ridge, Ark., Mar. 1862
Grant	A.S. Johnston	Island No. 10, Apr. 1862
Grant	A.S. Johnston	Shiloh, Apr. 1862
Commodore David Farragut, Gen. Benjamin F. Butler		New Orleans, Apr. 1862
Gen. Don Carlos Buell	Gen. Braxton Bragg	Perryville, Ky., Oct. 1862
Grant		Vicksburg, Miss., July 1863
Gen. William Rosecrans	*Bragg*	Chickamauga, Ga., Sept. 1863
Gen. George H. Thomas	Bragg	Lookout Mountain, Tn., Nov. 1863
Thomas	Bragg	Missionary Ridge, Tn., Nov. 1863
Gen. William T. Sherman	J.E. Johnston	North Georgia, 1864
Sherman	Gen. John Bell Hood	Atlanta, Ga., Sept. 1864
Sherman	Hood	Savannah, Ga., Dec. 1864
	Hood	Franklin, Tn., Dec. 1864
	Hood	Nashville, Tn., Dec. 1864
Sherman		Columbia, S.C., Feb. 1865

and for all. By this time almost all northerners blamed the war on that institution, and Yankees did not mind ending slavery — especially if it would help the war effort and hurt slaveholders, mostly Confederates, whose power inside a restored Union was feared.

Lincoln's position had been ambivalent. In 1861 he had written Horace Greeley, "If I could save the Union without freeing *any* slaves, I would do it, and if I could save it by freeing *all* the slaves, I would do it, and if I could save it by freeing some and leaving others alone, I would also do that."

As public opinion shifted, Lincoln's policy changed. He considered issuing a proclamation abolishing slavery in the South by emergency wartime presidential decree. Frequently discussed in the cabinet, the proclamation had been held back until after a Union victory. Because Lee had retreated after Antietam, Lincoln decided on September 23, 1862, to make a preliminary announcement.

The president, at that moment, freed no slaves but warned that he would do so shortly if the war continued. On January 1, 1863, Lincoln issued the **Emancipation Proclamation.** This document did not actually free any slaves. It touched neither those in the loyal border slave states nor those in portions of the Confederacy already under Union control. It promised freedom to any slave in areas then under Confederate control, but this promise would be meaningless unless Federal troops advanced.

Lincoln, however, understood that the North could no longer stomach slavery. Already, Congress was preparing to abolish the institution in the District of Columbia, and Lincoln urged the border slave states to adopt plans for **compensated emancipation.**

The war had thrown slavery into crisis. From the beginning northerners noticed that the Confederates used slave labor to build fortresses and other military facilities. In 1861, when Union troops invaded parts of the Confederacy, slaves frequently fled into the northern lines. A few commanders gave the blacks freedom, while others respected property rights and returned slaves to their owners. Both policies caused political problems, and finally the army decided to treat the slaves as **"contraband,"** like captured enemy guns or ammunition.

The contrabands, as the runaway slaves were called, would not be returned to the enemy. Nor would they be free. Rather, the army would hold them in camps until a later date. Meanwhile, they could dig ditches and build **breast-works** and perform other useful labor for the Union cause.

More and more northerners questioned this limited use of black manpower. If the war was about slavery, why not arm the blacks and send them into battle to fight for their own freedom? Many Yankees, however, hesitated to adopt this policy. Some feared that the blacks would make poor soldiers. Others worried that using black soldiers would enrage white southerners and prolong the war. As casualty lists grew, many white northerners concluded that freeing the slaves and arming black soldiers were necessary to win the war.

BOTH SIDES DRAFT SOLDIERS. In April 1862 the South had adopted a military **draft** in order to raise larger armies. This draft law provoked resistance. It also contained occupational deferments, and the South suddenly sprouted many new schoolmasters and parsons. The greatest bitterness, however, was caused by a provision that allowed any planter who owned 20 or more slaves to claim an exemption. By war's end perhaps a million men, some more willingly than others, had donned Confederate gray.

In 1862 the North decided to recruit black soldiers in place of a draft. By war's end about 180,000 Union soldiers were black. Half were recruited from the Confederacy, but some were under northern sponsorship, as in the case of the famous Massachusetts 54th Regiment. As Frederick Douglass predicted, willingness to die for the Union gave African-Americans a stronger claim to citizens' rights.

In 1863 the North enacted a draft, which lacked the South's occupational deferments but did provide an exemption upon payment of $300. Poor men pooled money to protect themselves. The draft did not apply to the western states or territories, to which some men escaped. Willingly or not, more than 1.8 million men served in the Union army.

After Antietam, the war had not gone well for the Union. In the West, Confederate General Braxton Bragg invaded Kentucky, and although stopped at Perryville in October 1862, he had challenged northern control of that state. Bragg's army continued to threaten Tennessee, and the Federals had to station troops there that distracted from the Union effort to take the Confederate river stronghold of Vicksburg, Mississippi.

In the East, Union General Burnside in December launched costly and stupid frontal assaults at Fredericksburg, Virginia. Watching the slaughter, Lee observed, "It is well that war is so terrible — we should grow too fond of it." Lincoln replaced Burnside with General Joseph Hooker. Hearing that "Fighting Joe" Hooker thought the country needed a dictator, presumably himself, Lincoln wrote him, "Only those generals who gain success can set up dictators." The president continued to look for a general who could outwit Lee. As the year ended, southerners still hoped for independence, and northerners wondered if victory would ever come.

The Key Year, 1863

Abroad, diplomacy prevented recognition of the Confederacy, but at home the Federals made no progress in defeating Lee in Virginia, even as Grant captured Vicksburg and the Mississippi River. Lee entered Pennsylvania and fought General George G. Meade at Gettysburg. This battle, the largest ever fought in North America, marked a turning point in the war. Never again would Confederate troops threaten the North, and, as Lee knew, a purely defensive Confederate strategy made a northern victory likely. Lincoln's Gettysburg Address brilliantly expressed Union war aims. The home front witnessed labor restlessness, strained family life, alienated intellectuals, and sustained support for the war.

WAR RESUMES ON ALL FRONTS. Although the British had not recognized the Confederacy, they had allowed the South to build naval raiding ships in Britain. Two raiders, the *Florida* and the *Alabama,* destroyed much northern shipping in the Atlantic Ocean, and when the American government learned that the Confederates were about to launch another newly built ship in Britain, the American ambassador, Charles Francis Adams, protested and persuaded the British government to block its sailing. British courts, however, eventually released the ship to its Confederate owners, thus again straining Anglo-American relations.

Spring 1863 brought a resumption of the war in Virginia. On May 2, Hooker's 130,000 Federals advanced against Lee's 60,000 Confederates at Chancellorsville on the Rappahannock River halfway between Washington and Richmond. Lee sent Stonewall Jackson's army to attack Hooker's right through an area of tangled vines and briars called the Wilderness. Taken completely by surprise, Union troops retreated in confusion. Before Hooker could reorganize his right, Lee engaged Hooker's main and left forces while they tried to cross the river. Lee's artillery controlled the high ground; on May 5 Hooker withdrew to the river's north bank.

Although the battle saved Richmond, the Confederates paid dearly. More southerners than Yankees were killed, and among the dead was Stonewall Jackson, accidentally shot by his own men. Of Jackson, Lee said, "I have lost my right arm."

Meanwhile, Union General Ulysses S. Grant had marched his troops past the Confederate stronghold at Vicksburg on the opposite, western side of the Mississippi River. His supply boats ran the river under Confederate guns in the middle of the night, picked up Grant's men, and ferried them to the Vicksburg side.

Then Grant began a siege that forced the 30,000 Confederates inside the city to the brink of starvation. Eating dogs, cats, and rats and hopelessly penned in, the Vicksburg defenders surrendered on July 4. Within a few days the last Confederate outpost on the Mississippi fell, leaving the river totally in Union hands. The Confederacy had been sliced in two. "The Father of Waters," said Lincoln, "flows unvexed to the sea."

Aware of the desperate situation in the West, Lee decided to be bold in the

East. In June, Lee's troops, always in need of supplies, moved north through the Shenandoah Valley, crossed the Potomac, and advanced into southern Pennsylvania, a lush agricultural area previously untouched by the war. Jeb Stuart's cavalry rounded up livestock for Lee's army, but while Stuart was busy seizing provisions, Lee lost track of Hooker's Federal army, which had moved into Maryland to protect Washington.

Although Hooker wanted to attack Richmond, which was no longer defended, panic in Washington over Lee's possible moves against Washington, Baltimore, or Philadelphia made that idea impossible. "Lee's *army,* and not *Richmond,*" an exasperated Lincoln wrote to Hooker, "is your true objective." Bickering inside the military led Lincoln to replace Hooker with General George G. Meade.

Neither army knew the exact location of the enemy's main force. Then on June 30 a small portion of each army made a chance contact at Gettysburg, Pennsylvania, and set the stage for a great battle — the greatest ever fought in North America, with 150,000 combatants.

LEE FIGHTS MEADE AT GETTYSBURG, 1863. On July 1, 1863, the Confederates drove the Union troops out of Gettysburg into defensive positions atop Cemetery Hill and Culp's Hill. Across the way Lee's troops occupied Seminary Ridge, which was somewhat lower. Meade had 15,000 more soldiers, better **artillery,** and a better geographical position. Union forces repelled Confederate attacks and won the day. Lee, however, remained on the field.

By July 2 Lee's remaining forces had reached the site, and he attacked. Fresh Union troops had also arrived, and the Confederates lost the crest of Seminary Ridge.

On July 3 Confederate assaults on Culp's Hill and Little Round Top failed. The latter position, which nearly fell, would have enabled Confederate artillery to have raked the entire Union army. In a last, desperate attempt to gain victory, Lee ordered General James Longstreet to attack the Union center. Lee hoped to break through, split the Union forces in half, and march directly into Washington.

After laying down heavy artillery fire to knock out the Federal guns, three **divisions,** including one led by General George E. Pickett, assaulted the Union position. As they approached the Union high ground, the Federal artillery and troops opened fire and mowed them down. Much of Pickett's 5,000-man division literally disappeared, leaving only tiny pieces of cloth, bone, and blood on the ground.

Gettysburg, more than any earlier battle, revealed the new, harsh reality of war. No longer did soldiers prove courage in fierce hand-to-hand fighting with bayonets fixed. No longer did individual marksmanship with a rifle count, although Americans had long exaggerated the importance of such skills. Soldiers no longer even saw the enemy, as they fired rifles that shot faster and more accurately up to half a mile. Now generals commanded vast hordes of men, called armies, to be slaughtered impersonally by distant artillery, beyond sight but no less deadly. Before the war's end mechanized **Gatling guns** would vomit such streams of hot, sharp metal that no human being could survive. These facts favored the defense, if entrenched. Taking the offense led to casualties of 50 percent or more.

Lee, a soldier of the old school, had mistaken the silence of the Union artillery as proof that his own guns had destroyed the enemy's pieces. It was a fantasy he wanted to believe. In fact, the Confederate artillery had overshot the Union guns, causing little damage. Then Lee had ordered Pickett's

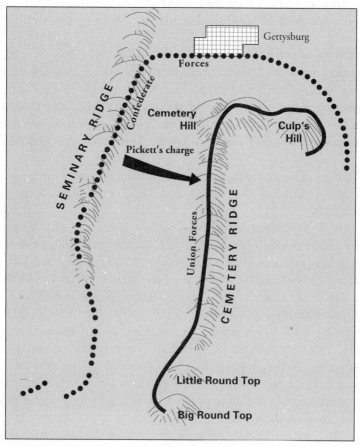

Map 14.3. Gettysburg

charge. That gesture — deeply rooted in Lee's romanticism — had cost him the battle, many of his best soldiers, and, indirectly, the war.

THE AFTERMATH OF GETTYSBURG. On July 4 Lee retreated to the Potomac River, which was flooding. Meade followed but did not attack. The river subsided, and in the middle of the night Lee fled back to Virginia. At Gettysburg the more than 7,000 dead were still being buried. More than 40,000 men from the two armies had been wounded or were missing.

On November 19 a national cemetery was dedicated at Gettysburg. Lincoln spoke for five minutes. His Gettysburg Address, widely printed in the newspapers, expressed northern resolve to see the war to its conclusion. It also showed Lincoln's unusual devotion to "government of the people, by the people, for the people."

Most important, however, was the president's understanding of the sacrifices that had been made at Gettysburg. Neither sentimentalizing nor trivializing what had happened, Lincoln stated that the true meaning of these deaths would be defined by the subsequent devotion that Unionists showed for their cause.

Gettysburg marked a turning point. Never again did the Confederates have a large enough army to threaten the North. Lee was forced to adopt a more defensive strategy that both inhibited his own daring and predicted a war of attrition that the North would ultimately win. After Gettysburg, the South also lost its hope for diplomatic recognition by Britain or France, and the British government confiscated Confederate ships being built in British shipyards.

Gettysburg, however, did not conclude the war, and the North had to win on the ground. On September 19 at Chickamauga, Georgia, just outside Chattanooga, Tennessee, General Braxton Bragg's Confederates produced a panic in General William Rosecrans's Union ranks. Federal troops retreated to Chattanooga and were all but surrounded.

Grant, in command in the West, replaced the luckless Rosecrans with General George H. Thomas, whose stand at Chickamauga had prevented a rout. Thomas, now called the "Rock of Chickamauga," drove the Rebels from Lookout Mountain and on November 25, in an unusually successful frontal attack, off Missionary Ridge. Chattanooga was secure. As both armies settled in for the winter, Chattanooga looked like a Union dagger pointed at the Confederacy's heart.

THE WAR AT HOME. As the war dragged on, it changed the way people lived, worked, and thought. By 1863 the North had more than 900,000 men in arms; the South, half that many. Tremendous labor shortages developed in

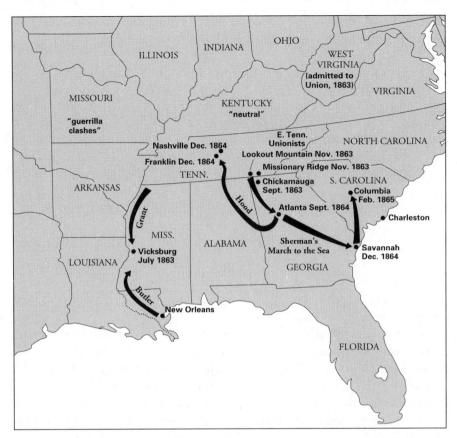

Map 14.4. The Civil War in the West, 1863-1865

both regions, and wages soared. Apprentices left unpaid labor to be hired as journeymen, and skilled workers, threatening to strike, demanded and got large pay raises. Many previously unorganized northern workers set up unions, and the Republican party, a coalition of business and labor hostile to slavery and cheap imports, cultivated workers.

Northern workers, however, became frustrated, because wage increases did not keep up with rising prices. Their standard of living declined. With so many skilled workers in the army, economic productivity lagged, even though women joined the workforce in unprecedented numbers as seamstresses, as teachers, and as **munitions** workers. In the South, Richmond and other cities had food shortages and bread riots. **Speculators** in both sections made fortunes illegally trading southern cotton for northern food.

Both North and South had trouble financing the war. Taxes were raised, including higher **tariffs** and the first federal income tax in the North and a tax of 10 percent payable "in kind" on all agricultural production in the South. Revenues, however, proved insufficient, and both sides resorted to selling bonds and the Revolutionary War expedient of printing paper money. The Confederates issued $1 billion in paper money, which brought hyperinflation and eventually became a bad joke. The North's **greenbacks** greatly increased the money supply and caused prices to double by war's end, when the national debt had reached $2.8 billion.

AMERICANS EXPRESS THOUGHTS AND FEELINGS ABOUT THE WAR. Compassion grew with the casualty lists, as both northern and southern women organized hospitals for the soldiers. They wrapped bandages, cooked meals, and nursed the wounded or sick. Told about the horrible suffering on the battlefields, the nurse Clara Barton and others took nursing directly to the front, where soldiers were most in need. All but ignored by the army and the federal bureaucracy, Barton received official recognition for her services only late in the war. In 1881 she founded the American Red Cross.

During the war northern intellectuals noticed that many soldiers died in army camps from disease. In fact, twice as many died in this way as in battle. Soldiers ignored regulations requiring them to dig and use latrines remote from water supplies. Unsanitary conditions, spoiled food, and lack of proper clothing in harsh weather led to many deaths.

A group of intellectuals, many of them pacifists and almost all abolitionists, set up the United States Sanitary Commission to inspect military camps. This body, led by the urban park planner Frederic Law Olmsted, collected health statistics and made practical recommendations that the Union army generally adopted.

Many Americans believed that civil war had been visited upon the nation as a just punishment for the sin of slavery. According to this view, which grew as the war raged on, both North and South had to pay a price for redemption. The South suffered for maintaining slavery, the North for not opposing slavery sufficiently in earlier years.

The songwriter Julia Ward Howe expressed this idea in her great war song, "The Battle Hymn of the Republic." According to Howe, Yankee soldiers battled at God's side, "trampling out the vintage where the grapes of wrath are stored," marching on with "His Truth." War, evangelical religion, and politics had become intertwined.

The South replied with "Dixie," a jaunty minstrel tune written by Dan Emmett, a Yankee, just before the war. The Confederacy's unofficial anthem, "Dixie" bouyed southern hopes even as it romantically and nostalgically portrayed a landscape dominated by cotton. This song stressed patriotism based on attachment to a locale. The Yankees, it suggested, had no right to invade the South. "I'll take my stand," went the lyrics, "to live and die for Dixie." This song's popularity led the South to be called Dixie.

In 1863 southerners took hope less from the battlefield than from signs of strain evident in the North. The Yankees might, after all, give up and go home. The first Union army draft had provoked serious riots, especially in New York City, where mobs of Irish immigrants spent four days in July attacking draft officials, demolishing abolitionists' homes, and lynching blacks. Lincoln was forced to send Federal troops to put down the disturbance.

Southerners incorrectly concluded that the ethnically diverse North would unravel. In fact, most northern immigrants strongly backed the war. Immigrants, mostly German and Irish, made up one-quarter of the Union army and composed such units as New York's famous "Fighting Irish" 69th Regiment.

The Confederacy Crumbles, 1864-1865

In 1864 Grant's slow movement toward Richmond and Sherman's capture of Atlanta provided visible proof of Union success. It came just in time to save Lincoln's otherwise doubtful bid for reelection. Sherman's march to Savannah and through South Carolina, a string of Confederate defeats, and Lee's evacuation of Richmond in April 1865 brought the war to a rapid close. Within days Lincoln was assassinated. Victory had not been cheap, and outwardly intense nationalism masked a dark undercurrent in the reunited country.

GRANT AND SHERMAN MOVE SOUTH, 1864. Noting Union success in the West, Lincoln at last called Grant to command Federal forces in the East. As the spring 1864 campaign opened, Grant's forces slogged on from Washington toward Richmond. Although the Union controlled the Shenandoah Valley and had plenty of troops along the James River southeast of Richmond, Grant's 100,000 Federals found it difficult to move against Lee's 60,000 Confederates.

In May in the Wilderness and at Spotsylvania Lee outmaneuvered the larger Union army and inflicted heavy casualties. Grant, unlike McClellan, calmly accepted these losses. Amid this grim war of attrition, Grant said, "I propose to fight it out along this line, if it takes all summer." On June 3 Grant's army failed in an assault at Cold Harbor. In one month Grant had suffered 60,000 casualties. Lee, however, had lost as many as 30,000 men.

While more Yankees would soon join Grant's force, Lee's casualties could not be replaced.

Changing his strategy, Grant moved his forces south of the James River and rushed to capture Petersburg, 25 miles south of Richmond. The Federals were unable to avoid tipping off the Confederates, and Lee reinforced Petersburg. In mid-June a Union attack failed, and Grant laid siege to Petersburg. The Confederates, however, were not trapped as they had been at Vicksburg. Southern forces controlled the railroad to Richmond, and one line there remained open to supplies from southwestern Virginia. In July the Union's attempt to blow up the Confederate forces at Petersburg by an underground mine produced what was called the war's single biggest explosion, but this experiment did not break the siege.

The Union enjoyed greater success in the West, where in May General William Tecumseh Sherman's 100,000-man army had marched from Chattanooga through north Georgia toward Atlanta. Already eyeing Savannah and the Atlantic Ocean, Sherman intended to split the remaining Confederacy in two and destroy so much property that Georgia could no longer provision southern forces. After southern General Joseph E. Johnston's 60,000-man army failed to check Sherman's advance, President Jefferson Davis replaced Johnston with General John Bell Hood. The key city of Atlanta, an industrial and rail center, fell on September 2, 1864. The southern diarist Mary Chesnut wrote, "There is no hope."

ELECTION OF 1864. Throughout the summer and fall, presidential politics engaged people both north and south. Confederates believed that high northern casualties might lead to Lincoln's defeat by a candidate willing to open peace negotiations with the South. Unionists looked desperately for military successes to plead for Lincoln's reelection. At times, the president himself doubted that he could be reelected.

To improve his chances, Lincoln agreed to accept as his running mate Andrew Johnson of Tennessee. The only senator from a seceded state who had remained loyal to the United States and had stayed in Congress when other southerners resigned, Johnson was a conservative War Democrat. In putting him on the ticket, Republicans dropped their party name and adopted a pro-war, bipartisan Union ticket.

The Democrats nominated McClellan on an antiwar platform. He accepted the nomination but rejected the platform. He dodged the issue because northern Democrats were divided. Nevertheless, Lincoln's defeat would have been such a repudiation of the war that it could hardly have been continued. In some parts of the North, especially in sections of the Midwest where southerners had settled, opposition to the war had been growing. Clement Vallandingham, a popular Democratic orator from Ohio, led the Copperheads, a faction of the Democrats who sought a peace treaty recognizing the Confederacy. Vallandingham endorsed McClellan.

Republican party leaders took this threat seriously. Nineteen states gave Union soldiers the right to vote by absentee ballot. Lincoln got three-quarters of the soldier vote. As it turned out, Grant's determination at Richmond's door and Sherman's success in Georgia, along with McClellan's lack of political skills, tipped the balance to Lincoln, who won reelection, though by a fairly narrow popular margin.

THE CONFEDERACY DISAPPEARS, 1864-1865. While the presidential campaign proceeded, Hood's Confederates harassed Sherman's long supply line, and Sherman sent part of his army to protect Tennessee. Vowing to "make war so terrible . . . that generations would pass before they could appeal to it," Sherman marched through Georgia to the sea in a path 60 miles wide, foraging off the land and burning cotton, factories, warehouses, and bridges along the way. "The fields were trampled down," wrote one Georgia woman, "and the road was lined with carcasses of horses, hogs, and cattle that the invaders, unable either to consume or to carry away with them, had wantonly shot down to starve our people and prevent them from making their crops."

Sherman entered Savannah on December 22, 1864, and gave the city to Lincoln as a Christmas present. Meanwhile, Hood's Confederates had been defeated at Franklin, Tennessee, and two weeks later at Nashville, when his army essentially disintegrated.

As the area controlled by the Confederacy shrank further, food shortages developed, rail transport failed, and up to half the South's soldiers deserted. Sherman marched and burned his way through South Carolina, which as the initiator of secession, was singled out for harsh treatment. On February 17, 1865, the Federals burned the capital city of Columbia. Sherman planned to proceed through the Carolinas and link up with Grant near Richmond.

Events then occurred with dizzying speed. On April 2, 1865, Lee abandoned Petersburg and Richmond, taking his army westward. Three days later Lincoln reasserted federal civilian authority by visiting Richmond. Blacks swarmed around him while Confederates remained indoors. Then on April 9, realizing the hopelessness of the military situation, Lee surrendered his army to Grant at Appomattox Courthouse, eighty miles west of Richmond.

Lincoln and his cabinet discussed postwar policies, and on April 14 a warweary president went to Ford's Theater, where the actor and Confederate sympathizer John Wilkes Booth shot the president. Lincoln died the next day.

Booth's act had been part of a conspiracy, and Secretary of State William Henry Seward had also been attacked, although he survived. After a wild escape on a horse, Booth was trapped in a barn and, refusing to surrender, was killed by the army. Nine suspects were arrested, and four were hanged.

On April 18, Johnston surrendered to Sherman in North Carolina, and on May 26 a final surrender took place in New Orleans. Meanwhile, Jefferson Davis had been captured while fleeing through Georgia. A favorite Union song promised, "We will hang Jeff Davis from a sour apple tree," but he was not hanged.

CALCULATING THE FINAL BALANCE. The Civil War ended both the idea of secession and slavery. Of the 2.8 million men who fought in the war, 620,000, more than one-fifth, had died. Perhaps more astonishing than the total number of deaths — greater than in all other American wars combined —was the high rate of military service. In the frontier state of Iowa, for example, half of all white males of military age fought, creating 46 separate **regiments.** The South — facing invasion, with a small white population, with a long military tradition including the recent Mexican War, and with an early draft —had both greater participation and a higher death rate. In that region, one-quarter of the white males of military age died in the war. Nationally, the figure was close to one-sixth. This is a death rate similar to that Germany or France suffered in World War I.

After the war Harriet Beecher Stowe wrote that on every block in every town, at least one person had died. Not a family in the United States had escaped. Everyone had lost a father, a son, a husband, a brother, or at the least an uncle, a nephew, or a cousin. Many families, of course, had lost more than one member. Stowe herself was not untouched. One son, badly wounded, had been given morphine for the pain, became an addict, and destroyed himself. The death lists do not include those who died later from wartime injuries, amputated limbs, or psychological trauma.

Nor do casualty rates reveal the way the war seared the American soul. Before the war, since Andrew Jackson's time, Americans had seen their society as a perfect model for the world. The war, however, had revealed deep flaws in this particular model of democracy. After the war, Americans outwardly expressed optimism, but deep, dark forebodings had entered the American psyche. Serious people found it difficult to reconcile the national calamity with prospects for a brighter tomorrow. Cynicism grew and the nation behaved as though it had entered a permanent period of mourning.

Throughout the North, intense nationalism masked these anxieties. Yankees concluded that the nation could accomplish any difficult task, if only it put its mind to it. This "can-do" spirit reaffirmed that Americans were a special, "go-ahead" people. Noticing that the war had been won by vast armies commanded with discipline and backed by ingenious inventions and staggering industrial capacity, Americans concluded that the nation's future demanded large-scale organizations with power concentrated at the top. Individuals must sacrifice both themselves and their rights to the nation's greater needs. Giant corporations, like large armies, could achieve spectacular success. The purpose of government, then, was to foster and encourage such organizations.

Rejecting Jefferson's idea of minimal government, Americans now accepted that government, and particularly the federal government, must play a large role in national life. At the same time, Americans, like Jefferson, retained their innate suspicion of putting power into the hands of a single person. Thus, increasing federal power took the form of a weakened presidency and a stronger Congress and larger bureaucracy. Americans favored the popularly elected House of Representatives, which for the only time in history assumed prominence.

After the war, the federal government built two buildings in Washington, D.C., that revealed these new attitudes. The Pension Building, which housed an army of bureaucrats hired to manage veterans' affairs, featured an exterior **frieze** portraying thousands of real Union soldiers. The large, lavishly decorated Library of Congress both glorified the nation and offered the learning found in books as the key to America's future.

A simpler, more innocent United States had vanished. Americans no longer saw expansion as a way to resolve or postpone resolution of political differences, as they had during James K. Polk's presidency. They recognized that states' rights, a doctrine originally invented to protect the individual from centralized federal power, had so weakened the federal government during James Buchanan's presidency that southerners adopted the delusionary view that they could unilaterally break up the Union.

The Constitution's checks and balances had failed to prevent secession, and the war had been won by at times putting the national interest ahead of a **strict construction** of the Constitution. Legal mechanisms had validity only when credibly defended upon the battlefield. A government existed only when people sacrificed and died for its existence. In the end, both secession and slavery ceased because Americans were willing to die in order to kill those ideas.

Conclusion

The Civil War decided the issues of secession and slavery, and in doing so, greatly diminished states' rights and enhanced national power. Before the Civil War, many Americans said, "The United States are . . . " After, they said, "The United States is . . . " The war's high price, however, did much to temper American idealism and optimism. Southerners found the war a bitter experience from which they did not fully recover, either psychologically or economically, for a hundred years. Northerners discovered common bonds that eased class, ethnic, and racial tensions. Industry and labor had both rallied to the Union, and immigrants' strong support for the war caused a sharp decline in nativist sentiments. Black participation in the war helped African-Americans win new rights.

Politically, Republicans emerged as the nation's guardians, while Democrats remained tainted with treason for a generation. The Republicans, a crazy-quilt coalition glued together by wartime solidarity, became the dominant political party for two generations. Even before the war's end, they had passed laws to build a transcontinental railroad from Omaha to Sacramento, to give free western land to settlers (Homestead Act, 1862), and to use federal money to support colleges (Morrill Act, 1862). These actions symbolized the growth of northern, federal, and business power as the nation remade itself. The old federation of states had died, and a new nation had been born.

Recommended Readings

DOCUMENTS: Mary Chesnut, *Mary Chesnut's Civil War* (1981); U.S. Grant, *Personal Memoirs* (2 vols., 1885); Thomas W. Higginson, *Army Life in a Black Regiment* (1870); Sam R. Watkins, *Co. Aytch* (1962).

READINGS: (GENERAL) Shelby Foote, *The Civil War* (3 vols., 1958-1974); James M. McPherson, *Battle Cry of Freedom* (1988); Phillip S. Paludan, *A People's Contest* (1988); Emory M. Thomas, *The Confederate Nation* (1979); (THE WAR) Thomas L. Connelly, *The Marble Man* (1977); James L. McDonough, *Shiloh* (1977); William S. McFeely, *Grant* (1981); Reid Mitchell, *Civil War Soldiers* (1988); Charles Royster, *The Destructive War* (1991); Robert G. Tanner, *Stonewall in the Valley* (1976); (RACE) Herman Belz, *Emancipation and Equal Rights* (1978); V. Jacque Voegeli, *Free But Not Equal* (1967); (WAR AT HOME) Iver C. Bernstein, *The New York City Draft Riots* (1990); Allan G. Bogue, *The Congressman's Civil War* (1989); Adrian Cook, *The Armies of the Streets* (1974); George M. Frederickson, *The Inner Civil War* (1965); Mary E. Massey, *Bonnet Brigades* (1966), and *Refugee Life in the Confederacy* (1964); David Montgomery, *Beyond Equality* (1967); Arnold M. Shankman, *The Pennsylvania Antiwar Movement* (1980).

15

——— ✖ ———

RECONSTRUCTION, 1863-1877

CHAPTER OVERVIEW: Wartime chaos forced the adoption of Reconstruction policies even before the Civil War ended. In 1865-1866, President Andrew Johnson and the Radical Republican majority in Congress fought bitterly over policy. Congress won and in 1867-1868 it imposed harsh Reconstruction policies on the South. Blacks gained political rights but lacked economic security, and southern whites responded with anger, intimidation, and violence. By the early 1870s Republican rule in the South began to fail, and the last Radical governments were sold out in the bargain over the presidential election of 1876.

Wartime Reconstruction, 1863-1865

Reconstruction began in 1863 as a wartime experiment at Port Royal, South Carolina, when thousands of slaves came under Union army control. Late in that year President Abraham Lincoln proposed formal rules for readmitting the southern states to the Union, but Radicals in Congress found these rules too mild and in 1864 passed harsher requirements, which Lincoln pocketvetoed. At the end of the war, in 1865, thousands of ex-slaves wandered throughout the war-torn South, unwilling to work on white-owned plantations.

EXPERIMENTING AT PORT ROYAL, 1863. Long before the Civil War came to an end, Americans began to rebuild their war-ravaged country. As the war raged, President Abraham Lincoln, who understood the importance of symbols, ordered workers to finish the huge dome towering over the Capitol building. The Republicans also broke ground for a **transcontinental railroad**. Representatives and senators from the Confederate states, with the exception of Senator Andrew Johnson, had resigned, and the northern-dominated Congress easily designated a northerly route from Omaha to San Francisco.

Northerners believed that this railroad would keep the West in the Union, even if the South did win independence.

The most strenuous efforts toward Reconstruction, however, involved parts of the South that the Union army had occupied. By 1862 **Yankees** controlled New Orleans, Louisiana's sugar **plantations**, and coastal South Carolina, where thousands of blacks, abandoned by their former masters, lived inside Union lines. Lincoln had to govern these areas, and he recognized that, if the North won the war, his policies would become models for postwar Reconstruction throughout the South.

Union commanders in coastal South Carolina tried a number of policies that became known as the Port Royal Experiment. Confederate landholders had fled, and black residents, who acted as if they were free even before the **Emancipation Proclamation,** took over the plantations.

The blacks resisted planting rice or cotton, the normal cash crops, and refused to work in the usual gangs. Instead, they divided the land among themselves and, turning to family-based subsistence agriculture, primarily raised corn. Although the blacks demanded ownership of the land they farmed, the army lacked the authority to make such a grant. The army could only recognize the right of black residents to use the land while the war continued. In some cases, white landowners did lose land for failure to pay property taxes, but most of these owners successfully reclaimed their property after the war.

Experts from the U.S. Sanitary Commission traveled to Port Royal, offered technical advice about agriculture, and then brought in dozens of northern female schoolteachers, both black and white. These teachers, who included the black Charlotte Forten, found both children and adults eager to learn to read and write.

The teachers also introduced a version of **evangelical** Christianity into the African-American community, which quickly chose its own black preachers. The black church became the community's most important organization, performing social, economic, and political functions as well as religious ones, and it survived to thrive after the end of Reconstruction.

Although residents prospered, supporters noted the lack of legal authority for the Port Royal Experiment. Technically, the blacks remained slaves, and absentee whites held legal title to the land. Many doubted that this new order in South Carolina would survive the end of the war. Few believed that such a change could be imposed across the entire South, due both to massive white resistance and to an inability to supply northern help on such a large scale. As feared, at the end of the war white landowners returned to Port Royal to demand that blacks either resume plantation-style agriculture or leave.

LINCOLN AND CONGRESS DEBATE RECONSTRUCTION, 1863-1864.
Louisiana, with a population about half white and half black and with a large
number of free blacks in New Orleans, proved more troublesome than coastal
South Carolina to the occupying Union army. To free the army from contro-
versy surrounding the occupation, Lincoln wanted to establish a new, pro-
Union government as soon as possible.

In December 1863, he announced a plan for Reconstruction. Louisiana,
or any other Confederate state, could rejoin the Union under simple
terms. Residents who had participated in the rebellion could take a loyalty
oath and then would be given amnesty. Lincoln would recognize a new
state government after 10 percent of the number of men who had voted
in the 1860 election had taken the oath, provided the state accepted **slavery's** end.

At first Lincoln did not propose political rights for blacks, but after some of
Louisiana's numerous articulate free blacks protested during a visit to the
White House, he privately asked the new state government to give literate
blacks the vote. The state's white Unionists, however — some of whom still
defended slavery — declined. In 1864 Lincoln recognized governments in
Arkansas and Louisiana under these terms, but Congress refused to seat their
representatives.

Radical Republicans in Congress found Lincoln's plan too mild. They also
resented the president's attempt to increase the power of the executive branch
at their expense. In 1864 Congress passed its own plan for Reconstruction,
the Wade-Davis Bill. This measure required a majority of the voters in each
seceding state to take an oath pledging both past and future loyalty. Under
this procedure some southern states were likely to remain out of the Union for
a long time.

Believing such harshness to be unwise, Lincoln declined to sign the bill,
which failed since it had been passed at the end of the session. (A bill becomes
law without the president's signature if passed during a session, but an un-
signed bill fails without the signature if Congress adjourns. This is called a
pocket veto.) The Radicals attacked Lincoln, but he postponed further consideration of Reconstruction until after the 1864 election.

SLAVERY DIES, 1865. As the Confederacy collapsed in 1865, Union army
officers and slaveholders throughout the region informed blacks that slavery
was dead. Blacks hardly needed to be told. One said to his former master, a
defeated Confederate soldier passing by, "Hello massa; bottom rail top dis
time!"

Heralded as the Day of Jubilee, slavery's end brought joyous, even riotous celebration. After the excitement of the moment had waned, blacks often tested their newly won freedom by traveling — sometimes in search of lost relatives, but often just to prove to themselves that they had actually gained freedom. The ability to meander unchallenged by slave patrols gave freedom vivid meaning.

Many blacks, including previously loyal houseservants, deserted the plantations and farms where they had always lived in search of better opportunities, or at least different whites with whom to deal. **Freedmen,** as the ex-slaves were called, shrewdly calculated that whites who remembered particular African-Americans from slavery days would never treat them with respect. Better to trust a stranger.

The result was a kind of chaos. Many blacks moved to southern towns and cities, which quickly developed slums at their edges. Before the war, African-Americans had generally been banned from cities. Now they enjoyed the anonymity of city life, which provided escape from watchful whites. Concentration of population also discouraged the kind of sporadic violence against blacks often found in rural areas. White city residents — used to slavery, slave patrols, and harsh laws prohibiting black residency — grew fearful.

Blacks also wandered through the countryside, sometimes dazed by their freedom and seemingly uninterested in work. Confederate soldiers returned home and, finding their labor force gone, seethed when passing blacks declined offers to work on plantations. Blacks resented and resisted traditional modes of labor, and agriculture suffered. For example, production on Louisiana's sugar plantations dropped to 10 percent of the prewar level.

Blacks did not wish to work for whites on white-owned plantations. Rather, they wanted to acquire land for their own family farms. At the time, few blacks had either the capital or the valuable labor skills that would enable them to get the capital in order to buy land. Indeed, the postwar South was a sorry place for anyone, white or black, to make money. Many years passed before the region regained its prewar number of farm animals or acres planted. As late as 1880 the per capita income in the South was only one-third of the national average.

Nor were blacks educated. In 1860 more than 90 percent could neither read nor write. Most southern states had prohibited teaching a slave to read. During Reconstruction blacks demanded that the South establish public schools. Eager for education, African-Americans reluctantly accepted white insistence that schools be **segregated.** Within a generation half of all blacks were literate.

Johnson and Congress Quarrel, 1865-1866

In 1865 President Andrew Johnson surprised the Radical Republicans in Congress by adopting conservative Reconstruction policies. The Constitution was amended to end slavery, but the southern states enacted Black Codes that all but reinstated slavery under another name. In 1866 Americans debated four distinct theories of Reconstruction, the harshest of which became congressional policy. Congress passed radical laws over Johnson's veto as well as the fourteenth amendment to the Constitution. In 1866, northern voters backed the Radicals' program, and white southerners organized the Ku Klux Klan to intimidate blacks.

JOHNSON ADOPTS CONSERVATIVE RECONSTRUCTION POLICIES. After Lincoln's assassination, Andrew Johnson became president. An obscure former Tennessee senator, he had been a lifelong Democrat. Born into poverty in North Carolina, he became an apprentice tailor and then ran away to the mountains of East Tennessee. There he married, and his wife taught the ambitious but illiterate young man to read. A naturally good stump speaker with the common touch, Johnson successfully practiced law and politics.

In the prewar years he denounced slaveholding planters, even though he owned five slaves, and when Tennessee seceded, he became the only senator from a Confederate state who remained in office. He was a racist. "Damn the Negroes," he said during the war, "I am fighting these traiterous aristocrats, their masters." Hating both planters and slavery, this quarrelsome and eccentric man welcomed emancipation. He had been put on the Republican ticket in 1864 to help win Democratic votes. Most Republicans knew little about him, except that he was a southern Unionist and had been drunk at his inauguration.

Johnson told Radical Republican leaders that he favored harsh measures against the South. Almost immediately, however, Johnson shocked the Radicals by adopting Lincoln's mild policies. The new president, with support from most of his cabinet, concluded that the country should heal the war's wounds by moving rapidly to restore power in the South to conservative whites.

Johnson believed that the Confederacy's leaders had been discredited and lacked a constituency. Instead, he expected onetime Unionists to gain control, create stable governments, and generate the confidence that would produce postwar economic development. Though he was relieved at the way the war had destroyed slavery, he opposed extending any rights to the freed blacks.

In mid-1865 Johnson issued a proclamation to recognize conservative white-only governments in all eleven former Confederate states. He also granted amnesty to most Confederates who took an oath of allegiance. One important exception involved persons who held more than $20,000 worth of property. These wealthy planters were required to apply to Johnson personally for a pardon. They did so and found the president generous. Johnson spent much of his time signing pardons, more than 13,000 in two years.

Conservative state governments organized along these lines accepted the abolition of slavery by approving the thirteenth amendment to the Constitution, repudiated Confederate war debts, and made provisions for sending representatives to Congress. In December 1865, the thirteenth amendment was declared **ratified**.

THE SOUTH ENACTS BLACK CODES. These same state governments also passed laws called the Black Codes regulating the conduct of the newly freed blacks. To northerners, the harsh Black Codes looked suspiciously like attempts to continue slavery under another name. Indeed, some states merely took old laws regulating slaves and changed the word "slave" to "freedman." Under these laws blacks were treated as noncitizens without the right to vote, to serve on juries, or to testify against whites.

Furthermore, blacks had to sign annual labor contracts and could not change employment while under contract. In some states employers had the right to whip employees, who could be forced to work in gangs. Blacks, but not whites, who lacked labor contracts or large sums of cash could be charged with **vagrancy.** The penalty for this crime was having the right to one's labor sold, with preference given to a former owner.

The Black Codes infuriated northern whites and southern blacks, including a good many Union army veterans. When Johnson accepted the southern white view that such laws were necessary to maintain order in the South, Radical Republicans in Congress became the president's bitter enemies.

CONFLICTING THEORIES OF RECONSTRUCTION, 1865-1866. In Congress most Republicans, especially those from evangelical, moralistic New England, had become Radicals. Deeply offended by Johnson's behavior, they feared both that the long, bloody war had changed little inside the South and that arrogant white southern planters would soon be running the federal government. In the North, Republicans faced a large and growing opposition from immigrant-oriented Democrats, and many Radicals worried that a coalition of white southerners and immigrant northerners might gain control of the national government. Indeed, southerners had dared to elect ex-Confederate officials to represent them in Congress. Georgia sent the former Confederate vice-president, Alexander Stephens, to the Senate. The Radicals responded by refusing to seat representatives from any of the ex-Confederate states.

At this point a great national debate on the South took place, and four distinct theories of Reconstruction emerged:

• *States' Rights:* According to this view, held by most white southerners and a few conservative northerners, including General William Tecumseh Sherman, the war had proved, as the North had contended, that secession was illegal. Therefore, the Confederate states had never left the Union and merely had to elect representatives to rejoin. The country would be restored more or less as it had been, except for slavery, which had collapsed during the war. Because this position enjoyed little support among the victors, it had no chance of being adopted.

• *Presidential:* Andrew Johnson took a similar but slightly different approach. He, too, believed that **secession** was illegal and that the southern state governments had not actually left the Union. On the other hand, their officials certainly had committed acts inconsistent with loyalty to the federal government. While the states had remained intact, the leaders had rebelled, and the proper way to restore harmony was for the president to use his constitutional power to pardon individuals. Had Johnson used his power carefully, he might have generated support for this view, but his almost giddy signing of pardons had angered many people. In the end, most Americans rejected this theory, because it merely enhanced the power of an inept president.

• *State Suicide:* Charles Sumner, Massachusetts's Radical senator, also believed secession unconstitutional, but he argued that the actions of the southern state governments in trying to secede had constituted a form of suicide. When those states had withdrawn from the Union, they had ceased to exist as far as the federal government was concerned. The federal government now had the obligation to restore those states to life. Thus, Congress could act aggressively to bring about new governments in the South that harmonized with the northern victory. Sumner's view, tinged with the flavor of evangelical religion embracing ideas of redemption and resurrection, enjoyed much popular support in the North.

• *Conquered Provinces:* Thaddeus Stevens, Pennsylvania's Radical representative, offered a similar theory. According to Stevens, it mattered little whether the southern states had or had not actually seceded from the Union. In fact, the Union army had conquered them. As conquered territory, the South could be dealt with however the North wished. Congress could treat the Confederate states and their residents any way that it wanted, and military occupation might be used to guarantee compliance with northern desires. "The foundations of their institutions," warned Stevens, "must be broken and relaid, or all our blood and treasure have been spent in vain."

The harshest theory, this one rang closest to the truth in the minds of most northerners and became the basis for congressional policy.

CONGRESS BEGINS RADICAL RECONSTRUCTION, 1866. In early 1866 Congress passed a bill expanding the powers of the Freedmen's Bureau, which had been established a year earlier to distribute food and clothes to the former slaves in the South. The new bill placed 900 federal agents, mostly former Union soldiers, in those southern counties with large black populations for the purpose of monitoring race relations and negotiating disputes between whites and freedmen. This was, except for the post office, the first massive federal bureaucracy. Although the bureau could not stop white harassment, it did put such action under a watchful federal eye. Citing cost and states' rights, Johnson vetoed the bill. The angry Radicals quickly overrode the veto and showed that they had more than a two-thirds majority in Congress.

Congress then passed the Civil Rights Act. This law directly overturned both the 1857 Dred Scott ruling that had denied citizenship to blacks and the Black Codes by granting citizenship to blacks and all other persons born in the United States. The measure could also be interpreted to prohibit racial discrimination in public facilities, such as trains or restaurants. The bill, however, did not provide for voting rights. At this time most northern states did not grant the vote to blacks, and Radicals did not wish to irritate northern voters.

The Radicals passed this bill over Johnson's veto. The provisions concerning public accommodations were seldom enforced, and in 1883 the Supreme Court ruled the act unconstitutional.

PROPOSING THE FOURTEENTH AMENDMENT, 1866. Worried about a possible loss of power in the future, Radicals decided to use their overwhelming majority in Congress to guarantee black rights with the fourteenth amendment to the Constitution. The longest and vaguest of all amendments, this measure repealed the Dred Scott decision by granting citizenship to all persons born in the United States. Citizens were guaranteed "due process of law" and "equal protection of the laws." The federal government, in other words, would intervene if the southern states mistreated the freedmen. In the long term, the Supreme Court would apply these two clauses to all sorts of situations and greatly expand the power of the federal government.

To pressure the South to give blacks the vote, the amendment provided for reduced representation in Congress if the vote was denied. This provision was never enforced. The amendment also barred most former Confederates from federal office unless pardoned by *Congress,* and the southern states were prohibited from paying off Civil War debts.

To ensure the fourteenth amendment's adoption, Radicals indicated that representatives from each ex-Confederate state would be admitted to Congress only after that state had ratified the amendment. Congress was determined to take control of Reconstruction away from Johnson. Tennessee ratified and was readmitted, but the other ten ex-Confederate states rejected the amendment and waited for the fall 1866 congressional elections. The southerners, along with Johnson, believed that the Radicals had misjudged public opinion.

NORTHERN VOTERS BACK THE RADICALS, 1866. Taking his case for milder measures directly to the people, Johnson used the midterm congressional election of 1866 to make a campaign "swing around the circle" to the Northeast and across the Midwest and then south to St. Louis.

Although Johnson's trip went well at first, Radicals quickly organized an all-out attack. Radicals "waved the bloody shirt," a reference to wartime flags carried by the Union army in battle, by reminding northern voters of how much the war had cost in treasure and lives, and of how the southern-born president now proposed yielding power to the former rebels.

By focusing on the war, by associating the Democrats with treason, and by linking the Republicans to the Union cause, the Radicals secured an overwhelming election victory. This success totally discredited Johnson's policies, and the already large Radical majorities in Congress actually increased.

CHAOS AND KU KLUX KLAN VIOLENCE ARISE IN THE SOUTH. Slavery had collapsed, but nothing had been put in its place. Blacks believed that the federal government would seize land owned by Confederate planters and give it to the freedmen, and some northerners encouraged this belief. "Forty acres and a mule!" cried some Radicals, including Thaddeus Stevens. Blacks quickly learned that this idea had little support. Northern property holders saw no advantage in endorsing a proposal that questioned the sanctity and permanence of private property. A government that confiscated land from planters today might take away someone else's property tomorrow.

In addition, few northerners wanted to create a politically powerful, property-owning black society in the South. On the other hand, neither did most northerners want the planters to regain their prewar national political influence. The North's policy, then, was to keep the South poor, to maintain northern dominance of the country politically and economically, and to divide southern whites and blacks. Radicals accomplished this result by the par-

Thomas Nast, America's greatest political cartoonist, portrayed the Democrats' White League as being in collusion with the Ku Klux Klan to oppress blacks in the South during Reconstruction. (CULVER PICTURES)

adoxical policy of giving blacks political rights while denying them the means to economic self-sufficiency.

Southern whites were self-confident, resourceful, educated, skilled, and well-connected, and they retained ownership of almost all the land, buildings, and tools but frequently lacked political rights. Insecure, illiterate, and ignorant blacks had political rights, granted through northern pressure, but lacked economic security. Blacks had no land, and whites had no labor. Both fell into dependency upon outside northern forces, especially Yankee-controlled railroad companies, which came to dominate the South's economy and politics.

Almost immediately, southern whites lashed out in violence. Infuriated by ex-slaves daring to assert their rights, frightened planters and ex-Confederate soldiers organized the Ku Klux Klan in 1866 in Pulaski, Tennessee, to force the freedmen to become docile, pliant tools. The Klan, which rapidly spread across the South, favored midnight visits to black homes, where they rousted blacks from bed, dragged them outside, and then took them into the woods to be beaten or killed. The Klan's whippings were designed, more than anything else, to remind freedmen of slavery.

The organization especially targeted African-Americans perceived to be leaders in the campaign for rights, or those who lacked proper humility in white eyes, or those known to be literate and therefore more capable of making trouble, such as by writing complaining letters to federal officials. The Klan, even more than the Black Codes, led Radicals to seek federal intervention in the South.

At the same time, both races began to move toward a new relationship. Blacks insisted that they would not work as gang laborers on plantations. Instead, they rented land from planters and farmed in family units. Prewar slave housing, which had been built in dense blocks, gave way to freestanding family cabins in the middle of fields. Black tenant farmers adopted the white view that women should not work in the fields.

In desperate poverty, black tenants brought little except labor to this system, and they usually had to be financed by the planter or by a merchant at a nearby general store. Many of these creditors, in turn, were themselves in debt to railroad corporations. The planter or merchant usually got half of the tenant's crop. Many tenants found that their living costs exceeded their earnings. Tenancy and the system of **sharecropping** quickly became ways of life in the rural South for poor whites as well as blacks.

Radicals Continue Reconstruction, 1867-1873

In 1867-1868 Radicals in Congress continued Reconstruction with stern new laws, and tiring of Johnson's opposition, impeached the president but failed by one vote to convict him. Black votes in the South enabled the Radical Republican candidate, U.S. Grant, to win the 1868 presidential election narrowly. Blacks in the South gained some political power under Radical rule, but radical power faded quickly. Conservative white southerners already were regaining control when Grant won a second term in 1872. The postwar years in the North brought immigration, factories, and the purchase of Alaska in 1867, but also labor strife and a depression beginning in 1873.

CONGRESS PASSES STERN MEASURES, 1867-1868. In 1867 the Radicals moved to impose the kind of harsh military Reconstruction long advocated by Thaddeus Stevens. The Reconstruction Act, passed over Johnson's veto, established five military districts covering ten ex-Confederate states (Tennessee had been readmitted). Under this law and several supplementary measures, 20,000 federal troops, including a number of black units, occupied the South. Military rule replaced the conservative state governments previously recognized by Johnson.

To be readmitted to the Union, the southern states had to adopt new state constitutions to be drafted by conventions elected by universal male **suffrage**. There was, however, a catch. Most ex-Confederates were barred from voting. This rule was consistent with the fourteenth amendment, which awaited ratification. Thus, in many southern states the freedmen's vote exceeded the white vote.

To guarantee fair elections, the United States army registered voters. In all ten southern states 703,000 blacks and 627,000 whites were registered. Blacks formed a majority of the registered voters in Alabama, Florida, Louisiana, Mississippi, and South Carolina. African-Americans were more than half of the population in South Carolina and Mississippi. Congress also required that the new state governments guarantee blacks the right to vote and ratify the fourteenth amendment. The Radicals reserved to Congress all final decisions about what constituted compliance and when a state could regain its representation in Congress.

Throughout the South the Radicals used military rule, the Freedmen's Bureau, and the black vote organized through Union League Clubs to create a powerful Republican party. In the upper South, including parts of Virginia and North Carolina, white Unionists formed an important Republican core to which were now added black voters from the former plantation districts.

This biracial Republican coalition proved inherently unstable. Blacks demanded protection for civil rights and massive increases in spending on public education to be paid with substantially higher property taxes on white landowners. On average taxes rose to ten times the prewar level. Although poor white Republicans from the mountains disdained planters, they usually opposed black rights and resisted higher property taxes. Relatively quickly, this unnatural Republican political alliance collapsed, and the planters regained their prewar political power.

In the Deep South the situation was different. These states had large black populations, and most whites had supported the Confederacy and could not vote. In South Carolina, Mississippi, and Louisiana the Republicans prevailed due to large black majorities among the electorate.

On the other hand, in these states most Republican party leaders were white. Some were **"scalawags,"** that is, southerners who had been Unionists or who now believed that personal advantage came from the Republicans. Others were **"carpetbaggers,"** that is, northerners who had moved to the South, usually with initial hopes for economic gain, and who had subsequently turned to politics.

In 1868 the Radicals in Congress approved the new state constitutions for seven states and readmitted them into the Union in time for the coming presidential election, in which they were expected to vote Republican.

Georgia's white Republicans, however, then proceeded to join with the few Democrats in the legislature to expel all 28 black Republican members of the legislature. This action — which contradicted the pledges that Georgia had made to the Radicals concerning black rights — enraged the Radicals. They withdrew recognition, reinstated military rule, and demanded that the state reseat the black legislators and ratify the fifteenth amendment to the Constitution before being restored to the Union. Georgia was readmitted a second time in 1870.

CONGRESS IMPEACHES JOHNSON, 1868. Meanwhile, the Radicals had decided to **impeach** President Johnson and remove him from office. Thaddeus Stevens, leader of the Radicals in the House of Representatives, eagerly pushed the impeachment through the House. The Radicals charged Johnson with a number of violations, including the attempted removal of Secretary of War Edwin Stanton in defiance of a dubious prohibition passed by Congress, but in reality the issue was more political than legal.

Although the Radicals had a two-thirds majority in the Senate, seemingly enough votes to convict Johnson, public opinion began to question the proceedings. Business leaders disliked the impeachment because it made the government look unstable and upset the financial markets. In addition, the next person in line for the presidency was the president pro-tem of the Senate, Benjamin Wade of Ohio, a widely disliked, angry Radical. Johnson was acquitted, 35-19, one vote short of conviction. Seven Republicans joined the Democrats in opposing removal.

ELECTION OF 1868. For the 1868 presidential election the Republicans nominated General Ulysses S. Grant on a platform supporting Radical Reconstruction. The Democrats picked Horatio Seymour, a colorless New York governor. Public opinion had shifted away from the Radicals, and Grant won only a narrow victory. Due to an overwhelming vote among southern whites, Seymour won a majority among white voters, but Grant carried most of the electorally rich North. His margin was enhanced by Radical control with black voters in six southern states. The Radical-dominated Congress barred three southern states suspected of Democratic tendencies from participation in the election.

The narrowness of this victory made the Radicals more determined to maintain control of the South. In 1869 Congress passed the fifteenth amendment to the Constitution specifically guaranteeing the black vote. Congress brushed aside attempts by women's groups, led by Elizabeth Cady Stanton and supported by Senator Charles Sumner, to use the amendment to give women the vote, too. Mississippi, Texas, and Virginia were finally readmitted to the Union in 1870, after they had banned ex-Confederate voters and ratified the fifteenth amendment.

BLACKS GAIN POWER BRIEFLY IN THE SOUTH. Mississippi became staunchly Radical and was the first and only state to elect two blacks to the U.S. Senate, Hiram Revels and, later, Blanche K. Bruce. Of the 14 blacks from the South who served in the House during Reconstruction, four were Union army veterans. The most flamboyant was Robert Smalls, a former South Carolina slave who, after the Emancipation Proclamation, had stolen a steamboat and sailed it through the Confederate navy to the federal fleet.

Although blacks provided about four-fifths of the Republican vote in the South, they accounted for less than one-fifth of the officeholders. Most blacks served in city and county offices or in state legislatures. South Carolina's legislature was the only one with a black majority. Black officials tended to be well-educated and light-skinned. Many had been free before the war. Only a few held statewide office, and none was elected governor. In 1872-1873, P.B.S. Pinchback, who had been elected lieutenant governor, served briefly as governor of Louisiana.

RECONSTRUCTION EBBS PRIOR TO THE ELECTION OF 1872. Radical Reconstruction, however, was already in decline. Georgia and Virginia slipped quickly under conservative control, and northerners resisted using federal troops to maintain Radical rule. At the same time, scandal had hurt the Grant administration. A number of officials had taken bribes, and in 1872 numerous prominent Republicans in Congress were revealed to have accepted stock from the Crédit Mobilier, a front for the Union Pacific Railroad, to which Congress had given huge land grants.

By 1872 many Republicans, including Horace Greeley, loathed both Radical Reconstruction and the era's sleazy, crooked politics. Organizing themselves as Liberal Republicans, they nominated Greeley for president. The Democrats endorsed Greeley, as did the German immigrant reformer and former Union General Carl Schurz, and two crusading journalists, E. L. Godkin of *The Nation* and Henry Adams. Grant, the regular Republican nominee, won by an increased majority, and a broken-hearted Greeley died suddenly. Grant, corruption, and Reconstruction lurched forward uneasily.

THE POSTWAR NORTH, 1867-1873. The immediate postwar years brought even more rapid change in the North than in the South. Fueled by the paper greenback currency issued during the war, the postwar northern economy boomed, along with considerable **inflation,** and industrialists converted factories from military to civilian production. Union army veterans returned home to resume farming, business, and handicrafts, but many soon made their way west along the newly built rail routes, including the transcontinental railroad to California, which opened in 1869. Massive immigration from Europe, largely stopped during the war, resumed. Irish, Germans, and Britons were joined by Scandinavians, who settled on farms in the upper Midwest.

Dynamic growth even led to a renewed interest in territorial expansion. In 1867 Secretary of State Seward learned that the Russians, pressed for cash, wanted to sell Alaska. Partly to keep the territory out of the hands of the British, who controlled Canada, and partly out of an unproven faith that a land as large as Alaska must contain valuable resources, Seward resolved to buy the frozen northland. The Russians demanded $7.2 million, generally considered an outrageous price, and the secretary had to cajole and bribe Congress to pay. Popularly scorned as "Seward's Folly," the territory of Alaska more than paid for itself within a few years in timber and salmon alone.

Change was not always kind. Many workers had organized successful unions during the war, but returning soldiers and immigrants now enlarged the labor pool and made it possible for employers to break strikes. Workers also discovered that the Republican party, which had rallied both business and labor to the antislavery cause, fell more and more under the control of business interests eager to pursue antilabor policies, including the outlawing of strikes. Labor newspapers that had started during the war collapsed, leaving only the probusiness partisan press.

By 1873, which brought the collapse of Jay Cooke's Philadelphia bond firm and the beginnings of a depression, many northerners were bored by the Republicans, by Reconstruction, and by talk about northern wartime sacrifices.

Conservatives Regain Power in the South, 1868-1877

Conservative white southerners used both sophisticated political tactics and economic power to overthrow the Radicals and regain control of the political system. Violence and intimidation also played a role. In the disputed presidential election of 1876, a Republican-southern Democratic deal gave the Republicans the presidency and the Democrats the South. The last Reconstruction state governments were sold out.

WHITE REDEEMERS USE POLITICS AND ECONOMICS. White southerners, especially ex-Confederates, had never accepted the legitimacy of Reconstruction. Many resisted the end of slavery, and even those who accepted slavery's death found the freedmen's right to vote bizarre. Perhaps a few might have conceded the merit of universal suffrage as a theory, but allowing blacks to vote while depriving whites of the ballot enraged white southerners.

The enforcement of these rules by the military, by the Freedmen's Bureau, and by Radicals in Congress embittered white southerners into sour contempt. Determined to restore what they considered to be the natural order of southern society — that is, white supremacy — they swore to use any and all means to achieve their goal.

Although most conservative white southerners were Democrats, some, like the opportunist Governor Joe E. Brown of Georgia, joined the Republicans. In addition to plotting the expulsion of black Republicans from the legislature, Brown sought to reduce black influence by moving the state capital from Milledgeville in the heart of the black belt to Atlanta, where railroad companies willingly paid legislators for votes. Brown, like many other white Republicans, emphasized economic development over civil rights. Southern Democrats soon realized that they, too, could make this same appeal to northern business interests.

Conservatives in South Carolina, where blacks had a legislative majority as late as 1876, felt they could regain control only by rallying virtually all the white vote and winning a share of the large black vote. That state's Radical Republican regime self-destructed with weak leadership, internal bickering, and charges of corruption. The conservative Democrat Wade Hampton, an **antebellum** planter and ex-Confederate general, won election as governor in 1876. Hampton pledged to retain black voting rights and act honorably toward blacks. One wonders if he made the pledge with a wink.

Economics worked against black political power. Whites owned virtually everything and had a **monopoly** of the most valuable job skills. In 1876 only 5 percent of blacks in the Deep South owned land. Economic intimidation, if not outright vote-buying, was used to produce a black electorate effectively controlled by whites. In those few areas where blacks had achieved a degree of landownership, such as parts of coastal South Carolina, economics tended to reinforce black political power, which remained potent for another generation. The last southern black congressman until modern times left office in 1901.

USING VIOLENCE TO INTIMIDATE BLACKS AND GAIN WHITE RULE. Conservative white southerners called themselves Redeemers, because they said that they were redeeming or saving the South from Radical misrule. Most significant in the Redeemers' movement to reclaim the power of government for conservative whites, however, was the use of intimidation and violence against blacks. Although southern whites learned that the high visibility of organizations such as the Ku Klux Klan generated unfavorable publicity in the North and threatened to bring a resumption of northern intervention, the Klan's mere existence acted to intimidate blacks.

The Klan was not the only means to reclaim white rule. Other militant white supremacist political organizations such as South Carolina's Red Shirts and Alabama's White League countered the Republicans' Union League Clubs. Mississippi Democrats took the motto: "Carry the election peaceably if we can, forcibly if we must."

Most important were individual threats or acts of violence directed at politically active blacks and white Republicans. Campaigns of arson and assassination took place throughout the South. These were little publicized, since Democrats had no reason to advertise undemocratic methods, and Republicans knew that publicity only revealed their own weakness.

Blacks sometimes responded to the tension by deciding to move. Some talked about Africa, and a few actually went there, although most returned in disillusionment. Others looked to **homesteading** on federal land in the West. A number, collectively known as the Exodusters, founded new black communities in Kansas. Others migrated to Texas or to western mining towns. Most blacks, however, remained in the South and increasingly under conservative white control.

By 1876 conservative white Democrats had, by one means or another, regained control of most southern states. When Democrats won state power, they routinely destroyed black power in predominantly African-American counties by requiring that officials in those counties be appointed by the governor rather than locally elected. In 1876 only South Carolina, Louisiana, and Florida remained under Republican rule, and Radical control in those states faced serious challenges, electoral and otherwise.

THE DISPUTED ELECTION OF 1876. Grant's second administration had been dogged by more scandals, including the Whiskey Ring, where distillers had bribed high officials to evade liquor taxes. Worse, the economy had slipped into a **depression** following the Panic of 1873. In 1876 Democrats recognized that scandal and hard times gave them an excellent chance to win the presidential election.

The Republicans nominated Rutherford B. Hayes, an Ohio politician and the husband of a leading **temperance** reformer, and the Democrats picked Samuel J. Tilden, a wealthy Wall Street lawyer. Although Tilden won the popular vote, the **electoral vote** was quite narrow. Indeed, Republicans quickly realized that if South Carolina, Florida, and Louisiana could be counted for Hayes, he could win, 185-184.

The actual vote in the three southern states will never be known. Black voters had been intimidated into staying away from the polls, ballot boxes had been stuffed or burned, and two sets of votes had been collected in some communities. Incumbent Radical administrations in all three states declared both Hayes and new Republican state governments victorious. Democrats challenged those outcomes, organized their own vote counts, and announced victories for Tilden and themselves.

No one could say for sure who had won the southern "elections," but it was clear that southern white Democrats were prepared to seize power in the three states and could be stopped only by federal military authorities. Grant, Tilden, and Hayes opposed such a use of force, each for his own reason.

Controversy about the election continued into early 1877, as Congress deadlocked. Democrats controlled the House, Republicans the Senate. Finally, Congress arranged a grand compromise. Republicans got the presidency, Democrats control of the three southern states. Northern Republicans stood aside as the last Radical governments in the three southern states fell to conservative Democrats. Amid reassurances from Hayes that he would withdraw remaining federal troops from the South, Congress sent the presidential election to a special commission composed of five Democrats, five Republicans, and four specified Supreme Court justices. These four were to choose a fifth justice. David Davis, an independent expected to be tapped, suddenly resigned from the court to take a Senate seat, and the justices were forced to pick from among the court's remaining justices, all of whom were Republicans.

After a secret meeting between Republican and southern Democratic leaders at the Wormley House hotel in Washington in February 1877, the commission's eight Republicans and seven Democrats followed their leaders' orders and by a strict party vote awarded all the disputed electoral votes to Hayes, who won, 185-184. Tilden, fearing civil war, seemed relieved.

Reconstruction was over. Although slavery had ended, the right to vote and the other rights blacks had won and exercised during Reconstruction would be lost during the 1890s. Modest gains survived, including segregated schools and black colleges, such as Howard, Atlanta, and Fisk.

In part, white racism and the white southern desire for a political system based upon white supremacy was to blame. In part, the failure to provide the freedmen with land created economic dependency that made it difficult for blacks to keep political rights. A measure of economic security, if not actual equality, is necessary to maintain democratic politics. And in part northern Republicans, having concluded that Reconstruction had brought their party few benefits, were prepared to sell out the southern Radical Republicans. In the new order, men of wealth from all sections had much in common.

Conclusion

Reconstruction cast a long shadow across the country and especially the South. Much more than the Civil War, the era generated great bitterness among honor-driven southern whites, who looked upon northern-imposed black rights with seething anger. Maintaining white supremacy became a hallmark of southern politics for almost a hundred years. Blacks, too, grew bitter. Promised much by northern Radicals, they had been handed modest amounts of power only to be abandoned in the end for political convenience. Never again did blacks entirely trust Republicans. Reconstruction produced only losers and goes far toward explaining the tawdry politics that followed for a generation.

Recommended Readings

DOCUMENTS: W.E.B. DuBois, *The Souls of Black Folk* (1903); Whitelaw Reid, *After the War* (1866); Albion W. Tourgée, *A Fool's Errand* (1879).

READINGS: (GENERAL) David Donald, *Charles Sumner and the Rights of Man* (1970); Eric Foner, *Reconstruction* (1988); Leon F. Litwack, *Been In the Storm So Long* (1979); (WARTIME) Louis S. Gerteis, *From Contraband to Freedman* (1973); Willie L. Rose, *Rehearsal for Reconstruction* (1964); (BLACKS) Carol R. Bleser, *The Promised Land* (1969); Edmund L. Drago, *Black Politicians and Reconstruction in Georgia* (1983); Robert F. Engs, *Freedom's First Generation* (1979); Jacqueline Jones, *Soldiers of Light and Love* (1980); Nell I. Painter, *Exodusters* (1976); Donald Spivey, *Schooling for the New Slavery* (1978); Clarence E. Walker, *A Rock in a Weary Land* (1982); (POLITICS) Michael L. Benedict, *The Impeachment and Trial of Andrew Johnson* (1973); Steven Hahn, *The Roots of Southern Populism* (1983); William C. Harris, *The Day of the Carpetbagger* (1979); Thomas Holt, *Black over White* (1977); Peggy Lamson, *The Glorious Failure* (1973); Jonathan M. Wiener, *Social Origins of the New South* (1978); (REDEEMERS) Michael Perman, *The Road to Redemption* (1984); George C. Rable, *But There Was No Peace* (1984); Terry L. Seip, *The South Returns to Congress* (1983).

16

———— ✖ ————

THE DREAM OF THE FRONTIER
WEST AND ITS REALITIES

CHAPTER OVERVIEW: In the aftermath of the Civil War, Americans in general were caught in a mania to get rich—in the new industrial development in the North, in the railroads spanning the continent, in silver and gold mining throughout the West, in cattle ranching in the Southwest, and in land speculation in the nation's fast growing cities. Out of this rush for riches came national myths—the New South, the Old West, the Freedman, the Captains of Industry. Behind these myths lay the reality of defeated Indians, disheartened ex-slaves, and the broken dreams of those who failed to find their fortunes. Those who did make it fostered new myths that riches were possible for any American, if opportunity and hard work coincided with good luck. Others, however, found disappointment, failure, and bitterness.

The West Settled: Illusion and Reality

Following the Civil War, thousands of Americans moved west across the Mississippi River to better their lives. They came for land and what the land held—a chance to settle, to own property, and to exploit its riches. Miners followed every lead to strike it rich. These westward settlers perceived themselves as individualists, but their efforts were made possible only with favorable legislation and free land by the federal government.

THE ILLUSION OF FORTUNE IN A LAND OF CONTRASTS. In late 1872 the citizens of Denver heard extraordinary news: two miners had discovered diamonds in a remote corner of northwestern Colorado. Reports of diamonds immediately stirred the imaginations of Denverites who had heard news of diamonds being found in South Africa. If South Africa, why not Colorado? After all, the territory's rich mountains had yielded precious gold and silver.

305

Its gold and silver rushes were over, and the people of Colorado found themselves caught up in the new craze.

Within days 25 companies capitalized at $250 million were formed. Diamond stock trading became rampant. At the same time, miners prepared to rush off to this remote section of the state—with little concern that winter was approaching. Before long, though, a geologist exposed what became known as the "Great Diamond Hoax": the two miners who had first reported the discovery had salted the area with diamonds in hopes of selling stock to the unwary.

The Diamond Hoax of 1872 revealed the acquisitive instinct and speculative temper of many who moved west in hopes of a better future. Their settlement of the West in turn, in the late nineteenth century seemed to symbolize the national dream of fortune. For many this dream proved to be a hoax, for some a tragedy; yet others found new opportunities and better lives in the West.

In the three decades following the Civil War, wave after wave of pioneers swept across the Mississippi River intent on finding wealth or the simple life in the West. The movement was part of a demographic explosion: from 1860 to 1900 the national population grew from 31 million to 76 million people. What the West offered, beyond all else, was land. It was the land that held gold, silver, and top soil that gave the promise of prosperity. There was only one appropriate way to treat the land: divide it, distribute it, and register it. The American experiment rested on land ownership.

That the land was often held by others—by native Indians or Hispanic peoples—did not hinder acquisition. The land was contested and taken from these groups. The hostilities that ensued were by no means limited to whites against all others. Indians had fought over land among themselves and with Hispanics long before the mass movement of whites into the West following the Civil War.

Ethnic conflict was not limited to different races. Tensions also arose among the English, French, Germans, Greeks, Irish, Jews, Polish, Russians, and Scandinavians. The problems of the East were played out in the West, as these European-American groups encountered Indians, Hispanics, and Asians. In the midst of these ethnic and racial tensions, class tensions also arose, giving rise to radical **unionism.** A strange amalgam of these conflicts was the **nativist** campaign to expel the Chinese laborers who were seen as tools of the **monopolists.**

Miners, ranchers, farmers, and the U.S. army battled and beat the Indians of the Great Plains, of the mountains, and of the Southwest. In this way, the frontier gave way to cities, farms, ranches, and industry. And as the land between Kansas and California was settled, new states were created—Colorado in 1876; North and South Dakota, Washington, and Montana in 1889; Idaho and Wyoming in 1890; Utah in 1896; Oklahoma in 1907, and Arizona and New Mexico in 1912.

The West is a region of geographic extremes. As the settlers left their homes and moved west, they first encountered the vast rolling prairies of the Great Plains which stretched from West Texas to Canada. Here approximately 300,000 Indians lived and hunted the 13 million buffalo that roamed the region. On the far side of the plains, the pioneers confronted the Rocky Mountains. Beyond the Rockies lay the Great Basin, a vast desert lowland that included the briny Great Salt Lake. To the south they would encounter the hostile Sonoran desert, one of the world's major deserts, stretching across southern New Mexico, Arizona, and California and into northern Mexico. And if the settlers pushed on further they confronted the forbidding Sierra Nevada or the Cascade Mountains before reaching California or the northern Pacific Coast.

INDIVIDUAL PURSUIT AND FEDERAL AID. Those who came west remained fiercely independent—individualists in spirit and sentiment. Westerners generally distrusted the government in Washington. Nonetheless, the federal government played an essential role in the development of the West through important legislation.

In 1862 Congress opened western land for settlement with the passage of the **Homestead** Act. The intent of the bill was to distribute government-owned land to individuals for farming. The act offered 160 acres of public land to any person over 21 or the head of a family if the person resided on the land for five continuous years. A homesteader also could purchase the land after six months for $1.25 an acre. From 1862 and 1900, nearly 400,000 families received free homesteads through the homestead act. While the vast number of these purchases were honest, some land **speculators** took advantage of the law by sending in dummy entrymen to make claims. In any case, nearly two-thirds of the homesteads failed before 1890.

This act was followed by the Timber Culture Act (1873) that allowed farmers to apply for an additional land if they planted one-fourth of it with trees within four years. During the 15 years this law remained on the books, individuals planted over 10,000 acres with trees.

The Desert Land Act (1877), in turn, benefitted settlers. This measure allowed a rancher to secure tentative title to 640 acres in the Great Plains or the Southwest for an initial payment of twenty-five cents an acre. If after three years it was proved that a portion of this land had been irrigated, the settler's title to the land became permanent for an additional dollar an acre. The price was a bargain and openly invited fraud. Many settlers simply dumped a bucket of water on the land—calling it irrigation—and purchased the land. Under this single act, the federal government gave away over two and half million acres.

Timber interests took note of this act and lobbied for their own special act, the Timber and Stone Act (1878). This extraordinary piece of legislation allowed them to buy rich forests in California, Nevada, Oregon, and Washington for $2.50 an acre—about the price of one good log. By 1900 almost 3,600,000 acres of potentially valuable forests had been sold under this law.

The largest federal giveaway program in the West came through the subsidizing of railroad construction, especially the **transcontinental railroad.** Through the Railroad Acts of 1862 and 1864 Congress freely awarded large tracts of land to railroad corporations to encourage construction of a transcontinental line. From 1850 to 1871 railroad interests received 181 million acres. Most of this land was given directly to the transcontinental lines. Individual states copied the federal policy. As a consequence, railroads became— and remain today—the largest private landowners in the West.

The railroad companies gained much, but so did the nation: the railroad system proved crucial to western development. The building of the first transcontinental railroad in the 1860s was one of the world's great engineering endeavors. The discovery of gold in California in 1849 had brought settlers into the Pacific coast region, but to reach the distant territory a complex transportation and communications system needed to be built. Although many in the West distrusted eastern financial interests and the federal government, western interests joined eastern **capitalists** to pressure Congress to grant subsidized stagecoach lines, telegraph corporations, and, most importantly, railroads to the West.

The **secession** of the South allowed Republican congressmen to pass legislation to build a transcontinental railroad along a central route. On July 1, 1862, Congress chartered the Central Pacific Railroad to begin construction from Sacramento through the Sierra Nevadas. At the same time Congress chartered a second company, the Union Pacific Railroad, to build westward from Omaha, Nebraska. Each company was offered 20 odd-numbered sections of land for each mile of track they constructed. Congress also loaned the railroads from $16,000 to $48,000 per mile, depending on the nature of the terrain in which the line was built.

Building the first transcontinental railroad in the 1860s was one of the world's great engineering endeavors. The proposal to build a line through the Sierras had been the dream of a California engineer, Theodore D. Judah. On his own, he surveyed a path through the nation's largest mountains. Judah enticed to his project four Sacramento promoters—Leland Stanford, Collis P.

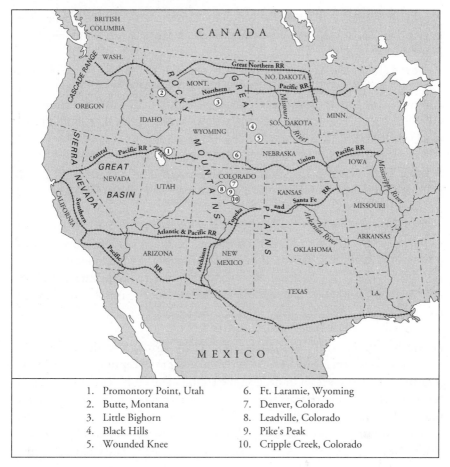

Map 16.1. The West in the Late 1800s

1. Promontory Point, Utah
2. Butte, Montana
3. Little Bighorn
4. Black Hills
5. Wounded Knee
6. Ft. Laramie, Wyoming
7. Denver, Colorado
8. Leadville, Colorado
9. Pike's Peak
10. Cripple Creek, Colorado

Huntington, Mark Hopkins, and Charles Crocker—to form the Central Pacific Railroad.

Construction of the line began in California in 1864 and proceeded slowly eastward at a rate of only about 20 miles per year. The company had difficulty finding labor. This was solved when the company began importing Chinese workers called "coolies."

The first transcontinental railroad was matched by a second line—the Atchison, Topeka and Santa Fe—crossing the southern route in the early 1880s. Henry Villard's Northern Pacific line linked Lake Superior and Puget Sound in 1887. The Southern Pacific connected Texas with Los Angeles, and James J. Hill's Great Northern provided another northern route along the

Canadian border. Hill's was the only line constructed without federal land grants. Dozens of other companies provided feeder lines, creating one of the best railroad systems in the world.

At the end of the Civil War there were only 35,000 miles of track, mostly east of the Mississippi River, dominated by local lines that used different track widths. By the end of the century, there were 240,000 miles of interconnected railroads. America's rail system impressed the world, and well it should have: the United States alone held one-third of the world's total railroad mileage.

The completion of five transcontinental railroads by the 1890s linked the Atlantic to the Pacific. In doing so, these lines allowed settlers to fill in the continent. The railroads also gave farmers access to midwestern and eastern markets.

The first continental line allowed the annihilation of the buffalo herds in a short period by affording hunters easy access to the land. The movement of settlers into the Great Plains and the elimination of the buffalo set the conditions for an inevitable confrontation with the Indians who depended on buffalo for their livelihood. The federal government once again played an essential role, by providing the army to police the territory.

MINING FOR RICHES, STRIKING REALITY. Mining also drew people to the West. No other industry—with the possible exception of the cattle industry—had as great an impact on the region. The Gold Rush of 1849 had brought miners, merchants, speculators, and others to California. Soon mines, camps, towns, mills, and **smelters** appeared across the countryside.

The California strike was followed by discoveries of gold and silver in Colorado, Nevada, and British Columbia, Canada, in 1858. The Colorado strike was particularly exciting. Hundreds of Indians and frontiersmen explored for gold along the Arkansas River in Colorado. After months of searching, just as the expedition was beginning to give up and drift apart, **paydirt** was struck near present-day Denver.

By the spring of 1859 the wildest rush in the nation's history was underway in Colorado, as nearly 100,000 gold miners rushed toward Pike's Peak. In the 1860s other rich **lodes** of gold were discovered near Boulder. More discoveries were still to come. In the 1870s silver was discovered in Leadville, and a short while later gold was struck at Cripple Creek. These strikes accelerated the development of Colorado, which became a state in 1876.

The richest find was in Nevada. In 1859 two Irish miners discovered flake gold in the eastern foothills of the Sierra Nevada. They were joined by a third partner, Henry T. P. Comstock, who gave his name to the lode. In the next four years over $15 million worth of pure gold and silver was taken from these mountains. In October 1864, Nevada became a state. In the next decade mine after mine opened, producing $24 million annually. Paupers became millionaires overnight before the boom ended in 1890.

In 1880 rich copper ore was discovered in Butte, Montana. The industrial revolution in the East demanded copper, which Montana's mines readily provided. Thousands of miners, many of them immigrants, were employed in Butte's mines. The miners were vulnerable, for the **Anaconda** copper barons controlled the state. They often battled one another for political control of the state.

In 1898 the battle between William Clark and Marcus Daly for the U.S. Senate seat ended with Clark bribing members of the state legislature to elect him. When the Senate refused to seat him, Clark claimed in his defense, "I never bought a man who was not for sale."

Gold was found in the Black Hills of the Dakotas in the 1870s. Full exploitation of the area was retarded by the fierce Sioux Indians, who were protected by federal troops intent on keeping all intruders from the lands. In 1874, however, with rumors circulating of riches of gold to be found in the hills, thousands of prospectors began to force their way into the forbidden territory. Under pressure, the military decided to send its own expedition into the territory to disprove the rumors. When this force of 1,200 soldiers and scientists—led by General George Armstrong Custer—instead discovered more gold in the Black Hills, a new rush began.

In October 1875 the military, without the agreement of the Sioux, opened the Black Hills to these goldseekers. That spring prospectors flooded into the territory, establishing such "Wild West" towns as Deadwood Gulch. Among the miners were gunmen, gamblers, and camp followers—men and women such as Wild Bill Hickock, California Jack, Poker Alice, and Calamity Jane— who left their indelible mark on the mythic West.

Miners brought their own order to the mining towns of the West. Even before governments were formed, miners established claim clubs, citizen courts, and vigilante committees. They were quite willing to use "stretched hemp" (a hanging rope) on desperados who proved to be too unrestrained. One of the first acts of the Colorado territorial legislature in 1859 was to pass an act that gave legal status to decisions made by local miners' courts and meetings.

Following the Civil War, Nevada Senator William Stewart pushed through Congress the Mining Law of 1866. This act, revised in 1872, declared that all mineral lands in the public domain were free and open to prospectors. The law also gave precedence to local customs and miners' rules. This act revealed the miners' preference for frontier law and minimal federal involvement. Miners called for law and order as long as it was on their own terms.

By the 1880s eastern capitalists had turned Idaho and Montana mining into a commercial enterprise that employed a permanent workforce. The commercialization of mining changed the nature of work and social relations in the West. Mines changed from individual enterprises to consolidated, industrialized businesses. By the 1890s corporate mining dominated the industry. Often these corporations had absentee owners. In these circumstances, the miners shared much in common with the workers in the industrialized East. This led to social tensions between employers and hired laborers, who replaced the individual prospector of the romantic West.

Work in the underground mines became increasingly dangerous. Cave-ins and rockfalls were common as hastily rigged timbers and shafts gave way. Dynamiting accidents were frequently caused by premature or delayed blasts.

Miners found little protection from either mine owners or the courts. Liability laws favored the employer. For instance, when Joseph Adams, working in Montana, drilled into a buried dynamite charge, the explosion blinded his left eye, damaged his right eye, fractured his jaw, knocked out most of his teeth, and blew off his left hand. The courts ruled that the company was not responsible and need not pay compensation. The risk of working in the mine was understood and was assumed by the miner.

In these conditions, labor radicalism gained a foothold in the industry, giving rise to a bitter industrial struggle by the turn of the century. In 1893, the Western Federation of Miners was formed and quickly became a major force in mining areas in Montana, Idaho, and Colorado.

Thus for many the dream of striking it rich faded into a reality of hard and unrewarding labor. Towns that were hurriedly erected in these rushes were quickly abandoned once strikes dried up.

American Indians Resist the Westward Flood

In the decades following the Civil War, white settlers flooded into Indian lands. Native Americans fought back, but they were outnumbered and overpowered. As Euro-Americans broke one agreement after another, Indians tried negotiation, appeals to reason, war, and even escape into Canada, but nothing would stop the settlers' relentless drive for even more land. Reservations were given to Indians, then taken back. Indians also suffered from Euro-Americans' diseases and the destruction of the buffalo herds on which Indians depended.

Eastern reformers took up the Native American cause, but their efforts did little good in improving the condition of the

Indian. The Dawes Act (1887) was meant to help Indians, but resulted in even further loss of their land.

CONQUEST OF THE WEST AND AMERICAN INDIAN LIFE. A great migration occurred as Euro-Americans moved westward. Older immigrant groups were joined by new arrivals. The Irish settled throughout the Great Plains states. Germans, already established in the upper Mississippi region, migrated into Kansas, Nebraska, and the Dakotas. Scandinavian immigration began in 1865, reaching a peak in 1882 when over 105,000 arrived from Norway, Sweden, and Denmark. Thousands of freed slaves—known as Exodusters—left the South following Reconstruction to establish settlements in Kansas.

The westward movement caused population booms in established states such as Kansas, Nebraska, and Texas. By 1880 Kansas boasted nearly a million inhabitants, while Nebraska had 450,000 people.

As Euro-Americans moved westward, they confronted an Indian population remarkable in its diversity of language, culture, and economy. Tribes made contact with Euro-Americans at different rates and in different circumstances. As a result, Indians drew different experiences from these encounters. Native American culture, even before the arrival of the Euro-Americans, had been dominated by intertribal rivalry. Indian life, for all its simplicity and closeness to nature, was a world of raids, counterraids, and alliances kept or broken. Often the arrival of whites appeared to play a peripheral role in this world, as whites were seen as either allies or enemies taking sides in this intertribal warfare.

Nevertheless, contact with whites transformed Native American culture. The Indian population had been devastated by European diseases, including smallpox, cholera, typhus, influenza, malaria, measles, and yellow fever. By the middle of the 1800s, the Native American population had fallen to less than 500,000. In 1860 approximately 1.4 million Americans lived in the West; by 1890 over 8.5 million did. The lands once dominated by Indians were now finally in the hands of the whites.

Whites transformed Indian culture in many ways. Western tribes acquired horses from the Spanish, while eastern Indians encountering whites gained metal knives, muskets, and rifles. Replacing dogs with horses as the primary beast of burden offered mobility. As horse culture moved north from Mexico and rifle culture westward, they converged on the Great Plains, creating a buffalo hunting culture.

Native peoples found themselves contesting the land not only with European Americans moving westward, but also with Hispanics moving north from Mexico after the Civil War. In some of the northern states of

Mexico, governors in fact established scalp bounties on Apaches to discourage raids.

The Failure of Federal Indian Policy

Following the Civil War, the federal government sought to place Indians in one large reservation called Indian Territory. Indians were to be confined to these reserved lands through negotiation, if possible, and through brutal force as necessary. This policy became known as Grant's "peace policy." The failure of the policy and the horrid condition of Indians by the late 1880s led reformers to call for a new policy of assimilation expressed in the Dawes Act (1887), which called for the division of tribal lands into private property. In implementing these policies, the federal government plunged the West into another period of brutal warfare that destroyed Indian society and life, leaving a people decimated, demoralized, and defeated.

AMERICAN INDIANS RESIST INTRUSION. Warfare against Indians was especially brutal in California, where miners and ranchers found peaceful, pastoral "Digger" Indians who lacked even weapons of war. Whites launched a merciless war on these Indians, often spending their weekends in parties hunting down these unarmed people. Approximately 4,500 California Indians were killed this way. By the time the federal government moved to protect the California Indians, disease and violence had spared only a handful them to protect. Campaigns were carried out against the Snake and Bannock in Oregon and Idaho, and the Ute in Utah.

Southwestern and Plains Indians showed fiercer resistance. In the Southwest the Apache and Navajo battled the white settlers. Conflict reached a peak in New Mexico during the Civil War. Led by Kit Carson, the military launched an all-out attack against the Navajo. The Navajo fought more than 143 battles against Carson, but in the end they were forcibly removed to a **reservation** on the Pecos River in eastern New Mexico.

The Plains Indians—from the Sioux in the north to the Kiowa and Comanche in the Southwest—fought hard to resist white migration. Particularly fierce were the Sioux, who had continued to expand their hunting grounds at the expense of the Crow and the Pawnee. This caused intertribal warfare that continued even as whites entered Indian lands.

In 1851, at a meeting at Fort Laramie, Wyoming, with federal officials, the chiefs of the Sioux, Crow, Cheyenne, and Arapaho were guaranteed land

George Armstrong Custer inflicts a crushing defeat on the Cheyenne Indians camped along the Washita River, Oklahoma, in November 1868. Civil War veterans like Custer brought a ruthlessness to Indian fighting. Custer himself was defeated at the Little Big Horn in June 1876. (CULVER PICTURES)

stretching from the foothills of the Colorado to the Platte River in the Dakotas. Here, they were promised, they could live for all time. The federal government's Indian Office forcibly removed Indians from Kansas and Nebraska, organized as territories in 1854.

Trouble resumed with the discovery of gold near Pike's Peak, Colorado, in 1859. Fighting began in Colorado when over 100,000 miners crossed the Plains in 1859 and moved into Cheyenne and Arapaho lands. Federal agents only exacerbated troubles when they demanded that the two tribes abandon all claims to land—contrary to promises made at Fort Laramie—in exchange for a small reservation in eastern Colorado. In the summer of 1862, Indian hostilities intensified when the eastern Sioux in Minnesota went on the warpath after the district Indian agent refused to distribute food to the starving Indians. One white trader expressed the sentiment of many: "So far as I am concerned, if they are hungry let them eat grass or their own dung."

By 1864 Colorado was ablaze. Indians had murdered settlers, burned homes, destroyed mail stations, and attacked travelers. The countryside lay in ruins; Denver itself appeared threatened. Outraged settlers undertook a fierce military campaign against the Indians. When one Cheyenne chief—Black Kettle, a gentle, wise chief who embodied the Cheyenne peace spirit—tried to surrender, the local militia instructed him to take his 700 followers to Sand Creek. There, on November 28, 1864, the Colorado militia under Colonel J.

M. Chivington surrounded the Indians' camp and launched an attack. Black Kettle at first raised an American flag, then a white flag, but the attack continued. The warriors were pushed to the river, while women and children fled to the caves, only to be dragged out and slaughtered. Within a few hours, over 450 Indians were killed. Black Kettle and a few young warriors escaped.

The Sand Creek Massacre was applauded in Denver. Indian scalps were later put on display at the opera house in Denver. In the East the attack was widely condemned as a symbol of government mistreatment of Indians. A congressional report later condemned Chivington's militia for indulging "in acts of barbarity of the most revolting character." The Sand Creek Massacre inspired even greater resistance by the Cheyenne and Arapaho. They were now joined by Kiowa and Comanche uprisings in the Southwest. Meanwhile, the northern Sioux in Montana went on the warpath. At issue was the federal government's attempt to link Montana with the east by building a road through the Powder River territory. The Bozeman Trail cut through the favorite hunting grounds of the Sioux up to the rolling hills of the Big Horn. By 1866 federal troops were under constant attack, culminating in the massacre of 82 troopers under William Fetterman.

The massacre stunned the nation and once again brought the Indian question to public attention. General William Tecumseh Sherman, fresh from his march through Georgia, declared, "We must act with vindictive earnestness against the Sioux, even to the point of their extermination, men, women, and children."

THE FAILURE OF RESERVATION POLICY. Continued warfare with American Indians sharpened divisions on how to deal with the issue. The War Department, hardened by its experience in waging war against civilians during the Civil War, advocated a military campaign to bring the Indians to their knees.

On other side, the Interior Department, housing the Indian Office, sought to negotiate peace treaties that would establish small reservations where Indians could be protected from white intrusion, could practice agriculture, and could enjoy private ownership of property.

Those federal officials who advocated negotiations found support among certain tribal chiefs. These chiefs and their followers met with a federal peace commission at Medicine Lodge Creek in late 1867. In the end, almost every chief of importance on the southern plains was represented. The final treaty negotiated with the peace commission established new reservations south of the Arkansas River for the southern Cheyenne, Arapaho, and Sioux. In turn, the Kiowas and Comanche were forced to relinquish all claims to lands in central Texas, western Kansas, and eastern New Mexico.

A year later, the treaty of Fort Laramie brought temporary peace with the Sioux. The treaty cost the Sioux, as well as the Winnebagos, their traditional lands in Minnesota when they were forced to move west into a great reserve set aside for them in the Dakotas. The one tribe that particularly welcomed the peace were the Navajo. They had suffered severely on their Pecos River reservation from Comanche raiders, drought, floods, and disease. Following the treaty of Fort Laramie, they were finally returned to their traditional lands in New Mexico. There they flourished and became the largest tribe in the twentieth century.

In October 1867 the Medicine Lodge Creek treaty was shattered when a party of young Cheyenne warriors and a few Arapahos and Sioux went on a rampage in Kansas. A winter campaign headed by Generals William Tecumseh Sherman and Philip Sheridan crushed the uprising. In this campaign General George A. Custer attacked the sleeping Cheyenne village of Black Kettle, killing more than a hundred, including Black Kettle and his wife. They were shot in the back while fleeing to the river. In Texas the Kiowas and Comanches continued raids that lasted until 1875, when the last hostile Indians were transported to Florida as military prisoners.

The Sioux mounted the greatest challenge to peace. The treaty of Fort Laramie in 1868 had established the Great Sioux Reserve west of the Missouri River in the Dakota territory. Although many Sioux were lured to this reservation with promises of food and annuities, some warriors headed by Sitting Bull remained off the reservation.

In 1874 tensions were heightened when gold was discovered in the Black Hills and prospectors overran the area. Finally, in 1876 the secretary of the interior declared that all Indians not on the reservation—such as Sitting Bull—would be considered hostile. General Sheridan directed three military expeditions against the Sioux and their Cheyenne allies.

One of these columns, led by General Custer, launched a premature attack on the headquarters of Sitting Bull at the Little Bighorn on June 25, 1876. Some 2,500 warriors led by Crazy Horse slaughtered 300 cavalrymen in one of the most dramatic episodes in American history.

In response, the army sent in heavily armed reinforcements to Montana to hunt down the hostile Sioux and Cheyenne. Finally, in early May 1877, Crazy Horse surrendered. Sitting Bull, who had fled into Canada with his followers, was finally forced back to the reservation in 1881.

Not all white assaults on Indians were so direct. For example, the building of the Union Pacific Railroad in 1867-1868 had divided the Plains buffalo into two herds. When commercial tanners in the East found a market for buffalo hides, hunters (including whites, blacks, and Indians) began slaughtering buffalo. Others shot buffalo for sport. Between 1867 and 1883, they killed three million annually, removing a major food source for Indians. By 1878 the southern herd had been obliterated. By 1883, a scientific expedition could find only 200 buffalo in all the West. As a consequence, Native Americans were forced into a life of dependency based on government handouts.

Moreover, most Indian lands were unsuitable for subsistence agriculture. The Indians' attempts at self-sufficiency were further hampered by corrupt Indian agents, inefficient suppliers, and incompetent bureaucrats.

Struggles by Indians in this period revealed the tragedy of reservation policy. The most dramatic example of resistance came in the mid-1870s when Chief Joseph led his band of Nez Percé on a heroic attempt to escape into Canada from their reservation in Oregon. Joseph skillfully maneuvered his band east into Montana, down into the Yellowstone valley. The Nez Percé had almost reached Canada when they were trapped by General Nelson Miles, who promised them that they could return to Idaho, but not Oregon.

But higher army officials overruled the decision and instead moved Joseph and his followers to the unhealthy lowlands of the Missouri River. As he watched his people die slowly of disease and starvation, Chief Joseph went to Washington to plead his case for returning to Idaho. In 1879 he declared, "I see men of my race treated as outlaws and driven from country to country, or shot down like animals. I know that my race must change. . . . We only ask an even chance to live as other men live. We ask to be recognized as men." Under pressure from reformers who took up Chief Joseph's cause, 33 Nez Percé women and children were returned to Idaho in 1883, followed by another hundred two years later. Chief Joseph died before his wish to return to Oregon was fulfilled.

The treatment of the Ponca, a small peaceful Plains tribe, gave further witness to the shortcomings of reservation policy. In the treaty of Fort Laramie, the United States had ceded the entire reservation of the Ponca to the Sioux, the Ponca's traditional enemies. The plight of the Poncas became a rallying point for critics of federal reservation policy.

The crusade for Indian rights took a dramatic turn when Standing Bear, bearing the body of his son who had died of malaria, returned with his band from South Dakota to Nebraska in 1879. The Ponca chiefs, Bright Eyes and Standing Bear, took their cause to the general public. Appearing in their full tribal regalia, they spoke to assemblies of reformers throughout the country. When army officials arrested Standing Bear, who was appearing in Omaha, townspeople hired lawyers to defend the chief. In the celebrated case of *Standing Bear v. Crook,* the federal district court ruled in 1879 that "an Indian is a 'person' within the meaning of the laws of the United States." This important case guaranteed the right of **habeas corpus** to Indians.

REFORMING INDIAN POLICY. By 1880 the plight of the Indians on reservations had reached urgent, even apocalyptic proportions. Fearful that Native Americans were on the verge of extermination, eastern reformers had begun a campaign to overturn reservation policy and "detribalize" the Indian.

The key group in this campaign was the Indian Rights Association, founded in Philadelphia in 1882. This organization was made up of **evangelical Protestants** who opposed federal subsidies and welfare for Indians as degrading. Instead, these reformers called for a new policy of individual land ownership and the protection of Indians through law and education. This policy prescription was based upon the evangelical ethos that called for individual salvation.

Just as military leaders drew from their Civil War experience, Indian reformers advocated a program similar to what they had demanded for freed blacks during Reconstruction: citizenship, equal protection under the law, and education aimed at adjustment to a democratic culture and a market economy. That the program remained unrealized for blacks in the South, or that it might be unsuitable for Indians, simply was not considered by most Indian reformers.

The reformers sought to promote "Americanism." As one reformer declared, the Indians needed to have "broader desires and ampler wants." This meant that federal policy should be aimed at getting the "Indian out of the blanket and into trousers, and trousers with pockets in them, and with a pocket that ache[d] to be filled with dollars."

Only the small and uninfluential Indian Defense Association, headed by Dr. Thomas A. Bland, defended Indians ways. He warned that the dissolution of Indian tribes would be a disaster, but he was dismissed as a romantic and a reactionary.

Many Indian reformers were women. Mary L. Bonney, a Boston educator, organized the Women's National Indian Association, which became a key lobbying group in Washington. This organization brought others into the reform movement, including Alice C. Fletcher, an ethnologist who had spent much of her life among the Omahas, Winnebagos, and other Indians. The woman who gained the greatest fame was Helen Hunt Jackson. In 1881 she published *A Century of Dishonor*, a sentimental overdramatization of the Indian problem that fitted perfectly the mood of eastern reformers. Three years later she wrote *Ramona*, a moving account of the plight of the California Mission Indians.

These reformers led the fight in Congress to "detribalize" Indians. They found a champion in Massachusetts Senator Henry L. Dawes. The Dawes Severalty Act (1887) divided tribal land. It provided 160 acres to each head of a family, 80 acres to every single person over 18, and 40 acres to those under 18. Where farming was impossible, this allotment was doubled. Adult Indian males who received grants were given United States citizenship. Senator Dawes worried that the transfer to private ownership was too rapid. His fears proved prophetic. Remaining Indian lands were quickly reduced. In 1881 Indians held approximately 155.5 million acres; by 1900 their lands had been halved to 77.8 million acres. Married Indian women were not protected under the law and could be turned out of the homesteads by their husbands. Only after 1890 would these women be offered any protection.

Many Indians lacked work animals or agricultural implements to work the land. During the disastrous droughts of the 1880s, many Indians slaughtered their work animals and cattle for food. In addition, attempts to educate Indians often failed. Efforts to educate Native American children suffered from sectarian fights between Catholic and Protestant missionaries. Richard Pratt's Indian Industrial School at Carlisle, Pennsylvania, won fame for playing football against Harvard, Cornell, and Pennsylvania, but generally failed in its education program.

Year after year, thousands of Native Americans left the reservations permanently and became absorbed into the larger society. Still, a highly visible minority remained on reservations. For those Native Americans remaining on reservations, dependence on government rations and subsidies continued. At the same time, government agents moved to suppress the nomadic life of the Indian, to replace native religions with Christianity, and to replace Indian languages and oral traditions with written and spoken English.

In the summer of 1890 the Sioux made a last effort to distance themselves from the hostile outside world. Their cattle and crops had been destroyed by drought, and epidemics of measles, influenza, and whooping cough swept through their reservation. In the midst of this devastation, a religious revival appeared among the Sioux. Introduced by a Paiute medicine man in Nevada who called himself the Messiah, the revival centered around a Ghost Dance that promised salvation. By the time the dance reached the Dakotas, the Sioux turned it into a more militant demonstration. Concerned that Sitting Bull might join the demonstrations, the Indian agent at Pine Ridge sent tribal police to arrest Sitting Bull. When a crowd of angry Indians gathered to prevent the arrest, a melee broke out. Both sides fired their weapons. When the smoke and noise cleared, Sitting Bull and seven braves lay dead.

Major General Nelson A. Miles then sent the Seventh Calvary to round up 300 braves who had gathered at Wounded Knee. A confrontation occurred.

Promised by their medicine men that their Ghost shirts would protect them from bullets, the young Sioux braves charged into army artillery and machine guns. In less than an hour 150 braves had been killed and 50 wounded.

The end result of Indian reform was astutely summarized by one old Sioux warrior who sadly observed, "They [the whites] made us many promises, more than I can remember, but they never kept but one: they promised to take our land and they took it."

Creating a Community

Euro-Americans settled into the land once inhabited by the American Indian. Settlers came with their own dreams, grandiose and modest. All sought to impose new order on the land. They erected new communities, established families, and cultivated "civilized" mores and tastes. In doing so, they often looked eastward toward the regions they had left.

CIVILIZING THE WEST. By the 1880s, as Native Americans had been swept from the plains, Euro-Americans had built a huge cattle empire—half the size of Europe—that stretched from Texas through Colorado, Wyoming, Montana, the Dakotas, Kansas, and Nebraska. The profits from buying cattle in Texas for $6 to $7 a head and selling them in Kansas for $50 to $60 had led to widespread speculation in cattle ranching. Capital flowed in from the East and Europe. In Wyoming alone in 1883, 20 cattle corporations, capitalized at $12 million, were formed.

By 1885, however, it was clear the bubble was ready to burst. Costs escalated and prices fell. In 1885-1886 the cold winter and hot dry summer killed off many herds. The severe winter of 1886-1887 brought final disaster to the industry. In one of the worst winters in the West, carcass piled upon carcass. Hungry animals stripped trees bare in order to feed themselves. Cattle froze standing upright. In Wyoming the numbers of cattle declined from 9 million in 1885 to 3 million by 1895. Many cattle companies were forced into bankruptcy.

Still settlers continued to move west—sheep ranchers, farmers, and merchants. These pioneers found life hard. Many early plains settlers lived in sod houses—dirty, cramped, and wet. Grass roots grew through the ceilings, bringing in mud and water during rains and snows. Women in particular found life hard and lonely. As guardians of the home—the haven from the outside world of corruption—these pioneer women sought to maintain traditional values. Frontier life had a way of breaking down family life, however.

Wife beating, child abuse, and divorce were common on the frontier. This, combined with high mortality rates, meant that many frontier children grew up in single-parent homes.

To counter the frontier's corrosive influence, pioneers sought to cultivate eastern values in the West—through genteel learning, manners, and religion. Schools and churches were often the first public structures erected in a community. In Seattle, for example, **Yankee** pioneers created the University of Washington in 1861. At the time there were no buildings, no professors, no books—and no students. Pioneers knew that education was important. As a consequence, learning rates in the West stood above those in New England and equalled those in the Ohio Valley.

TECHNOLOGY AND THE WEST. Westerners were aided in their efforts to bring civilization to the frontier by railroads, the telegraph, and an improved national mail service that brought letters, books, periodicals, and religious tracts from the East. In this way the settlement of the West was very much a part of the Industrial Revolution that transformed the entire nation after the Civil War.

The Industrial Revolution proved to be key to Western development. The very expanse of western lands forced farmers to mechanize. James Oliver had introduced a smooth surfaced plow that easily slipped through the rich soils of the plains without clogging up. The seated plow followed. Other technological breakthroughs included reapers, seed scatterers, grain drills, and mowing machines. A wheat **combine** that harvested and tied wheat was developed in the 1880s by Cyrus McCormick. Such machinery freed farmers from much of the drudgery of manual labor. At the start of the Civil War, a farmer could plant and harvest no more that seven and half acres of wheat; by 1890 he could plant and harvest 135 acres.

Agricultural chemists persuaded farmers to use more fertilizers than ever before, thereby increasing productivity significantly. While most farms and ranches remained small and were operated by single families, huge "bonanza" farms emerged in the northern plains states. Some of these farms occupied tens of thousand of acres, employed hundreds of migratory workers, and used heavy equipment to harvest vast amounts of wheat or corn. One North Dakota farm produced some 600,000 bushels of wheat in 1881.

Similarly, wheat farmers in California's Central Valley harvested huge quantities of hard winter wheat. California farmers readily accepted technological advances by using steam driven harvesting combines that could thresh and bag as much as 450 pounds of wheat a minute. In the early 1880s wheat prices remained high and farmers profited.

Farmers found a ready market for their wheat. They exported 153 million bushels of wheat to England each year in the 1880s. Railroads, grain elevators, and shipping companies prospered. Hard spring wheat thrived in Minnesota and the Dakotas, while Kansas and Nebraska proved to be ideally suited for a hard kernel red wheat. The development of new processing methods allowed advanced flour mills to be built in Minneapolis, Kansas City, and St. Louis.

To protect their lands from roaming cattle and trespassers, westerners strung barbed wire, an invention of Joseph F. Glidden of DeKalb, Illinois. Produced in mass quantities by a Massachusetts manufacturing firm, barbed wire transformed much of the western landscape. Similarly, mechanical refrigeration and assembly line slaughtering transformed the meatpacking industry by allowing mass quantities of processed beef to be shipped from Chicago to eastern cities. Refrigeration also allowed California to ship fruits, nuts, and vegetables to eastern markets.

As farmers settled the West, cities emerged as commercial and cultural centers. These cities brought a rich mix of peoples and religions together into a common society. This diversity itself created social tensions. On the West Coast and especially in San Francisco, these feelings were expressed in an anti-Chinese movement that spilled over to state politics when Dennis Kearny, leader of the Workingman's party, forced a clause in the revised state constitution of 1879 that read "no native of China, idiot, insane person, or person convicted of an infamous crime . . . shall ever exercise the privileges of this state."

The dream of the romantic West had in the end led to a region marked by social tensions that had once been thought of as uniquely eastern.

Conclusion

Two years after Wounded Knee a young historian from the University of Wisconsin, Frederick Jackson Turner, appeared before the annual meeting of historians in Chicago, to read his essay, "The Significance of the Frontier in American History." In this seminal paper he declared that the frontier had passed, replaced by civilized society. By the 1890s the plains and the mountains between the Mississippi River and the Pacific Ocean had been settled by people streaming westward from the Missouri River and eastward from the Pacific shore. They had come seeking wealth in gold and silver, timber and agriculture, commerce and politics. In doing so they displaced and nearly destroyed native peoples, united a continent, and prepared the nation for its destiny.

Recommended Readings

DOCUMENTS: Samuel Clemens (Mark Twain), *Roughing It,* (1871); Mari Sandoz, *Old Jules* (1935); H.G Merriam, ed., *Way Out West: Recollections and Tales* (1969); Sallie Reynolds Matthews, *Interwoven: A Pioneer Chronicle* (1982); Wallace Stegner, *Wolf Willow: A History, a Story, and a Memory of the Last Plains Frontier* (1983).

READINGS: Ray Allen Billington, *Westward Expansion: A History of the American Frontier* (1967); Dee Brown, *Bury My Heart at Wounded Knee* (1970); Albert Camarillo, *Chicanos in a Changing Society* (1976); Richard Griswold del Castillo, *La Familia: Chicano Families in the Urban Southwest* (1983); David Dary, *Cowboy Culture: A Saga of Five Centuries* (1981); Arnoldo de Leon, *They Called Them Greasers: Anglo Attitudes Toward Mexicans in Texas* (1983); Robert K. Dykstra, *The Cattle Towns* (1968); Elizabeth Hampsten, *Read This Only to Yourself: The Private Writings of Midwest Women, 1880-1910* (1982); Howard Robert Lamar, *The Far Southwest* (1966); Patricia Nelson Limerick, *The Legacy of Conquest: The Unbroken Fast of the American West* (1987); Robert Mardock, *Reformers and the American Indian* (1971); Sandra L. Myres, *Westering Women and the Frontier Experience* (1982); Rodman Wilson Paul, *Mining Frontiers of the Far West* (1963); Francis Paul Prucha, *American Indian Policy in Crisis* (1976); Robert J. Rosenbaum, *Mexicano Resistance in the Southwest* (1981); Lillian Schlissel, *Women's Diaries of the Westward Journey* (1982); Richard Slotkin, *The Fatal Environment* (1985); Robert M. Utley, *The Indian Frontier of the American West* (1984) and *The Last Days of the Sioux Nation* (1963); Elliot West, *Growing Up With the Country: Childhood and the Far West Frontier* (1989); Richard White, *"It's Your Misfortune and None of My Own," A New History of the American West* (1991).

17

GILDED AGE POLITICS: THE PERCEIVED FAILURE OF DEMOCRACY

CHAPTER OVERVIEW: Americans entered the late nineteenth century confident in their democratic government. From 1877 through 1900, Americans participated in politics in increasing numbers, with voter turnout reaching unprecedented numbers. Divided along ethnic, religious, and regional lines, well-organized political parties battled to control government. While Republicans generally controlled the White House, Congress remained divided between the Republicans and Democrats. Because the presidency remained weak in this period—given the nature of the office and the mediocrity of those who held it—Congress proved to be the more important institution.

As the century drew to a close, however, many middle-class Americans felt that democratic government had failed. Democratic politics seemed to be dominated by corruption, run in the interests of unscrupulous machine politicians who showed flagrant disregard for any notion of public morality. The nineteenth century appeared to be, above all else, an age of excess where the politics of privilege had subverted the public interest.

Party Politics Stalemated

In the late nineteenth century, Americans displayed fierce partisan loyalty and deep involvement in politics, even though politicians often proved corrupt and special interests dominated. Though the age lacked great statesmen, voters marched to the polls in record numbers. Sharply divided along ethnic and regional lines, political parties espoused nationalism; mired in past embitterment, they promised a better future; controlled by myopic self-interest, they spoke of broad vision. Little wonder that politics in the late nineteenth century appeared stalemated.

MACHINE POLITICS AND THE RULES OF THE POLITICAL GAME.
Clearly, the late 1800s were not characterized by notable American statesmen. While European politics in the late nineteenth century was dominated by William Gladstone and Benjamin Disraeli in England and Otto Von Bismarck in Germany, the United States witnessed a parade of singularly unimpressive presidencies after the death of Abraham Lincoln. Ulysses S. Grant (1869-1877) proved to be easily fooled by self-serving associates; Rutherford B. Hayes (1877-1881) left office with a bitterly divided party; James Garfield (1881) was assassinated before he accomplished anything; Chester A. Arthur (1881-1885) won a modest place in history with the passage of a civil service **bill;** Grover Cleveland (1885-1889) tackled the hard questions of the **tariff** and civil service, and Benjamin Harrison (1889-93) frequently capitulated to the special interests.

National politics itself often faced stalemate as the two political parties sought control of the White House and Congress. Although the Democrats won the presidency only once in this period, when they elected Grover Cleveland in 1884, they were by no means a weak party. Indeed, they won a **plurality** or a majority of the popular vote in the five presidential elections between 1876 and 1892. They lost the elections of 1876 and 1888 only because they did not win in the **electoral college.** They retained strength in the South and won the loyalty of urban Irish Catholics and midwestern Germans.

The Republicans were strong in New England, Pennsylvania, and the upper Midwest. Their strength lay among the native-born Protestants of British descent. The Republicans—also called the Grand Old Party or GOP—continued to play on their Civil War record by nominating a number of former Union army generals for the presidency and voting for generous veterans benefits supported by such lobbying groups as the Grand Army of the Republic (GAR).

Neither party, however, dominated national politics. In the 20 years between 1874 and 1894 Democrats controlled the House of Representatives for 16 years while Republicans controlled the Senate for 14 years. Indeed, only twice did a single party control both the presidency and the Congress: the Republicans from 1889-1891 and the Democrats from 1893-1895. This meant that radical shifts in policy, even if desired by either party, were impossible. Politics became a matter of filling constituent needs largely revolving around the tariff, the "money question," and pensions.

Because the Republicans and Democrats found themselves evenly matched, certain swing states took on special significance. States such as Connecticut, New York, New Jersey, Indiana, and Illinois—where the voters could "swing" to either party—were given added attention during elections. In turn, most presidential and vice-presidential candidates came from these states.

State and local parties had a significance of their own. They selected candidates, financed and organized campaigns, and mobilized the voters. Even presidential campaigns relied on state and local organizations to carry the party standard. These state and local party organizations were dominated by party bosses. For example, in Pennsylvania the father and son team of Simon and Don Cameron dominated the state. In some states, most notably in the West, economic interests prevailed, such as the Anaconda Copper Corporation in Montana and the Union Pacific Railroad in California. **"Political machines"** dominated major cities. These political machines, usually centered around a party "boss" or a group of leaders, mobilized voters at election time and dispensed government appointments **(patronage)** or government contracts to party loyalists.

These machines successfully mobilized voters to turn out on election days. Throughout this period, voter turnout soared to over 80 percent. Campaigns took on a fierce excitement comparable to a military battle. Voters were seen as soldiers to be aroused to fight the enemy. A continual barrage of rallies, speeches, torchlight parades, and mass demonstrations kept the soldiers of both armies excited. Although women and children were excluded from voting, they were eager participants in these rallies. Independent voters were ignored as the two armies confronted one another. Ballots were printed by the parties, reinforcing intense partisan loyalties when each voter revealed his party affiliation by displaying a party ballot at the polling booth on election day.

These political machines proved to be highly efficient organizations, often keeping detailed records on thousands of voters. In this age before computers and television, newspapers could predict the outcome of an election based on the earliest returns.

Victory meant more than putting one's candidate into office. It also meant the winner rewarding his supporters by giving them government jobs (see Chapter 10 on the **spoils system**). In federal elections over 100,000 government jobs were available to be doled out by the winner. While most federal workers were honest, a notable few were not. The rewards for those few were tremendous. Positions in the Post Office or foreign consuls were often sold. For instance, in New York, the winner could give out 1,000 jobs in the New York Customs House alone. Charged with collecting tariff duties on imports, customs officers had opportunities to extort millions of dollars from businesses. One common practice was to undervalue a shipment, then discover the mistake at a later date. Under the law, the entire value of an import that was falsely declared was forfeited, with half the total going to the head of the customs house. Businessmen willingly paid bribes to protect their goods. In 1874, Phelps, Dodge, and Company paid $50,000 to a group of

Republican officeholders that included the future president, Chester A. Arthur.

EXCLUDING IMMIGRANTS, BLACKS, AND WOMEN. Politics at the grassroots generated cultural and ethnic warfare. Democrats since Jackson's time had attracted Germans, Irish, Jews, Catholics, and white Protestants in the South. Republicans drew older white immigrant groups, usually of British, Scandinavian, and Dutch descent.

Evangelical Protestant groups in the Midwest tended to be Republican. They interjected their fears and prejudices toward Catholics into the political arena. Often these anxieties were expressed in **nativist** campaigns that called for cultural uniformity and the exclusion of Catholics from the political and social life of the nation. Anti-Catholic and nativist (anti-immigrant) sentiments were also expressed in campaigns against immigration, gambling, prostitution, and alcohol. **Prohibition** aroused passions on both sides. Antiliquor campaigns offended Irish whisky drinkers, German beer drinkers, and Italians who felt that dinner without wine was like song without music—possible, but less pleasurable.

In July 1848, the first women's rights convention met in Seneca Falls, New York. By 1918 women had acquired the vote in 15 states. The ratification of the nineteenth amendment in 1920 marked the final victory of the long campaign for suffrage. (BROWN BROTHERS)

For women and blacks, the late nineteenth century was an age of exclusion. Although after the Civil War the nation had conferred rights of citizenship and voting on freed black men through the passage of the fourteenth amendment (1868) and fifteenth amendment (1870) to the Constitution, blacks found that state and local laws prevented them from *exercising* their federal rights. These laws—known as **Jim Crow** laws—set up an array of barriers that kept blacks from the voting place.

Women too found themselves excluded from voting in national elections. Some localities granted women the right to vote; Nebraska in 1867 and Colorado in 1876 permitted women to vote in school elections. By 1910 four states—Idaho, Wyoming, Utah, and Colorado—allowed women full voting rights. Nonetheless, there was fierce resistance to women's **suffrage** on a national level. This led women such as Elizabeth Cady Stanton, Susan B. Anthony, and Lucy Stone to organize political campaigns to pressure Congress to approve a constitutional amendment extending voting rights to women. Divided by sectarian rivalry, opposed by the leadership of both parties, and unsupported by the majority of the male electorate, woman suffrage made little headway in the late nineteenth century.

For all the corruption, cultural conflict, and exclusion of the late nineteenth-century politics, the nation and its leaders did confront important issues. Americans debated the tariff, money, and the civil service. These were complex questions, yet voters proved to be remarkably knowledgeable about them, often willing to listen for hours to long and intricate speeches on the tariff and money question. (Before radio and television and mass spectator sports, politics served as mass entertainment and attracted people's concentrated attention). Questions concerning the rapid growth of corporate business, however, were generally ignored except for the passage of the Interstate Commerce Act (1887) and the Sherman **Antitrust** Act (1890).

Presidential Players, Washington Games, and the Politics of Division, 1877-1885

The worst aspect of late nineteenth-century democratic politics seemed to be embodied in the presidency. The Grant presidency had been marred by corruption and ineptitude. The presidencies that followed offered little better. Republicans controlled the presidency throughout the late nineteenth century, except for the election of Grover Cleveland in 1884 and 1892, but neither party offered much in way of presidential leadership.

HAYES TAKES OFFICE AND CONFRONTS LABOR, 1877. The election of 1876, as noted in Chapter 15, had ended in the Grand Compromise of 1877. In this compromise, Republican Rutherford B. Hayes stepped into the White House even though he had lost the popular vote by 250,000 votes. (Of course, these results excluded the hundreds of thousands of black supporters who were prevented from voting for Hayes).

As a Civil War hero and devoted family man, Hayes personified the values of Victorian America. His wife, Lucy Webb, was highly intelligent and college educated. She brought a moral earnestness to the White House that offended some and bored others. A supporter of the Woman's Christian Temperance Union (WCTU), Lucy refused to serve alcohol at the White House.

Hayes undermined his own position from the start when he declared he would not accept a second term in office. Instead he called for a constitutional amendment for a single six-year presidential term. He barely survived his four years.

In the summer of 1877, Hayes confronted his first great crisis, a railroad strike. A **depression** in 1873 had created massive unemployment and had led employers to cut workers' wages, as much as 35 percent on some railroads.

In July 1877, employees of the Baltimore and Ohio Railroad went on strike. Rioting led to hundreds of deaths and injuries and an estimated $10 million in damage, finally forcing President Hayes to use federal troops to suppress the strike. (CULVER PICTURES)

Railroad owners also used the depression to attack the unions of engineers, firemen, and conductors. When the Baltimore and Ohio Railroad (B&O) management sought further wage cuts in the summer of 1877, workers at Martinsburg, West Virginia, refused to operate the trains. Both the local militia and the governor refused to interfere in the strike, so Hayes sent in federal troops to quell it. The B&O strike quickly spread to other lines and cities, reaching as far as California.

Local militia often refused to intervene. In Philadelphia, full-scale rioting broke out when the city attempted to use the local militia. In Reading, Pennsylvania, ten people were killed. Miners, mill hands, unemployed workers, women, and children joined the strike. In St. Louis and Cincinnati, socialists became prominent strike leaders. In these circumstances Hayes called out federal troops. Before the strike ended, rioters had caused $10 million worth of property damage.

Hayes's action finally brought order to a shocked nation. The 1877 strike dwarfed any previous labor disturbance in the nation's history. Editorials compared it to the Paris Commune of 1871. The irony, of course, was that Hayes, who had campaigned for office calling for states' rights and the removal of federal troops from the South, had been forced to use these same soldiers against American workers in the North.

THE MONEY QUESTION PERPLEXES POLITICAL PLAY. Hayes's next challenge came in form of the money question. On the surface the issue revolved around how to supply enough money to meet the needs of a rapidly growing economy. Beneath the surface lay deep social and political questions concerning classes, wealth, and political influence.

From 1865 to 1908, two economic trends prevailed: the economy was growing (over 4 percent a year on average), while prices were falling. This decline in prices (called deflation) generally benefitted consumers. (Falling prices allowed consumers to buy goods more cheaply.) But deflation hurt others, especially farmers in the West and South. (In turn, falling prices meant that farmers sold their crops for less money.) In a period of deflation, farmers' fixed debts loomed larger each year. Southern and western farmers were most vocal in calling for a variety of measures to reverse the long-term trend of deflation. One measure that attracted their attention was increasing the money supply. (Adding more money to circulation tends to raise prices—called inflation.) Farmers claimed that the money supply was not keeping up with the growth of the economy. In fact, both the money supply and industrial production grew at parallel rates. The real problem was that the rate of growth for both money supply and production was erratic. This uneven pace of economic activity brought periods of hardship to great numbers of people—farmers as well as unemployed immigrants and displaced workers.

In general, bankers, business leaders, and creditors sought to stabilize the growth of the money supply by basing money on a **gold standard:** the money supply could grow only at the rate at which new gold was mined. (By limiting the supply of money in circulation, business leaders sought to prevent inflation.) Debtors and some manufacturers favored expanding the money supply by issuing **greenbacks** (government paper or fiat money) or by allowing more silver-based currency to circulate. Greenbacks were paper notes that had been issued by the federal government during the Civil War. People were legally bound to accept greenbacks during the war, but the value of greenbacks quickly fell below the price of gold. In 1865 it took $144.25 in greenbacks to buy $100 of gold.

As the war drew to a close, business interests wanted the federal government to withdraw greenbacks from circulation. For a time Congress ordered the government to buy up greenbacks to take them out of circulation, but the Panic of 1873 ended this policy. After the depression Congress again returned to a policy of limiting greenbacks.

This marked a victory for the conservative, hard-money (non-paper greenback) forces, but the fight about money was hardly over. By the mid-1870s the money question was again interjected into the political debate with the formation of the Greenback party. The party appealed to debtor farmers in the South and the West by calling for the expansion of the money supply through the issuing of greenback dollars. The Greenback party gained strength following the labor upheavals in 1877. In the first **midterm elections** of Hayes's presidency, the Greenbacks got over one million votes and sent 14 men to the House of Representatives.

Just as quickly as the Greenback party came onto the scene, though, it faded. The rise of wheat prices in 1878, due to crop failures in Europe, allowed American farmers to prosper. As a consequence, in the North the Greenback party lost support.

While the greenback issue died down, the issue of money did not. As soon as the greenback question faded, the silver question became even more heated. By demanding that money be based on both silver and gold, farmers and other groups sought to inflate the economy. If the base of the money supply could enlarged by silver, it was argued, prices farmers received for their crops would rise. Prior to 1873, the U.S. Treasury regularly coined silver and gold dollars. In 1873, however, little silver was being sold to the Treasury. Congress therefore instructed the Treasury Department through the **Coinage** Act (1873) to cease issuing silver coins. But just then, new discoveries of silver in Nevada increased the supply. Inflationists—debt-ridden farmers—now sought to expand the money supply through the making of silver coins. They denounced the Coinage Act as the "Crime of '73."

In 1878 Congress passed the Bland-Allison Silver Purchase bill. The bill had been first introduced in 1877 by Representative "Silver Dick" Bland of Missouri, who called for the "free and unlimited coinage of silver." The House of Representatives knew that Bland represented the small silver producing interests of Missouri, but it nonetheless overwhelmingly passed the measure. After all, economic self-interest was the stuff of politics. Only the efforts of Senator William Allison from the farm state of Iowa tempered the measure when he amended the bill to limit the coinage of silver each month to no more than $4 million in silver bullion.

Although Hayes opposed even this amended bill, he signed it because he feared the possibility of a stronger measure. Hayes need not have worried. John Sherman, secretary of treasury, sabotaged the act by instructing his agents to purchase only a minimum quantity of silver—and then refusing to circulate the silver dollars once they were minted.

REPUBLICANS DIVIDE INTO FACTIONS: STALWARTS V. HALF-BREEDS V. LIBERALS. While the money question became increasingly controversial, dividing both Republicans and Democrats, the Republicans divided into warring factions in which ideological lines became blurred. Divisions within the Republican party occurred less over principle than over personality and quarrels about the spoils of public office. On one side stood New York's handsome, egotistical Senator Roscoe Conkling, who led a group called the Stalwarts. Conkling's rival was Maine's Senator James G. Blaine, who led the Half-Breeds.

Throughout the Grant presidency, Conkling and his Stalwarts dominated Congress and controlled patronage in New York. These Stalwarts lacked a distinctive political philosophy. Their single interest in national government was to protect and strengthen their Republican political machines to win elections and distribute spoils in their home states.

Under Grant, Conkling and the Stalwarts gained control of New York's patronage, but the tall, charming Blaine captivated many Republicans, who saw in him a future president. He was elected to Congress from Maine in 1863 and quickly rose to become the speaker of the House six years later. Blaine, as leader of the Half-Breeds, opposed continuing Reconstruction, but he also sought to weaken Conkling's control over New York so that he could gain control of New York patronage for his followers.

Although Blaine's Half-Breeds and Conkling's Stalwarts shared a desire for patronage, a fundamental difference separated the two factions. Whereas the Stalwarts saw business interests in terms of serving the machine, the Half-

Breeds sought to establish a new relationship with business interests. Under Blaine the Half-Breeds sought to encourage cooperation between the party and business interests. The Half-Breeds favored promoting industrial growth, expanding foreign markets, raising tariffs to protect industry, and improving American workers' standard of living.

Standing outside these two factions was a smaller, although significant, grouping within the Republican party. The reform-minded Liberal Republicans had emerged in opposition to the Grant administration. In 1872 they broke with the party to form a separate Liberal Republican party which nominated Horace Greeley. After Greeley was soundly defeated, the Liberal Republican faction returned to Republican party.

Many reform-minded men and women focused their efforts on ending the corrupt patronage system by establishing a professional civil service based on merit, education, and training. As early as 1865, Representative Thomas A. Jenckes of Rhode Island had begun calling for competitive examinations for government posts. Civil service reform gained further momentum when British Prime Minister William Gladstone, the idol of American liberals, successfully reformed British government administration in the 1870s. In 1876 both political parties endorsed civil service reform in their platforms—a sure sign that reformers had gained some recognition within the parties.

Liberal Republicans included Carl Schurz, the German-born senator from Missouri, E. L. Godkin, the editor of the influential *The Nation,* and the social reformer Josephine Shaw Lowell. They formed the Civil Service Reform League in 1881. Calling for reform in government administration, they saw partisan politics as corrupt and inefficient. Always ill-at-ease within the Republican party, they would break again with the Republican party in 1884 over the nomination of James Blaine for the presidency.

Even with their intense dislike of Blaine, Liberal Republicans shared with the Half-Breeds an even greater dislike of Conkling. He insulted reformers by calling them "snivel service reformers" and offended Hayes by publicly referring to him as "His Fraudulency, the President," an allusion to the election of 1876. It was said that Conkling had many followers, but no friends.

By the time the 1880 election approached, the Republican party was severely divided.

Reform Simmers, 1881-1893

Elected in 1880 in a particularly bitter campaign, Garfield came into office promising reform. His assassination in 1881 stirred reform sentiment. Under Garfield's successor, Chester A.

Arthur, a modest civil service system was established under the Pendleton Act. The election of Grover Cleveland in 1884, the first Democrat elected since the Civil War, brought calls for reform, but special interests continued to block meaningful change. The election of Benjamin Harrison in 1888 revealed it was "politics as usual."

GARFIELD ATTACKS THE STALWARTS. To humiliate Hayes, the Stalwarts sought to renominate Grant in 1880. The Half-Breeds turned to Blaine. The ensuing convention deadlocked. On the 32nd ballot the Republicans turned to a **dark-horse** candidate, James A. Garfield, a leading congressman and former Civil War general and college president from Ohio. The **ticket** was balanced politically and geographically with Chester A. Arthur, formerly of the New York Customs House.

The Democrats also turned to a former Union general, Winfield Scott Hancock of Pennsylvania. Both Hancock and Garfield were men of high integrity, but the campaign took a bitter turn when the Republicans warned that Hancock's Catholic wife would allow Catholic influence in the White House. The Democrats counterattacked by charging Garfield with being dominated by big business. During the campaign Garfield cultivated businessmen. John D. Rockefeller sent 500 Standard Oil agents to closely contested Indiana to canvass the state for the Republican ticket. The election proved to be one of the closest in American history. Of the nine million votes cast, Garfield won by only 39,000.

In many respects Garfield was an unusual choice for president. Although he maintained close relations with business, Garfield had a reputation for honesty. He was a self-taught scholar who could speak both German and French and who could write Latin with one hand and Greek with the other at the same time. A one-time professor of mathematics, he is still remembered for inventing a proof in geometry. After one month in the White House he exclaimed, "My God! What is here in this place that a man should ever want to get in it?"

Following the election, Garfield, acting on Blaine's advice, attacked the Stalwarts at the base of their support, the New York Customs House with its 1300 patronage jobs, by seeking to appoint men loyal to his administration. When Conkling saw that his voice was not going to be heard in making patronage appointments, he played his single most important card: along with his colleague in the Senate, Tom Platt, he resigned. Conkling and Platt rushed home where they expected the New York legislature to reelect them. To their chagrin, the Half-Breeds and Democrats blocked their reelection. For six weeks this coalition held off Platt and Conkling. Then acting on a journalist's tip, a group of Half-Breeds carried a step ladder into the hotel home of Tom Platt and peered through the transom into his room. They found Platt locked in the embrace of "an unspeakable female." The public was regaled with the facts of his sex life, and Platt withdrew his candidacy.

The same day that Platt withdrew from the Senate race, July 2, 1881, Garfield went to the railroad station in Washington to travel to his Williams College reunion. As he stood on the platform listening to Blaine expound on the virtues of trade with Latin America, he was approached by Charles Guiteau, a disgruntled office seeker and religious fanatic. Suddenly Guiteau pulled a pistol and shot the president in the back. As he struggled with his captors, Guiteau was heard shouting, "I am a Stalwart, and Arthur is president now."

For three months Garfield lingered. The bullet that entered his back lodged in a muscle. The best surgeons in the country were called in to probe for the bullet. The clumsy probes did little good, and Garfield died on September 19, 1881. Chester Arthur now stepped into the White House.

A FIRST SMALL STEP TOWARD CIVIL SERVICE REFORM, 1881-1885.

Many feared that the presidency of Chester Arthur might mean the return of the Stalwarts. Former President Hayes warned that they would be "the power behind the throne, superior to the throne." Few had confidence in Arthur. He was best known for his vanity. Always impeccably dressed, he owned 80 pairs of pants. But Arthur proved to be more than a foppish follower of fashion. He brought an unexpected independence into the White House. The office transformed the man.

Garfield's assassination brought a crusade for civil service reform. Congress encountered a barrage of letters, petitions, editorials, and mass meetings calling for reform. Throughout the summer, while Garfield had lingered, Congress had investigated the corrupt mail services. The investigation centered on Star Route contracts (special mail routes), which had been given by an assistant postmaster general in exchange for bribes. The investigation revealed that dishonest contractors had overcharged the government $4 million. When the Star Route trial ended in a hung jury, public anger was further fueled.

Amid the **Star Route scandal,** public opinion was further inflamed when the newspapers published a letter from Jay A. Hale, chairman of the Republican congressional campaign, soliciting contributions from civil servants. The letter revealed that it was customary for government employees to contribute between 2 percent to 6 percent of their salaries to the party.

In a **lame duck** session, Congress finally passed civil service reform with the Pendleton Act. Introduced by Senator George Pendleton from Garfield's home state of Ohio, the bill established a civil service commission to examine candidates for federal jobs. It also made it illegal for political candidates to solicit contributions from government workers. The bill itself was relatively weak, covering only 12 percent of all federal jobs. The newly created Civil Service Commission got jurisdiction over only the custom houses and post offices in large cities. Arthur later expanded offices covered under the act, a practice followed by later presidents.

Reform, however, changed only the nature of corruption. Businessmen increased their influence in the 1880s. The Senate became known as the Millionaires Club. Many senators developed close links with the economic interests of their states. For example, George Hearst from California represented gold and newspapers. Philetus Sawyer served lumber interests in Wisconsin. Calvin Bruce attended to banks and railroads. H. B. Payne was known as Standard Oil's man in Congress. Many of the new senators were corporate lawyers, including John Spooner of Wisconsin, Arthur Gorman of Maryland, and Orville Platt of Connecticut.

By nature these men were cautious. Platt was especially known for hedging his bets. Once while traveling in his home state, he was stopped at the crossroads by a flock of sheep. His traveling companion observed, "The sheep have been shorn." Platt cautiously replied, "'Pears so—at least on this side."

A REFORMER BEATS A SPOILSMAN: GROVER CLEVELAND ELECTED, 1884. Arthur had pleased neither reformers nor conservatives in the party, so in 1884 Republicans nominated Blaine for president. A proponent of the high tariff, Blaine openly sought to make Republicans the party of business.

The nomination of Blaine outraged Republican reformers. Deciding "enough was enough," they bolted the party to endorse the Democratic candidate, Grover Cleveland. They were quickly denounced by party regulars as **"mugwumps"**—an Algonquian Indian word meaning "little chiefs," too proud of themselves. For these mugwumps the Republican party was in decline: the heroic struggle against slavery had been replaced by the fight over the spoils of office. These mugwumps sought a nonpartisan government run by experts. Thus there was no "Republican" or "Democratic" way of government, no party way of building sewers, no party way of educating children.

In many ways this bolt from the Republican party pointed to a new political consciousness that was to emerge in the next century: partisan loyalty was not as important as independent thought and choosing the best candidate. Yet while the mugwumps may have foreshadowed future political changes, in 1884 they were fiercely denounced as arrogant traitors and patrician elitists. Such charges against the mugwumps—most of whom were college educated urban northeasterners—were easily made at a time when only 2 percent of Americans between the ages of 18 and 21 were enrolled in institutions of higher learning.

In choosing Cleveland, a reformer who had been mayor of Buffalo and governor of New York, Democrats shrewdly sought to highlight the contrast with Blaine's reputation as a spoilsman. Cleveland brought to the campaign a strong belief in public morality and a fierce sense of independence. Son of a Presbyterian minister in western New York, Cleveland grew up on the ideals of Jacksonian democracy. As a Jacksonian Democrat, he shared his political hero's belief in a strong executive and weak federal government. Throughout his political career as the reform mayor of Buffalo and governor of New York he had expressed a deep anxiety that the American **polity** was being exploited by the wealthy and powerful for their own ends. For this reason he opposed protective tariffs and easy money. He saw the Republican party as embodying special privilege.

Blaine was no white knight. In the 1877 election he had been accused of taking a $64,000 bribe from the Union Pacific Railroad. Blaine and the Union Pacific denied the charge, but a railroad bookkeeper, James Mulligan, stepped forward with letters that supported the accusation of corruption. At a private meeting with Mulligan, Blaine artfully accepted the letters. Shortly afterwards he read excerpts from the letters on the floor of Congress in a way to convince his audience he was not guilty. He was exonerated, but the scandal continued to haunt him.

The presidential campaign of 1884 proved unusually bitter. Early in the campaign, Republicans revealed that Cleveland had fathered an illegitimate child with Maria Halpin, a attractive Buffalo widow. Cleveland had supported the child in an orphanage. When first revealed, Cleveland immediately admitted the charge. Democrats, in response, brought up the Mulligan letters. At rallies Republicans would chant, "Ma, Ma, where's my pa? He's gone to the White House, ha, ha, ha." Democrats would shoot back, "Blaine, Blaine, James G. Blaine, the continental liar from the state of Maine."

Neither side held a clear lead with the voters. In the closing days of the campaign, Blaine made several political mistakes. An extravagant fund raiser emphasized Blaine's ties with monied interests. That same day a Protestant minister in Blaine's presence denounced the Democrats as a party of "rum, Romanism, and rebellion," alienating Roman Catholic Irish voters in New York. Blaine's mother was in fact Catholic, but that made no difference. The damage was done.

New York proved difficult for Blaine in other ways. An active campaign by the Prohibition party cut into Blaine's support, especially in New York where the Prohibition ticket picked up over 16,000 votes, mostly drawn from Republicans. The loss of New York cost Blaine the election. When the New York votes were finally counted, Cleveland had carried the state by only 1,149 votes. Cleveland took the final **electoral vote** by 219 to 182, but he won the popular vote by fewer than 30,000 votes.

CLEVELAND TAKES ON THE SPECIAL INTERESTS, 1885-1889. Cleveland came to office with a clear political vision: reduce government activity, balance the budget, and free capital for private investment. He sought to limit government by severing what he perceived as its link to special interests. He specifically sought to cut government expenditures. In doing so, he incurred the wrath of many and won the hearts of few.

This no-win situation became apparent in Cleveland's confrontation with Civil War veterans who demanded larger pensions. Civil War pensions provided an elaborate welfare system that helped an estimated one in every four families in America. By 1886 pensions to Civil War veterans accounted for one-quarter of the federal budget. Congress also regularly passed special pensions for individual constituents. In the process, a small industry had emerged in Washington in which individuals hired lobbyists to push their petitions through Congress. The system was wide open for abuse. For example, one bill provided a pension for a man who had never served in the army: on the way to enlist he had fallen and was crippled. Another was for an army captain who had died from a heart attack in 1883: his widow claimed that his death had been brought on by a wartime hernia. Another widow received a pension on behalf of a husband who had drowned while in the process of deserting.

In 1887 Congress extended pensions with the Invalid Pension Act. The measure awarded pensions to all disabled veterans, whether their injury had been incurred in war or not. Cleveland vetoed the act. In so doing he ensured the wrath of veterans in the next election. Cleveland's support came largely from northern immigrants and ex-Confederates, neither of whom were eligible for pensions, so perhaps he did not fear the veterans lobby.

In his first year in office Cleveland showed similar disregard for another block of voters—farmers. Two actions especially hurt him with agricultural interests: his attack on the misappropriation of public lands in the West by ranchers, and his unwillingness to support farm relief for drought-stricken farmers. Cleveland worried that the West was being plundered. He therefore instructed Secretary of Interior Lucius Lamar and Land Commissioner W. A. J. Sparks to investigate land claims being made by cattle ranchers and mine owners in the West. He ordered the return of 81 million acres of public lands given to railroads for purposes of construction.

As the 1888 election approached, Cleveland further alienated the western farm vote. On February 16, 1887, he vetoed the Texas Seed bill, which appropriated a modest $10,000 to provide desperate farmers with seed. Cleveland declared, "Though the people support the government, the government should not support the people." He added that "Aid in such cases encourages the expectations of paternal care on the part of government and weakens the sturdiness of our national character."

Still, if Cleveland feared paternalistic government, he worried about the growing influence of **monopolies** and economic concentration in the republic. Cleveland had always endorsed the British notion of independent government commissions to regulate economic activity. Thus, when the Interstate Commerce Commission bill came before him in 1887, he willingly signed it into law. The act established the five-member Interstate Commerce Commission, with powers to oversee railroad rates. The ICC had little power outside of the courts to enforce its rulings.

CLEVELAND LOSES THE TARIFF BATTLE. That same year, 1887, Cleveland undertook his most daring action against the special interests: he spent his entire annual message to Congress discussing the tariff, which he thought was too high. The tariff was a tax on imported goods. In general, the higher the tariff, the more expensive foreign goods became, which protected domestic producers from foreign competition. At this time the tariff was the principal source of government revenue, and the treasury had a large and growing surplus. Cleveland hoped to balance the federal budget by reducing income from the protective tariff. Moreover, the millions of dollars generated by the tariff offered Congress a seemingly unlimited source of funds to distribute through **pork-barrel** projects like veterans pensions and expensive public works projects in their home districts. Cleveland attacked the protective tariff in the best Jacksonian rhetoric, claiming that the tariff benefitted the special interests while imposing a special burden on "those with moderate means and the poor." Many businessmen were divided on the tariff issue, depending on the nature of their business and region. For instance, a Rhode Island woolens manufacturer opposed the tariff on raw wool because it raised the cost of his raw materials without benefitting domestic wool producers. A large New Haven hardware manufacturer contended that high tariffs favored "coal and metal oligarchies" of Ohio, Pennsylvania, and Michigan, but not him and only raised his costs of production. Thus, aside from Cleveland's class rhetoric, many businessmen like financier John Murray Forbes supported Cleveland's attack on the protective tariff.

The House took up Cleveland's call to review the more than 4,000 items on the tariff list. A bill was passed reducing the average level of duties from about 47 percent of the value of imports to about 40 percent. When the bill reached the Republican Senate, it died in committee.

Cleveland was outraged. He warned that the values of hard work and sturdy enterprise were being subverted in favor of the manufacturers who made special arrangements with the government. **Trusts,** combinations, and monopolies had gained control of government, he said, while average American citizens were being "trampled to death beneath an iron heel." (This graphic phrase "iron heel" was taken up by the socialist Jack London, who in his novel of the same name described an America in open class warfare). Cleveland, carrying the banner of Jacksonian democracy, now took the issue to the voters in his campaign for a second term.

The 1888 Republican nominee, Senator Benjamin Harrison, accepted Cleveland's challenge to focus the election on the tariff. Harrison's record did him little harm—it was nearly nonexistent. He was a Presbyterian deacon and grandson of William Henry Harrison, the ninth president of the United States who had died a month into his term. His high cheekbones showed he was part Indian.

In the final vote, Cleveland took a plurality of the popular vote of 5,537,857 to Harrison's 5,447,129. Nonetheless, Cleveland lost three key states. Ohio, Indiana, and New York gave Harrison an electoral victory of 244 to 168.

OPPOSING CATHOLICS AND ALCOHOL. Benjamin Harrison and the Republican party played on rising resentment against immigrants and Roman Catholics that appeared with renewed strength in the mid-1880s. Concerned that the flood of immigrants coming from Europe was undermining the nation, nativists sought to restrict immigration and enact anti-Catholic legislation. Because many new immigrants were Roman Catholics, immigration and Roman Catholicism became linked in the minds of the nativists. In turn, nativists associated Roman Catholicism with labor radicalism, political corruption, and unemployment. Among these groups were the Minute Men, the United Order of Native Americans, and the Red, White and Blue. The most powerful organization was the American Protective Association (1887). The APA pledged never to hire nor vote for a Catholic. Within a short period of time the APA gained a half-million members. For a time these anti-Catholic groups gained influence in local and state Republican parties, as well as within the general populace.

Closely linked to nativism was the **prohibition** movement. Often new immigrants and the Roman Catholic Irish were associated with the sins of alcoholic drink. Throughout the Midwest, Republicans launched campaigns to eradicate the sale of alcohol. The influx of wine and beer drinking immigrants spurred the prohibition campaign. Alcohol became associated with crime, prostitution, vice, and personal degradation. Campaigns to outlaw the sale of alcohol, including beer, alienated Catholics and German Lutherans alike.

By the mid-1890s, however, this cultural conflict began to die down as Republican party leaders such as William McKinley of Ohio recognized the harm this antiimmigrant and anti-Catholic crusade was hurting the party. As a result, Republicans replaced antiimmigrant and anti-Catholic rhetoric with talk about economic prosperity and jobs.

HARRISON SUCCUMBS TO THE SPECIAL INTERESTS, 1889-1893.
Harrison was not a nativist, however. He was a strong nationalist who disliked both the British and the Irish. A devout Presbyterian, Harrison laid claim to a higher morality, yet did little to lead the party. He was small in stature and cold in manner. One story went that a visitor was told by Harrison's secretary, "I'm sorry sir, the president cannot be seen," the visitor replied, "Can't be seen! My God, has he got as small as that!" To many, Harrison seemed not only small in stature, but limited in vision as well.

Every group seemed to get its wish from what became known as the Billion Dollar Congress. Veterans pushed through the Dependent Veterans Pension bill in 1890. The list of pensioners doubled within four years. Veterans of only 90 days service who suffered from either physical or mental disabilities—whatever their cause—and their widows were provided with pensions if they could prove they had no other source of support.

Silver interests passed their measure to expand the money supply based on silver. Wheat, cotton, and corn prices had fallen catastrophically in 1889, which renewed silver agitation. Also, in 1889 four new states—South Dakota, North Dakota, Montana, and Washington—were admitted to the Union. The following year Idaho and Wyoming joined. These western states now became part of the silver bloc in Congress, which consisted of 17 Republicans and a single Democrat. Refusing to vote for a new tariff bill unless they got a new silver coinage bill, the block forced Congress to accept the Sherman Silver Purchase Act of 1890. It required the secretary of the treasury to purchase 4.5 million ounces of silver a month to mint into silver dollars.

Republicans had accepted the silver bill in order to get a new—and higher—tariff bill through Congress. Their new McKinley tariff raised general rates from 38 percent to 50 percent on imported goods. Tariffs on textiles and metal products were now so high that many people stopped buying these imported goods altogether. When Democrats protested that this tariff prevented poor people from buying cheaper European goods, Republican representative from Ohio, William McKinley responded, "Cheap is not a word of hope; it is not a word of inspiration. It is the badge of poverty; it is a symbol of distress."

Such rhetoric served Republicans poorly. In order to appease public opinion, they pushed through the Sherman Antitrust Act (1890). Few at the time, even Republicans, were willing to tolerate outright monopolies. The federal statue became the first antitrust legislation enacted in the nation's history. The act declared illegal any combination, trust, or conspiracy, "in restraint of trade."

This gesture, however, did little good to win back the voters. In the midterm elections, Republicans were swept out of Congress. Even leading Republican William McKinley of Ohio was defeated for his House seat in 1890. The new House had only 88 Republicans against 235 Democrats and 9 Populists, a new party on the scene. The harm had already been done, however. By 1892 Harrison had turned a $3 million dollar budget surplus into a deficit.

The election of 1892 was a rematch of Cleveland against Harrison. Cleveland organized his campaign around his opposition to the high McKinley tariff. This time he won a landslide victory, becoming the first president ever elected to a nonconsecutive second term. He carried the electoral college by 277 votes to Harrison's 145 votes. His popular plurality carried over to the congressional races, where the Democrats gained a majority in both houses of Congress for the first time since the 1850s.

The victory proved to be short-lived, however. In the spring of 1893 a stock market crash signalled the beginning of one of the worst depressions in history. As the economy sagged and people's suffering intensified, they turned on Cleveland and the Democrats with a vengeance. From this bitterness emerged a new politics, as many turned to the Republicans with renewed conviction.

Conclusion

Politics in the late nineteenth century offered a mixed record. Partisan politics excited enthusiastic participation that drew millions into local, state, and national elections. Voters listened attentively to intense debate concerning the tariff, the money question, and party reform. These were important issues, but at the same time politics often proved corrupt and politicians narrow-minded. As a result, major social issues concerning the emerging corporate economy, problems of the city, and labor relations were ignored, postponed for a later generation.

Recommended Readings

DOCUMENTS: Henry Adams, *Chapters of Erie, and Other Essays* (1871) and *The Education of Henry Adams: An Autobiography* (1907).

READINGS: Sean Dennis Cashman, *America in the Gilded Age* (1984); Carl Degler, *The Age of Economic Revolution* (1977); Ellen Carol DuBois, *Feminism and Suffrage* (1978); John Garraty, *The New Commonwealth 1877-1890* (1968); Richard J. Jensen, *The Winning of the Midwest: Social and Political Conflict, 1888-1896* (1971); Paul Kleppner, *The Cross of Culture* (1970); Morton Keller, *Affairs of State: Public Life in Late Nineteenth-Century America* (1977); Gerald W. McFarland, *Mugwumps, Morals and Politics* (1975); Michael E. McGerr, *The Decline of Popular Politics* (1986); H. Wayne Morgan, *From Hayes to McKinley* (1969) and *Unity and Culture: The United States* (1971); David J. Rothman, *Politics and Power: the United States Senate* (1966); Walter Nugent, *Money and American Society* (1968); Shelia Rothman, *Woman's Proper Place: A History of Changing Ideals and Practices* (1978); Mary P. Ryan, *Women in Public: Between Banners and Ballots* (1990); John Sproat, *"The Best Men": Liberal Reformers in the Gilded Age* (1968); Richard E. Welch, Jr. *George Frisbie Hoar and the Half Breed Republicans* (1971).

18

※

INDUSTRY AND LABOR IN THE
GILDED AGE

CHAPTER OVERVIEW: The late nineteenth century was an age of enterprise. Huge industrial combines flourished, creating wealth previously unimaginable. The country was on its way to becoming the wealthiest economic power in history. This second industrial revolution brought mass-produced goods and new technology to the average American consumer—thereby raising the nation's standard of living—while creating profound social tensions between labor and capital. Thus for many Americans who lived in this period, the United States appeared to be a study in contrasts.

An Industrial Giant Is Born

In the late nineteenth century the United States emerged as the world's most advanced industrial power. Economic growth during this period was unprecedented, greatly exceeding the growth of its European rivals. This second industrial revolution, following the earlier Market Revolution, transformed industry, manufacturing, transportation, and work itself. Factories doubled in size, hired more and more workers, and introduced more productive machinery. Railroad lines and telegraph systems linked isolated communities into a single society. Railroad lines cooperated in setting standards, but their unscrupulous business practices prompted the government to begin regulating private enterprise.

THE EMERGING MIDDLE CLASS. The economic transformation of the late nineteenth century brought uneven results for regions, groups, and individuals. While new technology displaced some, many other workers appeared to benefit from this economic revolution. Real wages climbed for both unskilled workers (31 percent) and skilled workers (74 percent) between 1860 and 1900. Moreover, most workers found new occupational mobility. At the same time, the rich seemed to grow richer, with 10 percent of America's families owning 73 percent of the nation wealth.

The greatest transformation brought about by the corporate revolution was the rise of the middle class. The corporation created new occupations for middle managers, accountants, service employees, and office workers. In 1870 less than 2 percent of the workforce was employed in clerical operations; by 1900 over 35 percent was white collar. Women were all but absent from this workforce in 1870, but by 1900 they held a quarter of all clerical jobs.

New white-collar occupations provided upward mobility for many. Prerequisites for working in the new corporate office were a solid foundation in English grammar and a proficiency in writing. Many managers came up through the ranks of labor. Others were drawn from the 8 percent of the population that graduated from high school. While they gave up some individualism to work in new bureaucratic structures, they gained new opportunities and a sense of challenge in participating in the creation of new forms of business.

LIFE IN THE LATE NINETEENTH CENTURY: TWO CONTRASTING VIEWS. While the industrial revolution benefitted the middle class, many differed over the extent of the benefits of the new economic order. Consider, if you will, the message of the railroad president Charles Perkins, who asked, "Have not great merchants, great manufacturers, great inventors done more for the world than preachers and philanthropists? Can there be any doubt that cheapening the cost of necessities and conveniences of life is the most powerful agent of civilization and progress?"

Then, contrast his opinion with the words of the socialist Eugene Debs, who declared, "The existing system is unspeakably cruel; the life currents of old age and childhood are the tributaries of the bottomless reservoir of private profit. The face of capitalism is blotched with the effects of a diseased organism."

How could two men differ so radically in their perspectives of American industry and labor in the late nineteenth century? Of course, one was a **capitalist** and the other a socialist, but how are we to judge their estimations? To answer this question we must examine the transformation of business and industry in this period. The social tensions expressed in the clash between labor and capital coincided with the emergence of an organizational revolution that affected both American business and American labor. In the process, social relations in the United States were also transformed, as a significant white-collar workforce developed that provided new opportunities and jobs for middle-class men and women. As a consequence, the United States did not become a society of haves and havenots (although disparities of wealth remained), but a society deeply rooted in middle-class values, **mores,** and aspirations.

As Americans appraised their natural resources after the Civil War, their estimation of themselves and their future seemed to be confirmed. The nation possessed two-thirds of the world's known coal deposits, high-quality iron ore in abundance, and enough precious metals, gold, silver, and copper to be the envy of the ancient pharaohs. The next decades were to reveal immense reserves of petroleum.

These resources provided the foundations of an economic revolution that transformed America from a second-rate power in 1860 to the world's most advanced industrial nation, far surpassing Great Britain, Germany, and France in industrial output. Indeed, from 1860 to 1900 the American economy grew 4 percent annually, one-third better than Germany's growth and nearly double Great Britain's. Fueling this expansion was the dramatic increase in population, which tripled between 1850 and 1900, from 23 million to 76 million.

PRODUCING AN ECONOMIC REVOLUTION. In this economic expansion, new steel and petroleum industries were created. Moreover, the factories that produced these new goods were transformed into gigantic enterprises. Manufacturing output soared from $1.8 billion in 1860 to $13 billion in 1900. Textile production and iron production doubled in this period.

Greater output meant larger factories. The average plant size in many industries doubled. Before the Civil War, a workforce of 400 employees in a firm was rare. By 1900 there were over 1,000 factories with more than 500 workers. The steel industry had 14 foundries that each employed 6,000 or more workers. Many industries introduced techniques of mass production. By the 1870s and 1880s, continuous production methods were in use in oil, sugar, and whiskey. These techniques allowed raw materials to be refined into finished products in a single factory.

New machines also created breakthroughs. For example, the introduction of a cigarette making machine in 1881 forever changed the tobacco industry. A single worker could make 3,000 cigarettes per day; by the mid-1880s one machine could make 120,000. New machinery also was introduced in the match, soap, and grain milling industries.

Still, the new economy brought new risks and hardships for many. Two sharp economic downturns in 1873 and 1893 scarred 14 out of the 25 years between 1873 and 1897. Business failure and unemployment were common to these decades. Furthermore, while real wages increased, disparity between classes worsened.

RAILROADS TRANSPORT A REVOLUTION. As manufacturing concerns grew larger and produced more, the United States was linked as a nation and a market by an extensive railroad and telegraph system. The railroads brought farm and factory, country and town closer together, while the telegraph and later the telephone, increased knowledge, business efficiency, and public debate. In 1860 the nation had only 30,000 miles of railroad track; by 1900 more track had been laid than in all of Europe including Russia. In 1866 the three leading telegraph companies merged to form Western Union. By 1915 this company operated 1.6 million miles of wire. This transportation and communications system linked every state and major city and integrated regions and isolated communities into a single society.

This railroad building spree also brought chaos. In the 1860s and 1870s, hundreds of small companies had accumulated insurmountable debt while building competing lines. Each had used widely different sizes for couplers, rails, track width, and engine size, so trains could not connect from one line onto another. Stock fraud and overspeculation were common. Order came slowly to the industry by the turn of the century. Financial interests led by railroad **magnate**s such as Jay Gould and Collis P. Huntington devoured these smaller lines. Out of this consolidation movement emerged four major trunk lines in the Northeast, five major lines in the South, and five west of the Mississippi.

To operate these lines, railroads developed new management structures and practices. For example, in the 1850s the Pennsylvania Railroad restructured its organization to enable regional superintendents to provide elaborate accounting and traffic reports to a central headquarters so that rates could be set and profits accurately predicted and measured. In linking their regional offices to the central office, railroads organized a complex communications system that relied on the telegraph.

Railroad managers brought uniform standards to the industry. In 1883 on their own they divided the country into four time zones. Now all Americans set their watches to a new standard uniform time. Through constant consultation and cooperation, managers also agreed to a standardized track gauge. They also entered into a cooperative billing system and accounting procedures that set uniform rates. By the 1880s and 1890s railway managers had adopted automatic couplers, air brakes, and block signal systems. Even with these improvements, railroads remained heavily in debt. The cost of building and consolidating the lines had been expensive. For example, in order to integrate its line, the Pennsylvania had bought more than 73 smaller companies. **Capitalization** for this expansion reached nearly $35 million. A similar story could be told for other lines. By 1900 the combined debt of railroads stood at $5.1 billion—nearly five times the debt of the federal government.

This cartoon depicts a Grange farmer warning a sleeping public that democracy will be crushed by railroad interests. The Grange, organized in 1867, helped push through state laws regulating railroads. (CULVER PICTURES)

Railroads were also marred by unscrupulous business strategies. Railroad barons earned reputations for offering kickbacks (rebates) to large shippers and dispensing favors to politicians. Many Americans, especially in the farmlands of the Midwest and plains states, questioned the high rates railroads charged for short trips. Although overall rates dropped in this period, large shippers pressured railroads to "kick back" money to them so they, in effect, received cheaper, wholesale rates than small shippers and farmers who paid retail.

Public pressure resulting from the abuses of the railroad industry pushed Congress to establish the Interstate Commerce Commission (1887), a five-member commission to oversee the practices of railroads. The creation of the ICC marked an important turning point in government-business relations in America. The federal government now exercised its power to regulate private enterprise in the public interest.

Railroads changed the law in other ways. One of the most significant changes came in bankruptcy law. In 1884 the federal district court of Missouri agreed to place Jay Gould's Wabash line into **receivership** before its actual default to its creditors. Moreover, the court agreed to appoint receivers friendly to Jay Gould. Many interpreted the ruling as the result of Gould's insidious influence on the courts, but the importance of the case rested in the court's implicit acknowledgement that a system of transportation was more important than its parts.

SPREADING THE REVOLUTION TO THE PEOPLE. The new corporate economy benefitted the average American. Overall price levels dropped in the late nineteenth century. The general price index fell dramatically in this period. Combined with a rise in real wages, falling prices enabled Americans to buy more for less. For instance, the price of one gallon of kerosene for lamps fell from 30 cents in 1866 to 5 cents in 1894.

At the same time, new household goods such as canned foods, vacuum cleaners, and sewing machines became available to the average consumer. Shopping itself changed. Before the Civil War, local stores bought their goods from middlemen called jobbers; following the Civil War, these stores were challenged by mass retailers who saved money by purchasing directly from manufacturers. By emphasizing speed and volume rather than high prices, retailers such as Macy's, Bloomingdale's, Marshall Field, Abraham & Strauss, Wanamaker's, Lazarus, and I. Magnin pioneered the modern department store.

Traditional stores were usually small, dark, dirty, and limited in the variety of goods they carried. Haggling over prices was common, and service was poor. The department store set fixed prices for brand names and standardized goods. Small-town and rural Americans found new ways of shopping through catalogue houses like Montgomery Ward (1872) and Sears, Roebuck (1886). At the same time, chain stores such as F. W. Woolworth's Five and Ten Cent Stores (1879) emerged.

This revolution in the production and sale of consumer goods transformed the American household. Homeownership itself increased. By the late nineteenth century, nearly 40 percent of all Americans owned their own home, although homeownership in some cities was quite small due to the transient patterns of many urban dwellers.

Houses could now be lighted with gas and electricity. Indoor plumbing, including toilets and bathtubs, became common. Central heating using coal furnaces was adopted. Cooking was made easier with a growing use of prepared canned foods. Common household tasks, such as sewing, became easier. By 1905 the Singer Sewing Machine Company, employing more than 90,000 employees at eight factories, sold 1.25 million sewing machines annually.

Class Differences Within the Revolution

The leaders of industry transformed how goods were produced and remade the entire economy. By driving out, buying up, or joining with competitors, they consolidated industrial power in a few hands. Steel manufacturer Andrew Carnegie, oil tycoon John Rockefeller, and financier J. P. Morgan symbolized the new power in industry.

BEING RICH IN AMERICA. The United States possessed only a handful of millionaires in the 1850s, but by 1892 there were over 4000. The new rich conspicuously displayed their wealth. They used private railroad cars and yachts to travel to resorts such as Saratoga Springs, New York. They gave ostentatious dinners and parties. At one such party, Mrs. Jay Gould wore $500,000 worth of jewels sewn onto her clothing. In their rivalry to outdo one another they sought more and more elaborate devices. At another dinner party the guest of honor was a chimpanzee dressed in a tuxedo.

Still, many millionaires were not driven by wealth alone and more often than not profits were reinvested in new growth. American business leaders combined ambition with a belief in the virtues of capitalism and a confidence that their work was for the betterment of the nation. John D. Rockefeller conveyed these sentiments when he recalled, "I saw a marvelous future for our country and I wanted to participate in the work of making our country great. I had an ambition to build."

Many Americans in the nineteenth century saw the American businessman as a success story of what hard work and moral values could accomplish. Indeed, Horatio Alger wrote popular children's novels expressing this idea. In reality, only a third of successful industrialists came from humble backgrounds.

American industrialists usually built their companies on the principles of mass production, intensive capital investment, and national (and later international) marketing. These men launched a revolution that transformed how goods were produced, how labor was organized, and how capital was spent. To build new industries they developed new structures such as the modern corporation. To finance their huge enterprises they created new financial institutions and markets to accumulate the vast amounts of capital to make the system work. And to ensure that this new corporate capitalism was more efficient than the system it replaced, they sought to rationalize the management and financial operations of the new corporate enterprise. As a result, a managerial revolution was an integral part of the economic revolution as a new professional class was created to manage American business and industry. With the creation of new white-collar jobs, a large middle class emerged which would affect the social and political life of the nation.

Certain men came to symbolize America—both in their success and in their excesses. Three men in particular captured the imagination of Americans—and earned both the admiration and hatred of the public. The careers of these men—Andrew Carnegie in railroads and steel, John D. Rockefeller in oil, and J. P. Morgan in finance—reveal much about the growth of American industry in the late nineteenth century. Two rose from humble backgrounds, while the third started out rich and became incomparably richer.

ANDREW CARNEGIE: MAN OF STEEL. For his contemporaries, Andrew Carnegie's rise to become what J. P. Morgan declared with some hyperbole the "world's wealthiest man" symbolized the American dream. He came to America as an immigrant fleeing poverty in Scotland. When he later traveled back to his birthland, he was a multimillionaire convinced he could redeem mankind through philanthropy.

The Carnegie family came to America from Scotland during the **depression** of 1848. The father was a skilled weaver who had been driven from his work by new textile machines and by a downturn in the economy. Arriving in Pittsburgh, the thirteen-year-old Andrew Carnegie was forced to go to work as a telegraph messenger. He worked his way up to become a telegraph operator who could read the telegraph by ear—a feat that amazed all, especially Tom Scott, the superintendent of the Pennsylvania Railroad in the Pittsburgh district. In 1853 Scott asked the 5'3", talkative, and affable Carnegie to join him as his personal telegraph operator.

Young Carnegie rose with the railroad industry. Following the Civil War, the young Carnegie watched the spectacular growth of the industry. His promotion to division chief of the Pennsylvania Railroad, following Tom Scott's promotion to a vice-presidency, placed Carnegie in touch with the leading businessmen and industrialists of the day. Carnegie used new cost accounting methods and more than quadrupled traffic in his district. He scheduled the first night trains, so that trains ran around the clock. He was a young man on the rise.

His activities did not stop with railroads, however. He began to invest heavily in stocks. He speculated in oil, in the manufacture of sleeping cars, in a telegraph company, and dozens of other enterprises. Finally, in 1865, he left the Pennsylvania Railroad to join an iron bridge construction company. From there his move to the steel industry was a natural.

Carnegie saw steel as the wave of the future. In 1866 he had learned of a

Andrew Carnegie (1835-1919), steel industrialist, devoted himself to
social and educational advancement in the United States and Great
Britain, funding the building of over 2,500 public libraries. World War I
shattered his dreams for international peace. (THE BETTMANN ARCHIVE)

new process for manufacturing steel, the Bessemer process. Developed by Sir
Henry Bessemer, an English engineer, the process used cold air blown into
steel to burn off the carbon. William Kelley of Kentucky discovered the process at the same time, but it was Carnegie who took advantage of the process.

Carnegie chose the depression of 1873 to begin large-scale manufacture of
Bessemer steel. Figuring costs were at a low point, Carnegie built a huge plant
outside Pittsburgh. He hired the best engineers and chemists in the country.
He also acquired expensive German open-hearth furnaces, which did not pay
for themselves until the 1880s.

Carnegie remained obsessed with costs. He spent hours pouring over division reports. He especially worked on labor costs. He drove his men hard,
insisting that they work 12-hour shifts even in July and August, when tem-

peratures would reach over 100 degrees. Work was scheduled every day, including Sundays, and industrial accidents were frequent.

Carnegie began buying up other steel companies. He sought to control the supply of raw materials as well as the sale of finished products. In short, he sought *vertical integration* of his firm. He purchased iron ore ranges in Michigan and coke fields in Ohio. His factories produced both finished steel products and ingots for others to shape.

Carnegie's success allowed him to expand his horizons. He established residences to New York and Scotland. He joined intellectual circles, ignoring New York's high society. He devoured the books of Herbert Spencer, an English intellectual who promoted "social Darwinism." Spencer saw competition as a natural law of nature and society. Only the fittest were destined to survive. Carnegie began to write essays expounding his own vision for bettering the world. In 1885, he collected his essays in his first book, *Triumphant Democracy.* He maintained that society must remain competitive, but if democracy was to triumph those who had benefitted from society, the wealthy, should serve as benefactors by distributing their wealth in the form of libraries and educational institutions that created opportunities for self-improvement. Acting on his principles, Carnegie endowed library, museum, and civic buildings. By the last decade of the century, Carnegie had become a household name in United States and Europe.

J. D. ROCKEFELLER: PORTRAIT IN OIL. While Carnegie was making his way in the world, so was another boy, John D. Rockefeller, from Cleveland, Ohio. Like Carnegie's father, Rockefeller's father was a failure. A wandering peddler of quack medicines and other products, the elder Rockefeller nonetheless taught his two sons how to succeed. Rockefeller's mother, a devout Baptist, instilled in her sons deep religious values that stayed with them throughout their lives.

Unlike the gregarious Carnegie, young Rockefeller was taciturn and sullen. In high school he studied bookkeeping and then took a job as a bookkeeper. He soon saved enough money to become a partner in a wholesale produce company in Cleveland.

Just as steel would make Carnegie, oil would make Rockefeller. In 1859 Edwin Drake struck oil in Pennsylvania. Crude oil could be refined into kerosene, which offered a cleaner and easier way of fueling lamps than did fats from whales or other animals.

Competition in the oil refining business became fierce. In 1863 there were over 300 refining companies, 31 in Cleveland alone. That same year Rockefeller entered the refining business cautiously while maintaining his produce business. The oil industry boomed and transportation facilities improved, so in 1867 Rockefeller turned his attention to oil refining. He poured capital into his refining plants, hired chemists to improve products and production, and accountants to watch costs. He built his own warehouses and barrel-making plant and bought a fleet of railroad tank cars. He brought Henry M. Flagler, a son-in-law of a major Cleveland whiskey distiller, into the business. Flagler was a good negotiator, especially with railroad people. He made a secret deal with the South Shore Railroad to ship Rockefeller's oil at a lower rate. When this deal became known, other refiners were up in arms, and the South Shore granted them the same deal. In 1870 Rockefeller formed the Standard Oil Company of Ohio.

That same year, Tom Scott of the Pennsylvania Railroad developed a plan to reduce competition and increase profits. He gathered the major railroads and oil refiners into a loosely defined organization called the South Improvement Company. Refiners who joined were given rebates, and railroads no longer had to compete for the business. Rockefeller used Standard Oil's interest in the South Improvement Company to force competitors out of business.

In the 1870s, Standard Oil began to expand nationally. Rockefeller pushed to control the wholesale trade by forcing dealers to buy from him. His tactics often broke all bounds of business propriety. In 1879 the courts ruled that Rockefeller's pooling arrangements were in restraint of trade. To get around this ruling, Rockefeller's lawyer devised a new form of organization, the **trust.** The proposed organization called for the various individually owned oil companies involved in this joint enterprise (called a **pool**) to turn their stock over to a board of trustees in exchange for trust certificates. In short, a union of corporations was to form the new trust. By 1890 Standard Oil controlled 90 percent of all oil refining in the United States.

J. P. MORGAN: CAPITALIST VISIONARY. Carnegie and Rockefeller consolidated the steel and oil industries, respectively. They were innovators who introduced modern practices to their businesses through cost accounting, expertise, and techniques of continuous production. In this way, they participated in the emergence of corporate capitalism, but it was their contemporary, financier J.P. Morgan, who brought a new vision of a corporate capitalism.

John Pierpont Morgan's background and career differed radically from Carnegie's and Rockefeller's. Born to wealth in 1835, he was the son of a well-known American financier based in London. His grandfather, for whom he was named, had founded the Aetna Fire Insurance Company. Although J.P. grew into a hulk of a man standing 6'2", weighing 230 pounds, he suffered from a skin disease which particularly affected his nose. It was so disfigured that some would turn away in disgust. Later, on Wall Street, his enemies called him "liver nose." Yet what Morgan lacked in looks, he made up for in brains. He received the best of educations, first in Switzerland and later at a German university.

Morgan distrusted the old days of cutthroat competition. Early in his career as an operator on Wall Street he had seen unscrupulous speculators bring disaster to business markets and financial markets alike. Morgan saw the market as a man-made institution. Because it was a creation of society, and not nature, he believed that it could be organized and rationalized. Because he believed that the market was not a God-given and unchanging institution, he sought to consolidate and stabilize capitalism by eliminating unnecessary competition and creating cooperation among corporations.

In 1856 he joined his father's firm in London, but relations between the two remained estranged. The following year Morgan returned to New York to work as a representative for both the prestigious George Peabody and Company and his father's firm. During the Civil War he speculated in army supplies and gold. In 1871 he formed, with Anthony J. Drexel, the investment company of Drexel, Morgan and Company. Through associates in Philadelphia, Paris, and London, Morgan's firm became one of the most powerful banking houses in the world. Following the collapse of Jay Cooke's company in 1873, the Morgan firm became the leading government financing agency.

One of his greatest triumphs came in 1895 when he formed an international syndicate that effectively halted a drain of gold from the federal treasury. Morgan's syndicate made approximately $300,000, but rumors placed profits in the millions. This incident only confirmed what many critics had claimed: Wall Street and the monied interests had a stranglehold on the federal government (see Chapter 20).

Morgan also showed a talent for financing and reorganizing American railroads. He understood that European investors wanted stability. He sought, therefore, to eliminate ruthless competition in order to maintain European confidence in American **securities.** When William Vanderbilt's New York Central Railroad threatened war with J. Edgar Thompson's Pennsylvania Railroad, Morgan brought the two parties together on his yacht, the *Corsair,* to resolve their differences.

His greatest triumph came in the depression of 1893, when he refinanced many American corporations and railroads that were on the verge of collapse. During the 1880s the railroads had overexpanded, laying over 75,000 miles of track in that decade alone. **Foreclosure** sales during the depression closed 40,000 miles of track. Morgan stepped in to refinance the Santa Fe, Erie, Northern Pacific, and Reading lines. The entire southern system was reorganized. The price he extracted was modest, though: he insisted on consolidation and placed his men on the boards of many of these corporations. When he was finished, nearly 1/8 of all lines had been consolidated. If his methods were seen as ruthless at the time, he nonetheless contributed to corporate stability in this new age of capitalism.

In 1900 he came head to head with Andrew Carnegie. Morgan had become interested in steel when he financed the Federal Steel Company and the National Tube Company. These firms challenged Carnegie in finished steel products. Carnegie prepared for war. He threatened to build new furnaces and plants to take on his rivals, including Morgan. Knowing full well what a fight with Carnegie meant, the other steelmakers urged Morgan make peace. Morgan and Carnegie met, and Morgan asked Carnegie how much he wanted for his company. Carnegie simply wrote on a napkin his price—$500 million. Morgan agreed. With the purchase of Carnegie Steel, Morgan consolidated his other steel interests and organized U.S. Steel, the first billion-dollar corporation.

The American corporate economy appeared triumphant, even as its critics worried about the growing concentration of industry. The rapid growth of big business in America over the course of one or two generations frightened many. Throughout the 1880s mergers had increased as independent companies were taken over and combined with other companies. Following the depression of 1893, merger activity accelerated. From 1895 through 1904 over 2,000 companies were merged into larger firms. Not all combinations worked, however: American Bicycle, National Cordage, U.S. Leather, American Glue, National Salt, and United Button were among the many that failed. Nevertheless, the common perception was that big business was driving out small business.

Morgan's own activities drew national attention. Morgan was personally involved in reorganizing U.S. Steel, General Electric, and International Harvester. The formation of U.S. Steel, for example, brought together 213 different manufacturing firms, 41 mines, over 1000 miles of railroad track, and 112 ore ships. This company alone controlled 43 percent of the **pig-iron** capacity and 60 percent of the steelmaking capacity in the United States. By 1912, Morgan interests held 341 directorships in 112 corporations.

The Backlash Against Industrial Abuses

Many industrialists made little effort to protect their workers from pay cuts, unemployment, or hazardous working conditions, and government often appeared to side with industry in these matters. So workers took matters into their own hands, forming local labor unions and going out on strike. Strikes were often violent. Some unions embraced political action, while others saw it as a distraction.

If Carnegie, Rockefeller, and Morgan symbolized business in the late nineteenth century, three men represented labor and its various organizational forms. Terence Powderly, head of the Knights of Labor, preferred arbitration over strikes. Samuel Gompers, founder of the American Federation of Labor, focused on immediate labor issues and established the basis of modern unionism. Eugene Debs, founder of the American Railway Union and later of the Socialist Party of America, rejected capitalism altogether.

REGULATING THE SECOND INDUSTRIAL REVOLUTION. Although Americans showed increasing anxiety about the growth of big business, efforts at regulating business were sporadic. In the 1870s farmers in the Midwest persuaded legislators to pass state laws regulating railroad traffic. While these laws were upheld by the U.S. Supreme Court in *Munn v. Illinois* (1877), the court reversed itself in *Wabash Railway v. Illinois* (1886). In the *Wabash* case, the court ruled that only Congress could regulate interstate traffic.

Still, little opposition to corporate consolidation appeared at the federal level. In 1887 Congress enacted the Interstate Commerce Act to regulate railroads, but the act lacked meaningful enforcement powers. In 1890 Congress declared through the Sherman Antitrust Act that "every contract, combination in the form of a trust or otherwise, or conspiracy, in restraint of trade or commerce" was illegal. Yet between 1893 and 1903 the government initiated only 23 cases under the act. Congress refused even to appropriate special funds for antitrust enforcement. When the Cleveland administration brought suit against sugar manufacturer E. C. Knight in 1895, its case was so shoddy that the court was forced to rule that manufacturing, as defined by the government, should not be considered interstate commerce and therefore fell outside the Sherman Antitrust Act. Four years later in the *Addyston Pipe and Steel Company* (1899) case, the court ruled that only the combination of *independent* companies to fix prices was illegal.

The second industrial revolution transformed work in modern America. Between 1860 and 1900 the number of industrial workers grew from 885,000 to 3.2 million, but the introduction of new production methods and new technology displaced thousands of semiskilled workers. While the new factory system and continuous production methods created jobs for skilled workers who could master the new equipment, many old-fashioned skilled jobs were replaced with lower paid, less-skilled workers. Nearly one-third of the 750,000 workers employed in steel and railroads were common laborers.

By 1910 nearly one-quarter of all children between the ages of ten and 14 had full-time jobs, often in less technologically advanced industries such as textiles in the South. Women entered the employment ranks in larger numbers as well, growing from 3.75 million in 1870 to nearly 8 million in 1910, making up 20 percent of the workforce. About 22 percent of these women were employed in manufacturing, although service sectors slowly attracted female labor.

Industrial accidents and unemployment continued to threaten workers in this period. The risk of industrial injury was high in the nation's factories, mines, and railroads. Unemployment rates increased following the Civil War and averaged 10 percent from the 1870s through the 1890s. Moreover, in any given year the unemployment rate might be higher. For instance, in 1890, a prosperous year, one out of every five nonagricultural workers was unemployed during at least one month.

Strikes and industrial violence were common. Indeed, during the two decades between 1876 and 1896 there were more strikes in America than in any other industrial nation. These strikes were particularly violent: more people were injured and killed in these labor protests than in any other nation. Often strikes involved mobs, property damage, and looting.

In these circumstances, many workers began to organize trade unions. Workers, however, remained undecided about the proper form and nature of these new unions. In a certain sense, the late nineteenth century was an age of experimentation and choice for workers, just as it was for industry and business.

TERENCE POWDERLY OVERSEES THE RISE AND FALL OF THE KNIGHTS OF LABOR. By the end of the Civil War, American labor had a well-developed union tradition, although only about 5 percent of workers were unionized. During the Civil War, organized labor grew rapidly. After the war, workers in many cities organized to demand an eight-hour work day. In Boston, Ira Steward organized an Eight-Hour League that drew national attention.

In 1866, this labor activity culminated in the organizing of America's first national union, the National Labor Union (NLU), under the leadership of William Sylvis. The NLU encouraged black workers to organize. Led by Isaac Meyers, a black ship caulker, black workers formed the National Colored Labor Union. The NLU became increasing involved with political reform through the Greenback movement. Greenbackism attracted reformers through its call for the federal government to issue inflationary paper money (greenbacks) not backed by gold. Sylvis's death in 1869 and the turn to political reform weakened the NLU. The depression of 1873 brought its demise.

The depression also temporarily killed the union movement in general. By 1877 only nine national unions remained. The breaking of a strike in the anthracite coal fields of Pennsylvania led to more violence. Following the strike a kind of **guerrilla** war broke out with a series of assaults and murders against strikebreakers and company officials. Finally, the company placed an undercover agent, James McParland, to spy on the Irish miners. He collected dubious evidence against an alleged secret society, the "Molly Maguires," which led to the arrest, conviction, and execution of 13 men.

Class tensions worsened. There was a general strike by workers in the summer of 1877. Only the calling out of federal troops by President Hayes quelled the rioting that left $10 million in damage (see Chapter 19).

In the midst of these events a new national labor organization emerged, the Knights of Labor. The Knights grew out of a Philadelphia shoe workers union—the Knights of St. Crispin—formed in 1869. In 1878 a national organization was formed under Uriah Stephens, half reformer, half religious mystic. One year later Stephens stepped down in favor of Terence Powderly, the son of Irish Catholic immigrants and the Greenback-Labor mayor of Scranton, Pennsylvania. Powderly now became Grandmaster of the Knights. Concerned with labor repression following the upheaval of 1877, the Knights instituted elaborate secret rituals. All workers and honest businessmen were welcomed into the Knights; professional gamblers, stockbrokers, lawyers, bankers, and liquor dealers were specifically excluded.

The Knights quickly grew into the nation's leading labor organization. At its peak it claimed 750,000 members, including some 60,000 black workers. Over 190 women's assemblies were organized for its 50,000 female members. The Knights created a woman's department and made its director a general officer of the union. Typical of its women activists was Leonara Marie Barry, who had become a millhand after the death of her husband. She joined the Knights in 1881 and became the first general investigator of the woman's department. Through her efforts, Pennsylvania passed the Factory Inspection Act (1899).

The Knights' willingness to include blacks and women, however, did not extend to the Chinese. Anti-Chinese sentiments were especially strong in California. The Knights actively joined in lobbying efforts for the Chinese Exclusion Act (1882), which placed a ten-year moratorium on Chinese immigration. Powderly denounced Chinese labor as "one of the greatest evils with which any country can be afflicted." Three years later Knights in Wyoming massacred 28 Chinese workers.

The Knights reached their peak strength when they successfully won strikes against the Union Pacific Railroad and the Southern Railway System in the early 1880s. In 1885 craft unions struck Jay Gould's Wabash railroad.

When Gould was forced to capitulate, Knights membership surged to 750,000 members.

Powderly, however, distrusted strikes. He viewed strikes as "acts of barbarism." Instead, he called for arbitration and the formation of producer and consumer cooperatives. Nonetheless, in the heady days that followed the victory over Gould, local unions called strike after strike. Without contracts between the union and management, locals were free to conduct strikes.

Gould bided his time. In 1886, he retaliated when the Knights attacked his Southwest line. Through the use of strikebreakers, state militia, and **Pinkerton** undercover detectives he smashed the union. The leadership of the Knights abandoned the striking workers. Within less than a half decade the Knights organization was but a shell of its former self.

SAMUEL GOMPERS STICKS TO THE BASICS. While industrial unionism and cooperatism failed, Samuel Gompers and the American Federation of Labor, founded in 1881, promoted a new form of organization, unique to the American situation: "pure and simple unionism." At a time when the labor movement was divided between political action versus trade unionism, **socialism** versus anarchism, cooperatism versus industrial unionism, Samuel Gompers and his associates developed the basis of the modern American movement.

Specifically, they dismissed talk of forming a labor party and taking political action. They also believed calls for workers to form producer cooperatives distracted labor from the real issues at hand: the struggle for union recognition and collective bargaining with management, and the need for better working conditions for all labor.

They also advocated a new form of organization—an international federation of labor that allowed individual unions and locals to set their own course of action, overseen by a central, or as they called it, an international office (so-called because it included Canadian locals). This international office was to be supported by high dues collected by local unions. In this way the international office could direct aggressive organizing campaigns in unorganized areas and support weaker locals. Gomper's organization, the American Federation of Labor (AFL), was a loose federation of international unions for skilled workers organized along craft lines. By organizing skilled workers into craft unions, the AFL explicitly rejected organizing both unskilled workers and skilled workers within single industries.

Gompers's outlook was shaped by his own experiences growing up in the slums of London. Although he attended a Jewish free school until the age of 10, he lacked further formal education. He continued his studies at night in order to learn to read Hebrew and French. In 1863 he emigrated with his family to the United States. There he joined his father as a roller in the cigar trade. Even as a young man, Gompers was a joiner. He became a member of the Odd Fellows, the Order of Foresters, and participated in a debate club. He also joined the cigar workers' union. There he met Adolph Strasser who convinced Gompers that socialism was not the answer to the plight of the workingman. Out of the cigar workers' union emerged in the early 1880s the Federation of Organized Trades, which in turn evolved into the American Federation of Labor.

In 1881 labor remained divided over political action. A large socialist group within the AFL called for more political involvement. A major turning point for organized labor came in 1886 in a strike against McCormick Harvester. When the police brutally attacked strikers demonstrating outside the McCormick plant, local anarchists called a mass demonstration at Haymarket Square in Chicago. That evening, just as the demonstration was about to break up, the police ordered the crowds to disperse. Suddenly from the crowd a bomb was hurled, killing two policemen. In the days that followed, eight anarchists were arrested on charges of conspiracy to commit murder. In court the defense showed that many of the defendants were not even present when the explosion occurred, although later evidence suggested anarchist involvement in the bombing. Nevertheless, all eight anarchists were convicted. Four were executed. Of the other four, one committed suicide, and the others were sentenced to prison.

Following Haymarket, employers took advantage of the national hysteria against radicals to attack labor. While this hastened the demise of the Knights of Labor, the AFL under Gompers steered a steady course by focusing on higher wages and the right to organize. Political activity remained limited to legislation protecting the rights of collective bargaining and bettering working conditions for all workers. The AFL also demanded the end of child labor. By 1892 the AFL emerged as the dominant labor organization in America.

Gompers remained president of the AFL until his death in 1924. The AFL survived largely because of this matter-of-fact, stubborn labor leader. He remained intensely loyal to the union cause and was willing to sacrifice his personal well-being for this cause. He was thoroughly honest and when he died he was by no means wealthy.

EUGENE DEBS RADICALIZES. Within the AFL, a large socialist faction continued to challenge Gompers for power. Socialists called for greater political involvement through the establishment of a labor party. Socialists also called for municipal ownership of public utilities and government ownership of railroads, telegraphs, and the telephone. They found an articulate spokesman for their cause in Eugene Debs, a native-born midwesterner of French ancestry. In many ways Debs cut a completely opposite figure from Gompers. Anyone looking only at their backgrounds would have predicted that Gompers would be the radical and Debs the conservative.

Raised in the railroad-dominated center of Terre Haute, Indiana, Debs grew up in the security of small-town America. He had worked for a railroad, moving up to fireman. He married the local physician's daughter, built a splendid home in the good section of town with his wife's money, and for a while dabbled in local Democratic party politics, winning a seat in the state assembly. He also became an active unionist. He helped organize in 1893 the American Railway Union (ARU), of which he became president. The union quickly gained a membership of 150,000.

The growth of the ARU frightened railroad owners. Through their General Managers Association, a half-secret combination of 24 railway companies, they decided to confront the ARU. As one spokesman declared, "We can handle the railway brotherhoods, but we cannot handle the ARU. We cannot handle Debs. We have got to wipe him out." Their opportunity came quickly.

Among those who joined the American Railway Union were the Pullman Palace Car workers. These workers lived in a town built by George Pullman, the company's owner. Pullman spoke with pride about this model town and the care he took of his employees. Many, even fellow businessmen, dismissed Pullman's rhetoric. Mark Hanna, a Cleveland industrialist, declared, "Model—go and live in Pullman and find out how much Pullman gets selling city water and gas ten percent higher to those poor fools."

Pullman responded to the depression of 1893 by cutting wages 25 percent. A year later a delegation of workers went to the company to ask for relief. Rents had increased—as had company profits—but wages had not been restored. When Pullman discharged three leaders of the delegation, the employees went out on strike. Against the warnings of Debs, the rank and file of the ARU railway unions decided to strike in support of the Pullman workers. By the summer of 1894, the entire railroad system of the United States had been effectively shut down.

The General Managers Association demanded action. They found a spokesman in Richard C. Olney, attorney general in the Grover Cleveland administration. A member of several railroad boards, Olney urged Cleveland to take action. He reported that the nation was on the verge of anarchy. Finally, he went to federal court to get an injunction based on the Sherman Antitrust Law, stating that the strike was in restraint of trade and was preventing the transportation of federal mail. Olney sent in 2,600 deputies to enforce this injunction and others that followed against picketing and boycotts. Three days of rioting followed. The strike was completely broken. Debs was arrested for disobeying the injunction and sentenced to prison.

In prison Debs was converted to socialism. Although he voted for the Democratic presidential nominee, William Jennings Bryan, in 1896, this would be the last time he would support the mainstream party system. Shortly after leaving prison in 1895, Debs joined Victor Berger, a Milwaukee socialist devoted to labor, and the handsome and eloquent Morris Hillquit, a Russian-born Jew and garment worker organizer, in organizing the Socialist Party of America.

The first two decades of the twentieth century were to be the "golden age" of socialism in America. Following the Civil War, many intellectuals expressed socialist and anticapitalist sentiments. In 1879 Henry George, a California newspaperman, attracted international attention with his book *Progress and Poverty*. He accused landlords of creating class division and poverty in America. To remedy the situation, he called for a "single tax" on landowners who speculated in land. Although simplistic, *Progress and Poverty* went through hundreds of printings and was read by millions in the United States, as well as in Great Britain, Australia, and New Zealand.

Equally popular was Edward Bellamy's bestselling utopian novel, *Looking Backward* (1887). Readers were attracted to the book's call to replace individualism and competition with a new social order that emphasized social cooperation and efficiency. Bellamy's new society would operate like a well-organized army. This regimented world appealed especially to the **Yankee** middle class, many of whom joined Nationalist Clubs based on Bellamy's program.

Other socialist books also gained attention. Henry Demarest Lloyd's *Wealth Against Commonwealth* (1894) attacked Standard Oil as an example of capitalism gone awry. That same year Robert Blatchford's *Merrie England* (1894) called for the establishment of a socialist society. In the next decade over two million copies of his book were sold in the United States and Great Britain.

Socialism in America also drew on European traditions brought by German, Finnish, and eastern European radicals, many of whom were influenced by the radical German economist, Karl Marx. Also, a native radicalism emerged among farmers in Oklahoma, Texas, and Arkansas. As a result, the Socialist party tapped many sources of radicalism in America and attracted followers from all classes in the United States.

In the next decade, the Socialists elected congressmen, state legislators, mayors, and an array of municipal officials throughout the United States. The party attracted many intellectuals and writers, including Upton Sinclair, Jack London, John Reed, and Helen Keller. However, faced with internal divisions, their inability to win the majority of Americans to their cause, and political repression during World War I, the Socialist party ultimately failed in the political arena.

The socialist critique of capitalism coincided with a general outburst against corporations that came from small entrepreneurs, labor leaders, and reformers who saw the new corporate order as a threat to freedom and their survival. Surely not all benefitted from the rapidly growing economy. In the hard decades of the 1880s and 1890s, many farmers became radicals, including those in the South, which continued to lag behind the rest of the nation in economic progress.

The New South Emerges

The South endeavored to get back on its feet by exploiting its natural resources and developing iron, steel, and textile manufacturing. African-American intellectuals such as Booker T. Washington and W. E. B. DuBois advocated improvements for blacks, while southern whites launched vicious attacks on blacks. Nevertheless, many African-Americans prospered, setting up businesses and entering the professions.

REPLACING PLANTATIONS WITH FACTORIES. Following Reconstruction a group of white southern editors, businessmen, and politicians began to call for the creation of a New South based on industrial development that would replace the old **plantation** system. Promoted by editors such as Henry W. Grady of the *Atlanta Constitution* and Henry Watterson of the *Louisville Courier,* and by Senator Wade Hampton of South Carolina, this New South ideology became widespread in the 1880s as many states sought to lure northern investment to their region through tax breaks, cheap labor, and the sale and leasing of mineral and timber rights.

Blessed with deposits of coal and iron ore, Alabama became a major producer of iron and steel by the turn of the century. Birmingham, Alabama became one of the nation's largest pig-iron producers. Other southern cities joined in this drive toward industrialization. Iron and steel plants attracted blacks from the countryside. By 1900, one-fifth of southern blacks lived in cities.

A textile industry emerged in the hilly piedmont region of the South. This region ran along the edge of the Appalachian Mountains from Lynchburg, Virginia, through North Carolina, northern Georgia to Birmingham, Alabama. Southern mill owners were able to purchase the latest machinery produced in the North. Southern white wages were oppressively cheap. Managers often paid teenage mill workers from 7 cents to 11 cents a day—30 percent to 50 percent less than wages in New England mills. Even with low labor costs, because of less efficient machinery cotton production in the piedmont remained just one-half of what mills produced within a 30-mile radius of Providence, Rhode Island. Southern per capita income was half of northern per capita income.

PLACING SOUTHERN BLACKS. The new southern economy did little for the majority of blacks in the South. Most remained tied to the land through the lien crop and **sharecropping** systems of the late nineteenth century. Black educators such as Booker T. Washington, president of the Tuskegee Institute in Alabama, called for young blacks to break from the past through industrial education and the dignity of efficient labor. Industrial education was promoted energetically by whites for their own race as well, but Washington gained national attention for his work. Eschewing black involvement in politics, he called for the immediate material improvement of blacks. He established the National Negro Business League and was involved in a number of conferences for self-improvement.

Other black intellectuals, such as W. E. B. DuBois, bitterly assailed Washington's program for industrial education for its lack of political consciousness and as a means of keeping blacks in virtual bondage. Instead, DuBois called for a political campaign to ensure civil rights for blacks.

Furthermore, white southerners sought to strengthen and maintain white supremacy. Fearing a growing pool of black laborers, many white workers in the South resorted to vicious racist attacks on blacks. A stereotype of blacks as sex-mad "beasts" emerged in public debates and in popular literature. Revisions of state constitutions in the late 1890s across the South stripped blacks, and sometimes poor whites, of the right to vote. In the civil rights cases of 1883, the Supreme Court ruled in favor of segregation in public accommodations. *Plessy v. Ferguson* (1896) held that "separate but equal facilities" for the races were acceptable.

Still, the period saw many blacks prospering. A growing number of self-employed blacks ran grocery and general merchandise stores, barber shops, and beauty parlors. Blacks also entered the printing and undertaking trades. In many communities, "buy black" campaigns were launched to encourage black capitalism. Throughout the South, black businessmen organized business associations and expositions. Black investors also formed banks, such as the National Freedman's Saving and Trust Company with branches throughout the South, but when that bank collapsed in 1874, it set black banking back until the 1880s.

Many blacks also entered the ranks of professionals by becoming clergy-men, doctors, dentists, lawyers, and schoolteachers. Nashville, for instance, became a center for black doctors largely because of the Meharry Medical Association. The Meharry Medical School provided opportunities for men like Dr. R. F. Boyd, who had been born a slave in 1858. By attending night school and teaching in rural areas for 12 years, Dr. Boyd was able to finance his medical degree at Meharry. He later earned degrees in chemistry and dentistry, and did postgraduate work at the University of Chicago on women's and children's diseases. He became one of the South's leading physicians.

Conclusion

The second Industrial Revolution created new industry and new organizations for businesses and labor. After the Civil War, manufacturing was transformed in iron, steel, oil, and consumer goods. Men such as Carnegie, Rockefeller, and Morgan transformed the way business was conducted in America. At the same time, labor experimented with new forms of organization: Terence Powderly led the Knights of Labor; Samuel Gompers established modern unionism with the American Federation of Labor; and Eugene Debs proposed a socialist program.

The second Industrial Revolution also changed the South. The "New South" which emerged created new manufacturing in steel, iron, and the textile industries. These new industries created opportunities for black workers who left southern farms to work in industrial cities in the South.

Any assessment of American capitalism in the late nineteenth century should acknowledge that the emergence of the new corporate order coincided with the creation of the largest middle class in history. And this middle class came to characterize and inform American politics and society in the twentieth century, as much as did the new corporate order and labor.

Recommended Readings

DOCUMENTS: Andrew Carnegie, *Autobiography* (1920); Eugene V. Debs, *Writings and Speeches of Eugene V. Debs* (1948); Thorstein Veblen, *The Theory of the Leisure Class* (1899).

READINGS: (LABOR) David Brody, *Steelworkers in America: The Nonunion Era* (1960); Melvyn Dubofsky, *Industrialization and the American Worker* (1975); Leon Fink, *Workingmen's Democracy: The Knights of Labor and American Politics* (1983); Herbert G. Gutman, *Work, Culture, and Society in Industrializing America* (1976); Gerald D. Jaynes, *Branches Without Roots: Genesis of the Black Working Class in the American South* (1986); Jacqueline Jones,

Labor of Love, Labor of Sorrow: Black Women, Work, and the Family from Slavery to the Present (1986); Susan E. Kennedy, *If All We Did Was to Weep at Home: A History of White Working-Class Women in America* (1979); Alice Kessler-Harris, *Out to Work: A History of Wage-Earning Women in the United States* (1982); Alexander Keyssar, *Out of Work: The First Century of Unemployment in Massachusetts* (1986); David Montgomery, *The Fall of the House of Labor* (1987); Daniel Nelson, *Managers and Workers: Origins of the New Factory System in the United States* (1975); John L. Thomas, *Alternative America: Henry George, Edward Bellamy, Henry Demarest Lloyd, and the Adversary Tradition* (1983); Daniel T. Rodgers, *The Work Ethic in Industrial America* (1974); Stephen J. Ross, *Workers on the Edge: Work Leisure and Politics in Industrializing Cincinnati* (1982); Nick Salvatore, *Eugene V. Debs* (1982). (INDUSTRY) Robert W. Bruce, *Alexander Graham Bell and the Conquest of Solitude* (1973); Alfred D. Chandler, Jr. *The Visible Hand: The Managerial Revolution in American Business* (1977); Carl Degler, *The Age of Economic Revolution* (1977); Samuel P. Hayes, *The Response to Industrialism* (1957); Thomas P. Hughes, *Networks of Power: Electrification in Western Society* (1983); Maury Klein, *The Life and Legend of Jay Gould* (1986); Naomi R. Lamoreaux, *The Great Merger Movement in American Business* (1985); Harold C. Livesay, *Andrew Carnegie and the Rise of Big Business* (1977); Alan Trachtenberg, *The Incorporation of America: Culture and Society in the Gilded Age* (1982); David O. Whitten, *The Emergence of Giant Enterprise* (1983); Olivier Zunz, *Making America, 1870-1920* (1990).

19

———— ✖ ————

IMMIGRANTS AND THE CITY TRANSFORM AMERICAN SOCIETY

CHAPTER OVERVIEW: In the late nineteenth century, Americans saw their society transformed as millions of immigrants poured into the United States. By 1910, more than 14 percent of America's entire population were immigrants. Most of these late arrivals (so-called "new immigrants") were from eastern and southern Europe. They did not speak English and brought with them customs viewed as strange in their new homeland.

Americans recognized the profound social consequences of this demographic movement and many found these changes disturbing. As one minister warned, the new industrial metropolis created by this influx of settlers was a "serious menace to our civilization." By 1890, Americans began using the phrase "the modern city" to denote this social transformation. Rapid urbanization created immense problems in transportation, housing, sanitation, crime, and poverty. City officials and reformers all sought solutions to these ills, with varying degrees of success.

Immigrant Experiences

Self-interested recruiters lured millions of immigrants to America with exaggerated promises of a better life. Immigrants after 1880 were more likely than earlier immigrants to be poor, single, and non-Protestant. Traveling to America was arduous, even with improvements in transportation, and new arrivals were poorly prepared for the harsh realities they found. Ethnic groups stuck together for comfort and protection.

DECIDING TO LEAVE HOME. The most noticeable change in late nineteenth-century America was the rich diversity created by the influx of immigrants. In the four decades between 1880 and 1920, more than 23 million immigrants came to America—80 percent from eastern and southern Europe. By 1890 adult immigrants outnumbered native adults in 18 of the 20 largest cities.

This massive migration was part of a global pattern in the late nineteenth century. People left their native lands to settle in South America, Canada, and Australia. Brazil and Argentina aggressively recruited immigrants by offering subsidized travel, duty-free entry of personal belongings, and full resident status upon arrival. These policies drew significant numbers of Germans, Italians, and Jews from Europe to South America.

The United States government did not offer travel subsidies or other direct inducements, in part because the United States already had a reputation as a haven for the politically oppressed and the religiously persecuted. Instead, recruitment to the United States was primarily the work of private companies seeking employees, steamships needing passengers, and states anxious for settlers. After the Civil War, most states and territories operated immigration bureaus in Britain, Germany, and Scandinavia.

Railroads actively sought immigrants to settle new western lands, which would promote expansion of the rail system. The Kansas Pacific, Missouri Pacific, Santa Fe, and Wisconsin Central railroads deluged Europe with pamphlets and brochures telling of the splendors of the Midwest and Great Plains states. Railroads offered reduced fares, provided low interest loans for purchasing farmland, and sometimes even built churches and schools. Promotional literature claimed that the Midwest and Great Plains states were ideal places to live. Stories were told of invalids miraculously getting well. Jay Cooke of the Northern Pacific went so far as to print fraudulent weather maps showing a deceptively mild climate in the Great Plains. These bogus maps, which were circulated throughout Europe, inspired some wits to rename the Northern Pacific Railroad the Banana Belt.

These newcomers came with widely divergent social, political, and religious views. Some were socialists, others Catholics. Among the German immigrants alone there were Catholics, Lutherans, Jews, and freethinkers.

Immigrants arriving after the Civil War joined the 4 million who had settled in America in the 1840s and 1850s. Before the 1880s most newcomers were northern Europeans. From 1860 to 1890 more than 7 million Germans came to the United States. They were joined by 2 million English, Scottish, and Welsh settlers, 1.5 million Irish, 1 million Scandinavians, and 800,000 French-Canadians.

Beginning in the 1880s, however, increasing numbers of eastern and southern Europeans—Slavs, Jews, Italians, and Greeks—crossed the Atlantic. More than 18 million "new immigrants," as they were called, came to this country before 1920. These new immigrants differed from the "old" immigrants. Old stock English speakers tripped over unfamiliar names such as Stanislawski and Alioto that ended in vowels. Many were Roman Catholics, Eastern Orthodox, or Orthodox Jews. They tended to be poorer than earlier settlers. Even immigrants from Germany and Britain who came after 1880 were often unskilled workers or displaced peasants. Furthermore, increasing numbers of young single men arrived, while before 1880 most immigrants came with their families.

These people left their home countries for a variety of reasons. Political and religious oppression pushed many eastern Europeans from their homes. Lack of land and jobs in Italy and Ireland forced others to leave. Mexican peasants pushed northward across the border after having been displaced by the growth of large sugar and coffee plantations.

While immigrant families came from a wide range of religious, cultural, and social backgrounds, most shared a strong belief in the primary importance of family and kinship. Leaving home was a well-considered family decision and a practical act for most.

These late immigrants came to the United States with differing aspirations. Some came seeking fortunes, many simply wanted jobs, while others dreamed of earning money and returning home. Over half of the Hungarians and southern Italians who came to the United States returned—often as planned—to their native lands. Forty percent of the Germans and Greeks did, as did nearly a third of the Poles. Many shuttled back and forth, going home and returning when they found work again in the United States.

Those immigrant families that remained in the United States were willing to experiment in creating new lives for themselves in the market economy of late nineteenth-century industrial America. Many had read about American life in promotional brochures, newspapers, and letters from friends and relatives, but those who left their homes entered into an essentially unknown world.

SAILING TO AMERICA. Improved land and sea transportation made the journey to America easier than it had been in the early nineteenth century, but travel still remained arduous. For example, Russians and east Europeans would hike for days or weeks with their belongings on their backs or in handcarts just to reach railroad terminals. Then they faced a long rail trip to major European seaports to board a steamship.

Immigrants favored certain ports and the busiest were Liverpool, England; Hamburg, Germany; Fiume, Austria-Hungary; and Palermo, Italy. Steamship companies vied with each other for passengers. By 1880, 48 steamship companies were competing for Atlantic traffic. This competition led steamships to make the transfer from the train to the ship as smooth as possible. Company employees met each train to ensure that emigrants were protected from thieves and confidence men. The Cunard steamship line built a huge complex that could house over 2,000 people in ten dormitories.

At the port of departure, company representatives who could speak a variety of eastern European languages were on hand. Conditions were kept comfortable and sanitary. Kosher food was available for Jewish travelers and fish was offered on Fridays for Catholics. Later the Hamburg-Amerika line constructed in Germany an entire immigrant village with its own railway station, churches, and synagogue. In 1891 American immigration law required that steamship companies vaccinate, disinfect, and give health exams to passengers before sailing. Often American physicians were assigned to European ports to help in this process.

Improvements in ship building and steam engines made travel across the Atlantic faster and easier. The voyage usually took eight to 14 days. In the 1870s and 1880s most immigrants traveled in **steerage,** below-deck compartments without portholes that had been used as cargo holds. In these steerage compartments, passengers were crammed into two or more tiers of narrow metal bunks. Travelers brought their own straw mattresses which they threw overboard on the last day of the trip. Men and women were segregated, sometimes only by a flimsy curtain of blankets.

Some ships carried as many as 2,000 passengers. Emigrants brought their own food, which they cooked on ranges, boilers, and vegetable cookers in the ship's galley. Ships usually provided herring, because it was inexpensive and helped combat seasickness. Toilet facilities were generally poor on pre-1890 ships. Some vessels provided only 21 toilets per thousand passengers.

Steamships continued to make marked improvements in accommodations throughout this period. By the 1890s steerage had been replaced by third-class cabins that accommodated two to six passengers. Outside walking promenades were constructed to allow exercise. Lounges and smoking rooms were provided. Meals were served in small dining areas, while concession stands sold beer, drinks, and tobacco. Many steamship lines employed nurses, physicians, and chaplains for the benefit of passengers.

ARRIVING IN AMERICA. Upon arrival in an American port, travel-worn immigrants were full of expectation and anxiety. Typical advice came from one immigrant who warned, "When you land in America you will find many who will offer their services, but beware of them because there are so many rascals who make it their business to cheat immigrants." American immigration officials sought to protect newcomers as much as possible from those who might prey on them, but their primary concern remained protecting America from potentially dangerous immigrants.

The busiest immigration port was New York. From 1855 to 1892, Castle Garden at the tip of Manhattan island served as the major entry facility. In 1893 Congress abandoned this facility for a new depot on nearby Ellis Island, close to the New Jersey shore. After the original wooden structure on the island burned in 1897, Congress began construction of an enormous red brick complex.

At its peak, Ellis Island processed hundreds of immigrants per day. The first floor housed the reception facilities, a railroad ticket office, food counters, and a waiting room. Other floors were used for administrative offices. An adjacent building offered new arrivals a restaurant, a laundry, and shower facilities. Here immigrants got their first taste of the new world. Sometimes their experience was humorous. As one immigrant later recalled, "I never saw a banana in my life and they served a banana. I was just looking at it." Others, she said, tried to eat their bananas with the skin on before they learned it should be peeled.

Under mandate from Congress, American immigration officials sought to keep out people considered dangerous. Throughout the late nineteenth century, Congress imposed more restrictive immigration policies. In 1882 Congress excluded "lunatics," convicted criminals, and persons likely to become public charges. Later restrictions barred prostitutes, "idiots," polygamists, and those suffering from contagious or "loathsome" diseases. Still, 80 percent of all entering immigrants were admitted without difficulty. Of those initially detained for further examination or questioning, over half were later admitted.

SETTLING IN AMERICA. An extensive network of private charities and benevolent societies were located at Ellis Island to aid the new arrivals. Immigrants were introduced to American life by Jewish, Irish, German and other mutual aid societies, by the Salvation Army, by the Women's Home Missionary Society, by the New York Bible Society, and by myriad other groups. Immigration officials instructed these groups to remain sensitive to the needs of the immigrant. One official cautioned Christian missionary groups to imagine themselves in the shoes of Jewish immigrants: "When they have Christian tracts—printed in Hebrew—put in their hands, apparently with the approval of the United States government, they wonder what is going to happen to them there."

From these ports of entry, immigrants spread throughout the nation. Many of the Irish and Jews remained in large cities, particularly in the Northeast. Many Poles, hoping to earn enough money to return home, opted to work for high wages in the coal fields of Pennsylvania, the stockyards of Chicago, and the steel mills of Buffalo.

Italians and Greeks also preferred the city, many taking jobs as menial laborers. Those with sufficient money started restaurants, fruit stores, or shoeshine parlors. Certain regions attracted specific immigrants. The Genoese Italians in Chicago and San Francisco often became saloon keepers, restaurant owners, or fruit vendors. Major enterprises such as the Del Monte corporation and Bank of America were launched by Genoese Italians. Many Germans and Scandinavians traveled to the Midwest to settle on farms or work in cities such as Racine, Wisconsin, Minneapolis and Duluth, Minnesota.

Immigrants usually emphasized close family bonds and ties of friendship within their own ethnic groups. Kinship provided protection and immigrant families tended to reinforce older traditions even as they encountered the New World. At the center of most families was the mother. As one Irish immigrant recalled, "Mother always handled the money; my father never even opened his pay envelope." Those wives who remained at home therefore enjoyed considerable influence within the family. Many of these women saw marriage as an act of independence from their original households. As mothers they now took charge of running the day-to-day tasks of the home. Much of their focus was on their children. Most immigrant families expected their children to go to work when they reached age 15. Children were asked to contribute their wages to the family and to help aging parents.

Those immigrants who settled in cities tended to congregate together. Although most large cities had Italian, Polish, German, or Chinese districts, usually no single neighborhood was composed exclusively of one ethnic group. Most ethnic neighborhoods contained a diverse population. Also, sharp regional, occupational, religious, and class differences often divided ethnic groups. In New York there was not a single "Little Italy." One could find Neapolitans and Calabarians on Mulberry, Genoese on Baxter Street, Tyrolese on 69th Street. Genoese Italians fought the newly arrived Sicilians. Poles divided along Prussian and Galician lines. Middle-class "lace curtain" Irish looked down on the "shanty" Irish. In St. Louis factionalism divided the German population. German Jews who had immigrated in the early nineteenth century seemed embarrassed by Jews from Eastern Europe and Russia.

Divisions also occurred between ethnic groups. Germans and eastern Europeans deeply resented Irish domination of the Catholic church hierarchy. In Buffalo, German Catholics joined forces with anti-Catholic legislators to oppose legal ownership and inheritance of church property by an Irish Catholic hierarchy. In Detroit, Poles became so upset when a Polish priest was dismissed by the local Irish Catholic bishop, that parish women actually blocked the newly appointed pastor from entering their church.

This Lewis Hine photo (1910) captures immigrant life in a tenement on the East Side of New York City. (Culver Pictures)

Exclusion and Assimilation

The new immigrants were not welcomed by many people already in America. Discrimination against them was sometimes overt, sometimes subtle. The immigrants themselves were torn between adopting American ways and preserving their old ways. They formed organizations to help their own people succeed in America. Public schools helped immigrant children assimilate into American society.

IMMIGRANTS ORGANIZE TO HELP EACH OTHER. Tensions within ethnic communities were tempered by deep loyalties toward the family, neighborhood, and Old World traditions. Immigrants also formed mutual aid societies, physical culture clubs, patriotic societies, foreign language newspapers, and churches and synagogues. Greeks and Turks opened coffee houses. German beer halls were found in every large city, catering not just to men but to entire families. To maintain ethnic values and pride, immigrants created such associations as the Polish National Alliance (1880), the (Irish) Ancient Order of Hibernians (1836), the (Greek) Pan-Hellenic Union (1907), and the Order of the Sons of Italy (1905).

Mutual aid societies offered low-interest loans to their members to start small businesses and buy homes. The New York Hebrew Free Loan Society, for example, enabled Jewish businessmen to become a dominant force in Harlem. Jews also established an array of other institutions, including the Hebrew Immigrant Aid Society, the Educational Alliance, and the Hebrew Sheltering Society.

Home ownership was particularly high among immigrant groups. In some cities, such as Detroit, it was higher among the immigrant working class than the native white middle class. In Cleveland, by 1910 more than 70 percent of Italian and Slovak immigrants owned homes.

Associations such as the Polish National Alliance and the Polish Women's Alliance invested well over 80 percent of their assets in home mortgages. Italians formed their own life insurance companies, while certain banks, most notably A. P. Giannini's Banca d'Italia (later Bank of America) served San Francisco's Italians. Japanese-American credit associations (Tanomashi) enabled members to pool money to buy and operate garden farms whose crops found a ready market in Los Angeles.

The church and the synagogue also served as a major source of social stability within immigrant communities. As early as 1860, there were 27 synagogues in New York City. As German Jews became Americanized, however, their attitudes toward religious life changed. A reform movement led by Isaac M. Wise made Cincinnati the center of Reform Judaism. Wise was joined by other German Reform rabbis who immigrated to the United States. By 1890 there were more members of Reform synagogues than Orthodox synagogues in the United States. Emphasis on religious education was evident in the establishment of 300 schools to teach Hebrew.

The majority of new immigrants were Roman Catholics. At the end of the Civil War there were 3,000 Catholic churches in the United States; by 1900 there were 10,000. Ethnic tensions between the Irish and other ethnic groups, especially Germans and eastern Europeans, troubled the Catholic church in the late nineteenth century. Tensions became so strained that in 1891 German Catholics asked the Vatican to allow each ethnic group to have its own priests and parishes. Officially the church denied the request, but tacitly it pursued a policy of appointing ethnic clergy. These churches played a key role in preserving ethnic family values. For example, the St. Stanislaus Kostka church in Chicago formed a mutual benefit association, women's groups, youth clubs and even a parish bank. Catholic immigrants also played an active role in creating an extensive parochial school system that included elementary and high schools and colleges. Non-Catholics also supported education. The Missouri Synod of the Lutheran Church established an extensive elementary and secondary school system throughout Illinois, Indiana, Missouri, Minnesota, and Ohio.

Still, many immigrant children dropped out of school to go to work. In 1910 fewer than 10 percent of Italian, Polish, and Slovak children in Chicago and Cleveland stayed in school beyond the sixth grade. Despite traditional Jewish educational values, only one-third of Jewish children completed high school in these cities.

LEARNING NEW WAYS AND PRESERVING OLD WAYS. Educational reformers encouraged immigrant children to attend public school in order to assimilate quickly into American culture. Most educators believed that learning English was the key to success in America. Schools also sought to further **assimilation** by offering personal health and grooming instruction. A key leader in education reform for immigrant children was William Wirt, who developed the Gary, Indiana, public school plan. His plan stressed basic reading and writing skills and provided for vocational training and moral instruction. Release time for religious instruction was built into the curriculum. In 1914 Wirt arranged with **Protestant** churches to set up a program of Bible study. Understanding the importance of the immigrant family, Wirt's plan encouraged children to take their Bible home for study. Wirt also established night schools to reach immigrant steel workers. The Gary plan became the model for schools in New York, Philadelphia, and El Paso.

Many religious leaders encouraged assimilation. Liberal Catholic clergymen such as Cardinal James Gibbons and Bishop John Ireland actively opposed the so-called "Cahensly Movement," which sought to appoint American bishops based in part on how well they represented various immigrant groups. Catholic leaders in Cincinnati and Louisville tried to discourage their parishioners from speaking German. In Chicago, Archbishop George Mundelein sought to undermine ethnic separateness and supported standardized education in Chicago parochial schools.

NATIVES OPPOSE THE NEWCOMERS. Many older Americans reacted negatively to the massive influx of immigrants. Ethnic jokes appeared regularly in newspapers and magazines. *Harper's, Atlantic Monthly, Puck,* and *Life* all published jokes about the "frugal Scottish," the "lazy Irish," the "cheap Jews," and the "ignorant Italians." Ethnic slurs could also take more malevolent forms. Italians, often considered "nonwhite," were frequent targets, sometimes maligned as criminals. One leading sociologist observed that Italians were prone to violence. He wrote that an Italian is "quite familiar with the sight of human blood as with the sight of the food he eats."

Anti-Italian sentiment took a particularly nasty turn in New Orleans in 1890. The popular police superintendent, David Hennessy, was assassinated shortly after announcing he had proof that a Sicilian mob was operating in the city. Public outcry over his murder led to the indictment of 19 Sicilians, but eight managed to flee and avoid prosecution. When the trial of the remaining 11 ended in a hung jury, an outraged mob stormed the jail, shot nine prisoners on the spot, and hanged two others from lampposts.

Discrimination against ethnic groups took more subtle forms as well. Social ostracism was common. As the number of Jews increased, hotels, clubs, and colleges began to exclude them. Many universities and colleges refused to accept Jews either as students or as faculty members. Some German Jews tried to counter this bigotry by arguing that Jews should not be judged by "the ignorant . . . bigoted, and vicious [Jewish] Poles and Russians arriving on the scene." Such strategies failed to overcome the ingrained prejudice of many native-born Americans.

Peopling the Modern City

The massive influx of immigrants transformed American cities, both physically and culturally. At the same time internal migration of people from rural to urban centers accelerated the growth of urban America. In this transformation, cities competed to become significant regional economic and cultural centers. The emergence of the industrial city also altered the social landscape as new urban spaces were created for living, work, and play.

CITIES GROW AND COMPETE. The growth of the urban population was startling, as immigrants from abroad and migrants from rural America flooded into cities. From 1860 to 1910 American cities absorbed nearly seven times the population they had in 1860. The population of Buffalo tripled, and Chicago's quadrupled. In 1870 New York City comprised only Manhattan and the small islands in the East River. In 1898 the city incorporated the five surrounding boroughs—including Brooklyn, the nation's third largest city in its own right—so that within a decade New York City's population reached 5 million.

The growth of the modern city transformed the cultural landscape. The fast pace of the city placed a premium on youthful energy. The latest fashions and fads took precedence over tradition and respect for elders. The diversity of people living in the new city challenged old patterns, while creating new expectations and anxieties.

The modern American city emerged from fierce competition by civic leaders to attract people, industry, and wealth. Most major American cities were founded before 1890. Among the most notable exceptions were Miami, Florida, established in 1896 on a new railroad line linking the west and east coasts of the state, and Tulsa, Oklahoma which emerged as a major city with the discovery of oil in 1901. New York remained the most populous city, while by the turn of the century many older cities, such as Philadelphia, Baltimore, Boston, and New Orleans, fell in the rankings as newer western and southern cities expanded.

Midwestern cities grew rapidly. By 1890 Chicago, despite a disastrous fire in 1871, had outdistanced its regional rival, St. Louis, to become the nation's second largest city. The rivalry with St. Louis for regional dominance had been fierce and left its mark on both cities. The English poet Rudyard Kipling described Chicago as a place of barbarism, boasting, and violence. "Having seen it," he said, "I urgently desire never to see it again."

Other cities in the Midwest vied to become regional centers. For example, in the 1870s many thought Leavenworth, not Kansas City, would dominate that region. Many thought Duluth, Minnesota, would become more important than Minneapolis. Similar competition occurred between Abilene, Texas, and Wichita, Kansas.

By 1900 the Midwest had emerged as a leading manufacturing region due to its natural resources and transportation facilities. Three-fourths of American manufacturing was concentrated there. Over three-fourths of American manufacturing workers lived in the belt east of the Mississippi River and north of the Ohio River. St. Louis, Cleveland, and Detroit ranked nationally as fourth, sixth, and ninth respectively in population. These cities were joined by Omaha, Nebraska; Kansas City, Missouri; and Minneapolis, Minnesota as major regional centers.

Western cities also grew quickly as shipping, finance, agriculture, mining, and tourism became major industries in the region. San Francisco remained the West's most prominent city, with its fine port and splendid vista overlooking the bay. By 1880 it had become the nation's ninth most populous city. Suburban communities across the bay such as Oakland and Berkeley enjoyed continued growth into the twentieth century.

Los Angeles was second to San Francisco in the West. The "City of Angels" grew when a rate war between competing railroads in the late 1880s brought an influx of people. Real estate **speculators** saw this boom as an opportunity to profit on rising land prices. Within a three-month period in 1887, as the railroads battled for passenger traffic, more than 20 town sites were laid out along the rail lines. Total real estate sales that year ranked below only Chicago and New York.

In this land frenzy, unscrupulous entrepreneurs inevitably entered the picture. Some developers deceived "greenhorns" from the East by hanging oranges on Joshua trees in the desert to make the land appear suitable for farming. Sidney Homberg sold 4,000 lots in the Mojave, which he claimed were in the cities of "Manchester" and "Border City." Manchester and Border City proved to be nonexistent. One wit observed that the desolate, roadless wasteland of the alleged Border City was most easily accessible by means of a balloon and as secure from attack as the home of the Cliff Dwellers. In this real estate boom less than 40 percent of the 100 towns mapped out for Los Angeles county between 1884 and 1888 were ever built. Still, some boom towns became permanent, including Burbank, Monrovia, and Azusa.

Seattle, located on the beautiful Puget Sound, had a port second only to San Francisco in the West. Its emergence as a major city, however, came largely as a result of the promotion tactics and business acumen of New England-born business leaders. In 1860 Seattle had persuaded the territorial legislature to locate the planned territorial university in the city. The community then built a hall and started classes. Despite this **Yankee** enterprise, Seattle languished until business leaders lured a major railroad terminus to the city. This "Seattle spirit" enabled the city to surpass its rival Tacoma, which came to emphasize its fine homes, genteel living, and preservation of tradition.

Again, regional competition between cities marked the development of the West. Salt Lake City competed with Ogden for economic dominance, while Denver struggled with a number of towns, including Cheyenne, Wyoming, for economic control of the mountain states.

The South, which remained primarily agricultural, did not show strong urban development. Although a number of interior cities did emerge— including Atlanta, Nashville, Louisville, Memphis, Dallas, and Birmingham—the South's population remained primarily rural. Even by the turn of the century, only 15 percent of southerners lived in urban areas.

Making the Modern City

Rapid urbanization created immense problems in housing, sanitation, and poverty. American cities were not prepared for the influx of millions of people. Cable cars and later electric streetcars improved transportation within cities and made suburbs possible. Residential building in cities were overflowing with people, and cities experimented with alternative housing approaches. Architects developed new ways of building and created skyscrapers, made possible by the development of elevators.

SOLVING CITY TRANSPORTATION PROBLEMS. Adequate public transportation quickly became a major problem, and many cities suffered daily traffic gridlock. In the 1850s horse-drawn street railways were introduced, so that by the 1880s most cities with populations over 50,000 had such streetcars. But the main means of transportation, the horse, was slow and messy. In 1880 an estimated 15,000 horses died in New York City. Horses fouled the city streets, and their droppings endangered public health. The city of Rochester figured that the daily excrement produced by horses there would be enough to fill a hole one acre in circumference and 175 feet deep.

City officials and private investors sought innovative solutions. By the 1870s city officials began experimenting with the steam engine to run cable cars. Chicago developed the first cable car. By 1887 it operated over 86 miles of track. The cable car was perfectly suited for San Francisco and Seattle, with their many hills.

In the 1890s many cities turned to electric trolley cars. The first electric streetcar system was installed in Richmond, Virginia, by Frank J. Sprague, an engineer who had worked for Thomas Edison. Electric car systems quickly spread to other cities. By the turn of the century ownership of electric streetcar companies and utility companies was increasingly concentrated as corporate **holding companies** were formed to extend their control regionally and in some cases nationally.

CRAMMING THE CITIES AND SPREADING INTO SUBURBS. The development of efficient transportation systems encouraged the growth of suburbs. American electric streetcar companies, unlike their European counterparts, charged a flat fee of a nickel for short or long trips, thus allowing commuters to live further from the city without having to pay more for transportation. In fact, many streetcar companies purchased land on the city's periphery in hopes of cashing in on suburbanization. Companies made more profits from land sales than from fares.

Other new transportation systems also encouraged the growth of suburbs. In 1864, Hugh B. Wilson, after studying the London underground railroad, proposed building a subway in New York City, but the state legislature defeated his proposal. He turned instead to building an elevated rail line for New York. Within a decade New York "El's" were carrying 175,000 passengers a day. New York became the model for other cities, including Kansas City, Brooklyn, and Chicago.

Suburban streetcar systems extended the freedom of urban life to women. The modern city provided opportunities for young women to become office workers and for middle-class women to shop at downtown department stores. (Library of Congress)

Although some suburbs had emerged as early as the 1820s, suburban sprawl came only in the late nineteenth century. The growth of suburbs allowed both the upper classes and the prosperous middle classes to move out to a safe, sanitary haven from city life. In this period, the wealthy began to move to fashionable suburbs—such as Bryn Mawr on the Pennsylvania Railroad "Main Line" west of Philadelphia, Brookline near Boston, and Shaker Heights near Cleveland. Suburbs also attracted the prosperous middle class, including both white-collar and skilled workers with family incomes of $600 to $1000 per year. Developers offered affordable homes for $1,000 to $4,000. In the 1890s a Chicago developer, Samuel E. Gross, built a subdivision outside the city that advertised houses for as little as $10 a month.

Those who remained in the city, however, faced a housing shortage. Builders failed to keep up with the demand. In most cities with populations over 100,000, urban dwellers usually rented. At first, older houses were divided into rooms for rent, or rooms were added. As early as the 1850s, five-story **tenement** buildings arose in New York. These buildings, which offered small rooms for rent, housed up to 500 people, as did the Gotham Court building. In New York in 1864, over 15,000 tenements housed 500,000 of New York's 800,000 people. Thousands of others lived in basements or damp, unfloored cellars within these buildings.

In 1877, James E. Ware won a magazine contest for a better designed tenement. Ware proposed a multiple-floor building with a ten foot by four foot air shaft on ᵉ h side to allow more light and ventilation. This type of building soon becaᵤₑ known as the "dumbbell" tenement because of its unusual shape. Stairs, hall, and common bathrooms filled the central parts of the building.

Tenements allowed cities to squeeze thousands of people into confined spaces. Some blocks housed as many as 10,000 people. This congestion was unhealthy because of inadequate sanitation and the increased exposure to contagious diseases like tuberculosis. In one Chicago district only 24 percent of the residents had access to bathrooms with running water. The rest relied on outhouses, called privy vaults, located in backyards or underneath porches.

If the poorest faced housing problems, so did the middle class. The shortage of living space led to the creation of the city apartment or flat. This new form of housing became socially acceptable only when Rutherford Stuyvesant built the first luxury apartment house in 1869 in New York, modeled on Paris structures. Soon "French flats," as middle-class and upper-class apartments were called, became fashionable in a few large cities.

BUILDING THE CITY. The confined space of the city placed restrictions on business as well. Strongly desiring central locations near business services, banks, and railroad stations, companies were forced to build upwards. Architects experimented with cast iron and later steel. Fireproof terra cotta tiles were used as façade. As early as the 1840s, James Bogardus, a New York watchmaker and ingenious inventor, developed an erector-set-like technique using cast-iron columns to construct an entire building. Others followed. In 1874 Richard Morris Hunt designed the New York Tribune Building with a cast-iron interior structure, and in 1884 William Le Baron Jenney pioneered the steel skeleton structure in his ten-story Home Insurance Building in Chicago.

The greatest contribution to the modern skyscraper came from Louis Sullivan, a Chicago architect. Sullivan gave form and substance to the skyscraper with his Wainwright Building (1891) in St. Louis. His designs, often associated with the Chicago School, set the style for American skyscrapers for the next half century. Sullivan's belief that a building should express its cultural purpose attracted other Chicago architects, including John W. Root, Daniel Burnham, Dankmar Adler, and Frank Lloyd Wright (who had once worked as Sullivan's draftsman).

Skyscrapers became feasible only with the development of the elevator, another American contribution to engineering. The elevator evolved through a series of innovations that began in 1853, when Elisha G. Otis's safety device was installed to protect passengers in case of a cable break. By the 1870s hydraulic power, gearing techniques, and electricity brought elevators into common use.

Reforming the City

In the late 1800s, filthy, overcrowded American cities were ravaged by disease, crime, fire, and poverty. Sanitation, health, police, fire, and social services emerged only slowly, and the police were often corrupt. In these conditions reformers sought to transform the city morally, socially, and politically. They set up public institutions to help the disadvantaged, fought vice, and worked to reclaim power from corrupt politicians. Women, finding new opportunities for education and employment, asserted independence and led many reform efforts. Despite all of its problems, city life gave diverse people something to share in common.

CLEANING THE CITY. Rapid population growth created its own problems, but the very density of the population aggravated conditions. A survey conducted in 1901 showed that one Polish section in Chicago had an average of 340 people per acre of land. One three-block area was home to 7,300 children. Trash, garbage, and manure littered the streets. Throughout the late nineteenth century outbreaks of cholera, typhus, and yellow fever plagued the cities. Tuberculosis, pneumonia, and dysentery brought early death to many children. Indeed, Pittsburgh had one of the world's highest mortality rates from typhoid.

Because many cities had grown along the nation's riverways, it was common to dump garbage, sewage, and waste in their rivers—which were, of course, the water supplies for cities downstream. The use of cesspools—holes for disposing waste—only worsened conditions. Washington, D. C. had 56,000 vaults (small private sewage pits), while Philadelphia had 82,000 such vaults and cesspools. The census of 1880 reported that New Orleans was literally saturated with the "oozings of foul private vaults." Baltimore had

80,000 cesspools that were absorbed by the city's porous soil and threatened to pollute water wells.

Despite such overwhelming problems of pollution, city officials throughout the nation responded slowly—although, on occasion, ingeniously. In 1889 the city engineer of Chicago, Ellis S. Chesbrough, persuaded the state legislature to create a 185-square-mile sanitary district to provide uniform, modern services for the city. In 1900 the Chicago Sanitary and Ship Canal helped reverse the flow of the Chicago River so that the city would be rid of the "menace of a contaminated water supply."

Water treatment and sewage treatment plants came slowly to most cities. A key figure in introducing new sanitation methods to the city was George Waring, Jr., a scientific farmer and engineer. When a yellow fever epidemic in 1878 killed nearly 5,000 people in Memphis, the city hired Waring to build a new sewage system. Ironically, Waring rejected the latest scientific theory that held germs responsible for disease, but instead asserted that filth was the cause. Nonetheless, Waring's work in Memphis earned him national acclaim. Later he served as New York City's first commissioner of street cleaning from 1895 to 1898, where he introduced regular garbage pick-up and street cleaning.

By the turn of the century, sewage and water treatment systems had been created in most large cities. By 1910 more than ten million residents in metropolitan areas drank filtered water. Such actions reduced mortality rates by a fifth in major cities. Even more dramatically, deaths from typhoid fever fell 65 percent for the nation.

PROTECTING THE CITY. The modern city also suffered from high crime rates. In Philadelphia the homicide rate tripled in the three decades following the Civil War. Gangs emerged in many cities, including Baltimore's Blood Tubs and New York's Bowery Boys. Gambling, prostitution, and public drunkenness became common sights in most cities. Cities had tried to cope with these problems by establishing volunteer or paid night watches, but they proved inadequate. The first modern police force in the United States was established in New York in 1845. New York provided the model for other cities including Philadelphia, Baltimore, and Boston. These police departments, staffed mainly by immigrants selected by local political bosses, usually performed additional city functions, including street cleaning, operating lodging houses for the indigent, and inspecting boilers and produce markets.

Some police proved vulnerable to corruption. An investigation of the New York City force by state senator Clarence Lexow in 1894 revealed that police were involved with gambling, prostitution, and liquor interests. In fact, one crooked New York cop boasted that his new precinct was so corrupt that bribes had allowed him to give up hamburger for tenderloin steak. Vice districts were soon renamed "Tenderloin" districts, a name that stuck in San Francisco.

Lexow's scathing report led New York to appoint Theodore Roosevelt as police commissioner. Between 1895 to 1897 Roosevelt introduced a number of reform measures—as well as the modern billy club—but the situation gradually eroded after he left office and corruption reappeared.

Fire continually threatened the modern city due to overcrowding, poor fire control service, and wooden buildings. Death due to fire was as great statistically as death from typhoid fever. In the 1870s fire took enormous tolls on life and property in New York, Boston, Pittsburgh, and Chicago. After the great Chicago fire of 1871, 64 insurance companies went bankrupt. The older volunteer fire companies had proven inadequate to meet the needs of the modern city. Cincinnati is given credit for creating the first municipal fire department. The development of new steam fire engines with automatic water pumps brought new technology to firefighting. By the turn of the century, American cities had some of the world's best fire departments.

CARING FOR THE CITY. While cities established and improved their public police and fire departments, addressing the needs of the urban poor was even more daunting. The lines between private and public charity often remained blurred. Many workers for private charities were distrustful of public relief and political influence. Nonetheless, the development of specialized public institutions to deal with poverty, mental illness, and other social ills marked a profound shift away from care in the home. The development of these local institutions coincided with the emergence of experts with specialized knowledge in the care and management of their clients.

Throughout the late nineteenth century, these experts sought to improve the institutional care of the poor, the mentally and physically afflicted, and the social deviate. One of the first relief efforts for the poor was Robert M. Hartley's organization of volunteers to visit the poor in their homes. Operating through the New York Association for Improving the Condition of the Poor, founded in 1843, volunteers went into the inner city to instruct the poor about sanitation, food preparation, and childcare. Following the Civil War, Hartley's association was a strong advocate for pure milk laws, public baths, and better housing.

There were similar efforts at reform on behalf of children. In 1853, Charles Loring Brace founded the New York Children's Aid Society. Brace's organization established dormitories, reading rooms, and workshops where young boys could learn work skills. Brace was also involved in a controversial foster care program that eventually transferred more than 90,000 boys from the city to foster homes and farms in Illinois, Michigan, and Wisconsin. Since many of these young boys were Roman Catholic, the Catholic church was particularly wary of Brace's efforts that often sent children to Protestant foster homes.

The late nineteenth century was a period of experimentation in addressing the needs of the poor and the indigent. The Salvation Army was one of the most interesting attempts to address social problems. Established in England in 1865 by a Methodist minister, "General" William Booth, the Salvation Army was a religious denomination organized along quasi-military lines to convert the poor to **evangelical** Christianity. Introduced to America in 1880, the Salvation Army provided food, temporary shelter and employment, and child care. The Salvation Army's lively street bands became a frequent sight in many large cities.

The Young Men's Christian Association (YMCA) also provided shelter to those coming to the city. The YMCA, which had strong support from the Methodist Church, then the leading Protestant denomination in the United States, was brought from England in 1851. By 1900 more than 1500 YMCAs and Young Women's Christian Associations (YWCAs) provided housing for many young people seeking a better life in the city.

After the Civil War, the creation of Boards of State Charities was a key effort to coordinate public relief on the local level. The Indiana Reform Law of 1895, which established a central state office to oversee local programs, further centralized local relief in the state. Still, the care of the poor and the afflicted largely remained local and voluntary. A Chicago directory in 1895 listed 57 asylums and hospitals, 28 infirmaries and dispensaries, 41 missions, 60 temperance societies, and hundreds of benevolent associations, camps, and lodges.

Leading the movement to make charity work more rational was the Charity Organization Society (COS) founded in 1882 by Josephine Shaw Lowell. Always dressed in mourning black for her husband who had died in the Civil War, Shaw brought scientific management to private charity in New York City. Under her direction, COS representatives compiled files on all who sought or received aid. COS representatives also visited the homes of the poor to encourage and advise them.

Other reformers attacked what they considered the foundations of poverty—liquor, gambling, and prostitution. Anthony Comstock and his New York Society for the Suppression of Vice (1872) undertook a vigorous campaign urging municipal authorities to close gambling houses and to censor obscene publications. Although his attacks against what he viewed as "obscene" literature and art led to controversy (the Comstock law is still federal law), his earlier activities against gambling made Comstock a powerful force in municipal reform.

While Comstock focused his attention on moral corruption in government and society, others probed the underlying values that contributed to poverty in America. In the 1870s Washington Gladden, a minister of a Congregational church in Columbus, Ohio, launched the Social Gospel movement. Applying Christian principles to society, he argued that the poor were victims of a society that created an environment which enabled poverty to exist. His call to bring Christianity to the streets was taken up by Walter Rauschenbusch, a Baptist minister in New York's notorious "Hell's Kitchen" district. He later described Hell's Kitchen as a place "one could hear human virtues cracking and crumbling all around." In a series of articles and books that included *Christianity and Social Crisis* (1907), Rauschenbusch influenced a generation of ministers and reformers who rejected older nineteenth-century views that blamed the poor for their misery.

WOMEN REFORMERS GET INVOLVED. Middle-class women played an important role in reform efforts such as the Social Gospel movement. The Victorian stereotype of the fragile, innocent woman was challenged by the changing role of women in the late nineteenth century. Working-class women displayed a sharp sense of independence by joining trade unions. By the first decade of the twentieth century, nearly 65,000 working women had joined over 500 trade unions. At the same time, women found whole new fields of employment opened to them with the development of the typewriter and telephone. Still, by 1900 almost 40 percent of working women were servants in private homes.

Middle-class women enjoyed new educational opportunities. Before the Civil War only a few colleges, such as Oberlin College and Emira College, admitted women. In the 1860s and 1870s, however, new women's colleges were founded, including Vassar, Smith, and Wellesley. State colleges and universities—beginning with those in Iowa in 1856—opened their doors to women.

Educated, middle-class women became active in a number of reform groups. The Woman's Christian Temperance Union (WCTU), under the leadership of Frances Willard, claimed a membership of 500,000 women. Although its primary focus was on banning liquor sales, it also campaigned actively for women's **suffrage**, labor legislation for women, and kindergartens in public schools. The General Federation of Women's Clubs, chartered by Congress in 1901, was a coalition of local societies of middle-class women who helped create better parks, recreational centers, and improved public schools in many cities.

Jane Addams of Chicago symbolized this concern with the social ills of the city. During a stay in England, Addams studied the settlement house movement in which reformers sought to introduce community centers—social settlement houses—to working-class neighborhoods to ease the harsh social conditions of the industrial inner city. Upon her return to Chicago, Addams joined her friend Ellen Gates Starr to open Hull House in Chicago in 1889. Hull House provided recreational, educational, childcare and health facilities to recent Italian and Greek immigrants. The daughter of a wealthy Illinois state senator, Addams sought not only to help the poor, but also to provide a role for educated women in society. She also became involved in the nonpartisan community reform movement in Chicago. In her *Hull House Papers* (1895), she surveyed housing and sanitation conditions in the city, providing an objective assessment of the need for reform in Chicago. Hull House became a model for other reformers, and by 1895 there were more than 50 settlement houses in other cities. The settlement houses flourished from 1895 to 1935, after which their functions were largely absorbed by government relief agencies.

REFORMING CITY POLITICS. Addams's involvement in nonpartisan reform politics occurred at a time when many middle-class activists called for an end to politics as usual. In the late 1890s, city bosses and machine politicians were targeted as the culprits in the growing social problems of the modern city. As the costs of running cities skyrocketed, reformers called for "efficiency and economy" in government. With burgeoning populations, many cities had gone into debt to meet normal services. Fifteen of the nation's largest cities saw their populations rise on average by 70 percent and their debts increase by 271 percent. At the same time, city bosses had links to utility and trolley interests which received lucrative franchises. Some cities, such as St. Louis, were profoundly corrupted by these utility interests.

As a consequence, middle-class nonpartisans called for a series of reforms. One was "home rule," a plan to take power from state legislatures and give it to city government. Reformers also advocated strong mayors to take power away from corrupt city councils. In the first decade of the twentieth century, reformers extended this concept further and advocated a powerful city manager working under a weak mayor to handle the city's business affairs. Reformers also demanded that nonpartisan regulatory agencies and boards be created to further weaken political control of city political bosses. One reformer quipped, "Whoever heard of a Republican park or playground, a

Democratic swimming bath, a Prohibitionist street clearing department, or a Populist mortuary?"

For many reformers, William Marcy Tweed's **political machine,** which dominated New York politics in the 1870s, symbolized "boss" government. Although the corrupt Tweed died in prison, there were other bosses like him: James McManes dominated Philadelphia politics from 1860 to 1880; "Blind" Alexander Sheppard ran Washington, D. C. from 1860 to 1873; "Boss" George B. Cox dominated Cincinnati from 1888 to 1910; and "Big Jim" Pendergast controlled Kansas City, Missouri, from 1910 to 1939. Political machines also ran Baltimore, Atlanta, San Francisco, and most other large cities.

In the 1880s reform movements took control of a number of cities. Reform mayors such as Grover Cleveland in Buffalo, Seth Low in Brooklyn, and James D. Phelan in San Francisco called for low taxes and more economy in city government. In the 1890s, other reformers emerged. In 1893 city reformers organized the National Municipal League to share programs and ideas.

The economic **depression** that marked the 1890s prompted many reformers to turn toward social issues. In city after city, reform-minded mayors were swept into office: Samuel M. Jones, the "Golden Rule" mayor of Toledo; Tom Johnson of Cleveland; Hazen S. Pingree in Detroit. Reform was in the air and would set the stage for the Progressive movement of the next decade.

SHARING CITY LIFE. Despite the social and political problems that troubled the modern city in the late nineteenth century, a rich, vibrant urban life emerged. Although the rich and the poor were divided into clearly defined neighborhoods, they shared the common experience of urban life. Cities were now tied together by better transportation systems. Communication was easier, because by 1900 there were nearly 800,000 telephones in the nation. New printing and production techniques allowed publishers such as Joseph Pulitzer and William Randolph Hearst to sell "penny" papers to a mass audience. As a result, dailies doubled in readership as newspapers developed well-defined editorial, news, sports, entertainment, and women's sections. The new metropolitan press introduced a distinct urban mentality to America.

Urban dwellers shared a common, democratic experience. Spectator sports such as baseball brought people from all walks of life together. Being a "fan" knew no social boundary. By the late 1870s there was a clear distinction between professional and an amateur baseball players, which only seemed to increase fan interest. Cities vied for major league teams. Even in the democratic experience of organized baseball, however, blacks remained excluded. In 1867 the National Association of Baseball Players barred blacks from membership.

The downtown was made more attractive in order to bring women shoppers to the city's new department stores. Across the nation department stores displaced the old dry goods stores. John Wanamaker's first success with his department store in Philadelphia became the model for Morris Rich in Atlanta, Adam Gimbel and Rowland H. Macy in New York, Marshall Field in Chicago, and Joseph L. Hudson in Detroit. Advertising developed by these stores urged urban people of all ranks to dress in the latest fashion. The development of the modern department store opened new job opportunities for women. Increasingly, they hired women on the sales staff, and provided one of the few opportunities for women to attain managerial positions. Still, consumption itself offered a shared, seemingly democratic experience.

Conclusion

The emerging modern city remained a disturbing and frightening place to some. The mass migration of immigrants from southern and eastern Europe transformed America socially and culturally. In America these immigrants created new communities around mutual aid societies, churches and synagogues, and social clubs. The diverse population and new manner of life threatened the old order and brought new dangers. With all its social ills and social divisions, the city appeared to embody the worst aspects of American capitalism. Yet for most Americans, especially immigrants and those who left rural farms to come to the city, urban life offered opportunities, excitement, challenge, and a radically new way of ordering their world.

Recommended Readings

DOCUMENTS: Jane Addams, *Twenty Years at Hull House* (1910); William L. Riordon, *Plunkitt of Tammany Hall* (1905); Lincoln Steffens, *The Shame of the Cities* (1904); and Josiah Strong, *Our Country* (1885).

READINGS: (THE CITY) Gunther Barth, *City People: The Rise of Modern City Culture in the Nineteenth Century* (1980); Susan P. Benson, *Counter Cultures: Saleswomen, Managers, and Customers in American Department Stores* (1986); Howard Chudacoff, *Evolution of American Urban Society* (1975); Clifford E. Clark, Jr., *The American Family Home, 1800-1960* (1986); Ruth S. Cowan, *More Work for Mother: The Ironies of Household Technology from the Open Hearth to the Microwave* (1980); Charles N. Glaab and A. Theodore Brown, *A History of Urban America* (1967); Dolores Hayden, *The Grand Domestic Revolution: A History of Feminist Designs for American Homes, Neighborhoods, and Cities* (1981); Daniel Horowitz, *The Morality of Spending* (1985); John F. Kasson, *Amusing the Millions: Coney Island at the Turn of the Century* (1978); Lawrence H. Larsen, *The Urban South* (1990); Terrence McDonald, *The Param-*

eters of Urban Fiscal Policy (1986); Blake McKelvey, *The Urbanization of America* (1962); Zane Miller, *Urbanization of America* (1975); Eric H. Monkkonen, *America Becomes Urban* (1988); Howard H. Rabinowitz, *Race Relations in the Urban South 1865-1890* (1978); Roy Rosenzweig, *"Eight Hours for What We Will": Workers and Leisure in an Industrial City* (1983); Stephan Thernstrom, *Poverty and Progress: Social Mobility in the Nineteenth-Century City* (1964); Sam Bass Warner, *Streetcar Suburbs: The Process of Growth in Boston* (1962) and *The Urban Wilderness* (1972). (IMMIGRANTS) Thomas J. Archdeacon, *Becoming American* (1983); Josef Barton, *Peasants and Strangers: Italians, Rumanians, and Slovaks in an American City* (1975); John Bodnar, *The Transplanted: A History of Immigrants in Urban America* (1985); Jack Chen, *The Chinese of America* (1980); Leonard Dinnerstein and David M. Reimer, *Ethnic Americans: A History of Immigration and Assimilation* (2nd ed., 1982); Mario Garcia, *Desert Immigrants: The Mexicans of El Paso, 1880-1920* (1981); Yuji Ichioka, *The Issei: The World of the First Generation Japanese Americans* (1988); John Higham, *Strangers in the Land* (1955) and *Send These to Me: Jews and Other Immigrants in Urban America* (1970); Frederic C. Jaher, *The Aliens: A History of Ethnic Minorities in America* (1970); Edward Kantowicz, *Polish-American Politics in Chicago* (1975); Alan M. Kraut, *The Huddled Masses: The Immigrant in American Society* (1982); Moses Rischin, *The Promised City: New York's Jews* (1962); William V. Shannon, *The American Irish* (1963); Barbara Solomon, *Ancestors and Immigrants* (1956).

20

DEPRESSION, PROTEST, AND POLITICS

CHAPTER OVERVIEW: Cleveland began his second term confident that his party's victory in 1892 promised reasoned reform. But within a year, an economic depression soured the national mood. Social tensions replaced complacency. Labor violence erupted; political radicalism spread like wildfire across the land. Farmers in the South and the Midwest broke ranks with the two-party system to form a third party, the Populist party.

Hopes ran high among the Populists that they could win the White House in 1896. These dreams were shattered when the Populist party fused with the Democratic party to support William Jennings Bryan, who called for a new monetary standard based on both silver and gold. The Republican candidate, William McKinley, overwhelmed Bryan at the polls, but America had been transformed. A new age of reform was about to begin.

The Depression of 1893: Labor Radicalizes, Cleveland Reacts

The depression of 1893 increased bankruptcies, unemployment, violent labor strikes, and class confrontation. Citizens marched on Washington to demand action. Class warfare seemed irreversible, but the new Democratic president, Grover Cleveland, did little to inspire confidence that the crisis was being met. Instead, he pursued a conservative strategy of trying to put the financial system back on a single gold standard. His efforts to increase the government's gold reserves convinced critics that monied interests were running the government. Cleveland lost even more support when the first income tax was passed, and was quickly declared unconstitutional.

393

CLEVELAND'S HOPES DASHED, 1893. In 1893 Cleveland reentered the White House as an extremely popular president. He had won a landslide victory with the solid Republican states of Illinois, Wisconsin, and California shifting to the Democratic party. Voters gave the Democrats majorities in both houses. For the first time since the Civil War the nation had swung Democratic. Republican businessmen seemed unperturbed. Henry Frick wrote to his boss, Andrew Carnegie, "I am very sorry for President Harrison, but I cannot see that our interests are going to be affected one way or the other by the change in administration."

The future seemed bright for Cleveland, the Democrats, and the nation. About to leave office in December 1892, Harrison declared, "There has never been a time in our history when work was so abundant, or when wages were so high."

Then shortly after Cleveland's inauguration, the nation plunged into one of its worst **depressions.** Signs of a faltering economy were evident in the collapse of a number of key railroad companies in 1893. Ten days before Cleveland assumed office, the Philadelphia and Reading Railroad entered federal bankruptcy court. That summer, only two months after Cleveland's inauguration, the New York stock market crashed. Other railroads, including the Erie and the Northern Pacific and Santa Fe, entered bankruptcy. People blamed the party in power—Cleveland's Democrats.

Economic distress snowballed. In 1894 more than 15,000 businesses failed. The rural banking system broke down, causing further strain on New York banks. Of 158 bank failures that year, 153 were in the West and the South. The number of unemployed soared, with estimates ranging from 2.5 to 4 million—one worker in five. Everywhere the crisis overwhelmed city authorities. Chicago reported 100,000 homeless people. Across the nation city officials opened jails and government buildings each night to shelter the unemployed who wandered the cities' streets. Although private charities were overextended, few believed that government should aid the unemployed in a systematic fashion. The governor of New York rejected such aid with the explanation: "In America the people support the government; it is not the province of government to support the people."

In this crisis, Cleveland did little to inspire confidence and much to elicit hostility. Always a reserved man, he now came across as unsympathetic to the plight of the nation.

CLASS VIOLENCE ERUPTS. Class tension filled the air. Shortly before the 1892 election labor violence erupted in Pittsburgh in July when steel workers at Andrew Carnegie's Homestead plant battled 3,000 strikebreakers brought in by the private Pinkerton Detective Agency under orders from plant manager Henry Frick. The clash broke out when strikers caught the Pinkerton strikebreakers attempting to sneak into the plant by floating down the river. The strikers, armed with guns, dynamite, rocks, and a small cannon, fought a twelve-hour battle with the **Pinkertons.** At the end of the battle, nine strikers and seven Pinkertons had been killed.

Some believed a revolution was at hand. Emma Goldman, an anarchist, later recalled that she and fellow anarchist, Alexander Berkman, were running an ice cream parlor in Worcester, Massachusetts, when they first heard of the Homestead strike. "To us," she wrote, "it sounded the awakening of the American worker, the long awaited day of his resurrection." The next day, upon hearing of the battle between the Pinkertons and the Homestead workers, Berkman headed to Pennsylvania and made a nearly successful attempt to assassinate Henry Frick.

Only a month after the Homestead strike, troops had to be sent into the Coeur d'Alene silver mines in Idaho when a private army of strikebreakers opened fire on strikers. While conservative and law-abiding observers abhorred violence on the part of labor, many were shocked and alarmed by management's use of private armies.

Economic depression further heightened class tensions. Many—radicals and conservatives alike—expected open class warfare. On May 1, 1894, the nation watched tensely as a grassroots movement, popularly known as Coxey's Army, marched on Washington, D. C. to confront the Cleveland administration concerning widespread unemployment across the nation. Jacob Coxey and his 400 veterans of the Commonweal of Christ gathered from across the country to bring attention to their demands for a federally sponsored public roads project to put people to work. In this "petition of boots," members of Coxey's Army spoke a visionary language of revolution.

That previous winter a "Jack the Ripper" had entered the White House, slashing the curtains and vandalizing furniture in the Green Room. The *Chicago Herald* expressed the fearful sentiments of the nation when it observed, "The air seems to breed cranks and the demon of destruction is abroad in the land." Reports of other armies on the march or in the process of being formed frightened Democrats and Republicans alike.

The protest ended when Coxey was arrested and armed policemen dispersed his "army" when it attempted to march on Congress to deliver its petition. During the following year 17 other armies would attempt to march on Washington. Many came from western cities—Los Angeles, San Francisco, Portland, Seattle, Tacoma, Salt Lake City, and Denver. In Butte, Montana, one "army" hijacked a train. In Chicago a Polish Coxey's Army was organized.

The summer following Coxey's march on Washington, even worse violence erupted when Eugene V. Deb's American Railway Union shut down the nation's railroads over a lockout of workers at the Pullman Palace Car Company. By the end of June 1894, more than 20,000 railroad men were on strike in and around Chicago. This strike was felt in 27 states. The use of the Sherman Antitrust Act to issue an injunction against Debs led to three days of rioting in Chicago. In the end more than 20 people were killed. Debs was arrested and convicted for disobeying the injunction. In *United States v. Debs* (1894), the Supreme Court upheld the use of the Sherman Antitrust law for the injunction against the strike.

CLEVELAND REACTS TIMIDLY, WALL STREET BARELY REASSURED. At no time since the election of 1876 had American democracy been so threatened. Cleveland believed that the origins of the depression was the collapse of the international monetary system. He believed that the first step toward recovery lay in balancing the federal budget and strengthening the monetary system through a strong gold standard. His policy reawakened the **"hard" money** controversy. Debt ridden farmers sought to raise prices for their crops through an inflationary scheme of issuing money based on a **bimetallic** gold and silver standard. Cleveland opposed this inflationary policy.

Instead, Cleveland asked Congress to repeal the Sherman Silver Purchase Act of 1890. Cleveland staked his presidency on this single goal. At the root of the crisis, he believed, lay fear for the nation's financial structure. As a Jacksonian, Cleveland favored hard money. He felt that if the nation's financial system could be placed back on a single **gold standard,** economic recovery was certain. In August, Cleveland called Congress into special session to repeal the Sherman Silver Purchase Act. What followed was one of the most bitter political battles since Reconstruction.

To understand Cleveland's actions, it is necessary to recall briefly the controversy over money that had cropped up in American politics after the Civil War (see Chapter 17). In 1873 Congress established that the price of one ounce of gold would be 16 times the price of one ounce of silver. At this ratio of 16 to one, silver was overvalued and little was minted. Those who would benefit from an inflationary monetary policy denounced the "crime of '73" and continued to press Congress for the coinage of more silver. Finally, in 1885 Congress gave in to this pressure with the passage of the Bland-Allison Act, which authorized minting silver in limited amounts of up to four million ounces each month at market value. Five years later, the Sherman Silver Purchase Act of 1890 nearly doubled the amount of silver to be purchased and minted by the government.

At issue was the proposal that the federal government expand the money supply by coining silver and issuing silver-backed paper money. This, in effect, meant placing the nation on a bimetallic money standard of gold and silver. The expansion of money in circulation would create **inflation**, which would increase the price of crops and aid debt ridden farmers.

Those who favored the **free coinage** of silver believed—with nearly religious fervor—that the issue was one of breaking the backs of monopolists and powerful financial interests who controlled government policy at the expense of American laborers and farmers. As one silverite argued, "the silver movement represented far more than merely free coinage. It was a complex of pent-up feelings against excessive power of great wealth." Opponents, on the other hand, viewed the free coinage of silver as hare-brained radicalism that threatened to disrupt international finances, the national economy, and the social order in America.

The proposal to place the nation on a bimetallic money standard suggested that government should be given expanded powers to intervene in the economy. To propose that government should play a hand in directing economic policy itself was a radical notion to those who believed in **laissez-faire** ("hands off") government. The free coinage of silver posed difficulties. First, the ratio of 16:1 overvalued silver. (Today, the gold-silver ratio is about 75 to 1). Those who demanded inflation, for all of their alleged radicalism, still did not accept the notion that the federal government should issue money unrelated to its stock of gold or silver.

Cleveland put all of his energy into repeal of the Sherman Silver Purchase Act. He was ruthless in his use of political pressure to get his way. He won easily in the House, but the vote for repeal barely passed the Senate.

Opponents bitterly assailed Cleveland. A young congressman from Nebraska, William Jennings Bryan, spoke extemporaneously from the House floor to declare that the silver issue represented the clash between the "corporate interests" and the ordinary people of America. Actually, not all **capitalists** supported the repeal of the silver act. Businessmen in debt and those who relied on foreign imports, for example, supported an inflationary monetary policy. Still, no other issue since the debate over race in 1866-1868 divided the nation as did the silver question.

The Cleveland administration was intent on maintaining a $100 million gold reserve. Cleveland feared a drain on gold reserves might create havoc in the international financial markets. Even before Harrison left office in 1893, this reserve had started to decline. The day the Senate repealed the Sherman Silver Purchase Act in 1893, the reserve had sunk to $84 million. By the start of 1894 it had fallen even further to $62 million.

When the government tried to sell $50 million in **bonds** at 4 percent interest, sales went slowly. When purchasers redeemed Treasury notes for gold to pay for the bonds, a further drain was placed on the Treasury. Politically, the bond sale further hurt the Cleveland administration. To Cleveland's critics it appeared, as one senator declared, that the president was "now fastened by golden cords to a combination of the worst men in the world."

Still intent on raising the gold reserve, the government issued more bonds which brought gold reserves past the magic mark of $100 million by December 1894. But by February 1895, the reserve had dropped again, this time to $42 million. Desperately, Cleveland turned to bankers J. P. Morgan and August Belmont to arrange for outside buyers to purchase $62 million worth of bonds. It was also agreed that over half of the money used for purchasing the bonds was to come from abroad. This arrangement only furthered talk of Cleveland's capitulation to "monied interests." In 1896 the Treasury issued another $100 million in bonds through public subscription. This loan finally stopped the gold drain, but the public attitude toward the Cleveland administration had soured completely.

Cleveland's handling of the **tariff** question did little to improve his standing. As a Democrat he had promised to lower import duties. Led by Democratic congressman William L. Wilson, the House passed a bill shortly before Christmas 1893 to reduce **import duties** by 20 percent. Moreover wool, coal, iron, hemp, and flax were placed on the duty-free list. Wilson's bill also created an income tax: a 2 percent tax on incomes over $4,000. In the Senate, high-tariff Democrats from industrial states joined Republicans to gut the bill. The final outcome was the Wilson-Gorman bill that Cleveland refused to sign, but it became law without his signature.

The new income tax, established in the tariff bill, aroused the wrath of many and was unanimously opposed by manufacturing executives across the country. Although the income tax was exceedingly modest, Senator John Sherman of Ohio denounced it as an "attempt to array the rich against the poor." He said the tax represented "socialism, communism, devilism." In *Pollock v. Farmers Loan and Trust* (1895), the Supreme Court ruled that the income tax was unconstitutional. Speaking for the court, Stephen Field warned that the income tax was only the beginning of an "assault upon capital." He declared, "It will be but the stepping stone to others, larger and more sweeping, 'til our political contests will become a war of the poor against the rich; a war constantly growing in intensity and bitterness."

The Democratic coalition established by Cleveland began to fall apart. In the congressional elections of 1894, the Republican party regained control of both houses of Congress in one of the most resounding victories in American political history. By 1895 Cleveland described himself as "a man depressed and disappointed." He was cut off from his cabinet, Congress, and party leadership. Cleveland wrote, "Think of it! Not a man in the Senate with whom I can be on terms of absolute confidence." Republicans now looked toward winning the White House in 1896. Cleveland remained in office with no prospect of winning another term. The Democrats had become the party of depression and economic chaos.

Farmers Revolt

The depression brought new winds of political change. Farmers outside the South became more productive, but low prices for their crops kept most farmers poor. Some farmers got trapped in no-win credit schemes, and many lost their land and had to lease land. Radicalism swept over them. They formed cooperatives to help themselves and political organizations to promote more favorable laws. By 1890, the farmers' movement had become a powerful political force in the South and West, culminating in the formation of the Populist party. Many Populist candidates won office, and one made a strong showing in the 1892 presidential election.

HARD TIMES BEFORE THE DEPRESSION OF 1893. The cruel winters of 1886 and 1887 and the harsh summer of 1887 ended the dreams of many farmers who saw themselves as the heirs of the Jeffersonian tradition of the independent **yeoman.** Throughout the plains, farmers quit their homesteads. From 1888 to 1892, 30,000 people in South Dakota vacated their homes, and in western Kansas nearly half the population abandoned their farms. Some left in wagons carrying signs that read, "In God We trusted, in Kansas we busted."

By the mid-1880s farmers found the traditional outlet for their wheat crops in Europe restricted because of tariff barriers and new competition from Argentina and Russia. The price of American wheat fell from $1.05 a bushel in 1875 to 67 cents in 1895. At the same time, improved agricultural machinery and better farming methods increased crop yield more than 250 percent. As a result, farmers raised more crops but earned less money. The consequence was a surplus of crops selling for less money in a buyer's market.

Farmers in the South faced additional problems. Following the Civil War, southern farmers had found themselves in a grim situation. Desperately short of capital, southern farmers continued older nonmechanized ways of farming. While the value of implements and machinery on northern farms more than doubled between 1861 and 1900, the value of southern farm machinery in

1900 was not even half of what it had been in 1861. Indeed, it was not until after World War II that mechanized cotton picking was introduced extensively in the South.

The scarcity of capital created further problems for the southern farmer. Many white and black farmers in the South entered into a new servitude brought about by a peculiar credit scheme—called the crop **lien** system—that emerged following the Civil War. Short of credit to buy seed for next year's crops, poor white and black farmers were forced to borrow money from local "furnishing" merchants. To receive this high-interest loan, a farmer pledged his unplanted crop. If the debt was not paid and if the crop failed, the merchant lost his money and placed a lien on the crop. In debt to the merchant even before his crop was planted, a southern farmer entered an oppressive cycle. As a result, when prices were low and he did not earn enough to pay off his debt, the farmer went deeper and deeper into debt year after year.

This system also imposed a one-crop system because the merchant only advanced cash for crops such as tobacco or cotton, which the merchant knew could be sold. In the end many impoverished farmers had to give up ownership of their land and rent it from the local merchant, who owned increasingly large amounts of land in the region. In this way some merchants exerted control over the economic and political life of a region. These merchants established close links to city bankers and railroad interests. This power was reinforced by their extensive links to railroad, banking, and financial institutions in regional centers such as Atlanta. Still, most Southern merchants remained poor. When cotton prices were low, everybody suffered.

THE GRANGE—1860S AND 1870S. Small farmers found themselves getting poorer. By 1900 well over a third of American farmers had become tenants forced to lease land, inevitably leading to social antagonism. As one South Carolina farmer declared, "All of us hated bankers and we hated merchants. We hated them because they robbed us."

Political organization of farmers started in the North with the formation of the National **Grange** of the Patrons of Husbandry in 1867. Initially organized as a group of social and cultural clubs by Oliver Hudson Kelley, a clerk at the Department of Agriculture, the Grange became a political force with more than 850,000 members by the mid-1870s. The Grange had its greatest strength in the states along the upper Mississippi River: Illinois, Iowa, Minnesota, and Wisconsin. The Grange especially targeted railroads and corporate-owned grain warehouses in their antimonopoly campaign.

In 1867 the Illinois Grange was able to get the state to enact the Warehouse Act, which required railroads to load grain from independent elevator

This Dakota sod hut captures a sense of early farm life on the Great Plains. In particular, women on the frontier endured both physical hardship and the lack of female companionship. (THE BETTMANN ARCHIVE)

operators. Other state laws supported by the Grange fixed railroad rates. The Supreme Court upheld these regulatory laws in *Munn v. Illinois* (1876). While some Grange members drifted to the Greenback party in 1876, a short upturn in agricultural prices weakened that party, whose candidate, James Baird Weaver, received only 308,000 votes in 1880.

THE ALLIANCE MOVEMENT—1880s. The 1880s revived militant farm protest through the Alliance movement. This movement evolved out of a Farmers' Alliance formed in the late 1870s in Lampasas county, Texas, to suppress horse rustlers. As this Alliance spread across the state, it became a rival to both the Greenback party and the Grange. The drought of 1885 and 1886 further accelerated the growth of the Texas Alliance.

In 1886 many Alliancemen turned to direct political action when they organized at the local Texas level. They formed at least 20 farmer-labor parties across Texas. These local parties—taking names such as the Human party—proved particularly successful on the county level.

These independent parties derived their power from ongoing antimonopoly and **soft-money** crusades by targeting "arrogant capitalists and powerful corporations." They called for the establishment of cooperative stores and marketing ventures to undermine the power of railroad and banking **monop-**

olies. Demands also included a corporate income tax, increasing the money supply by the unlimited coinage of gold and silver, establishing a federal interstate commerce commission, and limiting land companies owned by foreign (mostly British) syndicates.

Meanwhile, in early 1887 Charles Macune, recently elected state business agent of the Alliance movement, set about to organize a cooperative exchange that would provide supplies and credit to members who in return pledged to market their cotton through the exchange. In late 1887, the exchange opened in Dallas, which had generously provided cash and land. Yet the exchange was totally undercapitalized and was forced into bankruptcy by 1889. The notion of cooperative marketing found advocates in other southern states, but cooperative efforts usually failed because of underfinancing and poor management. So enthusiastic were some leaders to establish cooperative stores throughout the country that at one point the national Alliance approved a deal in which the National Cordage Company—a feared **trust**—financed a chain of Alliance cooperative stores with the promise of supplying everything from a "knitting needle to an elephant." The plan ultimately failed, but it showed the problems of trying to create alternatives to the market economy.

Macune advocated a new financial scheme—the subtreasury plan—to remedy farmers' reliance on banks for capital. Macune proposed that the federal government establish a system of financial lending institutions throughout the country (in effect, a sub-treasury) that would allow farmers to borrow money. Macune's proposals for economic cooperation helped promote the expansion of the Alliance movement throughout the South.

By the summer of 1887 Alliance organizers were at work in all the southern states. The Alliance movement, as one enthusiast observed, swept the South like a cyclone. Another organizer declared, "The farmers seem like unto ripe fruit—you can gather them by a gentle shake of the bush." Alliance rallies drew crowds of 20,000 to 50,000 people. By 1890 the Southern Alliance claimed 3 million members. A fervor had swept over the people and a culture of protest had emerged.

While the Southern Alliance grew, two other organizations had taken shape. In the mid-1880s, black farmers mobilized into a parallel organization, the Colored Farmers' Alliance. Although the Colored Alliance remained predominately black, a number of its key leaders were white. In 1888 and 1889, black and white recruiters of the Colored Alliance undertook an extensive drive throughout the South. By 1890 one key leader, Reverend Richard Manny Humphrey, a white Baptist, claimed that the Colored Alliance had a membership of 1.2 million. The actual membership was probably a third of this figure, but little doubt remained within the white Southern Alliance that this black organization was a force to be reckoned with.

In the Midwest, farmers organized another group, officially known as the National Farmers' Alliance. Under the leadership of Milton George, a Chicago farm journalist, this group gathered strength throughout the Midwest during the 1886-1887 agricultural depression. Illinois, the Dakotas, Minnesota, Kansas, and Nebraska emerged as key Alliance states. Ignatius Donnelly, a novelist and social critic, revived the defunct Minnesota Farmers' Alliance in 1889. By 1891 Alliance membership extended into 32 states from California to New York.

Although the Southern Alliance remained the largest of these organizations, the farmers' movement had emerged by 1890 as a powerful political force throughout the nation. Furthermore, over one thousand newspapers closely tied to the Alliance had been organized. These included the *Progressive Farmer,* the *Southern Mercury,* and Francis Wayland's *Appeal to Reason.*

THE POPULIST PARTY, 1892. By 1890, militant farmers had enough strength at the state level to conduct their own political campaigns. In the **midterm election** of 1890, militant Southern farmers gained significant influence in eight legislatures as well as winning four governorships. In Kansas, a newly organized local Peoples'—or Populist—party elected five congressmen and one senator. They also gained control of the lower house in the state legislature. In Nebraska, Populist Omar Kern was elected to Congress.

Alliance leaders began to speak of launching a national third party— Populist party—to challenge the Republican and Democratic parties in the 1892 presidential election. Many who favored third-party political action felt that economic schemes promoted by the Alliance movement such as cooperative exchanges and the subtreasury plan were not enough to challenge the existing political system. They wanted political representation. The drawback for many in the South was that a third party meant breaking with the Democrats, which brought up the race question. If whites abandoned the Democratic party, the Republican party and their black allies would gain a chance to resume control of state governments, reminiscent of Reconstruction. Also, when an individual farmer bolted the Democratic party, it was more than a political decision. It often meant breaking with one's neighbors, losing friends at the local church, or betraying party "tradition."

Meetings were held to bring northern and southern Alliances together. But Northern Alliancemen remained suspicious of the Southern Alliance movement. More important, they displayed little enthusiasm for Macune's subtreasury plan. Southern leaders continued to worry about breaking with the Democratic party. Still there was growing sentiment that a third party was needed by a nation that was, in the words of Ignatius Donnelly, on "the verge of moral, political, and material ruin."

Finally in July 1892, Alliance leaders met to form a national Populist party. Party leaders drafted the party's Omaha Platform that broke with "politics as usual." Although in hindsight many of the demands appear modest, at the time the Populist agenda challenged political and social thought. The platform demanded free and unlimited coinage of silver, a graduated income tax, and government ownership of the telegraph and railroads. It also demanded restrictions on immigration and the end of injunctions against labor unions.

In the election of 1892 the Populists nominated for president the old Greenback candidate, General James Baird Weaver. On a campaign trip to the West, Weaver did exceptionally well. His tour of the South proved less successful. Crowds hurling eggs made Weaver "a regular walking omelet," Populist leader Mary Lease observed. Still, the results of the election gave the Populists hope for the future. Weaver received over 1 million votes, 8.5 percent of the vote. He also received an absolute majority in three silver producing states and carried Kansas.

For the first time since the end of the Civil War a third party had broken into the **electoral college**. Moreover, Populists elected governors in Kansas, North Dakota, Colorado, and Washington. Washington's Populist governor, John Rogers, refused to take the train to his inauguration and instead arrived by riding a series of independent interurban streetcar lines. This ensured Rogers' popularity. Also, during the campaign Populist leaders with such colorful names as Mary "Raise Less Corn and More Hell" Lease, "Sockless Jerry" Simpson, "Whiskers" Peffer, and the "One Eyed Ploughboy" Ignatius Donnelly became national celebrities.

The election also revealed some of the serious problems of running a third-party campaign. In Alabama and Georgia, whites waged a campaign of terror against blacks to keep them from voting Populist. In Tom Watson's congressional race in Georgia, Democrats indulged in bribery, stuffed the ballot box, and counted votes fraudulently. The final vote showed twice as many votes as voters in the district. Those Populists who were elected found new difficulties once they took office. Davis H. Waite, the Populist governor of Colorado, faced a Republican-controlled lower assembly that systematically defeated his proposals for reform.

1896: The Populist Moment Fades, Republicans Triumph

Populist hopes ran high as the presidential election of 1896 approached. But Democrats stole the Populists' thunder by nominating William J. Bryan on a silver platform. After bitter debate, the Populist party endorsed Bryan, thereby fusing the Democratic and Populist parties. The Republicans turned to William McKinley, who used his well-financed and well-organized campaign to overwhelm Bryan on election day. The election was a turning point, marking the beginning of Republican domination of the White House, the return of prosperity, and the end of Populism.

POPULISTS FIND A SILVER LINING. The depression of 1893 led many Populists to believe that the future was theirs. Agriculture remained depressed, the downturn of 1893 had shaken the financial pillars of the nation, and the Cleveland administration and Congress appeared inept in confronting the crisis. Populist hopes were dashed when Kansas, Colorado, North Dakota, and Idaho went Republican in the 1894 midterm elections. Still, the Texas Populist party nearly doubled its vote. Moreover, splits had occurred within both the Republican and Democratic parties over the money question—the free coinage of silver. The silver issue in the 1890s became a symbol for both sides of the future of the nation.

As the election of 1896 approached, and the economic depression persisted, agitation for cheap money swept both Republican and Democratic parties. The issue surprised many as silverite propaganda flooded the country. William H. Harvey's series of silverite tracts, later issued as *Coin's Financial School,* immediately became a bestseller. In 1892, William Jennings Bryan, then a young politician from Nebraska who was soon to establish his reputation as a Silverite, declared, "The people of Nebraska are for **free silver** and I am for free silver. I will look up the arguments later." Four years later, the silver issue had become not just a political question, but a moral issue whose advocates on both sides viewed as a clash between the forces of light and the forces of darkness. And, as with all moral issues that enter into the electoral arena, compromise became impossible. As one journalist observed of the times, "It was a season of Shibboleths . . . . Reason slept; and the passions—jealousy, covetousness, hatred—ran amuck; and whoever would check them was crucified in public."

The silver forces proved particularly strong within the Democratic party. As a consequence, many Populists proposed joining forces with the Democrats. To the more militant Populists, though, fusion with the Democrats meant disaster. Southerners in particular, after having broken with the Democrats—sometimes under the threat of violence—often were the most critical of the notion of fusion. Tom Watson of Georgia and Henry D. Lloyd of Illinois led the opposition against merging with the Democrats. They were joined by Ignatius Donnelly of Minnesota who declared, "Narrow **Populism** to free silver alone and it will disappear in a rat hole." Still, many other Populist leaders saw fusion as a way of gaining real political power, especially since the midterm elections of 1894 had revealed the weakness of the Populists.

REPUBLICANS STAND BY GOLD, DEMOCRATS BY SILVER. All eyes now turned to the two major parties' nominating conventions in the summer of 1896. The Republicans named Governor William McKinley. In constant communication through a special telegraph and telephone wire from his home in Canton, Ohio to his operatives at the convention in St. Louis, McKinley conducted a brilliant campaign for the nomination.

Although a leading spokesman for high tariffs, he waffled on the silver question, and indeed he did not oppose free silver. The Republican party platform, however, revealed no ambivalence and strongly endorsed the gold standard. The platform also called for a high tariff, annexation of Hawaii, the construction of a canal through Nicaragua, a larger navy, and establishment of a labor arbitration board.

The Democratic convention went less smoothly. Sharply divided between western silver forces and eastern antisilver forces, the convention seemed unable to agree on a candidate. While Cleveland entertained no hopes that he could gain or control the nomination, he preferred that the party break up rather than go silver. The silver faction showed that it had strength in the Midwest and in the South where a number of former Confederates—all supporters of states' rights—supported free silver. To the bitter dismay of the conservatives, these forces quickly gained control of the convention.

Nevertheless, the silverites favored no single candidate. Initially the leading candidate was Richard Bland, but "Silver Dick," as many called him, at the age of 61 was considered too old and too dull. The names of a number of lesser figures were bantered about including William Jennings Bryan, but many considered this 36-year-old "silver-tongued" orator too young for the presidency.

Bryan rose to speak at the Chicago convention on its second day. His speech quickly galvanized the convention. Bryan had delivered much the same speech dozens of times in his extensive travels throughout the Midwest. Still, there was a fresh resonance when his rich, melodic voice rang out, "We will answer their demand for a gold standard by saying to them: You shall not press down upon the brow of labor this crown of thorns, you shall not crucify mankind upon a cross of gold."

Bryan electrified the convention. Nevertheless, it took him five ballots to win the nomination. In order to appease the conservatives, the convention selected as his running mate Arthur Sewall, a wealthy railroad owner from Maine. It did little good. Intransigent conservatives broke ranks to form their own National Democratic party. These "Gold Democrats" nominated Sena-

In the 1896 presidential campaign, William Jennings Bryan (1860-1925) traveled over 18,000 miles, making 600 speeches in 27 states — an unprecedented record. Although resoundingly defeated by William McKinley, Bryan set new standards for campaigning. (Brown Brothers)

tor John M. Palmer of Illinois. For many anti-Bryan Democrats who remained in the party, New York governor David B. Hill expressed their sentiments when he explained, "I am still a Democrat—very still."

POPULISTS JOIN THE DEMOCRATS (WITH SILVER SOLDER). The nomination of Bryan forced the Populists to confront the issue of fusion when they met at their convention a few weeks later. As Henry Demarest Lloyd, a leading Populist and author of the widely read indictment of Standard Oil, *Wealth Against Commonwealth* (1894), observed, "If we fuse, we are sunk; if we don't fuse, all the silver men we have will leave us for the more powerful Democrats."

At the Populist convention, the silver lobby exerted heavy pressure to endorse the Democratic candidate Bryan. Those in favor of fusion were not beyond the shenanigans of the older established parties. Rumors circulated that Bryan personally supported a Populist running mate. After what seemed like endless debate, the convention supported Bryan, while nominating their own vice-presidential candidate, Thomas Watson of Georgia. This unusual arrangement, which placed Bryan on the ticket with a Populist running mate (as well as a Democratic running mate), saved face and gave the Populists a sense of independence, but fusion with the Democrats spelled the end of the party.

THE CANDIDATES CAMPAIGN (TO VARYING DEGREES). Although Bryan and McKinley differed completely in their political program, they shared many characteristics. Both were midwestern lawyers who accepted the region's moralistic **Protestant** values. McKinley, from a relatively poor Ohio family, won fame as a Civil War hero. After the war, McKinley returned to Ohio, where he studied law and worked his way up through the ranks of the Republican party. The distant and reserved McKinley garnered respect from those who met him.

Bryan grew up in nearby Illinois. The son of a wealthy judge and well-known political figure, Bryan initially wanted to become a Baptist minister, but in college decided to pursue law. After graduating he moved to Nebraska and joined the Democratic party. He was elected to Congress in 1890, just as McKinley was voted out. Bryan brought moral fervor to his politics. A life-long **teetotaler** and fundamentalist who believed in a literal interpretation of the Bible, Bryan saw in the money question a division between the forces of good and the forces of evil. He remained essentially conservative, often looking to the past and the values of the yeoman farmer. Although a Jeffersonian, he was not a revolutionary.

Bryan brought a new style of campaigning to presidential politics. Since the time of Andrew Jackson, politicians had become increasingly democratic in style. Bryan took his message directly to the people. In three months he traveled over 18,000 miles to give 600 speeches to an estimated five million people in 21 states. While many thought his campaign vulgar, especially since financial constraints forced him to travel on commercial trains, Bryan introduced what became a regular formula for presidential politics: travel extensively, speak often (even if the same speech is always given), and show that you are a "man of the people."

McKinley and his campaign manager, Mark Hanna, conducted a campaign that played on Bryan's weaknesses. Even before he was nominated, McKinley had established an efficient organization. The Ohioan began by targeting groups worried about the consequences of Bryan's economic radicalism. As Hanna observed of Bryan's campaign, "He's talking silver all the time, and that's where we've got him." Playing on the theme of the Republicans as the party of prosperity, Hanna conveyed a sense of urgency when he asked businessmen throughout the nation to contribute one quarter of 1 percent of their assets to the campaign. Business responded generously. Two contributions alone, $500,000 each from J. P. Morgan and Standard Oil, totaled more than Bryan's entire campaign fund. In the end, Republicans spent more than $3.5 million on the campaign. Republican coffers were so full that many donors received refunds.

Republicans targeted urban voters in the Northeast and Midwest. Realizing that Bryan would probably win the Deep South and certain plains states, Republicans saw that midwestern states—Ohio, Indiana, Illinois, Michigan, and Wisconsin—were critical. Workers were told to vote their economic interests. More than 120 campaign documents and 275 pamphlets were sent to local and regional party leaders to distribute to voters. With titles such as "Advance Agent of Prosperity" and "Fill the Dinner Pail," this literature played on the fears of the average worker. Campaign manager Hanna cultivated the Catholic hierarchy to gain Catholic workers' support for McKinley. The case of John Ireland, the archbishop of St. Paul, is notable. He had been saved from bankruptcy through a loan from railroad financier James J. Hill. With Hill's assistance, Hanna won an explicit endorsement for McKinley from the archbishop.

McKinley's own strategy called for him to stay at home in Canton, Ohio, and speak to the voters. Each day trainloads of visitors—often traveling with free railroad passes issued by the Republican party—came to Canton to catch a glimpse of the candidate. On a single day on October 4, McKinley met some 30 delegations and made 14 formal speeches.

While McKinley remained at home, Theodore Roosevelt dogged Bryan throughout his travels denouncing the Democrats for "plotting a social revolution and the subversion of the American Republic."

ELECTION DAY, 1896: MCKINLEY WINS, POPULISM DIES, BRYAN SURVIVES. No other election since 1860 drew such national interest. Torchlight parades, picnics, and other public participatory events created excitement. Nearly 95 percent of the voters in the Midwest turned out, although in the South the turnout fell sharply to only 50 percent of the eligible voters. McKinley won an overwhelming victory. Economics mattered, but voters also split along clear religious lines. Often cultural issues such as **prohibition** of alcohol were crucial in determining how voters cast their ballots.

Bryan's vote equaled the combined Democratic and Populist vote in 1892. He received more popular votes in 1896 than Cleveland had in 1892. He won solidly in the South, some Great Plains states, and the mountain West. Still, McKinley's 7.1 million votes topped Bryan's total by 600,000. McKinley, swamping Bryan in the East and the Middle West, won 271 **electoral votes** to Bryan's 176. Twenty-two industrial states went Republican. Of 82 cities with a population of more than 45,000, 60 voted for McKinley. Bryan lost his own state, city, and precinct. In gaining the first undisputed majority since 1872, McKinley won support from the urban masses, industrial workers, and Catholics.

The election of 1896 marked a political turning point. For the next 16 years Republicans would control the White House, and well into the 1920s urban workers and Catholics voted Republican. At the same time, the Populists had frightened white elites in the South. Election laws and other devices were instituted to undermine future third-party efforts by making it more difficult to gain a place on the ballot. Moreover, the Republican party acquiesced in the disfranchisement of southern blacks. Attempts to pass a civil rights act in Congress in the 1890s had been overshadowed by the issue of free silver. In the 1880s and well into the 1890s, blacks continued to hold minor political offices, and elected black congressmen from southern states including North Carolina, Mississippi, and South Carolina.

Bryan continued to be a force within the Democratic party. After the election, he became a professional lecturer, still drawing large crowds who came to see the "Great Commoner," the "Peerless," and the "Boy Orator of the Platte." Yet as one wit of the day noted, "Bryan would rather be wrong than president."

McKinley's election also coincided with an upturn in the economy. Free silver died as an issue when gold discoveries were made in Australia, South Africa, and Alaska. At the same time, the United States snapped out of the depression and entered into a golden era of prosperity. On March 14, 1900, Congress made gold the single standard for the nation's money supply. The Populist party died with the silver issue. In 1900 the Populists ran a presidential candidate, Tom Watson, but hardly anyone noticed. Nevertheless, much of the Populist program including the direct election of senators, a graduated income tax, and closer regulation of business entered the political mainstream.

For the nation as a whole, interest turned to the business of prosperity. With prosperity middle-class Americans once again redirected their attention from politics to bettering their station in life. Basic values of individual rights, self-reliance, and pursuit of private gain had held throughout the turmoil of the nineties. And now with prosperity came a revived interest in world affairs and America's place among the nations of the world.

Conclusion

The depression of 1893 created a brief outburst of radicalism among farmers in the Midwest and the South. The rise of populism promised radical change, but the issue of silver dominated political debate. The Democrats attempted to capitalize on this radicalism by endorsing a silver platform and nominating Bryan in 1896. McKinley's triumph over Bryan ensured Republican control of the White House for the next decade. Still, change was in the air.

Recommended Readings

DOCUMENTS: Henry Demarest Lloyd, *Wealth Against Commonwealth* (1894); and William Allen White, *The Autobiography of William Allen White* (1946).

READINGS: (DEPRESSION) Stuart Bruchey, *Growth of the Modern Economy* (1975); Ray Ginger, *The Age of Excess* (1965); Harold U. Faulkner, *Politics, Reform, and Expansion, 1890-1900* (1959); Charles Hoffman, *The Depression of the Nineties* (1970); Edward C. Kirkland, *Industry Comes of Age: Business, Labor, Public Policy* (1961); Robert Wiebe, *The Search for Order, 1877-1929* (1968). (POPULISM) Peter Argersinger, *Populism and Politics: William Alfred Peffer and the People's Party* (1974); Chester M. Destler, *American Radicalism* (1946); Lawrence Goodwyn, *Democratic Promise: The Populist Moment in America* (1976); James R. Green, *Grass-Roots Socialism* (1978); Steven Hahn, *The Roots of Southern Populism* (1983); Sheldon Hackney, *Populism to Progressivism in Alabama* (1969); John Hicks, *The Populist Revolt* (1931); Robert C. McMath, *American Populism: A Social History* (1992) and *Populist Vanguard* (1975); Grant C. McConnell, *The Decline of Agrarian Democracy* (1953); Walter Nugent, *The Tolerant Populist* (1963); Bruce Palmer, *Man Over Money: The Southern Populist Critique of American Capitalism;* C. Vann Woodward, *Tom Watson: Agrarian Rebel* (1938) and *Origins of the New South* (1972). (ELECTION OF **1896**) Robert F. Durden, *The Climax of Populism: The Election of 1896* (1965); Ray Ginger, *Altgeld's America* (1958); Paul W. Glad, *McKinley, Bryan, and the People* (1964); J. Rogers Hollingsworth, *The Whirligig of Politics: The Democracy of Cleveland and Bryan* (1963); Samuel McSeveney, *The Politics of Depression* (1972).

21

    ⋈

AMERICA ACQUIRES AN EMPIRE

CHAPTER OVERVIEW: In his inaugural address to the nation on March 4, 1897, William McKinley focused primarily on domestic policy, much as he did throughout the campaign. Yet foreign relations dominated his first term. Within three years of McKinley's election, the United States had gained an empire that extended into the Caribbean and across the Pacific to Asia.

America's expansion came through a war with Spain that began in 1898. This three-month conflict gave the United States control of strategic islands in the Caribbean (Puerto Rico, Cuba, and the Dominican Republic) and in the Pacific, (the Hawaiian Islands, the Philippines, and Guam). America had acquired a foreign empire. Shortly afterward, the United States waged a bitter war of suppression against an insurgent Filipino movement demanding independence. Antiimperialists denounced American actions, but in the end imperialists triumphed. The United States emerged as a world power.

American Foreign Policy Between Two Wars, 1868-1897

American foreign policy throughout the late 1800s lacked a grand strategy. Presidents tended to move from crisis to crisis without a coherent vision. America got involved in disputes in Haiti, Chile, Venezuela, and Nicaragua, and Benjamin Harrison (1889-1892) made an abortive attempt to annex the Hawaiian Islands. A crisis in Venezuela revitalized the Monroe Doctrine's opposition to European interference in Latin America. Cleveland barely managed to maintain a policy of neutrality in Cuba's rebellion against Spain. Spain's brutal suppression of the rebellion and its mistreatment of American sailors strained relations with the United States.

FOREIGN POLICY BEFORE MCKINLEY: BETWEEN BELLICOSITY AND NEGLECT. Although McKinley spoke endlessly about the tariff and the international gold standard during the campaign of 1896, he entered office with little experience in foreign relations. In this way he was typical of most presidents of the late nineteenth century. American involvement in foreign policy was neither systematic nor well-informed. Indeed, American presidents seemed to fluctuate between bellicose involvement in foreign relations and neglect of day-to-day diplomacy.

During Ulysses S. Grant's tenure in office (1869-1877), the administration constructed a magnificent new home for the State Department. Begun 1871 and completed in the mid-1880s, the building had a profusion of Italian-style granite pillars, carved balconies, and ornate windows. Standing next to the White House, it covered more than ten acres, but housed only 50 clerks.

Grant showed a willingness to expand American influence abroad when he attempted to buy Santo Domingo — today known as the Dominican Republic. The Dominicans, in the midst of a debt crisis, tried to sell their nation. Grant offered $1.5 million, but the deal fell apart when Senator Charles Sumner of Massachusetts rallied fellow senators to oppose the bill.

Republican administrations after Grant pursued an activist role in international relations, but foreign policy in general remained a jumble of uncoordinated policies designed to meet crisis situations. James G. Blaine, secretary of state under both James Garfield and Benjamin Harrison, spoke of expanding American commercial ties with Latin America, but little came of his attempt to improve relations through a pan-American alliance. Indeed, the United States continued to display aggressive tendencies in Latin America that undercut cordial relations. In 1889 America tried to gain a foothold in Haiti when Harrison aided rebel Florvil Hyppolite, but the rebel leader rebuffed the United States once he gained power. Shortly afterward, Harrison threatened war with Chile when two American sailors on shore leave in the port of Valparaiso were killed in a drunken brawl with locals. War between the two nations was prevented only at the last moment when the Chilean government framed a conciliatory note apologizing for the incident.

Benjamin Harrison's most important diplomatic effort was his attempt to annex the Hawaiian Islands in 1893, after a group of American sugar planters overthrew Queen Liliuokalani's government. The United States minister to Hawaii openly aided the rebels by sending 150 marines to guard key locations in Honolulu. This action prevented the suppression of the rebellion. Only 30 days after the rebellion, Harrison sent a treaty to the Senate annexing the islands. Still, Harrison did not consider himself an imperialist. As he told Blaine, "You know I am not much of an annexationist, though I do feel that in some directions, as to naval stations and points of influence, we must look forward to a departure from the too conservative opinions which have been held heretofore."

Harrison's treaty to annex Hawaii bogged down in the Senate. Many members viewed American actions in the islands as a betrayal of American principles, and they feared bringing the islands into the republic. This treaty continued to languish in the Senate when Grover Cleveland, a foe of annexation, regained the White House. Although Cleveland refused to restore Queen Liliuokalani, he withdrew the treaty, explaining, "The mission of our nation is to build up and make a greater country of what we have instead of annexing islands."

CLEVELAND ARGUES FOR NATIONALISM AND AGAINST IMPERIALISM. Grover Cleveland knew that the late nineteenth century had become the age of **imperialism.** Like many Americans, he was dismayed as he watched European powers carve up the world in pursuit of power and profit. In Africa, Italy sought control of Ethiopia; Belgium, the Congo; Germany, Cameroon. In West Africa, France seized Guinea, the Ivory Coast, and Dahomey. England took Uganda and South Africa. Throughout Latin America, the influence of France, Britain, and Germany was growing. In Southeast Asia, France took Indo-China, what is now Vietnam, Laos, and Cambodia. Most of the European nations looked hungrily at China. Cleveland wanted America to be a world power, too, but not by betraying **republican** principles and so was fiercely opposed to European-style colonialism. His stance in foreign relations was that of a nationalist who took a defensive position rather than an imperialist pursuing an aggressive, well-calculated strategy.

The **depression** that started in 1893, however, led Cleveland to become increasingly aggressive, principally for political reasons, in the western hemisphere. In 1894 he sent American warships to Brazil, then in the throes of a revolution, to ensure that American goods were allowed to enter the harbor at Rio de Janeiro. A short time later, Cleveland protested when Great Britain sent soldiers to protect the Mosquito Indians, who claimed territory also claimed by Nicaragua. Cleveland's promise to protect these Indians' rights persuaded the British to withdraw and Nicaragua to incorporate the territory.

The stage was now set for Cleveland's boldest action in Latin America — his involvement in Venezuela in 1895-1896. Venezuela and Britain disputed the boundaries between Venezuela and the British colony of Guiana. At issue was control of the mouth of the Orinoco River, which many hoped was rich in gold. When Britain refused to accept arbitration over this dispute, Cleveland sought to weaken Britain's influence in Latin America by asking Congress in late 1895 to appropriate money for an American commission to examine the dispute. When aired by the press, the issue unleashed an outburst of **Anglophobia** (hatred of the British) and patriotism among the American people. A few talked of going to war. Britain, deeply involved in fighting the Boer War in South Africa, finally agreed to American arbitration. Ironically, the commission ruled in favor of Britain. Nonetheless, the crisis allowed the much neglected Monroe Doctrine — America's declared opposition to European involvement into Latin America — to be transformed into standard policy.

CLEVELAND AVOIDS WAR IN CUBA. Cleveland's strong stance in the Venezuelan crisis made it easier to be flexible when the colony of Cuba rebelled against Spanish rule in early 1895. He pursued a policy of neutrality without fear of a strong political backlash. Thus, even as Congress and the general public showed increasing sympathy with the rebellion, Cleveland refused to recognize the **belligerents.** Instead, Cleveland sought to pressure the Spanish into instituting reforms in Cuba. At the same time, Cleveland placed a strict **embargo** on arms and supplies being shipped to the rebels.

This policy differed markedly from the policy that had been followed 27 years earlier by Grant when a similar rebellion had occurred in Cuba in 1868. In that case Grant actively encouraged the rebels. American intervention in the crisis was prevented only by a cautious secretary of state. As a consequence, the Spanish government finally crushed the rebellion, but only after ten years of brutal warfare. Still, many Americans felt deeply about the plight of Cuba, a sentiment reinforced by strong commercial relations between the island's sugar producers and American sugar importers. A decline in sugar prices helped spark the 1895 rebellion. From 1894 to 1896 Cuban sugar exports to the United States fell by half.

Calls to "free Cuba" increasingly found their way into American politics. Nevertheless, Cleveland stubbornly refused to become actively involved in what he feared might become a long, devastating war in Cuba. Customs officials were told to prevent arms shipments to the rebels. As a result, of the 71 known shipments from New York to Cuba, only a third made it to the rebels. Cleveland's policy of neutrality struck many as overly cautious and inflexible.

Cleveland's call for reform found little sympathy in official Spanish circles. Instead, the Spanish government decided to crush the rebellion. By 1896 Spain had sent more than 150,000 soldiers to Cuba. As savage fighting continued, the Spanish intensified their campaign. Intent upon isolating **guerilla** rebels from their base of support among the civilian population, the Spanish undertook a campaign of terror against Cuba's peasants. In February 1896 the commander of the Spanish forces, General Valeriano Weyler, proclaimed a policy of reconcentration whereby peasants were forced to abandon their homes and were herded into "protected" towns and cities. In pursuing this policy, Weyler's troops laid waste to the land, destroying cane fields, butchering livestock, and razing sugar mills. One New York newspaper declared, "Weyler has turned the island into a prison."

Spain's hardline policy created a crisis with the United States. Between 1890 to 1896, American trade with Cuba fell to nearly a third of what it had been before the rebellion. Relations were further strained by Spain's policy of stopping and seizing ships on the high seas, and of ignoring the rights of Cubans who had become naturalized American citizens. Shortly before he left office, Cleveland warned Spain of America's growing impatience with Spain's conduct of the war and its arrogant treatment of American citizens.

McKinley Finds Himself Entangled in Cuba

McKinley entered the White House intent on focusing his attention of domestic policy. Foreign policy, especially the Cuban problem, quickly dominated his attention. Spanish atrocities in Cuba outraged Americans, who demanded intervention to stop the Spanish. At the same time imperialists, worried that America was declining, pressed for new export markets and colonies, and some saw military expansion as one way to get them. McKinley continued to pursue diplomatic alternatives, but to no avail. When an American battleship, the *Maine,* blew up in a Cuban harbor, Americans accused Spain of sabotage and demanded war.

The Spanish-American War was fought in the Caribbean islands of Cuba and Puerto Rico, and the Spanish-controlled Philippines in the Pacific. Neither side's military was prepared for war, and many troops died from disease. America won largely because of Spain's ineptitude. As a result of the war, though, the United States acquired an empire by gaining authority over Cuba, Puerto Rico, Guam, and the Phillipines. Theodore Roosevelt emerged from the war as a national hero and a leading political figure.

WASHINGTON FOCUSES ON DOMESTIC AFFAIRS. Throughout his campaign against William Jennings Bryan, McKinley generally focused on domestic policy, often linking tariff questions and the international money standard to prosperity at home. Nevertheless, at one point during the campaign he vowed, "We want to avoid wars of conquest. We must avoid the temptation of territorial aggression." McKinley's initial lack of concern for military and foreign affairs was revealed in his appointment of the cranky — and, some said, senile — John Sherman as secretary of state, and of an incompetent secretary of war. Still, McKinley was to learn diplomacy quickly, showing a flexibility and a sensitivity lacking in his predecessors.

McKinley entered the White House as the most popular president since Lincoln during a time of fierce patriotism. Throughout the 1890s, more patriotic societies, such as Patriots of America (1895), were founded than in any other decade. Children now began the ritual of saluting the flag in the nation's classrooms. Even socialist Edward Bellamy called his socialistic program "Nationalism". A heady confidence in America as God's chosen nation was evidenced in public ceremonies and public displays. Yet beneath this veneer of confidence lay deep insecurities concerning the nation's future. This insecurity was manifested in the spread of nativistic hostility to immigrants, especially newly arrived Catholics. Nativists, those who sought to exclude immigrants from American political and social life, pressured a number of city governments not to hire Catholics. In these conditions it was not surprising that **nativism** also brought **jingoism** (militaristic patriotism).

In general, however, Americans were more concerned with trade than with jingoism. Many businessmen agreed that the nation needed to expand its trade into foreign markets. As a result, many looked with renewed interest to Asia and Latin America. New markets offered a means for addressing the economic ills brought by the depression that began in 1893. A group of American businessmen in 1895 founded the National Association of Manufacturers to open markets in Latin America. Many companies involved in overseas trade shunned governmental assistance since they did not want to mix business with politics and the intrigue of foreign diplomacy. They thought that commercial growth could be accomplished without territorial expansion or European-style imperialism. Most American business leaders believed that colonies were expensive, unnecessary, and betrayed American democratic principles.

The national government focused on domestic affairs. Washington, D.C. remained provincial, displaying a confident insularity. The White House stood in ill-repair from years of neglect. Foreign dignitaries were often entertained in state dining rooms and reception areas with peeling paint and wallpaper. The furnishings of the house were old and shabby.

The White House staff itself remained small. McKinley increased the number to 80, but security was inadequate. The White House ignored the international terrorism that had emerged in Europe with the anarchist movement. Threats against the president were handled by the city police.

If Washington initially seemed isolated from the rest of the world, McKinley nevertheless brought new dignity to the White House. He saw himself as a model for the nation and its people. A lover of good cigars, he refused to smoke in public because he believed that he should not "let the young men of this country see their president smoking."

A Civil War veteran, he brought an understated firmness to the office that was not apparent to many upon first meeting him. McKinley's even temper led some to think that he lacked backbone, yet his experience as a leading congressman for 14 years had taught him the arts of self-control and compromise. He carefully cultivated relations with the cabinet and Congress. As one congressman noted, Harrison froze people out, Cleveland kicked them out, and McKinley kissed them out. Thus, McKinley gave the appearance of being wishy-washy, a man without firm ideas, but beneath this exterior was a shrewd politician with sound judgment and the ability to understand people accurately. He brought these strengths to the nation's growing involvement in international relations.

MCKINLEY HEARS THE VOICES OF IMPERIALISM. On the way to his inauguration the president-elect told Cleveland, "Mr. President, you are a happier man today than I am." Cleveland replied, "I am sure of that, Major." McKinley did not realize the full implications of the departing president's reply. He soon found himself confronting the seemingly insoluble Cuban problem.

As soon as he entered the White House, McKinley faced considerable pressure to intervene in Cuba. This pressure came from within his own party as well as from growing public sentiment that America could not stand by idly as witness to Spanish atrocities. Within the Republican party, McKinley faced an active group of imperialists who called for America to take its "rightful" place as a world power. Although differing over specifics, these imperialists presented an active voice in policy circles. They criticized McKinley's policies and laid the groundwork for American intervention in Cuba.

The imperialists proved particularly influential because of their ability to articulate — sometimes quite eloquently — their vision of America as a world power. For instance, Captain Alfred T. Mahan, teaching at the recently established Naval War College, presented a bold vision of the importance of naval strength and world power in his widely read *The Influence of Sea Power Upon History* (1890). Mahan's message was adopted by Theodore Roosevelt, assistant secretary of the navy in the McKinley administration, by Senator Henry Cabot Lodge of Massachusetts, and by John Hay, ambassador to England and later secretary of state. These men advocated larger navies and believed that American expansion would produce prestige, power, and wealth.

Their message was potent in a decade of economic depression in which many perceived declining opportunities and mushrooming social crises.

Many worried that America had begun to decline. The publication of Frederick Jackson Turner's essay, "The Significance of the Frontier in American History" (1893), which proclaimed the end of the American frontier, reinforced these pessimistic sentiments. A few interpreted Turner's message to mean that America must find new frontiers in export markets and colonies.

This expansionist message found a receptive audience in political circles — especially among congressmen from the Atlantic states. Certain newspapers and magazines advocated imperialist sentiment. Especially prominent were Whitelaw Reid's *New York Tribune,* Albert Shaw's *Review of Reviews,* and Walter Hines Page's *Atlantic Monthly.* The rhetoric of **expansionism** created growing support for American military intervention in Cuba.

Such journalistic reports created growing support for intervention in Cuba. The problems of economic depression and apparent social crises could be met through economic and, if need be, military expansion. Of course, those who advocated economic expansion by increasing business in new foreign markets did not necessarily agree with militaristic imperialists like Theodore Roosevelt, who wrote a friend in 1897, "In strict confidence . . . I should welcome almost any war, for I think this country needs one."

New markets appeared to offer an obvious solution for the hard times of the depression. Still, many in the upper class and in financial circles hesitated to pick up the imperialist banner. As a result, the call for military intervention in Cuba met stubborn resistance among the upper class. As one member of the New York elite recorded, he had not found one friend "who considers that we have any justifiable cause for war. Below that crust . . . the wish for war is almost universal."

Many American businessmen were naturally conservative and feared that a war would disrupt trade. For example, Mark Hanna, now a senator from Ohio, fiercely opposed military intervention in Cuba. Theodore Roosevelt replied, "We will have this war for the freedom of Cuba, Senator Hanna, in spite of the timidity of commercial interests." Other attacks on business's opposition to military intervention were less polite. Some newspapers used anti-Semitic language in attacking Wall Street and its antiinterventionist position. The *New York Journal* and *Sacramento Bee* published a poem which read, "Shall half a gross of merchants/ the Shylocks of the trade — / Barter your heart, and conscience, too/ While freedom is betrayed." This kind of language, while not pervasive, suited a time when nativism had reemerged in American politics with renewed vigor.

The emergence of sensationalist newspapers — the so-called **"yellow press"** — in New York City played upon public sympathy for the Cubans. Newspapers such as William Randolph Hearst's *New York Journal* and Joseph Pulitzer's *New York World* raised the specter of a cruel, oppressive, and decadent Catholic monarchy in Spain suppressing the democratic aspirations of the Cuban people. (It was rarely mentioned that Hearst and most Cubans were Catholics).

The influence of the yellow press reached beyond New York, as other newspapers picked up these atrocity stories. The nation's press demanded intervention and alarmed Congress. As an associate of McKinley observed, "Every Congressman has two or three newspapers in his district, most of them printed in red ink, shouting for blood."

MCKINLEY PURSUES QUIET DIPLOMACY, 1897-1898. McKinley tried to prevent war with Spain through diplomacy, while working to end the rebellion in Cuba. To help with both, he selected Stewart Woodford, a straightforward, honest man, to represent the United States to the Madrid court. In Cuba, he retained the Cleveland appointee, Fitzhugh Lee, a jingoistic southerner, who openly supported the Cuban rebels. McKinley hoped that he could pressure the Spanish government to accommodate the demands of the rebels through reform that would lead either to Cuban autonomy or independence. McKinley was distressed by Spanish policy. He openly denounced the policy of reconcentration and Weyler's strategy of waging war against civilians: "It was not civilized warfare. It was extermination."

McKinley's policy was aimed at liberalizing a **reactionary** — albeit democratic — Spanish government ruled by a weak queen regent. McKinley's policy seemed to be succeeding when in the fall of 1897 liberals won control of the Spanish government following the assassination of the conservative prime minister. Hopes for a diplomatic solution to the Cuban problem were furthered when the new government recalled General Weyler. Shortly afterwards, the queen regent proclaimed a new Cuban policy, but Cuban rebels refused to negotiate.

AMERICA DECLARES WAR, APRIL 1898. Although McKinley continued to press for a diplomatic solution, he became convinced that the Spanish military would never accept compromise. A greater shock came when Hearst's *New York Journal* published a stolen letter from the Spanish ambassador to the United States, Enrique Depuy de Lôme, which revealed deep cynicism within the Spanish government toward reform in Cuba. Dupuy de Lôme had written the confidential letter to a Spanish official in Havana, reassuring him not to worry about the United States. "McKinley," he wrote, "is weak and a bidder for the admiration of the crowd, besides being a would-be politician who tries to leave a door open behind himself while keeping on good terms with the jingoists of his party." Captured by guerrillas, the letter was turned over to Hearst, who published it in full under the headline,

"Worst Insult to the United States in Its History." As one "Cuban **Junta**" member remarked, "The Dupuy de Lôme letter is a great thing for us."

Indeed it was. War fever swept the country. Further trouble came on February 15, 1898. McKinley had sent the battleship *Maine* to Havana to demonstrate America's interest, while inviting a Spanish battleship to visit New York to assuage Spanish feeling. As the *Maine* rode in Havana harbor that night, an explosion onboard killed 260 sailors. Most Americans believed that the Spanish had sabotaged the ship, although later evidence suggested an internal engine explosion.

Americans demanded war. Only the Catholic and German-language presses remained neutral. On the other hand the Hearst papers declared, "Remember the *Maine* and to hell with Spain." Theodore Roosevelt accused Spain of "an act of dirty treachery." William Jennings Bryan, the Democratic leader, announced, "the time for intervention has arrived." Yet McKinley hesitated. He continued to press for arbitration, even though the new Spanish ambassador to the United States seemed unaware of the growing war fever in the United States. Irate mobs in Virginia and Colorado burned effigies of McKinley.

Finally, the Spanish replied in late March 1898. They promised arbitration of the *Maine* incident, the end of reconcentration, and Cuban autonomy. The reply, in fact, differed little from what had been offered in previous messages. A few weeks later, the queen offered to suspend hostilities, to implement autonomy, and to accept arbitration from the Pope. McKinley's cabinet rejected the offer in the belief that the Spanish government was unable or unwilling to fulfill its promises.

McKinley asked Congress to pass a resolution allowing him to intervene at his discretion. Both houses accepted an amendment offered by Senator Henry M. Teller of Colorado which ensured that the United States was "to leave the government and control of the Island [Cuba] to its people." On April 25 Congress declared war. Senator John Spooner of Wisconsin wrote, "possibly the President could have worked the business without a war, but the current was too strong, the demagogues too numerous, and the fall elections too near." McKinley believed he had little alternative. He sought a complete end to Spanish rule in Cuba. He viewed anything short of this as a betrayal of humanitarian impulses, economic interests, and geopolitical considerations. Spanish promises of autonomy had come too late.

A "SPLENDID LITTLE WAR" AGAINST SPAIN. The Spanish-American War proved to be the shortest in American history. It lasted only a hundred days. Americans celebrated the war as a great victory, but the it was won both because of Spanish ineptitude and plain good luck on the part of the Ameri-

This 1898 photograph of Theodore Roosevelt shows the colonel with his first voluntary cavalry regiment (Rough Riders) during the Spanish-American War. Roosevelt chronicled the unit's exploits in *The Rough Riders* (1899). (AP/WORLD WIDE PHOTOS)

cans. As one journalist concluded at the war's end, "God takes care of drunken men, sailors, and the United States."

The declaration of war sparked an outburst of patriotism throughout the nation. Even the wealthy rallied to the cause. Wall Street brokers organized a regiment, and Helen Gould, the wife of financier Jay Gould, gave her yacht and $100,000 to outfit another regiment. Theodore Roosevelt resigned as assistant secretary of the navy to become a lieutenant colonel in the Rough Riders, an elite regiment he helped found.

Patriotic outbursts aside, America was unprepared. The army was small, ill-equipped, and poorly managed. Only the navy appeared formidable. At the outset McKinley ordered Cuba blockaded and called for 125,000 volunteers. By the end of the war, the army had mustered some 270,000 men. Moreover, equipment was old and dated. Uniforms were so old that they had faded and many regiments appeared to be wearing different uniforms.

Command of the army fell to General William R. Shafter, a comic, over-weight figure. McKinley, wishing to integrate former Confederates, appointed Senator "Fighting Joe" Wheeler to a field command. The ex-Confederate general, however, had not fought for nearly 30 years. In Cuba, he reportedly once became so excited in battle that he shouted, "We've got the damn Yankees on the run."

The navy was more ably commanded and generally in better shape. In 1883 Congress had appropriated funds for rebuilding an obsolete navy left over from the Civil War, but the new fleet of lightly armored cruisers could not match most European battleships — except Spain's. In terms of size, the American navy ranked thirteenth, but was in better condition than Spain's. Although Americans initially feared a naval attack, Spanish ships were antiquated and ill-kept. Their gunners even lacked ammunition for target practice.

America's first victory came when Commodore George Dewey won a naval victory in the Spanish-held Philippine Islands on May 1, 1898, only six days after the declaration of war. Steaming into Manila Bay and easily destroying or capturing all ten of the Spanish ships anchored there, Dewey's fleet lost but one sailor; the Spanish 381. A month later Dewey was joined by army units sent to oust the Spanish troops already under attack from the Philippine guerilla leader, Emilio Aguinaldo. McKinley's fateful decision to send troops to the Philippines ensured further American entanglement in the islands.

Meanwhile, American troops who were supposed to invade Cuba remained in the staging area at Tampa, Florida. Lacking facilities and proper supplies, many soldiers fell ill. Transportation in and out of the port of Tampa proved inadequate. The single-track railroad was often used by tourists who wanted to see the ships, often preventing military supplies from being transported to the loading docks. After weeks of delay the troops were finally loaded onto transport ships, but reports of a Spanish cruiser sighted off the Florida coast further delayed the invasion. For five days the troops waited in hot steamy holds. Finally, when the convoy did set off, the 35 transport ships became so separated that they spread across a distance of 30 miles. Fortunately, the Spanish did not attack.

The Cuba expedition proved decisive. The Spanish made a crucial mistake in not stopping the Americans before they landed in Cuba at Daiquiri. Although it took nearly a full day to unload 6,000 American troops in this chaotic, ill-organized landing, within a month the troops had advanced to the outskirts of Santiago, the capital of Cuba.

At Santiago, American troops engaged in their bloodiest fight. Key to Santiago was control of San Juan Hill and Kettle Hill, overlooking the city. From

Map. 21.1. The Spanish-American War, 1898

this battle a new military hero emerged, Theodore Roosevelt. With his troops pinned down under fierce fire from seasoned Spanish soldiers, Roosevelt led a gallant charge up Kettle Hill. In the confusion, his Rough Riders and a regiment of black troops became mixed. In the midst of the battle, black and white troops were able to secure the hill together. As one Rough Rider later described the fight, "I joined a troop of the Tenth Cavalry, colored, and for a time fought with them shoulder to shoulder, and in justice to the colored race I must say that I never saw braver men anywhere."

Following this battle, American and Spanish troops became deadlocked in a trench war. Conditions were appalling. Plagued by flies and mosquitoes, rain and mud, soldiers on both sides began to fall to disease. Each day's rain washed up buried corpses of soldiers and mules.

While the campaign for Santiago had stalled to a gruesome impasse, on July 3 the American navy under Commodore Winfield Scott Schley and Admiral William T. Sampson defeated the Spanish fleet anchored in the city's harbor. The Spaniards made a desperate daylight run to escape the American fleet, and lost four ships and 323 sailors. The Americans lost 21 sailors. Once again, the Spanish ships proved ill-prepared for battle. Over 85 percent of their ammunition was defective.

On July 17, Santiago surrendered. Cuba had been liberated. The surrender of Santiago came just in time, as yellow fever, malaria, and dysentery had begun to sweep through the American camps. Within three days after the surrender, more than 4,000 American troops were on sick call. By the time the main American forces began to withdraw from Cuba, more than 500 soldiers had died of disease. More died in transport on the way home.

Taking the Spanish-held island of Puerto Rico proved easier than winning Cuba. There was only one significant battle, in which six Americans were wounded and six Spaniards killed. On Friday, August 3, 1898, Spain and the United States signed a **peace protocol.** The agreement gave Cuba its freedom, ceded Puerto Rico to the United States, and permitted the United States to occupy the former Spanish colony, the Philippines.

In December Spain and the United States agreed to a final settlement. Cuba became an American **protectorate.** In addition to Puerto Rico, the United States also acquired the former Spanish colony of Guam in the Pacific. Spain received a face-saving $20 million for ceding the Philippine Islands — 7,000 islands with 7 million inhabitants.

The United States had gained an empire. Even before the war's end, McKinley had signed a joint congressional resolution annexing the Hawaiian Islands, important as a naval base, to the United States. With the acquisition of the former Spanish colonies of Cuba, Puerto Rico, and the Philippines, the empire of the United States stretched from the Caribbean to the far Pacific.

Americans celebrated their victory in parades and demonstrations throughout the nation. Theodore Roosevelt returned home as a military hero and immediately won the governorship of New York. Roosevelt's success was rivaled only by Commodore Dewey's, whose ticker-tape parade up Fifth Avenue in New York drew thousands. In the midst of these celebrations, Theodore Roosevelt's close friend, John Hay, wrote, "It has been a splendid little war, carried on with magnificent intelligence and spirit, favored by the Fortune which loves the brave." Perhaps the spirit was better captured, however, by the wit of newspaper humorist Finley Peter Dunne, who speaking through his Irish character Mr. Dooley, declared, "We're a gr-reat people." Replied Dooley's friend Mr. Hennessey, "We ar-re that. An th' best iv it is, we know we ar-re."

The spirit of victory that united Americans proved short-lived. Its heroes — with the single exception of Roosevelt — were quickly forgotten. The magnificent arch commemorating Dewey's victory — initially made out of plaster before a marble monument was to be erected — soon fell in such disrepair that it had to be torn down.

America Becomes an Empire

Having fought the Spanish-American War to free an oppressed people from a colonial empire, America emerged from the war with a foreign empire of its own. Contrary to the wishes of an antiimperialistic bloc in Congress, McKinley was just as reluctant as the Spanish to grant independence to Spain's former colonies in the Caribbean and the Pacific. Believing the Filipinos unable to govern themselves and fearful that other nations might step in, America annexed the Phillippines. Filipinos revolted, and America brutally crushed the revolt. McKinley won reelection in a landslide and worked to keep China open as a market. He was soon assassinated, but his four years in office had transformed the United States into a world power.

AMERICANS DEBATE THE ANNEXATION OF THE PHILIPPINES. Americans now turned their attention to the consequences of empire. The signing of a formal peace treaty by the United States and Spain shortly before Christmas, 1898, brought into sharp relief the problems of ruling an empire that reached from the Caribbean into the western Pacific. Specifically at issue was McKinley's proposal to annex the Philippines.

Following Commodore Dewey's victory in the Philippines, McKinley could have simply withdrawn American naval forces and left the land war to the Philippine resistance leader, Emilio Aguinaldo. Still the president feared German and Japanese intervention if American troops withdrew. He also doubted the capacity of the Philippine people for self rule. As a consequence, he sent 11,000 American troops, double Dewey's initial request. On August 13, one day after the peace protocol had been signed, the Spanish garrison in Manila surrendered. American troops were instructed not to allow Filipino rebels to participate in the surrender of Manila.

Even with the large number of American troops occupying Manila, McKinley hesitated to take the next logical step — annexing the islands. His own cabinet was divided on the issue, and the politically astute McKinley realized that annexation would cause a political fight. Nonetheless, he found himself in a predicament. Some, including those in his cabinet, had suggested annexing only the principal island of Luzon and its capital, Manila. McKinley's military advisers warned him, however, that Luzon could not be defended without the other islands. On the other hand, McKinley believed the Filipinos were unprepared for independence. He considered Aguinaldo childlike in his infatuation with uniforms and courtly etiquette, even though both

Dewey and the commanding army officer in the Philippines had reported favorably on him. Relations between the American military and Aguinaldo began to sour with the first arrival of American troops. McKinley was not alone in his reservations about Philippine autonomy. Only a few radical antiimperialists in America believed that the Filipinos could maintain their independence. Most Americans felt that an independent Philippine Republic would lead to civil war or invite intervention by other foreign powers.

Specifically, McKinley worried that the British or the Germans might seize the islands. The British had already expressed an interest, and the Germans deployed naval forces to observe the American actions in the Philippines. Distraught over what course to take, the devout president got on his knees and prayed for divine guidance. He prayed so long his knees hurt. In the end, McKinley concluded, as he later told a meeting of religious businessmen, the United States must "uplift and civilize and Christianize them, and by God's grace do the very best we could for them, as our fellow-men for whom Christ also died."

ANTIIMPERIALISTS DECLARE BETRAYAL. Certain now as to which course to follow, McKinley sent a resolution to Congress calling for the annexation of the Philippines. His proposal unleashed a national debate. Many American businessmen who had long been acquainted with the islands believed that American interests in China could be sustained only through annexation of the Philippines. Although this view had wide support from the public and the press, an active group had organized against annexation under the auspices of the Anti-Imperialist League. As a result, the proposed annexation produced a full blown fight in the Senate.

Roosevelt acerbically denounced the antiimperialists as "little better than traitors." This barb, however, misconstrued the firm conviction that unified the antiimperialists' movement: annexation was alien to republican ideals and the American Constitution. Andrew Carnegie, a leading antiimperialist who financed the lobbying efforts against annexation, wrote to McKinley: "Our young men volunteered to fight the oppressor. I shall be surprised if they relish the work of shooting down the oppressed." He closed, "Your Bitterest Opponent."

Many members of the Anti-Imperialist League were liberal Republicans, or **"mugwumps"** (an Indian term meaning "Big Man"), who had broken with Grant and had supported Cleveland in 1884. They included such New England intellectuals as William James, the Harvard University psychologist and philosopher; E. L. Godkin, editor of the influential *Nation;* and the novelist William Dean Howells. Mark Twain, born a southerner but living in Connecticut, joined the antiimperialist crusade. Former presidents Grover Cleveland and Benjamin Harrison also opposed annexation. Some labor leaders and southern politicians opposed imperialism for their own vested interests. For example, Samuel Gompers, president of the American Federation of Labor, opposed annexation because he feared the admission of Filipino workers into the American workforce.

Antiimperialists revealed mixed motives. Although they united around the theme that imperialism was contrary to American democratic principles, deep divisions were apparent among the coalition's members when it came to specific reasons for opposing imperialism. Some opposed imperialism on humanitarian grounds. Others, however, displayed racial animosity toward accepting Filipinos into the United States. Many thought that Filipinos would never be prepared for democracy.

ANNEXATION OF THE PHILIPPINES SPARKS A NASTY LITTLE WAR. The fight in the Senate over the annexation treaty opened in earnest in December 1899. Throughout the fight, McKinley refused to compromise. He remained confident that he had the support of the American people and the necessary votes in the Senate to carry the treaty. In early February 1900, proannexation forces found their cause aided when Aguinaldo attacked American troops in the Philippines.

The president understood immediately that Aguinaldo had made a serious mistake. He observed, "How foolish these people are. This means the ratification of the treaty; the [American] people will insist on ratification." With American troops under fire, doubtful Republicans swung to **ratification**. McKinley used **pork-barrel** politics, **patronage,** and federal judgeships to win over those who wavered. The Democratic party's efforts to oppose the annexation treaty were hurt when their leader, William Jennings Bryan, decided to support the treaty. He hoped to make imperialism — along with **free silver** — an issue in the election of 1900. The treaty passed the Senate by a vote of 57 to 27, one vote more than the necessary two-thirds required to ratify a treaty.

During the debate one Republican senator warned McKinley that it would take 50,000 American soldiers to subdue the Filipino guerrillas and that Americans would find themselves committing the same kinds of atrocities for which that they had condemned the Spanish. This warning proved prophetic. It took three years to suppress the rebellion. Americans attacked civilian populations, pursued a policy of reconcentration, burned villages, and waged a brutal war against the insurgents. Estimates of Filipino deaths ranged from 10,000 to 60,000. The count may have been a half million. The fight against Aguinaldo and his guerrillas brought out the worst in the American soldiers.

McKinley felt that the insurgents had struck the first blow, so he declined negotiating with Aguinaldo until the rebellion was quelled. Initially, the American forces pursued traditional warfare. When newspaper reporters sent stories home telling of the slaughter of civilians and the killing of prisoners, the American commander ordered unfavorable news reports censored. Finally, in May 1900 a new general arrived — General Arthur MacArthur (the father of famed World War II commander Douglas MacArthur). He brought a new intensity to the war. At one point MacArthur ordered several Philippine prisoners of war executed in retaliation for the "murder" of American prisoners. In 1900 MacArthur asked for an additional appropriation of $100 million to conduct the war. This request led to inclusion of the Spooner amendment, proposed by Wisconsin Senator John C. Spooner, providing that once the Philippines were subdued the president would implement a system of self-government.

From the outset of the rebellion, American troops, who were mostly white, expressed deep prejudices against the Filipinos, usually referring to them in derogatory racial terms. In an early battle, American soldiers caught the Filipino guerrillas in a crossfire. One soldier described the battle as "more fun than a turkey shoot." From then on "the fun was fast and furious," as dead Filipinos piled up "thicker than buffalo chips." Brutality became a way of life. At one village more than a thousand men, women, and children were slaughtered. In the attack on the village, American soldiers became frenzied. As one soldier wrote, "I am probably growing hard-hearted, for I am in my glory when I can sight my gun on some dark-skin and pull the trigger." Another soldier wrote, "this shooting human beings is a 'hot game,' and beats rabbit hunting all to pieces. . . . We killed them like rabbits; hundreds, yes, thousands of them. Everyone was crazy."

The Filipino rebels also committed atrocities. Some of the fiercest fighting came on the island of Samar. A surprise attack by the insurgents took the lives of 50 members of one company. The mutilated bodies of the American soldiers were later discovered with their stomachs slit and stuffed with flour, jam, coffee, and molasses. The commanding officer Jacob "Hell Roaring Jake" Smith, a veteran of the battle of Wounded Knee, ordered his troops to take no prisoners. "I wish you to kill and burn, and the more you kill and burn the better it will please me." Reports of war atrocities in Samar finally led to a Senate investigation. While the committee was in session, reports arrived in Washington that American soldiers had executed 1300 Filipino prisoners of war on the main island, Luzon. Republicans on the Senate committee were able to whitewash these reports. So fierce was the Samar battle that for decades to come, when an American veteran from the Samar campaign entered a room, marines of all ranks would stand and salute.

Racial tensions also spilled over to affect black troops stationed in the Philippines. While many black American soldiers also looked down on the Filipinos by calling them "savages" and "half-civilized," blacks themselves experienced racism from white soldiers. At the same time that black regiments were arriving in the Philippines, race riots were breaking out in Chicago, San Antonio, rural Georgia, and Tennessee. The Philippines failed to offer an insularity to such racism. Whites refused to salute black officers and white soldiers jeered and spit at black soldiers.

Finally in late March 1901, American forces captured Aguinaldo. During the rebellion, Aguinaldo had shown dictatorial tendencies. Strong evidence suggests that he arranged the assassination of one rival. Upon his capture, Aguinaldo signed an oath of allegiance and retired to private life — living to the age of 96. The same month as Aguinaldo's capture, the American military government in the Philippines was replaced by a civilian commission headed by William H. Taft, a former circuit judge and future president of the United States.

The suppression of the Philippine rebellion required four times as many American soldiers as it had taken to invade Cuba and cost three times more American lives than had been lost in the entire Spanish-American War.

Shortly before the defeat of the insurrection, American courts had ruled that the United States Constitution did not extend to the Philippines or Puerto Rico. These islands, the court declared, were dependencies subject to congressional authority. As a result, the inhabitants of the Philippines and Puerto Rico were endowed with a curious mixture of civil rights and noncitizenship. However, Congress's promise to grant independence to the Philippines in the Jones Act (1916) was not fulfilled for 30 years.

Although critics accused the United States of betraying its anticolonial and republican principles by taking control of Spain's former colonies, American rule turned out to be humane. For example, American occupying forces in Cuba constructed roads, sanitation facilities, and schools. A commission of army surgeons working under Dr. Walter Reed identified the mosquito as the source of malaria (as first suggested by a Cuban physician, Dr. Carlos Finlay). In March 1901, Congress passed the Platt amendment to a military appropriation bill, which allowed the president to end the military occupation of Cuba, provided that Cuba consented to American future intervention if necessary to preserve its independence. The United States was also promised a naval base in Cuba at Guantanamo.

1900: MCKINLEY WINS AGAIN; BRYAN LOSES AGAIN. In 1900, William Jennings Bryan, as expected, again received the Democratic nomination. McKinley's nomination by the Republicans was a foregone conclusion. The great surprise at the convention came when party bosses led by New York's

Tom Platt selected Theodore Roosevelt to run as McKinley's vice-president. Fearing that Governor Roosevelt might gain control of the New York party, the bosses "kicked him upstairs." Neither McKinley nor Senator Mark Hanna favored Roosevelt, but the party bosses were too strong to be overturned.

Bryan hoped to rally voters against imperialism, but in the end prosperity decided the vote. McKinley won in a landslide. He was the first president to win a second consecutive term since Grant. The following years were to be a golden age for the Republican party. The **GOP** controlled the White House for the next three terms. In his second term, McKinley assumed an air of confidence that had been lacking in most administrations since the Civil War.

AMERICA TURNS EAST. In foreign affairs, Secretary of State John Hay forged a new Anglo-American alliance in keeping with America's new position as a world power. Under Hay's guidance, the United States also attempted to exert its modest influence in Asia by preventing China from being carved up by the European powers to the detriment of American business interests. The United States announced the **Open Door policy,** which demanded that China's market be open to all trading partners. Although American trade with China was relatively small, many saw the potential for a lucrative market. After all, exports to China had doubled from 1896 to 1899. This export trade was particularly significant for the American textile industry, which made nearly half of its foreign sales in China.

By the end of the 1890s, Germany, Britain, France, and Russia had gained spheres of influence, areas in China where they received key trading and commercial rights. In a series of diplomatic notes, Secretary of State Hay called upon these nations to maintain an open door policy in Chinese ports.

In 1900, the Boxer Rebellion, an uprising against foreigners and western missionaries, placed Peking's foreign population under siege. An international force to which America contributed 5,000 troops quelled the rebellion, but once again threatened Chinese sovereignty. On July 3, 1900, Hay sent a second Open Door note, which promised to uphold the territorial integrity of China. Although America was not willing to enforce this policy militarily, this new Open Door policy expressed America's new self-image as a first-class power.

MCKINLEY ASSASSINATED. In 1901 McKinley was at his height of popularity. In early September he traveled to Buffalo, New York, to address an industrial exposition. There, at a public reception, an anarchist named Leon Czolgosz shot McKinley. Czolgosz was seized immediately. McKinley, bleeding, was led to a chair. He told his aids, "My wife — be careful . . . how you tell her — oh, be careful." He then looked at his assassin and said, "Don't let them hurt him." Seven days later McKinley died.

Conclusion

William McKinley's presidency marked a transition for the American political order and the nation. McKinley had entered the White House primarily concerned with domestic economic problems. Nevertheless, his administration had directed most of its attention to international affairs. There was no turning back. America had emerged as a world power. McKinley set the stage for more dynamic leadership in the presidency as his successor, Theodore Roosevelt, turned to the problems created by the corporate order.

Recommended Readings

DOCUMENTS: Theodore Roosevelt, *The Rough Riders* (1899).

READINGS: (GENERAL DIPLOMATIC) Robert Beisner, *From the Old Diplomacy to the New* (1975); Charles S. Campbell, *The Transformation of American Foreign Relations* (1976); Foster Rhea Dulles, *Prelude to World Power* (1965); David Healy, *United States Expansionism: The Imperialist Urge in the 1890s* (1970); Walter LaFeber, *The New Empire: American Expansionism* (1963); Ernest R. May, *American Imperialism* (1968); H. Wayne Morgan, *America's Road to Empire* (1965); Thomas J. Osborn, *"Empire Can Wait": American Opposition to Hawaiian Annexation* (1981); Emily S. Rosenberg, *Spreading the "American Dream": American Economic and Cultural Expansion* (1982); William A. Williams, *The Roots of the American Empire* (1969). (THE SPANISH-AMERICAN WAR) Robert L. Beisner, *Twelve Against Empire: The Anti-Imperialists* (1968); Frank Freidel, *The Splendid Little War* (1958); W. B. Gatewood, Jr. *Black Americans and the White Man's Burden* (1975); Walter LaFeber, *Inevitable Revolutions: The United States in Central America* (1983); Gerald F. Linderman, *The Mirror of War: American Society and the Spanish-American War* (1974); Stuart Creighton Miller, *"Benevolent Assimilation": The American Conquest of the Philippines* (1982); David R. Trask, *The War with Spain* (1981); Richard E. Welch, *Response to Imperialism* (1979). (LATIN AMERICA/ASIA) Walter LaFeber, *The Panama Canal* (1979); David McCullough, *The Path Between the Seas: The Creation of the Panama Canal* (1977); Michael Hunt, *The Making of a Special Relationship: The United States and China* (1983); Akira Iriye, *Across the Pacific: An Inner History of American East-Asian Relations* (1967); Thomas J. McCormick, *China Market: America's Quest for Informal Empire* (1967); Marilyn B. Young, *The Rhetoric of Empire: American China Policy* (1968).

22

⚹

THE PROGRESSIVE YEARS

CHAPTER OVERVIEW: Between 1900 and American entry into World War I in 1917, the nation experienced an outburst of reform that extended into nearly all of its institutions and reached from local government to state and national government. Differing in vision, method, and goals, progressive reformers included wealthy industrialists, the middle class, and working people. Many were Republicans, but others were Democrats, Socialists, or independents. Progressivism took different forms in the Northeast, the South, and the West.

Whatever their differences, progressives shared a general belief that government had a new role to play in society. During the depression of 1893, President Cleveland had declared the opposite: people were to serve government. This view now changed. Progressives differed among themselves over the government's specific role, but clearly rejected older concepts of laissez-faire (i.e. do-nothing) government.

American Culture and Social Life Transformed

Technology introduced new products and conveniences that made life easier, healthier, and longer. Shorter work weeks gave people time to enjoy sports, music, and movies. New ideas in science and culture gave Americans a new view of the world: it was continually changing, and they themselves could force changes. The new corporate economy flourished. Giant corporations accumulated more wealth and economic power than ever, and their mass-production techniques transformed the nature of work while lowering the prices of goods. Nonetheless, many Americans lived in abject poverty and ethnic minority groups faced fierce discrimination.

TECHNOLOGY REVOLUTIONIZES AMERICAN LIFE. "Never in the history of the world was society in so terrific a flux as it is right now," declared the popular writer Jack London in 1907. "An unseen and fearful revolution is taking place in the fiber and structure of society."

While London expressed concern, most people welcomed the new age. Americans sensed the high drama of new businesses being organized, of new technologies being introduced, and of social life breaking with the past. American history is a record of changes, but never had change come so rapidly or so profoundly.

Most dramatic were technological changes that influenced people's daily lives. Ordinary Americans began to use electric lights, telephones, and aspirin. Technology imparted a sense of empowerment to the generation which came of age at the turn of the century. Chemistry provided new medicines to doctors, nitrogen fertilizers to farmers, and new products to consumers — from saccharin to the first plastics, including fashionable brush, comb, and mirror sets. Inexpensive red dyes allowed average people to wear brighter colors and decorate even modest homes in splendid colors.

As one English visitor exclaimed, "Life in the States is one of a perpetual whirl of telephone, telegrams, phonographs, electric bells, motors, lifts [elevators], and automatic instruments." By the turn of the century, Thomas Edison's inventions could be found in most American homes. The Wizard of Menlo Park had taken patents on electric lights and lighting systems, phonographs and movies, sewing machines and stoves, fans and flatirons. Telephones linked millions of homes. Electric streetcars tied together the city. And movies brought a shared popular culture that cut across class lines and regional divisions.

The American economy boomed. From 1896 to 1901 per capita income rose from $188 to $467. Manufacturing became the nation's pride, and exported goods made their way throughout the world. The Singer Sewing Machine Company had sales offices in a half dozen countries; Ford made cars in England and France; the American Tobacco Company produced cigarettes in China.

This was a golden age for American agriculture as well. From 1897 to 1920, American farmers enjoyed unprecedented prosperity. They raised more cotton, tobacco, wheat, and corn than ever. The introduction of irrigation opened western deserts to specialty crops, including citrus. Refrigerated cars allowed perishables to be sent east so that oranges, grapefruit, and lemons found their way into middle-class diets. Consuming more coffee, sugar, and cigarettes, the average American also dined on more red meat, fats, processed foods, and fewer cereals than in the past.

Although this diet might not be considered healthy by today's standards,

Americans were living longer due to better living conditions and improved health care. The acceptance of the theory that germs spread disease — and the consequent use of antiseptics in medicine, better personal hygiene, and improved public sanitation in the city — increased life expectancy. For white males alone life expectancy in the first two decades of the century grew from 46 years to 55 years. At the same time, the birth rate declined, so older people became a larger portion of the population during the century's first two decades.

Medicine itself experienced revolutionary changes brought about by new technologies. In these years American doctors began to use x-rays, better anesthetics, and blood transfusions. Medical research blossomed through private foundations such as the Rockefeller Institute for Medical Research and the Carnegie Foundation for the Advancement of Teachers. The Carnegie Foundation's study of medical education, issued as the Flexner Commission Report (1910), changed the way doctors were trained by upgrading educational standards.

AMERICANS RELAX. In these years American social life changed as well. The average work week had dropped from 66 hours in 1850 to 56 hours in 1900 and by 1920 it had fallen to 41 hours. Increased leisure time led to new forms of recreation. In larger cities, people might go to municipal zoos, playgrounds, or parks to walk, ride bicycles, rent canoes, or picnic. Commercial amusement parks like New York's Coney Island drew thousands. Baseball attracted spectators from both the working and middle classes. In 1903 the World Series was initiated. Football, popular in colleges, remained at first an upper-class sport, but soon spread to industrial towns in the Midwest.

Pianos could now be found in many homes, as mass production allowed thousands of middle-class Americans to buy on credit these once-expensive musical instruments. Songs such as "Take Me Out to the Ball Game" and "Daisy" thrilled the country. Phonographs further extended popular music to enable average Americans to hear recordings of professional singers in the privacy of their homes. The record industry helped change musical tastes. Songs such as "You Can Go as Far as You Like With Me in My Merry Oldsmobile" ridiculed older popular tastes.

The movie industry also became a major force in American popular culture. Thomas Edison had launched the movie industry with his invention of the kinetoscope, a machine that enabled viewers to look to through peephole to watch a moving film. Other entrepreneurs, mostly immigrants, began to project films on walls or large screens. They charged 5 cents admission and called their theaters "nickelodeons." Primarily aimed at urban working-class audiences these silent films attracted hundreds for shows that lasted only ten or fifteen minutes. Increasingly, movies became more daring in their approach and material. "The Great Train Robbery" (1903) introduced audiences to an action plot that included the first movie murder. People across social lines loved it. The movie industry moved from New York to Hollywood, California, largely to escape Edison's cartel of movie production and distribution. There film executives, often Jewish immigrants, produced more sophisticated fare. D. W. Giffith's "The Birth of a Nation" (1915) introduced such new techniques as the close-up, crosscutting, and shadows — even as its racist message provoked riots and stimulated the rebirth of the Ku Klux Klan.

Actors now became stars both on and off screen. Fans followed the careers and personal lives of comedians such as Harold Lloyd and Charlie Chaplin, cowboys Tom Mix and William S. Hart, and leading men such as Douglas Fairbanks. Gloria Swanson and Mary Pickford titillated the public. For the first time, America had an aristocracy, even if it was only made of tinsel. Movies introduced the public to new ways of talking, dressing, and behaving.

Many reacted negatively to the morality — or lack of it — projected on the silent screen. Critics complained that movies glorified criminals, ridiculed public authorities, and degraded women. Most large cities, such as Chicago and New York, appointed censors who cut scenes from hundreds of movies.

New styles in fashion and clothes were also evident. Cosmetics began to gain acceptance. At the same time, women began piling their hair high on their necks in a bun. Women discarded tight fitting corsets, cut their skirts shorter, and revealed their ankles — to the shock of their elders. Popular culture introduced exotic dances beginning with the fox-trot, which soon gave way to the ragtime rhythms of the bunny-hug, the grizzly bear, and the turkey-trot.

INTELLECTUAL LIFE TRANSFORMED. New theories in the natural sciences, the social sciences, art, and literature changed the way many Americans viewed the world. The general acceptance of Darwin's theory of evolution challenged world views based on an absolute, unchanging, and knowable Newtonian universe. Now the universe was seen as continually changing.

The emergence of the modern social sciences — economics, sociology, anthropology, history, and political science — also brought a new critical sensibility to Americans. If the natural world was in continual change, then society too could and must change. And men and women could change it for the better.

During this period, young professors — often trained in German universities — launched an attack on "formalism." They viewed the world as being relativistic and rejected truths based on a single absolute. Scholars such as William James, a Harvard psychologist and brother of the novelist Henry James, and philosopher John Dewey, believed that truth was "pragmatic" and could only be discovered in one's experience of the world. Historian Charles Beard attacked traditional assumptions about the United States Constitution in *An Economic Interpretation of the Constitution* (1913). Harvard Law Professor Roscoe Pound argued that law must take into account the nature of a changing society.

The shift from absolutes to relatives became most apparent in the visual art of the day. The New York Armory Show (1913) introduced such modern European painters as Picasso, Matisse, and Cezanne to America. Although to traditionalists such as Theodore Roosevelt they were the "lunatic fringe," European avant-garde artists influenced American artists, including Georgia O'Keeffe. Other American artists such as George Luks, John Sloan, and George Bellows became known as the Ash Can School for their realistic portrayals of drab, violent city life.

Literature changed, too. Mark Twain criticized society in his later novels, *The Man That Corrupted Hadleyburg* (1900) and *The Mysterious Stranger* (1906). So did William Dean Howells in *A Hazard of New Fortunes* (1890) and *A Traveler from Altruria* (1894). Novelists such as Frank Norris, Jack London, and Theodore Dreiser described a deterministic world where men or women lacked control over their fates.

Younger writers and artists consciously defined themselves as radicals eager to break with tradition. These "New **Bohemians**", as they were called, formed loose-knit artistic communities in Chicago and Greenwich Village in New York. They prided themselves in shocking middle-class society and the older generation's Victorian gentility. Small magazines such as Max and Crystal Eastman's *The Masses* published John Reed, Edna St. Vincent Millay, and Eugene O'Neill. In rebelling against the past, these intellectuals emphasized youth and its virtues. As one young writer declared, "It is the young people who have all the really valuable experience. . . . Very few people get any really new experience after they are twenty-five. . . "

AMERICA INCORPORATES. By the turn of the century, Americans had become more critical of corporations. While they welcomed prosperity, they also disliked the growing concentration of economic power of large corporations. A wave of mergers transformed the economy and resulted in more than 300 highly concentrated companies. These companies, which often held monopoly power over entire industries, controlled more wealth than did many nations.

Certain industries appeared especially concentrated. For example, just seven railroad groups controlled over 85 percent of all the nation's railroad mileage. John D. Rockefeller's Standard Oil dominated the oil industry. (Today its descendants include Exxon, Chevron, Mobil, and Amoco.) J. P. Morgan dominated national banking through his control of First National Bank of New York, National Bank of Commerce, the Chase National Bank, and many others. He also held a controlling interest in the nation's three largest insurance corporations, New York Life, Mutual of New York, and Equitable Life Assurance Society. United States Steel, cleverly created by Morgan, was a **holding company** that owned 11 other steel companies, operating nearly 800 mills, and controlling more than 60 percent of all steel production.

Major corporations created in these years included General Electric, National Biscuit Company (Nabisco), American Can, Eastman Kodak, United States Rubber, and American Telephone and Telegraph (AT&T). The legal framework for these enterprises had been formed under liberalized state laws in New Jersey and Delaware that allowed industrialists to incorporate vast corporate holding companies.

These new corporate entities changed the nature of work in America by forcing the development of new and more complex administrative and managerial structures. DuPont, General Electric, and International Harvester became models for other corporations. Heading these new corporate organizations were not owners, but new top managers such as Theodore Vail of AT&T, Elbert Gary of U.S. Steel, and George Perkins of International Harvester. Beneath them were an array of lesser managers — salaried employees who served from division heads down to supervisors.

Large corporations employed an increasing percentage of the nation's workforce. By 1910 just 5 percent of manufacturing firms employed over 60 percent of all workers in the United States. At the bottom rung of the employment ladder were new immigrants from southern and eastern Europe. Moreover, new techniques of mass production transformed the nature of work by upgrading highly skilled work, while downgrading semiskilled and unskilled labor.

The automobile industry presents a case in point. Henry Ford and his associates introduced continuous line production. By assigning workers to a moving assembly line and giving them only a limited, specific task to do, Ford cut the time to assemble an automobile from 12 1/2 hours to 1 1/2 hours. This allowed Ford to produce 500,000 Model T Fords a year. As a result he was able to lower the price of this automobile from $950 to $290. With mass production came mass consumption, but lost in the process were large numbers of older craft workers.

In addition to craft workers, the emergence of vast, powerful corporations threatened many farmers, small businessmen, and socially concerned citizens, including many women. The new corporate order appeared to subvert older democratic and individualistic values. Concentration at the expense of small business enterprise appeared to be the wave of the future. Few noted the failure of a number of **monopolies** including American Bicycle, U.S. Leather, and National Salt or other mergers that did not enjoy complete success. For example, because of its failure to adjust to new technology, U.S. Steel lost 20 percent of its market share from 1901 to 1920. Standard Oil's control of petroleum refining fell from 90 percent in 1900 to 50 percent by 1920, due to the growth of rivals Texaco, Gulf, and Union.

Although this new corporate economy brought cheaper goods into the marketplace, not everyone could afford them even at lower prices. In his study *Poverty* (1904), sociologist Robert Hunter estimated that 20 percent of the population in industrial states lived in abject poverty. Other sociologists, such as Thorstein Veblen, contrasted the plight of the poor with the "conspicuous consumption" and extravagant lifestyles of the rich. Fewer than 2 percent of the population owned 60 percent of the nation's wealth. Andrew Carnegie, for example, made a tax-free $23 million a year, while he paid the average steelworker $450 a year.

AMERICANS EXCLUDED. Some groups were clearly excluded from prosperity. The progressive era did little to benefit blacks. Blacks lost the right to vote through poll taxes, literacy tests, and outright intimidation. From 1900 to 1912 more than one thousand blacks were lynched or burned to death. Many Southern progressive politicians linked reform to the **disfranchisement** of black voters. For example, Hoke Smith, a leading Georgia progressive, ran for governor calling for the prohibition of child labor, **primary** elections, direct election of U.S. senators — all progressive causes — and taking the vote away from blacks.

The period also saw the outbreak of bitter race riots. Shortly after the 1906 gubernatorial election in Georgia, a riot broke out in Atlanta when rumors spread of black men attacking white women. A mob estimated at 10,000 to 15,000 white men roamed the city attacking any blacks found on the street before it was supressed by the state militia. One white and 25 blacks were killed. That same year, an entire battalion of black soldiers stationed at Brownsville, Texas, was dishonorably discharged after they fired on a crowd that had been goading them.

These incidents led a small group of mostly white reformers to organize the National Association for the Advancement of Colored People (NAACP) in 1911. Earlier, English Walling, a New York reformer and member of a wealthy Kentucky family, organized a small group around the "black question." Walling was joined by Mary White Ovington, who was compiling *Half a Man: The Status of the Negro in New York* (1911) and Oswald Garrison Villard, another wealthy New York reformer and descendant of abolitionist William Lloyd Garrison. Out of this group emerged the NAACP. The only high-ranking black was W.E.B. DuBois, the editor of the influential *The Crisis*. By 1930, however, the NAACP was predominately black.

In its early years, the NAACP targeted **segregation** and disfranchisement of black voters. In 1915 they persuaded the Supreme Court to overturn Oklahoma's grandfather clause, which prevented blacks from voting by setting difficult requirements that were waived if your grandfather had been a voter. (Because of slavery, most blacks did not have grandfathers who had voted). Two years later the court struck down Louisville's residential segregation ordinance. Still, these successes proved rather modest given the general climate for blacks.

Asians faced fierce discrimination as well, especially in the western United States. Legislation in 1882 prohibited the immigration of Chinese laborers, and because almost all of the early migrants were single men, the Chinese-American population gradually declined. Newly arriving Japanese farm workers replaced Chinese farm workers. Japanese immigrants tended to be more literate and came with their families. Work in the Hawaiian sugar fields had first attracted the Japanese in the 1870s. From there they moved to the mainland — especially California. Over 130,000 Japanese arrived in California in the first decade of the 1900s.

The arrival of so many Japanese upset many Californians. In 1905 San Francisco labor union leaders formed an Asiatic Exclusion League to prevent further immigration. Under pressure from this league, the city board of education ordered all Japanese children to attend a segregated school. Protests from the Japanese government created a diplomatic crisis that forced President Theodore Roosevelt to involve himself in the affairs of the city. In 1907, in return for a compromised agreement with city officials, Roosevelt negotiated the **Gentlemen's Agreement** with Japan which stopped any more Japanese laborers, unskilled or skilled, from migrating to the United States. Nevertheless, California Republican progressives made barring Japanese immigration a major part of their political platform.

Conditions for Mexicans in the United States also worsened in these years. The outbreak of revolution in Mexico in 1910 led thousands to flee north. Many Mexican refugees moved to cities and towns in the West where they created "barrios" or ghettos. Others became migrant farm laborers only to encounter horrible working conditions. In California, Mexicans replaced Japanese farm workers, after the Gentleman's Agreement (1907) barred further Japanese immigration. In 1903 farm laborers conducted a bitter strike against

California beet growers — one of the first agricultural strikes in the nation's history.

Reform Sweeps the Nation

Their willingness to break with the past set a context — and reflected a general mood — for Americans to rethink the political and social order. The women's movement revived around the turn of the century. While women's groups differed over agendas and tactics, together they pressed for the vote, birth control, social reform, and improved conditions for working women. Reformers worked to improve public health, housing, and sanitation. They made city governments more efficient and won control of many state governments.

WOMEN ORGANIZE. Women's roles within the American family began to change first among upper- and middle-class white Anglo-Saxon **Protestants**. Although a rising divorce rate alarmed traditionalists, others welcomed these changes as a sign that women were finally gaining greater independence. In 1880 only 1 in 21 marriages ended in divorce; in 1900 1 in 12 marriages had failed, and by 1915 the divorce rate had risen to 1 in 9. By this time the divorce rate among working-class families nearly equaled that of middle-class families.

A new reform mood swept over many American women, even those less militant than the organized feminists. As the newly elected president of the General Federation of Women's Clubs in 1904 declared, "I have an important piece of news to give you. Dante is dead. He has been dead for several centuries, and I think it is time we dropped the study of his *Inferno* and turned our attention to our own." By 1909 the traditional wife's promise "obey" had been dropped from civil marriage vows as well as some liberal Protestant vows. While most women continued to marry and become homemakers, the ideal of the "new women" was young, educated, and unmarried.

These women sought greater control of their personal lives, larger roles in society, and government protection in the workplace. Many demanded the right to vote. Margaret Sanger crusaded to introduce birth control devices, in the form of diaphragms, to working women. Trained as a nurse, Sanger argued that women had the right to determine for themselves "whether they shall become mothers, under what conditions, and when." She also saw in birth control a means to address social problems by allowing the poor to limit the size of their families. Influenced by Darwinian science and eugenics (the belief that the race could be improved through population control), Sanger believed that birth control could improve the American stock and liberate women.

The birth control movement illustrated only one aspect of women's involvement in reform in this period. Women became active in the **temperance movement,** social work, trade unions, consumer groups, and women's **suffrage** groups.

Many women campaigned against alcohol, with the Woman's Christian Temperance Union (WCTU) attracting the broadest support. Under the leadership of the dynamic Frances Willard, the Methodist-oriented WCTU linked its campaign to prohibit the sale of alcohol to "home protection" against drunkenness that broke up homes. By the 1880s, under a policy of "do-everything," the WCTU had accepted women's suffrage as necessary to enact of a federal constitutional amendment to ban alcohol. This campaign for **prohibition** led women to lobby for prison reform, workingmen's centers, and public health. The WCTU also worked with Native Americans and African-Americans.

The most militant expression of the women's movement appeared in the demand for female suffrage. Following the Civil War, the fourteenth amendment had granted **due process** and voting rights to black males, while excluding, in effect, white and black females. Opposition to the exclusion of women in the fourteenth amendment found its strongest voice in the National Woman Suffrage Association, headed by Elizabeth Cady Stanton and Susan B. Anthony. This position led to a bitter break in the women's movement when Lucy Stone and her husband, Henry Blackwell, formed the rival American Woman Suffrage Association based in New England.

These two groups remained divided until 1890, when they merged to form the National American Woman Suffrage Association. This new unified organization concentrated on over 400 campaigns to place woman's suffrage on state ballots. Women already voted in Wyoming and Utah. In only two states did women gain the right to vote in statewide elections — in Colorado (1893) and Idaho (1896). These state campaigns laid the groundwork for a national effort to secure woman's suffrage that continued throughout the progressive era.

In 1909 Carrie Chapman Catt organized the Women's Suffrage Party, which broke with the two major parties. Her efforts coincided with the winning of women's suffrage in California, Arizona, Kansas, and Oregon. Still, progress on the "women's question" remained too slow for some. Alice Paul, a Quaker influenced by her counterparts in England, organized the Congressional Union to undertake more militant activity. Although much smaller than the National American Woman Suffrage Association with its two million members, Paul's Congressional Union attracted considerable attention when it conducted a series of protests that led to arrests.

A new militant consciousness was also apparent in feminist writers such as Charlotte Perkins Gilman, who discussed the economic effects of marriage and labor in her sociological study, *Women and Economics* (1898). Her utopian novel, *Herland* (1916), envisioned a society without men and won a significant readership among women.

Middle-class female reformers actively aided working-class women. By 1900 over five million — nearly 21 percent of the female population — worked for wages. Most of these workers were young and unmarried. Nearly two million worked as domestic servants, another 900,000 were employed in clothing and textiles, and nearly a half million were professionals, many of them teachers.

Women factory workers were poorly paid and often worked in oppressive conditions. A number of groups campaigned to better the lives of working women. Leonora O'Reilly, a labor organizer, joined wealthy New York reformer Josephine Shaw Lowell to organize the New York Consumer's Society, which later became the National Consumers League (1891). The National Consumers League, under the able leadership of Florence Kelley, lobbied for laws limiting hours of working women and protecting them from unfair labor practices. Such groups ignored men's working conditions because the Supreme Court had ruled that laws could not be used to regulate male wages or working conditions. The progressives hoped that the court would accept regulation for women, on the grounds that "fragile" women needed protection.

Leonora O'Reilly also played a key role in organizing the Women's Trade Union League (1903). She was joined by a group of other reformers including William English Walling, Mary K. O'Sullivan, Jane Addams, and Lillian Wald. The Women's Trade Union League helped organize the Ladies Garment Workers Union in New York.

Attempts to organize women in the garment industry took a dramatic turn in 1909 when women workers in New York spontaneously organized a strike. Many of these women worked ten to 12 hour days for as little as $4 to $6 a week. Most were immigrants from eastern and southern Europe; many were Jewish. The city-wide strike began in October when the female workers at the Triangle Shirtwaist Company walked out. Joined by Mary Drier and the Women's Trade Union League, the strike spread to other garment companies. By December, between 20,000 and 30,000 workers were out on strike. Finally, in February 1910, garment factory owners agreed to a settlement proposed by Louis Brandeis, a lawyer representing the workers. The "Uprising of

This Lewis Hine photograph shows two boys working at midnight in the Indiana Glassworks. In 1910, 1.9 million children were part of the workforce. Of working children under the age of 15, 1.3 million were males and 305,000 were female. (AP/World Wide Photos)

Twenty Thousand" changed the course of labor relations in New York by recognition of the union by the garment industry.

In 1911, the Triangle Shirtwaist Company gained further notoriety when a fire broke out at its new plant, taking the lives of 146 female workers. Firemen found the charred bodies of many of these women piled up at doors that managers had locked to stop thefts. The public outcry against this tragedy led to the appointment of a commission composed of Frances Perkins (later to become secretary of labor in 1933 and the first woman cabinet member), Robert Wagner (later U.S. senator from New York), and Alfred E. Smith (later governor and presidential candidate for the Democratic party). Based on their report, the state legislature passed new legislation protecting women workers.

REFORM BEGINS ON THE LOCAL LEVEL. The reform movement began on the local level and moved through the states to the federal government. New conditions seemed to require new responses. Demands for more active government came from trade associations, professional groups, consumer

Jane Addams typified the reform spirit of many women involved in the settlement house movement. In 1889, Addams founded Hull House in a poor section of Chicago. A pacifist, she won the Nobel Peace Prize at 74. (AP/WORLD WIDE PHOTOS)

leagues, labor unions, and voters. This reform movement became a moral crusade, even as it demanded greater efficiency in private and public activities.

Reform-minded businessmen rejected **laissez-faire** government and unfettered competition when they organized the National Civic Federation (1900), an association promoting industrial arbitration in labor disputes. This reform spirit was also found in the organization of the National Tuberculosis Association, the Boy Scouts of America, the Women's League for Peace and Freedom, and local and federal research organizations such as the Brookings Institution — all established in these years.

Newspapers and magazines stimulated reform (and sold more subscriptions) by revealing public corruption and abuses of power. "Muckraking" gained notoriety when journalist Lincoln Steffens documented business payoffs to city governments in a series of articles in *McClure's Magazine.* Later reissued as a book, *The Shame of the Cities* (1904) showed how business interests had corrupted local governments virtually everywhere. Other magazines became even more persistent. *Cosmopolitan,* a Hearst magazine, published David Graham Phillips' investigative reports, "The Treason of the Senate," revealing corporate influence in the federal government.

The efforts at reform began on the municipal level with the **settlement house** movement. In 1889, Jane Addams, a wealthy social reformer, founded Hull House in a poor section of Chicago. Settlement houses sprang up in New York, Philadelphia, St. Louis, and other cities. Addams and other settlement house workers extended their efforts to improve public health, city sanitation, and public housing. Physicians and public health nurses fought against tuberculosis — "the white plague" — by urging the public, especially the working class, to boil milk. Other reformers such as Frederic C. Howe launched the "City Beautiful" movement to improve cities through planning. During these years cities built civic centers, tree-lined boulevards, fountains, playgrounds, and parks.

Many urban reformers blamed the plight of the city on political bosses. Reformers maintained that bosses controlled government through ignorant immigrant voters who were marched to the polls on election day and told how to vote. City bosses then willingly subverted the public good by selling out to local business interests who were given government contracts, licenses, and franchises. Reformers also accused bosses of giving jobs to political supporters, regardless of their competence to perform those jobs.

Some municipal reformers believed that control could be taken away from the bosses by bringing expertise to government. These reformers maintained that city governments should adopt a civil service under the direction of strong executive government, instead of hiring of employees by favoritism. Other new forms of government were also tried. In 1901, when local government failed to respond to a giant tidal wave that wiped out the port city of Galveston, Texas, leading citizens turned to a specially created commission form of government, which divided responsibility for city departments among three to five elected commissioners. The Galveston plan spread to other cities, and was refined into a city manager plan, in which a single administrator, appointed by an elected city council, operated the business affairs of the city. First adopted in Staunton, Virginia, the city manager plan was widely employed in other cities.

In city after city, reformers swept into office. Tom Johnson of Cleveland typified this reform sentiment. By the age of 30, he had made a fortune in streetcar companies. Then he read Henry George's bitter critique of wealth, *Progress and Poverty* (1883). He sold his stock and ran for mayor on a campaign to reduce streetcar fares. During his nine years in office, starting in 1901, he introduced clean, well-lighted streets, public baths, market inspections, public parks, and better sanitation.

Johnson's program became a model for municipal reform in many cities. Progressivism in the cities succeeded in improving municipal services and making city government more efficient. In many cities, public utilities and transportation services were taken over by publically owned companies.

The expansion of public services, however, often brought increased property taxes that alienated middle-class voters. Also, divisions among reformers over such issues as **prohibition** often led to political defeat at the polls. As a consequence, political bosses often regained control of government. For example, after being ousted briefly in 1901, New York City's dominant **political machine,** Tammany Hall under Charles Croker and Charles Murphy, regained power in New York City in 1903. William Vare controlled Philadelphia; Edward Crump dominated the Democratic machine in Memphis into the 30s; and the Pendergast brothers reigned in Kansas City.

REFORM MOVES TO THE STATE LEVEL. Nevertheless, the reform spirit rose from the cities up to the states. Reformers won control of many state governments. In California, Hiram Johnson became governor on a campaign to "Kick Southern Pacific Out of Politics." After leading an investigation of life insurance company abuses, Charles Evans Hughes became governor of New York in 1906. After enacting the first maximum hour law for women workers, Oregon elected William Uren as governor. Uren also established the first state laws for voters to govern directly through ballot **initiatives** and **referenda** and to remove officials through recall. Oregon adopted the first presidential primary in 1904. In the South, James Vardaman of Mississippi and Hoke Smith of Georgia led white farmers against corporate interests. During his three terms as governor of Wisconsin, Robert La Follette introduced the "Wisconsin idea" to restore democratic government through party **primaries** and to replace corrupt party conventions with primaries. La Follette also imposed the first state income tax, improved civil service, and regulated corporations.

Progressive reformers agreed on the importance of returning government to the people. In striving for this goal they sought to regulate economic activity, limit corporate influence in politics, and make government more economical and efficient. Yet a strong moral element in the progressive movement divided reformers. For example, after coming into office in 1910, California progressives achieved what Theodore Roosevelt described as the "greatest reform ever made by any state for the benefit of its people" through state constitutional amendments for the initiative, referendum, and legislation adopting women's suffrage and public utility regulation. Yet when they tried to legislate public morality by banning saloons, racetracks, and prostitution, California progressives became factionalized.

During these years, prohibition gained momentum in other states, particularly in the South and West. From 1906 to 1917, 21 states passed legislation prohibiting the sale and consumption of alcohol. By the time the eighteenth amendment to the Constitution was ratified in 1919 prohibiting the "manufacture, sale, or transportation" of intoxicating liquors, half the population already lived in dry areas.

The control of narcotics was another outcome of these years of reform. Many patent medicines contained narcotics. For example, opium could be found in "Mrs. Winslow's Soothing Syrup" for crying babies. Cocaine was used for hay fever medicine, and in small amounts in Coca-Cola until 1903, when it was replaced with caffeine. The Pure Food and Drug Act (1906) required most manufacturers to drop narcotics from their products. In 1909 Congress prohibited the importation of smoking opium, and in 1914 the Harrison Narcotics Control Act brought narcotics under federal control.

Theodore Roosevelt Brings Reform to the Nation, 1901-1909

Theodore Roosevelt's assertive leadership changed the nature of the presidency and made the federal government a more active player in the nation's economy. Though he accepted a place for large corporations, he opposed monopolistic control at the public's expense. Rather than serve the interests of industrialists, he believed government should be a broker between labor and management. He brought food and drugs under federal regulation and established programs to conserve the nation's natural resources.

William Howard Taft succeeded Roosevelt in the White House in 1909, but he proved to be a disappointment. Opposition to Taft split the Republican party and this rift enabled Democrat Woodrow Wilson to win the presidency in 1912. Wilson enacted the income tax, established a central banking system, and increased regulation of industry.

THEODORE ROOSEVELT ENTERS THE WHITE HOUSE, 1901. When Theodore Roosevelt catapulted into the presidency following the assassination of William McKinley in 1901, he focused the nation on progressive reform. Roosevelt quickly brought a vigorous, assertive leadership to the Executive Mansion, which he soon renamed the White House. Roosevelt promoted **antitrust** prosecution, consumer protection, conservation, and new industrial relations.

Roosevelt differed in many ways from previous presidents. Roosevelt had an exceptional personality. He had intellectual curiosity and expressed a conscious desire to be known in history as a prime mover. Afflicted as a child with a frail body and weak eyes, he was determined to prove he was physically equal to any man and intellectually superior to most. His well-publicized exploits and "charge" up San Juan Hill in Cuba during the Spanish-American War helped put him into the governor's mansion in New York, and then into the vice-presidency in 1901.

As president, Roosevelt first proceeded cautiously in his reform efforts. The Republican party was controlled by the "Old Guard" headed by Nelson Aldrich, senator from Rhode Island and an avowed spokesman for Wall Street, and Joseph B. Cannon, the autocratic speaker of the House. This Old Guard was self-consciously conservative and sought to protect the industrial, financial, and railroad interests of the country.

One of Roosevelt's first actions was to strike a deal with Aldrich. Following a visit to Aldrich's summer home in Rhode Island, Roosevelt agreed to leave alone the protective **tariff** and the monetary structure. In turn, he was allowed to propose railroad and antitrust legislation and enforcement. Roosevelt, who had earlier dismissed the trust question as Democratic partisan politics, understood that some action on this issue was necessary to appease an uprising in his own party from midwestern congressmen who became known as Insurgents. Led by men such as Robert La Follette (Wisconsin), George Norris (Nebraska), Albert Cummins (Iowa), and William Borah (Idaho), these progressive Republicans expressed a growing rebellion within the party.

Roosevelt immediately sought to strengthen the Interstate Commerce Commission (ICC), whose powers had been weakened in a series of court cases in 1896-1897 that limited its power to set rates. Roosevelt also moved to revise the Sherman Antitrust Act, which had also been weakened by the Supreme Court. In *United States v. E.C. Knight Company* (1895) the court had ruled that the Sherman Antitrust Act did not apply to manufacturing. To redress this situation, Roosevelt's administration filed 18 suits in the next few years against **trusts.** An investigation of Northern Securities, a holding company organized by J. P. Morgan that had brought together the Great Northern and Northern Pacific railroads, led to the first major antitrust suit. Shortly afterward, Roosevelt ordered the prosecution of the Swift, Armour, and Morris companies, the so-called Beef Trust, for organizing the National Packing Company. Successful antitrust actions were filed against Standard Oil in 1907 and the American Tobacco Company in 1908.

Even while conducting these actions against corporations, Theodore Roosevelt made a sharp distinction between good and bad trusts. He did not fear bigness *per se.* What he disliked was monopolistic control that thwarted the public interest. For this reason, Roosevelt later negotiated a series of gentlemen's agreements with Morgan interests. These arrangements occurred when Roosevelt initiated investigations into U.S. Steel and International Harvester. In both cases, Morgan agreed to open corporate books to the government with the stipulation that the president would have final authority on releasing the material to the public. It was also agreed that antitrust violations would be pointed out to the companies first, so they could correct the violation without going to court.

Roosevelt believed that government should serve the interests of neither labor nor capital. Rather, government was to be a broker between them. This attitude became evident in his first year in office when he confronted a national crisis brought about by a coal strike. In May 1902, 150,000 miners of the United Mine Workers Union under John Mitchell struck to gain a pay increase, an eight-hour day, and union recognition.

The mine owners fiercely resisted the union's attempts to break their hold on the coalfields of Pennsylvania, Ohio, and West Virginia. Represented by men such as George Baer, president of the Pennsylvania and Reading Railroad, they refused to bargain. Baer captured the attitude of his fellow owners when he told the press that capital had a religious duty to break the strike. "The rights and interests of the laboring men," he declared, "will be protected and cared for — not by labor agitators, but by Christian men to whom God in his infinite wisdom has given control of the propertied interest of the country."

Finally, Roosevelt forced mine owners to come to the table after a threat to call in federal troops. As a result, a commission granted the miners a substantial pay increase and a shorter work week. Although the union did not gain recognition, this episode marked the first time in the nation's history that a president had entered a dispute to defend the rights of labor.

In 1904 Roosevelt ran for the presidency in his own right by campaigning on what he described as a "square deal" for the American public. His task was made easier when the Democrats, tired of Bryan's defeats in 1896 and 1900, nominated conservative Alton Parker. Roosevelt's margin of victory was the greatest since Andrew Jackson's defeat of Henry Clay in 1832.

ROOSEVELT CAPITALIZES ON SOCIALIST STRENGTH. The election was significant in another respect: the Socialist party's nominee, Eugene Debs, increased his vote from 88,000 in 1900 to over 400,000 in 1904. The election showed the country moving leftward. Moreover, the party became a significant force in states as disparate as New York, Wisconsin, and Oklahoma. In 1911 Socialists won mayoral elections in 18 cities and towns, as well as state legislature seats in Rhode Island and New York. In all, 1,150 Socialists held office in 36 states. Socialist newspapers prospered. Julius Wayland's *Appeal to Reason,* published in Kansas, circulated 300,000 copies. Moreover, Socialist leaders gained control of a number of unions within the American Federation of Labor.

In 1905, Socialist party leaders, including "Big Bill" Haywood, played a key role in organizing a more militant union, the Industrial Workers of the World (IWW). The Wobblies, as they were known, prided themselves on "organizing the unorganized" — from lumberjacks in Louisiana to miners in Colorado. In 1912, the IWW gained national attention when Wobbly leaders assisted women strikers in their walkout against the American Woolen Company in Lawrence, Massachusetts. Although the strike ended in a victory for the workers, the IWW refused to sign a contract because contracts went against the union's radical principles.

The growth of radical politics in these years strengthened Roosevelt's hand in his second term. Playing on the fear of revolution, Roosevelt pushed reform legislation, including consumer regulation. In 1905 socialist Upton Sinclair wrote a series of muckraking articles exposing the sickening conditions in which sausages and cold cuts were processed in the Chicago meat plants (for example, floor sweepings were added to the sausage). As a consequence of Sinclair's exposé, which was the basis of a novel, *The Jungle* (1906), Roosevelt supported passage of the Meat Inspection Act (1906). The Pure Food and Drug Act (1906), through the Food and Drug Administration, sought to end fraud in patent medicines and the sale of adulterated foods and drugs. Much of this effort to reveal the use of dangerous chemicals and false advertising in drugs was credited to Dr. Harvey W. Wiley, chief chemist in the Agriculture Department.

Roosevelt's love and appreciation of nature led him to undertake a program to conserve the nation's natural resources. An avid lifelong birdwatcher and hunter, Roosevelt worried that the nation's timber and mineral resources were being rapidly depleted. In his first term, he secured passage of the National Reclamation Act (1902), which allowed proceeds from public land sales to be used for irrigation projects in the Southwest. He also appointed his friend Gifford Pinchot, a wealthy Pennsylvania environmentalist, to head the U.S. Forestry Service. In this position, Pinchot applied scientific resource management to federally owned lands. Following Pinchot's advice, Roosevelt designated more than 200 million acres of public lands, as national forests, mineral reserves, and potential water power sites. Roosevelt rejected the more radical ideas of John Muir, the founder of the California Sierra Club, who sought to preserve wilderness areas from any commercial development.

Still, Roosevelt avoided issues of tariff and monetary reform, in keeping with his agreement with Senator Aldrich. This decision had unfortunate consequences. A wave of bank failures in 1907 created a financial panic on Wall Street. Only assistance from J. P. Morgan and his associates prevented a complete financial collapse. Roosevelt's association with Morgan did little to hurt his overall popularity with the American people.

TAFT DROPS ROOSEVELT'S REFORM BANNER. Roosevelt's popularity remained so strong among the electorate that he was able to pick his own successor, William Howard Taft. In 1908, Taft easily won the Republican nomination and defeated William Jennings Bryan.

Taft perceived himself to be a progressive. Temperamentally, however, he was cautious and legalistic. Weighing well over 300 pounds, Taft presented a much different figure from the athletic Theodore Roosevelt. For this reason, many of Taft's contemporaries underestimated his abilities and later accomplishments. Although Taft misread the full momentum and emotion of the reform movement, he agreed to take on the issue of the tariff. He proved to be more active than Roosevelt on the matter of antitrust suits. With the Mann-Elkins Act (1910), he extended ICC control over telephone and telegraph.

Taft alienated the Insurgents in his own Republican party over the matter of tariff reform. He believed that the tariff should be lowered, and supported a bill to reduce rates. The bill passed the House, but when it came before the Senate, Nelson Aldrich drafted an alternative bill that raised rates on hundreds of items. The final bill that was signed into law in 1909, the Payne-Aldrich Tariff, was clearly **protectionist.** Taft nonetheless praised it as the "best tariff bill that the Republican party ever passed."

Taft's relations with the Insurgents became further estranged when progressive Republicans in the House revolted against the poker-playing, Old Guard Speaker of the House, Joseph G. Cannon of Illinois. Underestimating the power of the Insurgents, Taft sided with Cannon — a mistake soon revealed when the House stripped Cannon of his powers to appoint members to committees.

Taft's final break with the progressives came in 1910. Gifford Pinchot, head of the Forestry Service, accused Taft's Secretary of the Interior, Richard A. Ballinger, of collusion with Morgan interests in the sale of public land in Alaska. Ballinger was a conservative Seattle lumber baron in favor of private development of natural resources. Accusations of collusion involving Morgan immediately attracted national attention. Taft backed Ballinger and fired Pinchot. Theodore Roosevelt, now retired, openly broke with Taft. Any hope for reconciliation with Roosevelt disappeared when Taft filed an antitrust suit against U.S. Steel for the acquisition of the Tennessee Coal and Iron Company — an acquisition Roosevelt had personally approved during the Panic of 1907.

REPUBLICANS SPLIT: DEMOCRATS UNITE. The stage was set for an all-out fight between Taft and Roosevelt for the **GOP** nomination. Roosevelt formally entered the race in February 1912. He entered primaries in 13 states, winning primary after primary against both Taft and Insurgent Robert La

Follette. At the GOP convention that summer, however, Taft won the nomination by controlling delegates from New York, the South, and the nonprimary states. Nearly 300 delegates stormed out of the convention in protest. Shortly afterward they met to form the Progressive party.

The mood of the Progressive's convention was like that of a Protestant religious **revival.** The convention opened with the delegates singing the old Christian gospel song, "Onward Christian Soldiers." The party pledged itself to a minimum wage for women, child labor legislation, social security insurance, womer˙ suffrage, and national health insurance (which had been endorsed earlier ᴏy the American Medical Association). Theodore Roosevelt accepted the Progressive party's nomination, promising to roar like a bull moose during the campaign. Bull Moose stuck as a label for the newly formed party.

The Democrats also turned to a progressive, Woodrow Wilson, the former president of Princeton University who had startled political insiders when he won the governorship of New Jersey in 1910. Wilson received the nomination on the 46th ballot, only after Bryan threw his support to Wilson. A native Virginian raised in Georgia, Wilson appealed to the old Democratic South and the northern middle-class reform vote.

The Socialists turned to Eugene Debs, who advocated the restructuring of capitalism through government ownership of railroads, grain elevators, mines, and banks.

1912: THEODORE ROOSEVELT VERSUS WOODROW WILSON. The election of 1912 showed that the great majority of Americans were progressive, if not rebellious. With all four candidates favoring reform, the contest came down to Theodore Roosevelt versus Woodrow Wilson. At issue was the question of how to regulate corporate trusts. Theodore Roosevelt advocated a "New Nationalism" — a phrase coined by the editor of the *New Republic,* Herbert Croly. Roosevelt accepted the emergence of large industry, but called upon the federal government to regulate industry and protect consumers and workers. Wilson drew from the thinking of a young lawyer Louis Brandeis, in proposing what he called a "New Freedom." This program called for the break-up of large industry and the return to a competitive market economy. Roosevelt denounced Wilson's program as "Rural Toryism."

On election day Wilson received only 42 percent of the popular vote, but won 41 of the 48 states. Wilson won approximately six million votes, while Roosevelt received four million, Taft three million, and Debs nearly 900,000. Wilson won a majority of the popular vote in only 14 states, mostly in the South. The split in the Republican vote put the Democrats into the White House for the first time since Grover Cleveland.

WOODROW WILSON AND THE TRIUMPH OF PROGRESSIVISM. No other president had such a rapid rise as Woodrow Wilson, who rose from university president to governor of New Jersey and then to the presidency in three years. He now sought to use his good fortune to promote a progressive agenda. Wilson pressed for tariff reform, enacted a new income tax after the sixteenth amendment was ratified in 1913, sought to regulate industry through creation of the Federal Trade Commission, and established a central banking system, the Federal Reserve.

On his first day in the White House he called a special session of Congress to revise the much-reviled Payne-Aldrich Tariff. When protectionists threatened to defeat the new tariff, Wilson lashed out against the **lobbyists** and threatened to force senators to reveal their personal corporate holdings. The Underwood Tariff significantly lowered rates for the first time since the Civil War. To make up the lost revenue, Wilson turned to an income tax, made possible by the **ratification** of the sixteenth amendment. Through the efforts of a young congressman from Tennessee, Cordell Hull, a graduated income tax bill was enacted in 1913.

Wilson's next great reform measure was the Federal Reserve Act (1913). This act combined private control of local banks with federal, regulatory supervision. It also established the banking system still in use today, with a Federal Reserve Board and 12 district banks. This Federal Reserve system was given the right to issue paper currency. It also controls the nation's money supply by setting the amounts of money member banks must keep on hand and the interest rates at which member banks borrow from the system.

In 1914 Wilson turned to other questions of reform. The Clayton Antitrust Act (1914) prohibited competing firms from sharing holding companies and prohibited people from serving as directors of competing firms. That same year, Wilson's administration created the Federal Trade Commission to investigate unfair trade practices. During a threatened railroad strike, Wilson intervened to prevent a national shutdown of the lines and then signed the labor-supported Adamson Act that provided an eight-hour day for railway workers.

Wilson's reform record, however, was marred by his segregationist policies toward African-Americans. This was most evident in Wilson's support of his postmaster general, who issued orders to segregate black and white postal employees. Wilson also allowed his secretary of state, William Jennings Bryan, to appoint a white to the post of ambassador to Haiti, traditionally held by a black American.

As the election of 1916 approached, progressivism appeared to have spent itself. The outbreak of war in Europe in 1914 presented an ominous warning that foreign events were overwhelming domestic issues. Increasingly, Wilson's attention turned to international affairs — first in the western hemisphere and finally in Europe.

Conclusion

The activist years from 1901 to 1916 transformed Americans' expectations concerning government. During this period federal policy was actively extended in the areas of antitrust, consumer protection, conservation, banking, and industrial relations. In the process, a new relationship developed between government and business.

The growth of government — with its coinciding growth of bureaucracy and expertise — appeared necessary to protect democratic government. Ordinary Americans supported — and even demanded — activist government. Yet the emergence of big government created a deep ambivalence on the part of many people toward a federal government that seemed distinctly remote.

Recommended Readings

DOCUMENTS: W. E. B. DuBois, *The Souls of Black Folk* (1903); and William Allen White, *The Old Order Changeth* (1910).

READINGS: (GENERAL AND SOCIAL REFORM) Paul Boyer, *Urban Masses and Moral Order in America* (1978); Robert H. Bremmer, *From the Depths: The Discovery of Poverty in the United States* (1956); John D. Buenker, John C. Burnham, and Robert M. Crunden, *Progressivism* (1977); John Chambers II, *The Tyranny of Change: America in the Progressive Era* (1980); John Milton Cooper, Jr. *The Pivotal Decades* (1990); Susan Curtis, *A Consuming Faith: The Social Gospel and Modern American Culture* (1991); Allen Davis, *Spearheads for Reform: The Social Settlements and the Progressive Movement* (1967); Alfred Ekrich, *Progressivism in America* (1974); Samuel Hays, *Conservation and the Gospel of Efficiency* (1959); Richard Hofstadter, *The Age of Reform* (1955); Morton Keller, *Regulating a New Economy* (1990); Gabriel Kolko, *The Triumph of Conservatism* (1963); Richard L. McCormick, *Progressivism* (1983); William O'Neill, *The Progressive Years* (1975); James T. Patterson, *America's Struggle Against Poverty* (1981); Martin J. Sklar, *The Corporate Reconstruction of American Capitalism* (1988); Robert Wiebe, *Businessmen and Reform: A Study of the Progressive Movement (1962).* (WOMEN) Paula Baker, *Gender and the Transformation of Politics: Public and Private Life in New York* (1989); Ruth Bordin, *Women and Temperance* (1981); Nancy F. Cott, *The Grounding of Modern Feminism* (1987); Aileen Kraditor, *Ideas of the Woman Suffrage Movement* (1965); and David Morgan, *Suffragists and Democrats* (1972); William O'Neill, *Divorce in the Progressive Era* (1967); Robyn Muncy, *Creating a Female Dominion in American Reform* (1991). (PRESIDENTS) Donald Anderson, *William Howard Taft* (1973); John Blum, *The Republican Roosevelt* (1954) and *Woodrow Wilson and the Politics of Morality* (1954); John Milton Cooper, Jr. *The Warrior and the Priest: Woodrow Wilson and Theodore Roosevelt* (1983); Lewis Gould, *Reform and Regulation* (1978); Arthur Link, *Woodrow Wilson and the Progressive Era* (1954).

23

✛

GLOBAL POWER AND
WORLD WAR

CHAPTER OVERVIEW: Following the Spanish-American War, the United States emerged as a world power. Theodore Roosevelt and William Howard Taft extended American influence in Latin America and Asia. Prior to the outbreak of World War I, the United States intervened militarily in Haiti, the Dominican Republic, Nicaragua, Panama, and Mexico. With the outbreak of war in Europe, it proved difficult for Woodrow Wilson to maintain American neutrality and the United States was finally pulled into World War I.

War proved to be the nemesis of progressive reform. Wilson had called for "New Freedom" to restore the free market, but with war the economy became more centralized and regulated. Wilson called for a "war for democracy," but the very brutality of war led Americans to become disillusioned with reform at home and abroad. Wilson watched the repression of civil liberties at home in 1919, renewed conflict between labor and management, and the worst race riots in the nation's history.

Progressive Foreign Policy Before
the First World War

After the Spanish-American War, the United States became increasingly involved in the affairs of Latin America and Asia. As a world trade power, the United States wanted to streamline international shipping by linking the Pacific and Atlantic oceans with a canal in Central America. When Central American authorities balked, Theodore Roosevelt encouraged a revolution in Panama and quickly made a deal with the new government to build a canal there.

His successor, William Howard Taft, used American investment to encourage stability in the Caribbean and Latin America,

456

but did not hesitate to intervene in a Nicaraguan civil war. The next president, Woodrow Wilson, intervened in a Mexican civil war. His inept pursuit of the rebel Pancho Villa in northern Mexico showed how unprepared America was for war.

THEODORE ROOSEVELT CARRIES A BIG STICK AND WINS A PEACE PRIZE. In the early 1900s, American foreign policy focused increasingly on events in the western hemisphere. At the end of the Spanish-American War, the United States had acquired the Philippine Islands, Guam, Hawaii, Puerto Rico, as well as secured a protectorate over Cuba. In the ensuing years, the United States intervened in the affairs of Haiti, the Dominican Republic, Nicaragua, Panama, and Mexico.

America's place in the world seemed assured by the nation's economic position in international trade. In the two decades after the Spanish American War, American exports doubled. Manufactured goods outsold agricultural products as sewing machines, typewriters, automobiles, tractors, electric machinery, cigarettes, and soft drinks were shipped to every corner of the world. American investments in foreign countries quadrupled in these years. So prominent were American firms in Europe that many worried about the "Americanization" of the Old World.

America's prominent economic position imparted new meaning to Theodore Roosevelt's call for the nation to become a world power. Although Roosevelt quoted an African proverb — "speak softly and carry a big stick" — to describe his foreign policy, he was often given to saber-rattling rhetoric when discussing international affairs. While he proceeded cautiously in domestic affairs in his first term, he moved boldly abroad. Here he found a large enough arena to display his irrepressible energy, his need for action, and his vision of America as a global power.

The most dramatic episode in Roosevelt's presidency came in 1903, only two years after he entered the White House. The Spanish-American War had convinced many Americans of the need for a canal linking the Pacific and Atlantic oceans. During the hostilities, it had taken 68 days for the battleship *Oregon* to steam from San Francisco around the horn of South America to Cuba. Most Americans believed that Nicaragua offered the best opportunity for such a canal, although some preferred the isthmus of Panama, which then belonged to Colombia. In November 1901, Secretary of State Hay had negotiated a treaty with the British (the Hay-Pauncefote Treaty) that recognized American's plan to build a canal. (Britain also held claim to the territory through an earlier treaty).

The eruption of a volcano in Nicaragua confirmed the decision to build the canal in Panama. In 1881 a French company had started construction of

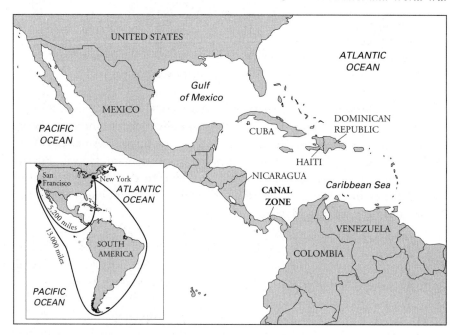

Map 23.1. The Panama Canal

a canal across Panama, but after the loss of 20,000 lives and $300 million, the company proposed selling its holdings to the United States for $40 million. At this point Roosevelt ignored the French offer and completed negotiations with Colombia through the Hay-Harran Treaty to purchase a six-mile strip across the isthmus for $10 million in cash, along with a lease of $250,000 a year. The U.S. Senate ratified the Hay-Harran Treaty while the Colombian government, under pressure from nationalists, balked. An outraged Roosevelt organized an insurrection in Panama against the Colombians and sent a battleship to prevent Colombian troops from suppressing the revolution. In 1903 the State Department recognized Panama only 40 minutes after hearing of the revolution. Twelve days later Panama's new ambassador to the United States signed a treaty stipulating that the United States pay $10 million in cash to Panama. The canal opened in 1914. Only after World War I did Colombia receive $25 million in compensation for the loss of the canal zone.

Roosevelt felt little need to justify his actions. Firmly believing that the nation should play a major role in world affairs, he asserted that the United States had a special mission in Latin America. He articulated this role in what became known as the Roosevelt Corollary to the Monroe Doctrine. Speaking in response to a threat by European powers to invade the Dominican Republic, which had defaulted on its loans, Roosevelt declared that the Monroe

Doctrine forbade European interference in Latin America. He emphasized that under certain circumstances the United States had the obligation to intervene in the internal affairs of Latin America if hemispheric interests were threatened. In this role, the United States operated the Dominican Republic's customs service from 1905 to 1907.

Roosevelt also extended American influence in Cuba. Under the Platt Amendment (1901) to the original United States protectorate over Cuba, American troops occupied the country from 1906 to 1909 and from 1917 to 1923. By 1920, American investment in Cuba had grown to $500 million.

While Roosevelt talked tough, his greatest legacy in foreign relations was as a peacemaker. In 1905, Roosevelt intervened on his own initiative to arbitrate the war that had broken out between Japan and Russia in 1904. Most observers believed that Russia, with its massive army and navy, would easily defeat Japan. Then, Japan caught the Russian fleet in a surprise attack at Port Arthur, Manchuria. European leaders began to worry that a Japanese victory would disrupt the balance of power in the Far East.

At this point, Roosevelt's personal diplomacy led the Russians and the Japanese to sign a peace treaty in Portsmouth, New Hampshire in 1905. The Portsmouth agreement recognized Japan's sovereignty over Korea and gave Japan territorial concessions in Manchuria. For his efforts, Roosevelt won the Nobel Peace Prize in 1906. Roosevelt favored Japanese claims in part because he hoped to turn Japan's ambitions away from the Pacific. Still, Japanese public opinion held that Roosevelt had sided with Russia during the negotiations. Lest the Japanese think America too weak, the following year Roosevelt sent American battleships — the "Great White Fleet" — around the world as a show of force to the Japanese government. Roosevelt also sent American representatives in 1907 to the Netherlands to an international disarmament conference at the Hague, and agreed to American participation in establishing the Permanent Court of International Arbitration, the Hague Tribunal.

TAFT PURSUES DOLLAR DIPLOMACY. From 1909 to 1913 Roosevelt's successor, William Howard Taft, continued the policy of exerting American influence in world affairs. Taft's "dollar diplomacy" sought to link American business with pro-American economic elites throughout the Caribbean and Latin America. He believed that American investment would usher in political and economic stability.

Taft showed he was even more willing than Roosevelt to use military power to protect American interests in the Caribbean and Latin America. When a revolt broke out in Nicaragua in 1909 against the anti-American government of José Zelaya, Taft supported the rebel Adolfo Diaz. Diaz overthrew the government, but when the new legislature refused to allow the

United States to manage its customs house and refinance its debt, Taft dispatched a warship to Nicaragua to ensure that the new government would be pro-American. When the "Zelayistas" launched a counterrevolution in 1912, Taft sent 2,500 marines to suppress the revolution. When the marines finally withdrew 21 years later in 1933, rebel resistance still had not been broken.

WILSON ESPOUSES IDEALISM IN FOREIGN POLICY. Woodrow Wilson sought to bring a new idealism to American foreign policy during his presidency (1913-1921). Wilson's first term reflected this idealism when he denounced dollar diplomacy as a guise for **imperialism.** Wilson, however, was no less interventionist than his predecessors: he sent troops to Haiti in 1915, extended American financial supervision over the Dominican Republic, and renewed controls over Cuba in 1917.

He intervened in the revolution in Mexico, where Americans had extensive investments. He sent warships to the waters off Veracruz in 1914 to halt arms shipments to the revolutionary government he opposed, then sent a detachment of marines to occupy the city. In March 1916, Mexican rebel General Pancho Villa led attacks against the U.S. cavalry stationed at Columbus, New Mexico, and killed 17 Americans. Wilson responded by ordering 11,000 troops under General John Pershing to cross the Mexican border to pursue Villa. For nearly a year, Pershing chased Villa and his army around northern Mexico before the rebels withdrew further south.

The American expedition proved to be a farce and revealed just how unprepared the United States was for war. Machine guns jammed, trucks and horse-drawn wagons were unavailable, and airplanes were in such poor repair that only two were in flying order.

America Reluctantly Enters
the First World War

When war erupted in Europe, Wilson tried to stay neutral, but the United States unofficially helped Britain and its allies. After Germany began attacking American ships near Britain, the United States protested and forced Germany to place a moratorium on submarine warfare. Americans were sharply divided over whether to enter the war or stay out. Wilson tried to improve military preparedness without alienating peace activists. After barely winning reelection in 1916, he tried unsuccessfully to broker peace in Europe. Finally, in April 1917, the United States declared war on Germany.

WILSON PLEDGES NEUTRALITY. In June 1914, a Serbian nationalist assassinated the heir to the Austro-Hungarian empire. A month later, Austria-Hungary declared war on Serbia. Soon every major power in Europe was in the war.

The nations of Europe divided into two warring alliances: the Triple Alliance, or Central powers, included Germany, Austria-Hungary, and Turkey; the Triple Entente, or Allied powers, included France, Great Britain, Russia, and Japan. Italy, initially linked with the Central powers, struck a bargain and joined the Allied powers in 1915.

German troops quickly drove through neutral Belgium in order to attack France. When the Germans, however, failed to crush France, the war in western Europe became a bloody stalemate. At this point each side sought to destroy the warmaking capabilities of the other. Britain imposed a naval blockade against Germany. Germany, realizing that Britain depended on overseas trade for military supplies and food, waged submarine warfare to sabotage British shipping lines.

Wilson favored the Allies but wanted to keep America out of the war. He therefore urged the American people to maintain their neutrality "in thought as well as action." This proved easier said than done. The war cut heavily into American exports. The situation worsened when English financial interests began dumping their American stocks, causing a drain on American gold reserves. Heavy trading forced the London Stock Exchange to close on July 31, 1914. This led to the closing of the New York Stock Exchange, which did not reopen until November. Unemployment, already high before the war, reached 11.5% by late 1914. By spring 1915, however, the Allies' demand for American supplies had created a wartime boom.

Wilson's policy of neutrality reflected deep divisions among the American people. Of the 92 million Americans in 1910, more than 32 million were of immigrant stock — either they or their parents had immigrated to the United States. Among those were 8 million German-Americans and 4 million Irish-Americans, who shared deep-rooted animosity toward England. Also 3 million Jewish-Americans had fled **anti-Semitism** in Russia and distrusted that country's participation in the Allied cause. A number of neutrality groups were organized to keep America out of the war. They included the Friends of Peace, the American Embargo Conference, the American Neutrality League, and the American Truth Society.

Allied demands for American goods placed a strain on Wilson's policy of neutrality. Loans were needed to buy American goods. In October 1914, Wilson began approving credits to the British and French. By 1917, American investors had advanced more than $2 billion to the Allies, while only $27 million had gone to Germany.

THE WEB OF WAR TIGHTENS. Wilson believed that even though the United States and Britain were tied together by a common culture and tradition, a policy of neutrality must be maintained, especially regarding the principle of freedom of the seas. This principle was deeply rooted in American foreign policy since at least the War of 1812. This principle was challenged, however, when the British declared the whole North Sea a war zone. As the war dragged on, Britain extended its **embargo,** warning that all ships suspected of carrying goods to enemy destinations would be liable to search and seizure. Britain also warned that vessels transporting goods via neutral ports were subject to being stopped. These actions provoked Wilson to declare, "I am, I must admit, about at the end of my patience with Great Britain."

In response to the British **blockade,** Germany declared in February 1915 that all ships entering the waters surrounding the British Isles were subject to attack by submarines, the German **U-boats.** Shocked by a new type of warfare that violated the traditional practice of stopping enemy vessels on the high seas and providing for the safety of passengers, Wilson warned that Germany would be held to "strict accountability" for any loss of American lives or property. In the spring of 1915, a series of German attacks on American ships created division in the administration about the proper response. Secretary of State Bryan believed that American citizens should be warned not to travel into the war zone. Other officials — including the State Department's Robert Lansing, Ambassador to Great Britain Walter Hines Page, and Wilson's advisor Colonel Edward House — demanded strong actions, including breaking off diplomatic relations with Germany if U-boat warfare continued.

The sinking of the British passenger liner, *Lusitania,* on May 7, 1915, provoked a crisis. Among the 1,198 passengers lost were 128 Americans. The outraged American public called for a strong response. The United States demanded that Germany stop unrestricted submarine warfare and pay reparations to American families who had lost relatives on the *Lusitania.* Germany denied responsibility, citing a German advertisement in the New York newspapers that warned Americans not to sail on the ship. Germany also charged that the ship had secretly carried military provisions — a charge proven true decades later. Secretary of State William Jennings Bryan refused to send a message he thought would lead to war and resigned from the cabinet. His successor, Robert Lansing, showed no hesitation. Fearing war with the United States, the German government finally announced that vessels would not be sunk without warning. The crisis seemed to pass. Wilson's strong stance won public confidence at a time when many doubted his understanding of international affairs because of the fiasco in Mexico.

Events in Europe prompted some Americans to champion "preparedness" through the building of a stronger army and navy, and a universal **draft.** In

December 1914, proponents of preparedness, including former Secretary of War Elihu Root and Theodore Roosevelt, organized the National Security League. Leading the charge, Roosevelt vociferously criticized Wilson's policy of neutrality and his reluctance to take a stronger stand against German imperialism. Once a close friend of the **kaiser** — the German emperor — Roosevelt now demanded that America enter the war on the side of the Allies to prevent autocratic rule in Europe. Bitterly assailing Wilson for his lack of leadership, Roosevelt suggested that moral cowardice lurked behind the proclamations of neutrality.

At the same time, antiwar sentiment gripped the rural South and West, while many northeastern liberals and pacifists opposed any measures that might lead to America's involvement in the European war. Playing a significant role in this peace movement was a group of women, including the social worker Jane Addams and the suffragist Carrie Chapman Catt. On August 29, 1914, these women organized the first significant peace march when they paraded down Fifth Avenue in New York dressed in mourning. Shortly afterwards they formed the Women's Peace Party.

The cause, however, drew public ridicule when Henry Ford, the automobile manufacturer, tried to bring peace to Europe. In November 1915, he joined Jane Addams and a group of one hundred men and women in chartering a peace ship — the *Oscar II* — to sail to Scandinavia in an attempt to mediate an end to the war in Europe. Newspapers lampooned the ill-fated cruise, and the warring Europeans ignored the earnest, albeit naive, Ford and his fellow passengers. Nevertheless, peace advocates were far from dismayed.

AMERICANS DIVIDE. With the approach of the 1916 election, the nation was divided on the issue of war. When Henry Ford ran as a presidential peace candidate in the Michigan and Nebraska primaries — and did well — peace activists were encouraged. At the same time, in Preparedness Day parades in Chicago and other industrial cities, thousands of workers marched, revealing strong support in the country for rearmament.

In the election of 1916, Wilson sought to steer a middle course between the peace and preparedness factions by pledging himself to a progressive program of social legislation, neutrality, and reasonable preparedness. He failed to endorse women's suffrage, but commended it to the states. Against his better instincts, he allowed his campaign managers to employ the antiwar slogan, "He kept us out of war." His Republican opponent, former progressive governor of New York, Charles Evans Hughes, ran as a progressive, endorsed women's suffrage, and promised peace.

Wilson won the election. Barely. He carried the Far West and the South, winning the popular vote 9 million to Hughes's 8.5 million, and the **electoral**

college by 277 to 254. He was the first Democrat to succeed himself since Andrew Jackson.

WAR DECLARED, JUNE 1917. Less than three months after the election, Germany announced a renewal of its policy of unrestricted submarine warfare. The German high command risked war with the United States to hurl a knockout punch in a major spring offensive against the Allies. On February 3, 1917, Wilson announced that the United States had severed diplomatic relations with Germany. Shortly afterward, the American press published a diplomatic note allegedly sent from the German Foreign Secretary Arthur Zimmermann to his minister in Mexico proposing an alliance between Germany and Mexico. The Zimmermann Telegram, which the British claimed to have intercepted but which was actually created by British intelligence, promised Mexico financial aid and the return of Texas, New Mexico, and Arizona if Mexico would support Germany. A brilliant act of espionage, the forged message terrified the American public.

A short time later, another bombshell exploded when revolution overthrew Russia's czar. In America, Russian Jews, Poles, and Scandinavians came out in support of the war to defend the new democratic government in Russia. Economic interests, traditional alliances with Great Britain, a fear of German imperialism, and democratic sentiment moved Wilson toward the Allies.

On April 2, 1917, Wilson asked Congress to declare war against Germany. He declared, "The world must be made safe for democracy." The war resolution overwhelmingly passed the Senate by a vote of 82 to 6. The dissenting votes included Republican progressives Robert La Follette and George Norris. The House concurred by a 373-50 vote. Among the opponents was Jeannette Rankin, a recently elected pacifist and feminist from Montana, a state that had enacted woman suffrage. Wilson signed the declaration of war on Good Friday, April 6. He privately admitted feeling depressed that the American people so willingly entered into war.

America Goes to War, 1917-1919

Once in the war, the United States went all-out to win it. Millions of men volunteered or were drafted into the military, but industrial and government inefficiency hampered the war effort. The government reorganized and centralized the economy. Women took jobs to fill labor shortages. Labor generally cooperated, but socialists and strikers were harassed. Dissent was forcibly suppressed through both legislation and vigilante groups.

The arrival of 500,000 fresh American troops in Europe in 1918 broke the military stalemate, leading to the surrender of Germany. Wilson tried to ensure an enduring peace by establishing the League of Nations, but opposition frustrated his idealistic plan. Economic readjustment after the war led to a series of bitter labor strikes, fears of a communist conspiracy, and race riots following the migration of southern blacks to the North.

AMERICA MOBILIZES FOR WAR. In late June 1917, the United States sent a token force to France. Shortly after he arrived, American commander General John Pershing requested an additional million troops by the following spring. In order to supply this manpower, Wilson had accepted the necessity of conscription through the Selective Service Act of May 1917. In June registration for the draft began for 9.6 million men. More than 300,000 failed to register. Before the armistice ending the war in Europe was signed in November 1918, the government had prosecuted 10,000 men for evading the draft.

The most dramatic instance of organized opposition to the draft occurred in Oklahoma in the "Green Corn Rebellion." Oklahoma was a hotbed of **populism** and western-bred **socialism.** On draft day a loosely organized army of 900 men gathered — mostly poor black and white **tenant farmers** — to march on Washington. They expected other "armies" of protesters to join them. The marchers, however, were rounded up by a local posse before much happened.

More than four million men served during World War I in the armed forces of the United States. Some army **regiments** gained fame, such as the "Fighting Sixty-Ninth," a New York Irish regiment that had been founded in the Civil War. African-American troops constituted 13 percent of those who served. Some black regiments, such as the "Ninety-Second," were as well-known as Irish and state regiments. General John Pershing, having commanded African-American troops in the Philippines, denounced racism, but black troops nevertheless experienced **segregation** and discrimination. A black officers' training program was created in May 1917 after students at black institutions like Howard University, Fiske University, and Tuskegee Institute demanded one.

Racism continued throughout the war. Black officers assigned to the "Ninety-Second" were prevented from rising above the rank of captain. Bringing together black troops and white southern troops also created tensions. On August 1917, members of the Twenty-Fourth Infantry's Third Battalion — an African-American unit — opened fire on white tormentors in Houston, killing 17 of them. As a consequence, 13 black soldiers were executed.

The United States committed huge numbers of men and quantities of resources to win the war. This was a total war involving armies, civilians, and
industry. Approximately 2 million Americans crossed the Atlantic, and 1.4
million saw combat. To finance its armed forces, the government spent $33.5
billion — $23 billion from loans and $10.5 billion from taxes. The United
States mobilized its industry and directed its resources for total war production.

Congress moved to mobilize American industry in 1916 when it created
the advisory Council of National Defense, composed of six cabinet officers
and seven civilian experts. Subsequently, the government began to extend its
control to a wide range of industries, creating what some would later call
"wartime socialism" (the coordination of industry by government during the
war). Although such a description misconstrues the key role private enterprise
played in the war effort, wartime controls did provide an experiment in government planning that was remembered in the 1930s.

The federal government built ships through the United States Shipping
Board, operated railroads through the Railroad War Board, managed agriculture through the Food Administration, and procured coal and oil through the
Fuel Administration. Under Herbert Hoover, the Food Administration encouraged farmers to expand production with guaranteed high prices for their
crops. During the war, land under cultivation increased by 203 million acres.
Hoover's Food Administration also popularized the slogan, "Food will win
the war," by urging Americans to economize through "Wheatless Mondays,"
"Meatless Tuesdays," and "Porkless Thursdays." Through the Lever Act
(1917), Hoover (who also served as head of the Fuel Administration) controlled the production, distribution, and price of coal and oil in the United
States.

An alarming rise in prices and production bottlenecks in certain strategic
industries in early 1918 led to more radical measures. Previously, in July
1917, Wilson established the War Industries Board (WIB) to oversee the war
effort. Finally, at the urging of Bernard Baruch, a Wall Street **speculator,**
Wilson expanded the powers of the WIB to fix prices and to set priorities for
the production and manufacture of goods. The War Industries Board became
the most important agency created during the war because of its overall powers to allocate resources and coordinate production.

Wilson also established the War Labor Board to arbitrate wages. Organized labor made great strides during World War I. Membership in the
American Federation of Labor increased from approximately 2 million members in 1914 to 3.2 million in 1919. While labor never relinquished its right
to strike, the AFL's president Samuel Gompers tried to ensure cooperative
relations with the Wilson administration to help win the war. During the war

wages increased, but so did food prices. Some companies experimented with cost-of-living increases. This caused later tensions between labor and management as the war drew to a close, but generally cooperation prevailed.

Labor shortages triggered by the vast numbers of men who joined the armed forces created new opportunities for women, who made **munitions,** operated elevators, and took on increased clerical duties in offices. Still, female workers earned less than men. For example, males earned between $2.24 and $2.64 a day in munitions plants while females doing the same job got $1.36 to $2.24 a day. Furthermore, gains made by women workers in employment disappeared at the end of the war when men returned to their civilian jobs. By 1920 fewer women worked for wages than in 1910.

The government also promoted the war effort through newspapers, newsreels, and public speakers. Wilson created the Committee on Public Information, headed by George Creel, a progressive Denver newspaperman who initially had opposed the war. Creel hired a remarkable group of journalists, artists, and entertainers to sell the war to the public. More than 75,000 "Four-Minute Men" were organized to sell Liberty Bonds, plead for fuel conservation, and promote patriotism.

DISSENT SUPPRESSED. Shortly before America's entry into the First World War in 1917, President Wilson declared "Once lead this people into war and they'll forget there ever was such a thing as tolerance." Wilson's words proved prophetic. As war approached, there was a spontaneous outburst of patriotism throughout the nation. Theodore Roosevelt denounced the "hyphenated American" — those Irish-Americans, German-Americans, and others who called for a policy of neutrality.

New patriotic groups were formed including the American Defense Society, the National Security League, and the Boy Spies of America. More than 250,000 people volunteered to aid the Justice Department watch immigrants from Germany, Austria, and Hungary. Fanatics randomly attacked German-Americans in Montana, Minnesota, and Wisconsin. German-sounding streets were renamed in Milwaukee, Chicago, and St. Louis. Bismarck, North Dakota, nearly lost its name. Public schools throughout the Midwest banned the teaching of German. Iowa outlawed speaking the German language. The New York Philharmonic stopped playing music by German composers. German measles became "liberty measles"; sauerkraut was renamed "liberty cabbage."

More drastic action came with the enactment of the Espionage and Sedition Acts (1917-1918). These acts made it unlawful to criticize the government or war policies. Accordingly, government denied mail privileges to Socialist party newspapers, including *The Masses* and the *Milwaukee Leader,* even though the party had split over the war. These laws also led to the prosecution of 1,500 dissenters for such acts as criticizing the Red Cross and the YMCA. One movie producer was sentenced to ten-years imprisonment for negatively portraying the English allies in a film about the American Revolution. In Chicago more than a hundred Industrial Workers of the World (IWW) leaders were put on trial for antiwar activity. Most were convicted. While awaiting appeal, radical labor leader Big Bill Haywood jumped bail and fled to the new Soviet Union. In 1918 the leader of the Socialists, Eugene Debs, drew a ten-year sentence for declaring that wars were fought by the working class in the interests of the **capitalist** class. In 1920 Debs ran for president and received nearly a million votes — while still in prison. The Supreme Court upheld the Espionage and Sedition Acts in *Schenck v. United States.* Free speech, the court ruled, could be restricted if it posed a "clear and present danger" to society.

AMERICAN TROOPS BATTLE IN EUROPE. The arrival of fresh American troops proved decisive. Russia's withdrawal from the war in November 1917, following the **communist (Bolshevik)** revolution allowed Germany to concentrate on the Western Front in France and Belgium. In mid-1918 the Germans launched an offensive against the French forces in the second Battle of the Marne. They failed and in September more than 500,000 American troops began to roll back a crumbling German army at St. Mihiel, Belgium. Two weeks later, American **divisions** broke through the German line in France in the Meuse-Argonne district. This action cost 117,000 American casualties, including 26,000 dead. By November 1918, the Germans were in full retreat.

THE WAR ENDS IN DISILLUSIONMENT. As the end of the war approached, Wilson set forth his program for peace. Speaking before a joint session of Congress on January 8, 1918, Wilson articulated his Fourteen Points for an enduring peace. He called for freedom of the seas, free trade, arms reduction, and self-determination for various nationalities. Point 14 expressed Wilson's greatest hope — the establishment of the League of Nations composed of all countries, great and small. The League, in Wilson's farsighted view, was to provide both a forum for the peaceful resolution of disputes and a global alliance to punish wrongful aggressors.

By the early fall of 1918, the Central Powers collapsed. The abdication of the German kaiser in November amid riots and revolutionary fervor finally brought an armistice on November 11, 1918. The war continued only in Russia where the Allied nations sent troops to aid the "White" forces attempting a counterrevolution against the Bolsheviks (the **"Red"** forces). Some

8,000 Americans joined the 100,000 Allied troop expedition, but this intervention failed. Not until April 1920 did Wilson withdraw American forces from Soviet territory.

Wilson insisted on attending the Paris peace conference that convened in January 1919. He became the first president to travel outside the United States while in office. Wilson wanted to ensure a lasting peace, but he became so absorbed in shaping the final peace treaty that he made crucial political mistakes. His relations with the Republicans in Congress were already strained. In 1918 Wilson had campaigned vigorously to keep a Democratic Congress, but the Republicans had won. He worsened matters when he selected a peace delegation that deliberately excluded prominent Republicans.

The huge European crowds that greeted Wilson upon his arrival in Paris in December 1918 also misled him. In Paris Wilson proved to be a skillful negotiator with the representatives of the leading victorious nations: Britain's David Lloyd George, France's Georges Clemenceau, and Italy's Vittorio Orlando. Wilson sought a forgiving peace, but to achieve his goals, Wilson first had to agree that Germany should pay high war **reparations** to Belgium and France, demilitarize the German Rhineland, and to accept ten years of French control of the coal-rich German Saar Basin. In return he gained self-determination for eastern European nations, including Poland, Hungary, and Czechoslovakia. His greatest victory was winning support for establishing the League of Nations.

WILSON FAILS TO ACHIEVE A LASTING PEACE. Wilson returned home in February 1919 with a draft of the League **charter**. He seemed impervious to rumblings from Republicans led by the powerful chairman of the Senate Foreign Relations Committee, Henry Cabot Lodge, who stated that the League charter was unacceptable "in the form now proposed." Wilson returned to Europe a month later to finish the negotiations. In June the Germans reluctantly signed the final treaty at Versailles, formally ending the war.

In July Wilson returned to present the Versailles Treaty to the Senate. He expected the Senate to accept "this great duty." After all, a third of the state legislatures and 33 governors had endorsed the League of Nations. In his absence, however, the Republicans had been brooding. Lodge personally disliked Wilson. He wrote, "I never thought I could hate a man as I hate Wilson." Moreover, many ethnic groups — the Germans, Italians, and Irish — disliked the final peace that had taken so much and given so little to their old countries. The Senate soon divided into three groups. Wilson loyalists backed the treaty, while the "irreconcilables" opposed any American participation in the League of Nations. Somewhere in the middle were the "reservationists" who called for amendments before accepting the treaty.

Wilson believed he spoke for the American people. In September he decided to take his case directly to them. In a whirlwind speaking tour by train that covered 8,000 miles in 22 days, he gave 32 major addresses. He was driven by passionate idealism, but the strain began to show. Finally in Pueblo, Colorado, signs of exhaustion became apparent. Ordered by his doctor to return home, Wilson on October 2 suffered a severe stroke that slurred his speech and paralyzed his left side. His active political career effectively ended, and while the government drifted, his wife Edith managed most of Wilson's affairs. In March, 1920, the Senate failed to muster the necessary two-thirds majority to **ratify** the treaty. Wilson, now an reclusive invalid, placed all hopes on the election of 1920.

AMERICA DEMOBILIZES ONLY TO SEE RED. The end of the war created additional problems at home. Wilson's administration had not prepared for the massive influx of job seekers as the troops returned home. Cancellation of war contracts hurt many businesses. Although pent-up consumer demand and overseas trade created a brief economic boom in 1919, consumers seethed as prices began to rise sharply. That year more than 4 million workers went on strike. These economic problems led congressmen to warn Wilson that the domestic economy was "far more important than the League of Nations."

The first signs of labor discontent occurred in Seattle, Washington, when 35,000 shipyard workers walked off their jobs. By early February the city was paralyzed as 60,000 other workers, influenced by the locally powerful IWW, went out in support of the shipyard workers. Seattle came to a standstill, and the business community was terrified. The week-long general strike was finally broken by imported nonunion labor and the vehemently antilabor mayor of Seattle, Ole Hanson, who called the strikers "Bolsheviks."

Strike activity throughout the country heightened fears of a communist conspiracy to incite labor violence. In September 1919, one of the most dramatic strikes took place in Boston, when most of the police force walked out demanding a union. After two days of looting, Governor Calvin Coolidge called out the National Guard to restore order. When the striking police offered to return to work, the police commissioner fired them all. Coolidge declared, "There is no right to strike against the public safety by anybody, anywhere, anytime." These words brought him national attention and later a vice-presidential nomination on the Republican ticket in 1920.

Also in September 1919, the steel workers went out on strike when Judge Elbert Gary, chairman of U.S. Steel, refused to discuss the union's demand for an eight-hour day. Led by a former **Wobbly** who had close ties to the newly organized Communist party, more than 600,000 workers were out on strike. Steel firms retaliated brutally. Police and strikebreakers broke up strikers' meetings and picket lines. By January the union admitted defeat and told its members to return to work.

The steel strike overshadowed developments in the railroad industry. Railroad unions had begun agitating for the "Plumb Plan," developed by union attorney Glenn Plumb, which called for federal ownership of the railways. The plan found few advocates outside the unions, and in 1920 Congress returned railroads to private operation under ICC regulation. With the defeat of the steel strikes and the failure of the Plumb Plan, unions began to experience a decline in membership, falling from more than 5 million workers in 1920 to a low of 3.4 million in 1930 — a mere 6.8 per cent of the nonagricultural work force.

Many Americans believed these labor strikes showed communist conspiracy at work. Following the Bolshevik revolution in Russia in 1918, American radicals split from the Socialist party to form two rival communist parties. The emergence of a communist movement in the United States frightened authorities and the general public. In the spring of 1919, paranoia increased when bombs were mailed to Ole Hanson, the antilabor mayor of Seattle, and to a former senator from Georgia. Shortly afterward, postal workers discovered 36 similar bomb packages destined for high officials.

United States Attorney General A. Mitchell Palmer, a former Quaker who entertained presidential aspirations, warned the nation of a communist uprising. Such rhetoric encouraged members of the American Legion and other groups to break up Labor Day parades and attack meetings of leftist groups including Socialist party headquarters in many cities. In November 1919, Palmer launched his most dramatic assault against the "Reds." Directed by J. Edgar Hoover, head of the Justice Department's new "alien-radical" division, federal officers rounded up thousands of "radicals," as well as innocent aliens caught in the dragnet. In December, 249 foreign-born radicals, including Russian-born anarchist Emma Goldman, were deported to the Soviet Union on a ship nicknamed the *"Soviet Ark."* Amid this excitement, the New York state legislature expelled those members who belonged to the Socialist party.

ETHNIC AND RACIAL TENSIONS MOUNT. In addition to labor troubles and fears of communism, the nation also experienced heightened racial and ethnic tensions. Signs of these tensions were evident even before American entry into the war. Most notable was the case of Leo Frank in Georgia. A Jew from the North who had become superintendent of a southern textile mill, Frank was accused of raping and murdering Mary Phagen, a 14-year-old factory worker. The case attracted the attention of northern liberals such as Jane Addams, who protested the trial. Despite inconclusive testimony, Frank was sentenced to death.

After much protest, the governor of Georgia commuted the sentence. White supremacists were furious. Tom Watson, the former Populist vice-presidential candidate, linked the war against the Germans to protecting southern white women at home. He warned, "When 'mobs' are no longer possible, liberty will be dead." On a summer night in 1915, 25 men broke into the Georgia jail where Frank was being held, kidnapped him, drove him 175 miles across the state, lynched him, and then mutilated the body. Less than two weeks later, a Methodist minister and longtime salesman, William J. Simmons, inaugurated a new **Ku Klux Klan** at a public ceremony on top of Stone Mountain, ten miles from Atlanta.

Tensions between whites and blacks became especially pronounced in northern industrial centers, which recruited heavily from the South to meet labor shortages. Between 1915 and 1917 close to a half million blacks moved from the South to the North. This migration followed the decline of cotton farming in the South, which was triggered largely by an infestation of boll weevils that destroyed the cotton crop. Those blacks who moved north aspired to better jobs and freedom from racial bondage. As one black wrote from Birmingham to a northern newspaper, "i am in the darkness of the south and i am trying my best to get out . . . o please help me get out of this low down county i am counted no more than a dog."

Most northern cities were ill prepared for this migration. Blacks could live only in certain segregated neighborhoods, but the new arrivals caused overcrowding and stimulated higher rents, which led some blacks to seek housing in white neighborhoods. Racial tensions sometimes erupted into fierce confrontations. In July 1917, a bloody race riot broke out in East St. Louis, Illinois, when whites, supported by the mayor and police chief, invaded the black district of town and burned houses with tenants still inside. An estimated 48 men, women, and children died. Shortly afterward, a similar riot occurred in Chester, Pennsylvania.

The year 1919 brought new racial troubles. That summer as many as 15 cities suffered race riots. The worst occurred in Chicago in July and claimed the lives of 23 blacks and 15 whites. The riot began on a hot day when a black boy strayed into a customary "white" bathing area along Lake Michigan and was stoned to death by a mob of white youths. Federal troops were called in to end the rioting.

Conclusion

As his second term drew to a close, Wilson was broken in mind, body, and spirit, no longer a leader of his generation, but a martyr for a future generation that was to emerge during a second world war. By 1920 the idealism of Wilsonian democracy had given way to disillusionment. The dream of a reformed society, with equitable distribution of wealth, harmony between the social orders, and peace in the world, had been displaced by a profound desire on the part of most Americans to return to what Republicans called "normalcy" — the traditional American values of family, capitalistic enterprise, and individualism.

Recommended Readings

DOCUMENTS: e. e. cummings, *The Enormous Room* (1934); Henry Berry, *Make the Kaiser Dance* (1978); Addie Hunton, *Two Colored Women with the American Expeditionary Forces* (1971).

READINGS: (NEUTRALITY) John Coogan, *The End of Neutrality* (1981); John Cooper, *The Vanity of Power: American Isolationism and the First World War* (1969); Patrick Devlin, *Too Proud to Fight* (1974); Ross Gregory, *The Origins of American Intervention* (1977); Roland Marchand, *The American Peace Movement and Social Reform* (1973); Ernest May, *The World War and American Isolationism* (1959). (WAR) Arthur Barbeau and Henri Florette, *The Unknown Soldier: Black American Troops in World War I* (1974); Edward Coffman, *The War to End All Wars* (1968); Frank Freidel, *Over There* (1964); Paul Fussell, *The Great War and Modern Memory* (1975); Maurine Greenwald, *Women, War and Work* (1980); N. Gordon Levin, Jr. *Woodrow Wilson and World Politics* (1968). (HOMEFRONT) Valerie Conner, *The National War Labor Board* (1983); Robert Cuff, *The War Industries Board* (1973); Ellis Hawley, *The Great War and the Search for Modern Order* (1979); Robert Haynes, *A Night of Violence: The Houston Riot of 1917* (1976); David Kennedy, *Over Here: The First World War and American Society* (1980); Frederick Luebke, *Bonds of Loyalty: German-Americans and World War I* (1974); Paul Murphy, *World War I and the Origins of Civil Liberties* (1979); Barbard Steinson, *American Women's Activism in World War I* (1982). (PEACE) Robert Ferrell, *Woodrow Wilson and World War I* (1985); Lloyd Gardner, *Safe for Democracy: The Anglo-American Response to Revolution* (1984); Thomas J. Knock, *To End All Wars: Woodrow Wilson and the Quest for a New World Order* (1992); Arno Mayer, *Politics and Diplomacy* (1965); Charles Mee, Jr., *The End of Order, Versailles, 1919* (1980); William Widenor, *Henry Cabot Lodge and the Search for an American Foreign Policy* (1980). (AFTERMATH) David Brody, *Labor in Crisis* (1965); Stanley Coben, *A. Mitchell Palmer* (1963); William Tuttle, Jr. *Race Riot: Chicago in the Red Summer of 1919* (1970).

24

———— ✖ ————

THE PARADOX OF THE 1920S

CHAPTER OVERVIEW: The 1920s appear full of contradictions and paradoxes. During this decade Americans supported the enactment of prohibition — outlawing the sale of alcohol — yet a significant subculture emerged around distributing and drinking illegal alcohol. In this decade of rapid social and cultural changes, conservative ethnic enclaves flourished around urban neighborhoods, social clubs, and religious institutions. While social scientists welcomed the "modern age," the Ku Klux Klan and religious fundamentalism attracted wide support.

Americans overwhelmingly elected Republicans to the White House, while, in general, displaying little interest in domestic politics and international affairs. The Harding administration (1921-1923) was marred by scandal, yet it achieved major domestic and foreign policy initiatives. President Calvin Coolidge (1923-1929) espoused the values of free enterprise, yet extended federal regulatory powers over business. Herbert Hoover (1929-1933) called himself progressive, but left office in the midst of an economic depression, denounced as a reactionary.

Americans Enjoy a Decade of Prosperity

Even though agriculture and certain industries suffered, the 1920s was a decade of prosperity. Americans enjoyed a higher standard of living and a better quality of life than ever before. Mass culture emerged through movies, radio, recorded music, and popular stage entertainment.

Though discrimination remained, minorities also found new opportunities. Women had won the right to vote and had begun to fill important places in politics and society.

AMERICANS PROSPER. Americans enjoyed the 1920s with a heady confidence. Evidence in 1928 seemed to confirm this optimism. The **gross domes-**

tic product rose 40 percent, per capita income rose 30 percent, and industrial production climbed 70 percent. Unemployment remained low, prices stable. As a result, real earnings increased 22 percent for the average American worker.

American consumers went on a buying binge. The availability of electricity allowed middle-class American households to use vacuum cleaners, refrigerators, and sewing machines. By 1929, 60 percent of all families owned a car. The automobile enabled people to live farther from downtown areas, thereby extending suburbs. The automobile became a symbol of the decade, offering new freedom particularly to the nation's youth and its women.

The extension of consumer credit allowed American families to buy new homes, automobiles, and appliances. By 1926, an estimated 15 percent of all retail goods sold annually were on installment. "Enjoy while you pay" became the slogan of the day.

Although prosperity characterized the decade, not all groups participated equally. Many workers experienced sporadic unemployment because of seasonal layoffs. Agriculture did not prosper, nor did many industries including cotton textiles, railroads, and coalmining.

Following a golden age from 1897 through 1920, agriculture once again experienced depression. After overexpanding production during the First World War, American farmers faced declining prices for their crops. The loss of European markets because of high **tariffs** and new competition in Europe only worsened matters. By 1929 the average per capita income for farmers stood at approximately $220, while it was $879 for the nonfarm population. Farmers tried cooperative marketing through the assistance of the American Farm Bureau Federation. They were aided in these efforts when they received **antitrust** exemptions from the federal government. The most successful of these marketing combines were the California citrus growers who formed Sunkist.

In this period, labor unions and collective bargaining also declined. Total union membership fell from 5 million to less than 3.5 million. Corporations encouraged this turn away from unions by instituting pension plans, disability and health programs, savings and credit institutions, and educational and recreational activities for their employees.

Most Americans overlooked the period's failures and were caught up in the frenzied prosperity. Bruce Barton's bestselling *The Man Nobody Knows* (1925) typified the obsession with success. Barton portrayed Jesus as a businessman who had "picked up twelve men from the bottom ranks of business and forged them into an organization that conquered the world." During this decade self-improvement "how-to-succeed-in-business" books flourished. Dale Carnegie (no relation to Andrew) became a millionaire selling his program on public speaking to aspiring businessmen. American advertisers played upon middle-class anxieties about getting ahead. President Calvin Coolidge expressed the sentiments of the age when he declared, "The business of America is business."

MINORITIES AND WOMEN FIND NEW OPPORTUNITIES. While this emphasis on "success" was parodied and satirized at the time, the 20s were a time of breakthrough for many. The growth of managerial positions opened opportunities for many to enter the expanding middle class. While the decade revealed deep-seated **nativist** and anti-Catholic prejudices within the culture, including religious quotas at many colleges, the 20s was a period when many Jews and Catholics began to enter the professions in large numbers. Also, despite the wretched poverty in which most blacks lived, they attended colleges and universities in larger numbers.

Women also enjoyed new opportunities. Although most women occupied a separate sphere as traditional homemakers, many gained recognition in this decade in sports, business, education, and politics. Following the **ratification** of the nineteenth amendment to the Constitution women finally gained the right to vote in 1920. Putting the new **franchise** to use, the year 1924 proved to be a banner year for women political candidates. In 1924 Nellie Taylor Ross became the first woman chief executive when she won the governorship of Wyoming. Ross later became the first woman director of the United States Mint under Franklin D. Roosevelt. That same year Miriam "Ma" Ferguson won the governorship of Texas.

MEDIA CREATES MASS CULTURE. The spread of a burgeoning mass culture through movies, radio, and advertising characterized this decade. Although mass culture tended to standardize the way Americans lived, it did not produce a fully homogenized society. Many working people and recent immigrant ethnic groups maintained older values and emphasized family relationships.

The popularity of movies was a key element in the emergence of mass culture. In 1922 more than 40 million movie tickets were sold each week. Seven years later, the introduction of sound, beginning with *The Jazz Singer* and *Don Juan,* attracted even larger audiences. Weekly attendance grew to 100 million. Blue-collar workers were particularly attracted to movies and spent a larger percentage of their incomes on "picture shows" than did the middle class.

Radio burst on the scene in 1920 when station KDKA in Pittsburgh broadcast the returns of the Harding-Cox presidential election. Few heard the broadcast since only a handful of people owned receivers. But radio quickly became popular.

Throughout much of the decade, small, independent radio stations dominated the market. Fundamentalists, those most opposed to modernism, ironically proved particularly aggressive in using the radio to evangelize the nation. The passage of the Radio Act of 1927 transformed the radio industry by requiring all radio stations to reapply for licenses under federal supervision, thereby driving out many of these independents. By the end of the decade, there were 8,000 broadcasting stations organized into two major networks, NBC and CBS, and two minor networks.

The growth of the record industry also characterized modern culture. Now all Americans could enjoy the same recording stars. The industry also allowed ethnic groups to preserve their heritage. For example, Italians listened to recordings of Italian opera sung by Enrico Caruso or folk songs recorded by ethnic bands. Ties to regional culture were preserved by country, "hillbilly," and "race" records performed by southern musicians. Jazz introduced whites to a black music form that had migrated from the South at the turn of the century. Whites enthusiastically took up black dances like the Charleston.

Mass journalism also grew with the introduction of the tabloid newspaper, syndicated features (including crossword puzzles and daily horoscopes), and news digests including *Reader's Digest* (1922) and *Time* (1923). Chain newspapers and national magazines encouraged mass advertising, which employed movie stars, radio personalities, and sports heroes to sell products to an audience which trusted and admired these popular figures. Advertising linked success and happiness to buying the right product. One ad told of how a businessman's career was being held back because of "faulty elimination" until he discovered Post Bran Flakes. Producers of Listerine mouthwash invented the word "halitosis" (bad breath) to exploit anxiety about personal hygiene.

Mass media made it possible for many to become national celebrities. Baseball stars such Babe Ruth became household names. American hearts went out to young Gertrude Ederle, who courageously swam the English Channel. The greatest of heroes, however, was Charles Lindbergh, who became the first person to complete a solo nonstop transatlantic flight from New York to Paris.

America Experiments with Prohibition

In 1920, the nation prohibited the sale and distribution of alcoholic beverages. This legislation received popular support, but Americans continued to drink. Widespread illegal drinking offered huge profits to the gangsters who provided alcohol, and organized crime permeated society. While many complained about the failure of prohibition, the law was not repealed until 1933.

AMERICANS OUTLAW THE SALE OF ALCOHOL—AND CONTINUE TO DRINK. The paradox of the decade was most evident in the era's boldest endeavor in moral reform, the **prohibition** of alcoholic beverages. Wartime prohibition came in 1917 and was written into the Constitution with the ratification of the 18th amendment. Although passed under a Democratic administration, prohibition found its greatest support within the Republican party, which campaigned throughout the decade on a platform of reducing the size of the federal government. Republicans did not see the contradiction in promoting prohibition, which involved greater government intervention, with a promise to reduce government.

In 1919 most Americans would have said that they favored prohibition. Indeed, the decade of the 1920s witnessed a decline in alcoholic consumption. Yet many Americans who favored prohibition did so on the grounds that other people should not drink. They intended to continue to drink themselves. Moreover, they took pride in their rebelliousness.

Most Americans continued to support prohibition, although with increasing reservations. The growth of organized crime and a popular culture that seemed to glorify drinking, gangsters, and having a good time caused many to change their minds about favoring prohibition. Many of the old industrial elite opposed prohibition. The banker J. P. Morgan laid by a personal supply of 1,000 cases of French champagne and prepared to wait out the law. These men argued that prohibition restricted private enterprise.

WOMEN DIVIDE OVER PROHIBITION. Women also split on the issue. Wives of many of these industrialists helped organize the Women's Organization for National Prohibition Reform, which sought to overturn prohibition. The principal proponent of prohibition, the Woman's Christian Temperance Union (WCTU), found itself isolated from elite opinion. Once an organization that attracted the socially prominent, the WCTU's membership increasingly became more middle class. Still the WCTU continued to uphold its prohibitionist principles with a kind of feminism. One well-known WCTU tract, Ella Boole's *Give Prohibition Its Chance* (1929), proclaimed that prohibition was women's chance to reorganize society.

The WCTU did not appeal to younger women, especially those in college and those who considered themselves part of the "smart" set. They saw prohibition as an expression of what they considered the repressive **Puritan** tradition. Alcohol, speakeasies, jazz — all represented freedom. Prior to prohibition, women were barred from saloons, which were part of male culture. In contrast, speakeasies opened their doors to women.

GANGSTERS THRIVE ON PROHIBITION. Behind the glamour of big-city nightclubs lurked gangsters and organized crime. These gangsters brought terror, murder, and corruption. These sinister aspects of American society were not new, but "modern" gangsters stimulated by huge profits became better organized. All parts of society were tainted. The chief of police in Chicago declared that "sixty percent of my police are in the **bootleg** business." As gangs struggled for control of illicit markets, war broke out in the streets. In Chicago between 1922 and 1926, 215 gangsters were killed by rivals. Police killed another 160.

Symbolizing this new era was Chicago's Al Capone. After killing seven members of Bugs Moran's rival North Side Gang on Valentine's Day 1929, Capone gained control of about 70 percent of Chicago's rackets. An estimated two-thirds of all labor unions paid Capone extortion. Grossing over $105 million a year, Capone's organization became a potent force in Chicago business and politics. Capone finally was brought to justice when the federal Prohibition Bureau set up a special team called the "Untouchables" headed by Eliot Ness. The Untouchables — so-called because they could not be "touched" by bribery — sent Capone to prison for income tax evasion.

The Rejection of Tradition

The emergence of mass culture coincided with a rejection on the part of many, especially in the city and among the young, of traditional culture. The 20s became characterized by youthful rebellion. In their search for freedom, many of the young found sexual freedom. Disillusioned by war and progressivism, young writers and artists encouraged this sense of rebellion by expressing disillusionment with tradition and idealism.

AMERICANS WORSHIP YOUTH AND SEX. Mass culture emphasized youth and sophistication. Closely linked to this culture was sex. In the 20s the "new woman" emerged. The new woman was independent, spirited, and slightly rebellious. She rejected the roles of both homemaker and of moral exemplar. Literary critic and essayist H. L. Mencken announced the arrival of the "American **Flapper**" in 1915, and in the 20s the flapper flourished. Noted for a distinct style that included blunt-cut short hair, left long at the front, often with bangs, dresses with hemlines above the knees and dropped waistlines, and caps pulled down over the ears, flappers captured the era's youthful rebellion.

The emergence of the new woman coincided with economic gains made by women. During World War I nearly 2 million women held jobs, a number that rose to 10 million by 1930. Some women revolted against traditional roles and masculine possessiveness. For some women, freedom did not mean sexual promiscuity, but the right to control their bodies. Margaret Sanger,

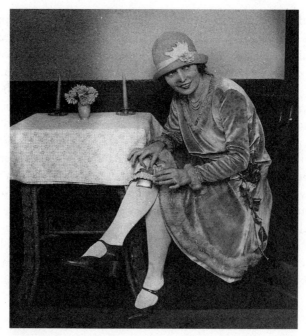

Novelist F. Scott Fitzgerald described the "flapper" as "lovely and expensive and about nineteen." In the Jazz Age, the flapper embodied a "boyish" look and rebellious youth's open rejection of Victorian morality. (Culver Pictures)

once sentenced to jail for advocating birth control (primarily condoms and diaphragms) now won approval for her promotion of birth control as a means of liberating women from the burdens of large families. Writer Charlotte Perkins Gilman warned, "Excessive indulgence in sex . . . has imperiled the life of the race."

For many younger women — and men — the search for freedom was often superficial. It meant little more than the right to enter a speakeasy or to smoke in public. Freedom became synonymous with sexual freedom. In throwing off Victorian restraint, Americans glorified sex.

WRITERS AND ARTISTS CHALLENGE TRADITION. The 20s marked a period when mass culture and high culture became closely intertwined. Mass culture was elevated through the Book-of-the-Month Club, regional theater, and middle-class art groups. For the first time, hundreds of cities established symphonies, and major orchestras were established in smaller cities such as Minneapolis, Rochester, and Atlanta.

Already disillusioned by World War I, American writers expressed their alienation from modern society and the progressive era's earlier confidence in human progress. In a group that Gertrude Stein called the "Lost Generation," novelists such as William Faulkner, F. Scott Fitzgerald, Ernest Hemingway, Sinclair Lewis, and John Dos Passos wrote about the limits of human progress, the futility of modern life, and their fear of the machine age. Only art seemed to be worth living for. The poet T. S. Eliot questioned even this conclusion in his poem "The Hollow Men" (1925).

The 1920 lso saw a renaissance among black writers, many of them associated with New York's Harlem. Langston Hughes, Claude McKay, Jean Toomer, and Countee Cullen expressed profound criticism of American society. By writing about the lives of blacks in northern cities and in the rural South, they introduced the general reading public to the problems of blacks in modern America.

The other arts continued to bloom from experimental roots that began before the war. Modern painting flourished with **cubists** such as Stuart Davis and Charles Shelter and **expressionists** such as Georgia O'Keeffe, notable for her large flower canvases and New Mexican desert scenes.

American culture in the 20s, contrary to its critics, was not a complete wasteland.

Changes Spark a Backlash

While many Americans welcomed social and cultural change, others looked to traditional values. Some Protestants turned to religious revivals, some to fundamentalism and antimodernist religious values. Fundamentalist efforts to outlaw the teaching of evolution in public schools climaxed in the "Scopes Trial." Some ethnic groups reacted to the homogenization of culture by asserting their ethnic identity. The Ku Klux Klan reformed to terrorize blacks, Jews, and Roman Catholics. Indians organized to protect their culture and African-Americans were inspired to promote their own businesses and culture.

TRADITIONALISTS DENOUNCE MODERNITY. Although most Americans welcomed the rapid transformation in social, cultural, and intellectual life in the 1920s, others, especially in more rural areas, resisted the change. They sought to restore traditional values, at least as they perceived them.

Religion in the 20s presented the greatest challenge to those who did not like the emerging order. Deep splits between religious liberals and conservatives only worsened the situation. Furthermore, church membership fell, especially among mainstream **Protestant** churches. Some Protestants reacted to this decline by undertaking **evangelical revivals.**

Conservative Protestants turned to **fundamentalism** — a literal interpretation of Bible. In their crusade, they saw the theory of Darwinian evolution as the corrupting force in the nation. They believed the Darwinian interpretation contradicted the Biblical view that the world was created in six days. Fundamentalists under the leadership of rural populist William Jennings Bryan won victories, restricting the teaching of evolution in Oklahoma, Florida, and North Carolina.

Their greatest success came in Tennessee in 1925 when the legislature passed a bill making it illegal for any teacher in a public school, including state universities, to teach a theory that denied the "divine creation of man as taught in the Bible." A high school biology teacher named John T. Scopes challenged the law to bring the issue before the court. The "Monkey Trial" in Dayton, Tennessee gained national attention when two of the most prominent lawyers in the country, Clarence Darrow (representing Scopes) and William Jennings Bryan (representing the state), confronted one another. Reporters flocked to Dayton, and the trial was broadcast nationally on radio.

The jury convicted Scopes, who was fined $100, but the real victory went to Darrow and other modernists. During the trial Darrow had made Bryan look foolish in the eyes of many Americans, especially when Bryan took the stand as an "expert witness" on the Bible. The 65-year-old Bryan died shortly after the trial. Fundamentalism, however, continued to thrive in parts of the South and the Midwest.

ETHNIC IDENTITIES STRENGTHENED. The reemergence of the **Ku Klux Klan,** which had emerged immediately following the Civil War and then declined, showed a pernicious desire to maintain the old ways. Reorganized in 1915 by a Methodist minister, William J. Simmons, the Klan grew rapidly after it was joined by two professional organizers, Edward Clarke and Elizabeth Tyler. From 1920 to 1925, the KKK grew from 2,000 to 2 million members. The KKK claimed to be for the "100 percent" native-born, white, gentile American. It was anti-black, anti-Jewish and anti-Catholic. Hiram Evans, who became head of the Klan, took the KKK into politics, where it gained a political foothold in many states. The Klan strongly supported prohibition. Scandals involving Klan members severely damaged the organization, so that by 1930 the KKK had dwindled to about 100,000 members.

While the Klan, with its lynchings and terrorist tactics, represented the worst aspects of an ethnic consciousness that swept over the nation, other groups experienced ethnic reawakening. In the Southwest, Native American

President-General of the Universal Negro Improvement Association, Marcus Garvey was 33 when this photo was taken at a Harlem parade. Garvey influenced other black nationalist leaders, including Malcolm X, in the 1960s. (AP/WORLD WIDE PHOTOS)

tribes in New Mexico organized to protect their culture from being weakened by white educators and missionaries. They protested the poor treatment of their children in government-run Indian schools and the attempts by officials to outlaw native religious practices.

An ethnic reawakening also occurred within the black community. Most prominent in this regard was Marcus Garvey, a Jamaican-born leader who promoted black nationalism through his Universal Negro Improvement Association (UNIA). Garvey's UNIA sponsored black-run commercial enterprises including the Black Star steamship line, a hotel, a printing plant, a black doll factory, grocery stores, restaurants, and laundries. His "Back to Africa" movement attracted tens of thousands of followers and large donations.

Garvey's program appeared radical, but it embraced capitalist standards of success. He promised "every Black Man, Woman, and Child the opportunity to climb the greater ladder of industrial and commercial progress." Garvey was convicted of mail fraud and deported in 1922 — he sold tickets for trips on a nonexistent line.

Black **capitalism** continued to expand in the African-American community, especially in the larger northern cities. Campaigns were launched to encourage blacks to shop at black-owned stores. This campaign particularly benefited undertakers, barbers, and beauticians, but also allowed for the creation of black-owned banks and insurance companies.

Harding Seeks "Normalcy," 1920-1923

Warren G. Harding swept into the White House in 1920 with his call for a "return to normalcy." Though the United States had become the world's leading economic power, Harding's administration reflected the nation's prevailing desire to isolate itself from international involvements and to promote narrow self-interest. Still, Harding played an instrumental role in international arms reduction and also arranged to reduce Germany's war reparations. Domestically, Harding pursued a probusiness program, for which critics accused him of soaking the poor to help big business.

Harding's inability to say no and his appointment of dishonest cronies to his administration resulted in extensive corruption and scandals. Just as these scandals were breaking, Harding died suddenly in 1923.

HARDING ELECTED, 1920. After a "war for democracy" that had seemingly left militarism and colonialism intact, Americans became **nationalistic,** ethnocentric, and conservative.

After nearly two decades of reform, Americans were tired of change. **Progressivism** as a political movement simply collapsed under the weight of a weary, disillusioned people easily distracted by popular diversions. As a consequence, progressives fragmented into special interest blocks including agriculture, labor, Indian reform, and **isolationism** in foreign affairs.

In 1920 the Republican convention became deadlocked and finally picked a weak compromise candidate, Senator Warren G. Harding of Ohio, who called for lower taxes, smaller government, and a "return to normalcy." He condemned the Democratic candidate James Cox and his running mate, Franklin D. Roosevelt, for their support of "Wilson's League." Instead, he proposed a new association of nations — a vague proposal that appealed to pro- and anti-League of Nations forces alike. On election day Harding won in a landslide, getting nearly twice as many votes as Cox.

HARDING PURSUES INTERNATIONALISM IN AN ISOLATIONIST PERIOD. In foreign policy, Harding sought peace and cooperation without involving America in the League of Nations. A deep fear of the outside world seemed to capture the American mind in this decade.

Nevertheless, World War I left America the world's leading economic power. By 1920 the United States had replaced Great Britain as creditor to the world. American trade accounted for some 30 percent of all international trade. As a result of its new status as a world power, the United States could not simply absolve itself from international problems. In October 1921, German-American relations were normalized with the ratification of the Treaty of Berlin. In the following years the United States developed an unofficial system of cooperation and consultation with the League of Nations, which had been organized without America's formal participation.

President Harding's greatest accomplishment in international affairs came in 1921 when Secretary of State Charles Evans Hughes brought the major world powers to Washington for a conference on arms reduction. Hughes called for scrapping warships and maintaining fixed naval ratios. As one observer remarked, in 30 minutes Hughes sank "more ships than all the admirals of the world had sunk in a cycle of centuries." By the close of the Washington Conference, three treaties had been signed pledging that the five leading naval powers (the United States, Great Britain, Japan, France, and Italy) would restrain the naval arms race by limiting the construction of battleships over 10,000 tons for ten years. The five powers also agreed to a fixed ratio that left the British and American navy at 525,000 tons, the Japanese navy at 315,000 tons, and the French and Italian navies at 175,000 tons each.

The Four Power Treaty pledged Britain, the United States, Japan, and France to respect each others' Pacific possessions. The Nine Power Treaty (the five major powers plus China, Belgium, Portugal, and the Netherlands) promised that the leading powers of the world would respect Chinese sovereignty and maintain an **"open door" policy** toward Chinese markets. Later critics found much to criticize in these treaties, especially after the outbreak of World War II, but at the time, Americans welcomed Harding's peacekeeping efforts.

Among the most serious problems confronting the Harding and subsequent Republican administrations in the 1920s were issues of war debts and war **reparations.** Allied war debts amounted to some $26.7 billion, mostly owed to the United States and Britain. France remained the principal debtor nation. To ease their debts the Allies, contrary to Wilson's wishes, had imposed heavy war reparations on Germany. Germany, however, found itself unable to make its reparation payments in 1922-1923. Finally, in January 1923 France and Belgium sparked an international crisis when they marched into the German Ruhr district to seize the coal mines.

In this crisis American and British pressure forced France and Belgium to withdraw their troops. Hughes then convened a commission headed by Charles Dawes, a Republican with close ties to Wall Street. After months of negotiations, France, Britain, and Germany accepted the Dawes Plan which reduced Germany's annual reparation payments and set a new payment schedule. American financial interests also agreed to extend loans to Germany. The United States still insisted on debt payments from the Allies — even though it maintained high tariff barriers that restricted their ability to sell goods to earn money to pay their debts. This created a circular arrangement: Americans extended loans to Germany, Germany made reparation payments to France and Great Britain, and France and Great Britain continued to make payments to the United States, which maintained a high tariff barrier.

HARDING FOLLOWS A MODERATE PATH DOMESTICALLY. Harding's domestic policy called for cuts in government expenditures and a probusiness program built around high tariffs and low taxes. While the federal budget was reduced, public activities were expanded in a number of areas. For example, Secretary of Commerce Herbert Hoover's department was enlarged, and federal mail subsidies for the fledgling airline industry were increased. Federal aid for state and local highway construction grew from $20 million in 1920 to $90 million in 1929.

Secretary of the Treasury Andrew Mellon, one of the country's richest men, actively advocated federal income tax cuts. The top rates, which applied to high-income Americans, were reduced in 1921, and again in 1924, 1926, and 1927. This trend led the Democrats to accuse the Republicans of following a policy of soaking the poor to finance big business. Mellon argued, however, that reduced taxes for the rich meant further capital investment in production and the creation of new jobs.

Harding's probusiness policies also entailed a general hostility to labor. In 1921 Harding approved the use of federal troops to restore order following a strike in West Virginia's coal mines. The following year the nation's railroads were shut down by a strike. Attorney General Harry M. Daugherty obtained sweeping court injunctions prohibiting strike activity.

Nevertheless, Harding's administration was far from **reactionary.** Harding opposed peacetime sedition laws and pardoned Eugene Debs, who had been convicted of sedition during World War I. Harding also refused to support white supremacy within the Republican party in the South. He chided southerners on their discriminatory practices toward blacks and urged the passage of a federal antilynching law. He also appointed a record number of women to his administration, including Mabel Willebrandt as assistant attorney general for prohibition enforcement. Lucille Anderson became the first woman to enter the diplomatic service. Still, Harding did not champion complete cultural **pluralism.** He declined to use the federal government to stop the terrorism of the Ku Klux Klan, and he opposed the equal rights amendment, which would have explicitly recognized equal rights to women under the U.S. Constitution.

HARDING'S ADMINISTRATION MARRED BY SCANDAL. Corruption finally overwhelmed Harding's administration. The president was jovial and a friend to everyone — he simply could not say "no." This inability proved to be his downfall. His administration was pulled into the spotlight after the assistant to Attorney General Harry Daugherty committed suicide. He ran a private house on K Street in Washington, where the so-called Ohio Gang — Harding and his associates — met to play poker and drink bootleg whiskey. His suicide prompted congressional investigations that revealed the depth of corruption in the administration. Investigators discovered that the attorney general had allowed the Department of Justice to sell hundreds of pardons to bootleggers, wartime **profiteers,** and tax evaders. The Office of Alien Property had arranged for confiscated property to be transferred to a bogus claimant. The director of the Veterans Bureau, Charles Forbes, was indicted for embezzling $200 million in departmental funds.

In the midst of these scandals, Senate investigations revealed that Secretary of the Interior Albert Fall had received payoffs in the form of "low interest loans" from oil executives who were leasing Navy-owned oil reserves. The Senate probe showed that oil executive Edward Doheny had given Fall a $100,000 "loan" shortly before he gained drilling rights to federal land in Elk Hills, California. In the case of Teapot Dome, Wyoming, Harry Sinclair had given Fall $223,000 in government bonds and $85,000 in cash. Although Sinclair and Doheny escaped conviction, Secretary of the Interior Fall went to prison.

The depth of the scandals shocked even the president. He told a confidant, "I have no trouble with my enemies . . . but my damn friends . . . they're the ones that keep me walking the floor nights!" Just as these scandals were breaking, the deeply worried and depressed Harding suffered a heart attack and died in July 1923. His death unleashed a flood of exposés about his drinking, gambling, and sexual affairs. A former mistress claimed that Harding had made love to her in a White House clothes closet and had fathered her illegitimate child.

Coolidge Calms the Nation, 1923

Calvin Coolidge (1923-1928) brought to the presidency stability after the debacle of the Harding era. He continued Harding's isolationist foreign policy, while bringing honesty to government. Domestically, he cut taxes and spending. Prosperity enabled Americans to feel removed from world affairs. An expression of this isolationist sentiment was the National Origins Act (1924), which limited non-Anglo-Saxon immigration. Coolidge's greatest foreign policy success was the signing of the Kellogg-Briand Pact, intended to outlaw war. He also intervened in Nicaragua to stop a civil war.

COOLIDGE OFFERS STABILITY. Republicans scrambled to dissociate themselves from Harding. Vice-President Calvin Coolidge, who stepped into the White House following Harding's death, appeared to be perfect for this task. Raised in Vermont, Coolidge seemed nearly a caricature of rural New England reserve. The honest, simple Coolidge believed that the duty of the citizen was to serve God and society, and that big business offered American society prosperity, social stability, and opportunity for individual advancement.

Coolidge moved quickly to clean up the scandals within the administration by forcing Harry Daugherty to resign as attorney general. Although once aligned with the moderate-progressive wing of the Republican party in Massachusetts, Coolidge pursued a conservative program of reducing taxes and expenditures, including military spending. He continued Harding's isolationist policies, modified by America's participation in international peace agreements.

In 1924 Coolidge sought the presidency in his own right. Easily nominated, he defeated Democratic rival John W. Davis, a conservative Wall Street lawyer who was nominated in a bitter fight after 104 ballots, and the Progressive candidate, Robert La Follette, senator from Wisconsin.

COOLIDGE FOLLOWS THE REPUBLICAN AGENDA. Coolidge articulated a conservative Republican philosophy but rejected **laissez-faire** economics. Coolidge supported Secretary of the Treasury Mellon's initiatives for further tax reduction and a program of cutting government expenditures.

President Coolidge also called for greater federal enforcement of prohibition as well as the "prevention and punishment against the hideous crime of [Negro] lynching." He asked Congress to expand agricultural and medical education for blacks. (Coolidge, however, appointed few blacks to federal offices, even though African-Americans continued to actively support the Republican party). Despite his professed belief in limited government, he supported federal regulation of Alaskan fisheries, coastal water pollution, radio broadcasting, and aviation. His administration supported additional funds for highways and reforestation. He also proposed to privatize the postal system.

On the other hand, Coolidge called for budget cuts, including reductions in defense spending. Defense expenditures fell so low that Colonel Billy Mitchell, an advocate of air power, accused the American high command of "incompetency, criminal negligence and almost treasonable administration of national defense." Mitchell was court-martialed for these statements and discharged from the service.

American's desire for isolation from world affairs found expression, in part, in the passage of the National Origins Act of 1924. Based upon a belief that the Anglo-Saxon stock was being weakened by immigration from eastern and southern Europe, as well as Asia, the law set ethnic quotas based upon the composition of the American population in 1890. The act excluded Asian immigration altogether. Outraged, the Japanese in Tokyo declared the day the act passed, July 1, 1924, "Humiliation Day."

Isolationist sentiment rested on a prospering economy that allowed Americans to remain self-satisfied and removed from world affairs. The Republican party encouraged this belief in "Coolidge prosperity." Yet agriculture presented a striking example that not all was well. Although California and Florida citrus farmers prospered, most American farms foundered after the war. Farm debts doubled from 1915 to 1922, while crop prices remained soft. Farmers on marginal land — especially in the northern Great Lakes states, the Ozarks, and Appalachian areas — felt the brunt of depressed conditions.

As American farming failed to come out of the doldrums, a "farm bloc" in Congress — drawn mostly from midwestern agricultural states — began to press for more radical measures to save agriculture. They pressed for a remedy that came to be called "McNary-Haugenism." Proposed by Senator Charles McNary (Oregon) and Representative Gilbert Haugen (Iowa), the plan called for the federal government to support domestic farm prices by purchasing surplus agricultural goods at **"parity"** (equivalence) to the pre-World War I price. These surpluses were to be sold abroad at lower prices. While Congress passed McNary-Haugen bills in 1927 and 1928, Coolidge refused to sign them into law.

Liberals enjoyed few successes in these years. Their plans for a Tennessee valley administration to bring cheap power to that region was defeated when Coolidge vetoed the measure. Their most important victory came in the area of federal Indian policy. After a well-organized campaign by Native Americans, Coolidge ordered an investigation of the federal Indian Service. The investigation's final report called for major reforms in Indian education, governance, and aid. This marked the beginnings of a major shift in Indian policy for the first time in 50 years.

COOLIDGE SEEKS WORLD PEACE. President Coolidge's greatest "triumph" came in the late summer of 1928, shortly before he left office, when his new secretary of state, Frank Kellogg, negotiated a treaty with France and 14 other nations to renounce war as an instrument of national policy except in cases of self-defense. The Kellogg-Briand Pact (1928) outlawed war. Coolidge rejoiced, as did isolationists such as Senator William Borah of Idaho. Republicans appeared to have fulfilled Wilson's dream of a world safe for democracy — without American participation in the League of Nations.

In Latin America, Coolidge sought to develop a pan-American alliance. But revolutionary upheavals in Mexico and Nicaragua led to calls for Coolidge to send in the marines. Coolidge finally capitulated to this pressure in 1927 when he ordered 5,000 marines into Nicaragua to put down a civil war. Coolidge's action unleashed a storm of criticism in the United States and Latin America, but a special diplomatic mission headed by Henry L. Stimson, who had been secretary of war for Taft, led to a truce and an agreement to hold democratic elections in Nicaragua. Only one small rebel band, under Augusto Sandino, refused to lay down their arms and accept the election results. American troops began withdrawing from Nicaragua in 1931.

Hoover Elected: Prosperity Collapses

Herbert Hoover easily defeated his Democratic opponent, Al Smith, in the presidential election of 1928 in a landslide. Smith, a Roman Catholic, a New York Democrat, and "wet", proved a poor match for Hoover, a Protestant, midwestern Republican, and "dry", running in a boom year for the economy. Within a year, however, the good times ended when the stock market crashed, marking the beginning of the Great Depression.

HOOVER WINS THE 1928 ELECTION. Finally after six years in office, the taciturn Coolidge announced, "I do not choose to run in 1928."

The Democratic convention proved raucous. The party remained divided between its urban and rural wings, north and south, and **"wets"** (those who opposed prohibition) and "drys" (those who favored prohibition. After a bitter floor battle, the party nominated Al Smith, outgoing governor of New York, an Irish Catholic, and a "wet." The Republicans turned enthusiastically to Secretary of Commerce Herbert Hoover.

Hoover personified the American success story. Orphaned at an early age, he grew up on a farm in Iowa and later lived in Oregon. Educated at public schools, he entered Stanford University, became a mining engineer, and amassed a fortune building hydroelectric dams. During World War I, Hoover won a reputation as a humanitarian, when as chairman of the American Relief Committee he worked to provide food to Belgium and other war-ravaged countries. As secretary of commerce, Hoover prevailed upon industry to standardize, simplify, and become more efficient. In 1928, many people saw Hoover as an engineer with a heart, a man of vision with a sense of the possible.

The religious issue haunted the campaign. In the fundamentalist Bible Belt, opponents organized, "Southern Protestants Against Smith." Protestant ministers denounced "Al-cohol Smith." He confronted a revived KKK that had gained strength in the South, Indiana, Ohio, Oklahoma, Oregon, and California. When Smith traveled to Billings, Montana, his train passed a fiery display of burning crosses that extended for miles outside the town.

On election day, Herbert Hoover's 21.3 million votes swamped Al Smith's 15 million votes. Still, Smith won the traditional Republican states of Massachusetts and Rhode Island and carried the urban vote for the Democratic party for the first time since 1896, suggesting a permanent shift among voters.

Hoover had little time to enjoy his victory. Within a year after Hoover's election, the American economy began a frightening spiral downward. Beginning on October 29, 1929, the stock market crashed. The crash abruptly shifted American's attention away from the politics of culture and the pursuit of individualism to economic concerns. The worst **depression** in modern history had begun.

Conclusion

As the economy declined and America slipped into the Great Depression, Americans began to reassess the 1920s. Many viewed the period as marred by corruption and self-indulgence.

History proves to be a stern judge. The onset of the Great Depression, and the push for reform that followed, allowed critics of American culture and society to have their day. Surely, Americans had been too complacent in celebrating economic growth, Republican political success, and cultural renaissance in the 20s. Still, there had been much to celebrate: the economy had boomed, the political order had remained stable, and the arts had flourished as never before. The crash of 1929, however, made it hard to celebrate.

Recommended Readings

DOCUMENTS: Bruce Barton, *The Man Nobody Knows* (1925); Frederick Lewis Allen, *Only Yesterday* (1931); Malcolm Cowley, *Exile's Return* (1934).

READINGS: (GENERAL) Paul Carter, *The Twenties in America* (1968) and *Another Part of the Twenties* (1977); John D. Hicks, *Republican Ascendancy* (1960); William E. Leuchtenberg, *Perils of Prosperity* (1970); Donald McCoy, *Coming of Age* (1973); Geoffrey Perrett, *America in the Twenties* (1982); David Shannon, *Between the Wars* (1979). (SOCIAL) Lois Banner, *American Beauty* (1983); Irving Bernstein, *The Lean Years: A History of the American Worker* (1960); David M. Chalmers, *Hooded Americanism* (1965); Norman H. Clark, *Deliver Us from Evil: An Interpretation of Prohibition* (1976); Robert Crunden, *From Self to Society: Transition in Modern Thought* (1972); James Flink, *The Car Culture* (1975); James Gilbert, *Designing the Industrial State* (1972); Nathan Huggins, *Harlem Renaissance* (1971); Kenneth T. Jackson, *The Ku Klux Klan in the City* (1967); J. Stanley Lemons, *The Woman Citizen: Social Feminism in the 1920s* (1973); Roland Marchand, *Advertising the American Dream* (1985); George Marsden, *Fundamentalism and American Culture* (1980); Lary May, *Screening Out the Past* (1980); Leslie W. Tentler, *Wage Earning Women* (1979); and Robert Zieger, *Republicans and Labor* (1969). (POLITICS) Kristi Andersen, *The Creation of a Democratic Majority* (1979); Robert Murray, *The Politics of Normalcy* (1973); Burl Noggle, *Teapot Dome* (1962); Eugene Trani and David Wilson, *The Presidency of Warren G. Harding* (1977).

25

THE GREAT DEPRESSION AND THE NEW DEAL

CHAPTER OVERVIEW: The economic downturn that began in 1929 shook American confidence, weakening the traditional belief in progress, historic destiny, and providential mission.

As a result, the depression led to a restructuring of the American economy and new government-business-labor relations. President Franklin Roosevelt's program, called the New Deal, modified democratic capitalism by placing new government regulations on business, labor, and society. The New Deal provided work for the unemployed, security for the elderly, legal rights for workers, and better lives for farmers.

In the process, American political life underwent a profound transformation as Roosevelt shaped the Democratic party into a majority coalition built around ethnic and racial minorities, organized labor, blue-collar workers, and large segments of urban dwellers and farmers. At the same time American social life experienced deep alterations.

Hoover Faces Depression

The stock market of the 1920s had encouraged speculation rather than investment in technology and improving factories, so stock prices rose to artificially high levels. Huge investment companies issued more and more stock, and prices went even higher. The house of cards finally collapsed in October 1929. Industrial production and sales dropped sharply, so business laid off workers. Unemployment reached 25 percent. Just a month after taking office, Herbert Hoover faced the worst depression in modern times.

Hoover believed in local solutions and American individualism, so he called on state and local governments and the private sector to help, but they were soon overwhelmed by the severity of the depression. Despite his reputation as a visionary, his responses revealed political ineptness in a crisis.

THE BUBBLE BURSTS. In early 1929, few worried that the bubble might burst. Presidents Harding and Coolidge had encouraged stock market **speculation** by maintaining low interest rates, which encouraged speculators to borrow money to purchase stocks. One of the major consequences of the stock market boom was that it directed money into speculation rather than into investment in new technology and plant renovation. The Wall Street boom — similar to that of the 1980s — coincided with an intensive merger movement that brought even more securities (stock issues) on the market. Mergers occurred particularly in utilities, food processing, and retailing.

The emergence of vast investment **holding companies** (a parent company holding stock in lesser companies) fueled this explosive situation on Wall Street. These huge companies, often controlling dozens of smaller companies, issued millions of dollars worth of stock. In the process, these investment houses built large paper pyramids that appeared attractive from the outside, but were structurally flimsy. This balloon popped in October 1929.

Hoover had just entered office when the system began to unravel. By the summer of 1929, industrial production went into a slump, although the stock market remained strong. By the fall, however, the market began to wobble. The first signs of the portending crash began on October 21, 1929. On Thursday, October 24, the market fell into complete disorder that soon gave way to panic as an unprecedented 12.9 million shares traded hands. The volume was so heavy that the reporting system completely broke down. People could not find out what had happened until hours after market closed. Rumors added to the confusion.

Finally, leading New York financiers stepped in to pledge $20 to $30 million dollars to bolster the market and calm fears. Thomas Lamont, a senior partner of J. P. Morgan and Company, assured reporters in a classic understatement, "There were technical difficulties, but these have been addressed." The market remained fairly calm until "Black Tuesday," October 29, 1929. By the end of that day stock prices fell 43 points — more than 10 percent in one day. Investment houses, brokers, and small investors were devastated. Tens of thousands of accounts were wiped out.

AMERICANS CAN'T FIND WORK, OR RELIEF. The singular feature of the stock market crash was that economic decline continued. As the economy plummeted downward, industrial production fell to nearly half of what it had been. This downward spiral was made worse by the policy of the **Federal**

Potatoes and cabbage are distributed in Cleveland in 1938 by the Federal Relief Agency. By 1938 the economy had begun to revive, but unemployment remained a serious problem until America's entry into World War II. (AP/WORLD WIDE PHOTOS)

Reserve Bank, which withdrew funds and shrank the money supply, at the exact moment when additional liquidity was needed. As sales dropped, businesses began laying off their workers. By 1932, an estimated 13 million to 17 million workers — about one-quarter of the labor force — had been laid off.

Unable to find regular jobs, casual work, or even relief — the unemployed became desperate. As many as two million young men (and a few women) took to the railroads and highways as tramps. Tens of thousands of the homeless slept in city parks, subways, or abandoned buildings. Others gathered in makeshift camps that sprang up on the outskirts of towns. These rough settlements of primitive tar and paper shacks were sardonically called Hoovervilles.

As conditions worsened, many families turned to private or local government charities for aid. Yet government at all levels simply lacked the administrative infrastructure to deal with the problems facing the nation. As a result, public officials relied on volunteer relief efforts to handle the growing numbers of those seeking relief. The numbers themselves reveal all too graphically the scale of the problem. More than half the families on unemployment relief were located in eight states, and more than a third were in four highly industrialized states: Pennsylvania, New York, Ohio, and Illinois. Forty percent of all persons on relief were children. Exact numbers are unknown because the government had never tried to collect unemployment statistics.

Initially, most social workers opposed federal involvement in local relief efforts. As people began to go hungry, social workers sought federal aid. Hoover refused. He saw America at a crossroads, declaring that the "American system" limited government "to protect the people." Hoover feared "that we shall directly or indirectly regiment the nation, the people, and the state."

The severity of the **depression** made the world seem irrational. Hamburgers sold two for 5 cents; still, people could not afford to buy them. Men worked for only 10 cents an hour, yet many businesses seemed unable to make a profit. Interest rates fell to below 1 percent; nevertheless few were willing to invest. Unable to sell their crops at decent prices, farmers allowed them to rot in the field while people went hungry. The world seemed topsy-turvy, and after a decade of general prosperity, Americans simply were not prepared to cope with the economic collapse that began on Wall Street in October 1929.

HOOVER RESPONDS RELUCTANTLY. In 1930 many Americans naturally looked to President Herbert Hoover, the great engineer and the great humanitarian, to duplicate his past feats when he had prevented Europe from starving at the end of World War I. From these early experiences, Hoover held fast to his belief that local voluntary cooperation, community effort, and federal encouragement would address the problems of the emergency.

Hoover had a reputation as a visionary. Like other progressives, he believed that economic stability and efficiency could be introduced in the formation of business and community associations. This associational vision held that voluntary groups of business, labor, and social leaders could provide rational, scientific planning to cope with the complex problems of a industrial society. These associations were touted by Hoover as the beginning of a new era in American **capitalism.** Destructive competition through unfair business practices, he argued, was a thing of the past.

Hoover addressed the national economic crisis in 1929 by calling on businessmen and labor leaders to maintain employment, prices, and wages. In 1930 he appointed an emergency commission to review unemployment, but when this commission recommended a federal public works program,

Hoover disbanded it to form the new President's Organization on Unemployment Relief. This committee also failed. Hoover also encouraged businessmen to undertake campaigns to "Buy American and Spend American." In 1931 Hoover persuaded Congress to pass the Smoot-Hawley Tariff, which raised **import duties** to the highest levels ever seen. Foreign trade almost stopped, as other nations pursued similarly foolish policies by raising their **tariffs** to protect their markets in the midst of what had become a world-wide depression.

Protectionism also extended to the domestic front. By late 1932, half of the states required their governments to buy goods from their own states and employ only residents of their states in public works contracts. Such policies, however, only caused trade to decline, introduced inefficiencies, raised costs, and did little to revive a plummeting economy.

Hoover continued to resist instituting a concerted federal program to address problems, even as those problems grew worse each day. Finally, in the summer of 1932, he capitulated to Congress and a distressed nation. About to stand for reelection, Hoover accepted a relief bill that allowed the newly created Reconstruction Finance Corporation to lend $1.8 billion to states and municipalities for relief and public works. Hoover continued to insist, however, that federal money should not undermine local relief efforts and American individualism.

As the depression worsened, Hoover reluctantly increased government spending. Money was appropriated to build Boulder Dam (later renamed Hoover Dam) along the Colorado River. The Emergency Relief and Construction Act gave federal grants to states for highway construction. The Reconstruction Finance Corporation continued to provide loans to banks and insurance companies. As a consequence, federal expenditures increased from 3 percent ($3.3 billion) of the gross national product in 1929 to 9 percent ($4.6 billion) of a smaller gross national product in 1932.

As federal expenditures increased and revenues fell (with declining corporate and individual earnings), the federal budget went into the red. A strong supporter of a balanced budget, Hoover hiked business taxes in 1932, a policy that dampened an already weakened economy.

Franklin D. Roosevelt Launches the New Deal

Franklin Delano Roosevelt easily defeated Herbert Hoover for the presidency in 1932. In his first hundred days in office, FDR targeted industrial and agricultural recovery through legislation which granted federal powers to control agricultural production and to set industrial prices and wages. These measures challenged fundamental American assumptions about the government's proper role in society and drew intense criticism. The economy recovered somewhat, but only temporarily.

FRANKLIN DELANO ROOSEVELT ELECTED, 1932. The presidential election of 1932 saw the desperate Republicans renominate a demoralized Hoover, while the Democrats, sensing that the depression would bring them victory, turned to Franklin D. Roosevelt, governor of New York.

Roosevelt brought to the campaign a bright personality and a cheerful manner that generated confidence wherever he traveled. His own fight against physical disability imparted courage to Americans. In 1920, political insiders saw Roosevelt as a future leader of the party when he won the Democratic nomination as vice-president. When polio struck him the following year, Roosevelt's political career appeared over. He was only 39. His mother urged him to retire, but his wife Eleanor encouraged him to fight his disability. From 1921 to 1928 she kept her husband's name alive by writing hundreds of letters to leading politicians in the country. She also established key contacts with women's groups, social welfare activists, and human rights advocates. Franklin Roosevelt eventually turned his disability into a strength. His fight against polio became a symbol of the nation's fight against a sick economy. His haughty laugh and cigarette jauntily dangled in a long holder became symbols of the nation's defiance against the depression.

While he attacked Hoover's spendthrift policies which had led to budget deficits, he also called for the federal government to put people back to work. For example, in a speech in Pittsburgh he declared, "I regard the reduction in federal spending as one of the most important issues of this campaign." Still, he pleaded on behalf of the "forgotten man at the bottom of the economic pyramid," and called for "bold, persistent experimentation."

Meanwhile, Hoover further offended people by his bungled handling of a protest by hundreds of World War I veterans who marched on Washington in the summer of 1932. They demanded that Congress give them pensions they were not due to receive until 1945. Some veterans set up a crude shanty town of tents and shacks at the edge of Washington, while others occupied unused lots along Pennsylvania Avenue. Feeling under siege and fearful of an angry mob, Hoover ordered the White House put under guard, the gates chained, and the streets cleared of people. Warned that communists had infiltrated this makeshift "Bonus Army" of protesters, Hoover ordered the military to drive the veterans away. General Douglas MacArthur led six tanks, four troops of cavalry with drawn sabers, and a column of steel-helmeted infantry to clear the camps. A thousand veterans and their wives and children

Franklin Delano Roosevelt, as president during the Great Depression and World War II, offered Americans reassurance that American democracy would survive and prosper. (The Franklin D. Roosevelt Library)

fled as troops attacked the colony and burned the shacks. Fires lit Washington that night. And Hoover's bid for reelection went up in smoke.

Roosevelt's election proved a foregone conclusion. Roosevelt received 22.8 million votes to Hoover's 15.7. FDR, as Roosevelt became popularly known, swept 32 states, carrying cities in the Northeast and the Midwest, the farm vote in the Midwest and the West, and the reliably Democratic South. Roosevelt's victory was the worst defeat for the Republicans since 1912. Memories of "Hoover's Depression" kept the Republicans out of the White House until 1952.

ROOSEVELT JUMPSTARTS THE NEW DEAL. Roosevelt faced a nation in crisis. In the four months between his election in November 1932 and his inauguration on March 4, 1933, the nation's entire banking system collapsed. (The Constitution's twentieth amendment changed inauguration day to January 20, beginning in 1937). By the eve of the inauguration, 30 states had closed or restricted their banks to discourage **runs** by depositors. In early 1933, business activity had reached an all-time low — half the 1929 level. In the Appalachian Mountains of Kentucky, unemployed coal miners ate wild greens from the fields and forests. Unemployment among blacks in Harlem, Philadelphia, Detroit, and Chicago reached 50 percent. In the Midwest, under the leadership of Milo Reno and his National Farm Holiday Association, farmers protested low prices and declared a farmers' holiday. Corn was so cheap in South Dakota that one county courthouse burned it as fuel. In an attempt to drive up farm and dairy prices, armed bands of farmers began blockading highways. In the cities, **communists** had successfully organized protest marches of unemployed. A thousand hungry men attacked two bakery trucks in New York. In Oklahoma 300 unemployed men raided food stores.

At his inauguration, Roosevelt reassured the American people. "The only thing we have to fear is fear itself, nameless, unreasoning, unjustified terror which paralyzes needed efforts to convert retreat into advance." Brave words, but Roosevelt knew that more than words were needed. The people, the nation, demanded action. FDR's plan of action was called the New Deal.

In the next hundred days, Congress was called into session by Roosevelt, and furiously enacted laws concerning banks, industry, agriculture, Wall Street, unemployment relief, and home mortgages. What emerged was neither planned nor comprehensive, but a series of practical responses generally informed by progressive concerns.

Roosevelt's first action was to resolve the banking crisis. On March 5, 1933 — the day after his inauguration — the president declared a "bank holiday" closing all banks. Although progressives within Congress called for the **nationalization** of the banking system, Roosevelt enacted the Emergency Banking Act which provided federal loans to distressed banks and set guidelines for reopening those banks considered solvent. Later banking legislation separated commercial banks that provided checking and saving accounts from investment banks handling stocks and bonds, and established the Federal Deposit Insurance Corporation (FDIC) to insure deposits in individual banks up to $5,000.

The keystones of the early New Deal were two measures aimed at agricultural relief and industrial recovery. Secretary of Agriculture Henry A. Wallace, son of Harding's former secretary of agriculture, cooperated with economists Rexford Tugwell and M. L. Wilson in 1933 in drafting an agricultural relief measure, the Agricultural Adjustment Act (AAA). This act transformed American farm policy by controlling the supply of agricultural goods placed on the market. Through a tax on food processing plants, farmers received subsidies not to plant certain crops (since oversupply of a given crop would drive prices down, limiting the supply would hold prices up). At the same time, new credit measures allowed farmers to receive funds for improving their farms. Shortly after the enactment of the AAA, Wallace ordered farmers to slaughter 6 million pigs and plow under 100 million acres of cotton — one-fourth of the entire 1933 crop. Few within the administration seemed to worry about plowing crops under while people went hungry. Nor did many worry about the long-term costs of subsidizing a special class of citizens — farmers.

The second keystone of the New Deal was the National Industrial Recovery Act (NIRA). Drafted by Raymond Moley, the NIRA called upon industry and labor to meet to set wage and price controls through cooperative codes overseen by a federal board — the National Recovery Administration (NRA). Modeled on the War Industries Board of 1919, the National Recovery Administration (NRA) oversaw the establishment of more than 500 industrial and trade associations to draft codes of fair competition. These codes determined production quotas, hours, business practices, standards of quality, and methods of competition. The act thus granted the federal government extensive and previously unheard of powers to set prices and wages in a peacetime economy.

That New Dealers often compared the depression to the nation's struggle during World War I seemed natural to many at the time. Yet NRA practices raised serious constitutional questions. Moreover, few within the administration seemed to notice the apparent contradiction of a policy that sought to maintain industrial wages through the NRA, while driving up agricultural prices through the AAA. Higher food prices inevitably meant higher costs for the industrial worker.

An important feature of the National Industrial Recovery Act, Section 7A, gave employees the right to form labor unions, as well as setting minimum wages and maximum hours for all employees. Section 7A pleased the American Federation of Labor and offered organized labor an impetus to regain ground lost during the 1920s.

The NIRA also appropriated $3.3 billion for the Public Works Administration (PWA) to be placed under Harold Ickes, secretary of the interior. Like many New Dealers, Harold Ickes, a former progressive Republican, remained cautious about spending government money. Because the PWA only undertook large projects, such as highways, bridges, and dams, that took meticulous and time-consuming planning, its funds were disbursed slowly and did little immediately to relieve the unemployed.

THE NEW DEAL TARGETS THE UNEMPLOYED. Roosevelt sought more direct relief for the unemployed with the Federal Relief Act of May 1933, which appropriated $500 million to the states for relief through the Federal Emergency Relief Administration (FERA). Headed by New York social worker Harry Hopkins, the FERA confronted an unemployment problem of historic magnitude: More than 4.7 million Americans were on relief by 1933. Impatient with bureaucratic red tape, Hopkins within a month disbursed over $51 million in matching grants to states. To manage the program and to control the aid, Hopkins created regional staffs throughout the country to oversee state and local agencies.

Federal relief dented the massive unemployment problem only slightly. As winter approached, Hopkins worried about the 12.5 million Americans still unable to find work. In November 1933, he convinced Roosevelt to establish a temporary Civil Works Administration (CWA) to undertake short-term, light construction in the public sector. Diverting funds from the PWA, the CWA put 4 million people to work. In its brief span during the winter of 1933-1934, the CWA built 500,000 miles of roads, 40,000 schools, 3,500 playgrounds, and 1,000 airports.

For all of its successes, the CWA drew political fire from conservatives within the administration — including Vice-President John Nance Garner, Budget Director Lewis Douglas, and others. Southern congressmen complained in particular that the program was luring black workers off farms. CWA policy of paying equal wages to black and white workers also drew resentment from some whites. As one small farmer wrote his senator, "The CWA's paying sorry no account Negroes 45 cents per hour . . . and I can't get any job." Concerned with these political attacks, as well as the high costs of the program, FDR ordered Hopkins in the spring of 1934 to start disbanding the program.

The Civilian Conservation Corps (CCC), established in 1933 to put the nation's unemployed youth to work, drew less political criticism. The CCC recruited 250,000 youths, including many blacks and Indians, to camps in national parks and forests. CCC members built roads, trails, campgrounds, and ranger stations, planted trees, cleared brush, and improved the environment. Paid $1 a day — the same as army wages — CCC workers were housed, fed, and clothed in uniforms. Most mailed their pay home to their desperate families. The CCC proved to be one of the New Deal's greatest success stories.

Other legislation created the Home Owners Loan Corporation to provide refinancing for homeowners facing foreclosure on mortgages, and the Tennessee Valley Authority (TVA) to bring federally sponsored electricity and flood control to the Tennessee River valley.

The fight over establishing the TVA had pitted progressive Republican Senator George Norris of Nebraska against conservative Republican administrations from Harding through Hoover. The federal government's entry into public utilities proved to many Republican and conservative opponents of the emerging New Deal that Roosevelt planned to take the country down the path of **socialism.** Conservatives were even more dismayed when

Roosevelt announced that he was taking America off the domestic gold standard. The price of gold was to be set at $35 an ounce, but Americans could no longer exchange their dollars for gold.

The accomplishments of Roosevelt's first hundred days offered some relief to a nation demoralized by the depression. Eventually the gross national product rose from $56 billion in 1933 to $72 billion in 1935. Wholesale prices jumped a third. People began to speak of an NRA recovery. In the congressional elections of 1934, Americans showed their enthusiasm for the New Deal by electing 322 Democratic congressmen, a gain of 13 seats for Roosevelt's party. The recovery proved only temporary, however. Early in 1935 the economy began to lapse again, and by midsummer it was clearly stagnant.

Left and Right React

Despite its early success, the New Deal came under increasing criticism from those who thought it went too far and from those who thought it did not go far enough. In 1935, the NIRA and the AAA were declared unconstitutional. As the depression wore on, Americans became more receptive to calls for radical action. A drive for old-age pensions won wide support. Senator Huey Long challenged FDR with a plan for a guaranteed income for everyone. Conservatives and big business opposed the New Deal, but attracted little popular support.

THE NRA AND AAA COME UNDER FIRE. In these circumstances critics on the left and the right voiced discontent. Once the symbol of success, the National Recovery Administration drew criticism from all sides. The NRA, under its director Hugh Johnson, had been launched with much fanfare. Those businesses that had participated in the drafting of the production codes willingly displayed the blue "NRA Eagle" emblem. Problems soon became apparent within the agency. Johnson, suffering from a severe drinking problem, often disappeared for days leaving the office in charge of his secretary (and mistress).

Discontent also arose concerning the program itself. Small business owners felt disadvantaged by big business, which played a key role in drafting the NRA's 600 production codes. Organized labor felt betrayed by the promise of the NRA when businesses formed company unions designed to keep out organized labor. Protesting that the NRA allowed discriminatory codes to be instituted, blacks denounced the NRA as the "Negro Run Around," the "Negro Removal Act," and the "Negro Rarely Allowed." Roosevelt's embarrassment over the NRA was finally relieved when the Supreme Court in *Schechter v. United States* (1935) ruled the NIRA act unconstitutional.

The Agricultural Adjustment Administration also drew fire. Early AAA efforts to cut food production had been aided by a drought that swept through the Great Plains in 1934. Without rain, much of the plains looked like a desert, swept by severe winds that blew blinding dust storms. Thousands began a mass exodus out of the Dust Bowl. Weather and the AAA caused wheat production to fall and prices to rise. Farmers' share of the nation's income rose from 11 percent in 1933 to 15 percent in 1935.

While the AAA benefited many farmers, the program hurt **tenant farmers** in the South. Large cotton planters, as major beneficiaries of the program, took federal money to remove land from production and then ordered tenant farmers to leave. Particularly hard hit were black farmers. Some experts estimated that the AAA displaced 200,000 black tenant farmers. Liberals in Congress and the AAA protested, while tenant farmers formed, under communist influence, the Southern Tenant Farmers Union. Pressure led President Roosevelt to increase the share of AAA payments to tenant farmers, but the Supreme Court in early 1936 in *United States v. Butler* (1936) ruled the AAA unconstitutional because of its tax on food processors.

Some critics of the New Deal found it too tame. The first signs of popular discontent came in the governor's race in California in 1934 when socialist and novelist Upton Sinclair, best known for *The Jungle,* won the Democratic nomination on a campaign to "End Poverty in California" (EPIC). Sinclair's call to establish cooperative farms and state-run industries frightened conservatives such as movie mogul Louis B. Mayer of Metro-Goldwyn-Mayer and young Oakland district attorney Earl Warren (later chief justice of the Supreme Court), who conducted a vicious media campaign against Sinclair. Sinclair lost the general election to the Republican candidate, but EPIC indicated widespread discontent among the electorate.

Others turned to Francis Townsend, a dentist from South Dakota who had retired to California. Townsend devised a scheme that would provide a federally funded monthly payment of $200 to any unemployed person over the age of 60 on the condition that this money be spent within the month. By 1935 the Townsend movement claimed 3.5 million supporters, helped win seats in Congress, and assisted lobbying efforts for state old-age pensions.

Another radical, the Roman Catholic priest Charles Coughlin, reached nearly 30 million listeners each week on a nationally syndicated religious radio program. He demanded inflation through a **free silver** policy. His increasingly vitriolic attacks charged that Roosevelt's Brain Trust (which he called the "Drain Trust") had been infiltrated by communists and Jews.

A more serious threat came from Louisiana's Huey P. Long. Although

Long supported Roosevelt in 1932, by 1934 he had broken with New Deal. Entertaining presidential aspirations of his own, Long proposed a "soak the rich" tax program which would enable every man to have a homestead worth $5,000 and an income of $2,500. He promised everyone a college education and a guaranteed income. His "Share Our Wealth Clubs" swept the nation, claiming 27,000 clubs with a mailing list of 7.5 million supporters. The Long threat ended on September 8, 1935, when he was assassinated in Baton Rouge by a relative of a recently discharged state judge.

Radicalism also led to a revival of the Communist party. In 1932 the party had backed William Z. Foster for president on a **Stalinist** platform calling for nationalizing all private enterprise and abolishing all political parties except its own. By 1935, however, the party had adopted the slogan, "Communism is Twentieth Century Americanism" and formed coalitions with liberal groups through what were called "popular fronts." For example, the Communist party sponsored the 1935 American Writers Congress, which attracted such distinguished authors as John Dos Passos, Theodore Dreiser, James T. Farrell, Richard Wright, and Ernest Hemingway. The Writers Congress issued a public statement declaring that "**communism** must come and must be fought for."

CONSERVATIVES ORGANIZE AGAINST THE NEW DEAL. The right appeared less well-organized than the left. The American Bund, a fascist organization, found support among a small group of German-Americans. **Fascism,** however, attracted few followers, although Lawrence Dennis, a Harvard graduate and former Foreign Service officer, drew considerable attention with his book, *The Coming of Fascism* (1936).

Mainstream conservative opposition to the New Deal led to formation of the Liberty League in 1935, financed by members of the DuPont family and New York financiers Winthrop Aldrich and Felix Warburg. Although membership remained small, the Liberty League was significant as an indicator that much of big business had broken with the New Deal. Roosevelt had become a "traitor to his class." On the other hand, Roosevelt made the Liberty League into a symbol of big business and its selfish opposition to the New Deal and helping the common citizen on the street.

Roosevelt Secures the New Deal

Roosevelt responded to attacks from the left and the right by pushing the New Deal forward. In doing so, he transformed the nature of the American welfare state. The Social Security Act

(1935) became the centerpiece of the second New Deal. Roosevelt also moved to secure new farm, public works, and labor legislation. After winning reelection in 1936, however, he found his administration embattled over his scheme to reform the Supreme Court and his failure to address another downturn in the economy.

ROOSEVELT TACKLES UNEMPLOYMENT. Under political attack from both the left and right, Roosevelt moved to redefine the New Deal. Denouncing the **dole** as a "narcotic, a subtle destroyer of the human spirit," Roosevelt disbanded the temporary Federal Emergency Relief Administration in December 1935. In its place he established a $5 billion employment program called the Works Progress Administration (WPA) directed by Harry Hopkins. In doing so he returned 1.5 million people — including the aged, disabled, orphaned — to state and local welfare agencies. The other 3.5 million "employables" were put to work on federally sponsored WPA projects, building more than 2,500 hospitals, 13,000 playgrounds, and 1,000 airports. The WPA also hired artists who decorated post offices with murals, actors who performed free plays in parks, and writers who turned out tourist guidebooks. Among the young authors employed were John Cheever, Richard Wright, and Conrad Aiken.

Congress also authorized the creation of a National Youth Administration (NYA). This agency paid stipends to a half million college students and offered part-time employment to 1.5 million needy high school students. Another 2 million youths received stipends in state-sponsored programs.

Nevertheless, of the 10 million unemployed, the WPA and the NYA employed a little more than 3 million. Even at its height, the WPA never employed more than one-third of the nation's jobless.

SOCIAL SECURITY AND LABOR LEGISLATION ENACTED, 1935. State governments were ill-equipped to meet the needs of the so-called unemployables — the aged, the disabled, and the sick. For this reason, Roosevelt called for a **social security** program. The Social Security Act (1935) marked a decisive turning point in the history of social policy in the United States by extending federal responsibility for care to the elderly, the poor, and the disabled. The act established a contributory system that provided pensions to all over age 65. The program also offered relief for the elderly poor, allowed matching grants-in-aid to states to assist dependent mothers and children, and the blind. In addition, it established a federal-state system of unemployment insurance.

Roosevelt also moved to address problems created for organized labor and farmers when the Supreme Court overturned the National Industrial Recovery Act. The court's ruling meant that the right to collective bargaining embodied in Section 7A no longer had a basis in law. To redress this situation, the Wagner Act (1935) granted collective bargaining rights to organized labor, and established the National Labor Relations Board (NRLB) to oversee relations between labor and industry.

The Wagner Act came just in time. Workers were restless. In 1934, the nation had been rattled by a series of violent strikes, often led by radicals. Taxi drivers rioted in Philadelphia and New York; communist-led farm workers struck in California's Salinas valley; textile workers in 20 states had walked out; violence broke out in Minneapolis when a **Trotskyist**-controlled truckers union went on strike. Harry Bridges, a follower of the Communist party, launched a general strike in San Francisco to support dock workers.

The Wagner Act protected workers' rights to collective bargaining, while creating a more stable environment for labor and management. Shortly after the passage of the act, John L. Lewis, who believed in organizing unskilled workers, led the United Mine Workers Union, into the newly formed Committee for Industrial Organization (CIO). Supported by representatives of various garment workers unions including Sidney Hillman, David Dubinsky, and Max Zaritsky, the Committee for Industrial Organization tried to unionize the unorganized. Expelled by the AFL in the summer of 1936, the committee formally changed its name into the Congress of Industrial Organizations as it moved to organize unskilled workers in auto, rubber, textile, steel, and other heavy industries.

Congress also passed laws about public utilities. The Holding Company Act (1935) broke up many utility holding companies, while the Federal Power Act (1935) created the Federal Power Commission to regulate interstate rates for electricity and natural gas. More important, the Rural Electrification Act (1935) encouraged loans for local farm cooperatives to build electric lines. This law alone transformed the American farm, especially in the South. In 1933 only 10 percent of southern farms had electricity, but by 1943 more than 80 percent of the region's farms did.

ROOSEVELT REELECTED, 1936. Roosevelt entered the 1936 presidential race in a strong position. Although the depression continued, the federal government had moved aggressively in providing work for the unemployed, security for the elderly, legal rights for organized labor, and in improving the lives of farmers. Republicans fumed that these measures were socialistic and antibusiness, and they nominated Alf Landon, the governor of Kansas, to head the Republican ticket. Landon lost. In fact, Roosevelt carried every state except of Vermont and Maine. In winning, he forged a new Democratic coalition that added urban white ethnics in the industrial Northeast, organized labor, and blacks, to the party's traditional white southern base. The election revealed sharp polarization along class lines. Upper-income groups went overwhelmingly Republican, while those with lower incomes, especially the poor on relief, voted Democratic.

ROOSEVELT BATTLES THE COURT AND ECONOMIC RECESSION. Victory gave Roosevelt a mandate to move forward with the New Deal, but he quickly made a key mistake: he tried to change the composition of the Supreme Court. The Supreme Court's overturning of the National Industrial Recovery and Agricultural Adjustment Acts, as well as unfavorable rulings against other New Deal measures, caused Roosevelt great consternation. The president feared that the court might overturn the Wagner Act protecting workers' rights to collective bargaining and perhaps even the Social Security Act. Confident that he had the support of the people, the president proposed the Judicial Reorganization Bill (1937) that would have allowed him to appoint a new judge to the Supreme Court for each present justice over the age of 70. Under this bill, Roosevelt would have been able to add six handpicked justices to the nine-member Court — enough to ensure support for his programs.

Roosevelt's "court packing" scheme caused a fury. Newspapers warned of dictatorship, protesters marched, citizens signed petitions, and Republicans described Roosevelt as another Mussolini, the Italian fascist leader. Many prominent Democratic congressional leaders opposed the measure, and Roosevelt withdrew it. Ironically, within two years four justices died or retired, which allowed Roosevelt to appoint replacements and gain control of the court.

Roosevelt's second mistake was an attempt to balance the budget by cutting government expenditures when the economy still remained weak and dependent on federal expenditures. Although Roosevelt had reluctantly accepted budget deficits as necessary in his first term, he remained essentially a fiscal conservative. Roosevelt believed, however, that the economy was recovering and that continued deficit spending might release runaway inflation. As a consequence, in late 1935 and early 1936 Roosevelt began systematically to slash the federal budget including the WPA. The WPA had come under attack by Republicans who denounced the program as creating makeshift, nondemanding jobs for people who really did not want to enter the labor force. Moreover, the middle class had turned against the program. Humor of the day captured the general mood. Even Roosevelt told WPA jokes. The president told Alf Landon about a WPA poison: "We don't guarantee it to kill rats, but it'll make them so damned lazy you can catch 'em."

Just as the budget appeared to be nearing balance, economic disaster struck. The rapid decline in income and production in the nine months from September 1937 to June 1938 was without precedent in American economic history.

Roosevelt once again took the offensive. He rejected fiscal conservatives and accepted the advice of a group of young economists (followers of the English economist John Maynard Keynes) who urged the government to undertake a deliberate policy of deficit spending during economic slumps. Roosevelt proposed a $4.5 million package to finance a public housing, highway construction, and agencies that had been targeted for cuts the previous year. A new farming bill, the Agricultural Adjustment Act (1937) was enacted. It allowed the federal government to pay farmers not to plant crops under the guise of preventing soil erosion. The government made it possible for tenant farmers to borrow money to buy and improve their own farms. The Fair Labor Standards Act (1938) set minimum wages and maximum hours for the nation's workers.

ROOSEVELT SWINGS TO THE LEFT. Swinging to the left, Roosevelt openly targeted big business. On the advice of Supreme Court Justice Louis Brandeis and Harvard law professor Felix Frankfurter, Roosevelt revitalized the **antitrust** division in the Justice Department. He also appointed a commission to investigate **monopolies** in the nation's major industries. He imposed new federal regulations on the trucking and airline industries. The Fair Trade Act (1937) required retailers to sell products at prices set by manufacturers. Finally, the government imposed new corporate taxes and increased taxes on upper-income groups.

With the outbreak of war in Europe that began on September 1, 1939 when Germany invaded Poland, the president accelerated the American build-up, pressuring a reluctant Congress to increase defense **appropriations.** Later, it would become common wisdom that the war brought America out of the depression. Of course, what people meant was that *spending* on the war effort had ended the economic slump. Roosevelt's spending program had begun before the war, but the war did allow Roosevelt to accelerate the government's spending program.

The Cultural Fabric of Depression

American writers and artists remained social critics, but celebrated American culture and American themes.

At the same time, social life changed for women and minorities during the depression years. Women entered the workforce and politics in increasing numbers. The New Deal's record on the behalf of African-Americans proved mixed. During the depression years, thousands of immigrants from Mexico entered the United States, where they often met hostility and violence. The New Deal promoted tribal control of Indian lands, but life on reservations remained deplorable for most Native Americans.

DEPRESSION CULTURE. The bestselling novel of the decade was Margaret Mitchell's *Gone With the Wind* (1936), a romantic epic about the Old South far removed from the Great Depression. Still, social criticism found expression in such works as James T. Farrell's trilogy, *Studs Lonigan* (1932-1935), which described Irish-American working class life; John Dos Passos's trilogy *U.S.A.* (1930-1936), which satirized American capitalism; and Nathaniel West's *Miss Lonelyhearts* (1933) and *Cool Million* (1934), which told of alienation in modern America. Leftist writers such as Mike Gold, Jack Conroy, Howard Fast, and Josephine Herbst explored the theme of class struggle, but their works found only a limited audience.

By the mid-1930s writers, while remaining critical of society, displayed a more affirmative mood. For example, John Steinbeck, in his moving story of an uprooted dust bowl family, *The Grapes of Wrath* (1939), has Ma Joad declare, "They ain't gonna wipe us out. Why, we're the people — we go on."

The American stage also reflected a shift from radical social criticism to a celebration of American culture. Clifford Odets' *Waiting for Lefty* (1935) ended with the audience shouting "Strike! Strike! Strike!," but Thornton Wilder's *Our Town* (1939) celebrated small town life at the turn of the century.

Composers also celebrated American themes in their music. For example, George Gershwin turned to black life in Charleston for his enthusiastically received opera *Porgy and Bess* (1939). Although white and Jewish, Gershwin decreed that only African-Americans could be in the cast. This marked the first time an all-black cast appeared on Broadway.

SOCIAL LIFE IN THE DEPRESSION. The American family proved particularly resilient in the depression, even though the divorce rate began to climb in the mid-1930s. The role of women also showed signs of continuing change. During the depression, women entered the workforce and politics in increasing numbers. Enrollments of female college students grew throughout the period, reaching one-quarter of those attending. The number of single women increased, while the birth rate declined. Abortion rates also appear to have increased in this period.

Women took an active part in the New Deal. The Women's Division in the Democratic party, headed by Molly Dawson, lobbied for women to receive key positions within the New Deal. Secretary of Labor Frances Perkins gained high visibility as the first female cabinet officer, and other women attained leadership in the Federal Emergency Relief Administration and WPA. Grace Abbott, director of the Children's Bureau, played a key role in shaping social policy. The black educator Mary McLeod Bethune, a college president, served as Director of the Office of Negro Affairs for the National Youth Administration. In 1935 Bethune organized the National Council of Negro Women to coordinate the work of a hundred black groups representing 800,000 women.

During the 1930s, women continued as sport stars. The most notable sports figure was Babe Didrikson Zaharias who won two Olympic gold medals in track in 1932 and later became a professional golfer. Figure skater Sonja Henie won fame as an Olympic champion and became a popular movie star. Pilot Amelia Earhart, the first woman to fly solo across the Atlantic, led other women to follow her pioneering example.

THE NEW DEAL BENEFITS MINORITIES. During these years the Supreme Court showed growing liberalism on the issue of civil rights for African-Americans. In 1935 the Supreme Court questioned the absence of African-Americans from juries involving black defendants and reexamined the "separate but equal" doctrine upheld in *Plessy v. Ferguson* (1896). In 1938 the court, under Chief Justice Charles Hughes, ruled in *Missouri ex rel Gaines v. Canada* that a black applicant for law school must be admitted to the University of Missouri given the absence of a state-supported black law school.

In contrast to the Supreme Court, the New Deal's record on black civil rights was mixed. In large part because of FDR's need to win southern congressional support for his programs, he refused to back new civil rights legislation or antilynching bills brought before Congress in 1933 and 1939. Secretary of the Interior Harold Ickes **desegregated** the cafeteria at the Department of the Interior. He also insisted that the Public Works Administration reserve one-half of the housing projects for African-Americans. Moreover, all PWA construction contracts were required to hire blacks.

Some African-Americans grew increasingly militant. In 1934 the National Association for the Advancement of Colored People (NAACP) split when W.E.B. DuBois resigned as editor of the association's newspaper, *The Crisis,* over his belief that blacks should pursue a militant nationalist program. In many American cities strong nationalist tendencies became especially evident in "buy black" campaigns. At least 35 cities saw pickets and boycotts organized by "Don't Buy Where You Can't Work" campaigns. Some of these campaigns lasted for years, often engaging large segments of the black community and eventually securing a significant number of jobs for blacks. In Chicago and New York, nationalist leaders such as Sufi Abdul, Ira Kemp, and Arthur Reid conducted fairly successful campaigns to pressure white merchants to hire more African-Americans. This campaign often increased tensions between the black community and Jewish merchants, leading Jews to charge blacks with **anti-Semitism**.

Hispanics, although a less organized force in the 1930s, benefited from New Deal programs. The Mexican-American population increased rapidly during the depression as many Mexicans migrated to the United States. This migration occurred mostly in the West, but extended to Kansas, Illinois, and Michigan. As a result, many Hispanics enrolled in the Civilian Conservation Corps in Texas, New Mexico, and California. Mexican-American agricultural workers tried to organize labor unions in California, which often led to violent confrontations with local authorities and with well-financed owners' organizations such as the Associated Farmers of California and the California Fruit Growers Exchange (which markets Sunkist citrus).

Newly arrived Mexicans faced ethnic hostility in cities such as Los Angeles where white welfare officials offered to pay transportation costs to send them back to Mexico. In 1931 alone an estimated 70,000 Mexicans left Los Angeles to return home. Nevertheless, the first signs of the growing political power of Hispanics came with the election of Dennis Chavez in New Mexico to the U.S. Senate in 1934.

The New Deal also helped Native Americans when the Commissioner of Indian Affairs, John Collier, persuaded Congress to enact the Indian Reorganization Act (1934). Although Collier's program sparked opposition in western states, as well as from some Native American leaders, this law shifted American policy away from cultural **assimilation** of Native Americans and individual land ownership to tribal government and tribal control of Indian lands. Collier also encouraged the hiring of Native Americans by the bureau.

Even with this progress, however, most Native Americans continued to live in abject poverty. Infant mortality remained the highest of any group in the nation, life span the shortest, and educational levels the lowest. Suicide and alcoholism continued to be prevalent on Indian reservations.

Conclusion

The New Deal marked a major turning point in American politics. FDR forged a new coalition, while the federal government assumed new responsibilities for maintaining economic prosperity and caring for the elderly and the poor. At the same time the federal government extended its economic powers.

The New Deal accomplished much, even though its record at reform remained uneven. If its record on civil rights was poor, new hope had been offered to blacks, Hispanics, and Native Americans. Women had been given new roles in government. American democracy had been preserved and capitalism had survived. The nation did not experience an economic revolution, as some liberals claimed it would, nor did it take the road to socialism, as some conservatives warned it might.

Recommended Readings

DOCUMENTS: Robert S. McElvaine, *Down and Out in the Great Depression: Letters from the "Forgotten Man"* (1983); Studs Terkel, *Hard Times: An Oral History of the Great Depression* (1970); and Twelve Southerners, *I'll Take My Stand: The South and the Agrarian Tradition* (1937).

READINGS: (GENERAL) Frederick Lewis Allen, *Since Yesterday* (1939); James Burns, *Roosevelt: The Lion and the Fox* (1956); Alan Brinkley, *Voices of Protest: Huey Long, Father Coughlin, and the Great Depression* (1982); Lester Chandler, *America's Greatest Depression* (1970); Paul Conkin, *The New Deal* (1967); Frank Freidel, *Franklin D. Roosevelt* (4 vols., 1952-1976); John Garraty, *The Great Depression* (1937); John Kenneth Galbraith, *The Great Crash* (1960); Barry Karl, *The Uneasy State* (1983); William E. Leuchtenburg, *Franklin Roosevelt and the New Deal* (1983); Robert McElvaine, *The Great Depression* (1984); Gerald Nash, *The Great Depression and World War II* (1979); Arthur Schlesinger, Jr. *The Age of Roosevelt* (1957-1960). (SOCIETY AND CULTURE) Irving Bernstein, *Turbulent Years: A History of the American Worker, 1933-1941* (1969); Lizabeth Cohen, *Making of a New Deal* (1990); Sidney Fine, *Sit-Down: The General Motors Strike* (1969); Abraham Hoffman, *Unwanted Mexican-Americans in the Great Depression* (1974); Laurence Kelly, *The Assault on Assimilation: John Collier and the Origins of Indian Policy Reform* (1983); John Kirby, *Black Americans in the Roosevelt Era* (1980); Carey McWilliams, *North from Mexico* (1949); Harvard Sitkoff, *A New Deal for Blacks* (1970); Raymond Walters, *Negroes and the Great Depression* (1970); Susan Ware, *Beyond Suffrage: Women and the New Deal* (1981).

26

———— ❈ ————

A GLOBAL NATION:
WORLD WAR II AND THE
ORIGINS OF THE COLD WAR

CHAPTER OVERVIEW: Roosevelt entered the White House when the western democracies confronted the rise of ruthless dictators who threatened the world order.

Economic depression in the 1930s, however, only reinforced isolationist sentiments as Americans turned to domestic problems. Congress, reflecting this general sentiment, sought to isolate the United States from international events. The outbreak of World War II in Europe in 1939 led Roosevelt to tacitly support England and its democratic allies, against the wishes of a well-organized isolationist movement. Japan's attack on the U.S. Pacific fleet in Pearl Harbor, Hawaii, in 1941 ended the debate. America entered the war in full force.

In fighting a war for democracy, American society was transformed as a new era of prosperity began, characterized by the emergence of a military-industrial complex. Women and ethnic minorities were called to enter the armed services and the workforce at home. The war led to the emergence of the United States as an international power that would face a powerful foe, the Soviet Union.

The United States Isolates Itself from World Events

Preoccupied with the depression at home, Roosevelt tried to avoid involvement in international affairs. He pledged not to intervene in Latin America and kept that pledge even after Mexico seized American oil holdings. He worked to grant Philippine independence and responded with only a protest when Japan invaded China. He also opened relations with the

Soviet Union. Still, the nation — and Congress — remained deeply isolationist.

ROOSEVELT LIMITS INTERNATIONAL INVOLVEMENT. In the 1930s, Franklin Roosevelt favored reducing the nation's involvement in international affairs. As a result, he tempered his earlier commitment to **internationalism.** Although he ran as the Democratic party's vice-presidential candidate in 1920 on a platform that supported Wilson's League of Nations, once in the White House in 1933 Roosevelt retreated from Wilsonian internationalism.

Clear evidence of Roosevelt's backtracking came in 1933, when he undermined an international economic conference in London. During the conference he instructed Secretary of State Cordell Hull, who was representing the United States in London, to oppose any currency stabilization proposals, thereby derailing the conference. The message sent a clear signal to the European delegates: the United States would take care of its own problems; Europe should do the same.

Roosevelt did not retreat fully into **isolationism,** however. In November 1933 the United States recognized the Soviet Union. Although FDR's official recognition of the **communist** government caused great consternation among conservatives, Roosevelt believed that the Soviet Union should be brought back into the family of nations. He believed that the Soviet Union offered new business opportunities for depressed American industry. Nevertheless, the Soviet Union failed to live up to its promise to grant religious freedom in Russia, nor did it curb its international communist propaganda.

Roosevelt moved to establish new relations with Latin America when he announced the Good Neighbor policy and formally pledged the United States to pursue a noninterventionist policy in Latin America. He sought to lower **tariff** barriers through reciprocal trade agreements and he established the Export-Import Bank in 1934 to help stabilize the currencies of South American trading partners. (Roosevelt's willingness to stabilize Latin American currencies contrasted sharply with his refusal to participate in European monetary stabilization.) As a result, U.S. exports to Latin America rose more than 14 percent.

In pursuit of the Good Neighbor policy, Roosevelt abrogated the Platt Amendment, which had given the United States the right to intervene in the internal affairs of Cuba. In 1934 Roosevelt withdrew U.S. marines from Haiti — ending 19 years of military occupation. This noninterventionist policy was extended in 1936 when the United States signed a nonintervention treaty with 21 Latin American nations at the Inter-American Conference in Buenos Aires, Argentina.

The **nationalization** of American oil holdings by the Mexican government in 1938 tested Roosevelt's noninterventionist resolve, but the United States remained steadfast, despite the urging of one congressman to annex the Gulf of California and the call by American Catholic bishops for reprisals against the anticlerical Mexican government. As one Mexican magazine lamented, "Poor Mexico! So far from God, and so close to the United States."

In Asia, Roosevelt moved to grant the Philippines their independence. In 1934 Congress enacted the Tydings-McDuffie Act, which established the Commonwealth of the Philippines and offered full independence after a transition period of ten years. American sugar interests supported Philippine independence in order to place tariff restrictions on Philippine sugar. In this way, American policy in the Philippines reflected altruism carefully interwoven with economic self-interest.

Elsewhere in Asia, the United States confronted an increasingly aggressive Japan. In 1933, Japan seized disputed territory in northern China. The Japanese government ignored American protests against this clear violation of the Nine-Power Pact (1921) and the Kellogg-Briand Pact (1928). Isolationist sentiment in Congress, however, constrained Roosevelt from pursuing a stronger course of action.

ISOLATIONISTS CONTROL CONGRESS. With the **depression,** Americans withdrew deeper into isolationism. Ironically, the rise of militarism in Europe and Japan seemed to offer the American public further proof of World War I's failure. Pacifism ran high on college campuses and in intellectual and religious circles. Within Congress, isolationists such as Senators Hiram Johnson (R-California), Gerald Nye (R-North Dakota), and William Borah (R-Idaho) dominated the Senate Committee on Foreign Relations. In 1934 Nye chaired a special Senate committee that alleged a link between America's entry into World War I and the self-interests of the banker J. P. Morgan and the **munitions** making DuPont Corporation. Nye concluded that World War I had been fought "to save the skins of American bankers. . . ."

In 1935 when Roosevelt proposed that the United States join the World Court, thousands of hostile telegrams flooded into Washington. One senator declared, "To hell with Europe and the rest of those nations." Congress defeated Roosevelt's modest proposal.

Instead isolationists enacted the Neutrality Act (1935). The measure purported to be a compromise between Roosevelt and Congress over trade **embargoes.** Actually, the act favored Congress by limiting executive power. It prohibited American munitions sales to any nations at war. Roosevelt preferred a limited embargo applied only to aggressor nations. Roosevelt reluctantly signed the bill, nevertheless, and quickly implemented it by placing an arms embargo on Italy when Mussolini invaded Ethiopia in October 1935. Roosevelt called for a "moral embargo" restricting all trade with Italy, but the embargo failed. Indeed, oil exports to Italy tripled within a matter of months.

Further troubles came in the summer of 1936 when civil war broke out in Spain. There, rightist General Francisco Franco led an army revolt against the leftist democratic-Loyalist government. Aided by **fascist** Germany and Italy, by 1939 Franco's army had overwhelmed the Loyalists, who were supported by the Soviet Union. The three-year Spanish Civil War divided American public opinion. The hierarchy of the Roman Catholic Church supported Franco, while liberals and those close to the Communist party backed the Loyalists. American leftists organized the Abraham Lincoln Brigade, which sent 2,000 to 3,000 volunteers to fight in Spain. The majority of Americans remained neutral, but when Roosevelt imposed a U.S. embargo on Spain, the effect favored Franco, who continued to be well supplied by his allies, especially Germany.

In 1937, Congress enacted a stricter neutrality act that provided an embargo on oil and other products to nations at war, extended neutrality laws to cover civil wars, and banned American loans to warring nations. The act also imposed a **"cash and carry"** clause that forced belligerents who did buy American war goods to pay for them in cash and transport their purchases on their own vessels. Shortly afterward, Japan invaded China in July 1937. Outraged by the invasion, Roosevelt favored imposing a "quarantine" on aggressor nations through trade **sanctions** on all goods, but the isolationists forced him to retreat. As a consequence, Japan's invasion went unchecked.

Indeed, isolationists sought stronger measures to keep the United States out of war. In late December 1937, Indiana Representative Louis Ludlow introduced a resolution that called for a constitutional amendment requiring a national **referendum** before any declaration of war. Only Roosevelt's intervention prevented Congress from approving the measure. That same month, Japanese war planes attacked an American patrol boat, the *USS Panay,* and three Standard Oil tankers along the Yangtze River in China. A crisis was averted when the Japanese government agreed to pay an **indemnity** for the attack.

Despite such provocation, antiwar sentiment continued to run high in Congress. Isolationists refused to increase defense **appropriations.** From 1933 to 1937, the armed forces only received on average $180 million annually. Experts rated the American army equal to that of Poland's army. Poverty-stricken army units were forced to drill with wooden rifles.

World War Erupts in Europe, 1939

Before the outbreak of World War II, French and British leaders sought to appease Hitler by giving in to his demands to regain German territory lost during the First World War. He soon revealed his brutality by seizing all of Czechoslovakia, and, on September 1, 1939, invading Poland. In the spring of 1940, Hitler swiftly conquered most of western Europe leaving only England to oppose him.

After winning an unprecedented third term, Roosevelt increased aid to England. Meanwhile, American-Japanese relations deteriorated. On December 7, 1941, Japan bombed America's Pacific fleet in Pearl Harbor, Hawaii. The United States entered the Second World War on the side of the Allies.

BRITAIN AND FRANCE SEEK TO APPEASE HITLER, 1938-1939. In the immediate aftermath of World War I, antiwar sentiment also ran high in Europe. As a result, European leaders sought to avoid war through a policy of **appeasement** which recognized Adolf Hitler's claims to former territory lost by Germany in the Versailles peace treaty that ended World War I. British Prime Minister Neville Chamberlain and French Premier Edouard Daladier became Europe's most eloquent and avid spokesmen for appeasement. While Chamberlain and Daladier sought peace, Hitler saw weakness.

This policy found tragic expression when Chamberlain and Daladier met with Hitler in Munich in September 1938 amid a crisis caused by Germany's demand to **annex** the Sudeten region of Czechoslovakia. Hitler's troops had already rolled into Austria earlier in 1938. Chamberlain fervently believed that appeasement might contain Hitler's appetite for expansion. He therefore accepted Hitler's "right" to the Sudetenland.

Chamberlain's hopes were short-lived. That November Hitler launched a vicious attack against Jews in Germany that included burning and looting synagogues and shops. This campaign of terror led to an exodus of Jewish and non-Jewish intellectuals, scientists, and artists. Still, Congress refused to open the immigration quota system to allow more Jewish refugees into the United States. As a result of this policy, thousands of Jews remained in Germany. Most were destined to die in wartime **Nazi** extermination camps.

Less than six months after the Munich Conference, Hitler launched a full-scale invasion to annex the remainder of Czechoslovakia. Nevertheless, Chamberlain continued to espouse appeasement even as Mussolini invaded Albania, Franco won in Spain, and Japan proclaimed its intention to create a

Greater East Asia Co-Prosperity Sphere in China and Manchuria. On August 23, 1939, the Soviet Union and Germany — previously bitter enemies — shocked the world when they entered into a defense pact. The pact included a secret agreement to partition Poland between them. Still, many European leaders believed that war could be prevented.

Hitler's invasion of Poland on September 1, 1939, shattered this illusion. Two days after the invasion, England declared war on Germany; six hours later the French government, more reluctantly, followed. The Poles valiantly resisted, but their fate was sealed when the Soviet Union's **Red** army attacked from the east. Warsaw fell in less than a month.

ROOSEVELT HELPS ENGLAND BUT AVOIDS WAR, 1940. After Poland's defeat, a six-month lull in the war occurred — which the press quickly called the "Phony War." The Soviet Union's treacherous attack on Finland on November 30, 1939, still did not convince some that war had come to Europe. Following this winter of illusion, Hitler quickly conquered most of western Europe beginning with his invasion of Norway and Denmark in early April 1940. The next month, Hitler's tanks surprised French, Belgian, and British troops when they rolled through the hilly and wooded Ardennes — an area the Allied High Command had considered impassable to tanks. Caught from behind, the British army barely escaped by sea from Dunkirk, France. A week later, on June 22, 1940, the remaining French forces surrendered. Britain now stood alone against Nazi Germany.

Germany's rapid conquest of most of Western Europe swung American public opinion toward the cause of the **Allies,** but isolationist sentiment remained strong. As a consequence, Roosevelt pursued a cautious policy of aiding England, while promising to keep America out of the war. Three weeks after the invasion of Poland, FDR asked a special session of Congress to replace the arms embargo with a cash-and-carry principle that provided munitions and raw materials to England. Roosevelt's request set off a storm of criticism. Thousands of telegrams flooded into Congress pleading to "keep America out of the blood business." After six weeks of bitter debate, Congress finally agreed to allow England to buy munitions, if bought with cash and transported on British ships.

With England tottering at the brink of defeat, Roosevelt now called for an additional $1 billion for a massive defense program, including the production of 50,000 airplanes a year. (The urgency of the program was all too apparent: the army had only 350 serviceable infantry tanks, 2,806 mostly outmoded aircraft, and no antiaircraft ammunition). Under fierce air attack, England pleaded for American aid. Chamberlain had been replaced as prime minister by Winston Churchill, who warned Roosevelt that the situation was critical.

On September 2, 1940, Roosevelt offered Britain 50 rusting World War I navy destroyers in exchange for a 99-year lease on naval and air bases in Newfoundland and the Caribbean. In October Congress enacted the first peacetime conscription law in American history.

ISOLATIONISTS OPPOSE ROOSEVELT. These military measures outraged isolationists who found support among Irish and German ethnic groups, college students, and elements in the Republican party. In the summer of 1940, isolationists organized the America First Committee to oppose Roosevelt's defense program. Led by a group of midwestern businessmen, including Robert Wood of Sears, Roebuck, the meat packer Jay Hormel, and Robert McCormick, publisher of the *Chicago Tribune,* the America First Committee found its most eloquent spokesman in the aviator hero Charles Lindbergh. Lindbergh's wife, Anne Morrow Lindbergh, had revealed profascist sympathies in her widely read book, *The Wave of the Future* (1939). Charles Lindbergh drew thousands to America First rallies throughout the nation, filling stadiums throughout the Midwest and the Hollywood Bowl in California. Lindbergh's accusations that America was being led into war by a Jewish conspiracy caused a backlash in mainstream America, but isolationist passions continued to find expression in Congress, especially as the election of 1940 approached.

ROOSEVELT WINS, LENDS AID TO ENGLAND, 1940. To ensure Republican support for his program and counter the isolationists, Roosevelt appointed two Republicans to his cabinet, Henry Stimson as secretary of war and Frank Knox as secretary of the navy. Roosevelt's appointments stole thunder from the Republicans on the eve of their national convention. Believing that FDR would not break the time-honored tradition of not serving more than two terms, the Republicans nominated former Democrat and anti-New Dealer Wendell Willkie to head their presidential **ticket**. In a bitter campaign, Roosevelt won, but with only 55 percent of the vote.

After the election, Roosevelt confidently pursued a forthright policy of aiding the Allied cause. In December 1940 Churchill reported to Roosevelt that Britain faced its darkest hour. Financially broke, Britain could no longer afford to purchase war materials. Roosevelt acted swiftly. In the spring of 1941, Roosevelt requested Congress to establish the **lend-lease** program to provide $7 billion for production and export of military supplies. The Lend-Lease Act (1941) empowered the president to lend Britain money to lease military arms. With the passage of the bill, Roosevelt announced that the United States was determined to become the "arsenal of democracy."

JAPAN ATTACKS PEARL HARBOR, 1941. In late 1940, Roosevelt shifted his attention increasingly toward Japanese **imperialism** in Asia. In September 1940, Japan entered into the Tripartite Pact with Germany and Italy to create the **Axis** alliance.

The Axis' opportunity for expansion came in June 1941 with Germany's invasion of the Soviet Union. Expecting England's imminent surrender, Hitler broke Germany's nonaggression pact with the Soviet leader Stalin and launched a surprise attack on the Soviet Union on June 22, 1941.

Japan took advantage of Allied problems in Europe by occupying the southern portion of French Indochina. Japan's wanton attack on Indochina outraged Roosevelt, who placed an embargo on aviation oil and scrap metal to Japan. As United States-Japanese relations deteriorated, a faction within the Japanese government advocated avoiding war through negotiation.

American and Japanese negotiators, however, found little common ground between the two nations. For example, Japan offered to refrain from armed aggression in Southeast Asia, if the United States restored trade and recognized its position in China. The United States, on the other hand, demanded that Japan withdraw from China and Indochina. By September 1941, negotiations appeared stalemated. Japanese militarists began drafting secret war plans, and in October an extremist faction headed by Admiral Hideki Tojo took over the government. Final negotiations were underway in Washington when Japan launched a surprise attack on the Pacific fleet stationed at Pearl Harbor, Hawaii, on December 7, 1941. Within hours Japanese aviators had disabled or sunk eight battleships, three cruisers, and three destroyers. Simultaneously, Japan attacked the Philippines, Hong Kong, Thailand, Malaya, and Wake and Midway islands.

The next day, December 8, 1941, President Roosevelt appeared before Congress. "Yesterday, December 7, 1941 — a date which will live in infamy — the United States of America was suddenly and deliberately attacked by naval and air forces of the empire of Japan," he declared. "We will gain the inevitable triumph, so help us God." After Congress declared war on Japan, Italy and Germany brought the Axis pact into play by declaring war on the United States. The United States had entered the Second World War.

The War Transforms the Home Front

Once the United States entered the war, it went all-out to win. Roosevelt created a myriad of federal agencies to manage the war effort. As production boomed so did the economy. Despite re-sentiment of rationing, Americans widely supported the war effort. The government sought to protect civil liberties of dissenters, but this policy was marred when the government relocated Japanese-Americans into special camps.

The war created labor shortages that created new employment opportunities for African-Americans and women. Blacks moved north to take jobs, but found discrimination and racial hostility. Native Americans and Mexican-Americans joined in the war effort.

AMERICANS MOBILIZE FOR WAR. The global nature of the war entailed the total **mobilization** of the United States as a military and industrial power. More than 16 million men and women served in the armed services during the war: 11.2 million in the army, 4.1 million in the navy and coast guard, 670,000 in the marines, and 216,000 women in the auxiliary services. Of those 16 million who served in the armed services, 291,000 died in battle — less than half the total during the Civil War.

The war unleashed an industrial giant that had slept through the Great Depression of the 30s. American production skyrocketed. In 1944 the United States produced more munitions than all of the Axis nations combined. America supplied 45 percent of the total arms used by all nations during the war.

ROOSEVELT ORGANIZES WARTIME GOVERNMENT. Roosevelt pursued the war in much the same way he had confronted the depression. He created myriad agencies (more than 45) that often competed with one another for resources and power. Before the outbreak of war, he created the War Resources Board (WRB) and the Office of Production Management (OPM). Without extensive powers to mobilize war production, the agencies faced massive shortages of steel, copper, rubber, and other vital raw materials. Finally, in January 1942, Roosevelt established the War Production Board (WPB), headed by the Sears, Roebuck marketing executive Donald Nelson.

The government's war effort proved to be a remarkable success. Although war **profiteering** occurred, leading to congressional investigations spearheaded by a special Senate committee chaired by Missouri Senator Harry S. Truman, war production boomed. By 1944 unemployment fell to 1.2 percent. In many cities **skid rows** vanished overnight.

With war production in full swing by 1943, there was a shortage of labor. As a consequence, pay rates soared as average weekly wages increased from $24.96 in 1940 to $45.70 in 1944. Workers changed jobs frequently. Strikes were kept to a minimum, however, through the cooperation of organized labor. Unions expanded from 10 million to nearly 15 million members, primarily among industrial unions organized by the Congress of Industrial Organizations. The demand for labor drew women, blacks, and older workers into the workforce.

AMERICAN CONSUMERS COPE WITH RATIONING. American industrial capability was so vast that even in wartime half of its production continued to go to consumer goods. Unlike their counterparts in England and Russia, American civilians experienced little **rationing.** In April 1941, Roosevelt established the Office of Price Administration (OPA) to set prices and wages. By imposing wage and price controls, wartime **inflation** was kept at a minimum, well below the rate of inflation during the First World War. Controls also created lucrative black markets.

Nevertheless, even limited rationing created an undercurrent of resentment in the American electorate. Because there was a shortage of imported rubber used in making tires, the government sought to conserve tires by imposing gasoline rationing, setting a national 25 mph speed limit, and setting up road blocks to stop Sunday driving. A shortage of leather forced the government to limit consumers to three pairs of leather shoes a year. War also brought forced the rationing of nylon hose, sugar, coffee, and meat.

The planting of 20 million "Victory Gardens" by homeowners, city officials, and businesses produced nearly 40 percent of all vegetables grown in the country and created an excess of green vegetables for the American consumer. Also, the emergence of a "black market," where goods could be bought at higher prices without ration cards, made most goods available. Yet it also encouraged crime. Hijacking of trucks carrying liquor, nylon stockings, and shoes became common, and in the West cattle rustling revived.

Despite their resentment against limited rationing, Americans generally rallied to the war effort and purchased over $156 billion in war **bonds,** accounting for nearly half of the $389 billion spent by the government during the war. The other half of the war's cost was raised through significantly higher taxes. Many more people had to pay income tax, and the top bracket was raised to 98 percent. In order to expedite tax collection, the government instituted a "pay-as-you-go" taxation scheme by withholding income tax from current paychecks. Prior to the war, income taxes were due in one annual lump-sum payment.

ROOSEVELT LEAVES A MIXED RECORD ON CIVIL LIBERTIES. The war unified the American nation as never before. In the war against fascism, few Americans dissented. Less than one-fifth of one percent of the 34 million who registered for the draft declared themselves **conscientious objectors,**

who opposed war on religious grounds. These were mostly members of Quaker, Mennonite, and Brethren sects. Although some Jehovah's Witnesses went to jail because they refused any involvement in the war, most consciousness objectors were treated fairly.

The Office of War Information, headed by newsman Elmer Davis, promoted American patriotism through radio broadcasts, pamphlets, and posters. Unlike the Creel Committee, the government information agency during the First World War, the Office of War Information did not suppress dissent or target "un-American" antiwar opponents.

Furthermore, the Supreme Court showed a strong determination to uphold the right of free speech. Court decisions upheld the right to criticize the draft and the war effort. When the government tried to prosecute 25 members of the fascist German-American Bund (a pro-German political organization), the court threw out the case.

This fine civil liberties record, however, was severely tarnished by the federal government's actions against people of Japanese ancestry in California, Oregon, and Washington. The government ordered the evacuation of Japanese-Americans — citizens and aliens alike — without trial to "relocation" camps in the interior of the nation in a flagrant disregard for civil liberties. The evacuation of the Japanese was undertaken under executive orders signed by Roosevelt in early 1942. Over 112,000 Japanese-Americans were forced, under great emotional and economic stress, to leave their homes and farms to move into military-run camps surrounded by barbed wire. The Supreme Court upheld this relocation policy in the *Hirabayashi* case (1943) and the *Korematsu* and *Endo* cases (1944). In his dissent to the *Korematsu* case, however, Justice Frank Murphy argued that this interpretation pushed constitutional power to the "ugly abyss of racism."

AFRICAN-AMERICANS EXPERIENCE THE WAR AT HOME. The employment of blacks and women created new demands for equality and fair treatment in the work place. In this way, the American home front portended the transformation of postwar life and society.

New economic opportunities encouraged large numbers of African-Americans to move north. Once in the North, however, they found that employers often hesitated to hire them. Confronted by seemingly impenetrable racial barriers, black leaders demanded federal intervention to ensure that the war against fascism meant democratic participation for all races at home. In the summer of 1941, the black **socialist** and labor leader A. Philip Randolph called for a march on Washington to pressure FDR into taking action. Under mounting political pressure, Roosevelt issued an executive order establishing the Fair Employment Practices Committee with powers to investigate complaints of employment discrimination. By 1942, African-Americans were entering the northern urban workforce in large numbers.

Black migration transformed northern cities. The massive influx northward created a volatile situation in many cities. For example, more than 500,000 people had flooded into Detroit between 1940 and 1943. Here, 60,000 African-Americans found themselves living in some of the worst housing in the nation. Local white ethnic groups, mainly Poles and Irish, bitterly resented the new arrivals. Tension reached a boiling point when rumors began to spread both among blacks and whites of incidents of rape and assault. On June 23, 1943, black and white teenagers clashed at a Detroit recreation park. Blacks then began attacking unsuspecting white workers returning from the night shift, and bands of whites poured into the street randomly attacking blacks. The next day full-scale rioting erupted as whites rampaged through the black ghetto. With violence spreading, Governor Frank Murphy called out 6,000 national guardsmen to quell the riot. The episode left 25 blacks and nine whites dead.

That August a riot in Harlem ended in the deaths of six blacks and 300 people injured. To restore order the New York police deputized 15,000 blacks, who quickly contained the riot. These incidents shocked the nation and became ready propaganda for the Nazis who broadcast reports of the riots to Allied troops.

Nevertheless, the war brought new opportunities to many black Americans. More than 800,000 African-Americans served in the armed forces during the war. The fight for democracy abroad encouraged African-Americans to seek civil rights at home. In 1942, militant black leaders formed the Congress of Racial Equality (CORE) to sponsor nonviolent protest to achieve civil rights. In 1943, CORE conducted a series of **sit-ins** in a number of major cities to integrate restaurants and movie theaters. At the same time, the National Association for the Advancement of Colored People (NAACP) quadrupled its membership. Young lawyers such as Thurgood Marshall planned a judicial strategy to challenge the "separate but equal" doctrine that had been used to justify **segregation** and had shaped racial policy since the end of the nineteenth century.

HISPANICS AND NATIVE AMERICANS AT WAR. The war brought changes to other ethnic minorities as well. Native Americans actively supported the war effort. With the outbreak of the war, the Pueblo Indians retreated to their ancient shrine where they prayed for victory. The Indians of the Six Nations of the Iroquois Confederacy declared war on the Axis. Over 29,000 Native Americans joined the armed services. A contingent of Navaho fighting in the Pacific formed a special communications unit, the Code Talkers, who used their native language to communicate on the battle front. More than 100,000 Native Americans migrated to cities to take war jobs.

Hispanics displayed deep patriotic feelings by volunteering in the armed forces in disproportionate numbers. Mexican-Americans gained fame fighting for the 200th and 515th Coast Artillery in the campaign for the Philippines. During the war, 17 Mexican-Americans won Congressional Medals of Honor.

Mobilization also opened new opportunities for Hispanics at home. Discrimination against Mexican-Americans in the copper mines of Arizona and the shipyards and oil refineries on the Pacific coast led FDR to appoint Carlos Castaneda, a prominent political leader, as assistant to the chairman of the Fair Employment Practices Committee. The Spanish-speaking People's Division was created in the Office of Inter-American Affairs to confront problems of discrimination against Hispanics. This office played a key role in reducing segregation in public schools in Texas and California.

The labor shortage during the war led the federal government to renew a program of importing Mexican farm labor to the United States through the "bracero" (worker) program. These guest workers alleviated the shortage of agricultural workers during the war. The war, however, worsened ethnic tensions, especially in large western cities. In Los Angeles, some young Mexican-Americans formed *Pachuco* (a slang term for "newcomers") gangs that led to confrontations with soldiers and sailors on leave. Noted for their "zoot suits" — a distinctive suit characterized by large shoulder pads, trousers ballooning at the knee with narrow ankles, accompanied by broad-brimmed felt hats — these *Pachuco* gangs often roamed the streets engaging in acts of vandalism and assault. Following a series of attacks on servicemen, a group of angry sailors stationed at the Chavez Ravine Naval Base entered East Los Angeles and attacked these gangs. Their attack sparked a two-day riot involving 1,000 youths before order was restored. During the spring of 1943, smaller disturbances erupted in San Diego, Long Beach, Chicago, Detroit, and Philadelphia.

WOMEN CHALLENGE TRADITION. At the war's outset, many employers hesitated to hire women. Labor shortages and efforts by the Women's Bureau of the Department of Labor soon overcame this initial resistance. Between 1940 and 1945 the number of women in the workforce spiraled upward from 12 million in 1940 to 18.6 million in 1945, making women workers a third of the work force. These women performed every job from welding to operating heavy equipment. As a result, many unions promoted women to leadership positions, called for federal child care centers, and demanded "equal pay for equal work."

The federal government responded positively to these demands. The War

Production Board and the War Manpower Commission accepted an equal-pay policy. Under the Lanham Act (1940) the federal government established federally funded day-care centers for children of working mothers.

Because many of these women took jobs formerly held by men, they presented an implicit challenge to traditional notions of women. At the same time, disruptions to family life caused by the war reinforced beliefs that women should subordinate personal ambition for the benefit of the family. Nonetheless, the war marked a turning point in making it acceptable for women to combine their role in the home with paid employment. Three-fourths of working women were married. After the war, many women quit their jobs, but by 1950 the percentage of women working outside the home still was 29 percent, higher than it had been a decade earlier.

The war also encouraged greater involvement of women in government. The number of women entering the civil service rose from 200,000 in 1939 to 1 million in 1944, making up 38 percent of all federal office workers. Women's groups, such as the American Association of University Women and the National Federation of Business and Professional Women's Clubs, lobbied for legislation to prevent discrimination. State campaigns were launched to protect women from job discrimination, make women eligible for jury duty, and eliminate legal restrictions on married women. Although women divided on the issue of an equal rights amendment to the Constitution, 11 states endorsed such an amendment. Women also entered political office in greater numbers. By 1945, 228 women had been elected to state legislatures, up from 144 the previous year.

Nevertheless, poor housing, inadequate child care services, long working hours, and single-parent households strained the American family. Juvenile delinquency increased, leading many experts to decry the breakdown of the American family. Everywhere, school truancy and juvenile arrests for loitering and petty crimes appeared on the rise. Sexual promiscuity and venereal disease rose dramatically. Teenage girls, called "Victory girls" by the press, provided "companionship" to lonely servicemen.

The United States Fights in Europe and the Pacific

The United States fought on five fronts — a vicious war in the Pacific, a fierce naval war in the North Atlantic, an involved campaign against the Germans in North Africa, an air war over Europe, and a major military operation in western and central Europe.

The war occurred in three phases from 1942 through 1945. The first phase, in 1942, was primarily defensive in the Pacific and in Europe. The second phase, during 1943, turned the Allied tide with a costly island campaign in the Pacific, massive bombing raids on German industry, and a Middle East campaign. The last phase brought victory in Europe beginning with the Allied landing in France on June 6, 1944, and the final defeat of Japan.

THE UNITED STATES ON THE DEFENSIVE, 1942. Following the attack on Pearl Harbor, the Japanese swept through the Pacific. In March 1942, the Japanese navy inflicted heavy losses on an Allied fleet in the Battle of the Java Sea. Two months later, in May 1942, the Japanese army in a well-executed campaign finally broke the valiant resistance of American troops under Generals Douglas MacArthur and Jonathan B. Wainwright in the Philippines. The Japanese onslaught was stopped only by American victories in the battles of the Coral Sea and Midway. The loss of four Japanese aircraft carriers at Midway Island, located through breaking Japanese codes, ended the Japanese army's control of the air and spelled Japan's ultimate doom.

In the Atlantic, German submarines, called **U-boats**, sank Allied ships nearly at will throughout 1942. The Allies lost an average of three boats a day, which kept vital supplies from reaching Europe. Ships sank faster than shipyards could replace them. Only the introduction of newly developed British radar equipment which could detect lurking German submarines and the use of elaborate convoys of hundreds of Allied vessels restored Allied shipping in early 1943. As the year drew to a close, the United States had been able to cut its losses to less than 1 percent of its traffic in the Atlantic.

The German Afrika Korps under General Erwin Rommel (known as the "desert fox") swept through North Africa and threatened to seize the Suez Canal, crucial to Allied shipping and oil supplies. An extended American, British, and Free French offensive finally forced Rommel's withdrawal from North Africa in the spring of 1943.

THE ALLIES TURN THE TIDE, 1943. In 1943 the Allies took the offensive. American industrial production, now in full swing, provided the ships, planes, tanks, trucks, and munitions that overwhelmed both Japan and Germany. Beginning in 1943, British and American air forces initiated massive bombing raids on German industrial centers. Employing from 1,000 to 1,500 bombers, these raids rained destruction on Germany.

Despite Allied efforts, German production increased throughout 1942. In

Map 26.1. World War II in Europe

January 1943, the Allied command ordered intensified raids on Germany to undermine the "morale of the German people." The destruction wrought by Allied air attacks was horrendous. Within the year, a total of 200,000 tons of bombs destroyed city after city in Germany.

THE ALLIES ENTER INTO THE FINAL PHASE OF WAR, 1944. By 1944 the defeat of Germany and Japan was certain. The only question was when. On the eastern front, the Soviet army courageously withstood the German siege of Stalingrad (now called Volgograd) from September 1942 to February 1943. Thousands died and the city was devastated before the German forces finally withdrew. The Red army then began a long offensive that drove the Germans back. By 1944 the Russian army moved at will, checked only by the limits of its own supply lines. The Russians launched their final offensive against the Germans in June 1944 to coincide with the British-American landings in Normandy, France. By late July the Russian army had driven the Germans back to Warsaw, Poland. There the Russians halted their advance, allowing the Germans to crush a rebellion by the Polish resistance. By autumn 1944, the Russians were once again on the march.

On June 6, 1944 — D-Day — American and British forces under the Supreme Allied Commander Dwight D. Eisenhower launched their long-awaited campaign on the European mainland by massive landings of troops on the beaches of Normandy, France. More than 2 million troops stormed Hitler's "Atlantic Wall," including a force of 58 divisions in the west of France, which included ten panzer tank divisions. Within weeks the American army broke through German lines and sped to liberate Paris on August 25, 1944.

In the spring of 1945 the Russian and American armies met inside Germany. As the American army under General George Patton approached Berlin, Eisenhower ordered him to withdraw to Prague, Czechoslovakia, to allow the Soviets to enter Berlin first — an agreement reached by FDR, Churchill, and Stalin. On April 30, as the German army waged a desperate street-by-street resistance to the entering Russian army, Hitler and his recent bride, Eva Braun, committed suicide. On May 8, 1945 the war in Europe officially ended with Germany's unconditional surrender.

The liberation of Germany revealed the stark horror of the Nazi regime and its extermination program against the Jews. Reports of death camps had first arrived in Washington in late 1942, but nothing could have prepared American soldiers for what they discovered when they entered these camps. In mid-April 1945, Eisenhower visited an extermination camp. Accompanied by top staff officers, Eisenhower moved in silent horror through the barracks where naked and emaciated bodies of Jewish inmates were piled. Following the tour, Eisenhower told his officers, "I want every American unit not actually in the front lines to see this place. . . . Now, at least, he will know what he is fighting against."

As other camps were liberated by Allied troops, the full extent of the extermination program became obvious. Of the 8 million Jews living in German-occupied territory only 2.3 million escaped. Six million non-Jews, including Polish Catholics, gypsies, communists, homosexuals, or anyone else the Nazis disliked, also died in the camps.

Planning the Postwar World

Roosevelt, Churchill, and Stalin coordinated strategy for ending the war and shaped the postwar order. Roosevelt held fast to his overriding priority: creating a new international organization, the United Nations. In order to secure Roosevelt's assent to Soviet influence in eastern Europe, Stalin withheld his acceptance of the United Nations until late in the war. These wartime compromises became the basis of the Cold War, which would dominate world affairs for the next 45 years. Roosevelt died before either the end of the war or the founding of the United Nations.

DESIGNING A GREAT ALLIANCE. Roosevelt began preparing for the postwar world even before the United States entered the war. In August 1941, Roosevelt and Churchill met off the coast of Newfoundland. The meeting concluded with a joint declaration known as the Atlantic Charter, which promised a world without war "after the final destruction of the Nazi tyranny." The Atlantic Charter envisioned a new postwar international organization to replace the League of Nations, and affirmed democracy's adherence to the Four Freedoms — freedom from want, freedom from fear, freedom of speech, and freedom of religion.

Soon after the attack on Pearl Harbor, Roosevelt announced the formation of the United Nations alliance, composed of nations opposed to the Axis powers. These nations pledged themselves through the Declaration of the United Nations, issued on January 1, 1942, to support the principles of the Atlantic Charter (1941) and not to conclude a separate peace with the Axis powers. (Even so, rumors circulated throughout the war that the Soviet Union was prepared to sign a separate peace with Hitler).

Both Roosevelt and Churchill shared a profound faith in the British-American democratic tradition. This sense of cooperation led the United States and Britain to establish during the war the Combined Chiefs of Staff, composed of ranking military commanders of each nation. This body shaped military strategy, conducted joint operations, and allocated supplies and resources. Although inevitable tensions arose between rival commanders, the Combined Chiefs of Staff functioned remarkably well.

Roosevelt believed that China, under military dictator Chiang Kai-shek, should be treated as an equal power, but Chiang often seemed more interested in resuming the civil war against the communists than engaging the Japanese. General Joseph W. Stilwell reported widespread corruption in Chiang's army, including selling American supplies to the Japanese. Nevertheless, FDR authorized more than $4 billion of lend-lease aid and provided an additional $100 million in loans to Nationalist China.

COMPROMISING WITH STALIN. The most difficult relationship within the alliance remained the Soviet Union. The Soviet regime continued to be tightly controlled by its ruthless dictator, Josef Stalin. Stalin remained fiercely nationalistic and suspicious of the western democracies. Nevertheless, in order to gain American supplies through the lend-lease program, Stalin agreed to mute communist propaganda against the West. As a consequence, the United States sent more than $11 billion in supplies to help the Soviet Union in its war against Hitler.

Relationships became severely strained in 1942, however, when Stalin insisted that a western front be opened in France. At Churchill's urging, however, Roosevelt postponed an Allied landing in France and instead launched an invasion of North Africa in January 1942. Shortly afterward, British, American, and Free French leaders met in Casablanca, Morocco, to discuss the next phase of the military campaign. Here, Churchill, Roosevelt, and France's Charles DeGaulle decided to invade Europe through Italy. This decision precluded a second major front against Germany. To assuage the angry Stalin, Roosevelt and Churchill agreed to meet with Stalin in Teheran, Iran, in late November 1943.

The Teheran meeting marked the height of Allied cooperation. Churchill, Roosevelt, and Stalin reached an accord on a number of key points. The United States and Britain accepted a date for an invasion of France. The Allies also agreed to the principle that Germany would never again be a military power. At Stalin's urging, Roosevelt agreed to send military aid to the communist underground leader Tito in Yugoslavia. Churchill and Roosevelt also accepted Stalin's demand that Poland's western and eastern borders be radically shifted to the west. Questions, however, concerning democratic elections in Poland divided the Allies. In particular, Churchill sought recognition of the London-based Polish government in exile, while Stalin wanted recognition for his communist-controlled Polish government. As a bargaining chip, Stalin refused to make a commitment to the new international organization that Roosevelt and Churchill wanted.

THE BIG THREE BARGAIN IN YALTA. Shortly after his election to a fourth term in 1944, Roosevelt flew in February 1945 to Yalta in the Russian Crimea where he met once again with Churchill and Stalin. The looming defeat of Germany set the context for the final meeting of the **Big Three.** Roosevelt came to Yalta with one primary goal: the creation of a new international or-

Map 26.2. World War II in the Pacific

ganization, the United Nations. Roosevelt seemed willing to subsume all other questions to achieve Stalin's acceptance for a postwar United Nations organization.

The Big Three turned first to the German question. Stalin proposed that Germany be divided into three separate states. He stated bluntly that Germany's heavy industry should be destroyed and that Germany should pay a huge **reparation** of $20 billion (half of which was to go to the Soviet Union). The final resolution of reparations and other questions concerning postwar Germany, however, were left to a later joint commission.

Before Yalta, British, American, and Soviet representatives had agreed to a basic structure for the new United Nations, but could not agree on voting procedures. Soviets wanted veto power over the Security Council (the executive committee of the organization) and demanded that the 16 Soviet republics be given separate voting powers in the organization's general body, the General Assembly. At Yalta, Roosevelt now conceded the principle that each permanent member of the Security Council hold a veto power. In return, Stalin dropped his demand for General Assembly representation from 16 to three seats (Ukraine, White Russia, and the Soviet Union). With Stalin's acceptance of the United Nations, Roosevelt felt he had achieved a major diplomatic victory.

Next came the question of establishing a postwar government in Poland. Roosevelt and Churchill accepted Stalin's claim to land in eastern Poland. There was little choice: Stalin's army had been there since 1939. In return, Stalin agreed to free Polish elections, although the mechanics of these elections were never decided. One aide warned Roosevelt that the Polish agreement was "so elastic that the Russians can stretch it all the way from Yalta to Washington without technically breaking it."

Finally, Stalin agreed to declare war on Japan "in two or three months after Germany surrendered." (The Soviet Union and Japan had agreed tacitly not to fight, so each could avoid fighting on a second front.)

Shortly after the Yalta meeting, on April 12, 1945, Roosevelt died of a cerebral hemorrhage. Throughout the war, Roosevelt had kept foreign policy in his own hands. His death brought into the White House his vice-president, Harry S. Truman, a man of little experience in world affairs.

The United States Defeats Japan

Despite decisive Allied victories in the Pacific and deadly fire-bombing of Toyko, Japan refused to surrender. In order to avoid a bloody land invasion of Japan and end the war quickly, the new American president, Harry Truman, ordered atomic bombs — the most powerful weapons ever invented — dropped on two Japanese cities. Japan surrendered.

JAPAN CONTINUES TO FIGHT. With Germany's surrender and a new president, Americans turned to the defeat of Japan. The war in the Pacific proved especially fierce. By early 1944 the Japanese had been driven out of the central Pacific islands. The Japanese, however, showed no signs of surrendering.

Chief of Staff George C. Marshall and Pacific Commander General Douglas MacArthur concluded that only an invasion of Japan could end the war. Calculations indicated that such an invasion would be costly — perhaps as high as one million American casualties. On March 9, 1944, an American air raid on Tokyo using incendiary bombs took approximately 185,000 lives and destroyed 267,000 buildings. In the battle for Okinawa, an island between Formosa and Japan that the Japanese considered part of their homeland, the Japanese had put up a fierce defense from April 1 through mid-May 1945. In the battle for Okinawa, Japanese planes undertook **"kamikaze"** suicide attacks, sending 700 pilots to crash their planes on American ships. During the three-month campaign, Japan lost an estimated 110,000 soldiers, while America experienced 49,000 casualties.

THE WAR ENDS. Japan's continued resistance created deep anxiety among Truman's military chiefs. Although Tojo's militarist government had been replaced, signs of surrender still had not appeared. Seeking a quick solution to the end the war, Truman turned to atomic weapons, developed by American and British scientists at Los Alamos, New Mexico. These weapons were more powerful than any other developed in human history. Although leading American scientists expressed opposition to using the bomb, military advisers felt that the bomb offered a "merciful abridgement of the slaughter in the East." Concerned with the further loss of American lives, Truman ordered the bomb dropped.

On August 6, 1945 a single atomic bomb leveled the city of Hiroshima with casualties of 130,000. When the Japanese military leaders did not immediately surrender, Truman ordered a second bomb dropped on the city of Nagasaki, wounding and killing approximately 75,000 people on August 9. On August 15th a stunned Japanese nation listened to their emperor announce the end of the war.

In the context of war, in which an estimated 45 million people lost their lives, the atomic bomb appeared to be just another weapon — a weapon that had mercifully ended a terrible war. The bomb also revealed the extent of American military power to a Soviet Union whose relations with the United States were already appearing strained.

Conclusion

The Second World War taught Americans an important lesson: never again would the United States be caught with its guard down, unprepared for war. Never again would the nation turn its back on world events. Never again would aggression be appeased. And, it was this new consciousness that would lead the United States to counter the Soviet Union at every turn in the postwar world. The nation had entered into a new era.

Recommended Readings

DOCUMENTS: Omar N. Bradley, *A Soldier's Story* (1951); Dwight D. Eisenhower, *Crusade in Europe* (1948); and Phillip McGuire, ed., *Taps for a Jim Crow Army: Letters from Black Soldiers in World War II* (1982).

536   26 • *A Global Nation: World War II and the Origins of the Cold War*

READINGS: (GENERAL) A. Russell Buchanan, *The United States and World War II* (2 vols., 1964); Robert A. Divine, *Roosevelt and World War II* (1969); B. H. Liddell Hart, *History of the Second World War* (1970); Martha Byrd Hoyle, *A World in Flames: The History of World War II* (1970); Gordon Wright, *The Ordeal of Total War* (1968). (COMING OF WAR) Robert Dallek, *Franklin D. Roosevelt and American Foreign Policy* (1979); Robert Divine, *The Reluctant Belligerent* (1979); Gordon Prange, *At Dawn We Slept* (1981); John Toland, *Infamy* (1982); David Wyman, *The Abandonment of the Jews* (1984). (MILITARY) John Dower, *War Without Mercy: Race and Power in the Pacific War* (1986); Kent R. Greenfield, *American Strategy in World War II* (1963); Akira Iriye, *Power and Culture: The Japanese-American War* (1981); John Keegan, *Six Armies in Normandy* (1982); Robert Leckie, *Delivered from Evil* (1987); Charles B. MacDonald, *The Mighty Endeavor* (1969); Bernard C. Nalty, *Strength for the Fight: A History of Black Americans in the Military* (1986); Ronald H. Spector, *Eagle Against the Sun: The American War with Japan* (1984); and John Toland, *The Rising Sun* (1970). (HOMEFRONT) Robert Abzug, *Inside the Vicious Heart: Americans and the Liberation of Nazi Concentration Camps* (1985); Karen T. Anderson, *Wartime Women* (1981); John M. Blum, *"V" Was for Victory* (1976); David Brinkley, *Washington Goes to War* (1988); Roger Daniels, *Concentration Camps U.S.A.* (1971); Leonard Dinnerstein, *America and the Survivors of the Holocaust* (1982); Susan Hartman, *The Home Front and Beyond: American Women in the 1940s* (1982); Clayton Koppes and Gregory Black, *Hollywood Goes to War* (1986); Nelson Lichtenstein, *Labor's War at Home* (1982); Richard Lingeman, *Don't You Know There's a War On?* (1970); Mauricio Mazon, *The Zoot Suit Riots* (1984); Gerald Nash, *The American West Transformed* (1985); Richard Polenberg, *War and Society* (1972); Harold Vatter, *The American Economy in World War II* (1984).

27

✖

THE COLD WAR HAUNTS THE "FABULOUS FIFTIES"

CHAPTER OVERVIEW: The postwar years after 1945 brought renewed prosperity to the American people. Looming over this era of abundance, however, was the threat of the Soviet Union. The development of nuclear weapons and the emergence of the Soviet Union as a world power affected nearly every aspect of American politics — foreign and domestic. The ideological conflict between the Soviet Union and the United States, and the ensuing arms race, became known as the Cold War.

President Harry S. Truman (1945-1953), who had stepped into the White House following Franklin Roosevelt's death, sought to extend New Deal reform at home in what he called the Fair Deal and to contain communism abroad. His Republican successor Dwight D. Eisenhower (1953-1961) undertook moderate domestic reform, while continuing Truman's policy of containment.

American popular culture, too, reflected this mix of complacency and anxiety. Prosperity brought new leisure time, opportunities for greater consumption, higher standards of living, and better prospects for education and worldly success. As the "fabulous fifties" drew to a close, however, Americans began once again to question where their society was headed.

Truman Confronts Communism Abroad and at Home, 1945-1952

Following the death of Franklin Roosevelt, Harry S. Truman came into the presidency under the shadow of his predecessor. In international relations, Truman was slow to find his own voice. He shifted American foreign policy toward a policy of containment of Soviet expansionism. Truman called for rebuilding Europe through the Marshall Plan and for organizing regional defense through the North Atlantic Treaty Alliance (NATO).

In 1950 Truman's attention turned to Asia when the communist North Korean army invaded South Korea. Truman succeeded in having the United Nations pass a resolution to send troops to Korea in a "police action." The Korean War still had not been resolved by the time Truman left office.

Tensions with communism abroad created anticommunist sentiment at home. Republican Senator Joseph R. McCarthy of Wisconsin became a leading force in this anticommunist crusade by attacking opponents, often without any evidence of communist involvement.

FACING TENSIONS WITH THE SOVIET UNION, 1945. Upon hearing of Roosevelt's death, Truman told reporters, "The moon, the stars, and all the planets fell on me." Truman stepped into the White House as World War II was drawing to a close. FDR, as was his style with subordinates, had kept his vice-president generally uninformed about his plans for the postwar world.

Many in Washington viewed Truman as a small-time politician lacking the ability or stature to lead the nation. Cabinet members remained loyal to FDR and compared Truman unfavorably to his predecessor. (All but three cabinet members were gone by the end of 1945.) As Truman stumbled from one diplomatic problem to another, many perceived him as a failure.

No doubt a large part of Truman's problems came from a personal style that clashed with eastern New Deal liberals. He was from Missouri, a state that combined the characteristics of the Midwest and the South. (Truman's mother was an unreconstructed Confederate). Although Truman had won election to the U.S. Senate in 1938 as a loyal New Dealer, he was placed on the 1944 presidential **ticket** as a running mate to Roosevelt at the insistence of mainstream Democrats who disliked FDR's liberal vice-president, Henry Wallace. (The popular Wallace became secretary of commerce in early 1945 during Roosevelt's fourth term). The Democrats won an unprecedented fourth term in 1944 against a Republican ticket headed by the New York reformer, Thomas Dewey. Truman had just come into the vice-presidency, when Roosevelt's death in 1945 placed him in the White House.

As Truman surveyed the postwar world, he saw an America unrivaled as an economic and military power. Western Europe had been shattered by the war. England no longer stood as a preeminent imperial power. Germany was devastated. The only threat to world order came from Josef Stalin's Soviet Union. Tensions between the United States and the Soviet Union were already evident before FDR's death in April 1945. The struggle between Russia and the United States soon assumed global dimensions.

Liberals hoped to continue the wartime alliance of the **Big Three** — the United States, Great Britain, and the Soviet Union. Truman, too, wanted to maintain cordial relations with the Soviet Union. At the same time, however, he saw clear signs of Stalin's willful disregard for agreements reached at Yalta, especially those pertaining to eastern Europe. Most apparent was the Soviet Union's brazen suppression of political opposition in Poland. The Soviet Union dominated **coalition** governments in Bulgaria and Hungary. Only in Finland did the Soviets accept genuinely independent leaders.

Other problems between the United States and the Soviet Union exacerbated tensions. At first, the Soviets refused to withdraw their occupation troops from northern Iran, an issue made even more significant by Iran's strategic location in the oil-rich Middle East. The Soviet Union finally agreed, under pressure from the United States, to withdraw from northern Iran in May 1946, but by then relations had already deteriorated.

In Asia, Truman confronted a full-scale civil war between the reactionary and corrupt nationalist government of Chiang Kai-shek and communist insurgents led by Mao Zedong. Americans supported the nationalists, but called for Chiang to institute meaningful political and economic reform. In late 1945, Truman sent General George Marshall as a special **envoy** to settle the conflict. By the spring of 1946 negotiations had collapsed. At home, many liberals held that a **Red** Chinese victory was for the best. Misunderstanding the nature of Chinese **communism,** one liberal journalist declared that the Red Chinese were no more communistic "than the farmers of Minnesota and North Dakota."

Liberals sensed a hardening against the Soviet Union within the administration that included Chief of Staff Admiral William D. Leahy, Secretary of the Navy James V. Forrestal, and Ambassador to the Soviet Union W. Averell Harriman. From mid-July through August 1, 1945, Truman met with Britain's Prime Minister Clement Atlee (the Labor party leader who had just defeated Churchill in the general election) and Stalin at Potsdam, Germany, to discuss postwar problems. The code name of the conference — TERMINAL — proved appropriate; this would be the last time top leaders of the three countries would meet together for a decade.

TRUMAN DECIDES TO "CONTAIN" THE SOVIET UNION, 1946-1949. Relations only worsened in early 1946. In February, George F. Kennan, a long-time State Department official stationed in Moscow, sent Washington officials a closely reasoned analysis of Soviet foreign policy in a 10,000 word telegram. The "long telegram," as it was called, argued that the Soviet Union remained historically and ideologically hostile to democratic government and expansionistic by nature. **Appeasement** would not work; instead, the United States should keep Soviet **expansionism** in check through a policy of containment. He warned, however, that the United States should only defend those places vital to American strategic interests. Kennan later published a shorter version of his memorandum in the influential *Foreign Affairs* magazine, under the pseudonym "X", so as not to reveal his official status in the State Department. Containment remained the general American policy toward the Soviet Union for the next four decades.

Shortly after the Kennan memorandum, former prime minister Winston Churchill, speaking at Westminster College in Fulton, Missouri, asserted that an "iron curtain" had fallen across eastern Europe, dividing the Soviet bloc from western Europe. Many Americans, however, were not ready to accept a prolonged **Cold War** with the Soviet Union. Liberal Senator Claude Pepper, (Democrat-Florida) denounced Churchill's speech as a lame attempt "to make America the great defender of [British] imperialism." Liberals became further alarmed in September 1946, when Truman fired Henry Wallace as secretary of commerce after he spoke in favor of recognizing Soviet dominance in eastern Europe.

With relations rapidly deteriorating, Truman attempted to ease Stalin's suspicions by offering to place atomic weapons under the control of the United Nations. Stalin, calculating that he could build bombs better than he could control the pro-American United Nations, immediately rejected the proposal. Only Stalin knew how close the Soviets were to becoming a nuclear power.

United States-Soviet tensions intensified in 1947, setting a course for relations between the two nations for the next 40 years. Responding to a direct threat to Greece, where communist insurgents had launched a civil war against a military government, Truman appeared before Congress on March 12, 1947 to enunciate the Truman Doctrine — a commitment by the United States to support democratic nations threatened by communist aggression. He specifically requested $450 million in aid for Greece and Turkey to resist such aggression. Although conservative Republicans led by Robert Taft (Ohio) questioned this massive foreign-aid package, the Greek-Turkish aid bill passed Congress by a narrow vote. Truman continued to worry that war-devastated western Europe was ripe for Soviet-backed communist revolution.

In response, Secretary of State George C. Marshall announced a bold economic recovery program to aid western democracies in Europe. The Marshall Plan called for massive economic assistance to aid European economic recovery. The program would bolster Europe's economies, while providing important market and investment opportunities for American business. The Soviets predictably denounced the program as imperialistic.

In February 1948, communists ruthlessly seized power in Czechoslovakia. The Soviet takeover shocked many in the West. Czech foreign minister Jan Masaryk, son of the founder of the republic and a much-admired figure, mysteriously "fell" from a window in his apartment, likely a victim of assassination. The coup in Czechoslovakia confirmed Truman's worst perceptions of Stalin's intentions.

Truman moved to unite American, British, and French military zones in occupied Germany into the Federal Republic of Germany (West Germany). A politically and economically strong West Germany could present a powerful buffer against further Soviet expansion into Europe. In spring 1948, a unified West Germany was created. Berlin now stood divided physically and symbolically into noncommunist West Berlin and communist East Berlin.

The Soviet Union retaliated by blockading all surface traffic into West Berlin. This challenge prompted Truman to initiate a massive airlift to provide West Berlin with food and other provisions. Nearly a year later, in May 1949, Russians finally lifted the blockade; two days later the formation of a West German democratic government was announced. Americans now spoke of a "Cold War" between the United States and the Soviet Union.

Truman pressed for stronger defensive measures against the Soviet Union. Shortly after the 1948 election, the United States and 12 other nations entered the North Atlantic Treaty Organization (NATO), a regional defense alliance that linked Europe and America. In 1949 Truman substantially increased the defense budget and approved the development of a hydrogen bomb. The arms race was on.

TRUMAN SENDS TROOPS TO KOREA, 1950. In the Far East, Truman's attention remained focused on China. By 1949 communist forces led by Mao Zedong had defeated the American-backed nationalist government, forcing its leader, Chiang Kai-shek, to retreat to the island of Taiwan. The new Chinese communist government quickly aligned itself with the Soviet Union. At home, the loss of China created a backlash as conservative Republicans denounced Truman and State Department "liberals" for "losing" China. Fearing further losses in Asia, the Truman began aiding the French in their war against a communist insurgency in Vietnam.

Truman's fears of further communist intrusion in Asia were confirmed when the communist North Korean army launched a full-scale invasion of South Korea in June 1950. (At the end of World War II, Korea had been taken from Japanese control and divided at the thirty-eighth parallel into zones of occupation by the Soviet Union and United States). The Soviet-backed leader of North Korea, Kim Il Sung, had informed Stalin of his intentions and had not been discouraged from the attack. Although the invasion caught the Americans by surprise, Truman moved within hours to prevent the total collapse of South Korea. He ordered additional American troops to Korea and then succeeded in securing a United Nations' Security Council mandate for a "police action." (The Soviet Union failed to veto the U.N. resolution, as might have been expected, because their ambassador had undertaken a poorly timed boycott of the Security Council just at that moment).

In the war's first weeks, the North Koreans overwhelmed Americans fighting under the United Nations banner led by General Douglas MacArthur. Surrounded at Pusan at the southeastern corner of the Korean peninsula, MacArthur executed a brilliant maneuver with an amphibious landing behind enemy lines on the west coast of Korea. Within a week, the North Korean army was routed. Of 400,000 North Korean troops sent south, at least 280,000 were killed.

Overjoyed by the victory, Truman approved MacArthur's request to drive north to unseat the Soviet-backed North Korean government and reunify Korea. MacArthur crossed the thirty-eighth parallel that divided North and South Korea and by mid-October 1950 had captured the North Korean capital of Pyongyang. He boasted, "The boys will be home by Christmas." Disobeying presidential orders, MacArthur decided to advance further north toward the Yalu River bordering China. MacArthur seemed oblivious to reports of a Chinese build-up. On October 27, 1960, waves of Red Chinese troops (previously assembled for an invasion of Taiwan) crossed into North Korea. The Americans retreated, attacked, and retreated again. Only the use of massive air bombing saved American forces from disaster.

By the spring of 1951, Americans and North Korean-Chinese troops had entered into a prolonged stalemate. When MacArthur denounced the administration's handling of the war, an outraged Truman relieved MacArthur of his command. MacArthur returned home a hero among conservatives, but a movement to draft him as the Republican presidential nominee in 1952 soon fizzled. "Old soldiers," said MacArthur, "never die. They just fade away."

Meanwhile, truce talks, which opened in July 1951, bogged down over America's refusal to send back to the north communist prisoners who wished to remain in South Korea.

THE COMMUNIST SPECTER HAUNTS THE NATION, 1947-1950. The struggle with the Soviet Union created profound fears of communist subver-

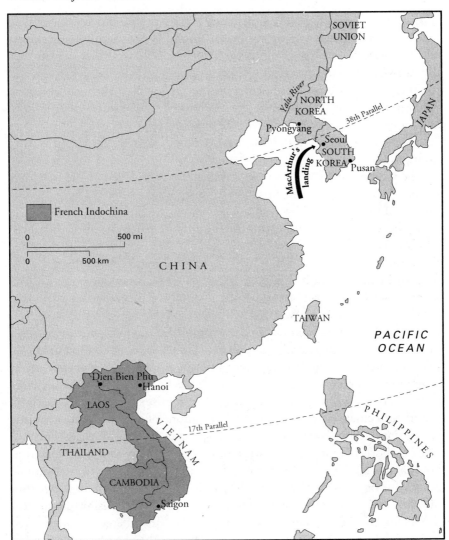

Map 27.1. Asia in the 1950s

sion at home. While genuinely concerned with the communist issue, Republicans also astutely saw political advantages of an anticommunist crusade that targeted liberal groups once tied to communists. The House Un-American Activities Committee (HUAC) opened hearings into communist influence in the United States. Witnesses were instructed to disclose known communist associates. Uncooperative witnesses found themselves harassed at work and home by HUAC and the FBI.

In March 1947, Truman, under increasing pressure, ordered the FBI to investigate all federal employees. In this probe, more than 300 employees resigned, largely for "personal" reasons such as homosexuality, which they did not want publicly revealed. Others quit because they had leftist ties and felt their careers would be ruined if this became public. So began the great witch hunt, which soon extended to Hollywood, universities, labor unions, and industry. For those questioned, the only way to prove their loyalty was to "name names." Many reputations and livelihoods were lost, as gossip and lies multiplied.

The Communist party also came under attack as dozen of the top party leaders in America went to prison for their political beliefs. The party was infiltrated by the FBI and was all but destroyed.

In the summer of 1948, former Communist party members Elizabeth Bentley and Whittaker Chambers shocked the nation by testifying that they had been involved in a Russian spy ring in Washington. Chambers, a *Time* magazine editor, identified Alger Hiss, a former high-ranking State Department official who had accompanied Franklin Roosevelt to Yalta, as a key figure in this ring. Working with Richard Nixon, a young congressman from California, Chambers led the committee and journalists to his farm in Maryland and produced microfilm — hidden in a hollow pumpkin — that appeared to many to implicate Hiss in a scheme to transmit secret government documents to the Russians. A technicality prevented a charge of espionage, but the "pumpkin papers" led to Hiss's conviction on perjury.

Other accusations of communist infiltration followed. In late 1949 the British intelligence service uncovered a spy ring headed by Klaus Fuchs, a German-born atomic scientist with British citizenship who had worked at Los Alamos, New Mexico, on the Manhattan Project building the first atomic bomb during World War II. Fuchs's trail led to the arrest in New York of Julius and Ethel Rosenberg, who were charged with transmitting nuclear secrets to the Soviet Union. Convicted, the Rosenbergs were executed in 1953 despite intense controversy over whether they had been given a fair trial.

Fears of further communist infiltration came in February 1950, when Republican Senator Joseph R. McCarthy told a Republican Women's Club in Wheeling, West Virginia, that he had compiled a list of 205 communists employed in the State Department. Later, he narrowed his list to 57 known communists, but he refused to reveal his evidence. It did not matter. His power was such that he forced a number of key State Department officials, including the Asian specialist Owen Lattimore, to resign. President Truman called these smear tactics **McCarthyism,** a name that stuck.

Truman Announces the Fair Deal, 1945-1953

At the conclusion of World War II, American policymakers confronted the problem of converting the war economy into a peacetime economy by providing veterans with loans to attend college and buy homes. Truman also proposed a Fair Deal program extend the New Deal social program. Republicans countered this program by enacting legislation such as the Taft-Hartley Act (1947) that restricted union activity. Truman won the 1948 election, but his proposal for national health failed. Congress did enact new Social Security legislation, however.

EXTENDING BENEFITS TO RETURNING GIS. When Truman stepped into the White House in April 1945, he faced a major problem of converting the basis of the economy from war to peace. Policymakers, worried that a **depression** might be caused when returning World War II soldiers flooded into the labor force. The **GI Bill** cleverly kept millions of ex-soldiers out of the labor market and sent them to college. The bill also provided low interest loans for veterans to buy houses, which created jobs in construction and began a postwar suburban housing boom.

Congress sought to extend federal economic power with the enactment of the Employment Act (1946) which established the Council of Economic Advisers and vaguely committed the federal government to maintain high employment.

Truman also called for a permanent Fair Employment Practices Commission (FEPC), a wartime agency temporarily created to end employment and housing discrimination. Nevertheless, the racial riots of 1943 had created a backlash against civil rights legislation. As a result, when the FEPC measure came before Congress in 1946, a group of southern legislators **filibustered** and forced the bill's withdrawal.

Republicans countered the Fair Deal with their own agenda, including antiunion legislation. In 1947 a coalition of Republicans and conservative southern Democrats pushed through the controversial Taft-Hartley Act. Enacted over Truman's veto, Taft-Hartley authorized use of antistrike court injunctions against labor unions. The legislation also outlawed secondary union boycotts (e.g. one union picketing a business involved in a dispute with another union) and closed shops (a union agreement with an employer to hire only union workers). This new law also allowed states to adopt so-called

"right-to-work" laws that prohibited union contracts from requiring employees to join the union. Most southern states quickly adopted such laws to lure
industry from the North. Denounced by liberals and organized labor as a
"union busting" measure, a campaign was launched to repeal Taft-Hartley,
but to no avail.

TRUMAN WINS THE ELECTION OF 1948. By 1946, Republicans, capital-
izing on war weariness and campaigning under a slogan of "Had Enough?
Vote Republican!", gained control of both houses of Congress for the first
time since 1928. Amid a wave of strikes and rising prices, Republicans looked
forward to taking the White House in 1948. As the 1948 presidential election
approached, however, Truman revealed unexpected political tenacity.

Harry Truman entered the 1948 election hampered by a divided Democratic party. Indeed, liberals had asked war hero General Dwight D. Eisenhower to run. He declined. (The general had not yet publicly declared himself
a Republican). When Truman won renomination, Henry Wallace, the
former vice-president, sought an anti-Cold War alternative by forming a new
third party, the Progressive party. In turn, conservative southern Democrats
bolted to support South Carolina's Governor J. Strom Thurmond and his
States' Rights ("Dixiecrat") party in their opposition to the party platform on
civil rights. Truman's defeat appeared inevitable when the Republicans nominated the popular New York reformer, Governor Thomas Dewey.

Truman's opponents underestimated his resolution. As his 30,000-mile
railroad tour wound its way across the country, Truman began to hear cries of
"give 'em hell, Harry."

On election night, contrary to the polls and pundits, Democrat Truman
squeaked by Republican Dewey. Truman polled 24.1 million votes to
Dewey's 22 million, while Dixiecrat Strom Thurmond, won 1.1 million
votes and carried only four southern states. Henry Wallace's Progressive
party, which called for friendly relations with the Soviet Union, failed to win
a single state. Still, Truman won less than half the total vote.

Following the election, Truman proposed a far-reaching legislative agenda.
The centerpiece of his Fair Deal was comprehensive national health insurance. Although a public majority initially favored the idea, the bill stalled
in Congress when the American Medical Association denounced it as
"socialized medicine." On the other hand, Truman's proposal to expand the
Social Security system found widespread support among both Democrats and
Republicans who extended coverage to 10 million additional workers in
1950. On the whole, Truman's call for a "Fair Deal," became, in effect, a
small deal.

Dwight D. Eisenhower Seeks Moderation, 1952-1960

Dwight D. Eisenhower came to the presidency in 1953 as one of America's most popular figures. Still in the midst of a war in Korea that had become brutally stalemated, the country turned to the former military commander of the Allied forces in Europe. In foreign policy, Eisenhower and Secretary of State John Foster Dulles sought to turn back communism in eastern Europe, Asia, the Middle East, and Latin America.

In domestic policy, the moderate Eisenhower, critical of the welfare state, favored limited expansion of federal activity in housing, medical care, education, and highway construction. In 1957 his administration enacted the first civil rights legislation since Reconstruction. In the end, Eisenhower's administration offered an interlude rather than a new beginning.

ELECTION OF 1952. While the Democrats nominated Adlai E. Stevenson, a relatively unknown liberal governor of Illinois, in 1952, the Republicans picked the immensely popular Dwight D. Eisenhower, a moderate. In doing so, the party rejected conservative senator Robert Taft ("Mr. Republican"). After being out of the White House for 20 years, the **GOP** cared more about victory than ideology.

Eisenhower's appeal was broad and deep. His own modest beginnings in Abilene, Kansas, and his success as a West Point graduate who had become commander of the Allied forces during World War II made Eisenhower a hero. In order to appease the right, Eisenhower selected Richard Nixon, the well-known anticommunist senator from California, as his running mate.

Nixon nearly got bumped from his vice-president slot on the Republican ticket due to a controversial political bank account, but successfully defended himself on television in what became known as the "Checkers speech." Nixon asked for sympathy by declaring that his family would not return one gift, a puppy named Checkers, even if the dog proved to be an illegal campaign donation. Other than this, the campaign offered little excitement. Eisenhower won by a landslide, carrying every state except a few border states and the Deep South. Moreover, the Republicans regained control of Congress.

EISENHOWER ADDRESSES FOREIGN POLICY, 1953-1960. Eisenhower and his secretary of state, John Foster Dulles, promised a new foreign policy.

While Truman had pursued a policy of Soviet containment, Eisenhower and Dulles rhetorically claimed they would liberate communist-dominated countries in Eastern Europe. They also shifted American defense policy toward nuclear weapons development which they called the "new look." In practice, Eisenhower's foreign policy differed little from Truman's. Eastern Europe was not liberated, and the United States continued to be involved in limited engagements — often **covert** — against perceived communist threats.

By threatening nuclear war, Eisenhower was able to end the war in Korea on July 27, 1953, when a final truce once again divided North and South Korea near the thirty-eighth parallel. After three years of fighting, the United States had prevented the communist takeover of South Korea, but over 50,000 American lives had been lost.

Eisenhower believed firmly that communist aggression must be thwarted, that a communist takeover in one country might lead to a **"domino effect"** in nearby countries. Eisenhower especially worried about Vietnam, where the French colonial army was engaged in an eight-year struggle (1946-1954) against a communist nationalist insurgency led by Ho Chi Minh. The situation became critical in 1954 when communist forces surrounded a French garrison at Dien Bien Phu. The French pleaded for direct American military assistance, but Eisenhower declined to commit troops to another Asian war.

Peace negotiations opened in Geneva, Switzerland, in April 1954. Shortly after the conference convened, the French surrendered at Dien Bien Phu. This defeat led the French and the Vietnamese to sign the Geneva Accords that partitioned Vietnam at the seventeenth parallel between the communist North and the pro-French South. Reunification of the country was to be achieved through democratic elections, but the United States refused to sign the agreement, fearing that Ho Chi Minh would, in all likelihood, win such a nationwide election. Instead, the United States sought to strengthen South Vietnam by arranging for Ngo Dinh Diem, a fiercely anticommunist Catholic, to head a new government in South Vietnam.

At the same time, Secretary of State Dulles organized a regional defense alliance, the Southeast Asia Treaty Organization (SEATO), that eventually included the United States, Britain, France, Australia, New Zealand, the Philippines, Pakistan, and Thailand. Dulles also instructed the Central Intelligence Agency (CIA) to become more active in the region.

The Korean peace might have led to better relations with communist China, but Dulles adamantly refused, unlike Britain and France, to recognize "Red China," which he described as "demonstrably aggressive and treacherous." Tensions worsened in 1955 when mainland China began shelling islands off its coast controlled by Taiwan. Eisenhower acted decisively to align

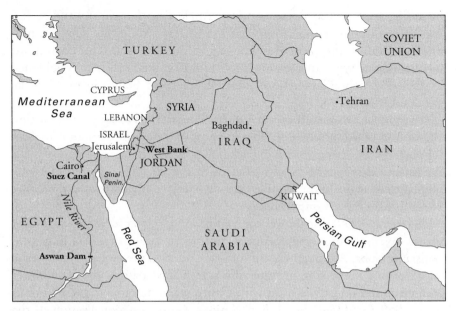

Map 27.2. The Middle East in the 1950s

the United States with the nationalist government on Taiwan through a mutual defense treaty. The crisis passed when the Chinese abruptly ended the shelling.

The Middle East presented Eisenhower with another series of crises. Shortly before Eisenhower came into office, nationalist forces in Iran under Mohammed Mossadeq overthrew the repressive government headed by Shah Mohammad Reza Pahlavi. The British and the French, concerned with Mossadeq's **nationalization** of western oil interests, undertook an economic boycott of the country. Viewing the action as naked colonialism, Truman had refused to join the boycott, but Eisenhower reversed American policy and sided with the British and French. At his instructions, the CIA orchestrated a coup against the Mossadeq government and returned the shah to power in 1954. Ironically, even as Mossadeq was being overthrown, his party was engaged in a campaign against the small Iranian Communist party.

By the mid-1950s **nationalism** had emerged as a potent force in Middle Eastern politics. The creation of Israel in 1948 fueled much of this nationalism. In Egypt, Gamal Abdel Nasser flamed anti-**Zionist,** nationalist passions. When it was discovered that Nasser had undertaken an **adventurist** policy of accepting American aid while purchasing weapons from eastern-bloc countries, the United States punished Nasser by withdrawing its promise to build the huge hydroelectric Aswan Dam on the Nile River. Nasser boldly retaliated by seizing the Suez Canal from a private Anglo-French company and declaring its tolls would be used to pay for the construction of the dam. In mid-October 1956, in the midst of an uprising in Hungary against the communist regime, Egypt, Syria, and Jordan entered into a military alliance. Frightened by the new Arab alliance, Israel joined Britain and France in retaking the canal in October 1956.

To the chagrin of its allies, the United States refused to support this action and instead called for a negotiated settlement of the crisis. Without American support, the allies were forced to back down. Nasser remained in power, and the canal was reopened to all nations with the notable exception of Israel. Nonetheless, many in the Middle East viewed the United States as the leader of pro-Israeli western **imperialism.**

In January 1959, Eisenhower confronted a crisis closer to home when Fidel Castro overthrew the corrupt, American-supported government of Fulgencio Batista in Cuba. Although Castro initially criticized the Cuban Communist party for not supporting his **guerrilla war** against Batista, the Eisenhower administration refused to meet with Castro when he came to New York in April 1959 to address the United Nations. Castro's nationalization of the sugar industry and of other American-owned companies in Cuba convinced Eisenhower that Castro was a threat to American interests. When Castro signed trade agreements with the Soviet Union and China, Eisenhower approved covert plans to overthrow the Castro government.

MCCARTHY ACCUSED, 1953-1954. While confronting communism abroad, Eisenhower faced a powerful conservative wing in his own party that demanded an even stronger anticommunist stance. The right focused much of its attention on China, forming the so-called "China Lobby" that called for the "liberation" of the mainland. A potent force in ultraconservative circles was Wisconsin's Senator Joseph R. McCarthy. By 1952, McCarthyism was in full swing, and the politically cautious Eisenhower refused to confront the volatile senator.

By 1953 many believed McCarthy himself was a threat to the nation. McCarthy said the schools, the churches, the CIA, and the Eisenhower administration were infested with communists. The end came when McCarthy accused the army of harboring communists. (The accusation came when army officials revealed that McCarthy had sought special privileges for his former aide Private G. David Schine). The Senate decided to hold special televised hearings concerning McCarthy's charges. For 35 days, nearly 20 million Americans watched the Army-McCarthy hearings, witnessing McCarthy's bully tactics. In November 1954, the Senate voted 64 to 25 to censure McCarthy. Three years later he died of alcoholism.

EISENHOWER QUIETLY SEEKS LIMITED GOVERNMENT. Many Americans continued to equate "big government" with **socialism.** In this atmosphere, Eisenhower accepted a limited role for the federal government. He endorsed the Saint Lawrence Seaway Act (1954) for a canal system to link the Atlantic Ocean with the Great Lakes. He supported the Federal Highway Act (1956) to construct 40,000 miles of interstate highways and freeways across the nation. In other matters Eisenhower believed that federal responsibilities should be given back to the states and private interests. He approved a measure to return offshore tideland oil wells to states bordering the Gulf of Mexico. His proposal to privatize the Tennessee Valley Authority, however, failed when it came under public scrutiny. Only in 1957 when the Cold War spilled over to a debate on education, after the Russians launched the world's first space satellite, the *Sputnik,* would the administration show strong support for federal aid to public education.

Still, while Eisenhower warned of "creeping socialism," he accepted gradual enlargement of the welfare state. The number of people receiving Social Security increased dramatically, from 1.3 million in 1945 to 14.8 million in 1960. The number of women and children receiving welfare benefits through Aid to Families with Dependent Children (AFDC) nearly tripled. The percentage of poor people fell in the 1950s, however, because of an expanding economy.

Learning to Live with the Bomb

American society in the 1950s reflected the fears of the atomic age and the smugness promoted by economic abundance. Following the war, the nation experienced the longest sustained period of economic prosperity in its history. During the war the gross domestic product more than doubled. Even minor recessions during the decade did little to dispel a sense of never ending affluence.

ANXIETY RADIATES IN THE ATOMIC AGE. The Cold War introduced new fears to America as the arms race accelerated. Atmospheric testing of atomic weapons was conducted quite openly. During the 1950s the United States tested 122 nuclear bombs, the Soviet Union 50 bombs, and Great Britain 21 bombs.

Military authorities, overseen by the Atomic Energy Commission, downplayed the seriousness of this testing. They conducted the first tests in Nevada without warning the small populations in surrounding areas. One rancher later said it was quite common on test days to wake up at the break of dawn to see a "nuclear sunrise" as a bomb exploded. The military showed even less regard for its own personnel. Sometimes soldiers and sailors were less than 30 miles away from a bomb site.

While military officials treated nuclear devices as ordinary weapons, civil authorities prepared the nation for war. One government pamphlet, "You Can Survive" (1950), told Americans to "Know the bomb's true dangers; know the steps you can take to escape them." And what steps were recommended in case of nuclear attack? First, take refuge inside a house or get inside a car, "rolling up the window." And what happened if you could not find a shelter? The pamphlet said you would get sick to your stomach and then two weeks later your hair might fall out. But in spite of it all you stood a good chance of making a complete recovery.

Only a few publicly opposed the arms race. Scientists such as Linus Pauling, a Nobel Prize winner, became leading spokesmen for a "ban the bomb" movement that called for nuclear disarmament. The "ban the bomb" movement was joined by a group of religious and moral pacifists led by A. J. Muste and **Protestant** activists.

DEFINING THE GOOD LIFE. Most Americans learned to live with the threat of nuclear war. They found security in a well-paying job, in home ownership in the suburbs, and in family life. At no time did middle-class values shape the country as a whole more than in the years after World War II.

Ignoring contemporary problems was made easier by the extraordinary affluence enjoyed by average Americans. Life was to be enjoyed, along with hard work. Americans went on a shopping spree and filled their homes with the latest labor-saving devices, including dishwashers, electric can openers, and garbage disposals. By 1960, most American households had a television. Suburbanites might have as many as two roomy cars — often with electric powered windows, power brakes, and power steering.

Much of this good life resulted from federal efforts on behalf of veterans. The "G. I. bill" provided educational grants, home and business loans, and imposed employment preferences for veterans. The act encouraged the immense expansion of higher education following the war. By 1948 the Veterans Administration paid the college expenses of about half of all male students enrolled in college. Approximately 2.5 million students attended college under the first "G.I. bill," as it was popularly called. In turn, returning veterans changed campus life.

Veterans' loans also changed how Americans lived. These loans financed nearly one out of every five houses sold in the 1950s. At the start of World War II, about 45 percent of American families owned their own homes; by the end of the 1950s, over 60 percent did.

This rise in homeownership paralleled the shift in population to the West and South. The good life also meant moving to the suburbs. Large old cities like Detroit, Baltimore, St. Louis, and Washington, D. C., lost population in the 1950s. In the process, suburbs gained almost 4 million jobs, while central cities lost 3 million jobs, mostly in manufacturing. This movement from the city also meant that large cities lost much of their **tax base.**

Americans lived not only better, but longer in the postwar years. In 1940 the average life expectancy was about 61 years for men and 65 for women. Better medical treatment contributed significantly to longevity after the war, largely due to the invention of antibiotics such as penicillin. By 1950 it had risen to 65.5 for men and 71 for women. These figures remained significantly lower for blacks — 59 for men and 63 for women.

AMERICANS FOCUS ON FAMILY. While Americans lived longer, they also married more readily and at younger ages than ever before in modern history. The United States had one of the highest marriage rates in the world. By 1950 almost 70 percent of males and 67 percent of females over 15 were married. Furthermore, the divorce rate dropped to only 10 percent in 1950. Because of this marriage boom, more children were born. The rising birth rate reflected economic prosperity — people could afford children, and the middle class wanted more children. Surveys showed that most Americans thought three or four children "ideal."

Within the family, the happy housewife became a symbol of postwar America, featured prominently on television comedies, such as "I Love Lucy," and in advertising. In part, this ideal reflected a reaction against women working at men's jobs during the war, when approximately 5 million new women workers had joined the labor force. Although the war effort had encouraged "Rosie the Riveter," Rosie was told she was a temporary expedient necessary only until Rosie's husband returned from the war. As one unenlightened government pamphlet declared, "A woman is a substitute — like plastic instead of a metal."

Surveys showed that many women did not want to give up their jobs after the war, and as the war drew to a close many women began lobbying for equal pay for equal work and federally funded child-care centers. This movement for job equality led the Democrats to endorse an equal rights amendment in 1944, backed earlier by the Republicans in 1940. As male veterans returned home, however, many women were forced from jobs.

Still, many women continued to work, contrary to the idealized vision of the happy housewife. Indeed, the decade of the 1950s marked one of the largest increases in female employment. This did not mean, however, better

The 1950s offered unparalleled stability to the American family. By 1950, approximately 70 percent of people older than 15 were married. The divorce rate fell to about 10 percent, where it remained until 1968. A generation of "baby boomers" was born. (H. Armstrong Roberts)

careers for women. Except for low-paid jobs as teachers, nurses, and social workers, women generally could not gain higher level positions in most professions. Many worked part time as secretaries or sales clerks. The percentage of postgraduate degrees for women fell in the 1950s from a high mark in the 1930s. For example, only 10 percent of the Ph.D.s in history were awarded to women in the 1950s.

During this decade, American society nevertheless saw a significant rise in single-family households headed by women. The number of women under 55 who headed households jumped from 2.5 million in 1940 to 4.4 million in 1962. Nearly half of these families were poor, and many were black.

OF SEX AND GOD. In the 1950s a new sexual consciousness occurred even as Americans expressed greater feelings of religiosity. This clash between changing sexual mores and traditional values indicated mounting tensions within American culture.

Americans showed a new awareness about sex, as many states repealed laws prohibiting homosexual activity between consulting adults. Moreover, the publication of Alfred Kinsey's *Sexual Behavior in the Human Male* (1948) introduced to the public for the first time a broad portrait of American sexual behavior. Crammed full of charts, tables, and graphs, this study gave every appearance of being dry and scientific, but quickly became a bestseller. Other changes in attitude were evidenced in 1953 with the publication of Hugh Hefner's *Playboy* magazine, which offered readers revealing photographs of Playboy "Bunnies." At the same time out-of-wedlock births nearly quadrupled from 1940 to 1970. The number of abortions, rarely legal, increased in the 1950s.

Many contemporary observers were struck also by what they described as a religious revival in the 1950s. In 1942, less than 50 percent of the population belonged to churches. By 1956, 65 percent did. Evangelists such as the Baptist Billy Graham organized **revivals** that drew tens of thousands of people to his rallies often held in football stadiums. Bible sales skyrocketed 140 percent from 1949 to 1953. Vendors reported that one out of every ten books were religious.

The Social Order Starts to Crack

For all the signs of stability, society revealed deep anxieties about where the culture was headed. African-American civil rights leaders demanded the end to segregation. In 1954 the Supreme Court declared segregation unconstitutional in *Brown v. Topeka School Board.* This decision unleashed a black civil rights movement that openly protested segregation and struggled to integrate public schools, buses, and other public facilities. Signs of discontent with society also appeared among writers, artists, and intellectuals. Teenagers also showed a youthful discontent with American society. As the decade drew to a close, Americans had begun to reevaluate their society.

THE BLACK CIVIL RIGHTS MOVEMENT BEGINS, 1953-1957. The transformation of the American economy in the immediate postwar period laid the groundwork for the civil rights movement that emerged in the late 1950s and early 1960s. The high demand for labor in a burgeoning economy opened new opportunities for African-Americans. A new, although small, black middle class, largely created by the G.I. education bill and housing loans for World War II veterans, emerged and soon demanded political rights and equal treatment before the law. At the same time, however, a poor urban class emerged among blacks in the inner city.

In these circumstances, the National Association for the Advancement of Colored People (NAACP) undertook a legal campaign to overturn the "separate but equal" doctrine embodied in *Plessy v. Ferguson* (1896). Their opportunity came in 1952 when the Supreme Court decided to hear a school case involving a suit by Reverend Oliver Brown against the school board in Topeka, Kansas. Because of the crazy quilt system imposed to ensure **segregation,** Brown's daughter was forced to travel more than two miles to school, even though her home was only five blocks from an all-white grade school. The NAACP was represented by Thurgood Marshall, later the first black appointed to the Supreme Court.

On May 17, 1954, reporters were called into the Court Chambers. Here newly appointed Chief Justice Earl Warren read the opinion, only ten pages long. He read tonelessly for 15 minutes and then concluded, "We come then to the question presented: does segregation . . . deprive the children of the minority group of educational opportunities? We believe that it does." *Brown v. Topeka Board of Education* (1954) marked a historic moment in the court's history and in race relations in the country.

Eisenhower worried that the ruling would create a white backlash. Nevertheless, he deplored segregation and ordered federal agencies to end financial support for segregated facilities. He pushed the armed services to speed up integration and appointed Vice-President Richard Nixon to draft new civil rights legislation. In 1957, largely through the efforts of Senate Majority Leader Lyndon Johnson, Congress enacted the Civil Rights Act (1957), the first civil rights legislation since 1875. The act established the Civil Rights Commission and a civil rights division in the Justice Department. The act proved modest in its powers, but significant in its symbolism.

The emergence of a black civil rights movement showed that change had arrived. By the 1950s black Americans were earning four times more than they had earned in 1940. Yet black median income of $3,000 was well below the white median of $5,000. Despite *Brown v. Topeka Board of Education,* school integration moved slowly. Southern states devised schemes to delay or stop integration. In many parts of the South segregationists organized White Citizen's Councils to intimidate black activists. A campaign of terror spread across the South.

African-Americans fought back. In 1955 the struggle for black civil rights gained national attention when civil rights activists launched a campaign to end segregation on city buses in Montgomery, Alabama. That campaign was sparked on December 1, 1955, when a well-dressed black seamstress, Rosa

Parks, a long-time local civil rights activist, refused to give up her bus seat to a white man and was arrested. Local black religious leaders launched a boycott of the Montgomery bus system, which largely served black patrons.

Leadership quickly fell to a 26-year-old Baptist minister, Martin Luther King, Jr. The boycott lasted nearly a year, before the Supreme Court ruled that segregation on Montgomery buses was unlawful.

President Eisenhower hesitated to interject federal power into local conflicts. Events in Little Rock, Arkansas, forced Eisenhower's hand, however. In September 1957, the federal courts ordered Central High School integrated. Hoping to win reelection on the issue, Governor Orville Faubus ordered the state-controlled National Guard to prevent the "forcible" integration of the school. When a lone black child mistakenly appeared at the school, a white mob attacked her. The ensuing national outcry forced Eisenhower to put the guard under federal control and send a thousand army troops to Little Rock to protect the nine black children who entered Central High that year.

Massive resistance to integration continued in much of the South, but blacks countered this opposition. Martin Luther King, Jr., the socialist Bayard Rustin, and Ralph Abernathy organized the Southern Christian Leadership Conference (SCLC) to press for an end to segregation. As King crossed the nation organizing communities and students, especially in black colleges, the nation sensed that a new era was about to dawn.

INTELLECTUALS REBEL. Intellectual circles showed signs of rebellion. Writers also criticized conformity and praised rebellion. Playwrights such as Arthur Miller and Tennessee Williams wrote about humanity's tragic struggle against the norms of society.

A new generation of "beat" poets and writers in New York and San Francisco proclaimed their disgust with American civilization — its values, obsession with materialism, and the legacy of puritanism. Jack Kerouac's *On the Road* (1957) became a bible for many of these beat writers. The romantic ethos of the beat poets, who spoke in the language of free verse, was captured in Allen Ginsberg's collection, *Howl and Other Poems* (1955). Ginsberg wrote of individualism and sexual liberation.

Liberal society came under criticism from the right and the left. Friedrich von Hayek, an Austrian emigré economist, warned that the liberal welfare state offered *The Road to Serfdom* (1944). As the end of the 1950s approached, radical leftists also attacked the liberal society. One of the most notable critics was Texas-born sociologist C. Wright Mills, a Columbia University professor who zoomed around New York on his motorbike. In *The Power Elite* (1956) and other books he laid the intellectual foundation for the New Left that emerged in the 1960s.

REBELS WITH A CAUSE. Tensions were evident in the emerging teenage subculture based on rock-and-roll music, fast cars or motorcycles, and a unique style of dress. Rebellious males wore duck-tailed haircuts, low jeans with the cuffs rolled up, white teeshirts,and motorcycle boots. Females put on bright lipstick and lowcut blouses. The most daring wore tight skirts and high heels. For music, teens turned to the pulsing beat of Elvis Presley, the frenetic sounds of Jerry Lee Lewis and black performers such as Little Richard and Chuck Berry. For the first time black music found a large white audience, and white pop music was almost entirely derived from black rhythm and blues. While parents listened to "The Man Upstairs," teenagers turned to "Blueberry Hill," "Great Balls of Fire," and "Honey Love."

Conclusion

The Truman-Eisenhower years hid profound changes taking place in American society — changes in the family, in roles for women and youth, in sexual consciousness, and in race relations. As the 1950s closed Americans began to reevaluate where they were and where they were headed as a nation. Many people sensed profound changes to come.

Recommended Readings

DOCUMENTS: Dean Acheson, *Present at the Creation* (1969); Daniel Bell, *The End of Ideology* (1960); George Kennan, *Memoirs,* 2 vols. (1967 and 1972); David Riesman, *The Lonely Crowd* (1950); William Whyte, *The Organization Man* (1956).

READINGS: (GENERAL) John P. Diggins, *The Proud Decades* (1988); James Gilbert, *Another Chance* (1981); Eric Goldman, *The Crucial Decade and After* (1960); Alonzo Hamby, *The Imperial Years* (1976); Godfrey Hodgson, *America in Our Time* (1976); Martin Jezer, *The Dark Ages* (1982); William Leuchtenburg, *A Troubled Feast* (1979); William O'Neill, *American High* (1986). (FOREIGN POLICY) Stephen Ambrose, *The Rise to Globalism* (1983); John L. Gaddis, *The United States and the Origins of Containment* (1982) and *Strategies of Containment* (1982); Gregg Herken, *The Winning Weapon* (1980); Michael Hogan, *The Marshall Plan* (1987); Hugh Thomas, *Armed Truce: The Beginnings of the Cold War* (1987); Adam Ulam, *The Rivals* (1983); Daniel Yergin, *Shattered Peace* (1977). (ANTICOMMUNISM AT HOME) David Caute, *The Great Fear* (1978); Stanley I. Kutler, *The American Inquisition: Justice and Injustice in the Cold War* (1982); Michael Oshinsky, *A Conspiracy So Immense: The World of Joe McCarthy* (1983); Ronald Radosh and Joyce Radosh, *The Rosenberg File* (1983); Ellen Schrecker, *No Ivory Tower: McCarthyism and the University* (1984); Athan Theoharis, *Seeds of Repression* (1971); Allen Weinstein, *Perjury: The Hiss-Chambers Case* (1978). (POLITICS IN THE TRUMAN-EISENHOWER ERA) Stephen Ambrose, *Eisenhower the President* (1984); Larry Burt, *Tribalism in*

Crisis: Federal Indian Policy (1982); Robert Donovan, *Conflict and Crisis* (1977); Fred Greenstein, *The Hidden Hand Presidency: Eisenhower as Leader* (1965); Alonzo Hamby, *Beyond the New Deal* (1973); Donald McCoy, *The Presidency of Harry S. Truman* (1973); Elmo Richardson, *The Presidency of Dwight D. Eisenhower* (1979). (AMERICAN SOCIETY) Erik Barnouw, *Tube of Plenty* (1975); Paul Carter, *Another Part of the Fifties* (1983); William Chafe, *The American Woman* (1972); Carl Degler, *At Odds* (1980); John D'Emilio and Estelle Freedman, *Intimate Matters: A History of Sexuality in America* (1988); James Gilbert, *A Cycle of Outrage* (1986); Kenneth Jackson, *Crabgrass Frontier* (1985); Elaine May, *Homeward Bound* (1987); Richard Pells, *The Liberal Mind in a Conservative Age* (1985); and Jon C. Teaford, *The Rough Road to Renaissance: Urban Revitalization in America* (1990).

28

DECADE OF ILLUSION, 1960-1969

CHAPTER OVERVIEW: The 1960s, which began with the high hopes of John F. Kennedy's presidency, were soon marred by the growing controversy over race and civil rights, and took a sudden, alarming turn with Kennedy's assassination in 1963. Suddenly elevated to office, President Lyndon Baines Johnson launched the Great Society, including a "war on poverty", new civil rights laws, and federal aid to education, to welfare, and to health care. Johnson's programs failed to meet the rising tide of black expectations and anger, which produced militants by decade's end. Other racial and ethnic groups, women, and homosexuals soon joined in demanding rights. Radicalism within black communities and on college campuses led to a backlash among the white middle class and in blue-collar families. As a consequence, politics became increasingly polarized. Meanwhile the United States had gradually become involved in a large, growing, and controversial war in Vietnam. By the end of the 1960s some young people had adopted radical politics, while even more created a subculture, which they called "counterculture," based on drugs, rock music, and easy sex.

Kennedy Fights the Cold War on the New Frontier, 1961-1963

Young, charismatic John Fitzgerald Kennedy won the presidency in 1960 by narrowly defeating his Republican rival, Richard Nixon. A staunch Cold Warrior, Kennedy believed that communism fed on poverty and advocated new foreign assistance programs. Early crises in Cuba, Berlin, and Laos nearly ruined the administration, and the Cuban missile crisis (1962) almost led to a nuclear war. At home Kennedy proposed an ambitious liberal domestic program called the New Frontier, but

560

his proposals stalled in Congress. The rising civil rights movement worried Kennedy, and only in 1963 did he propose a civil rights bill. His administration ended abruptly with his assassination.

ELECTION OF 1960. In 1960 Americans appeared restless, ready for change. Eisenhower's "middle way" brought economic prosperity to many and political stability to the nation, but anxieties were triggered by mild economic **recessions** in 1957-1958 and in 1960-61. There was also a fear that America was losing the arms race and the space race. The Republican nominee, Richard M. Nixon, who had loyally served Eisenhower through two terms, offered political continuity. Kennedy, a **Cold Warrior** in foreign policy and a tempered liberal domestically, conveyed youthful energy, wit, and the promise of change.

From the outset, the race was close. Nixon made a strategic mistake by promising to campaign in all 50 states. While he exhausted himself flying all over the country, Kennedy focused on key states with large blocks of electoral votes. In hindsight, Nixon's greatest mistake was to accept Kennedy's challenge to meet him in four nationally televised debates. The first debate proved crucial. More than 70 million Americans, the largest audience in history to that time, tuned in to the nation's first televised encounter between presidential candidates. Many believed that Nixon, an experienced college debater, would trounce his rival, but the photogenic, energetic Kennedy more than held his own against the perspiring and tired-looking Nixon.

Kennedy gained further momentum when he telephoned the civil rights leader Martin Luther King, Jr., who had been sentenced to prison by a Georgia court on a trivial charge. Kennedy's supportive call stopped the erosion of black votes, which had begun to drift to the Republicans in 1956.

Kennedy's popularity among Catholics and blacks proved crucial. Kennedy barely won. A shift of fewer than 33,000 votes in both Illinois and Texas would have brought Nixon to the White House. Charges of massive Democratic voter fraud in Chicago, Texas, and Missouri clouded the election, but Nixon chose not to challenge the outcome.

Table 28.1. Election of 1960

Candidates	Parties	Popular Vote	Percent	Electors	States
Kennedy	Democrat	34,227,096	49.9	303	23
Nixon	Republican	34,107,646	49.7	219	26
Byrd	Independent	285,820	.4	15	1

MEETING THE COLD WAR CHALLENGE, 1961. When Kennedy took office in 1961, the **Cold War** appeared at its iciest. The Soviet Union, led by the truculent Nikita Khrushchev, had emerged as a superpower and began to pursue an aggressive foreign policy in Latin America, Africa, and Asia. As a committed Cold Warrior, Kennedy prepared to meet the Soviet challenge.

Believing that **communism** fed on poverty, Kennedy sought to promote a "peaceful revolution" in the world's developing countries through the creation of the Peace Corps. Established in 1961, the Peace Corps offered young Americans an avenue to put idealism into practice by serving two years as teachers, engineers, agricultural experts, and health workers in 40 developing nations. Kennedy also established the Agency for International Development (AID) to oversee foreign aid to these countries and established a foreign assistance program, the Alliance for Progress, for Latin America.

TESTING IN CUBA, BERLIN, AND LAOS, 1961. Kennedy tended to view foreign policy as a series of tests posed by the Soviet Union, mainland China, and other communist countries. The first foreign policy test came in April 1961, when the United States Central Intelligence Agency (CIA) trained a group of 1400 anti-Castro exiles to invade Cuba and overthrow Fidel Castro's communist government. The exiles landed at Cuba's Bay of Pigs, but when Kennedy refused to provide the outnumbered invasion force with American air support, they were forced to surrender within days. Although the Eisenhower administration had planned the Bay of Pigs invasion, Kennedy took full responsibility for the fiasco. After this episode, he became suspicious of the CIA and the foreign affairs bureaucracy within the State Department.

Kennedy's next test came in Berlin. When Kennedy met with Khrushchev in Geneva in June 1961, the Soviet leader crudely demanded that the United States immediately withdraw its troops from West Berlin. The Soviets were determined to stop the flood of East German refugees seeking **asylum** in West Berlin. Kennedy refused to budge, returned home, and called up 150,000 reservists and national guardsmen, increased the defense budget, scheduled maneuvers, and started a crash program of building nuclear fallout shelters.

In mid-August 1961 this tense atmosphere worsened when the Soviet-backed East German government began building a wall to separate East Berlin from West Berlin. The Soviets countered by withdrawing from a voluntary agreement to ban nuclear testing. The Berlin Wall came to symbolize a world divided by superpowers capable of destroying the other with their nuclear arsenals.

Meanwhile, Kennedy confronted another crisis in the Southeast Asian nation of Laos. In this small, landlocked country bordering China, a communist insurgent movement, the Pathet Lao, appeared near victory. Shortly before leaving office, Eisenhower had encouraged Kennedy to intervene militarily, but Kennedy concluded that intervention would be a mistake logistically and diplomatically. Instead, he supported a Soviet proposal for negotiations between the unpopular rightist government in Laos and the Pathet Lao. Finally, both sides agreed to restore a neutralist government to power, although the insurgents continued to make gains in the countryside. Deciding that the communists should not be allowed to make any further gains in Southeast Asia, Kennedy resolved to provide military assistance to South Vietnam, which also faced a communist-backed insurgent movement in North Vietnam. Ironically, the Laos settlement convinced the North Vietnamese that American resolve to protect South Vietnam was weak.

FACING THE CUBAN MISSILE CRISIS, 1962. In August 1962, rumors began to circulate that the Soviet Union was installing offensive nuclear missiles in Cuba. In October intelligence photos taken by American's high-flying U-2 spy planes revealed the construction of medium- and intermediate-range missile sites in Cuba.

On October 22, Kennedy went on national television to reveal the missile sites in Cuba. He demanded the missiles' immediate removal and ordered a naval "quarantine" of Cuba to block Soviet ships that might be carrying missiles to Cuba. For the next five days, with the American military on full alert, the world tottered on the edge of nuclear war. Anxious Americans began hoarding canned goods in preparation for war. After a week of confusing diplomatic messages, proposals, and counterproposals, Radio Moscow announced on October 28, two days before Kennedy's deadline, that the Soviet Union was withdrawing its missiles from Cuba. The Soviets and the Americans had confronted one another, "eyeball to eyeball," and the Russians had blinked first. Kennedy appeared to have won a diplomatic victory. Privately, Kennedy promised the Soviets that he would remove American missiles from Turkey in exchange for the Cuban withdrawal. He also pledged that the United States would not invade Cuba. The crisis led to the ousting of Khrushchev two years later because of his **"adventurist"** foreign policy. Humiliated, the Soviet Union began a massive armaments build-up to gain **parity** with America's nuclear arsenal.

The Cuban missile crisis led the administration to reevaluate American defense policy. During the presidential campaign, he had attacked the Eisenhower administration for allowing the United States to fall behind the Soviet Union in nuclear missiles. In reality, there was no "missile gap," and the United States held a technological lead. Following the missile crisis, defense strategists such as Secretary of Defense Robert McNamara convinced

Kennedy that nuclear war could best be avoided if the Soviet Union developed nuclear parity with the United States. According to the Mutually Assured Destruction theory — called MAD — if both superpowers could destroy one another equally, the threat of a nuclear **holocaust** would cause each side to think twice about pressing the "red button" launching a first strike against the other.

On McNamara's advice, Kennedy proposed that *both* sides enter *mutually* into a formal treaty banning nuclear testing. In July 1963, Kennedy sent a delegation headed by W. Averell Harriman to Moscow to negotiate a test ban treaty. The the final treaty, ratified in September 1963, only banned atmospheric testing and not underground testing, but other agreements set up a direct telephone "hot line" to link the White House and the **Kremlin** and arranged for American wheat to be sold to the Soviet Union. Kennedy, the Cold Warrior, had eased tensions between the two rival nations.

KENNEDY QUARRELS WITH CONGRESS, 1961-1963. Kennedy failed to develop good relations with key congressional members. Kennedy's style, while winning public approval, proved ineffectual with powerful committee chairmen, many of them older, conservative southerners who noted the president's inexperience, tiny margin of victory, and rumored playboy escapades. His vice-president, Lyndon Baines Johnson, a politician with deep ties in Congress, felt underutilized and observed that the White House won the support of the congressional minnows, but not the whales.

As a result, Kennedy's major proposals for education, health, and welfare became stalled in Congress. As a consequence, Kennedy focused his attention on a proposed tax cut. Inheriting a recession that left unemployment at 6.7 percent in 1961, Kennedy needed to show that he could offer an economic program that promoted a high rate of economic growth without unleashing **inflation.** Kennedy moved to stimulate the economy by lowering top tax rates and providing an investment credit that provided corporations with a generous tax break. By the time the measure passed Congress, economic recovery was well underway, but the tax break further stimulated economic growth. This tax cut measure became a hallmark of Kennedy's administration.

Kennedy also enjoyed success with environmental legislation. In 1963, Rachel Carson's *Silent Spring* became a bestseller with its sobering account of the toxic effects of DDT and other pesticides on wildlife in America. Carson's exposé set off a national furor that led Kennedy to establish an advisory committee on pesticides that eventually produced tough new federal regulations. In 1963, Congress passed the first major Clean Air Act, regulating automobile and industrial emissions. These measures marked the awakening of a new environmental consciousness among Americans.

CIVIL RIGHTS HAUNT KENNEDY, 1961-63. Civil rights troubled Kennedy. He correctly feared that new civil rights legislation would split the Democratic party. While he appointed an unprecedented number of African-Americans to high office and encouraged the Department of Justice to speed desegregation of southern schools, he named well-known white racists as federal judges in the South. During his campaign he argued that discrimination in federally financed housing could be eliminated with "a stroke of the pen," but only in his second year in office did Kennedy issue a weak executive order to remedy housing discrimination.

Black and white civil rights activists became increasingly impatient with Kennedy's timidity. In 1961, the Congress of Racial Equality (CORE) dramatically undertook "freedom rides" to integrate buses and bus terminals throughout the Deep South. Attacks on these freedom riders by hostile white mobs forced Kennedy to send federal marshals to end the violence. In the fall of 1962, a riot broke out when James Meredith, a black air force veteran, attempted to enroll at the University of Mississippi. Backed by defiant Governor Ross Barnett, a mob attacked federal marshals escorting Meredith, and in the ensuing riot two died and hundreds were injured.

Each incident left civil rights leaders increasingly determined to push Kennedy toward action. In early 1963 a confrontation between civil rights activists, led by Martin Luther King, Jr., and officials in Birmingham, Alabama finally moved the conscience of the nation. This episode began when over 15,000 blacks and activists attempted to march on city hall, demanding the end of **segregation.** The police commissioner, Eugene "Bull" Connor, unleashed state troopers armed with fire hoses, dogs, and nightsticks. After witnessing this savage assault on national television, Kennedy went on the air to declare, "Are we to say to the world that this is the land of the free, except for the Negroes. . . . Now the time has come for this nation to fulfill its promise." He called for a civil rights law to protect blacks.

In August 1963 the movement's leaders organized the March on Washington to support civil rights legislation. Martin Luther King, Jr. electrified the audience. "I have a dream," he declared, that someday "all of God's children, black men and white men, Jews and gentiles, Protestants and Catholics, will be able to join hands and sing the words of the old Negro spiritual: Free at last, free at last, thank God almighty, I'm free at last." That next summer, under Lyndon Johnson, the Civil Rights Act (1964) was passed, outlawing discrimination on the basis of race, creed, sex, or age.

Kennedy's actions hurt him politically in the South, although national polls ranked his popularity high in the fall of 1963. In November 1963, the president traveled to Dallas, Texas, to shore up his southern political support. On November 22, as Kennedy rode with his wife in an open car past the cheering crowds, shots burst through the air, leaving the president mortally wounded. Two days later, a stunned nation witnessed on television the shooting of the accused assassin, Lee Harvey Oswald, by a Dallas bar owner with underworld connections. These events led many to suspect a conspiracy, although no conclusive proof has ever been offered to confirm this. Stunned by this event, the nation turned to Vice-President Lyndon Baines Johnson, to whom the burdens of leadership now fell.

Lyndon Johnson Launches the Great Society, 1964-1965

Following Kennedy's death, President Lyndon Baines Johnson launched a crusade to bring racial equality and economic opportunity to all Americans. He called his program the "Great Society." In his five years in office, Johnson saw more legislation enacted than any other president including civil rights, education, and medical care for the elderly and the poor. Johnson presided over the further extension of the welfare state, but when his programs failed to fulfill the high expectations he had raised, the national mood turned to resentment.

JOHNSON DECLARES WAR ON POVERTY, 1964. "We have suffered a loss that cannot be weighed," Johnson told the nation on the day of Kennedy's assassination. "I will do my best. That is all I can do." The new president swore to carry on the Kennedy legacy, but his predecessor's image haunted him.

After three years of neglect and humiliation in the Kennedy administration, Johnson remained resentful and defensive. Johnson knew that many on Kennedy's staff, including his brother, Attorney General Robert Kennedy, had opposed Johnson's selection as vice-president.

Johnson represented the old Democratic party with its base in the South and the congressional committee system. Johnson rose through Congress to become the Senate majority leader in 1953 by carefully cultivating older, more powerful men such as Speaker of the House Sam Rayburn, a fellow Texan.

An obsessive man, Johnson alternatively flattered and badgered other politicians. He rarely slept and wore down opponents with late night phone calls and ample supplies of liquor. A large man physically, Johnson intimidated fellow senators and was so hard on his staff that most quit from exhaustion within a year.

When Johnson stepped into the presidency, he found approximately 50 pieces of Kennedy's legislation stalled in Congress. He quickly moved to cajole a sympathetic Congress to fulfill the Kennedy dream. After pushing through a Kennedy-proposed tax cut, Johnson led Congress to enact the most comprehensive civil rights bill since Reconstruction — despite a 57-day **filibuster** by a group of southern Democrats. The Civil Rights Act (1964) provided safeguards for voting; prohibited discrimination in public places; offered assistance for the desegregation of public schools; and outlawed discrimination in employment on the grounds of race, color, religion, sex, or national origin. Although Congress was assured that the law did not require quotas, the Equal Employment Opportunity Commission, established under the legislation, later defined "equal opportunity" in such terms, thereby provoking further legal and political argument.

A former history teacher, Johnson sought to impart historic meaning to his administration by waging a "war on poverty." He remained convinced that poverty could be eliminated in his lifetime. At his urging, Congress voted to establish the Office of Economic Opportunity (OEO), the centerpiece of this war on poverty. Headed by Sargent Shriver, Kennedy's brother-in-law and former director of the Peace Corps, OEO was charged with overseeing job training, work relief, remedial and adult education, rural assistance, small business loans, a domestic Peace Corps, and a Community Action Program (CAP) that would enlist the poor in the war against poverty.

The Community Action Program became the most visible program in the war against poverty by its mandate to organize poor communities. Community organizing, however, generated political **factionalism** among the groups claiming to represent the poor and antagonized vested interests. It quickly became a lightning rod for attacks from both right and left.

Middle-class whites reacted hostilely to a program that in their eyes fostered welfare and radicalism. Increased racial tensions and growing involvement in the war in Vietnam led the politically astute Johnson to distance himself from his own war on poverty by 1965, less than a year after declaring this war.

JOHNSON WINS, RAISES EXPECTATIONS. In 1964, Johnson seemed certain to win a second term when the ideologically divided Republican party nominated conservative Arizona senator, Barry Goldwater. Promising "a choice, not an echo," Goldwater chose as his campaign slogan, "In Your Heart You Know He's Right." Critics replied, "You Know He's Too Far Right," or "In Your Head You Know He's Nuts."

With Goldwater on his right, Johnson moved toward the political center by downplaying his support for the welfare state and civil rights, even though his running mate, Senator Hubert Humphrey of Minnesota, was a well-known liberal. The president portrayed Goldwater as a danger to the world, a man who would not hesitate to use atomic weapons if necessary. On election day, Johnson won over 43 million votes (61.1 percent) to Goldwater's 27.1 million (38.5 percent). Johnson's landslide victory provided **coattails** as Democrats gained 37 seats in Congress, ensuring that liberals would dominate both ends of Pennsylvania Avenue.

In 1965 Congress passed unprecedented social legislation, including Medicare and Medicaid, which provided national health insurance for the elderly and the needy. Other legislation provided massive federal aid to education from kindergarten to graduate school, funds for urban development, housing, and transit, and established the National Endowments for the Arts and the Humanities to promote culture, as well as public television and public radio. Congress also liberalized immigration and approved the Voting Rights Act (1965), which provided federal examiners to register voters in the South.

The rhetoric of the Johnson administration only further raised expectations. Johnson promised to eliminate poverty in ten years, to rebuild American cities and beautify its highways (a special project of Johnson's wife, Lady Bird), to educate all Americans, to provide meaningful jobs to everyone who desired work, and to improve racial relations. He thus offered dreams that left the impatient unfulfilled and the realistic skeptical.

Americans Struggle for Equality, 1961-1971

After 1963 many African-Americans became increasingly militant. While Martin Luther King, Jr. continued to press the Democratic administration for new civil rights legislation, young blacks, influenced more by Malcolm X and the Black Muslims, turned to black nationalism and separatism. Other militant black leaders, such as Stokely Carmichael and H. Rap Brown, emerged within the civil rights movement to denounce nonviolent protest for revolutionary struggle. Racial riots in 1965 and 1966 caused a white backlash and further exacerbated racial tensions. Inspired by black activism, Native Americans,

Hispanics, and Asians likewise asserted their ethnic identity and rights. Women organized their own liberation movement.

THE BLACK CIVIL RIGHTS MOVEMENT MARCHES, 1965. Following the Civil Rights Act (1964), Johnson felt that further civil rights legislation should be delayed to give Americans a chance to assimilate the profound changes brought about by that bill. Social conditions for African-Americans had improved. Between 1947 and the late 1960s, black household income more than doubled. With segregation in the South tottering on the brink of collapse, Martin Luther King, Jr. and other civil rights leaders demanded a new voting rights bill that would extend federal protection to the polling booth.

To apply political pressure, King targeted Selma, Alabama, as the focus of the Southern Christian Leadership Conference (SCLC) campaign to register black voters. Local white officials resisted, and in March 1965 civil rights marchers faced a brutal attack by state troopers swinging clubs from horseback. More than 90 blacks were hospitalized in the attack. Shocked by the brutality of "Bloody Sunday," as the day came to be called, ABC television interrupted its Sunday night movie, *Judgment at Nuremberg,* to report the assault. The events at Selma moved the nation and the president, and in August 1965, Johnson signed the Voting Rights Act.

MILITANTS SPEAK OUT, 1963-1966. Many African-Americans, however, turned militant. In an increasingly tense atmosphere, some looked to the Black Muslims, also called the "Nation of Islam." The Nation of Islam had been founded in 1931 in Detroit by Elijah Muhammad, who urged blacks to practice self-discipline and reject integration. In the early 1960s Malcolm X, who had rejected his "slave name" of Malcolm Little, gained national attention as a spokesman for the Muslims. He called upon African-Americans to separate from "white devil" culture and to free themselves "by any means necessary." He told audiences that with John F. Kennedy's violent death "the chickens have come home to roost" because whites had perpetuated centuries of violence on blacks. After a pilgrimage to Mecca, Saudi Arabia, however, Malcolm X declared that cooperation among people of different races was possible, but shortly after this startling reversal he was assassinated in 1965.

In August 1965 a confrontation between police and young blacks in the Watts section of Los Angeles led to six days of rioting. Thousands of rioters battled police officers, firefighters, and national guardsmen. In the end, an estimated $30 million worth of property was destroyed, 34 people killed, 900 injured, and nearly 4,000 arrested. Riots followed in Chicago and Springfield, Massachusetts.

The following summer, in 1966, racial riots broke out in 38 cities. Cleveland experienced the most sustained outbreak, but the police and national guardsmen were also called out in San Francisco, Chicago, Dayton, and Milwaukee. Cries of "Get whitey" and "Burn, baby, burn" were heard through the conflagrations.

Young militants within the civil rights movement espoused "black power." The main black youth group, the Student Nonviolent Coordinating Committee (SNCC), expelled that organizations' whites. Its leader, Stokely Carmichael, declared, "The only way we are gonna stop them white men from whuppin us is to take over. . . . What we gonna start saying now is Black Power." Carmichael's successor in SNCC, H. Rap Brown, used even more inflammatory language by declaring, "Don't be trying to love that honky [white man] to death. Shoot him to death."

In Oakland, California, Huey Newton and Bobby Seale organized the Black Panther party in 1967 to urge blacks to undertake "armed self-defense." They quoted the Chinese communist leader Mao Zedong who stated, "political power comes through the barrel of a gun."

RACIAL PRIDE GROWS. As the black power movement spread, other ethnic communities took up the call for "Red Power," "Brown Power," and "Yellow Power." Militant American Indian leaders began organizing protests that moved from **reservations** into the cities.

Native-American activists clashed with state officials in Washington over fishing rights on the Columbia River and Puget Sound. A group of Native Americans from various tribes invaded the recently closed federal prison on Alcatraz Island in San Francisco Bay and claimed the island as their own. This intertribal cooperation led to the organization of the militant American Indian Movement (AIM), which battled tribal elites, entrenched interests, and the Bureau of Indian Affairs.

Mexican-Americans took up the cry of "Brown Power." Farm workers, led by Cesar Chavez and his United Farm Workers union, called a strike in the grape fields of California in 1965. When growers hired strikebreakers, Chavez and other labor leaders organized for a nationwide boycott of grapes that eventually forced growers to recognize the union. Still, less than 20 percent of farm workers were ever organized.

Mexican-American militants demanded that bilingual and bicultural education be instituted in public schools. In response, the Bilingual Education Act (1968) provided funds for bilingual education to public schools. In New Mexico, Hispanics organized the militant — and sometime violent — Alianza movement. Emphasizing that their ancestors had lived in New Mexico for 400 years, they demanded that the territory taken from them by Anglos be returned. Mexicanos organized the Crusade for Justice in Colorado and La Raza Unida in Texas.

REDEFINING GENDER RULES AND ROLES, 1963-1971. The rise of a new feminist movement also reflected the emergence of a radical consciousness concerning self-identity. Kennedy assisted this new feminist awareness when he established the President's Commission on the Status of Women. The commission's final report, *American Women* (1963), documented that women were still denied many rights and opportunities enjoyed by men. As a consequence, many states established commissions on the status of women.

During this same time, Betty Friedan published *The Feminine Mystique* (1963), a bestseller that questioned cultural assumptions that women could find fulfillment only as wives and mothers. This "mystique," argued Friedan, left women feeling trapped without independent careers. In 1966, Friedan helped organize the National Organization of Women (NOW).

More militant feminists called for "women's liberation" by openly criticizing the Black Power movement and the New Left for its "male chauvinism." Across the country radical feminists organized "consciousness raising" groups to discuss ways in which women were oppressed and measures needed to overcome their oppression. These feminists established health groups, day care centers, abortion-counseling services, and a range of **collectives.** In August 1970 feminists organized the largest women's rights demonstration in American history, when tens of thousands of women across the nation paraded under the banner of the Women's Strike for Equality. Demonstrations called for equal employment opportunities and legal abortions. Underneath this appearance of solidarity, however, an ideological rift became evident between liberals and radicals within the movement.

Some feminists announced their lesbianism and demanded rights as homosexuals. By the early 1970s, female and male homosexual lifestyles enjoyed a kind of fashion in certain circles, and "coming out" gained ground as homosexuals discovered that they, too, could claim to be a minority long discriminated against by majority culture. In 1969 male homosexuals rioted against abusive police officers at New York's Stone Wall bar. The Stone Wall riot marked an important turning point in the homosexual liberation movement.

These liberation movements challenged the traditional vision of the American "melting pot" in which all groups are assimilated into one culture. Later critics, however, accused these radical movements of heading toward a "cult of otherness" which envisioned a society made up of subgroups — African-Americans, Hispanics, Asians, women, and homosexuals who only identified with their own cultures. Proponents of these new movements responded by arguing that American society needed to acknowledge and encourage the existing diversity of cultures within the nation.

Vietnam: The United States Begins Its Longest War, 1961-1968

In the early 1960s, the United States sent a few thousand military advisers to South Vietnam to help suppress a communist guerrilla insurgency (the Viet Cong) in that country. In August 1964, though, following an alleged attack on two American ships patrolling in North Vietnam's Gulf of Tonkin, Johnson escalated the war. Although Johnson pledged to limit America's involvement, he launched a military campaign in Vietnam.

Reports of atrocities by Americans intensified domestic opposition to the already unpopular war. The Tet offensive, a major campaign by the Viet Cong and North Vietnamese in 1968, discredited Johnson's assurances that the United States was on the verge of victory. When antiwar Democrats challenged Johnson for the 1968 presidential nomination, he was forced to announce his retirement.

AMERICA GETS ENTANGLED IN VIETNAM, 1961-1964. When Kennedy took office, 2,000 American military "advisers" were in South Vietnam aiding the government in its efforts to suppress a well-organized **guerrilla** movement, the Viet Cong. Kennedy hoped to avoid American involvement in a full-scale land war in Southeast Asia through a counterinsurgency program organized around "strategic hamlets." This strategy called for peasants to be relocated by South Vietnamese troops into fortified villages. Americans also urged South Vietnam's government, headed by the Catholic leader Ngo Dinh Diem, to undertake serious social and economic reform. Continued corruption and political repression by Diem's government, however, brought other groups, especially from among the country's Buddhist majority, into open opposition.

Finally, in October 1963, South Vietnamese generals, with American encouragement, staged a coup and the following day executed Diem. Three weeks later, John F. Kennedy was assassinated in Dallas. By then, the United States had 16,000 "advisers" in Vietnam.

Johnson came into the White House with a reputation as a **"hawk,"** that

Map 28.1. Vietnam

is, one who sought greater American involvement in Vietnam. In August 1964, the president found an opportunity to widen the war when two American destroyers patrolling in the Gulf of Tonkin off North Vietnam's coast were allegedly attacked by North Vietnamese patrol boats. (Due to fabricated evidence, the real nature of the incident remains unclear.) Johnson asked Congress for a resolution granting authority to "take all necessary measures to repel any armed attack against the forces of the United States." The Senate passed the so-called Gulf of Tonkin Resolution 88 to 2. The House passed the resolution without a single dissenting vote.

In lobbying for the Gulf of Tonkin Resolution, Johnson assured Congress that he sought to contain the present conflict, but he used the resolution to justify a rapid escalation of United States involvement. In doing so, Johnson failed to anticipate a prolonged and brutal conflict that would severely divide public opinion.

Although Ho Chi Minh, the leader of North Vietnam, was a ruthless communist who purged opponents, many American antiwar dissenters perceived him as the George Washington of his country — a nation conceived in revolution against a colonial power. On the other hand, various leaders in South Vietnam were often corrupt and incompetent.

JOHNSON EXPANDS THE WAR, 1965-1967. What began as a limited engagement in a distant land soon escalated into a full-scale war without clear objectives and of uncertain morality. During early 1965 Americans remained confused as the war continued, several South Vietnamese governments fell, and American casualties rose. In 1965 Johnson ordered sustained bombing of North Vietnam through operation "Rolling Thunder." Johnson hoped that bombing selective sites in North Vietnam would force Ho's government to negotiate. From 1965 to 1968, the United States dropped 800 tons of bombs daily on North Vietnam. When North Vietnam refused to talk, Johnson sent additional American troops into Vietnam. There were 184,000 troops there by the end of 1965.

By 1967, the United States had nearly a half million troops in Vietnam. General William Westmoreland, the American commander, asserted that the United States was winning the war. Seeking to draw a highly mobile, lightly equipped enemy into open battle, Westmoreland evacuated huge areas, declaring them "free fire zones" in which all remaining inhabitants were declared hostile. Bombing **sorties** caused an estimated half-million civilian casualties. Surrounding areas were cleared through spraying **defoliants** such as "Agent Orange" that caused the lush green jungles to turn brown. Crops, livestock, and homes were systematically obliterated. As one American officer commented after surveying the destruction of one such village, "We had to destroy the town in order to save it."

By its guerrilla nature, the war meant that both sides terrorized peasants. While insurgents undertook land reform in villages they controlled, the Viet Cong also conducted a systematic campaign of brutal assassination against enemies. Village chiefs who opposed the communist-controlled National Liberation Front (NLF) were often beheaded and dismembered. The destruction and burning of Vietnamese villages by American soldiers was also brutal. Americans used deadly napalm, a flammable jelly-like substance that stuck to clothing and skin. Finding it impossible to distinguish between "friendlies" and the Viet Cong, some American soldiers fired indiscriminately at Vietnamese peasants. "A gook is a gook" was the attitude used to justify this brutality. One of the worst cases of indiscriminate slaughter occurred on March

16, 1968, when an American combat unit captured the small village of My Lai and systematically executed 400 civilians, mostly old men, women, and children. The My Lai massacre fueled further outrage against the war at home.

TET TOPPLES JOHNSON, 1968. Still, Johnson believed the war was being won. Then, on January 30, 1968, the beginning of the Vietnamese New Year (Tet), North Vietnam's regulars and their allies, the Viet Cong, launched a major offensive that startled the Americans. Attacking 36 of 44 provincial capitals, the communists seized the old imperial capital of Hué and occupied it for a month. In Saigon, a suicide squad penetrated the American diplomatic-military compound before being driven off. The Tet offensive was contained in a matter of weeks. An estimated 42,000 communists were killed during the offensive.

Afterward, General Westmoreland claimed a military victory, but the communists nevertheless had won an important political victory. Their offensive revealed unexpected strength and determination throughout South Vietnam. Even reports of the massacre of 2,000 Vietnamese civilians by communist troops in Hué did little to persuade a growing number of Americans that the war was worth fighting. In addition, the Johnson administration's rosy portrayal of a quick, easy victory was completely discredited. Even Johnson's top advisers, including Secretary of Defense Robert McNamara, until then a hawk, concluded that the United States needed to extricate itself from the Vietnam **quagmire.** His opposition to the war led to his replacement by Clark Clifford. The Tet offensive bolstered the political strength of the **"doves"** (opponents of the war) within the Democratic party.

While liberal senators such as William Fulbright of Arkansas and Robert Kennedy of New York denounced the war, other leaders, including Martin Luther King, Jr. and influential pediatrician Dr. Benjamin Spock, called for more direct action by resisting the **draft**. Increasing draft calls in 1965 had ignited a protest movement on American college campuses. In the spring of 1965 some 20,000 people, far more than organizers expected, attended the first major antiwar rally in Washington, D. C. Opposition to the war spread from pacifists and leftists to members of the clergy, liberal Democrats, and the general public. As the war escalated, the antiwar movement itself split, as segments turned radical and violent. Many spoke of not changing the system but overthrowing it. Protest led some into revolutionary rhetoric or violence.

Opposition to the war spilled over into the Democratic party. Johnson's approval rating dropped to 35 percent, the lowest since Truman. By the spring of 1968, polls showed the nation equally divided between those who described themselves as "doves" and "hawks." This antiwar sentiment allowed Senator Eugene McCarthy of Minnesota to challenge Johnson in the Democratic presidential primary in New Hampshire. His campaign drew 5,000 students from across the country, who cut their long hair and shaved their beards to ring doorbells for McCarthy. This "clean for Gene" campaign paid off when McCarthy won nearly half the votes cast in the March primary. At this point, Robert Kennedy, who had hesitantly stayed on the sidelines, entered the presidential race.

On March 31, 1968, Johnson appeared on evening television to announce a bombing halt in the North as a first step to end the conflict. He then added, "I shall not seek and I will not accept the nomination of my party." Johnson left office a disappointed man who realized that war in Vietnam had marred his presidency. Years later he explained in his homespun way that the Great Society was a beautiful lady and his true love, yet he had felt compelled to embrace war, ugly old whore that she was.

Young People Seek Solutions

One refrain from Stephen Stills' popular rock song of the period, "For What It's Worth" (1967), was "Something's happening here, but it ain't exactly clear. . . ." These lyrics captured the mood of the times. It was clear to most people, radicals and traditionalists alike, that "something" was happening to popular culture, especially among the youth, although "what" remained unclear. On college campuses angry students turned to "New Left" radical politics to bring social change and stop the war in Vietnam.

Many youths expressed political cynicism and rejected materialist values, and began a search for intensity of experience through alternatives such as drugs, mysticism, and sexuality. The result was a loose counterculture based on inarticulate feelings and unclarified sentiment.

ORGANIZING THE NEW LEFT. In the late 1950s a number of college students had protested against nuclear weapons testing. Many of these student leaders sought to create a new radical politics that broke with Cold War alignments. In 1962 several dozen students, sponsored by the socialist League for Industrial Democracy, met at Port Huron, Michigan, to draft a charter for a new organization, Students for a Democratic Society (SDS). Largely written by Tom Hayden, a student at the University of Michigan, the Port Huron Statement rejected both American **capitalism** and Soviet-style communism

In April 1968 New York City's Columbia University was under siege by students. Radical politics fused with the drug culture, embodied by the student with a marijuana "joint." The Columbia strike was followed by other student strikes across the country. (BURK UZZLE/THE PICTURE GROUP)

for an envisioned "participatory democracy" in which citizens directly controlled political decisions that affected their lives.

Two years later, in the fall of 1964, students at the University of California, Berkeley, organized a massive protest against the university's decision to ban political groups from setting up tables on campus to distribute their literature. Organized into the Free Speech Movement (FSM), the students held a massive sit-in leading to nearly 800 arrests and conducted a strike that closed down classes. The strike garnered sufficient faculty support to pressure the university administration into backing down and opening the campus to political activity.

In January 1966 the government abolished automatic draft **deferments** for college students, a move that mobilized campus protest across the country. Activist students burned draft cards, disrupted Reserve Officers' Training Corps (ROTC) classes, and protested war-related corporate recruiting efforts on campus. Dow Chemical, which manufactured napalm, was singled out for angry protests. In 1967 SDS urged more militant resistance through open acts of civil disobedience. That spring nearly a half-million antiwar protesters, mostly young and long-haired, converged on New York's Central Park in the largest demonstration against the war. As protesters chanted, "Hell, no, we won't go," and "Hey, hey, LBJ, how many kids did you kill today," many waved signs reading "Make love — not war."

Not all American youth participated in the protest movement. Indeed, most students remained middle of the road politically. Surveys at the time revealed that the vast majority of college students believed that the United State should either win the war or get out. Antiwar sentiment was strongest at the most elite colleges and universities. Furthermore, the number of students who identified themselves as conservatives, members of such organizations as Young Americans for Freedom, equalled the number of radicals on campus.

MAKING THE COUNTERCULTURE. Most political activists separated themselves from the larger youth counterculture represented by "hippies" — those youths who sought an alternative life style through rejecting political involvement, taking drugs, wearing their hair long, and living communally. Most middle-class adults failed to distinguish between the two, however, especially since many activists also wore long hair, listened to rock music, and took drugs. Hippies followed a path of noninvolvement, heeding to varying degrees the dictum of counterculture's high priest, Timothy Leary — a former Harvard psychologist — "tune in, turn on, drop out." The widespread use of drugs contributed to this ethic.

In the early 1960s young people listened to antiwar and civil rights protest songs by folksingers such as Joan Baez, Peter, Paul, and Mary, and Bob Dylan. In 1964, the English rock group, the Beatles, swept the United States with such innocuous songs as "I Want to Hold Your Hand." On top of the charts for more than two years, the Beatles' music took a decidedly different turn with *Sgt. Pepper's Lonely Hearts Club Band* (1967). This album, some believed, glorified drugs. To others it broke open a whole new musical world and in the process challenged traditional culture in fundamental ways. Other performers who boldly innovated were Jimi Hendrix, Janis Joplin, and Jim Morrison. All three died of drug overdoses.

Closely associated with youth culture was a sexual revolution that brought changes in how people perceived and practiced sex. Promiscuity became common, and increasing numbers of young couples chose to live together outside of marriage. Homosexuality became more open and accepted. While many welcomed the new sexual liberation, others feared that the erosion of traditional values would lead to the decline of the family, a rise in divorce and abortion, and erosion of the social order. Ironically, while many proponents of the counterculture decried the negative influence of technology and mass society, they also benefited from technology. The sexual revolution was made possible with the development of artificial contraception — "the pill."

Conclusion

As the decade drew to a close, Americans appeared polarized over politics and culture. The idealism of American youth in the first part of the decade had given way to anger, frustration, and despair. Americans in general — and young people in particular — found political involvement meaningless, distrusted politicians, and considered participation in the "establishment" (American business and government) as selling out. In these circumstances, many felt that American society was coming apart and that Americans had lost control of their future.

Recommended Readings

DOCUMENTS: Joan Didion, *Slouching Towards Bethlehem* (1968); Todd Gitlin, *The Sixties* (1987); Anne Moody, *Coming of Age in Mississippi* (1968); Theodore Roszak, *The Making of a Counter Culture* (1969).

READINGS: (GENERAL) John Morton Blum, *Years of Discord* (1991); William Chafe, *Unfinished Journey* (1986); Godfrey Hodgson, *America in Our Time* (1976); Allen Matusow, *The Unraveling of America* (1984); Charles R. Morris, *A Time of Passion: America, 1960-1980* (1988). (KENNEDY AND JOHNSON) James N. Giglio, *The Presidency of John F. Kennedy* (1991); Paul Conkin, *Big Daddy from the Pedernales: Lyndon Baines Johnson* (1986); Greg Davis, *Years of Poverty, Years of Plenty* (1984); Hugh Davis Graham, *Uncertain Trumpet* (1984); Jim Heath, *Decade of Dillusionment* (1975); Lyndon Johnson, *Vantage Point* (1971); Doris Kearns, *Lyndon Johnson and the American Dream* (1976) and *JFK — The Presidency of John F. Kennedy* (1983); Walter McDougall, . . . *The Heavens and the Earth: a Political History of the Space Age* (1985); Charles Murray, *Losing Ground: American Social Policy* (1984); Gerald Rice, *The Bold Experiment: JFK's Peace Corps* (1985); Tom Wicker, *JFK and LBJ* (1968). (FOREIGN POLICY) Graham Allison, *Essence of Decision: Explaining the Cuban Missile Crisis* (1971); Loren Baritz, *Backfire: A History of How American Culture Led Us into Vietnam* (1985); Larry Berman, *Planning a Tragedy* (1982); Frances Fitzgerald, *Fire in the Lake* (1972); Leslie Gelb and Richard Betts, *The Irony of Vietnam;* Mike Gravel et al., *The Pentagon Papers* (1975); David Halberstam, *The Best and the Brightest* (1972); George Kahin, *Intervention: How America Became Involved in Vietnam* (1986z); Stanley Karnow, *Vietnam* (1983); Gabriel Kolko, *Anatomy of a War* (1985); Kathryn Marshall, *In the Combat Zone: An Oral History of Women in the Vietnam War* (1987); Norman Podhoretz, *Why We Were in Vietnam* (1982); Al Santoli, *Everything We Had: An Oral History of the Vietnam War* (1981); Neil Sheehan, *A Bright Shining Lie* (1988); Harry Summer, Jr., *On Strategy: A Critical Analysis of the Vietnam War* (1981); Wallace Terry, *Bloods: An Oral History of the Vietnam War by Black Veterans* (1984); James S. Olson and Randy Roberts, *Where the Domino Fell* (1991); Glen Seaborg, *Kennedy, Khrushchev, and the Test Ban* (1981). (CIVIL RIGHTS) Michael Belknap, *Federal Law and Southern Order* (1987); Taylor Branch, *Parting the Waters* (1988); Carl Brauer, *John F. Kennedy and the Second Reconstruction* (1980); Stokely Carmichael and Charles Hamilton, *Black Power* (1967); Clayborne

Carson, *In Struggle: SNCC and the Black Awakening* (1981); William Chafe, *Civilities and Civil Rights* (1980); David Garrow, *Bearing the Cross* (1986); Steven Lawson, *Black Ballots* (1976) and *In Pursuit of Power* (1985); Malcolm X (with Alex Haley), *The Autiobiography of Malcolm X* (1966); August Meier and Elliot Rudwick, *CORE* (1975); Harvard Sitkoff, *The Struggle for Black Equality* (1981); Nancy J. Weiss, *Whitney M. Young, Jr., and the Struggle for Civil Rights* (1989). (SOCIETY AND CULTURE) John Patrick Diggins, *The Rise and Fall of the American Left* (1992); David Farber, *Chicago, '68* (1988); Maurice Isserman, *If I Had a Hammer* (1987); James Miller, *Democracy Is in the Streets* (1987); William O'Neill, *Coming Apart* (1971); Kirkpatrick Sale, *SDS* (1973); Ed Ward et al., *Rock of Ages: The Rolling Stone History of Rock and Roll* (1986); Lawrence Wittner, *Rebels Against the War* (1984).

29

THE TUMULTUOUS YEARS: NIXON-FORD-CARTER, 1968-1980

CHAPTER OVERVIEW: In 1968 the Vietnam war raged and violence erupted at home. Martin Luther King, Jr. and Robert F. Kennedy were assassinated. That summer at the Democratic national convention in Chicago police battled protesters. Republican Richard Nixon defeated Democrat Hubert Humphrey for the presidency on the promise to restore law and order and end the war.

Nixon pressured the North Vietnamese into a negotiated settlement, while he pursued a policy of detente with the Soviet Union and opened diplomatic relations with China. At home he proposed to reform the welfare system, to give federal funds to the states through "new federalism," and to control inflation. Nixon easily won reelection in 1972, but the Watergate scandal, involving a break-in at the Democratic National Committee headquarters during the 1972 campaign, forced his resignation from office. His successors to the presidency, Gerald Ford and Jimmy Carter, failed to win public confidence. By 1980 many Americans believed that the "American century" — the promise of continued American prosperity and international leadership — had ended in dismal failure.

1968: The Year of Disarray

In 1968 unprecedented violence haunted the nation. Martin Luther King, Jr. and Robert F. Kennedy were assassinated, and race riots and violent protest became commonplace. With King's death, advocates of black violence became more influential. Radical students at elite universities turned increasingly to violence. Political protest climaxed at the Democratic convention in Chicago, where vicious police attacks on protesters eclipsed Hubert Humphrey's nomination. Repelled by the turmoil and the extremist rhetoric of young radicals, the white middle class and blue-collar workers deserted the Democratic party to elect Richard Nixon, who promised "peace with honor" in Vietnam and "law and order" at home.

VIOLENCE ESCALATES. The year 1968 brought escalating violence — often seemingly pointless — to American cities and political life. In March 1968, the National Advisory (Kerner) Commission on Civil Disorders reported on race riots that had occurred the previous three years. Blaming "white racism," the commission called for a "massive" economic program targeted at the inner city to relieve tensions within the black community. Less than a month later, on April 4, 1968, the civil rights leader Martin Luther King, Jr. was assassinated in Memphis, Tennessee.

King had gone to Memphis to support a group of black sanitation workers who had been on strike for nearly a month. The night before he was slain, King had prophetically announced in a speech to supporters that his struggle on behalf of civil rights had placed his life in danger. He passionately declared, "I've seen the Promised Land. I may not get there with you. But I want you to know tonight that we as a people will get to the Promised Land."

Following news of the assassination, rioting broke out in cities across America. In Washington, D.C., flames of burning buildings crackled only three blocks from the White House. In Chicago, Mayor Richard Daley ordered police to "shoot to kill" looters. By week's end, 46 people had died in rioting across the nation. In total, riots from 1964 through 1968 destroyed an estimated $200 million in property, left 200 dead, 7,000 injured, and 40,000 arrested.

King's death marked a major setback for the civil rights movement. Many within the movement now rejected King's strategy of nonviolence and denounced King for not being militant enough. The rhetoric of revolutionary violence replaced King's message of nonviolent resistance in certain circles. H. Rap Brown proclaimed that violence was "as American as cherry pie." Other black militants spoke ominously of robbery and rape as "revolutionary" acts against oppressive white society.

The antiwar movement turned increasing violent as well. Following the Tet offensive in late January 1968, the antiwar movement became increasingly militant. Students for a Democratic Society (SDS), the principal radical student group, splintered into warring factions, each claiming to be truly revolutionary. In the spring of 1968, student protest turned violent. Much of this activity involved only a small number of students concentrated at elite universities such as Harvard, Cornell, Columbia, Berkeley, Michigan, and Stanford.

In April 1968 radical students at Columbia University, led by SDS leader Mark Rudd, seized control of the administration building to protest the construction of a student gymnasium in a park in neighboring Harlem. When police — who were mostly from the outraged working class — brutally attacked the students and recaptured the buildings, other students joined a general strike that closed the campus. The Columbia strike inspired student radicals across the country.

ELECTION OF 1968. The presidential election of 1968 focused on the war in Vietnam. After the antiwar candidate Eugene McCarthy showed surprising strength in the New Hampshire primary, Robert Kennedy entered the race. President Johnson withdrew as a candidate, leaving McCarthy and Kennedy bitterly struggling for the peace vote. Vice-President Hubert Humphrey made it a three-way race.

McCarthy embodied the moral fervor and idealism of the peace movement. A devout Catholic given to reading philosophy and writing poetry, he appeared to eschew politics. Robert Kennedy also spoke of peace, but appealed to working-class ethnic voters and minority groups. As a result, while McCarthy was a one-issue candidate (peace), Kennedy was cheered by blacks in New York, Hispanics in Phoenix, poor whites in Appalachian West Virginia, and Irish-Americans in Chicago. He appeared on his way to gaining the Democratic nomination, when tragedy struck. After winning the important California primary on June 5, Kennedy was assassinated by an Arab nationalist.

The death of another Kennedy in less than five years, as well as the second major assassination in 1968, shocked the nation. Within the Democratic party, Humphrey stepped forward to claim his party's nomination. Students in the antiwar movement felt embittered and frustrated by the democratic process and turned to the politics of the streets. When the Democrats met in Chicago for their convention, antiwar protesters gathered outside the convention hotels to battle the police. While Chicago's mayor Richard Daley shouted obscenities at delegates protesting on the floor of the convention hall, his police went after the protesters outside with a viciousness that shocked the nation. As television cameras panned them, the bloodied protesters chanted "the whole world is watching." After the convention, Humphrey's nomination elicited little excitement from an alienated and hostile electorate.

The disarray of the Democratic party opened the way for a third-party candidate, conservative Democratic Governor George Wallace of Alabama, running on the American Independent **ticket.** Wallace appealed to less-educated white voters who welcomed his attacks on "pointy-headed intellectuals and bureaucrats," black militants, hippies, welfare mothers, and "beard-

Table 29.1. 1968 Presidential Election Results

Candidates	Parties	Popular Vote	Electoral Vote
Richard M. Nixon	(Republican)	31,785,480 (43.4)	301
Hubert H. Humphrey	(Democrat)	31,275,166 (42.7)	191
George C. Wallace	(American Independent)	9,906,473 (13.5)	46

ed anarchists." His running mate, retired Air Force General Curtis LeMay, terrified many when he spoke of dropping "nukes" on Vietnam. Nonetheless, September polls estimated Wallace's support among the electorate at more than 20 percent — close to Humphrey's 28 percent.

The Republicans turned back to their center by nominating former Vice-President Richard Nixon. Many believed that Nixon's political career had ended following his failed presidential bid in 1960 and subsequent loss in his run for governor of California in 1962. Nevertheless, Nixon easily won the 1968 Republican nomination on the first ballot.

Nixon hoped to cut into the Democratic majority by courting southern whites, working-class white ethnics, and the suburban middle class. This strategy entailed supporting law and order, reforming the "welfare mess," and promising a "secret plan" to end the war in Vietnam.

By 1968 the white working class, as well as poor whites, identified the Great Society with black militants and race riots. As a result, Humphrey received just 38 percent of the white vote. Instead, former Democratic loyalists including white southerners, ethnic Catholics, and union members switched to either Wallace or Nixon. The Sunbelt — including the South — shifted toward the **GOP** as well. Concerned with law and order, disdainful of welfare programs, and opposed to forced **busing,** these voters declared themselves ripe to become Republicans. In so doing, they gave the Republicans a chance to build a clear majority that would dominate American presidential politics for the next two decades.

Nixon Pursues a Pragmatic Foreign Policy, 1969-1973

Richard Nixon sought to end America's involvement in Vietnam through a negotiated settlement that would save as much face as possible for the United States. To do so, he intensified air strikes, while withdrawing American ground troops. He intensified bombing to pressure North Vietnam to negotiate and tried to replace American troops with South Vietnamese troops. Seeking to break the back of communist forces, he launched in the spring of 1970 a major offensive in Cambodia, which unleashed violent protests at American colleges. Finally, secret negotiations conducted in Paris by foreign policy adviser Henry Kissinger led to a break through that brought peace to Vietnam in late 1972. Two years later, North Vietnam conquered South Vietnam.

In resolving the war in Vietnam, Nixon also sought to stabilize relations with the Soviet Union and China. This led to nuclear arms reduction with the Soviet Union and the diplomatic recognition of mainland China. Nixon, the anticommunist, showed his instinct for diplomatic compromise.

NIXON: THE MAN AND THE FOREIGN POLICY LEADER. Nixon's skill in diplomacy reflected his instinctive political cunning, his sharp sense of himself as a poor boy who had fought his way to the top, and a broad knowledge of the world and international relations unequaled by most other presidents in the twentieth century.

Nixon had built a political career as an anticommunist crusader. He had supported the prosecution of Alger Hiss and had defeated the liberal Democrat Helen Gahagan Douglas for the Senate in an especially dirty campaign, in which he declared, "Douglas is **pink** right down to her underwear." His visibility in the Republican party led him to being placed on the presidential ticket as Eisenhower's running mate.

Secretive, obsessed with politics, and concerned with his place in history, Nixon came to the presidency in 1969 intent on making a name in foreign policy. He viewed himself as a "tough guy" who needed to take an aggressive line against the North Vietnamese. He appointed William Rogers to head the State Department and Henry Kissinger, a former adviser to Nelson Rockefeller, to chair the National Security Council. In the end, Kissinger eclipsed Rogers and later became secretary of state.

THE WAR IN VIETNAM GRINDS ON, 1969-1973. By the time Nixon came to office in 1969, the war in Vietnam had become a hot moral issue. Nixon, however, was far too pragmatic to view the war in terms of morality. He sought to get the United States out of Vietnam as expeditiously as possible, with the minimal cost to American prestige. To do so he decided to upgrade South Vietnam's military capacity through a policy of "Vietnamization." This entailed gradually turning the fighting over to the South Vietnamese and withdrawing American ground troops, while at the same time intensifying the bombing of the North to bring Ho Chi Minh to the negotiating table.

Although Nixon intensified the bombing of the North, he realized that LBJ's air offensive, Rolling Thunder, had failed to break the back of the North Vietnamese. He therefore sought a new option, a major offensive against the Ho Chi Minh Trail in Cambodia. Kissinger reported that the **communists** were using the trail through Cambodia to provide a steady source of replacement troops and supplies into Vietnam. Nixon also was told by army intelligence of a secret central headquarters in Cambodia that the communists used to prepare a major offensive in the South.

On April 30, 1970, Nixon announced a major U.S. ground offensive and air raids into Cambodia. The Cambodian invasion unleashed a fury of angry protest on American college campuses. While radicals smashed windows and attacked police, campus leaders organized a nationwide student strike.

In Ohio, Governor James Rhodes ordered 3,000 national guardsmen to restore order at Kent State University. On May 4 a squad of inexperienced and nervous guardsmen fired wildly into a group of rock-throwing protestors, killing two demonstrators and two bystanders. Reports of the Kent State killings only heightened tensions on campuses. Eleven days later state police killed two black students and wounded 11 at Jackson State College in Mississippi. Most campus demonstrations remained nonviolent, but the Cambodian invasion encouraged ultraradicals to undertake acts of terrorism. There were fire bombings on at least ten campuses. Sixteen governors called out the national guard to quell unrest on 21 campuses. In California, Governor Ronald Reagan closed the 28 campuses in the state university and college systems.

The war ground on. In February 1971 the South Vietnamese army invaded Laos to cut off supplies flowing to communists in the South. The North Vietnamese army easily routed the invaders, who fled in disarray back to South Vietnam.

Negotiations with the North Vietnamese dragged on. Nixon sent Henry Kissinger to Paris to negotiate secretly with North Vietnam's foreign minister, Le Duc Tho. In Paris, Kissinger faced an intransigent North Vietnam. Le Duc continued to reject various proposals made by Kissinger, when in the fall of 1971 the North Vietnamese launched an offensive in the South that led to the fall of the provincial capital of Quang Tri. An American counteroffensive recaptured the city, but negotiations in Paris still proceeded slowly.

The war entered its final phase in 1972. Negotiations between Kissinger and Le Duc moved forward, albeit ever so slowly. By October 1972, with the American presidential elections fast approaching, Kissinger and Le Duc reached a secret agreement. It provided for a cease fire, the formation of a coalition government in South Vietnam, free elections, the withdrawal of the remaining American troops, and the release of all prisoners. When the South Vietnamese refused to accept the peace plan, the North Vietnamese angrily broke off further negotiations. Following his reelection in November, Nixon put additional pressure on the North with massive bombing from December 18 to 29. The "Christmas bombing" strategy brought Le Duc Tho back to the table.

Finally, on January 22, 1973 — the day Lyndon Johnson died of a heart attack on his Texas ranch — Nixon announced that a cease-fire agreement had been signed in Paris which would allow U.S. troops to withdraw. Kissinger and Le Duc Tho won the Nobel Peace Prize for their efforts. Nixon had extricated America from Vietnam, but at a heavy cost. Nearly 60,000 Americans had been killed — more than half during Nixon's presidency — 300,000 wounded, and $146 billion spent on the war. In April 1975, the war finally ended in a communist victory when the North Vietnamese captured Saigon, soon renamed Ho Chi Minh City, and quickly absorbed South Vietnam into the single country of Vietnam.

NIXON SEEKS DETENTE WITH COMMUNIST POWERS, 1969-1973. During the Vietnam negotiations, Nixon also sought to achieve peaceful coexistence with the Soviet Union and recognition of mainland China, a policy called **detente.** Nixon felt that ideology should be subordinated to a pragmatic acknowledgement that recognized that the United States and the communist countries had a self-interest in maintaining a competitive balance of power in the world.

In 1968 relations between the United States and the Soviet Union worsened when Russian tanks rolled into Prague, Czechoslovakia, to suppress local communist-led liberalization. Soviet leader Leonid Brezhnev asserted the "Brezhnev Doctrine," which upheld the right of unilateral Soviet intervention in any "socialist" state in Eastern Europe. United States-Soviet tensions did not improve when American intelligence discovered that the Soviets were building a naval base for atomic submarines in Cuba. The Soviets ceased construction of the base only after strong U.S. protests.

Nixon believed that a balance of power entailed mending relations with mainland China, the People's Republic of China. Nixon and Kissinger believed that **rapprochement** with China would pressure the Soviet Union to stabilize relations with the United States. The **Sino**-Soviet dispute had become particularly ominous with the development of nuclear weapons in China. (On a number of occasions Russian officials had suggested to their American counterparts that a **preemptive strike** by the Soviet Union against China's nuclear facilities would be desirable.)

President Richard Milhous Nixon surprised liberal opponents when he renewed trade with communist China. In 1972, while the war in Vietnam continued, he visited China for a week, meeting with Chinese leader Mao Zedong. (AP/WORLD WIDE PHOTOS)

Since the Truman administration the United States had refused to extend diplomatic recognition to the People's Republic. This refusal had been made easier by Chinese leader Mao Zedong's devout adherence to communist revolutionary ideology and by China's vituperative anti-American propaganda. The widening Sino-Soviet split, however, created a diplomatic opening for Nixon to establish relations with Mao. Armed clashes in 1969 between Soviet and Chinese troops along their border further encouraged reestablishing United States-China relations.

Nixon, the old anticommunist, journeyed to communist China on February 22, 1972. American television showed Nixon touring the Great Wall and toasting Mao Zedong and the Chinese premier, Zhou Enlai. Although full diplomatic relations were not established until 1979, Nixon's visit marked a milestone in **Cold War** history. The idea of a monolithic, global communism gave way to a recognition that the Soviet Union and China were rivals who could be played against one another.

American public opinion toward communist China seemed to shift overnight. Shortly after Nixon's visit, actress Candice Bergen, returning from a carefully supervised tour of the mainland, declared she had been most impressed by the pervasive respect for human life she encountered in China.

This praise for mainland China was joined by a chorus of serious journalists and government officials who returned from tours during the next several years.

The road to detente (establishing peaceful relations with the Soviet Union) proved rocky. While relations with the Soviet Union went through fits and starts, Nixon struck his boldest stroke in 1972 when he concluded an agreement to sell American wheat and technology to the Soviet Union. Nixon and Brezhnev then signed the first Strategic Arms Limitation Talks (SALT I) agreement. It limited both nations to a maximum of 200 antiballistic missiles (ABM) and two ABM systems. A separate agreement froze for five years the number of intercontinental ballistic missiles (ICBM) and submarine-launched missiles. These treaties formalized a strategy of mutual-deterrence, the view adopted by both sides that the surest guarantee against nuclear attack came through **parity.**

In pursuing the SALT agreement, Nixon pressured reluctant liberals in Congress to support the development of new weapons systems. Nixon gave the go-ahead to develop a new kind of missile called a multiple independently targeted reentry vehicle (MIRV). Each of these missiles carried three to ten separately targeted warheads, so fewer missiles could launch more bombs.

Nixon's belief that American foreign policy needed to be realistic — not ideological or idealistic — sometimes led the United States to support repressive regimes considered important to American economic and strategic interests. As a consequence, the Nixon administration enthusiastically supported the brutal government of Iran headed by the shah, Reza Pahlavi. The administration also backed the corrupt Ferdinand Marcos in the Philippines and the repressive white-only government in South Africa. Nixon also backed repressive regimes in Argentina, South Korea, Brazil, and Nigeria. Nixon's foreign policy came under criticism in 1973, when he used the Central Intelligence Agency to help overthrow Chile's **Marxist** president, Salvador Allende, who had been democratically elected in 1970.

Nixon Baffles Liberals in Domestic Policy

Though liberals despised Nixon, he turned out to be a reformer. His proposal to transform the welfare system failed, but he did push through a variety of measures to help the poor, aged, blind, and disabled. A record volume of environmental legislation was passed during his administration. His New Federalism program aimed to shift power back to states and local communities. A restructuring and then elimination of the draft in 1972 took the steam out of the antiwar movement. He had a mixed record on civil rights and women's issues.

REFORMING WELFARE, ENVIRONMENT, AND THE ADMINISTRATION, 1969-1970. Although Nixon remained less interested in domestic affairs, he sought new policy initiatives in welfare, health care, federal aid to states, and executive reform. At the same time, Nixon — ever the politician — believed that Republicans could emerge as the majority party by luring white southerners and blue-collar voters away from the Democrats. He therefore espoused "law and order," appointed conservatives to the federal courts (including the Supreme Court), and opposed busing children to achieve school integration.

During the presidential campaign of 1968, Nixon attacked the "welfare mess." He knew that many Americans disliked the Great Society's welfare measures, but he also wanted to beat the liberals at their own game, by doing them one better. He proposed in 1969 to transform the welfare system by offering direct benefits to welfare recipients through the Family Assistance Plan (FAP). The centralized program, however, drew fierce opposition from liberals and fiscal conservatives alike. Liberals conducted a "ZAP-FAP" campaign that denounced Nixon's proposal as the "Family Annihilation Plan."

Nixon withdrew the proposal and replaced it with a food stamp program, which allowed the poor to purchase food with vouchers. In October 1972, Nixon signed the Supplemental Security Income Act, which led the government to assume responsibility for aid to the aged, the blind, and the disabled. The act also increased Social Security benefits, extended subsidized housing, and expanded the Job Corps program.

The Nixon administration also extended the federal government's role in protecting the environment. When a burst oil well off the California coast at Santa Barbara spewed tons of sludge on the beaches in 1969, environmentalists demanded new legislation. Congressional Democrats led by Senators Edmund Muskie (Maine) and Henry Jackson (Washington) pushed for support of the National Environmental Policy Act (1969). Declaring that the environment must be protected and restored, this historic law required that every federal construction project have an environmental impact study done before beginning work.

Shortly after the passage of this act, Nixon consolidated all antipollution programs through the establishment of the Environmental Protection Agency (EPA). The EPA under William Ruckleshaus became an activist agency that brought scores of criminal actions against polluters. Nixon also called for drinking water standards, mass transit, stronger land use policies, the protection of coastal wetlands, and the preservation of endangered species. The National Oceanic and Atmospheric Agency consolidated research in these areas. The Clean Air Act (1970) established national emission standards for automobiles and factories, while the Occupational Safety and Health Administration (OSHA) protected worker safety.

Congress pushed the environmental agenda further when it enacted legislation over Nixon's **veto** that provided funds to clean the nation's polluted waterways. More environmental legislation was passed in Nixon's administration than under any previous presidency.

Following the 1970 congressional elections, Nixon moved to cut federal expenditures, vetoing dozens of bills passed by a Democratic-controlled Congress. When these vetoes were overridden, Nixon refused to spend ("**impound**ed") the funds authorized by Congress. The Supreme Court eventually outlawed impounding. Nixon announced a New Federalism that promised to shift power back to the states and to local communities. To fulfill this objective, Nixon pushed through a revenue-sharing act in October 1972, that reallocated certain federal revenues back to the states with no strings attached. At the same time, the federal government used revenue sharing to consolidate 130 grants concerned with urban community development, education, law enforcement, and manpower training.

MIXED RECORD ON CIVIL RIGHTS AND WOMEN'S ISSUES. An essential part of Nixon's strategy to keep the white southern vote that had helped him win office meant taking a low profile on civil rights.

The Nixon record on civil rights, however, proved to be more mixed than his rhetoric might have implied. While his administration challenged "forced" busing, the Justice Department quietly presided over desegregation of southern schools, which brought the proportion of black children in the South attending all-black schools from 68 percent in 1968 to 8 percent in 1972. At the same time, the Equal Employment Opportunity Commission (EEOC) under Nixon imposed targets for the hiring of minorities and women on federal projects. In 1972 Congress passed an equal employment practices law covering all federal, state, and municipal governments, educational institutions, and businesses or unions with more than eight employees.

The inclusion of women in federal hiring guidelines set by the EEOC followed legally from civil rights legislation passed in the Johnson administration. In 1968 women accounted for only 8 percent of scientists, 7 percent of physicians, 3 percent of lawyers, and 1 percent of engineers. Progress was slow, but the number of women appointed to military academies, embassies, and the federal courts increased rapidly.

In 1970 Congress passed the Equal Rights Amendment (ERA) to the Constitution, which had first been suggested by Alice Paul in the 1920s. The ERA ran into strong opposition, especially in the Sunbelt states. Many fundamentalist Christians campaigned against the amendment, as did Phyllis Schlafly, an antifeminist activist, who argued that it would destroy the American family. In the end, 34 states **ratified** it, but the amendment failed to win the 38 states needed for ratification.

During the presidential campaign of 1968, Nixon had promised to fill the Supreme Court with conservatives. In late May 1969, Nixon nominated and the Senate quickly confirmed federal judge Warren E. Burger to the position of chief justice, following Earl Warren's retirement. Nixon also appointed Harry Blackmun, Lewis F. Powell, and William H. Rehnquist to the court; among these appointments only Rehnquist proved to be consistently conservative.

This Supreme Court issued one of its most important decisions in 1973: *Roe v. Wade* struck down a Texas law that made abortion a crime except to save the life of the mother. In the 1960s a number of states, including California under Ronald Reagan, had legalized abortion. In *Roe*, Justice Harry Blackmun wrote the majority opinion that made abortion within the first three months of pregnancy a constitutional right. Later court cases restricted this right, but *Roe* marked an important turning point in American constitutional law.

Nixon's Excesses and Economic Failures

Facing a deteriorating economy in 1971, Nixon announced a variety of sweeping economic reforms. These reforms proved rigid and unworkable. To win over the conservative South and the white working class, Nixon emphasized law and order, but he launched a campaign of harassment, infiltration, and sabotage against dissidents, using an assortment of legal and illegal tactics.

CURING STAGFLATION WITH WAGE AND PRICE CONTROLS. Nixon approached the 1972 election convinced that only a weak economy might cost him reelection. The war in Southeast Asia had led to an inflationary spiral that seemed uncontrollable. By 1970 **inflation** had risen to an annual rate of more than 5 percent, and was still growing, while unemployment — partly caused by the winding down of the war's defense contracts — reached 6 percent. The Democrats blamed Nixon for the worst of all possible worlds: stagnant employment and high inflation — dubbed stagflation.

The state of the economy continued to deteriorate through 1971. Under pressure, Nixon went on television on August 15, 1971, to announce how he was reshaping the economic system.

He took the United States off the **gold standard** — Roosevelt had pegged the dollar at $35 to one ounce of gold in the 1930s. Now, Nixon declared, the dollar would no longer be tied to gold. This unleashed pressures to increase the money supply and greatly increased inflation during the rest of the 1970s. For the first time since the late 1940s, Nixon also placed the dollar on the international market, allowing the exchange rate of the dollar and foreign currencies to be set by market conditions. This had tremendous implications for world trade and prices.

He also announced a 90-day freeze on wages and prices. In November 1972 Nixon announced Phase II of the wage and price controls strategy that established firm federal guidelines for increases in wages, prices, and interest rates. There was a lingering suspicion among business executives that exemptions from the guidelines could be obtained in exchange for large campaign contributions to Nixon. Although economic conditions improved only marginally (indeed, inflation soared 9 percent in 1972), the American electorate was temporarily reassured.

NIXON PREACHES LAW AND ORDER WHILE VIOLATING CIVIL LIBERTIES, 1969-1973. Nixon knew that the middle class feared the breakdown of law and order in America. New Left revolutionaries, hippie counterculturists, pornography, and crime in the streets seemed to be inexplicably linked. Thus, while Nixon had campaigned in 1968 on a slogan of "bring us together," he used the presidency to denounce protesters, attack crime, and promote "law and order." Nixon worked to win over southern and suburban Americans to the Republican party.

Nixon encouraged Attorney General John Mitchell to pursue a "war on crime" and take a tough stand on drugs. The Justice Department also attacked domestic dissidents through the use of wiretaps without court approval, a practice the Supreme Court prohibited in 1971. Meanwhile the Justice Department obtained conspiracy indictments against several groups of radical political activists. Working closely with local police, the FBI and the Justice Department targeted the militant Black Panthers in a number of police raids. Shoot-outs with the police led to the deaths of more than 40 members of the Black Panthers.

The Central Intelligence Agency (CIA), in violation of its charter, was instructed in 1970 to compile dossiers on thousands of American dissidents. Nixon wanted to intensify this antiradical campaign through a scheme known as the Huston Plan that proposed using the CIA and FBI in an extensive program involving wiretaps, electronic surveillance, break-ins, and **covert** operations against radical groups. Although many were indicted, convictions were rare.

These indictments were part of a larger policy of harassment, infiltration, and sabotage of organized dissent called COINTELPRO (counter-intelligence program). Never had civil liberties been so systematically violated by the United States government. Activities included destroying dissenters' property, planting lies in the media to ruin reputations, and controlling political nominations.

Concerned with government "leaks" to the press, the White House established a secret group — the "plumbers" — to ensure that sensitive information remained secret. Headed by ex-FBI agent G. Gordon Liddy and former CIA agent E. Howard Hunt, the plumbers undertook a campaign to discredit radicals. Their first target was Daniel Ellsberg, a former analyst for the Defense Department who had turned over to the press the Pentagon's secret history of the Vietnam War. When the *New York Times* began publishing the *Pentagon Papers,* as they were called, in the summer of 1971, the administration obtained a court injunction preventing further publication. After the Supreme Court lifted the injunction on first amendment grounds, Nixon ordered the Justice Department to indict Ellsberg. In August 1971, the plumbers broke into the office of Ellsberg's psychiatrist in hope of finding information that might be used to discredit the antiwar movement's new hero.

While attacking antiwar dissenters and student radicals, the administration sought to defuse confrontations by undertaking a long overdue reform of the Selective Service System. The military **draft** was modified through a national lottery system. The goal, however, was an all-volunteer army — finally achieved in 1972. The decline and then the end of the draft effectively took the steam out of the student antiwar movement.

Nixon Wins Reelection and Loses the Presidency, 1972-1974

Though his opponent, George McGovern, appeared to have little chance of beating him in 1972, Nixon undertook a "dirty tricks" campaign which involved — without his knowledge — an attempted break-in by his campaign workers to tap the phones at the Democratic headquarters in the Watergate office complex in Washington. When the burglars were caught by the police, Nixon and his aides attempted to cover-up White House involvement. Nixon's illegal obstruction of justice became a more important issue than the original crime. In 1973 when presidential tapes recording conversations in the White House were released — after much resistance by Nixon — he was forced to resign from the presidency under threat of impeachment.

ELECTION OF 1972. Approaching the 1972 election, the Democrats remained in disarray. They nominated the liberal senator from South Dakota, George McGovern, who capitalized on the prevailing antiwar sentiment within the party. At the convention, new party rules required every state delegation to include a proportionate number of minority, female, and youthful delegates, which startled television audiences used to seeing conventions dominated by older, affluent, white males. This convention stood well to the left of the American electorate.

McGovern proved an easy target for Nixon. When third-party candidate George Wallace had to withdraw from the race in the spring of 1972 after a would-be assassin's bullet left him paralyzed, Wallace's "law and order" vote was left to Nixon. McGovern called for defense cuts, immediate withdrawal from Vietnam, **amnesty** for draft dodgers who had fled to Canada, and income redistribution. Nixon attacked McGovern as an inept radical who wanted "abortion, acid [LSD], and amnesty." When it became known that McGovern's vice-presidential running mate, Thomas Eagleton, had received electric-shock therapy for mental depression, McGovern confirmed this image of incompetence by first declaring his "1,000 percent" support for Eagleton and then dumping him.

In these circumstances, Nixon's reelection seemed certain. Nevertheless, he left nothing to chance. His Committee to Reelect the President (CREEP), operating independently of the Republican party, raised millions of dollars — often delivered in briefcases stuffed with untraceable cash — by targeting corporations and executives with ties to government contracts. The chairman of CREEP, former Attorney General John Mitchell, also approved a campaign of "dirty tricks" against the Democrats. The extent of these tricks became known after agents of Nixon's reelection committee, supervised by G. Gordon Liddy and H. Howard Hunt, were arrested on July 17, 1972, while breaking into the Democratic National Committee headquarters in the Watergate office complex in Washington. Shortly afterward, the police arrested James McCord, the security coordinator of CREEP, for his involvement in the break-in.

Immediately, Nixon's White House began to cover-up its links with the break-in by announcing that "no one in the White House staff, no one in this administration . . . was involved in this bizarre incident." Nixon also ordered that the White House telephone directory be changed to delete the name of

E. Howard Hunt. Moreover, Nixon secretly provided $400,000 to buy the silence of those arrested. The administration pressured the FBI to halt its investigation of the Watergate break-in on the pretext of national security. By these actions, Nixon committed an illegal act by trying to cover-up a crime.

McGovern's campaign was in such shambles that the Democrats could not capitalize on the issue. The *Washington Post* was one of the few newspapers that even mentioned Watergate. Nixon swamped both the popular vote, polling over 60 percent, and the **electoral college,** 520 to 17. McGovern won only Massachusetts and the District of Columbia.

WATERGATE FORCES NIXON TO RESIGN, 1973-1974. The Watergate scandal, however, continued to haunt Nixon. The trial of the Watergate burglars in spring 1973 brought further troubles to Nixon when federal judge John Sirica encouraged James McCord to confess that highly placed White House aides knew of the break-in. Then, two young, enterprising *Washington Post* reporters, Bob Woodward and Carl Bernstein, wrote a series of front-page stories linking the Nixon administration with the break-in. Using an unnamed informant in the Nixon administration, nicknamed "Deep Throat" (after the then-popular pornographic film), Woodward and Bernstein kept the Watergate story alive.

In February 1973, the Senate established the Special Committee on Presidential Campaign Activities under Democratic Senator Sam Ervin of North Carolina to investigate the matter. Feeling the heat, Nixon forced top White House aides, John Ehrlichman and H. R. Haldeman, to resign and also fired John Dean, the president's special counsel, who had engineered the original cover-up. Pledging "no whitewash at the White House," Nixon appointed a new attorney general, Elliot Richardson, to oversee the investigation and named Archibald Cox, a Democrat and Harvard Law School professor, as special prosecutor to conduct the investigation.

In May 1973, the Ervin committee began nationally televised hearings. When the Senate committee and the special prosecutor learned that Nixon had installed a secret taping system in the White House that recorded all conversations in the oval office, they demanded the tapes. Claiming "national security," Nixon resisted Cox in court, and after losing, ordered Attorney General Richardson to fire Cox. When Richardson and his deputy, William Ruckelshaus, refused to do so, Nixon fired both of them and ordered Solicitor General Robert Bork to dismiss Cox. The firings, timed too late to make the Sunday newspapers, were dubbed the "Saturday Night Massacre." Thousands of telegrams pushed the House Judiciary Committee to initiate **impeachment** proceedings against Nixon.

Later that October, Vice-President Spiro Agnew was forced to resign in a plea bargain after being charged with income tax evasion and with accepting bribes while governor of Maryland. Members of Congress from both parties forced President Nixon to select Representative Gerald R. Ford, a Republican, to replace the disgraced Agnew.

In April 1974, Nixon released edited transcripts of many tapes, while withholding the tapes themselves. Far from restoring confidence, the transcripts showed Nixon to be foul-mouthed, mean-spirited, anti-Semitic, manipulative, and cynical. His approval rating plunged. Nixon did not release everything, and after the new special prosecutor, Leon Jaworski, persuaded the Supreme Court, 9-0, to order that he turn over additional tapes, the jig was up. The end became certain when congressional Republicans, led by Barry Goldwater, informed Nixon that he would be convicted in the impeachment proceedings. On August 9, 1974, Nixon became the first president of the United States to resign from office.

Gerald Ford Tries to Heal a Troubled Nation, 1974-1977

As the new president, Gerald Ford attempted to end the Watergate saga by pardoning Nixon. An Arab oil embargo made a bad economy worse, driving up inflation and contributing to a severe recession. Ford's handling of the economy showed him to be an inept leader.

He continued Nixon's foreign policy course and generally served as little more than a caretaker. The war in Vietnam had drained the public interest in Southeast Asia, so Ford could do little when communists took control of Cambodia and South Vietnam. By 1976, voters were fed up with Washington and replaced Ford with an outsider, Jimmy Carter.

FORD FUMBLES DOMESTIC POLICY. On August 9, 1974, Gerald Ford was sworn in as the first president to have reached the highest office in the land without having been elected either president or vice-president. Ford brought to the presidency a calm, reassuring manner, a sense of confidence, and a deep faith in traditional values. A former football player on a winning team at the University of Michigan, Ford enjoyed success in Republican politics, working his way up through the ranks to become minority leader in the House.

As president, Ford sought desperately to reconcile a divided nation. One of his first acts, just 30 days after assuming the presidency, was to pardon Richard Nixon for "any and all crimes" committed while in office. This action did little to restore confidence in Washington and severely hurt Ford politically. He defended his decision, made with little input from advisers, as being in the best interest of the nation.

The economy remained Ford's greatest concern, and his actions further reinforced his image as an inept leader. Arab oil producers imposed an **embargo** against the United States in early 1973, then raised prices through the Organization of Petroleum Exporting Countries (OPEC). This sent oil prices spiraling upward, which in turn produced runaway inflation. Ford attempted to thwart inflation through persuasion, by promoting a voluntary program of wage and price freezes called "Whip Inflation Now" (WIN). The president frequently wore a WIN button. The Federal Reserve Board tried to cool inflation by raising the **discount rate** at which banks borrowed money. The resulting high interest rates led to a severe economic **recession** in 1974-1975 as money became tight. By 1974 unemployment reached nearly 11 percent — the highest rate since the Great Depression of the 1930s.

Faced with expensive gasoline, consumers increasingly brought more fuel efficient imported autos, which hurt the American car industry. Domestic producers were slow to respond to changing demand with new, competitive models. As domestic automobile sales plunged, General Motors, Ford, and Chrysler were forced to lay-off more than 200,000 workers.

FORD CONTINUES NIXON'S FOREIGN POLICY. In foreign policy, Ford sought to continue Nixon's initiatives by retaining Henry Kissinger as secretary of state (a job Kissinger had taken following Nixon's 1972 reelection). In his first year in office, Ford faced the final collapse of anticommunist resistance in Southeast Asia. In April 1975, Cambodian communists under Khmer Rouge leader Pol Pot defeated the pro-American government. The ensuing campaign by the communist Pol Pot government forced millions of Cambodians from the towns to the countryside and led to genocide on a scale unseen since the Nazi **holocaust.** More than a million Cambodians died.

In the spring of 1975, the North Vietnamese openly violated the 1973 truce and invaded South Vietnam, whose army and corrupt government quickly collapsed. In March, the North Vietnamese communists took Saigon, imposing a harsh rule on those who had opposed them.

By this time, most Americans did not want anything more to do with Southeast Asia. This widespread sentiment limited Ford's response to the communist takeover of Cambodia and South Vietnam. This became evident when the new communist government of Cambodia seized a U.S. merchant marine ship, the *Mayaguez*, shortly after the fall of Saigon. Ford ordered a military rescue of the 39 crewmen, and a massive bombing of Cambodia, but the raid cost the lives of 41 U.S. marines.

Ford also drew criticism from the right wing of his party for his diplomacy with the Soviet Union. Meeting with the Soviet leader Leonid Brezhnev in Vladivostok, Siberia, in late 1974, Ford made progress toward a new arms control treaty. The following year, Ford and Brezhnev signed an accord in Helsinki, Finland with 31 other nations recognizing Europe's post-1945 political boundaries and agreeing to respect human rights. The Helsinki agreement drew further criticism from conservatives who felt that Ford had given the Soviets too much for little in exchange. Even Kissinger expressed doubts about the agreement.

CARTER WINS THE ELECTION OF 1976. Ford's strength among conservatives was challenged when the former governor of California, Ronald Reagan, entered the Republican primaries. Ford barely defeated Reagan for the nomination, and the contest left the GOP severely divided.

Vietnam and Watergate had shaken the public's faith in Washington and anyone associated with it. As a result, the Democrats turned to an outsider, Jimmy Carter, an engineer, Annapolis graduate, ex-nuclear submarine officer, former governor of Georgia, and wealthy peanut farmer. Proclaiming opposition to "politics as usual," Carter promised to restore virtue and trust to government. He pledged a government as good as the American people. Cynics worried about any government that "good."

Carter narrowly won the election with 49.9 percent of the popular vote to Ford's 47.9 percent. The Georgian swept the South, but gained only 297 votes to Ford's 240 votes in the electoral college. As a consequence, Carter entered the White House without strong Washington ties, without much party support, and without a strong mandate to lead the nation.

Carter Disappoints a Nation in Malaise, 1977-1981

Jimmy Carter brought to the White House a welcome downhome style but no clear vision of where to lead the nation. His inability to work with Congress sank many of his proposals and convinced Americans that he was the wrong person for the job. Inflation reached record levels, and Carter's measures to fight it were ineffective. His greatest achievement was brokering a peace treaty between Israel and Egypt in 1979. He signed a new arms control treaty with the Soviet Union, but Congress refused to ratify it.

Carter entered the 1980 election campaign having made many enemies and few friends. His chances for reelection declined further when Islamic militants took over the U.S. embassy in Iran and held its diplomats hostage. For over a year, Carter was unable to free them by diplomacy or by military rescue. Few should have been surprised when Carter was trounced in the election by Ronald Reagan.

CARTER FLUNKS POLITICAL SCIENCE. Carter entered the White House as an outsider. His promise to change the "imperial presidency" that marked the Johnson-Nixon years was reflected in a down-to-earth style he brought to the office. On inauguration day, he and his wife, Rosalyn, walked more than a mile from the Capitol to the White House to demonstrate the beginnings of a "people's presidency." He insisted on being called Jimmy Carter, not James Earl Carter, Jr. He brought to the White House a group of young advisers from Georgia who prided themselves on their lack of experience in Washington.

At first the public welcomed the down-home Carter style, but his inability to work with a liberal Congress only accentuated his growing image as a nice man out of his depth. He seemed overly concerned with the details of government — including such matters as assigning times at the White House tennis courts — while lacking a broader vision to set an agenda or guide his administration along a particular path. As a result, Americans began to view his unpretentiousness as staged and indicative of a man unable to lead the nation.

In 1977, the administration succeeded in persuading Congress to enact a tax cut and a public works program that reduced unemployment to 5 percent by late 1978. Yet Carter's attempts at welfare reform by reactivating Nixon's FAP proposal failed miserably, as did his proposal for national health insurance.

Inflation haunted his administration even more than it had Nixon's or Ford's. A boost in oil prices by the OPEC nations further worsened inflation. By 1979 inflation was more than 13 percent per year. Carter relied, as Ford had, on voluntary curbs on prices and wages. To slowdown the spiral, the Federal Reserve Board also pushed interest rates higher, so that by 1980 mortgage and business loans reached an unheard-of 20 percent.

Carter created a new Department of Energy to deal with oil prices. He also proposed a comprehensive energy bill, but due to his poor relations with Congress, his initiative was watered-down in 1978. By 1979, Carter's approval rating had fallen below Nixon's during the Watergate scandal.

In the midst of growing political despair, Carter retreated to the presidential country house at Camp David in Maryland to consult with some 130 public figures. Then he emerged from his retreat to deliver a remarkable television address in which he proclaimed that Americans were suffering from a "malaise," and a "crisis of confidence." By 1979, however, most Americans concluded that the problem lay not with the national spirit, but with Carter himself.

FOREIGN POLICY DOOMS CARTER. Carter enjoyed some success in foreign policy. He made human rights a priority. Through Secretary of State Cyrus Vance, the administration applied pressure on the governments of Chile, Argentina, Ethiopia, South Africa, and the Philippines to correct human rights violations.

Carter successfully persuaded a reluctant Congress to ratify a treaty gradually transferring the Panama Canal and the Canal Zone to the Panamanians. He also established full diplomatic relations with the People's Republic of China in early 1979.

His greatest achievement came in the Middle East when he invited Israeli Prime Minister Menachem Begin and Egyptian President Anwar al-Sadat to Camp David in September 1978 to hammer out a basis for a peace treaty between the two antagonistic nations. After 13 days of prolonged negotiations the three leaders announced a "framework" for a peace treaty. Carter's moral fervor, especially concerning the Biblically significant Middle East, gave him confidence in the power of personal diplomacy. The president saw his own generosity and will, rather than political calculation, as the basis of this foreign policy success. In March 1979, Begin and Sadat signed a formal peace treaty at the White House establishing diplomatic relations between the two nations.

The Middle East accord marked a high point in the Carter administration. It was quickly followed by SALT II, a new arms control treaty with the Soviets. His image as a peacemaker seemed assured. When Carter submitted this treaty to Congress, however, he ran into strong opposition from conservatives who argued that the Soviets had not lived up to either the earlier SALT I agreement or the Helsinki Accords. Warning that the treaty offered the Soviets a means of achieving nuclear supremacy, Senate conservatives blocked SALT II's ratification.

In December 1979 the Soviet Union invaded neighboring Afghanistan to support a weak pro-Soviet regime against anti-Soviet rebels. Washington felt obliged to demonstrate its outrage. Carter withdrew the SALT II agreement from the Senate and ordered American athletes to boycott the summer Olympic games to be held in Moscow in 1980. Acting on the advice of his national

The American embassy in Iran was seized in November 1979 by radical Iranian students demanding the extradition of the deposed shah. The hostage crisis helped elect Ronald Reagan, who secured the release of 90 prisoners in January 1981. (AP/WORLD WIDE PHOTOS)

security adviser, Zbigniew Brzezinski, Carter endorsed the development of a very expensive nuclear-missile system, the MX. (Though SALT II was never ratified, the United States and the Soviet Union informally agreed to abide by it anyway.)

As the 1980 election approached, Carter was in political trouble. Matters only worsened in January 1979, when America's long-time ally, Reza Pahlavi, the shah of Iran, was overthrown by militant Islamic leader, Ayatollah Ruhollah Khomeini. Within a year, zealots seized the American embassy in the Iranian capital, Tehran, and held more than 50 Americans hostage. For the next 444 days, American television showed angry Iranian mobs parading blindfolded American hostages through the streets. While running for reelection, Carter tried desperately to explore every diplomatic avenue to secure the release of the hostages. Finally, in April 1980, Carter ordered a secret military mission to rescue them. The mission failed disastrously when an American helicopter and a transport plane crashed, leaving eight servicemen dead. Carter's approval rating sank to the lowest of any president since polling began in the 1930s.

REAGAN ELECTED IN 1980. By 1980 Carter's presidency was in deep trouble. Although the president fought off a challenge by Senator Edward

Kennedy — the youngest brother of John and Robert — in the Democratic primaries, the Democratic party was unenthusiastic about Carter. Few predicted, however, the severity of his defeat at the hands of his Republican challenger, Ronald Reagan — ex-Hollywood actor, former governor of California, and long-time presidential hopeful. In a single presidential debate, Reagan challenged Carter by asking the American voter, "Are you better off now than you were four years ago?" For most the answer was "no."

On election day the voters soundly rejected Carter. Reagan received almost 51 percent of the popular vote to Carter's 42 percent. John Anderson, a moderate Republican running as an independent, got 7 percent. Reagan received 489 **electoral votes** to Carter's 49. For the first time since the 1920s, a self-proclaimed conservative stepped into the White House. Jimmy Carter became the fifth consecutive president after Dwight D. Eisenhower to fail to gain and complete two terms.

Conclusion

The 1970s appeared to have ended in political and economic failure. The early confidence Americans had placed in the Nixon presidency had been betrayed, and the Ford and Carter presidencies seemed to be only brief and disillusioning interludes in a downward spiral. The office of president was left tarnished and weakened. In all, America — at home and abroad — seemed less vital, less confident, and less certain of its place in history than ever before.

Recommended Readings

DOCUMENTS: Henry Kissinger, *The White House Years* (1979) and *Years of Upheaval* (1982); and Bob Woodward and Carl Bernstein, *All the President's Men* (1974) and *The Final Days* (1973).

READINGS: (GENERAL) Peter Calleo, *The Imperious Economy* (1982); Jim Hougan, *Decadence: Radical Nostalgia, Narcissism, and Decline in the 1970s* (1975); Christopher Lasch, *The Culture of Narcissism* (1978); J. Anthony Lukas, *Common Ground* (1986); Kim McQuaid, *The Anxious Years* (1989); Martin Melosi, *Coping with Abundance* (1985); Lester Thurow, *The Zero-Sum Society* (1980). (NIXON-DOMESTIC) John Dean, *Blind Ambition* (1976); John Ehrlichman, *Witness to Power* (1982); Stanley I. Kutler, *The Wars of Watergate* (1990); J. Anthony Lukas, *Nightmare: The Underside of the Nixon Years* (1988); Patrick Moynihan, *The Politics of a Guaranteed Income* (1973); Richard Nixon, *RN* (1978); Leon Panetta and Peter Gall, *Bring Us All Together* (1971); Jonathan Schell, *The Time of Illusion* (1975); Garry Wills, *Nixon Agonistes* (1970). (NIXON-FOREIGN POLICY) Seymour Hersh, *The Price of Power: Kissinger in the Nixon White House* (1983); Roger Morris, *Uncertain Greatness: Henry Kissinger and American Foreign*

Policy (1977); William Shawcross, *Sideshow: Nixon, Kissinger, and the Destruction of Cambodia* (1978). (FORD-CARTER) Zbignew Brzezinski, *Power and Principle* (1983); Jimmy Carter, *Keeping the Faith* (1982); Erwin C. Hargrove, *Jimmy Carter as President* (1988); Charles O. Jones, *The Trusteeship Presidency: Jimmy Carter and the United States Congress* (1988); Clark Mollenhoff, *The President Who Failed* (1980); Richard Pipes, *U.S.-Soviet Relations in the Era of Detente* (1981); James Reichley, *Conservatives in an Age of Change: The Nixon and Ford Administrations* (1981). (SOCIETY AND CULTURE) Mary Frances Berry, *Why ERA Failed* (1986); Alice Echols, *Daring to Be Bad: Radical Feminism in American Society* (1989); John D'Emilio, *Sexual Politics, Sexual Communities: The Making of a Homosexual Minority in the United States* (1983); Sara Evans, *Personal Politics: The Roots of Women's Liberation in the Civil Rights Movement and the New Left* (1979); Jo Freeman, *The Politics of Women's Liberation* (1975); Samuel Hayes, *Beauty, Health, and Permanence: Environmental Politics in the United States* (1977); Steven Mintz and Susan Kellogg, *Domestic Revolutions: A Social History of American Family Life* (1988); Marc Reisner, *Cadillac Desert: The American West and Its Disappearing Water* (1986); Robert Stobaugh and Daniel Yergin, *Energy Future* (1979); Donald Worster, *Rivers of Empire* (1985).

30

※

THE REAGAN REVOLUTION
AND ITS AFTERMATH

CHAPTER OVERVIEW: The United States presented many contradictions in the 1980s. The decade witnessed astonishing technological and social changes accompanied by political and, to a lesser extent, cultural conservatism. Presiding over this paradox was Ronald Reagan (1981-89), who redefined the tone and nature of political discourse in this decade.

During his first term, Reagan initiated a rapid arms build-up that challenged detente with the Soviet Union, arms control, and mutual nuclear deterrence. In his second term, Reagan used the stronger American military position to reopen negotiations with the Soviet Union. These negotiations preceded the break-up of the Soviet bloc and the collapse of communism in Russia and eastern Europe. At the same time, Reagan pursued aggressive policies in the Middle East, Central America, and the Caribbean. Swapping arms for hostages in Iran and a covert war in Nicaragua led to the Iran-Contra Affair, which rocked the administration in 1986-1987.

Reagan's popularity was so high that he was able to pass the presidency on to his vice-president, George Bush (1989-1993). Bush sought moderation in domestic policy and a strong foreign policy that led to American involvement in Panama and the Middle East. A lingering economic recession which continued into the 1992 election led to Democrat Bill Clinton's victory over Bush that year.

Peoples of Paradox

The 1980s saw striking economic and social changes that contrasted with the political conservatism of the decade. The computer revolution, demographic changes, the transformation of the traditional American family, rising ethnic consciousness, and foreign immigration characterized the decade.

605

OF COMPUTERS AND CONTRADICTIONS. No change affected Americans' lives in the 1980s more than computer-based technology. During the 1980s new companies, such as Apple and Microsoft, joined the Fortune 500. "Silicon Valley," south of San Francisco, became a major high-tech center with more than 400,000 computer-related manufacturing jobs — more than in steel and autos combined. The rise of the computer industry accelerated a shift of jobs, profits, wealth, and power to the South and West "sunbelt."

Computers changed the way the country did business. Large corporations, insurance companies, banks, and retail merchants laid off thousands of middle managers. Decisions could now be made directly by senior management employees or sales staffs who had access to the relevant data on computers.

The decade of the 1980s was a contradictory mix of high-tech advances, social progress, and social decay. For example, the communications revolution brought on by cable television, satellites, and computers allowed unprecedented access to information, yet illiteracy rose to historic highs.

WOMEN IN THE 1980S: DIFFERING SPHERES. Women entered the workforce in increased numbers and in better jobs, but at the same time growing numbers of women also entered the ranks of the poor — a process described as the "feminization of poverty." By 1988 approximately 60 percent of women worked outside the home, although much of this work remained part-time. Most significantly, women now held more than a third of all corporate management positions and accounted for nearly one-fourth of all doctors and lawyers. Half of the students in law school were women, while close to 40 percent of university graduate students were women.

As a result of these economic gains, the big winners in the 1980s were women. While median annual salaries for men slid 8 percent in the 1980s, comparable salaries for women rose to 10 percent, although they still made less on the whole than men. Unlike World War II, when women achieved temporary increases in pay, gains in the 1980s and 1990s reflect solid, enduring trends. Women have chosen to stay in school longer and train for higher-paying occupations. Since the mid-1980s more women have received bachelor of arts degrees than men. Moreover, women entered male-dominated professions from medicine and law to law enforcement to construction. Still, women's wages remained only 70 percent of men's earnings.

By 1990 nearly 50 percent of all marriages ended in divorce. Associated with this increase was the growing number of single-parent households headed by women. By 1990 close to half of women workers were single either because they had never married or because they were divorced. At the same time, almost 25 percent of the nation's children were being raised in single-parent households.

AFRICAN-AMERICANS GAIN AND LOSE. The 1980s also marked a period of upward mobility for many African-Americans. During the decade large numbers of African-Americans entered the middle class as professionals. Over 40 percent of African-American workers held white-collar jobs, and nearly half owned their own homes. Moreover, median family income for African-Americans rose in the 1980s, while the number of those in poverty fell.

While social conditions had improved, many blacks remained poor, unemployed, and vulnerable to violence. More than 1 in 3 blacks remained in poverty, compared to 1 in 10 whites. Moreover, the inner city created an environment of social isolation for African-Americans. As middle-class blacks left for the suburbs, a hard core of inner city poor was abandoned. Unemployment in poor neighborhoods often reached over 60 percent, and nearly half of the residents failed to graduate from high school. This environment created its own pathology of an underclass plagued by joblessness and lawlessness.

In this world violence prevailed. Murder became the largest cause of death among young black males. Blacks accounted for about half of all crimes of violence. The growth of black gangs such as the Bloods and the Crips of Los Angeles further contributed to the problem of violence in the city.

AMERICA DIVERSIFIES. In the 1980s the United States experienced a significant influx of Hispanic and Asian immigrants. Hispanics became the fastest growing ethnic group as Mexican-Americans settled in the Southwest and West, Puerto Ricans and Dominicans migrated to the East Coast, and Cubans made homes in Florida. Newcomers from Vietnam, Thailand, Korea, Hong Kong, Taiwan, and the Philippines created new communities, especially in California. Demographers predicted that by the year 2010 whites of European ancestry would be a minority in California. During the 1980s, the number of residents for whom English was a foreign tongue jumped by more than a third to 31.8 million. As a result, about 14 percent of all residents grew up speaking a language other than English.

As the United States became more ethnically diverse, American religion reflected this change. While the majority of Americans remained within the Judeo-Christian tradition, this tradition revealed greater variety. By 1990 Roman Catholics, reflecting in part the growing Hispanic immigrant population, constituted 24 percent of the American population. At the same time, Protestantism became more diverse as **evangelical** sects attracted new followers.

Quasi-Christian movements, such as the Korean-based Unification Church (the Moonies) under the leadership of Sun Myung Moon, drew wide attention. By 1990 Islam had become the eighth largest denomination in the United States, larger than the Episcopal church, the Presbyterian church, and the Assemblies of God.

Even as religion grew more diverse, many Americans declared themselves secularists, expressing "none" when questioned about religious preference, thereby making secularists the fastest growing segment within American religion.

Reagan Charts a Domestic Revolution, 1981-88

As a candidate, Reagan had promised Americans a "new sunrise." As president he cut taxes, reduced social spending, and placed greater reliance on state, local, and community efforts. Easily reelected in 1984, Reagan reformed taxes but faced criticism over several scandals.

REAGAN UNLEASHES A CONSERVATIVE REVOLUTION. After a career as a Hollywood actor from the 1930s through the 1950s, Reagan entered politics in the 1960s as a conservative Republican who promised less government and lower taxes. He served two terms (1966-1974) as governor of California, while he continued to build a conservative following. He won the Republican nomination for president in 1980 on the promise to implement his conservative agenda.

Reagan promised to unleash American **capitalism** by cutting taxes and deregulating business. During his administration, **inflation** abated, unemployment fell, and the economy experienced the longest peacetime expansion in history. The government also ran record budget **deficits**. By 1986 a series of tax cuts had benefitted the wealthy by reducing top personal income tax rates to 28 percent, and cutting capital gains, inheritance, and gift taxes.

To compensate for the lost revenue, Reagan proposed massive spending cuts. Conservatives argued that the nation could no longer afford the expensive social programs established in the 1960s. Conservative southern Democrats — nicknamed **"boll weevils"** — joined Republicans in slashing more than $40 billion from domestic spending in 1981. Reagan's Omnibus Budget and Reconciliation Act (1981) proved to be a milestone in welfare policy. It shifted greater responsibility for maintaining social programs to state and local governments. Between fiscal years 1981 and 1984, Reagan drastically cut spending for youth training, school lunches, child nutrition, food stamps, preventive health, and Aid to Families with Dependent Children (AFDC).

Reagan and his advisers believed that tax cuts and deregulation would spur economic growth. Growth, it was argued, would increase government revenues and thus make up for money lost from lower tax rates. Cutting taxes to increase federal revenues appeared paradoxical, but a similar policy had been followed in the Kennedy administration. Reagan's tax strategy — labeled **"supply-side economics"** — called for unprecedented tax cuts. The theory assumed that consumers, freed from the burden of taxes, could both spend and save more, and businesses could both invest and produce more, leading to overall greater economic activity and hence larger tax revenues. Reagan also tried to shift spending from social programs to the military. The defense budget burgeoned, but Congress refused to cut social spending by enough to offset the increase. As a result, by 1986 the budget deficit had soared to more than $200 billion.

Reagan's new environmental policies drew the most criticism. In his campaign, Reagan captured a strong antienvironmental sentiment among western ranchers, miners, lumber interests, and farmers. This "sagebrush rebellion" called for an end to regulatory control of the western states, where the federal government owned the majority of the land, timber, and mineral resources. Reagan's first secretary of the interior, James Watt, proposed selling public lands. He also favored oil and gas exploration off the California coast and placed a **moratorium** on further federal land purchases.

Environmental groups filed dozens of lawsuits against federal agencies for not enforcing environmental regulations or laws. More damaging, however, was the criticism that Watt's program drew from conservatives. Sagebrush ranchers wanted grazing rights on federal land, not land auction in competition with wealthy oil and mineral companies. Conservatives attacked Watt's land sale program as economically improvident and environmentally unsound.

These criticisms took their toll on Watt. Then in 1983, Watt's appointee to the Environmental Protection Agency, Anne Gorsuch Burford, resigned following disclosure of her mishandling of the $1.6 billion "superfund" intended to clean up toxic-waste sites. She was replaced by William Ruckelshaus, a proenvironmentalist. The final nail was put in Watts' political coffin when he made a derogatory racial remark and was forced to resign.

Environmentalists generally blasted Reagan and Watt, although the administration scored some notable environmental successes including a renewed Endangered Species Act (1982) and several dozen wilderness laws (1984). Still, environmentalists remained sorely disappointed by Reagan's international record, which included reduced support for the United Nations' environmental and population control programs. He also opposed international treaties on global cooperation for environmental protection of the seas and the atmosphere.

Reagan quickly began deregulating the economy. Deregulation, in fact, had begun in the Carter administration with the airline industry. Reagan accelerated this movement by reducing federal regulatory power in areas such as broadcasting, transportation, and occupational safety and health. Early in Reagan's administration, Secretary of Transportation Drew Lewis reduced automobile safety and pollution regulations.

In the summer of 1981, Lewis confronted the Professional Air Traffic Controller's Organization (PATCO) when they illegally went on strike. Reagan broke this walk-out by firing all 11,500 striking workers and hiring replacements. Reagan's victory set a tone for the rest of his administration, and the destruction of PATCO marked a devastating defeat for organized labor.

Reagan's administration also sought to change federal policy toward civil rights. Conservative Republicans believed that many white Americans resented affirmative action and preferential hiring programs for minorities. As a consequence, the Justice Department opposed school busing and sought to overturn prohibitions against tax deductions for contributions to non-integrated religious schools. The budget for the Civil Rights Division of the Justice Department was cut and the number of African-Americans appointed to major government positions declined.

Reagan's record on appointing women to federal positions was marginally better. Women served in the cabinet and in the Republican party. He named Jeane Kirkpatrick as ambassador to the United Nations. His most notable appointment came in 1981 when he nominated Sandra Day O'Connor as the first female justice on the United States Supreme Court.

In late 1981, Reagan faced his greatest challenge when the economy went into a severe **recession**. The Federal Reserve Board, trying to fight the double-digit inflation that was plaguing the country, allowed interest rates to soar. Rates for home mortgages shot up to double-digit figures. Very high interest rates created an abrupt and deep slowdown of the economy. By late 1982 unemployment had risen to 10 percent — the highest in 45 years. A decline in American exports led to a worsening trade deficit, fueled by huge increases in imports of Japanese televisions, stereos, and automobiles. The trade deficit rose from $31 billion in 1981 to $111 billion in 1984.

Reagan's program appeared doomed. In the 1982 **midterm elections**, Democrats gained 26 House seats, although the Republicans held on to a narrow Senate majority. The break-up of the Middle East's oil cartel (OPEC) and a decline in world oil prices, however, fueled a recovery. Inflation dropped to 4 percent; unemployment fell, and the gross domestic product rose nearly 10 percent. American auto manufacturers reported record sales. This economic boom lasted until 1990.

Ronald Reagan, elected at age 69, was the oldest man and first professional actor chosen president. While the economy boomed and the Cold War cooled, budget deficits skyrocketed during his two terms. (UPI/BETTMANN)

REAGAN REELECTED, 1984. Reagan's personality seemed to mesmerize the American people. His aura was enhanced on March 30, 1981, when a mentally disturbed man shot him. Wounded in the chest, Reagan was rushed to the hospital. As he was wheeled into surgery he told the physicians, "Please tell me you're all Republicans." This jaunty ability to joke under pressure ingratiated him with the public. He possessed a natural ability to communicate with the American people. Opponents called him the "Teflon president" because nothing negative seemed to stick to him. Supporters called him "the Great Communicator."

In 1984 Reagan enjoyed the highest popularity rating since Dwight D. Eisenhower. He brought to his reelection campaign an economy that was booming. As promised, Reagan revived the economy, conquered inflation, rebuilt the military, and reestablished America's place "standing tall" in the world. Reagan said it was "morning in America." In the 1984 election he and Vice-President Bush beat Democrat Walter Mondale, Carter's former vice-president, and running mate Representative Geraldine Ferraro, the first woman placed on a major-party **ticket.** In a landslide, Reagan swept 49 states for 525 of the 538 **electoral votes.** He won the popular vote 59 percent to Mondale's 41 percent.

CONSERVATISM AT HIGH TIDE, 1986-88. Reagan entered his second term intent on a major overhaul of the tax system. The president's main goal was to reduce rates, especially on higher incomes. He achieved that goal with the Tax Reform Act (1986), which provided the first fundamental reform of the modern federal income tax system since World War II. The act both lowered rates and simplified the tax code, closing many loopholes and eliminating a variety of **tax shelters.** Moreover, the law removed 6 million poor Americans from the federal income tax rolls. The act also lowered the tax burden for the majority of taxpayers, although those with high incomes benefitted the most. Some of the tax burden was shifted to corporations by eliminating some tax **write-offs** and exemptions.

Reagan promised that this supply side tax reform would bring a booming economy and control of a mounting federal deficit. This proved half right. The economy prospered, with growth rates averaging 3 to 4 percent annually. Corporations enjoyed record sales and profits, the stock market reached new heights, and consumer spending and confidence remained high. Nevertheless, federal deficits continued to soar, reaching a high of $200 billion in 1986 and settling at $150 billion by 1988. Congress attempted to balance the budget with the Gramm-Rudman Act (1985), which tried to limit spending. Gramm-Rudman failed, however, to balance the budget when Congress found myriad ways to circumvent the law and the Supreme Court found key provisions unconstitutional.

Next to tax reform, Reagan believed that his most enduring legacy might come by remaking the Supreme Court in a conservative fashion. His appointment of moderate Sandra Day O'Connor in 1981 pointed in this direction. Following the retirement of Chief Justice Warren Burger in 1986, Reagan elevated conservative William Rehnquist to chief justice and appointed the equally conservative Antonin Scalia to the bench. In 1988, after a bitter fight which led to the rejection of Robert Bork, a well-known judicial conservative, California federal judge Anthony Kennedy joined the court.

Reagan also tackled the difficult problem of illegal immigrants. He was successful when Congress enacted a landmark immigration bill in October

1986. The law offered **amnesty** for current illegal aliens, while providing tougher rules to stop future illegal immigration by requiring employers to verify the citizenship of job applicants. Designed to stem the tide of illegal immigration by cutting access to jobs, it nonetheless failed to halt the thousands of illegal aliens entering the United States, especially from Mexico and Central America. Often employers neglected to enforce the rules, and illegal immigrants forged documentation verifying citizenship.

SCANDALS PLAGUE REAGAN'S SECOND TERM. Reagan promised new integrity in government, but a series of scandals tarnished his second term. After a two-year investigation, the Justice Department in June 1988 revealed widespread corruption in the Pentagon involving bribes taken from defense contractors. Other officials came under investigation. In July 1988 Attorney General Edwin Meese, a close friend of Reagan's, resigned after allegations of having used his influence to secure a billion-dollar contract for friends to build an oil pipeline in Iraq. Reagan advisers were convicted of influence peddling after leaving their positions in the White House. One of the worst scandals occurred in the Department of Housing and Urban Development, where developers paid hundreds of thousands of dollars in bribes for federal contracts.

While Reagan remained personally and politically immune from these charges, critics maintained that the get-rich quick atmosphere of the Reagan years contributed to influence peddling and corruption in government.

The Reagan Revolution around the World, 1981-1988

Ronald Reagan entered the White House convinced that detente with the Soviet Union had failed and that communism remained a threat to international stability. Taking a hard line, he ordered a massive defense program, while taking a tougher stance toward arms control with the Soviet Union. Reagan displayed a willingness to use American military forces, as evidenced when U.S. marines were sent to Lebanon in early 1983. The Reagan administration provided covert support to rebels in Soviet-occupied Afghanistan and rebels seeking to overthrow the leftist government in Nicaragua. This involvement in Nicaragua led to the Iran-Contra scandal when administration officials entered into a secret deal to supply the Iranian government with arms.

While foreign policy under Reagan often appeared blundering, his administration witnessed the end of the Cold War as major arms treaties with the Soviet Union were reached and the Soviet Union began to withdraw from Eastern Europe.

REAGAN CHOOSES MORE MUSCLE, LESS TALK. Reagan and his advisers found **detente** wanting. They believed the Soviet Union had taken advantage of American goodwill and desire for cooperation and had given little in return. Instead, the Soviet Union had invaded Afghanistan, Soviet and East German generals commanded Cuban troops in Ethiopia, and the Soviet Union was supplying and encouraging a revolutionary, anti-American regime in Nicaragua. Reagan denounced the Soviet Union as an "evil empire" intent on undermining American power around the globe.

Under Reagan the Pentagon's budget swelled from $171 billion in 1981 to more than $300 billion in 1985. Secretary of Defense Caspar Weinberger warned that the Soviet Union might be able to undertake a first strike nuclear attack against the United States. This sort of advice pushed Congress to approve the MX missile system, a new strategic bomber, and an expanded navy with 600 ships. In 1983, the United States deployed more than 500 Cruise and Pershing II missiles in Europe to counter the Soviet Union's intermediate missiles in eastern Europe. The placement of these missiles set off peace demonstrations in both the United States and Europe. Activists called for a **unilateral** "nuclear freeze" to halt the new arms race.

Reagan showed little faith in arms control. Nevertheless, his administration proposed to the Soviet Union a dramatic "zero option" plan, which offered to cancel the U.S. deployment of intermediate missiles in western Europe if the Soviets withdrew missiles from eastern Europe. When this proposal was rejected, the United States entered into new negotiations — called START — with the Soviet Union. Meeting in Geneva, American negotiators proposed that both sides scrap one-third of their nuclear warheads. The Soviet Union rejected the proposal outright. When intermediate missiles sent from the United States began arriving in Great Britain and West Germany in 1983, the Soviet Union broke off the START talks.

Following the break-up of the START talks, Reagan approved the Strategic Defense Initiative (SDI), a complex antimissile system that would use high-powered lasers in space to destroy Soviet missiles launched at the United States. Quickly denounced as a fanciful and impractical "Star Wars" by critics, SDI was seen as an expensive and destabilizing escalation of the arms race that might encourage a preemptive first strike.

Reagan's tough stance appeared to have little effect on the Soviet Union. In late 1981 the Soviet Union ordered a crackdown in Poland against the militant Solidarity trade union movement. Following the declaration of **martial law** by the communist government, Reagan sought to isolate the Soviet

Union by imposing an economic boycott on Poland. In 1982, Reagan tried to block the building of a natural gas line linking the Soviet Union and western Europe, but Reagan's efforts were stymied by western European leaders.

Efforts to aid anti-Soviet rebels in Soviet-occupied Afghanistan proved more successful. The Central Intelligence Agency arranged to supply high-tech weapons to the rebels through an extensive **covert** operation based in Pakistan. Rebel forces were able to bog down Soviet forces in a **guerrilla war** reminiscent of America's involvement in Vietnam a decade earlier.

EXPANDING TRADE WITH ASIA. The Reagan administration worked to expand trade with Asia. The population of China exceeded one billion — a potentially vast market for American goods. In addition, the economies of Japan, South Korea, Taiwan, Hong Kong, Malaysia, and Singapore were booming, largely fueled by trade with the United States.

While the United States sought to develop new markets in China, the administration faced a serious challenge from aggressive Japanese manufacturers who flooded America with their high-quality, low-priced products. The trade imbalance between Japan and United States, unfavorable to the United States, rose from $10 billion in 1980 to $35 billion in 1984. A large part of this deficit was due to imported Japanese cars. In the 1970s American auto manufacturers had lost 25 percent of their home market to Japanese auto-makers. Under pressure the Japanese agreed to a "voluntary" reduction in auto shipments to the United States.

DEALING WITH SOUTH AFRICA AND THE PHILIPPINES. The administration faced growing problems in South Africa, where the militant African National Congress (ANC) organized protests against an oppressive system of racial segregation and white supremacy known as **apartheid** (an Afrikaner word for "apartness"). In the mid-1980s, government security forces began a serious crackdown against ANC demonstrators. When violence followed, American civil rights groups called for American corporations and institutions to withdraw investments in South Africa. Fourteen states and scores of cities refused to own stocks of any corporations that did business in South Africa, and college students across the country demonstrated against their universities' investment policies.

The Reagan administration pursued what it called "constructive engagement." This policy applied diplomatic pressure through State Department channels, while refraining from open criticism of apartheid. Under mounting public pressure, Congress in 1986 overrode a presidential veto and imposed an economic boycott on South Africa.

In 1986 Reagan's attention also turned to the Philippine Islands, where

Corazon Aquino challenged military dictator Ferdinand Marcos for political power. Fearing a communist revolution in the islands, the United States had backed the Marcos government until Aquino emerged to challenge what had become the Marcos **"cleptocracy"** (government of theft). America pressured Marcos to hold democratic elections in early 1986. Although he claimed victory, the people believed the results had been rigged. Massive protests forced him to flee the country and Mrs. Aquino assumed power. The new democratic government continued to face communist insurgency, a stagnant economy, and political pressure from the military.

MUDDLING THROUGH THE MIDDLE EAST. In the Middle East, the Reagan administration sought to continue the peace process begun in the Carter years. Nevertheless, Secretary of State Alexander Haig appeared to encourage Israel's policy of gradually taking over the West Bank, considered by the Palestinians as their homeland. In 1982 Israel invaded Lebanon to destroy refugee camps controlled by the Palestine Liberation Organization (PLO), a long-time foe of Israel. The Reagan administration sent Philip Habib, an **envoy** of Lebanese descent, to arrange for the safe withdrawal of PLO forces and refugees under attack from the Israelis. In September 1982, Christian Lebanese forces allied with Israel invaded two refugee camps and slaughtered hundreds of unarmed Palestinians.

The United States sent 1,500 troops to Beirut to help restore peace. Syrian forces, backed by the Soviet Union, occupied eastern Lebanon, while Israel controlled southern Lebanon. Militant Muslim factions despised the American troops, who remained isolated and in a poor defensive position. Early on the morning of October 23, 1983, a Muslim terrorist drove a truck filled with explosives directly into the U.S. marine compound. The explosion killed 241 sleeping marines — the worst military disaster since the Vietnam War. By early 1984 Reagan quietly withdrew the remaining marines from Lebanon. Reagan had achieved nothing.

INTERNATIONAL TERRORISM AND THE MIDDLE EAST. International terrorism haunted the government. The State Department estimated that there were 700 terrorist assaults around the world in 1985 alone. Most of these attacks came from Arab extremists committed to the destruction of Israel. In 1986, pro-Libyan terrorists, with cooperation from the communist government in East Germany, bombed American military installations in West Germany. In retaliation, Reagan ordered an air strike on Libya. Public opinion supported this action, although some critics called the strike ineffective and counterproductive because it accomplished little militarily.

The situation in the Middle East became extremely explosive in 1987 when it looked like the United States might be drawn into the Iraq-Iran war. This grueling six-year war between Iraq and Iran had begun in 1981 and claimed an estimated 600,000 lives. When the Iranian navy began attacking Kuwaiti oil shipments destined for the United States, western Europe, and Japan, Reagan ordered a U.S. naval fleet into the Persian Gulf. Tensions between the United States and Iran heightened when the destroyer *USS Vincennes* mistakenly shot down an Iranian airliner, killing 290 passengers. A series of clashes between the Iranian navy and American fleet ensued. The Iraq-Iran war finally ended in the summer of 1988 in a negotiated stalemate, but tensions remained between Iran and the United States.

THE CENTRALITY OF CENTRAL AMERICA. Two small nations — Nicaragua and El Salvador — became the focus of U.S. policy in Latin America during the 1980s. The administration remained intent on rolling back pro-Soviet **socialism** in Nicaragua and on defeating an insurgent movement in El Salvador. United States policy in Latin America was designed to thwart Marxist revolutions in the southern hemisphere.

Evidence gathered by the CIA revealed that Marxist **Sandinista** supporters in Nicaragua were aiding communist rebels across the border in El Salvador. Following the murder of several American Catholic nuns by right-wing Salvadoran government forces, President Carter had cut off financial aid to El Salvador. In 1984 Jose Napoleon Duarte, a moderate democrat, was elected president. He initiated reforms curbing the right-wing "death squads" that had murdered thousands of civilians. Duarte's army, however, was unable to defeat the left-wing guerrillas or bring them to the negotiation table.

While civil war raged in El Salvador, Reagan authorized $19 million in late 1981 to arm 500 rebel troops in Nicaragua. This counterrevolutionary army — called the "Contras" — became the focus of Reagan's foreign policy in Central America. Composed of anti-Sandinista Nicaraguans, including former supporters of the deposed dictator Anastasio Somoza Debayle — the Contras conducted raids and sabotage in Nicaragua. Congress remained skeptical of Reagan's support of the Contras and in December 1982 enacted the Boland Amendment, which barred the CIA or the Pentagon from directly funding these anticommunist insurgents.

Although the administration conducted a proxy war in Nicaragua and El Salvador without deploying U.S. troops, Reagan was not opposed to using direct force. In 1983, he sent U.S. marines to help overthrow a Marxist dictator on the tiny Caribbean island of Grenada. Deployed shortly after the debacle in Lebanon, the marines quickly overran the island and captured several hundred Cuban military advisers who appeared to have been hurriedly constructing a Soviet air base. The United States installed a friendly government and granted $30 million in financial assistance. While both Congress and the Organization of American States condemned the invasion, public opinion polls in the United States and Grenada showed Reagan receiving wide support.

THE IRAN-CONTRA AFFAIR, 1986-1988. Relations with Iran proved more enigmatic than met the eye. In early November 1986, a Beirut magazine reported that in 1985 the United States had shipped more than 500 antitank missiles to Iran. The article sparked accusations of a scandal. Reagan, however, claimed that the missiles were sold to Iran as a means of persuading pro-Iranian radical groups to release American hostages they were holding in Lebanon.

More bizarre details soon followed, including a report that Colonel Oliver North, a National Security Council aide, had used profits from the missile sales to help fund the Contras in Nicaragua. The diversion subverted the congressional directive embodied in the Boland Amendment. Congressional investigators also revealed that North had arranged a deal with the Saudi Arabians to sell them 400 U. S. Stinger antiaircraft missiles if they would donate $10 million to the Contras. North also persuaded Israel, as well as private donors, to back the rebels. Just before the FBI arrived to seal the office for investigation, North and his secretary shredded documents that might have incriminated other high officials, including Central Intelligence director William J. Casey.

A joint House-Senate investigative committee convened in the summer of 1987 to investigate the Iran-Contra affair. In nationally televised hearings, more than 250 hours of testimony were taken. The committee's final report roundly criticized the administration for its flagrant disregard for the law. An independent prosecutor continued the investigation through 1992 in an attempt to unravel the whole story of "who knew what, and when". In late 1992, shortly before leaving office, President George Bush pardoned key Reagan officials, including former Secretary of Defense Caspar Weinberger, implicated in the affair.

THE COLD WAR ENDS. In his second term, Reagan dramatically shifted his foreign policy toward negotiation with the Soviet Union. Shortly after the 1984 election, Reagan surprised his leading advisers — as well as his critics — by resuming negotiations with the Soviets. In late 1985, Reagan traveled to Geneva to meet with the new Soviet leader Mikhail Gorbachev for a three-day summit meeting. At the meeting, Reagan insisted on America's right to develop the Strategic Defense Initiative (SDI). This position precluded any major agreements being reached, but Reagan and Gorbachev pledged to accelerate arms control negotiations in future meetings.

Finally, in 1987 Gorbachev flew to the United States to sign the historic Intermediate Nuclear Forces Treaty (INF), the first major arms control agreement that called for the destruction of deployed nuclear weapons systems. The treaty provided that inspectors from both nations would observe the destruction of intermediate-range missiles. Soviet and American leaders also announced that they would seek further arms reductions through the Strategic Arms Reduction Treaty (START) talks, which had been temporarily broken off in Reagan's first term. Gorbachev also began to withdraw Soviet troops from Afghanistan, to end support to the Sandinista government in Nicaragua, and to reduce commitments to Cuba and Vietnam. Moreover, Gorbachev urged Soviet-backed governments in eastern Europe to undertake political and economic reform.

Reagan's success with the Soviet Union helped overcome setbacks related to the Iran-Contra scandal. Following that debacle, these successful negotiations with the Soviet Union proved decisive for restoring public confidence in Reagan, the longtime **Cold Warrior.** As Reagan's administration drew to a close, the **Cold War** appeared to have ended. These negotiations marked one of the great diplomatic feats since World War II.

Bush Fails to Fill Reagan's Shoes, 1988-1993

Reagan passed the mantle of power to his vice-president, George Bush, who easily won the 1988 presidential election. Domestically, Bush pursued a moderate program that called for less government intervention in the economy, modest social reform, and reduction of the deficit. His willingness to work with congressional Democrats led him to break a campaign pledge not to raise taxes. The Bush presidency coincided with the disintegration of the Soviet Union, whose rivalry with the United States had dominated international relations since World War II. The Soviet Union's demise transformed American foreign policy and defense strategy. The United States now exerted its strength in confronting dictators in Panama and Iraq.

An economic recession, however, marred the last two years of Bush's administration, weakening his popularity and enabling Bill Clinton to unseat him in the 1992 election.

BUSH STRUGGLES WITH THE DEFICIT. The Republicans picked Reagan's vice-president, George Herbert Walker Bush, to head their ticket in 1988. Bush appeared to have no clear ideological vision of his own and was seen as someone who would continue the Reagan agenda. He promised at the Republican Convention, "read my lips — no new taxes." In a particularly nasty campaign Bush defeated his Democratic opponent Michael Dukakis by assailing him for opposing legislation requiring school children to recite the Pledge of Allegiance, for failing to clean up pollution in Boston Harbor, and for allowing a convicted rapist and murderer to be furloughed from prison — during which time he committed other heinous crimes. Bush won the election with 54 percent of the popular vote and 426 **electoral votes**, to Dukakis's 46 percent and 112 electors.

Once in office, Bush promised to make America a "kinder, gentler nation." In a subtle reprimand of the Reagan administration, Bush expressed a willingness to be a "hands-on" president who would cooperate with Congress. Although he sought few domestic initiatives, he expressed a concern that the budget be balanced. The national debt stood at nearly $3 trillion when Bush took office.

Bush proposed sharp reductions in military spending by slashing $2.7 billion from Reagan's defense budget, including severe cutbacks in funding for the SDI ("Star Wars") program. Despite his campaign pledge to be an "education president," he requested $3 billion less for education than Reagan had in his last budget. He proposed, however, additional funding for child care, clean air, and AIDS (a disease that attacks the immune system) research. Declaring a new war on drugs, he called for increased funding for law enforcement.

Rising budget deficits dominated Bush's administration. By 1991 the budget deficit had risen to $268 billion, the largest in U. S. history. Finally, under pressure from Congress, in July 1990 Bush reneged on his campaign pledge not to raise taxes. The backlash from conservatives and working-class Reagan Democrats was immediate. Conservatives accused Bush of having broken his firm pledge on taxes. The break with conservatives within his party proved irreversible.

Bush sought to shore up conservative support by continuing the Reagan agenda of transforming the Supreme Court. Reagan's appointments had appeared to shift the court in a decidedly more conservative direction. In *Webster v. Reproduction Health Care Services* (1989) the court had upheld a Missouri law that limited a woman's right to an abortion. Yet the court had also showed an independence that set it apart from any set conservative position when it ruled in *Texas v. Johnson* (1989) that first amendment rights allowed flag burning.

In 1990, following the retirements of William Brennan and Thurgood Marshall, Bush appointed David Souter, a federal judge from New Hampshire, who easily won Senate approval. Bush's second appointee, Clarence

Thomas, a conservative African-American, ran into serious problems when Anita Hill, an African-American former employee of Thomas, accused him of sexual harassment when she worked for him at two federal agencies in 1982 and 1983. Following televised hearings, the Senate narrowly confirmed Thomas's nomination.

In the midst of the Thomas fight, Bush signed the Civil Rights Act of 1991, which he had denounced earlier as a "quota bill." The civil rights bill only compounded a sense of betrayal among conservatives and Reagan Democrats.

THE SOVIET UNION COLLAPSES. The collapse of the Soviet Union, beginning in 1989 with the crumbling of the communist government in Poland, soon spread throughout eastern and central Europe as communist regime after regime fell with a domino-like effect. Republicans claimed that Reagan's aggressive anticommunist foreign policy brought about the demise of the Soviet empire. Many Soviet leaders agreed that this was a contributing factor, although any full analysis of the collapse of communism must acknowledge the role played by the economic failure of Soviet-style communism.

During the Reagan administration, Mikhail Gorbachev became leader of the Soviet Union. Gorbachev called for economic restructuring *(perestroika)* and political openness *(glasnost)*. A deteriorating Soviet economy forced Gorbachev to accept political reform in eastern Europe. Without Soviet support, communist regimes fell in Poland, Czechoslovakia, Hungary, Bulgaria, and Romania. The most dramatic event came when East Germans were allowed to cross the border at the Berlin Wall, separating East and West Germany, on November 9, 1989. Later, West Germany absorbed East Germany into a single nation. The Cold War had ended.

The Chinese government also reacted harshly against a prodemocratic movement that had been unleashed by the events in the Soviet Union. Inspired by reform movements in eastern Europe, thousands of Chinese students and their supporters occupied Tiananmen Square in the Chinese capital of Beijing in a massive demonstration calling for political reform. On the morning of June 4, 1989, Chinese leader Deng Xiaoping ordered the army to crush the dissident movement. A least a thousand demonstrators were killed when the army ruthlessly attacked the unarmed students. Bush condemned the attack but refused to sever diplomatic ties with China.

The crisis in the Soviet Union soon affected Latin America. Shortly after the Soviet Union announced that it would no longer continue to subsidize the Marxist Sandinista government in Nicaragua, the Sandinistas permitted the first democratic elections in Nicaragua in 60 years. To their surprise, a coalition of anti-Sandinista forces swept into office.

The Soviet decline left the United States as the world's only superpower. Bush remained determined to assert America's military power by shaping what he described as the "new world order." Determined to overthrow the drug-dealing dictator Manuel Noriega in Panama, Bush ordered military forces into Panama in December 1989. Most Panamanians welcomed the invasion of 25,000 American troops, who subsequently seized Noriega on charges of drug trafficking. Noriega was returned to the United States, where he was tried and convicted for his involvement in the international drug trade.

Most Americans cheered Bush's move against Noriega. This use of force in Panama set the stage for further U.S. action when Iraq invaded its oil-rich neighbor, Kuwait, in August 1990. Fearing an Iraqi invasion of Saudi Arabia and subsequent threat to American oil interests, Bush forged an international coalition under United Nations' auspices to force Iraq to withdraw from Kuwait. When an economic boycott appeared to have little effect on the Iraqi leader Saddam Hussein, Bush ordered a massive air and ground assault that eventually totaled 700,000 Allied troops against Iraqi-occupied Kuwait and southern Iraq.

In a six-week campaign, Operation Desert Storm, led by U.S. General Norman Schwarzkopf, overwhelmed Saddam's army. An estimated 50,000 to 100,000 Iraqis were killed. Kuwait was liberated, although Saddam continued in power. Bush's popularity soared to 91 percent, the highest ever recorded for any president. In the fall of 1991 Bush's reelection for a second term seemed certain.

ECONOMIC DOWNTURN, RIOTS, AND THE ELECTION OF 1992. The record-long business expansion that began in 1983 halted in 1990 as the United States entered a recession that lasted until mid-1991. Even as signs of growth appeared, the economy continued to hover in limbo between recession and recovery. Unemployment rose to 7.5 percent in 1992. As the economy spiraled downward, so did George Bush's popularity. Convinced that he would easily win reelection, though, he accepted the advice of his advisers and refused to push new legislation to improve the economy.

Lingering economic recession and growing discontent among the electorate created a volatile political situation as the presidential race opened in 1992. While Republicans under Reagan had made significant inroads among traditional Democratic blocs — white southerners, Catholics, and blue-collar workers — only 29 percent of the electorate expressed strong identification with either political party. A walloping 26 percent of the electorate considered themselves "independents." Surveys revealed deep cynicism among voters toward professional politicians.

In this situation, the Democrats turned to Bill Clinton, governor of Arkansas, who campaigned as a moderate intent on returning the party to the middle class. In a departure from typical political wisdom, Clinton did not try for regional balance but rather selected another southerner as his running mate: Tennessee Senator Albert Gore, a strong environmentalist.

Confident of his own reelection, Bush nonetheless faced a sputtering economy and an array of social problems. The national debt had doubled in the Reagan-Bush years to $4 trillion. The banking industry, especially savings and loan institutions, was in disarray caused by heavy debt. Unemployment hovered intractably at 7 percent. One American in ten was on food stamps, while one in eight lived in poverty.

The situation seemed ripe for an explosion. On April 29, 1992, that eruption came when a jury in Simi Valley, California, acquitted four white Los Angeles policemen accused of beating a young black man named Rodney King. The beating had been videotaped by a passing witness, providing what many considered obvious proof of their guilt.

For the next four days Los Angeles experienced the worst riot in its history. Protestors targeted a section of south-central Los Angeles where 200,000 Koreans had settled and opened small businesses in a neighborhood called "Koreatown." At one point, the smoke over Los Angeles caused by the upheaval forced the airport to close all but one runway.

The national guard finally restored order, but estimates of property damage in Los Angeles varied from $750 million to $1 billion. Approximately 50 people died. More than 15,000 were arrested. Critics blamed the riot on the failure of the Reagan-Bush administrations to address the needs of the inner city.

The political situation became complicated when a Texas billionaire, Ross Perot, declared he was entering the presidential race as an independent. Polls showed him winning 30 percent of the vote in a three way race — but then in July he abruptly withdrew from the race. The Clinton-Gore **ticket** continued to hammer Bush on the economy, portraying Republicans as out of touch with the needs of the middle class. Republicans countered by raising issues of trust, charging that Clinton had dishonestly avoided the **draft** during the Vietnam War. Bush portrayed Clinton as a liberal who would raise taxes, increase social spending, and enact a radical cultural agenda. In mid-October Perot had a change of heart and reentered the race, conducting his campaign largely through controlled television advertising rather than direct contact with reporters or the public.

On election day, Clinton swept the **electoral college,** winning 370 **electoral votes** with 43 percent of the popular vote. Bush won 168 electoral votes

Table 30.1. 1992 Presidential Election

Candidate	Popular Vote	Electoral Vote
Bill Clinton (Democrat)	43,726,375	370
George Bush (Republican)	38,167,416	168
Ross Perot (Independent)	19,237,247	0

with 38 percent of the vote. Perot failed to carry any state, but won 19 percent of the popular vote, the largest vote received by any third-party since Theodore Roosevelt ran as a Progressive in 1912.

For the first time in 16 years, the Democrats had won the White House. The election of Bill Clinton promised historic change. The first president born after the Second World War, the 46-year-old Clinton promised a generational transfer of power. He received particularly strong support among blacks, the very poor, the elderly, and some groups of women.

The 1992 election proved to be a breakthrough for women and minorities. Five of 11 women running for the Senate won. Democrat Carol Moseley Braun became the first African-American woman ever elected to the Senate. California became the first state ever to be represented in the Senate only by women, when Barbara Boxer and Dianne Feinstein were elected. The first American Indian to sit in the Senate in 60 years was Democrat Ben Nighthorse Campbell of Colorado.

Conclusion

The United States, a society founded on immigration, had become one of the most ethnically diverse nations in the world, home to people of European, African, Latin American, and Asian descent. American religions now included Protestants, Catholics, Muslims, Buddhists, Hindus, and secularists. Single-parent families became more common. In this social transformation, women increasingly entered professions formerly closed to them. Gender roles, too, changed as homosexuals — male and female — sought recognition and acceptance.

The American political system reflected this diversity as more women, as well as African-Americans, Hispanics, and other minorities were elected to office. At the same time, confidence in democratic government and the two-party system appeared shaken as voter participation declined and the elector-

Bill Clinton was elected president after 12 years of Republican rule by hammering the issue of a stagnating economy. He proposed deficit reduction, economic growth, health care and welfare reform, and defense conversion. (Pam Price/The Picture Group)

ate expressed disillusionment with "politics as usual." The end of the Cold War left the United States as the preeminent military and economic power in the world, but many wondered if American civilization was not itself in decline. Americans remained an optimistic people, but, as always, skeptical about the future and anxious about the noble experiment, American democracy.

Recommended Readings

READINGS: (REAGAN/BUSH) Steve Bruce, *The Rise and Fall of the New Christian Right: Conservative Protestant Politics in America, 1978-1988* (1988); Lou Cannon, *Reagan* (1982) and *President Reagan: The Role of a Lifetime* (1991); Robert Dallek, *Ronald Reagan* (1984); Lawrence Freedman and Efraim Karsh, *The Gulf Conflict* (1993); Steven M. Gillon, *The Democrats' Dilemma: Walter F. Mondale and the Liberal Legacy* (1992); Alexander Haig, Jr., *Caveat* (1984); Jerome L. Himmelstein, *To the Right: The Transformation of American Conservatism* (1990); J. David Hoeveler, Jr., *Watch on the Right: Conservative Intellectuals in the Reagan Era* (1991); James Davison Hunter, *Culture Wars: The Struggle to Define America* (1991); Charles O. Jones, ed., *The Reagan Legacy: Promise and Performance* (1988); Jonathan Lash, *A Season of Spoils: The Story of the Reagan Administration's Attack on the Environment* (1984); Jane Meyer and Doyle McManus, *Landslide: The Unmaking of the President* (1988); Peggy Noonan, *What I Saw at the Revolution: A Political Life in the Reagan Era* (1990); Robert Pastor, *Condemned to Repetition: The United States and Nicaragua* (1987); Nicol C. Rae, *The Decline and Fall of the Liberal Republicans: From 1952 to the Present* (1989); Adolph Reed, *The Jesse Jackson Phenomenon* (1986); Kirkpatrick Sale, *Power Shift: The Rise of the Southern Rim and Its Challenge to the Eastern Establishment* (1975); Peter Steinfels, *The Neo-Conservatives* (1979); David Stockman, *The Triumph of Politics* (1987); Strobe Talbott, *Deadly Gambits* (1984) and *The Russians and Reagan* (1984); F. Clifton White, *Why Reagan Won* (1981); Garry Wills, *Reagan's America* (1986). (SOCIETY) John Crewden, *The Tarnished Door: The New Immigrants and the Transformation of America* (1983); Todd Gitlin, *Inside Prime Time* (1985); Kenneth Keniston, *All Our Children: The American Family Under Pressure* (1977); Reynolds Farley and Walter Allen, *The Color Line and the Quality of Life in America* (1987); David Reimers, *Still the Golden Door: The Third World Comes to America* (1985); Alan Wolfe, *America's Impasse: The Rise and Fall of the Politics of Growth* (1981).

The Declaration of Independence

IN CONGRESS, JULY 4, 1776. *The unanimous Declaration of the thirteen United States of America.*

When in the Course of human events, it becomes necessary for one people to dissolve the political bands which have connected them with another, and to assume among the powers of the earth, the separate and equal station to which the Laws of Nature and of Nature's God entitle them, a decent respect to the opinions of mankind requires that they should declare the causes which impel them to the separation.—

We hold these truths to be self-evident, that all men are created equal, that they are endowed by their Creator with certain unalienable Rights, that among these are Life, Liberty and the pursuit of Happiness.—

That to secure these rights, Governments are instituted among Men, deriving their just powers from the consent of the governed,—

That whenever any Form of Government becomes destructive of these ends, it is the Right of the People to alter or to abolish it, and to institute new Government, laying its foundation on such principles and organizing its powers in such form, as to them shall seem most likely to effect their Safety and Happiness. Prudence, indeed, will dictate that Governments long established should not be changed for light and transient causes; and accordingly all experience hath shown, that mankind are more disposed to suffer, while evils are sufferable, than to right themselves by abolishing the forms to which they are accustomed. But when a long train of abuses and usurpations, pursuing invariably the same Object evinces a design to reduce them under absolute Despotism, it is their right, it is their duty, to throw off such Government, and to provide new Guards for their future security.—

Such has been the patient sufferance of these Colonies; and such is now the necessity which constrains them to alter their former Systems of Government. The history of the present King of Great Britain is a history of repeated injuries and usurpations, all having in direct object the establishment of an absolute Tyranny over these States. To prove this, let Facts be submitted to a candid world.—

He has refused his Assent to Laws, the most wholesome and necessary for the public good.—

He has forbidden his Governors to pass Laws of immediate and pressing importance, unless suspended in their operation till his Assent should be obtained; and when so suspended, he has utterly neglected to attend to them.—

He has refused to pass other Laws for the accommodation of large districts of people, unless those people would relinquish the right of Representation in the Legislature, a right inestimable to them and formidable to tyrants only.—

He has called together legislative bodies at places unusual, uncomfortable, and distant from the depository of their public Records, for the sole purpose of fatiguing them into compliance with his measures.—

He has dissolved Representative Houses repeatedly, for opposing with manly firmness his invasions on the rights of the people.—

He has refused for a long time, after such dissolutions, to cause others to be elected; whereby the Legislative powers, incapable of Annihilation, have returned to the People at large for their exercise; the State remaining in the mean time exposed to all the dangers of invasion from without, and convulsions within.—

He has endeavoured to prevent the population of these States; for that purpose obstructing the Laws for Naturalization of Foreigners; refusing to pass others to encourage their migrations hither, and raising the conditions of new Appropriations of Lands.—

He has obstructed the Administration of Justice, by refusing his Assent to Laws for establishing Judiciary powers.—

He has made Judges dependent on his Will alone, for the tenure of their offices, and the amount and payment of their salaries.—

He has erected a multitude of New Offices, and sent hither swarms of Officers to harrass our people, and eat out their substance.—

He has kept among us in times of peace, Standing Armies without the Consent of our legislatures.—

He has affected to render the Military independent of and superior to the Civil power.—

He has combined with others to subject us to a jurisdiction foreign to our constitution, and unacknowledged by our laws; giving his Assent to their Acts of pretended Legislation:—

For quartering large bodies of armed troops among us:—

For protecting them, by a mock Trial, from punishment for any Murders which they should commit on the Inhabitants of these States:—

For cutting off our Trade with all parts of the world:—

For imposing Taxes on us without our Consent:—

For depriving us in many cases, of the benefits of Trial by Jury:—

For transporting us beyond Seas to be tried for pretended offences:—

For abolishing the free System of English Laws in a neighbouring Province, establishing therein an Arbitrary government, and enlarging its Boundaries so as to render it at once an example and fit instrument for introducing the same absolute rule in these Colonies:—

For taking away our Charters, abolishing our most valuable Laws, and altering fundamentally the Forms of our Governments:—

For suspending our own Legislatures, and declaring themselves invested with power to legislate for us in all cases whatsoever.—

He has abdicated Government here, by declaring us out of his Protection and waging War against us.—

He has plundered our seas, ravaged our Coasts, burnt our towns, and destroyed the lives of our people.—

He is at this time transporting large Armies of foreign Mercenaries to compleat the works of death, desolation and tyranny, already begun with circumstances of Cruelty & perfidy scarcely paralleled in the most barbarous ages, and totally unworthy the Head of a civilized nation.—

He has constrained our fellow Citizens taken Captive on the high Seas to bear Arms against their Country, to become the executioners of their friends and Brethren, or to fall themselves by their Hands.—

He has excited domestic insurrections amongst us, and has endeavoured to bring on the inhabitants of our frontiers, the merciless Indian Savages, whose known rule of warfare, is an undistinguished destruction of all ages, sexes and conditions.

In every stage of these Oppressions We have Petitioned for Redress in the most humble terms: Our repeated Petitions have been answered only by repeated injury. A Prince, whose character is thus marked by every act which may define a Tyrant, is unfit to be the ruler of a free people.

Nor have We been wanting in attentions to our British brethren. We have warned them from time to time of attempts by their legislature to extend an unwarrantable jurisdiction over us. We have reminded them of the circumstances of our emigration and settlement here. We have appealed to their native justice and magnanimity, and we have conjured them by the ties of our common kindred to disavow these usurpations, which would inevitably interrupt our connections and correspondence. They too have been deaf to the voice of justice and of consanguinity. We must, therefore, acquiesce in the necessity, which denounces our Separation, and hold them, as we hold the rest of mankind, Enemies in War, in Peace Friends.—

We, therefore, the Representatives of the United States of America, in General Congress, Assembled, appealing to the Supreme Judge of the world for the rectitude of our intentions, do, in the Name, and by Authority of the good People of these Colonies, solemnly publish and declare, That these United Colonies are, and of Right ought to be, Free and Independent States; that they are absolved from all Allegiance to the British Crown, and that all political connection between them and the State of Great Britain, is and ought to be totally dissolved; and that as Free and Independent States they have full Power to levy War, conclude Peace, contract Alliances, establish Commerce, and to do all other Acts and Things which Independent States may of right do.—

And for the support of this Declaration, with a firm reliance on the protection of divine Providence, we mutually pledge to each other our Lives, our Fortunes and our sacred Honor.

John Hancock
(MASSACHUSETTS)

NEW HAMPSHIRE
Josiah Bartlett
William Whipple
Matthew Thornton

MASSACHUSETTS
Samuel Adams
John Adams
Robert Treat Paine
Elbridge Gerry

DELAWARE
Caesar Rodney
George Read
Thomas McKean

NEW YORK
William Floyd
Philip Livingston
Francis Lewis
Lewis Morris

NEW JERSEY
Richard Stockton
John Witherspoon
Francis Hopkinson
John Hart
Abraham Clark

NORTH CAROLINA
William Hooper
Joseph Hewes
John Penn

MARYLAND
Samuel Chase
William Paca
Thomas Stone
Charles Carroll of Carrollton

SOUTH CAROLINA
Edward Rutledge
Thomas Heywood, Jr.
Thomas Lynch, Jr.
Arthur Middleton

RHODE ISLAND
Stephen Hopkins
William Ellery

CONNECTICUT
Roger Sherman
Samuel Huntington
William Williams
Oliver Wolcott

PENNSYLVANIA
Robert Morris
Benjamin Rush
Benjamin Franklin
John Morton
George Clymer
James Smith
George Taylor
James Wilson
George Ross

VIRGINIA
George Wythe
Richard Henry Lee
Thomas Jefferson
Benjamin Harrison
Thomas Nelson, Jr.
Francis Lightfoot Lee
Carter Braxton

GEORGIA
Button Gwinnett
Lyman Hall
George Walton

The Constitution of the United States of America

WE THE PEOPLE OF THE UNITED STATES, in Order to form a more perfect Union, establish Justice, insure domestic Tranquility, provide for the common defence, promote the general Welfare, and secure the Blessings of Liberty to ourselves and our Posterity, do ordain and establish this Constitution for the United States of America.

ARTICLE I LEGISLATIVE DEPARTMENT

Section 1. All legislative Powers herein granted shall be vested in a Congress of the United States, which shall consist of a Senate and House of Representatives.

Section 2. The House of Representatives shall be composed of Members chosen every second Year by the People of the several States, and the Electors in each State shall have the Qualifications requisite for Electors of the most numerous Branch of the State Legislature. No Person shall be a Representative who shall not have attained to the Age of twenty-five Years, and been seven Years a Citizen of the United States, and who shall not, when elected, be an Inhabitant of that State in which he shall be chosen.

Representatives and direct Taxes shall be apportioned among the several States which may be included within this Union, according to their respective Numbers, which shall be determined by adding to the whole Number of free Persons, including those bound to Service for a Term of Years, and excluding Indians not taxed, three-fifths of all other Persons. The actual Enumeration shall be made within three Years after the first Meeting of the Congress of the United States, and within every subsequent Term of ten Years, in such Manner as they shall by Law direct. The Number of Representatives shall not exceed one for every thirty Thousand, but each State shall have at Least one Representative; and until such enumeration shall be made, the State of New Hampshire shall be entitled to chuse three, Massachusetts eight, Rhode Island and Providence Plantations one, Connecticut five, New York six, New Jersey four, Pennsylvania eight, Delaware one, Maryland six, Virginia ten, North Carolina five, South Carolina five, and Georgia three.

When vacancies happen in the Representation from any State, the Executive Authority thereof shall issue Writs of Election to fill such Vacancies.

The House of Representatives shall chuse their Speaker and other Officers; and shall have the sole Power of Impeachment.

Section 3. The Senate of the United States shall be composed of two Senators from each State, chosen by the Legislature thereof, for six Years; and each Senator shall have one Vote.

Immediately after they shall be assembled in Consequence of the first Election, they shall be divided as equally as may be into three Classes. The Seats of the Senators of the first Class shall be vacated at the Expiration of the second Year, of the second Class at the Expiration of the fourth Year, and of the third Class at the Expiration of the sixth Year, so that one third may be chosen every second Year; and if Vacancies happen by Resignation, or otherwise, during the Recess of the Legislature of any State, the Executive thereof may make temporary Appointments until the next Meeting of the Legislature, which shall then fill such Vacancies.

Source: House Document #529. U.S. Government Printing Office, 1967. [NOTE: *The Constitution and the amendments are reprinted here in their original form. Amended or superseded portions are underlined.*]

No Person shall be a Senator who shall not have attained to the Age of thirty Years, and been nine Years a Citizen of the United States, and who shall not, when elected, be an Inhabitant of that State for which he shall be chosen.

The Vice President of the United States shall be President of the Senate, but shall have no Vote, unless they be equally divided.

The Senate shall chuse their other Officers, and also a President pro tempore, in the absence of the Vice President, or when he shall exercise the Office of President of the United States.

The Senate shall have the sole Power to try all Impeachments. When sitting for that Purpose, they shall be on Oath or Affirmation. When the President of the United States is tried, the Chief Justice shall preside: And no Person shall be convicted without the Concurrence of two thirds of the Members present.

Judgment in Cases of Impeachment shall not extend further than to removal from Office, and disqualification to hold and enjoy any Office of Honor, Trust or Profit under the United States: but the Party convicted shall nevertheless be liable and subject to Indictment, Trial, Judgment and Punishment, according to Law.

Section 4. The Times, Places and Manner of holding Elections for Senators and Representatives, shall be prescribed in each State by the Legislature thereof; but the Congress may at any time by Law make or alter such Regulations, except as to the Place of chusing Senators.

The Congress shall assemble at least once in every Year, and such Meeting shall be on the first Monday in December, unless they shall by Law appoint a different Day.

Section 5. Each House shall be the Judge of the Elections, Returns and Qualifications of its own Members, and a Majority of each shall constitute a Quorum to do Business; but a smaller number may adjourn from day to day, and may be authorized to compel the Attendance of absent Members, in such Manner, and under such Penalties as each House may provide.

Each House may determine the Rules of its Proceedings, punish its Members for disorderly Behavior, and, with the Concurrence of two thirds, expel a Member.

Each House shall keep a Journal of its Proceedings, and from time to time publish the same, excepting such Parts as may in their Judgment require Secrecy; and the Yeas and Nays of the Members of either House on any question shall, at the Desire of one fifth of those Present, be entered on the Journal.

Neither House, during the Session of Congress, shall, without the Consent of the other, adjourn for more than three days, nor to any other Place than that in which the two Houses shall be sitting.

Section 6. The Senators and Representatives shall receive a Compensation for their Services, to be ascertained by Law, and paid out of the Treasury of the United States. They shall in all Cases, except Treason, Felony and Breach of the Peace, be privileged from Arrest during their Attendance at the Session of their respective Houses, and in going to and returning from the same; and for any Speech or Debate in either House, they shall not be questioned in any other Place.

No Senator or Representative shall, during the Time for which he was elected, be appointed to any civil Office under the Authority of the United States, which shall have been created, or the Emoluments whereof shall have been encreased during such time; and no Person holding any Office under the United States, shall be a Member of either House during his Continuance in Office.

Section 7. All Bills for raising Revenue shall originate in the House of Representatives; but the Senate may propose or concur with Amendments as on other Bills.

Every Bill which shall have passed the House of Representatives and the Senate, shall, before it become a Law, be presented to the President of the United States; If he approve he shall sign it, but if not he shall return it, with his Objections to that House in which it shall have originated, who shall enter the Objections at large on their Journal, and proceed to reconsider it. If after such Reconsideration two thirds of that House shall agree to pass the Bill, it shall be sent, together with the Objections, to the other House, by which it shall likewise be reconsidered, and if approved by two thirds of that House, it shall become a Law. But in all such Cases the Votes of both Houses shall be determined by Yeas and Nays, and the Names of the Persons voting for and against the Bill shall be entered on the Journal of each House respectively. If any Bill shall not be returned by the President within ten Days (Sundays excepted) after it shall have been presented to him, the Same shall be a Law, in like Manner as if he had signed it, unless the Congress by their Adjournment prevent its Return, in which Case it shall not be a Law.

Every Order, Resolution, or Vote to which the Concurrence of the Senate and House of Representatives may be necessary (except on a question of Adjournment) shall be presented to the President of the United States; and before the Same shall take Effect, shall be approved by him, or being disapproved by him, shall be repassed by two thirds of the Senate and House of Representatives, according to the Rules and Limitations prescribed in the Case of a Bill.

Section 8. The Congress shall have Power to lay and collect Taxes, Duties, Imposts and Excises, to pay the Debts and provide for the common Defence and general Welfare of the United States; but all Duties, Imposts and Excises shall be uniform throughout the United States;

To borrow money on the credit of the United States;

To regulate Commerce with foreign Nations, and among the several States, and with the Indian Tribes;

To establish an uniform Rule of Naturalization, and uniform Laws on the subject of Bankruptcies throughout the United States;

To coin Money, regulate the Value thereof, and of foreign Coin, and fix the Standard of Weights and Measures;

To provide for the Punishment of counterfeiting the Securities and current Coin of the United States;

To establish Post Offices and post Roads;

To promote the Progress of Science and useful Arts, by securing for limited Times to Authors and Inventors the exclusive Right to their respective Writings and Discoveries;

To constitute Tribunals inferior to the supreme Court;

To define and punish Piracies and Felonies committed on the high Seas, and Offenses against the Law of Nations;

To declare War, grant Letters of Marque and Reprisal, and make Rules concerning Captures on Land and Water;

To raise and support Armies, but no Appropriation of Money to that Use shall be for a longer Term than two Years;

To provide and maintain a Navy;

To make Rules for the Government and Regulation of the land and naval Forces;

To provide for calling forth the Militia to execute the Laws of the Union, suppress Insurrections and repel Invasions;

To provide for organizing, arming, and disciplining the Militia, and for governing such Part of them as may be employed in the Service of the United States, reserving to the States respectively, the Appointment of the Officers, and the Authority of training the Militia according to the discipline prescribed by Congress;

To exercise exclusive Legislation in all Cases whatsoever, over such District (not exceeding ten Miles square) as may, by Cession of particular States, and the acceptance of Congress, become the Seat of the Government of the United States, and to exercise like Authority over all Places purchased by the Consent of the Legislature of the State in which the Same shall be, for the Erection of Forts, Magazines, Arsenals, dock-Yards, and other needful Buildings;—And

To make all Laws which shall be necessary and proper for carrying into Execution the foregoing Powers, and all other Powers vested by this Constitution in the Government of the United States, or in any Department or Officer thereof.

Section 9. The Migration or Importation of such Persons as any of the States now existing shall think proper to admit, shall not be prohibited by the Congress prior to the Year one thousand eight hundred and eight, but a tax or duty may be imposed on such Importation, not exceeding ten dollars for each Person.

The privilege of the Writ of Habeas Corpus shall not be suspended unless when in Cases of Rebellion or Invasion the public Safety may require it.

No bill of Attainder or ex post facto Law shall be passed.

No capitation, or other direct, Tax shall be laid, unless in Proportion to the Census or Enumeration herein before directed to be taken.

No Tax or Duty shall be laid on Articles exported from any State.

No Preference shall be given by any Regulation of Commerce or Revenue to the Ports of one State over those of another; nor shall Vessels bound to, or from, one State, be obliged to enter, clear, or pay Duties in another.

No Money shall be drawn from the Treasury, but in Consequence of Appropriations made by Law; and a regular Statement and Account of the Receipts and Expenditures of all public Money shall be published from time to time.

No Title of Nobility shall be granted by the United States: And no Person holding any Office of Profit or Trust under them, shall, without the Consent of the Congress, accept of any present, Emolument, Office, or Title, of any kind whatever, from any King, Prince, or foreign State.

Section 10. No State shall enter into any Treaty, Alliance, or Confederation; grant Letters of Marque and Reprisal; coin Money; emit Bills of Credit; make any Thing but gold and silver Coin a Tender in Payment of Debts; pass any Bill of Attainder, ex post facto Law, or Law impairing the Obligation of Contracts, or grant any Title of Nobility.

No State shall, without the consent of the Congress, lay any Imposts or Duties on Imports or Exports, except what may be absolutely necessary for executing its inspection laws; and the net Produce of all Duties and Imposts, laid by any State on Imports or Exports, shall be for the use of the Treasury of the United States; and all such Laws shall be subject to the Revision and Control of the Congress.

No state shall without the consent of Congress, lay any duty of Tonnage, keep Troops, or Ships of War in time of Peace, enter into any Agreement or Compact with another State, or with a foreign Power, or engage in War, unless actually invaded, or in such imminent Danger as will not admit of delay.

ARTICLE II

Section I. The executive Power shall be vested in a President of the United States of America. He shall hold his Office during the Term of four years, and, together with the Vice President, chosen for the same Term, be elected, as follows:

Each State shall appoint, in such Manner as the Legislature thereof may direct, a Number of Electors, equal to the whole Number of Senators and Representatives to which the State may be entitled in the Congress: but no Senator or Representative, or Person holding an Office of Trust or Profit under the United States, shall be appointed an Elector.

The Electors shall meet in their respective States, and vote by Ballot for two persons, of whom one at least shall not be an Inhabitant of the same State with themselves. And they shall make a List of all The Persons voted for, and of the Number of Votes for each; which List they shall sign and certify, and transmit sealed to the Seat of the Government of the United States, directed to the President of the Senate. The President of the Senate shall, in the Presence of the Senate and House of Representatives, open all the Certificates, and the Votes shall then be counted. The Person having the greatest Number of Votes shall be the President, if such Number be a Majority of the whole Number of Electors appointed; and if there be more than one who have such Majority, and have an equal Number of Votes, then the House of Representatives shall immediately chuse by Ballot one of them for President; and if no Person have a Majority, then from the five highest on the List the said House shall in like Manner chuse the President. But in chusing the President, the Votes shall be taken by States, the Representation from each State having one Vote; a quorum for this Purpose shall consist of a Member or Members from two-thirds of the States, and a Majority of all the States shall be necessary to a Choice. In every Case, after the Choice of the President, the Person having the greatest Number of Votes of the Electors shall be the Vice President. But if there should remain two or more who have equal votes, the Senate shall chuse from them by Ballot the Vice President.

The Congress may determine the time of chusing the Electors, and the Day on which they shall give their Votes; which Day shall be the same throughout the United States.

No person except a natural-born Citizen, or a Citizen of the United States, at the time of the Adoption of this Constitution, shall be eligible to the Office of President; neither shall any Person be eligible to that Office who shall not have attained to the Age of Thirty-five Years, and been fourteen Years a Resident within the United States.

In Case of the Removal of the President from Office, or of his Death, Resignation, or Inability to discharge the Powers and Duties of the said Office, the same shall devolve on the Vice President, and the Congress may by Law provide for the Case of Removal, Death, Resignation or Inability, both of the President and the Vice President, declaring what Officer shall then act as President, and such Officer shall act accordingly, until the Disability be removed, or a President shall be elected.

The President shall, at stated Times, receive for his Services, a Compensation, which shall neither be encreased nor diminished during the Period for which he shall have been elected, and he shall not receive within that Period any other Emolument from the United States, or any of them.

Before he enter on the Execution of his Office, he shall take the following Oath or Affirmation:—"I do solemnly swear (or affirm) that I will faithfully execute the Office of the President of the United States, and will to the best of my Ability, preserve, protect and defend the Constitution of the United States."

Section 2. The President shall be Commander in Chief of the Army and Navy of the United States, and of the Militia of the several States, when called into the actual Service of the United States; he may require the Opinion in writing, of the principal Officer in each of the executive Departments, upon any subject relating to the Duties of their respective Offices, and he shall have Power to Grant Reprieves and Pardons for Offenses against the United States, except in Cases of Impeachment.

He shall have Power, by and with the Advice and Consent of the Senate, to make Treaties, provided two thirds of the Senators present concur; and he shall nominate, and by and with the Advice and Consent of the Senate shall appoint Ambassadors, other public Ministers and Consuls, Judges of the supreme Court, and all other Officers of the United States, whose Appointments are not herein otherwise provided for, and which shall be established by Law; but the Congress may by Law vest the Appointment of such inferior Officers, as they think proper, in the President alone, in the Courts of Law, or in the Heads of Departments.

The President shall have Power to fill up all Vacancies that may happen during the Recess of the Senate, by granting Commissions which shall expire at the End of their next Session.

Section 3. He shall from time to time give to the Congress Information of the State of the Union, and recommend to their Consideration such Measures as he shall judge necessary and expedient; he may, on extraordinary Occasions, convene both Houses, or either of them, and in Case of Disagreement between them, with Respect to the Time of Adjournment, he may adjourn them to such Time as he shall think proper; he shall receive Ambassadors and other public Ministers; he shall take Care that the Laws be faithfully executed, and shall Commission all the Officers of the United States.

Section 4. The President, Vice President and all civil Officers of the United States, shall be removed from Office on Impeachment for, and Conviction of, Treason, Bribery, or other high Crimes and Misdemeanors.

ARTICLE III   JUDICIAL DEPARTMENT

Section 1. The judicial Power of the United States, shall be vested in one supreme Court, and in such inferior Courts as the Congress may from time to time ordain and establish. The Judges, both of the supreme and inferior Courts, shall hold their Offices during good Behaviour, and shall, at stated Times, receive for their Services, a Compensation, which shall not be diminished during their Continuance in Office.

Section 2. The judicial Power shall extend to all Cases, in Law and Equity, arising under this Constitution, the Laws of the United States, and Treaties made, or which shall be made, under their Authority;—to all Cases affecting Ambassadors, other public Ministers and Consuls;—to all Cases of admiralty and maritime Jurisdiction;—to Controversies to which the United States shall be a Party;—to Controversies between two or more States;— between a State and Citizens of another State;—between Citizens of different States;—between Citizens of the same State claiming Lands under Grants of different States, and between a State, or the Citizens thereof, and foreign States, Citizens or Subjects.

In all Cases affecting Ambassadors, other public Ministers and Consuls, and those in which a State shall be Party, the supreme Court shall have original Jurisdiction. In all the other Cases before mentioned, the supreme Court shall have appellate Jurisdiction, both as to Law and Fact, with such Exceptions, and under such Regulations as the Congress shall make.

The trial of all Crimes, except in Cases of Impeachment, shall be by Jury; and such Trial shall be held in the State where the said Crimes shall have been committed; but when not committed within any State, the Trial shall be at such Place or Places as the Congress may by Law have directed.

Section 3. Treason against the United States, shall consist only in levying War against them, or in adhering to their Enemies, giving them Aid and Comfort. No Person shall be convicted of Treason unless on the Testimony of two Witnesses to the same overt Act, or on Confession in open Court.

The Congress shall have Power to declare the Punishment of Treason, but no Attainder of Treason shall work Corruption of Blood, or Forfeiture except during the Life of the Person attained.

ARTICLE IV   RELATIONS AMONG THE STATES

Section 1. Full Faith and Credit shall be given in each State to the public Acts, Records, and judicial Proceedings of every other State. And the Congress may by general Laws prescribe the Manner in which such Acts, Records and Proceedings shall be proved, and the Effect thereof.

Section 2. The Citizens of each State shall be entitled to all Privileges and Immunities of Citizens in the several States.

A Person charged in any State with Treason, Felony, or other Crime, who shall flee from Justice, and be found in another State, shall on demand of the executive Authority of the State from which he fled, be delivered up, to be removed to the State having Jurisdiction of the Crime.

No Person held in Service or Labour in one State, under the Laws thereof, escaping into another, shall, in Consequence of any Law or Regulation therein, be discharged from such Service or Labour, but shall be delivered up on Claim of the Party to whom such Service or Labour may be due.

Section 3. New States may be admitted by the Congress into this Union; but no new State shall be formed or erected within the Jurisdiction of any other State; nor any State be formed by the Junction of two or more States, or parts of States, without the Consent of the Legislatures of the States concerned as well as of the Congress.

The Congress shall have Power to dispose of and make all needful Rules and Regulations respecting the Territory or other Property belonging to the United States; and nothing in this

Constitution shall be so construed as to Prejudice any Claims of the United States, or of any particular State.

Section 4. The United States shall guarantee to every State in this Union a Republican Form of Government, and shall protect each of them against Invasion; and on Application of the Legislature, or of the Executive (when the Legislature cannot be convened) against domestic Violence.

ARTICLE V   AMENDING THE CONSTITUTION

The Congress, whenever two thirds of both Houses shall deem it necessary, shall propose Amendments to this Constitution, or, on the Application of the Legislatures of two thirds of the several States, shall call a Convention for proposing Amendments, which, in either Case, shall be valid to all Intents and Purposes, as part of this Constitution, when ratified by the Legislatures of three fourths of the several States, or by Conventions in three fourths thereof, as the one or the other Mode of Ratification may be proposed by the Congress: Provided that no Amendment which may be made prior to the Year One thousand eight hundred and eight shall in any Manner affect the first and fourth Clauses in the Ninth Section of the first Article; and that no State, without its Consent, shall be deprived of its equal Suffrage in the Senate.

ARTICLE VI   GENERAL PROVISIONS

All Debts contracted and Engagements entered into, before the Adoption of this Constitution, shall be as valid against the United States under this Constitution, as under the Confederation.

This Constitution, and the Laws of the United States which shall be made in Pursuance thereof; and all Treaties made, or which shall be made, under the Authority of the United States, shall be the supreme Law of the Land; and the Judges in every State shall be bound thereby, any Thing in the Constitution or Laws of any State to the Contrary notwithstanding.

The Senators and Representatives before mentioned, and the Members of the several State Legislatures, and all executive and judicial Officers, both of the United States and of the several States, shall be bound by Oath or Affirmation, to support this Constitution; but no religious Test shall ever be required as a Qualification to any Office or public Trust under the United States.

ARTICLE VII   RATIFICATION

The Ratification of the Conventions of nine States shall be sufficient for the Establishment of this Constitution between the States so ratifying the Same.

DONE in Convention by the Unanimous Consent of the States present the Seventeenth Day of September in the Year of our Lord one thousand seven hundred and eighty-seven and of the Independence of the United States of America the Twelfth. In Witness whereof We have hereunto subscribed our Names.

G° Washington
Presid' and deputy from
VIRGINIA

Attest: *William Jackson,* Secretary

DELAWARE
Geo: Read
Gunning Bedford, jun
John Dickinson
Richard Bassett
Jaco: Broom

MARYLAND
James McHenry
Dan: of St Thos Jenifer
Danl Carroll

VIRGINIA
John Blair
James Madison Jr.

NORTH CAROLINA
Wm Blount
Richd Dobbs Spaight
Hu Williamson

SOUTH CAROLINA
J. Rutledge
Charles Cotesworth Pinckney
Charles Pinckney
Pierce Butler

GEORGIA
William Few
Abr Baldwin

NEW HAMPSHIRE
John Langdon
Nicholas Gilman

MASSACHUSETTS
Nathaniel Gorham
Rufus King

CONNECTICUT
Wm Saml Johnson
Roger Sherman

NEW YORK
Alexander Hamilton

NEW JERSEY
Wil: Livingston
David Brearley
Wm Paterson
Jona: Dayton

PENNSYLVANIA
B Franklin
Thomas Mifflin
Robt. Morris
Geo. Clymer
Thos. FitzSimons
Jared Ingersoll
James Wilson
Gouv Morris

Amendments

AMENDMENT I (1791)

Congress shall make no law respecting an establishment of religion, or prohibiting the free exercise thereof: or abridging the freedom of speech, or of the press; or the right of the people peaceably to assemble, and to petition the Government for a redress of grievances.

AMENDMENT II (1791)

A well regulated Militia, being necessary to the security of a free State, the right of the people to keep and bear Arms, shall not be infringed.

AMENDMENT III (1791)

No Soldier shall, in time of peace, be quartered in any house, without the consent of the Owner, nor in time of war, but in a manner to be prescribed by law.

AMENDMENT IV (1791)

The right of the people to be secure in their persons, houses, papers, and effects, against unreasonable searches and seizures, shall not be violated, and no Warrants shall issue, but upon

[The date following each amendment number is the year of ratification.]

probable cause, supported by Oath or affirmation, and particularly describing the place to be searched, and the persons or things to be seized.

AMENDMENT V   (1791)

No person shall be held to answer for a capital, or otherwise infamous crime, unless on a presentment or indictment of a Grand Jury, except in cases arising in the land or naval forces, or in the Militia, when in actual service in time of War or public danger; nor shall any person be subject for the same offence to be twice put in jeopardy of life or limb; nor shall be compelled in any criminal case to be a witness against himself, nor be deprived of life, liberty, or property, without due process of law; nor shall private property be taken for public use, without just compensation.

AMENDMENT VI   (1791)

In all criminal prosecutions, the accused shall enjoy the right to a speedy and public trial, by an impartial jury of the State and district wherein the crime shall have been committed, which district shall have been previously ascertained by law, and to be informed of the nature and cause of the accusation; to be confronted with the witnesses against him; to have compulsory process for obtaining witnesses in his favor, and to have the Assistance of Counsel for his defence.

AMENDMENT VII   (1791)

In suits at common law, where the value in controversy shall exceed twenty dollars, the right of trial by jury shall be preserved, and no fact tried by a jury, shall be otherwise reexamined in any Court of the United States, than according to the rules of the common law.

AMENDMENT VIII   (1791)

Excessive bail shall not be required, nor excessive fines imposed, nor cruel and unusual punishments inflicted.

AMENDMENT IX   (1791)

The enumeration in the Constitution, of certain rights, shall not be construed to deny or disparage others retained by the people.

AMENDMENT X   (1791)

The powers not delegated to the United States by the Constitution, nor prohibited by it to the States, are reserved to the States respectively, or to the people.

AMENDMENT XI   (1798)

The Judicial power of the United States shall not be construed to extend to any suit in law or equity, commenced or prosecuted against one of the United States by Citizens of another State, or by Citizens or Subjects of any Foreign State.

AMENDMENT XII   (1804)

The Electors shall meet in their respective states and vote by ballot for President and Vice-President, one of whom, at least, shall not be an inhabitant of the same state with themselves; they shall name in their ballots the person voted for as President, and in distinct ballots the person voted for as Vice-President, and they shall make distinct lists of all persons voted for as President, and of all persons voted for as Vice-President, and of the number of votes for each, which lists they shall sign and certify, and transmit sealed to the seat of the government of the United States, directed to the President of the Senate;—The President of the Senate shall, in presence of the Senate and House of Representatives, open all the certificates and the votes shall then be counted;—The person having the greatest number of votes for President, shall be the President, if such number be a majority of the whole number of Electors appointed; and if no person have such majority, then from the persons having the highest numbers not exceeding three on the list of those voted for as President, the House of Representatives shall choose immediately, by ballot, the President. But in choosing the President, the votes shall be taken by states, the representation from each state having one vote; a quorum for this purpose shall consist of a member or members from two-thirds of the states, and a majority of all the states shall be necessary to a choice. And if the House of Representatives shall not choose a President whenever the right of choice shall devolve upon them, before the fourth day of March next following, then the Vice-President shall act as President, as in the case of the death or other constitutional disability of the President.—The person having the greatest number of votes as Vice-President, shall be the Vice-President, if such number be a majority of the whole number of Electors appointed, and if no person have a majority, then from the two highest numbers on the list, the Senate shall choose the Vice-President; a quorum for the purpose shall consist of two-thirds of the whole number of Senators, and a majority of the whole number shall be necessary to a choice. But no person constitutionally ineligible to the office of President shall be eligible to that of Vice-President of the United States.

AMENDMENT XIII (1865)

Section 1. Neither slavery nor involuntary servitude, exceptas a punishment for crime whereof the party shall have been duly convicted, shall exist within the United States, or any place subject to their jurisdiction.

Section 2. Congress shall have power to enforce this article by appropriate legislation.

AMENDMENT XIV (1868)

Section 1. All persons born or naturalized in the United States, and subject to the jurisdiction thereof, are citizens of the United States and of the State wherein they reside. No State shall make or enforce any law which shall abridge the privileges or immunities of citizens of the United States; nor shall any State deprive any person of life, liberty, or property, without due process of law; nor deny any person within its jurisdiction the equal protection of the laws.

Section 2. Representatives shall be apportioned among the several States according to their respective numbers, counting the whole number of persons in each State, excluding Indians not taxed. But when the right to vote at any election for the choice of electors for President and Vice-President of the United States, Representatives in Congress, the Executive and Judicial officers of a State, or the members of the Legislature thereof, is denied to any of the male inhabitants of such State, being twenty-one years of age, and citizens of the United States, or in any way abridged, except for participation in rebellion, or other crime, the basis of representation therein shall be reduced in the proportion which the number of such male citizens shall bear to the whole number of male citizens twenty-one years of age in such State.

Section 3. No person shall be a Senator or Representative in Congress, or elector of President and Vice-President, or hold any office, civil or military, under the United States, or under any State, who, having previously taken an oath, as a member of Congress, or as an officer of the United States, or as a member of any State legislature, or as an executive or judicial officer of any State, to support the Constitution of the United States, shall have engaged in insurrection or rebellion against the same, or given aid or comfort to the enemies thereof. But Congress may by a vote of two-thirds of each House, remove such disability.

Section 4. The validity of the public debt of the United States, authorized by law, including debts incurred for payment of pensions and bounties for services in suppressing insurrection or rebellion, shall not be questioned. But neither the United States nor any State shall assume or pay any debt or obligation incurred in aid of insurrection or rebellion against the United States, or any claim for the loss or emancipation of any slave; but all such debts, obligations and claims shall be held illegal and void.

Section 5. The Congress shall have power to enforce, by appropriate legislation, the provisions of this article.

AMENDMENT XV (1870)

Section 1. The right of citizens of the United States to vote shall not be denied or abridged by the United States or by any State on account of race, color, or previous condition of servitude.

Section 2. The Congress shall have power to enforce this article by appropriate legislation.

AMENDMENT XVI (1913)

The Congress shall have power to lay and collect taxes on incomes, from whatever source derived, without apportionment among the several States, and without regard to any census or enumeration.

AMENDMENT XVII (1913)

The Senate of the United States shall be composed of two Senators from each State, elected by the people thereof, for six years; and each Senator shall have one vote. The electors in each State shall have the qualifications requisite for electors of the most numerous branch of the State legislature.

When vacancies happen in the representation of any State in the Senate, the executive authority of such State shall issue writs of election to fill such vacancies: *Provided,* That the legislature of any State may empower the executive thereof to make temporary appointments until the people fill the vacancies by election as the legislature may direct.

This amendment shall not be so construed as to affect the election or term of any Senator chosen before it becomes valid as part of the Constitution.

AMENDMENT XVIII (1919)

Section 1. After one year from the ratification of this article, the manufacture, sale, or transportation of intoxicating liquors within, the importation thereof into, or the exportation thereof from the United States and all territory subject to the jurisdiction thereof for beverage purposes is hereby prohibited.

Section 2. The Congress and the several States shall have concurrent power to enforce this article by appropriate legislation.

Section 3. This article shall be inoperative unless it shall have been ratified as an amendment to the Constitution by the legislatures of the several States, as provided in the Constitution, within seven years from the date of the submission hereof to the States by the Congress.

AMENDMENT XIX (1920)

The right of citizens of the United States to vote shall not be denied or abridged by the United States or by any State on account of sex.

Congress shall have power to enforce this article by appropriate legislation.

AMENDMENT XX (1933)

Section 1. The terms of the President and Vice-President shall end at noon on the 20th day of January, and the terms of Senators and Representatives at noon on the 3d day of January, of the years in which such terms would have ended if this article had not been ratified; and the terms of their successors shall then begin.

Section 2. The Congress shall assemble at least once in every year, and such meeting shall begin at noon on the 3d day of January, unless they shall by law appoint a different day.

Section 3. If, at the time fixed for the beginning of the term of the President, the President elect shall have died, the Vice-President elect shall become President. If a President shall not have been chosen before the time fixed for the beginning of his term, or if the President elect shall have failed to qualify, then the Vice-President elect shall act as President until a President shall have qualified; and the Congress may by law provide for the case wherein neither a President elect nor a Vice-President elect shall have qualified, declaring who shall then act as President, or the manner in which one who is to act shall be selected, and such person shall act accordingly until a President or Vice-President shall have qualified.

Section 4. The Congress may by law provide for the case of the death of any of the persons from whom the House of Representatives may choose a President whenever the right of choice shall have devolved upon them, and for the case of the death of any of the persons from whom the Senate may choose a Vice-President whenever the right of choice shall have devolved upon them.

Section 5. Sections 1 and 2 shall take effect on the 15th day of October following the ratification of this article.

Section 6. This article shall be inoperative unless it shall have been ratified as an amendment to the Constitution by the legislatures of three-fourths of the several States within seven years from the date of its submission.

AMENDMENT XXI (1933)

Section 1. The eighteenth article of amendment to the Constitution of the United States is hereby repealed.

Section 2. The transportation or importation into any State, Territory, or possession of the United States for delivery or use therein of intoxicating liquors, in violation of the laws thereof, is hereby prohibited.

Section 3. This article shall be inoperative unless it shall have been ratified as an amendment to the Constitution by conventions in the several States, as provided in the Constitution, within seven years from the date of the submission hereof to the States by the Congress.

AMENDMENT XXII (1951)

Section 1. No person shall be elected to the office of the President more than twice, and no person who has held the office of President, or acted as President, for more than two years of a term to which some other person was elected President shall be elected to the office of the President more than once. But this Article shall not apply to any person holding the office of President when this Article was proposed by the Congress, and shall not prevent any person who may be holding the office of President, or acting as President, during the term within which this Article becomes operative from holding the office of President or acting as President during the remainder of such term.

Section 2. This article shall be inoperative unless it shall have been ratified as an amendment to the Constitution by the legislatures of three-fourths of the several States within seven years from the date of its submission to the States by the Congress.

AMENDMENT XXIII (1961)

Section 1. The District constituting the seat of Government of the United States shall appoint in such manner as the Congress may direct:

A number of electors of President and Vice-President equal to the whole number of Senators and Representatives in Congress to which the District would be entitled if it were a State, but in no event more than the least populous State; they shall be in addition to those appointed by the States, but they shall be considered, for the purposes of the election of President and Vice-President, to be electors appointed by a State; and they shall meet in the District and perform such duties as provided by the twelfth article of amendment.

Section 2. The Congress shall have power to enforce this article by appropriate legislation.

AMENDMENT XXIV (1964)

Section 1. The right of citizens of the United States to vote in any primary or other election for President or Vice-President, for electors for President or Vice-President, or for Senator or Representative in Congress, shall not be denied or abridged by the United States or any State by reason of failure to pay any poll tax or other tax.

Section 2. The Congress shall have power to enforce this article by appropriate legislation.

AMENDMENT XXV (1967)

Section 1. In case of the removal of the President from office or of his death or resignation, the Vice-President shall become President.

Section 2. Whenever there is a vacancy in the office of the Vice-President, the President shall nominate a Vice-President who shall take office upon confirmation by a majority vote of both Houses of Congress.

Section 3. Whenever the President transmits to the President pro tempore of the Senate and the Speaker of the House of Representatives his written declaration that he is unable to discharge the powers and duties of his office, and until he transmits to them a written declaration to the contrary, such powers and duties shall be discharged by the Vice-President as Acting President.

Section 4. Whenever the Vice-President and a majority of either the principal officers of the executive departments or of such other body as Congress may by law provide, transmit to the President pro tempore of the Senate and the Speaker of the House of Representatives their written declaration that the President is unable to discharge the powers and duties of his office, the Vice-President shall immediately assume the powers and duties of the office as Acting President.

Thereafter, when the President transmits to the President pro tempore of the Senate and the Speaker of the House of Representatives his written declaration that no inability exists, he shall resume the powers and duties of his office unless the Vice-President and a majority of either the principal officers of the executive department or of such other body as Congress may by law provide, transmit within four days to the President pro tempore of the Senate and the Speaker of the House of Representatives their written declaration that the President is unable to discharge the powers and duties of his office. Thereupon Congress shall decide the issue, assembling within forty-eight hours for that purpose if not in session. If the Congress, within twenty-one days after receipt of the latter written declaration, or, if Congress is not in session, within twenty-one days after Congress is required to assemble, determines by two-thirds vote of both Houses that the President is unable to discharge the powers and duties of his office, the Vice-President shall continue to discharge the same as Acting President; otherwise, the President shall resume the powers and duties of his office.

AMENDMENT XXVI (1971)

Section 1. The right of citizens of the United States, who are eighteen years of age or older, to vote shall not be denied or abridged by the United States or any state on account of age.

Section 2. The Congress shall have the power to enforce this article by appropriate legislation.

AMENDMENT XXVII (1992)

No law, varying the compensation for the services of the Senators and Representatives, shall take effect, until an election of Representatives shall have intervened.

U.S. Population Characteristics for Selected Years (in thousands)

	1790	1840	1890	1940	1990
White	3,172	14,196	55,101	118,215	199,686
Black	757	2,874	7,489	12,866	29,986
(slave)	(698)	(2,487)			
Other minorities*	—	—	358	589	9,805
(Hispanic)**	—	—	NA	NA	(22,354)
Urban***	202	1,845	22,106	74,424	NA
Women	NA	8,381	30,711	65,608	127,470
Median age	NA	17.8	22.0	29.0	32.9
Total	3,929	17,069	62,980	132,165	248,710

*Definitions varied in different census years.
**Hispanics may be of any race.
***Defined as living in a place with 2500 inhabitants.

Population for Selected Large Cities for Selected Years (in thousands)

	1800	1850	1900	1950*	1990*
New York	60	696	3,437	12,912	18,087
Los Angeles	—	2	102	4,152	14,532
Chicago	—	30	1,699	5,586	8,065
San Francisco	—	35	343	2,136	6,253
Philadelphia	70	409	1,294	3,671	5,899
Detroit	—	21	286	3,016	4,665
Boston	25	137	561	2,411	4,172
**Washington	3	40	279	1,464	3,924
**Dallas	—	—	43	744	3,885
**Houston	—	2	45	807	3,711
**St. Louis	NA	78	575	1,755	2,444
**Baltimore	27	169	509	1,405	2,382
Cincinnati	1	115	326	1,023	1,744
**New Orleans	NA	116	287	712	1,239

*Metropolitan area population.
**City with slavery before the Civil War.

Presidential Elections

Year	Presidents	Party	Electoral Vote	Popular Vote (000s)	Losing Candidates	Party	Electoral Vote	Popular Vote (000s)
1788	Wash-ington	F	69	—	unopposed			
1792	Wash-ington	F	132	—	unopposed			
1796	J. Adams	F	71	—	Jefferson	D	68	
1800[1]	Jefferson	D	73	—	Burr	D	73	—
					J. Adams	F	65	—
					Pinckney	F	64	—
					Jay	F	1	—
1804	Jefferson	D	162	—	Pinckney	F	14	—
1808	Madison	D	122	—	Pinckney	F	47	—
					G. Clinton	D	6	—
1812	Madison	D	128	—	D. Clinton	F	89	—
1816	Monroe	D	183	—	King	F	34	—
1820	Monroe	D	231	—	J.Q. Adams	D	1	—
1824[2]	J.Q. Adams	D	84	114	Jackson	D	99	153
					Clay	D	37	47
					Crawford	D	41	47
1828	Jackson	D	178	647	J.Q. Adams	NR	83	508
1832	Jackson		219	702	Clay	NR	49	484
					Wirt	A	7	} 101
					Floyd	D	11	
1836	Van Buren	D	170	764	W. Harrison	W	73	} 738
					White	W	26	
					Webster	W	14	
					Mangum	W	11	

Year	Presidents	Party	Electoral Vote	Popular Vote (000s)	Losing Candidates	Party	Electoral Vote	Popular Vote (000s)
1840	W. Harrison	W	234	1,275	Van Buren	D	60	1,129
1841[3]	Tyler	D						
1844	Polk	D	170	1,339	Clay	W	105	1,300
					Birney	L		62
1848	Taylor	W	163	1,361	Cass	D	127	1,223
					Van Buren	FS		292
1850[3]	Fillmore	W						
1852	Pierce	D	254	1,608	Scott	W	42	1,387
					Hale	FS		155
1856	Buchanan	D	174	1,836	Frémont	R	114	1,342
					Fillmore	AM	8	873
1860	Lincoln	R	180	1,866	Douglas	D	12	1,380
					Breckinridge	D	72	848
					Bell	CU	39	591
1864	Lincoln	R	212	2,218	McClellan	D	21	1,813
1865[3]	A. Johnson	D						
1868	Grant	R	214	3,014	Seymour	D	80	2,709
1872	Grant	R	286	3,598	Greeley	D	66	2,835
1876	Hayes	R	185	4,034	Tilden	D	184	4,289
1880	Garfield	R	214	4,454	Hancock	D	155	4,445
1881[3]	Arthur	R						
1884	Cleveland	D	219	4,875	Blaine	R	182	4,852
1888	B. Harrison	R	233	5,440	Cleveland	D	168	5,540
1892	Cleveland	D	277	5,557	B. Harrison	R	145	5,176
					Weaver	P	22	1,041
1896	McKinley	R	271	7,112	Bryan	D	176	6,509
1900	McKinley	R	292	7,220	Bryan	D	155	6,358
1901[3]	T. Roosevelt	R						
1904	T. Roosevelt	R	336	7,629	Parker	D	140	5,084
1908	Taft	R	321	7,679	Bryan	D	162	6,409
1912	Wilson	D	435	6,293	T. Roosevelt	PR	88	4,119
					Taft	R	8	3,486
					Debs	S		900

Year	Presidents	Party	Electoral Vote	Popular Vote (000s)	Losing Candidates	Party	Electoral Vote	Popular Vote (000s)
1916	Wilson	D	277	9,130	Hughes	R	254	8,538
1920	Harding	R	404	16,153	Cox	D	127	9,133
1923[3]	Coolidge	R						
1924	Coolidge	R	382	15,720	Davis	D	136	8,387
					La Follette	PR	13	4,833
1928	Hoover	R	444	21,437	Smith	D	87	15,007
1932	F. Roosevelt	D	472	22,830	Hoover	R	59	15,761
1936	F. Roosevelt	D	523	27,757	Landon	R	8	16,680
1940	F. Roosevelt	D	449	27,313	Willkie	R	82	22,348
1944	F. Roosevelt	D	432	25,613	Dewey	R	99	22,018
1945[3]	Truman	D						
1948	Truman	D	303	24,179	Dewey	R	189	21,991
					Thurmond	SR	39	1,176
					H. Wallace	PR		1,157
1952	Eisenhower	R	442	33,936	Stevenson	D	89	27,315
1956	Eisenhower	R	457	35,590	Stevenson[4]	D	73	26,023
1960	Kennedy	D	303	34,227	Nixon	R	219	34,108
					Byrd	I	15	286
1963[3]	L. Johnson	D						
1964	L. Johnson	D	486	43,130	Goldwater	R	52	27,178
1968	Nixon	R	301	31,785	Humphrey	D	191	31,275
					G. Wallace	AI	46	9,906
1972	Nixon	R	520	47,170	McGovern	D	17	29,170
1974[3]	Ford	R						
1976	Carter	D	297	40,831	Ford[4]	R	240	39,148
1980	Reagan	R	489	43,904	Carter	D	49	35,484
					Anderson	I		5,720
1984	Reagan	R	525	54,455	Mondale	D	13	37,527
1988	Bush	R	426	48,881	Dukakis	D	112	41,805
1992	Clinton	D	370	43,682	Bush	R	168	38,117
					Perot	I		19,217

AM = American; AI = American Independent; A = Antimason; CU = Constitutional Union; D = Democrat;
F = Federalist; FS = Free Soil; I = Independent; L = Liberty; NR = National Republican; P = Populist; PR = Progressive;
R = Republican; S = Socialist; SR = States Rights; W = Whig

[1] Jefferson and Burr tied in electoral votes, and the House of Representatives elected Jefferson.
[2] No candidate had an electoral majority, and the House of Representatives elected Adams.
[3] Vice-presidents who succeeded to the presidency.
[4] One elector strayed and cast an independent vote.

Chronology

B.C.	38,000	Ice Age land bridge migration from Asia
	6000	Central Americans raise corn and beans
A.D.	300-900	Mayan civilization
	700-1600	Southeastern moundbuilders
ca.	1000-1010	Vikings in Vinland
	1300-1500	Aztec civilization
	1492	Columbus discovers America
	1534-1542	Cartier in Canada
	1539-1542	DeSoto in Southeast
	1585-1590	Roanoke Colony
	1607	Virginia founded
	1618	Virginia headright system
	1619	First slaves in Virginia
		Virginia House of Burgesses
	1620	Pilgrims go to Plymouth
	1624	Dutch found New Netherland
	1629	Dutch patroon plan
	1630-1642	Puritan migration to Massachusetts
	1632	Maryland chartered to Lord Baltimore
	1636	Roger Williams flees to Rhode Island
		Thomas Hooker founds Connecticut
	1638	Massachusetts banishes Anne Hutchinson
	1649	Maryland Toleration Act
	1651-1696	English Navigation Acts
	1663	Carolina chartered to eight lord proprietors
	1664	English capture New Netherland (renamed New York)
		New Jersey split from New York
	1675-1676	Bacon's Rebellion in Virginia
		King Philp's War in New England
	1676	New Jersey split into East and West Jersey (reunited 1702)
	1682	William Penn founds Pennsylvania
	1686-1689	Dominion of New England
	1689	Leisler's Rebellion in New York
	1692	Salem Village witchcraft trials
	1704	Delaware split from Pennsylvania
	1729	North Carolina split from South Carolina
	1732	Gen. James Oglethorpe founds Georgia
	1733	John Peter Zenger wins libel trial
	1741-1742	Jonathan Edwards leads Great Awakening
	1754-1763	French and Indian War
	1764	Sugar Act
	1765	Stamp Act
	1767	Townshend Acts
		Tryon's Palace built
	1771	North Carolina Regulators

1773	Tea Act
1774	Coercive Acts
	Shakers arrive
1775	Battles of Lexington, Concord, and Bunker Hill
1776	Declaration of Independence
1777	Battle of Saratoga
1780-1846	North abolishes slavery
1781	Cornwallis surrenders at Yorktown
1781-1789	Articles of Confederation
1783	Peace treaty grants independence
1785	Land ordinance
1786	Shays's Rebellion in Massachusetts
1787	Northwest Ordinance
	Constitutional Convention (ratified 1788)
1789-1797	George Washington's presidency
1789	Bill of Rights
1790s	Second Great Awakening
1790	Assumption of war debts
	Slater's spinning mill
1791	Bank of the United States chartered
1793	Citizen Genêt
	Whitney's cotton gin
1794	Whiskey Rebellion in Pennsylvania
1795	Treaties with Britain, Indians, and Spain
1796	Washington's Farewell Address
1797-1801	John Adams's presidency
1797	XYZ Affair
1798	Alien and Sedition Acts
	Kentucky and Virginia Resolutions
1798-1800	Quasi-War with France
1801-1809	Thomas Jefferson's presidency
1803	*Marbury v. Madison*
	Louisiana Purchase
1804-1806	Lewis and Clark expedition
1807	Fulton's steamboat
1808	Embargo
	Congress abolishes slave trade
1809-1817	James Madison's presidency
1810	Macon's Bill No. 2
1811	Bank of the United States expires
1812-1815	War of 1812
1813	Waltham weaving mill
1816	Second Bank of the United States chartered
	African Methodist Episcopal Church founded
1817-1825	James Monroe's presidency
1817	American Colonization Society founded
1819	*Dartmouth College Case*
	McCulloch v. Maryland
1820s	Americans settle Texas

1820	Missouri Compromise
1822	Liberia founded
1823	Monroe Doctrine
	Lowell weaving mills

1825-1829	John Quincy Adams's presidency
1825	Erie Canal opens
1828	Tariff of Abominations

1829-1837	Andrew Jackson's presidency
1829-1832	Nullification
1830-1840	Indian removal
1830	Peggy O'Neale Eaton affair
	First railroads open in Baltimore and Charleston, S.C.
	Church of Jesus Christ of Latter-Day Saints founded
1831	*Cherokee Nation v. Georgia*
	Nat Turner Rebellion
	Garrison's *The Liberator* begins
1832	Second Bank of the United States recharter veto
	Worcester v. Georgia
1833	American Antislavery Society founded
1836	Specie Circular
	Texas independence

1837-1841	Martin Van Buren's presidency
1837-1845	Depression
1837	*Charles River Bridge Case*
1838	Frederick Douglass runs away
1839-1841	*Amistad Case*
1840-1860	Record Irish and German immigration
1840	Independent Treasury

| 1841 | William Henry Harrison's Presidency |
| | Brook Farm founded |

1841-1845	John Tyler's presidency
1844	Millerites
	Morse's telegraph
1845	Texas annexed
	Thoreau at Walden Pond

1845-1849	James K. Polk's presidency
1846	U.S.-Canada boundary settled
1846-1848	Mexican War
1846-1847	Wilmot's Proviso
1848	California and New Mexico acquired
	Seneca Falls Declaration of Female Independence
	Oneida Community founded

1849-1850	Zachary Taylor's presidency
1849-1852	California Gold Rush
1849-1860	Filibusterers

| 1850-1853 | Millard Fillmore's presidency |
| 1850 | Compromise of 1850 |

1851	Maine Prohibition begins
1852	Stowe's *Uncle Tom's Cabin*
1853-1857	Franklin Pierce's presidency
1854	Gadsden Purchase
	Kansas-Nebraska Act
	Ostend Manifesto
1854-1856	Bleeding Kansas
1856	Charles Sumner caned
1857-1861	James Buchanan's presidency
1857	*Dred Scott v. Sandford*
1857-1858	Kansas's Lecompton Constitution
1859	Brown's Harper's Ferry raid
1860	South Carolina secedes
1861	Confederate States of America formed
1861-1865	Abraham Lincoln's presidency
1861	Fort Sumter falls
	Upper South secedes
	Battle of Bull Run
1862	Battles of Shiloh, Antietam
1862-1863	Drafting soldiers
1863	Emancipation Proclamation
	Battles of Vicksburg, Gettysburg
	Port Royal experiment
1864	Battles of Petersburg, Atlanta
	Wade-Davis Bill veto
1865	Lee surrenders
1865-1869	Andrew Johnson's presidency
1865	Thirteenth amendment
	Black Codes
1865-1866	Freedmen's Bureau
1866	Civil Rights Act
	Fourteenth amendment
	Ku Klux Klan founded
1867	Reconstruction Act
	Alaska bought
1868	Johnson impeached (but not convicted)
1869-1877	U. S. Grant's presidency
1869	Fifteenth amendment
1872	Crédit Mobilier scandal
1873	Depression
1876	Disputed election
1877	Last Reconstruction government falls
1877-1881	Rutherford Hayes' presidency
1877	National railway strike
1877	Thomas Edison invents phonograph
1879	Bland-Allison Act requires silver purchase
1879	Terence Powderly elected head of Knights of Labor
1879	Edison invents electric light

| 1879 | F. W. Woolworth opens five-and-ten store |

| 1881 | James Garfield's presidency |
| 1881 | Garfield shot by disturbed office seeker and dies |

1881-1885	Chester Arthur's presidency
1882	Chinese Exclusion Act
1883	Pendleton Act passed

1885-1889	Grover Cleveland's presidency
1886	Haymarket riot and bombing
1886	Geronimo surrenders
1886	American Federation of Labor (AFL) founded
1887	Interstate Commerce Commission created

1889-1893	Benjamin Harrison's presidency
1890	Battle of Wounded Knee
1890	Sherman Antitrust Act passed
1890	Sherman Silver Purchase Act passed
1892	Populists organize
1892	Homestead strike

1893-1897	Grover Cleveland's presidency
1893	Financial panic begins depression
1894	Coxey's Army
1894	Pullman strike
1895	United States intervenes in Venezuela boundary issue
1896	*Plessy v. Ferguson* establishes "separate but equal" doctrine

1897-1901	William McKinley's presidency
1898	Spanish-American War
1899	Hayes "Open Door" policy
1899	Philippine guerilla war begins
1900	Boxer Rebellion in China
1901	McKinley shot by anarchist

1901-1909	Theodore Roosevelt's presidency
1901-1917	Progressive years
1901	U.S. Steel formed
1903	Panama declares independence; signs canal treaty
1903	Wright brothers' first flight
1906	Pure Food and Drug Act and Meat Inspection Act passed
1907	Financial panic
1908	Henry Ford introduces Model T

1909-1913	William Taft's presidency
1909	Payne-Aldrich Tariff passed
1910	Pinchot controversy
1911	Triangle Shirtwaist Factory fire
1912	Progressive party (Bull Moose) formed

| 1913-1921 | Woodrow Wilson's presidency |
| 1913 | Sixteenth amendment (income tax) and seventeenth amendment (direct election of senators) ratified |

1913	Federal Reserve Bank established
1914	First World War begins in Europe; Wilson declares neutrality
1914	Clayton Antitrust Act
1914	Federal Reserve Trade Commission created
1914	"Ludlow Massacre" in Colorado
1916	Wilson sends General John Pershing to Mexico
1917	Bolsheviks take power in Russia
1917-1918	United States fights in World War I
1918	Wilson's Fourteen Points
1918	Sedition Act
1918	War Industries Board created
1919	Race riots
1920	Red Scare
1920	Defeat of Versailles Treaty by Senate
1920	Eighteenth amendment (prohibition) and nineteenth amendment (women's suffrage)

1921-1923	Warren G. Harding's presidency
1921	Immigration restriction through national quota
1921	Limitation of Armaments Conference in Washington
1921	Ku Klux Klan begin revival
1923	Teapot Dome scandal
1923	Harding dies

1923-1929	Calvin Coolidge's presidency
1924	National Origins Immigration Act
1924	Nellie Taylor Ross elected governor of Wyoming, first woman governor
1925	Scopes trial
1926	National Broadcasting Corporation, first radio network, formed
1927	Charles A. Lindbergh Atlantic flight
1927	First "talkie" motion picture, *The Jazz Singer*
1928	Kellogg-Briand Pact outlaws war

1929-1933	Herbert Hoover's presidency
1929-1941	Great Depression years
1930	Smoot-Hawley Tariff raises protective barriers
1931	Japan invades Manchuria; Stimson Doctrine issued
1932	Bonus Army
1932	Reconstruction Finance Corporation founded

1933-1945	Franklin Roosevelt's presidency
1933	Frances Perkins U.S. Secretary of Labor, first woman in cabinet
1933	"100 Days" special session March 9-June 16
1933	Twenty-first amendment (repeals prohibition)
1933	Emergency Banking Act halts banking crisis
1933	National Industrial Recovery Act wage-price codes
1933	Agricultural Adjustment Act provides farm supports
1933	Glass-Steagall Act establishes Federal Deposit Insurance Corporation
1934	Father Charles Coughlin states National Union for Social Justice
1934	Francis Townsend proposes old age pensions
1935	Works Progress Administration begins

1935	Supreme Court strikes down NRA
1935	Wagner Act sets up National Labor Relations Board
1935	Social Security Act enacted
1935	Huey Long assassinated
1935	Congress of Industrial Organizations (CIO) founded
1936	Supreme Court strikes down AAA
1937	Roosevelt proposes court packing
1937	CIO expelled from AFL
1937	Japan invades China
1938	Munich Conference
1939	Germany invades Poland; World War II begins
1939	Germany and Soviet Union sign pact
1939	Neutrality Act
1940	Germany captures Belgium, Holland, and France
1940	Roosevelt wins third term
1941	Lend-Lease
1941	Germany invades the Soviet Union
1941	Japan attacks U.S. naval forces at Pearl Harbor; United States enters war
1942	United States evacuates Japanese from California
1942	Battle of Midway; North African invasion
1943	Race riot in Detroit
1943	Allied invasion of Italy
1944	G. I. bill enacted
1944	Allied invasion of France
1945	Yalta Conference
1945	Roosevelt dies

1945-1953	Harry Truman's presidency
1945	Germany surrenders
1945	Atomic bombs dropped on Hiroshima and Nagasaki; Japan surrenders
1946	Military demobilization
1947	Taft-Hartley Act
1947	Truman Doctrine announced
1947	Marshall Plan launches economic recovery in Europe
1948	Truman integrates armed forces
1948	Berlin airlift
1948	Alger Hiss found guilty of perjury
1949	North Atlantic Treaty Organization established
1950	U. S. sends troops to Korea
1951	Julius and Ethel Rosenberg sentenced to death
1951	MacArthur removed from Korean command
1951	Twenty-second amendment limits presidents to two terms
1952	H-bomb developed

1953-1961	Dwight Eisenhower's presidency
1953	Korean War ends
1954	*Brown v. Board of Education of Topeka* decision ordering integration
1954	Senate censures Senator Joseph McCarthy
1955	Montgomery, Alabama bus boycott

1956	Interstate highway system begins
1956	Suez crisis
1957	First civil rights law since Reconstruction
1957	National Guardsmen sent to Little Rock, Arkansas
1957	Soviet Union launches *Sputnik*
1960	Black students stage sit-in in Greensboro
1960	First birth control pill introduced in U.S.
1961-1963	John Kennedy's presidency
1961	Peace Corps established
1961	Bay of Pigs invasion of Cuba fails
1961	Freedom rides in South begin
1962	Cuban missile crisis
1963	Nuclear Test Ban Treaty ratified
1963	Betty Friedan publishes *The Feminine Mystique*
1963	Kennedy assassinated
1963-1969	Lyndon Johnson's presidency
1964	Gulf of Tonkin Resolution begins war in Vietnam
1964	Civil Rights Act enacted
1965	Racial riot in Watts
1965	Great Society begins including Medicare, federal aid to education, and urban renewal
1965	U. S. combat troops sent to Vietnam
1965	Voting Rights Act enacted
1967	Thurgood Marshall becomes first black appointed to Supreme Court
1967	Black riots in Newark, New Jersey and Detroit, Michigan
1968	Tet offensive in Vietnam
1968	Johnson withdraws from presidential race
1968	Martin Luther King, Jr. assassinated
1968	Robert Kennedy assassinated
1969-1974	Richard Nixon's presidency
1969	Nuclear Nonproliferation Treaty signed
1970	Environmental Protection Agency founded
1970	U. S. troops invade Cambodia; student strikes
1971	United States goes off international gold standard
1971	Twenty-sixth amendment lowers voting age to 18
1971	Pentagon Papers reveal U. S. involvement in Vietnam
1972	Nixon travels to China
1972	United States enters into Strategic Arms Limitation Treaty with the Soviet Union
1972	Equal Rights Amendment sent to states for ratification
1973	War ends in Vietnam
1973	Senate begins Watergate break-in hearings
1973	Supreme Courts upholds abortion in *Roe v. Wade*
1973	Arab oil boycott creates stagflation in U. S. economy
1974	Nixon resigns from the presidency
1974-1977	Gerald Ford's presidency
1974	Ford pardons Nixon
1974	Economic recession
1975	South Vietnam and Cambodia fall to communists

1976	United States celebrates bicentennial of independence

1977	Jimmy Carter's presidency
1977	Energy Department created
1978	Panama Canal turned over to Panama
1979	Chrysler Corporation federal bail-out
1980	Soviet invasion of Afghanistan
1980	Iranian hostage crisis

1981-1989	Ronald Reagan's presidency
1981	Iranian hostages released
1981	Tax cut
1981	Federal air traffic controllers strike broken
1981	Sandra Day O'Connor first women appointed to Supreme Court
1982	Equal Rights Amendment defeated
1982	Economic recession
1982	U. S. Marines sent to Lebanon
1983	Grenada invaded
1984	Central Intelligence Agency acknowledges mining of Nicaraguan harbors
1984	Reagan visits China
1985	Reagan and Soviet leader Mikhail Gorbachev meet
1986	William Rehnquist appointed as chief justice and Antonin Scalia appointed as associate justice of Supreme Court
1986	Tax Reform Act enacted
1987	First trillion dollar budget
1987	Iran-Contra hearings
1987	Arms limitation treaty with the Soviet Union
1988	Amnesty offered to 1.4 million illegal immigrants

1989-1993	George Bush's presidency
1989	Savings and loan bailout
1989	Supreme Court allows state laws restraining abortion
1989	United States invades Panama
1990	Physical and Mental Disabilities Act enacted
1990	United States sends troops to Saudi Arabia
1990	Clean Air Act passed
1990	Taxes increased
1991	United States and allies defeat Iraq in Gulf War
1991	Economic recession
1991	Clarence Thomas nominated to Supreme Court
1992	William Clinton elected to presidency

Glossary

abolition/abolitionist the policy of the government to end slavery; abolitionists were people who urged government action to end slavery

adventurist a term often used in foreign policy to connote a hazardous or dangerous undertaking or policy

Allies those nations that fought against the **Axis** powers (Germany, Italy, Japan) during World War II

amnesty the act of the government to pardon a large number of individuals

Anaconda a copper city in southwestern Montana; site of the world's largest copper smelter

Anglophobia hatred of England or English customs, people, manners, or institutions; used by certain American politicians to inflame voters, especially Irish voters

annex/annexation the process by which a government takes in new territory

antebellum literally, "before the war," usually before the Civil War

anti-Semitism intolerance of Jews or Jewish culture

antitrust federal and state statutes that limit the ability of businesses and unions to exercise monopolistic control or restrain trade, such as the Sherman Antitrust Act of 1890 (see also **trust**)

apartheid a policy of **segregation** and political and economic discrimination against non-European groups in the Republic of South Africa

appeasement/appease to bring peace by making concessions; a policy of appeasement was pursued by Neville Chamberlain, prime minister of Great Britain (1937-1940) in negotiating with the Nazis

apprenticeship a system for training youths for careers in skilled crafts

appropriations funds set aside by a legislature to pay for something authorized by law

aristocracy a hereditary ruling class; commonly found in Europe

Articles of Confederation the document that in the 1780s created the government of the United States before the U.S. Constitution; like Canada today, the United States under the Articles was a weak alliance of loosely associated states

artillery very heavy guns used to fire long distances in war

artisans skilled workers such as butchers, bakers, and candlestick makers

assimilation the process by which one group of people gradually becomes like another group of people by adopting the other group's language, religion, and culture

asylum a refuge, retreat, or shelter

Axis powers a **coalition** that developed from the Rome-Berlin Axis of 1936 and eventually included Germany, Italy, Japan, and others; opposed by the **Allies** in World War II

belligerent a person or nation engaged in warfare or fighting

Bible Belt those portions of the rural South and Midwest dominated from the early 1800s to the present by **evangelical Protestant** Christians

Big Three Franklin Roosevelt (United States), Winston Churchill (Great Britain), and Josef Stalin (Soviet Union)

bill draft of a proposed law not yet passed by Congress or signed by the president.

bimetallic standard the concurrent use of both gold and silver as the standard of currency and value; advocated by the Populist party in 1896

black nationalism the belief that African-Americans should form their own nation or society separate from white society

bohemian a person, usually of artistic or literary tastes, who lives in an unconventional manner; a term that became popular among intellectuals at the turn of the twentieth century

boll weevils a long-used term for southern Democrats in Congress, including those who supported Ronald Reagan during his presidency

Bolsheviks a political faction of **communists** who gained control of Russia in 1917 following the overthrow of the czar

bond in finance, an interest-bearing certificate of debt, usually issued by a government, municipality, or corporation; the federal government issues bonds to finance its debt

bootlegging/bootlegger the sale and distribution of illegal alcohol during **prohibition** in the 1920s

breastworks hastily built low barriers behind which gunners fire

burgess a legislator, specifically a member of Virginia's House of Burgesses during colonial times

busing a method of transporting students from one school district to another to ensure racial balance

Calvinism the religion of John Calvin and his followers, including Presbyterians, **Puritans,** and **Pilgrims,** which stressed that only certain people could be saved and go to heaven (compare with **universal salvation**)

capital wealth (money and property); an accumulated source of wealth used to produce more wealth; also, used to define capitalists collectively as distinguished from labor

capitalists/capitalism people who invest money in business enterprises in the hope of making profits; an economic system in which all or most of the means of production and distribution are privately owned and operated for profit

capitalization the total capital funds of a corporation, represented by stocks, bonds, undivided profit, and surplus

carpetbaggers northerners who moved south to assist Radical Republicans during Reconstruction (compare with **scalawags**)

cash and carry a system imposed by the Neutrality Act (1937) in which goods were to be paid in cash

charter an important government document; under English law, charters were more important than laws or court rulings; they could be granted either by the king or by **Parliament**; persons often gained great power through the land or privileges granted in a charter; colonies such as Virginia and Massachusetts were started under the authority of charters

checks and balances the principle in the U.S. Constitution, derived from colonial and English experience, that power should be divided rather than concentrated; the U.S. Constitution divides power among three branches of government, legislative, executive, and judicial

Church of England the official **Protestant** church in England founded when Henry VIII broke with the Catholic church; in America, it became the Episcopal church after the American Revolution

cleptocracy a form of government by theft

coalition an alliance of interests or groups; the New Deal coalition brought together urban ethnic groups with southern whites and blacks

coattails a political expression meaning to help win an election for a follower or supporter; a congressional candidate will sometimes win election on the coattails of a strong presidential candidate from the same party

coinage the act to make coins; free coinage meant unlimited use of certain metal, often used in the silver controversy in 1872-1900

Cold Warrior a person who supported the Cold War against the Soviet Union

Cold War war by other than military means; the hostile but nonlethal relations between the United States and the Soviet Union, 1945-1989

collective a body of people brought together in a common enterprise; the Soviet Union formed agricultural collectives under Stalin; in the 1970s, New Left students formed revolutionary collectives to challenge **capitalist** society

collectivism a general term often suggesting **socialism** or **communism**, as opposed to individualism

colonizationists/colonization people who favored abolishing slavery and resettling the ex-slaves from the United States to Africa; this movement was strongest from 1817 to 1830 (not to be confused with colonialism)

combine an agricultural machine that reaps, threshes, and cleans grain while harvesting it; invented and manufactured by Cyrus McCormick

communes groups living together on an equal basis, sharing work and leisure; there were many communes in the 1800s; the most successful had religious roots

communion a Christian ceremony commemorating Christ's resurrection using wine and bread; Christians often disagree on the ceremony's conduct and meaning

communist/communism a member of a Communist party; or one who supports communism, a theory and social system conceived by the German philosopher Karl Marx (see also **Bolsheviks, socialism, Marxism**)

compensated emancipation a system by which the government freed **slaves** by paying slaveholders for the value of their slaves

congregational churches churches governed by their congregations rather than by bishops or other outside groups; in New England both **Puritans** and **Pilgrims** governed their churches this way, and they became known by this name

conscientious objector an opponent to war on religious or moral grounds

contraband in warfare, any items valuable to an enemy which might therefore be seized; during the Civil War, the North for a time considered **slaves** to be contraband

conversion experience for some Christians, the process by which a person becomes a Christian; Puritans believed that a person had to undergo a rebirth of the spirit that could be described convincingly to others; later **evangelicals** found a statement of having had such an experience sufficient

cotton gin Eli Whitney's 1793 invention, no bigger than a breadbox, for easily separating cotton fibers from the seeds

covert not openly shown, as in "covert CIA operation"

cubism a movement of modern art about 1907-1925, concerned with abstract and geometric interpretation of form

customs duties (see **tariff**)

daguerreotype an early photographic process that did not use negatives; the pictures were remarkably clear and detailed, but the cost was high and no copies could be made

dark horse an obscure presidential candidate picked by a political party as a compromise to break a deadlock; James Polk and Warren Harding are examples of dark horses who won

deferment the act of delaying or postponing, especially used with the **draft,** such as a student deferment which allowed students to postpone entering the draft during the Vietnam War

deficit the amount by which expenditures exceed revenues

defoliant a chemical spray or dust applied to plants in order to cause leaves to drop off prematurely

depression a period marked by slackening business activity, widespread unemployment, falling prices and wages (compare with **recession**)

desegregate to end segregation, often practiced in schools, businesses, and public places against racial minorities (primarily African-Americans)

detente a relaxation of strained relations between two nations (pronounced *day-TAHNT*)

discount rate the interest rate paid by a commercial bank when it borrows from a Federal Reserve Bank; one of the tools of monetary policy used by the Federal Reserve System

disfranchisement removal of a person's right to vote; many southern states disfranchised African-Americans in the late 1800s

divisions military units usually composed of three **regiments;** in the American Civil War, about 5,000 soldiers

dole that which is distributed through charity in the form of a small gift of food or money; often used for those receiving public aid during the Great Depression in the 1930s

domino effect the theory that if a critically situated country falls to **communism,** its neighbors will soon follow; a rationale for American involvement during the Vietnam War

dove an advocate of peace; a term often used for those opposed to the war in Vietnam (compare with **hawk**)

draft compulsory military service; the practice of drafting people into military service is called conscription

due process the constitutional requirement that "no person shall be deprived of life, liberty, or property without the due process of law," a right guaranteed by the fifth, sixth, and fourteenth amendments to the U.S. Constitution

duties (see **tariff**)

egalitarian favoring absolute equality

electoral college the U.S. Constitution's method for electing presidents; the members of the electoral college, called electors, elect the president; the states determine how the members of the electoral college are picked (see also **electoral vote**)

electoral vote the votes cast for president and vice-president by the **electoral college** as established in Article II, Section 1, and Amendment XII and Amendment XXIII of the U.S. Constitution

elitism rule by an elite or dominant group

emancipate/emancipation a slaveholder voluntarily giving freedom to a slave

Emancipation Proclamation the executive order by President Abraham Lincoln in 1863 that freed the slaves inside the Confederacy on the grounds that slavery aided the Confederate military cause

embargo a federal law barring merchant ships from leaving or entering port and thus totally ending all foreign trade; imposed by Thomas Jefferson in 1807, the embargo prevented war with Britain but ruined the American economy (compare with **blockade**)

eminent domain the right of the government to take private property forcibly but with compensation for public purposes, such as building a road or railroad

enfranchise to give the right to vote

Enlightenment the movement prevalent in the 1700s that reason and logic determined all; it was highly favorable to science and suspicious of religion (see also **romanticism**)

envoy a diplomatic representative

evangelical a **Protestant** Christian who stresses the authority of the Bible, exhortation to faith, and usually the availability of **universal salvation**

expansionism the act of expanding the state

expressionist a movement in the arts, originating about 1914, that had as its object the free expression of the inner experience of the artist

factionalism the practice of dividing an organization or other body into contentious or self-seeking groups

fascism a political philosophy that advocates governance by a dictator to maintain a totalitarian, regimented society; fascism appeared in Italy and Germany in the 1920s and 1930s (pronounced FASH-izm)

Federal Reserve Bank the central bank of the United States created by the Federal Reserve Act (1913)

feudalism the political, economic, and social system emphasizing graded classes by which Europe was organized in the Middle Ages, circa 1000-1500

filibuster the use of a delaying tactic to prevent action in a legislative assembly, especially the U.S. Senate; the taking of foreign territory in a private war in the 1850s

filibusterers leaders of private armies who tried to seize territory in the 1850s for the purpose of adding it to the United States (not to be confused with **filibuster**)

flapper an informal name given to women trying to appear sophisticated in dress and behavior in the 1920s

flotilla a fleet of boats or ships

foreclosure to take away the right to redeem a mortgage when regular payments have not been made on a home, farm, or other property

49th parallel in the West, the boundary between the United States and Canada, which runs along this straight line of latitude

franchise the right to vote

free coinage the issuing of currency based on a silver or bimetallic standard

free love a celebration of sex and a rejection of traditional restrictions, including marriage; advocated by Frances Wright in New York in the 1830s

free silver the free and unlimited coinage of silver, particularly at a fixed ratio to gold

free soil the policy of keeping **slavery** out of the western territories without interfering with slavery in the South; Van Buren's position in 1848; the Republican party position in 1856 and 1860

free trade the right to buy or sell anything to anyone across national borders without regulation or taxes; free trade exists among states within the United States (see also **tariff**)

freedmen the name given to former **slaves** during Reconstruction

frieze a three-dimensional sculpture placed in a band around the top of a building

fundamentalism a movement organized in the early twentieth century to defend orthodox **Protestant** Christianity against the challenges of theological liberalism, evolution, and liberal interpretations of the Bible

Gatling guns machine guns invented and first used in the Civil War

Gentlemen's Agreement an agreement reached with Japan in 1908 by which the Japanese government promised to issue no more passports to peasants or workers coming directly to the continental United States

gentry in England, landowning farmers who enjoyed some wealth, some prestige, and some political power; in Virginia and the South, the owners of **plantations**

GI Bill Servicemen's Readjustment Act (1944) under which $13 billion was spent for veterans on education, medical treatment, unemployment insurance, loans for homes and business

gold standard a monetary system in which gold is used as the standard of value for the money of a country; inflationists in the late 1800s wanted a **bimetalic** standard of gold and silver; the United States remained on a domestic gold standard until 1933

GOP Grand Old Party, the Republican party

Grange laws state laws passed in the 1870s with the support of farmers, represented by the **Grange,** that strove to regulate railway rates and storage fees charged by railroads and by operators of warehouses and grain elevators; these laws were overturned when the Supreme Court decreed in the *Wabash* case (1886) that individual states had no power to regulate interstate commerce

Grange formally called the Order of Patrons of Husbandry, an association of U.S. farmers founded in 1867 to promote agricultural interests

Great Awakening a series of religious **revivals** that swept the colonies in the 1740s

greenbacks United States paper money, first issued during the Civil War, so called because the back side was printed in green ink (compare with **specie** and **hard money**)

gross domestic product the value of all the nation's goods and services in a given year

guerrilla/guerrilla warfare a combatant who fights secretly and with terrorism; a type of warfare carried on behind enemy lines through surprise raids, sabotage, and disruptive attacks; used in the Philippines against American troops following the Spanish-American War and later during the Vietnam War (1965-1973)

habeas corpus a court order requiring authorities to free a person held in custody

Halls of Montezuma Mexico City, captured by the U.S. marines in the Mexican War in 1847

hard money money issued in gold coins; the opposite of paper (or **soft**) money (see also **specie**)

hawk a person who supports a military action or war, as opposed to a **dove**

headright system the method in some colonies by which a person could gain free land in return for bringing laborers from England to America

hierarchy persons arranged by rank or status, often for political purposes; a king, for example, would be at the top of the hierarchy

holding company a company that invests in the stocks of one or more other corporations, which it may thus control

holocaust a thorough destruction, often used to describe Hittler's destruction of Jews in World War II or the result of using nuclear weapons

Holy Spirit God's presence in the third person of the Trinity; also called the Holy Ghost

homestead/homesteading a tract of land occupied under the Homestead Act (1862) that provided a person with 160 acres of free public land in return for settling and farming it

Huguenots French **Protestant** Christians who left France to avoid persecution after 1685

impeach/impeachment the U.S. Constitution's method for removing the president, vice-president, or judges from office before their terms have expired; used against Federalist judges in 1801, against Andrew Johnson in 1868, and against Richard Nixon in 1974; charges are brought by the House, and conviction requires a two-thirds vote in the Senate; Johnson was not convicted; Nixon resigned

imperialism the creation or extension of an empire, comprising many nations and areas; advocated in the late 1800s by certain social thinkers and policy makers

import duties (see **tariff**)

impound the withholding by the executive branch of funds authorized and appropriated by law

impressment the British policy, especially in the early 1800s, to stop American ships at sea and to seize sailors by claiming that they were British subjects, whether they were or not; this was a main method used to staff the British navy; impressment led to poor relations between Britain and the United States and helped produce the War of 1812

indemnity that which is given as compensation for a loss or for damage

indentured servants persons whose passage from England to America was paid in return for signing a written contract (called an indenture) agreeing to serve as laborers for a term of years, usually seven; a large number of whites used this method to migrate to the South and to the Middle Colonies in the 1700s; used in Texas in the 1830s as a disguised form of slavery

inflation rise in prices resulting from an increase in circulating currency and a mounting demand for available commodities and services

initiative a procedure that allows citizens, as opposed to legislators, to propose the enactment of state and local laws; promoted by progressive reformers in the early twentieth century

internationalism the belief that mutual understanding and cooperation among nations will advance the common welfare

isolationism the policy of curtailing a nation's international relations; isolationism was dominant in U. S. foreign policy during much of the 1800s and the two decades between the world wars

Jesuit a member of the Catholic religious order called the Society of Jesus; Jesuits were very active in missions and education throughout the world after 1600

Jim Crow a name given to racial **segregation;** the name comes from a popular dance tune in the 1830s performed by a black-faced white actor

jingoism an aggressive, highly nationalistic, foreign policy

journeymen skilled workers who had completed apprenticeships but lacked the means to go into business for themselves *journeyed* around working for other craftsmen; they used part of their wages to save the money needed to set up for themselves

junta a Central or South American legislative council, or a political body gathered together for some secret purpose; exiled Cuban rebels opposed to Spanish rule (pronounced HOON-tah)

kaiser title of German emperors, 1871-1918

kamikaze a suicidal Japanese tactic of ramming with a piloted airplane or boat carrying explosives in World War II; from Japanese *kami* (god) and *kaze* (wind) (pronounced kahm-i-KAHZ-ee)

Kremlin governing center of Russia

Ku Klux Klan a white supremacist group established in the South following the Civil War and revived in the early twentieth century

laissez-faire a hands-off style of governance that emphasizes economic freedom; the concept is associated with Adam Smith and his book *The Wealth of Nations* (1776) (pronounced le-say FAIR)

lame duck any office holder who has not been reelected and who waits for his or her successor to assume office

land grants land given to a person, usually by a government, often for political reasons

legal tender items defined by law as money, which must be accepted in payment of debts; governments have frequently made paper money legal tender; such paper money could be produced by the government in large quantities cheaply

lend-lease terms of the Lend Lease Act (1941) which furnished goods to Allied powers

lien a legal right to claim or dispose of property in payment for a debt (pronounced lean)

lobbyist a person, group, or organization that seeks to influence legislation or administrative action

lode a deposit of ore located between rock; also called vein

lyceum a series of well-organized public lectures, stressing self-improvement, held each year in most northern towns and cities in the 1840s-1850s (pronounced lie-SEE-um)

machine an informal political organization, often centered on a single politician, that controlled the formal process of government through corruption, **patronage,** and service to its constituents

magnate an important or influential person, often found in business, e.g., John Pierpont Morgan

Manifest Destiny the belief that Americans had the God-given right to own all of North America, and perhaps South America, too; common from 1844 to 1861

manors large tracts of land owned by wealthy, politically powerful New Yorkers during the colonial period; most manors were along the Hudson River

martial law the law administered by military forces that is invoked by a government in an emergency

Marxist a follower of German philosopher Karl Marx, a **communist** or socialist

masonic pertaining to Freemasons, whose lodges stress charity and sociability

McCarthyism extreme and irresponsible anticommunism; the use of unproven association with any individual, organization, or policy, which the accuser perceives as anti-American (see also **communism, Marxist**)

mercantilism an economic theory and practice popular from 1500 to 1800 that used government regulation and **monopolies** to control business, and especially to maintain colonies as part of a global system; the British empire is one example

midterm election an election held for Congress between presidential elections

militia ordinary citizens called to temporary duty as soldiers, especially from the colonial period to circa 1850; the equivalent today is the National Guard

mobilization to prepare for war by organizing industry, personnel, and national resources

monopoly the exclusive control of a commodity, service, or means of production in a particular market that allows the fixing of prices and the elimination of competition (see also **trust**)

moratorium a waiting period set by an authority

mores folkways that are considered conducive to the welfare of society (pronounced MOHR-ayz)

mugwump a Republican who bolted the party when James G. Blaine was nominated as the presidential candidate in 1884; a term used for any political independent

munitions guns, bullets, and other necessary war materiel

nationalism strong, sometimes chauvinistic, devotion to one's own nation (see also jingoism; not to be confused with **nationalization**)

nationalization to transfer ownership of land, resources, or industries to the federal government; advocated by various parties such as the Populist party and the Socialist party (not to be confused with **nationalism**)

nativism/nativist a belief in the superiority of Americans born in the United States and a rejection of the foreign-born

natural law the idea prevalent in the 1700s that nature operated according to rules laid down by God; discovering the rules was a major undertaking

naval blockade use of warships to close off trade to or from a seaport or coastline (see aso **embargo**)

Nazi a member or supporter of Adolf Hitler's National Socialist German Workers Party

New World North and South America; the term used by Europeans after Columbus's discovery in 1492

nullification the idea, promoted by John C. Calhoun, that a state could act to overrule a federal law inside its own borders; thus, laws would be declared unconstitutional by the states rather than by the Supreme Court; opponents pointed to the chaos caused by different states acting differently

Open Door Policy a policy or practice of giving to all nations the same commercial privileges in a region or area open to trade; the United States advocated an open door policy toward China in the late 1800s

out work in certain industrial processes, especially shoemaking, the practice of sending some work out of the main shop or factory, often to be performed in the home by women or children at low wages

papal edict a Catholic Pope's public proclamation carrying great authority both spiritually and politically among Catholics

parity a level for farm prices that gives to the farmer the same purchasing power that was averaged during each year of a chosen base period; also used during the Cold War to refer to the rough equivalence of missiles between the United States and the Soviet Union

Parliament the legislative body governing England

party ticket a political term used to pair presidential and vice-presidential candidates

patronage the system by which political winners fill all government jobs with their supporters (see also **spoils system**)

patroons wealthy, powerful landowners in Dutch New Netherland who received much land in the 1600s in return for bringing settlers to the colony

paydirt soil containing enough metal, especially gold, to be profitable to a mine

peace protocol the preliminary draft of an official peace treaty

Pentagon headquarters of the Defense Department; the U.S. military establishment

pig iron crude iron as it comes from the blast furnaces

Pilgrim a **Protestant** Christian who found the **Church of England** so corrupt that a new church must be formed; they migrated to Holland, then to Plymouth, Massachusetts (compare with **Puritan**)

pink a derogatory term often associated with a position or person accused of being sympathetic to a socialist or **communist (red)** position

Pinkerton a name given to employees of the Pinkerton Detective Agency, often used to infiltrate labor organizations and break strikes in the late 1800s

plantations large-scale farm units in the South usually devoted to one crop for sale in the world market and worked with **slave** or, less commonly, **indentured servant** labor; plantations began in the 1600s and lasted until the end of slavery in 1865

pluralism cultural diversity in a society stratified along racial lines; also, any political system in which there are multiple centers of legitimate power and authority

plurality the greatest number of votes cast for a candidate, but not more than half of the votes cast

pocket veto an indirect **veto** in which the president declines to sign a **bill** after Congress has adjourned (after adjournment, a bill passed by Congress does not become law without the president's signature)

polarized broken up into opposing groups

political machine an informal organization, often centered on a single politician, that controlled the formal process of government through corruption, **patronage**, and service to its constituents

polity an organized society, such as a state; governing structures of a political community

pool the combined investment of a group of persons or corporations, and the sharing of responsibility for a joint enterprise; employed by John D. Rockefeller in development of the oil industry in the late 1800s

populism a political movement which grew out of a farmers' protest movement in the 1890s

pork barrel favoritism by a government in the distribution of benefits or resources; legislation that favors the district of a particular legislator, often through public works

preemptive strike a military attack aimed to prevent aggressive military action by an opponent or enemy

primary a state or local election held before a general election to nominate a political party's candidates for office

privateer/privateering a private ship commissioned by a government in time of war to act as a warship against an enemy country's merchant ships

profiteer/profiteering a person who obtains excessive profits during times of shortages, frequently during wartime

progressivism a designation applied to reform in the decades between 1890 and 1920, a period of rapid urbanization and industrialization

prohibition legally forbidding the manufacture, transportation, or sale of alcoholic beverages; adopted by some cities and counties in the 1840s and by some states beginning with Maine in 1851; enacted nationally in the eighteenth amendment (1919), repealed with twenty-first amendment (1933); (compare with **temperance movement**)

proprietary colony a colony owned by one person, called a proprietor, such as Lord Baltimore's Maryland or William Penn's Pennsylvania; a few proprietary colonies, such as North and South Carolina, had multiple owners

protectionist one who favors high **tariffs** to protect a domestic market from foreign trade competition

protectorate a country or region under the protection or political domination of another

Protestant a Christian belonging to any number of groups that rejected the Catholic church

Puritan a **Protestant** Christian who wished to purify the **Church of England** but did not wish to form a separate church; some stayed in England, others went to Massachusetts (compare with **Pilgrim**)

quagmire literally, soft mucky ground which, once stepped in, is difficult to get out of; a difficult or dangerous situation; the war in Vietnam was often described as a quagmire

rapprochement establishment or state of peaceful relations (pronounced *ra-prosh-MAHN*)

ratify/ratification the power of a legislature to approve or reject treaties, constitutional amendments, or a new constitution

rationing a fixed allowance or portion of food, fuel, or goods allotted during times of scarcity and war

reactionary one who favors political and social reaction and is hostile to radicalism or rapid political change

receivership a legal term in which a business enterprise is placed in the hands of a court-appointed administrator

recession a period of reduced economic activity, less serious than a **depression** (compare with **depression**)

Redcoats British soldiers in the American Revolution; this nickname came from the color of the soldiers' uniforms

reds a name given to **communists**; the Red Scare in 1919 expressed anxiety among the public and politicians concerning communist influence in America (see also **pink**)

referendum a procedure for submitting proposed laws or state constitutional amendments to voters for their direct approval or rejection; favored by **progressive** reformers at the turn of the twentieth century (compare with **initiative**)

regiments military units of 1,000-2,000 soldiers; the most common Civil War unit (see also **divisions**)

reparations compensation paid by defeated countries for acts of war; following World War I, the Allied powers, especially France and Great Britain, insisted that Germany pay war reparations

republican a democratic, constitutional form of government, such as that established by the U.S. Constitution; not to be confused with the Republican party

reservations land set apart by the government for a particular use, as, for example, Indian reservations

revival a large, popular gathering for religious purposes, especially among **Protestants**; revivals have been common in America at periodic intervals since the 1740s

romanticism/romantic movement in the early 1800s, the rejection of the rational **Enlightenment** in favor of seeing emotion and the need for its expression as the central element in life; many romantics were poets and artists (see also **transcendentalism**)

run (on a bank) a panic in which all of a bank's customers try to withdraw all of their deposits at the same time, thereby causing the bank to fail; bank runs often occurred during a **depression** or a panic

salt pork pork stored and preserved without refrigeration by packing the meat in barrels filled with salt

salvation the Christian idea that people could be saved spiritually and go to heaven (see also **Calvinism** and **universal salvation**)

sanctions coercive measures adopted, usually economic and usually by several nations at a time, to force a nation to stop violating international law

Sandinista a member of a revolutionary group that came to power in Nicaragua in the late 1970s; named after Cesar Augusto Sandino, a Nicaraguan rebel who resisted U.S. marines sent into the country in the 1920s

scalawags white southerners who supported Radical Republican rule during Reconstruction (compare with **carpetbaggers**)

secession a state formally declaring that it is leaving the United States

securities any evidence of debt or ownership, especially stocks and bonds

segregate/segregation to separate by race, often imposed by law (see also **apartheid**)

separatism a belief that white and black races should be separated physically, culturally, and socially

settlement house a welfare institution established in a congested part of a city, having a resident staff of workers to conduct educational and recreational activities for the community

sharecropper/sharecropping a **tenant farmer,** usually heavily in debt to a local merchant or bank, who rented land and paid the rent by splitting the money from the sale of the crop with the landowner; common in the South after the Civil War

Sino- Chinese (pronounced SIGH-no)

sit-in a demonstration of protest, as by African-Americans in the southern United States in the 1960s, in which participants entered and remained seated in a public place

skid row a district of a city inhabited by vagrants and derelicts (slang); originally, a road used to skid logs to a mill in Seattle

Slave Power Republican party phrase in the 1850s to describe slaveholders' political influence

slave/slavery a person totally owned and controlled by another person under the law; slavery became an important institution in colonial America, especially in the South

smelter a furnace used to reduce ores to obtain a metal

Social Security the popular name for the Old Age, Survivors, and Disability Insurance system established by the Social Security Act (1935)

socialism a system of government in which many of the means of production and trade are owned by the government and in which many welfare needs are provided directly by the government; an early advocate was Eugene Debs, leader of the Socialist party (see also **communism, Marxism,** and **Bolsheviks**)

soft money paper money, as opposed to **hard money** and coins (see also **specie** and **greenbacks**)

sortie one mission or attack by a single plane

sovereignty complete independence and self-government

specie gold or silver money, as opposed to paper money (see also **hard money** and **soft money**)

speculators/speculation persons who engage in risky business, often with borrowed money, in the hope of large profits; Americans have often speculated with land

spiritualism a movement founded in the 1840s whose followers believed the living could communicate with the dead, especially through seances with crystal balls

spoils system the widespread practice of awarding government jobs to political supporters without consideration of their qualifications for the jobs (see also **patronage**)

squatters frontier farmers who used land they did not own without anyone's permission; they moved frequently

Stalinist a follower of the Soviet dictator Josef Stalin, chief of state in the Soviet Union, 1924-1953

star route scandal a government scandal that emerged in the Garfield and Arthur administrations involving fraudulent postal contracts issued for special "star" routes by key Republican party officials

steerage a section in a passenger ship for passengers paying the lowest fare and given inferior accommodations

strict construction an interpretation of the U.S. Constitution that stresses the limited powers of government rather than the broad provisions; Thomas Jefferson first argued this view in the 1790s

subsistence farmers farmers who produced food and clothing for their own use and only rarely sold their produce in the market

suffrage the right to vote; by the 1830s most states had universal white male suffrage; the fifteenth amendment (1870) held that suffrage shall not be denied "on account of race"; the nineteenth amendment (1920) extended the right to vote to women in all states

supply side economics the belief that lower tax rates encourage capital to flow into the economy; an economic theory adopted by President Reagan and his advisers

tariff taxes placed on goods brought into the United States; in the late 1800s Republicans favored high tariffs and Democrats favored low tariffs or no tariffs **(free trade)**

tax base the value on which taxes are levied including individual income, real property, corporate income, and wealth

tax shelter an investment in which any profits are fully or partially tax-free

teetotaler one who abstains totally from alcoholic drinks

temperance movement in the 1790s, a movement urging people to use alcohol only in moderation; by the 1830s, a movement asking people to give up all alcohol voluntarily; strongly connected to **evangelical** religion; many female reformers were involved in this movement; especially well-known was the Woman's Christian Temperance Union (WCTU) (compare with **prohibition**)

tenant farmers farmers who lacked the means to buy land and therefore rented it; already common in colonial America, the practice grew in the late 1800s, especially in the South (see also **sharecropper**)

tenement an urban apartment building that is poorly constructed and maintained, typically overcrowded and often part of a slum

theocracy a government controlled by a church or church leaders

ticket a political term used to pair presidential and vice-presidential candidates

titled nobility the highest rank in British society, except for the royal family; examples are dukes or lords

Tories in the 1700s in England, the conservative political faction emphasizing the king and hierarchy; in 1776 Americans who opposed the American Revolution and sided with the British

transcendentalism the belief, associated with Ralph Waldo Emerson in the 1840s and 1850s, that doing good deeds, **romanticism,** and contemplating nature enabled people to transcend ordinary life and get close to God intuitively

transcontinental railroad begun during the Civil War under acts of 1862 and 1864, this railroad was completed in 1869 by the Union Pacific Railroad and Central Pacific Railroad, linking Omaha, Nebraska and Sacramento, California

Trotskyist a follower of the radical **communist** Leon Trotsky, an exiled rival to Soviet dictator Josef Stalin

trust a group of companies that work together to maintain an effective monopoly that inhibits competition, such as the Standard Oil Trust, developed by John D. Rockefeller to control the oil industry in the late 1800s

U-boat a German submarine or *Unterseeboot* (undersea boat); a popular term during World War I

Unilateral undertaken by only one of two or more people or parties

universal salvation the belief by some Christians that everyone could be saved as a Christian and go to heaven (compare with **Calvinism**)

vagrancy shiftless or idle wandering

veto the U.S. Constitution's method by which a president may stop a **bill** passed by Congress from becoming law; the House and Senate, each by a two-thirds vote, can overturn a veto

war hawks in 1812, supporters of war against Britain on the grounds that Britain had snubbed American rights

weir a fence or obstruction placed in a stream to catch fish; this technology was known and used by American Indians before white contact (pronounced weer)

wet a political term used to designate a person opposed to **prohibition**, especially in the 1920s; Al Smith ran for president in 1928 as a "wet" opposed to prohibition

Whig in the 1700s in England, the liberal political faction emphasizing rural interests and liberty; in 1776, a supporter of the American Revolution; in the 1830s-1840s, an American political party led by Henry Clay and favorable to a national bank

Wilmot's Proviso in 1846, Wilmot's amendment to a **bill** that sought to keep **slavery** out of any Mexican territory acquired by the United States in the Mexican War

Wobbly a slang term for a member of the Industrial Workers of the World (IWW), a radical labor group, circa 1900

write-off a tax deduction

Yankee in the narrow sense, a resident of New England; in the broad sense, any American; during the Civil War, any northerner

yellow press a type of journalism that features cheap, sensational news in order to attract readers, from the use of yellow ink in printing a cartoon strip, "The Yellow Kid" in the *New York Journal* (1896)

yeomen farmers who owned and operated small farms

zionism originally a movement to resettle Jews in Palestine; support for the state of Israel

Index

I-1